AF516151

Exclusion, Discrimination and Stratification

Exclusion, Discrimination and Stratification

Tribes in Contemporary India

Edited by

N.K. Das

Anthropological Survey of India

RAWAT PUBLICATIONS

Jaipur • New Delhi • Bangalore • Hyderabad • Guwahati

ISBN 978-81-316-0580-6

Published by
Prem Rawat for **Rawat Publications**
Satyam Apts, Sector 3, Jawahar Nagar, Jaipur 302 004 (India)
Phone: 0141 265 1748 / 7006 Fax: 0141 265 1748
E-mail: info@rawatbooks.com
Website: www.rawatbooks.com

New Delhi Office
4858/24, Ansari Road, Daryaganj, New Delhi 110 002
Phone: 011 2326 3290

Also at *Bangalore, Hyderabad* and *Guwahati*

Typeset by Rawat Computers, Jaipur
Printed at Nice Printing Press, New Delhi

Contents

Preface vii

Contributors xiii

Introduction — Exclusion, Discrimination and Stratification: Tribes of India 1
N.K. Das

1 Authority Pattern, Hybridization Process and Emerging Inequality in Nicobar Islands 42
A. Justin

2 Economic Deprivation, Occupational Innovations and Growing Social Stratification among the Lalungs of Assam 67
G.C. Ojha

3 Inter-Ethnic Competition, Deprivation and Changing Power Configurations: The Maans of Garo Hills 89
Sarit Kumar Chaudhury

4 Chieftainship, Vaishnavism and New Political System among the Noctes of Arunachal Pradesh 99
R.P. Athparia

5 Immigrant Encroachment, Economic Deprivation and Cultural Squeezing: The Lepchas of Sikkim-Darjeeling 126
J. Chakraborty

6 Matriliny, Christianity and Economic Inequality: The Khasis of Meghalaya 148
Bibhash Dhar

7 Changing Village Economy, Religious Conversion and Social Exclusion: The Mech-Bodo of North Bengal 161
Krishna Mandal

8 'Primitive' Economy, Politicization Process and Emerging Stratification among the Riangs of Tripura 179
Goutam Kumar Bera

9 Culture-Contact and Emerging Middle Class among the Santals 198
K. Mukhopadhyay

10 Economic Discrimination, Social Exclusion and Caste Hierarchy: The Mahalis of West Bengal 208
S. Chanda

11 Adivasi Economy, Slow Impact of Development and Discrimination: The Saora of Odisha 231
D.P. Biswas

12 Social Exclusion, Discrimination and Tribe-Caste Hierarchy: The Rajuars of Odisha 245
D.B. Mondal

13 Foraging to Agriculture: Nascent Class Formation among the Chenchus of Andhra Pradesh 265
Md. Azeez Mohidden and G.V. Ramana

14 Inter-Tribal Competition and Status Ranking among the Koya and Lambadi of Andhra Pradesh 285
M. Rajendra Prasad

15 Pre-Agricultural Economy, Deprivation and NGO induced Empowerment: The Soliga of Karnataka 301
S.N. Mahato

16 Pastoral Clanship, Regional Hierarchy and Social Exclusion: Changing Todas of the Nilgiris 318
Sibir Ranjan Das

17 Adivasi Solidarity, Social Movement and Empowerment: The Bhumia-Baiga of Madhya Pradesh 331
R.K. Sinha

18 Economic Deprivation, Adivasi Solidarity and Syncretic Religion: The Mawasi of Madhya Pradesh 352
Tamal Maity

19 Sectarian Movements, Changing Economic Relations and Inequality: The Dungri and Talat Warlis of Gujarat 365
Rajendra Sarkar

20 Poverty, Social Exclusion and Culture-Change: Emerging Inequality among the Bedias of Jharkhand 381
Tilak Bagchi

21 Changing Tribe-Caste Stratification and Secularization of a Kokna Tribal Village of Maharashtra 400
Debesh Roy

22 Bhotia Tribe-Caste Cluster, Religious-Secular Ranking and Social Exclusion in Uttarakhand 412
Mukul Hazra

23 Kinnaura Tribe-Caster Cluster, Status Ranking and Social Exclusion: Frontier Villages of Himachal Pradesh 418
Pranab Jyoti De

24 Ritual Hierarchy, Class Formation and Social Exclusion: The Gujjar of a Multi-Ethnic Village, Himachal Pradesh 441
R. Haider

Preface

Social exclusion has emerged as a key concept reflecting social disadvantages faced by weaker sections. Disadvantages arising out of exclusion in India have multiple forms – economic, social, and cultural. In India, tribespeople have been subjected to various forms of exclusion right from the colonial period when their rights over natural resources, lands, forests and hills came to be curtailed and derecognized. There are many tribes living in the midst of the castes in many parts of India. Caste remains the most obnoxious of exclusionary systems. Caste-centred exclusions are implicit in the hierarchical classification and ritual hierarchy-based commensality norms. Generally, the tribes living in midst of castes are accorded 'low' status. Hence, they encounter even more deeply embedded social exclusion and economic deprivation. Social exclusion indeed is entwined with inequality and social stratification. Social stratification is generally conceived as the presence of acknowledged differences in social status, political influence and wealth. Anthropological notions of 'inequality' are applied semantically in such divergent domains as political stratification, economic differentiation, class formation and the culture of honour. Social inequality refers to a situation in which individuals and groups do not have equal social status in terms of property rights, land possession, access to education, health care, housing and other social goods. Social inequality involves the belief that some individuals are socially defined as disadvantaged due to their life circumstances. Thus, social inequality and discrimination are fairly matching perceptions. Social inequality is dissimilar from economic inequality though the two are interlinked. Economic inequality refers to disparities in the distribution of economic assets and income. Gender also forms a type of social inequality. Women are less vocal compared to men in political activities and decision-making processes; hence, they suffer from deprivation in patrilineal systems.

The pattern of social stratification perceptible among the tribes located in homogenous tribal territories differs from disparity noticeable in areas where tribe and caste reside in the realm of ritual hierarchy and social exclusion. Indeed, tribes with their diverse social formations, dissimilar historical interactions and uneven economic types manifest inequality and discrimination in many distinguishing ways, as we have illustrated in this volume. While some tribes have pronounced chieftaincy, there are also tribes without chiefly clans. In many instances, village elders/clan/lineage headmen ensure enforcement of customary laws in tribal societies, though younger generation is challenging the traditional practices now more often. Tribes are referred to as 'tribes without rulers' although even such 'tribes', which pursued hunting-gathering largely, had certain positions of informal kind. Searching a non-stratified egalitarian or 'acephalous' stateless/headless 'tribe' will be a futile exercise today as all tribes of India (except a few in remote islands and hills of northeast) have been placed, at least theoretically, within federal legislative structure. Special provisions made in the Constitution of India indeed facilitate northeast tribes to remain outside countless laws and regulations. Thus, the feature of social stratification is studied at multiple levels in this book. At one level we have homogenous tribes occupying a particular space and at another level we find tribes living in mixed localities, with several other tribes and caste groups. Many tribes are divided into sub-tribes and considerable economic and cultural distinctions are often maintained between them. Tribes are divided and differentiated internally into clans and lineages, where age and sex differences guide the interpersonal relations. In some tribes status is accorded to individuals or families following some hereditary principle or the traditional norms of kinship. In the study of homogenous tribal villages we have fairly concentrated on descent system, clanship, lineage system, customary laws and headmanship/chieftainship, though the statutory councils and secular democratic institutions are making indoors steadily in tribal life. In fact, the need to observe social stratification among tribes led our scholars to look into the patterns of descent principles and statuses of descent groups (clans/lineages). Chieftainship emerges as an important feature in two case studies (Nocte and Nicobarese). The chiefs represent their privileged clan groupings vs. clans of the 'commoners'. We observed that the status and rights of the chiefs are derived from kinship/descent norms and customary laws. Since these 'chiefs' have been steward of village polity, their statuses have been accredited and they are suitably incorporated within the modern statutory village/regional administration.

Discourses of social exclusion, discrimination and inequality have emerged as defining characteristics of the 21st century social sciences. Social exclusion, discrimination and explicit inequality among the tribes in contemporary India are themes of vital significance. In Indian anthropological literature, nonetheless, there is serious lack of discussion focusing on these issues. In this volume, our descriptions of tribes in different parts of India demonstrate that the tribespeople have remained poor and are largely subjected to discrimination and exclusion variously. Twenty-four papers included in this volume are the result of village studies conducted in diverse ecological regions of India. In order to portray and discuss multifaceted features of deprivation, disadvantage and exclusion, we have also included in this volume case studies dealing with tribes representing a wide range of economies (hunting-gathering, pastoralism, shifting cultivation, terrace/wet settled agriculture, etc.). We have studied the tribes in numerous locations in order to elucidate concurrently intra-tribe, inter-tribe as also tribe-caste distinctions in rural India. Excepting some inaccessible and mountainous tribes, tribes living in multi-caste villages of peninsular India suffer from identical disadvantages which are meted out to the 'lower' castes. The contributors analytically show how multiple practices of discrimination and denial are deep-rooted and embedded in economic, social and ritual spheres. They also discuss how administrative indifference and negligence often augment deprivation and discrimination. As a result, tribespeople are restrained to liberally make use of sources of living, such as land, capital, governmental development subsidies as also basic needs like education, health and other amenities. Even though there are provisions of affirmative action in place as well as several reservations and special economic packages are provided to minimize discrimination and deprivation, the tribespeople in general and the poor and weak sections among them, in particular, fail to avail the benefits, as most of the authors have discussed in their articles. Indeed, the 'primitive' tribes especially fail to take substantial advantage of new sources of income and development subsidies pertaining to education, health and other amenities. Three 'primitive' tribes, viz., Riangs, Chenchus and Saoras, are studied in this volume. Some sections of primitive tribes, now designated as 'Particularly Vulnerable Tribal Groups' (PVTGs) in official parlance, have shown capacity to abandon their earlier practices and adopt new professions, which we have also discussed.

The tribes we discussed in this volume embody diverse social structures/descent systems, such as polyandry (Todas, Lepchas, Jaunsaris), matriliny (Khasi, Lalung) and patriliny (Santal). The fact remains that majority of the tribes of India broadly follow patrilineal principles. The Lalung tribe of Assam plains has adopted patriliny norms through contacts with Hindu castes, while the original Hills Lalungs pursue matriliny. Some Kinnauris, among whom fieldwork was conducted, claim to be the descendants of the Pandavas and thus they justified the practice of polyandry. We also observed that the polyandry is still practised in Jaunsar-Bawar though it is least preferred now. The Todas practise fraternal polyandry – a practice in which a woman marries all the brothers of a family. We observed the decline of polyandry among the Todas. The Lepchas practised monogamy, polygyny and polyandry forms of marriage and patrilocal residence in the past. Monogamy is the preferred practice among them now. There is decline of polyandry and polygyny among the Lepchas, though the patrilocal residence pattern is prevalent. Northeast tribes indeed retain strong kinship-based polities and clanship. Polyandry is now fast disappearing from tribal societies. It is observed that the institution of polyandry will die its natural death with increasing growth and spread of formal education, migration, social mobility, women's awareness of their rights, etc.

Ideally, tribes do not have any concept of property, even as some families were privileged to possess some wealth through their sheer fortune or hard efforts. Elsewhere we have noted how Naga tribes indulge in accumulation of surplus food articles which are afterwards distributed through 'feasts', so as to achieve some privileged status. Nevertheless, differences in terms of wealth leading to economic 'stratification' are now emerging among most tribes all over India in recent years. In some cases, as our case studies reveal, pronounced differentiation of statuses have appeared, and tribespeople now identify themselves increasingly as 'rich' and 'poor'. Most of our village studies reveal that tribespeople are generally small landholders and majority of them are landless. There are some families within tribes which have emerged as rich peasants through their efforts and by availing the available subsidies. Some contributors to this volume have focused on the tribal proprietary tenants, tenants-at-will and sharecroppers besides landless agricultural labourers and manual workers. It is seen that tribespeople have been attracted towards attaining education and thereby many of them are procuring government employment. Many among them have become senior bureaucrats and professionals. A few of the studies included in this volume have also revealed the emergence of diverse economic strata among tribespeople, formed by the agricultural labourers/poor cultivators, middle cultivators, rich cultivators and white-collar employees. In some instances we observed that an entire sub-tribe achieved prosperity in terms of wealth, income, occupation, education and political power.

Tribes pursuing diverse economies such as foraging (Chenchu), shifting cultivation along with hunting, gathering and fishing (Lanjia Saora, Koyas, Lalung), shifting cultivation with terrace cultivation (Riangs, Nocte), wet plough cultivation (Lepcha), terrace cultivation (Noctes) and settled agriculture (Lalung, Santal, Bedia, Saora, Koya) are portrayed in this volume. There are also pastoral (Gujjars, Todas) and artisan (Mahali) tribes discussed in this volume. It is observed that with passage of time and through slow impact of development projects and democratic institutions tribespeople in various parts of the country are coming forward to redefine their social and economic positions. There are sections within former foragers/pre-agricultural tribes who have left hills and settled in the plains regions (such as Saora, Chenchu) to pursue new economic ventures. Having settled in plains they have shown tendency to be part of the peasant economy, by learning better techniques of cultivation from plains people, even though culturally they are placed in the lower echelon of the local caste system. These neo-peasant tribespeople regard themselves as superior to their hills counterparts.

Tribes of Himalayan areas, hills of northeast and islands are generally better off than tribes/adivasis of peninsular India. Tribes in northeast have greater access over natural resources and smaller states and constitutionally granted autonomous councils better manage local administration. Awareness level is high in northeast. Hence, there are numerous ethnic/autonomy movements seeking self-governance units and development ventures. In northeast India the institution of 'village headman' (gaon-bura), established in colonial era, is retained. Headmen enjoy de facto recognition. Tribal customary laws and kinship-based jural polity often survive at village level. In most areas we find traditional and modern councils existing in harmonious manner. Elsewhere this author has discussed how identity politics had served to marginalize and exclude some tribes in north-east. These exclusions are reflected in twofold notions of majority-minority, tribal-non-tribal and hills-plains. It is argued that the tribal protests for autonomy and the demands of preservation of culture need to be viewed as a prerequisite for distributive justice (N.K.Das, 2009, www.gsdrc.org/social-exclusion/causes-and-forms-of-social-exclusion-identity). There have been numerous measures to establish de facto autonomy and self-rule among tribespeople, through Vth and VIth schedules, all over India, but their execution suffered variously in different regions. There are new regulations now in place such as the Panchayati Raj (Extension to the Scheduled Areas) Act, 1996 (PESA) and Scheduled Tribes and other Traditional Forest Dwellers (Recognition of Forest Rights) Act, 2006. They have raised hope and one may expect a drastic revamp of the mechanisms of the self-governance and economic empowerment in tribal areas in near future. Task is intricate as over 95 per cent of tribes live in rural, hills and island regions of India, and about 10 per cent depend on hunting and gathering practices to lesser or greater degrees. Discrimination and deprivation afflicting the tribes can be deduced from the reality that over 52 per cent among them still live below poverty line. These tribes also lag behind from general population in terms of maternal and child mortality, agricultural land possession, access to communication and electricity. There have been many malnutrition-related deaths among the tribes in India. There is acute shortage of health centres in tribal areas. Many tribal areas lack Anganwadi and other child development programmes. Rate of decline in poverty, particularly in peninsular India, is less. In terms of livelihood and employment the tribespeople are broadly differentiated into cultivators, agricultural labourers, white-collar/salaried workers and even shopkeepers/traders. In some parts of India they are also industrial workers. The bulk of tribal families that own some land often are just the marginal and small farmers. At all-India level majority of tribespeople depend on labour work for survival.

In more recent years through provisions of affirmative action and reservations, intensification of statutory councils and electoral politics, diffusion of secular values and democratization processes in rural areas, the tribespeople have shown determination and made efforts to fight for their rights. They are now conscious to avail constructive development endowments and subsidies. They are also educating their children. These are indeed positive indications. In some villages we studied it is seen that tribal numerical strength and accumulation of wealth among them have redefined the stratification pattern, and thus some tribes now enjoy elevated statuses in village hierarchy. However, there are still not many success stories. Tribes in contemporary India are increasingly becoming part of the democratic-secular nation-state. Tribespeople are now concerned about raising their economic conditions and shaping a new secular identity. We have reported in this volume how some tribes are giving up the adopted Hindu surnames and replacing with adivasi surnames. Adivasi deprivation was tied up with silencing of their voice in the past. Our findings reveal that they have steadily resisted the persistent repression and adopted strategies to defy mistreatment. The rising trend of adivasi awakening is a defining characteristic of contemporary India. Tribespeople are no longer silent spectators of coercion.

Indigenous movements worldwide have relevance for research in India. Hence, redefining the indigenous predicaments, this book illustrates simultaneously marginality and vulnerability and epitomizes resistance and agency.

This volume is the outcome of a research project, 'Stratification and Social Change in Tribal India', which was undertaken as component of a larger research scheme 'Tribal India: Structure, Pattern and Transformation' launched by the Anthropological Survey of India (ASI). All the regional centres of the ASI had participated in this project. The social anthropologists of the ASI conducted intensive field investigations and prepared these papers. The editor expresses his gratitude to the Director, ASI, for entrusting the tasks of coordination of the project and editing the volume. Views expressed by scholars in this book are their own. The editor is thankful to scholars who had attended our workshops where the reports were critically reviewed and consequently fresh field investigations were conducted to collect additional data.

N.K. Das

Contributors

Austin Justin, Superintending Anthropologist (Cultural), Andaman and Nicobar Regional Centre, Anthropological Survey of India, Port Blair

Bibhash Dhar, Superintending Anthropologist (Cultural), North East Regional Centre, Anthropological Survey of India, Shillong

D.B. Mondal, former Deputy Director, Eastern Regional Centre, Anthropological Survey of India, Kolkata

D.P. Biswas, Anthropologist (Cultural), Headquarters, Anthropological Survey of India, Kolkata

Debesh Roy, Anthropologist (Cultural), Central Regional Centre, Anthropological Survey of India, Nagpur

G.V. Ramana, Anthropologist (Cultural), Southern Regional Centre, Anthropological Survey of India, Mysore

Ganesh Chandra Ojha, Anthropologist, North East Regional Centre, Anthropological Survey of India, Shillong

Goutam Kumar Bera, Anthropologist, Eastern Regional Centre, Anthropological Survey of India, Kolkata

Kanchan Mukhopadhyay, Superintending Anthropologist (Cultural), Headquarters, Anthropological Survey of India, Kolkata

Krishna Mandal, Anthropologist, Eastern Regional Centre, Anthropological Survey of India, Kolkata

Jyotirmoy Chakraborty (Late), then Anthropologist, Headquarters, Anthropological Survey of India, Kolkata

M. Rajendra Prasad, Anthropologist (Cultural), Southern Regional Centre, Anthropological Survey of India, Mysore

Md. Azeez Mohidden, Anthropologist (Cultural), Southern Regional Centre, Anthropological Survey of India, Mysore

Mukul Hazra, former Anthropologist, Northeast Regional Centre, Anthropological Survey of India, Shillong

N.K. Das, former Deputy Director and Visiting Fellow, Headquarters, Anthropological Survey of India, Kolkata

Pranab Jyoti De, former Anthropologist, North Western Regional Centre, Anthropological Survey of India, Dehradun

R. Haider, Anthropologist (Cultural), Andaman and Nicobar Regional Centre, Anthropological Survey of India, Port Blair

R.K. Sinha, former Anthropologist (Cultural), Southern Regional Centre, Anthropological Survey of India, Mysore

Rajendra P. Athparia, former Superintending Anthropologist (Cultural), North East Regional Centre, Anthropological Survey of India, Shillong

Rajendra Sarkar, former Superintending Anthropologist (Cultural), Western Regional Centre, Anthropological Survey of India, Udaipur

S. Chanda, former Anthropologist, Eastern Regional Centre, Anthropological Survey of India, Kolkata

S.N. Mahato, former Anthropologist (Cultural), Southern Regional Centre, Anthropological Survey of India, Mysore

Sarit Kumar Chaudhury, Professor of Anthropology, Institute of Tribal Studies, Rajiv Gandhi University, Itanagar, Arunachal Pradesh

Sibir Ranjan Das, former Superintending Anthropologist (Cultural), North East Regional Centre, Anthropological Survey of India, Shillong

Tamal Maity, Anthropologist (Cultural), Central Regional Centre, Anthropological Survey of India, Nagpur

Tilak Bagchi, Western Regional Centre, Anthropological Survey of India, Udaipur, now with Census of India, Kolkata

Introduction

Exclusion, Discrimination and Stratification: Tribes of India

N.K. Das

Tribes of India have suffered grievously from the practices of social exclusion and discrimination in economic and social spheres. This phenomenon is not thrashed out comprehensively in Indian social science literature. The tribes of India, barring some isolated and hilly tribes, have experienced exclusion and marginalization in regions dominated by caste and other dominant groups, in different ways. Different factors caused deprivation and poverty among tribespeople variously. Articles dealing with different tribes of India in this volume analytically show how multiple practices of discrimination and denial are deep-rooted and embedded in economic, social and ritual spheres. Even after several decades of independence and considerable economic achievements, the tribes of India are subjected to injustice and social exclusion. Even when tribes have become part of multi-caste villages, through adoption of norms and practices of Hinduism, they are rarely treated with positive conduct. In most cases, as our studies reveal, tribes are kept at par with the 'lower' castes of the region and are made to suffer physical segregation, discrimination and elimination in several ways. This situation also reduced the opportunities for tribespeople to liberally take advantage of sources of income, such as land, capital and governmental development subsidies pertaining to education, health and other amenities. Even though there are provisions of affirmative action in place and several reservations are provided to minimize discrimination and deprivation, the tribespeople in general and the 'weakest section' within them, in particular, failed to avail the benefits. There are provisions for the scheduled people such as the tribespeople to nominate their representatives in local/regional statutory bodies, yet it is invariably seen that the powerful positions are always captured by the members of wealthy communities and higher castes, though there are some exceptions wherein members of some tribes have done well in economic and political spheres and emerged as privileged sections within the area. In more recent years, through greater secularization of village society and as a result of democratization process, the tribespeople have shown determination and made efforts to fight for their rights in rural areas. Growing awareness and aspiration are indeed positive indications. However, as our village studies show there are still not many success stories.

I

The 'tribe' is a colonial construction (Singh, 1982): 'A "tribe" in India is defined by certain criteria such as relative isolation, homogeneity, settlement in a well-defined habitat. The "more primitive" groups have been distinguished from the "less primitive". Implicit in this two-fold stratification has been the recognition of the fact that there is no one tribal system but that there are many tribal systems, that there is not one economy of the tribe but there are many economies of the tribes' (Singh, 1982: vii). The Anthropological Survey of India identified and located 635 distinct tribes in India. People of India project (1985–1995) identified 461 main tribes and 172 segments/minor tribes. Some territorial segments were also included. Hence, People of India project reported about 635 tribes (Singh, 1994). It is inaccurate to say that the project followed the list of Scheduled Tribes to identify the tribes. Native perceptions and local processes of segmentation and combination were described and several 'tribes' not part of the schedule during investigation were described (such as, Pochury Naga, Das, 1994). Tribes constitute 8.14 per cent of the total population of the country, numbering 84.51 million (Census, 2001) and cover about 15 per cent of the country's area. The tribes inhabit most parts of the country (except Punjab, Haryana, Delhi, Chandigarh and Puducherry (Pondicherry). In most parts of eastern, central and western India tribespeople are recognized as Adivasis. In view of their habitation in hills areas they came to be called as girijan and vanvasi/vanyajati – 'forest dwellers' (Srivastava, 2010). An immense concentration of the tribes/Adivasis is seen in central-eastern states of India, notably Chhattisgarh, Jharkhand, Odisha, West Bengal, Madhya Pradesh, and beyond the Western Ghats (hills) of Gujarat and Maharashtra and most parts of south India. However, the foremost concentration is found in the north-eastern states (Assam, Manipur, Nagaland, Mizoram, Tripura, Meghalaya, Sikkim and Arunachal Pradesh). The Indian government has a special programme for the welfare of 'primitive tribal groups' (now rechristened as 'particularly vulnerable groups'). These tribes are largely dependent on hunting and gathering and some pre-agricultural activity including shifting cultivation. The Sentinelese of the North Sentinel Island of the Andamans is the only tribe of India who live in complete isolation. The list of Scheduled Tribe (a legal and constitutional term) differs from state to state. It includes in the list the 'native tribes' and excludes such tribes who immigrated later, but who deserved to be declared as 'Scheduled Tribe'. Since many such tribes remain outside the Scheduled category, we find in this occurrence a form of discrimination and injustice. This situation also demonstrates that the concept of tribe as used in anthropology needs to be separated from the category 'Scheduled Tribe', an arbitrary phrase.

There is substantial debate concerning the indigeneity and ancestry of Indian tribes. It is generally accepted that the tribespeople are the original inhabitants of India (Ray, 1972; Thapar, 1966). The tribes speak over 700 languages belonging to language families of Austro-Asiatic, Dravidian and Tibeto-Burman. The proto-Australoid tribes, who speak dialects belonging to the Austric linguistic group, are believed to be the basic element of Indian population (Thapar, 1966). Anthropologists, historians and linguists

(Pattanayak, 1998; Risley, 1915) generally accept that the Austro-Asiatic speaking tribes could be the original inhabitants, while others (Buxton, 1925; Sarkar, 1958) regard the Dravidians as the original inhabitants. New genetic and genomic studies reveal the early ancestry of the Indian tribes, including tribes of the Andaman Islands. India has served as a major corridor for the dispersal of modern humans out of Africa (Cann, 2001). Myths and folklore of many tribes suggest that they had occupied much larger part of the subcontinent and were swamped by the dominant agricultural communities, previously through normal incursions and later under the patronage of the British. The colonial rulers introduced several oppressive laws and regulations; hence there were numerous 'tribal revolts' from the mid-nineteenth century onwards in several parts of eastern India. In view of growing unrest, the colonial administration barred the sale of tribal lands to non-tribes. However, in most cases, the alienated lands could not be restored. In fact, many of the new laws were widely disregarded and unscrupulous merchants and moneylenders found ways to circumvent them. The tribal/Adivasi problems still persist though the propensity of the exploitation seems somewhat changed.

II

It is widely asserted that the Indian anthropologists ignored the premise of tribal social stratification in the past primarily on account of their obsession with holistic ethnographic focus and their stress on cultural transformation and Hinduization. Ghurye (1963: 205) observed that the tribes who were described in the census as animists were 'backward Hindus'. N.K. Bose (1941) pointed to tribes being absorbed into Hindu society. He nevertheless provided an economic rationale for culture change. Surajit Sinha (1958) regarded the culture of tribespeople as a dimension of little tradition (within Indian civilization). Kosambi (1956) highlighted tribal elements being fused into the general society. He found adoption of the technology of Hindu castes by the tribes as the major route of absorption. Sanskritization indeed had been the most dominant code prevailing in large parts of India, in the past, if not now, for absorbing tribes into Hindu society (Srinivas, 1952). N.K. Bose distinguished two ideal types: 'tribal organization' and 'Hindu organization' (Bose, 1975, cited in Srivastava, 2010). These two models differed in terms of their technology of production. Since they lived in contiguity with caste Hindu communities, many tribes gradually absorbed Hindu traits and ways of living, in many cases ending up as a jati. Bose (1975) called this process 'Hindu method of tribal absorption'. H. Kulke (1993) has examined the historical writings on culture change in India. According to him, Alfred C. Lyall was first to point to the process of Hinduization among Indian tribes (Lyall, 1882). He mentioned about 'the gradual Brahminization of the aboriginal non-Aryan, casteless tribes' and their passing 'into the social scale of the composite population'. The next stage, according to Lyall, was 'the invitation of a Brahman to officiate at the rites de passage of the family'. Lyall further pointed out that 'if the converted families are of standing among their own people, the Brahman will usually discover for them a decent Hindu pedigree, or a miraculous incident which proves a half savage chief or rich outcaste to be really allied to one of the recognized castes'. According to A. Hofer, 1979, most probably, 'A. Lyall was the first to formulate a proto-theory of Sanskritization'. Risley also pointed to several processes which were involved in the transformation of tribes into castes: 'Mobility of "leading men of an aboriginal tribe" to a higher ranking, as among the Maharajas of Chota Nagpur and their recognition as Nagbansi Rajputs; Mobility of members of a tribe, who embrace the tenets of Hindu religious sects (Vaisnavas, Lingayat, Ramayats, etc.); A whole tribe or a large section enrolling in the ranks of Hinduism as a new caste by accepting Brahminical rites; A whole tribe or a section of it gradually converted to Hinduism without, however, losing its tribal designation or abandoning completely its tribal deities, etc.'. According to Kulke, it is quite evident that Risley's first two processes are identical with the two modes described by Lyall. It is also perceptible that a process of Rajputization was also indicated by Risley, which was later highlighted by Indian scholars. Max Weber was one of the earliest scholars to define Hinduization as 'transformation of tribes into castes' (1958: 15). The process of extensive Hinduization was initiated by the tribal ruling stratum (Herrenschicht) through imitation of specific Hindu customs. This process usually begins with abstention from meat and alcohol, the adoption of Hindu rites de passage. Later, the Brahmins intervene and they 'provide testimony to the fact that the section of the tribe was of ancient, only temporarily forgotten, knightly (Kshatriya) blood' (1958: 10). Hinduization of the tribal leaders was then completed by the performance of the sacred thread ceremony. Having achieved the change of status, these new 'Rajput' parvenus sought social intercourse through intermarriage with the equivalent social strata of the surrounding Hindu areas (1958: 11). H. Kulke says that Weber's distinction is a clear anticipation of two major concepts brought out about half a century later by Indian anthropologists ('Sanskritization', Srinivas, 1952; 'Rajputization', Sinha, 1962). Srinivas' concept of Sanskritization became an influential concept in the discussions on social change in Indian society. Kulke says the 'Kshatriya model' or Weber's 'extensive propaganda' had been taken up by Surajit Sinha in his article on 'State Formation and Rajput Myth in Tribal Central India'. Sinha stated that the process of acculturation, Hinduization and social stratification within the village could not be properly understood unless the data are examined in the broader context of the formation of the principality. He further adds that the formation of the state provided the decisive socio-political framework for the transformation of the tribal system into the regional caste system.

In social anthropological literature, peasant society has often been conceptualized and studied in contrast to tribal society (Xaxa, 1999; Das, 1987). The process of peasantization among tribes in Indian history is attributed largely to cultural contact with the non-tribal world. The theme of state formation and peasantization process among the tribes is explained by K.S. Singh. He says,

> The crucial factors of economic changes in the tribal regions were formation of state in the later medieval period and migration of peasant castes. The first phenomenon is witnessed all over the tribal territory extending from the Brahmaputra Valley to the Satpuras and the Godavari. The tribes could not generate surplus with their primitive technology, but

> peasant castes, (often invited by chieftains/kings) did so. There were also other factors. The Ahoms encouraged the extension of the Sali (wet land) cultivation, and of the 'new' transplantation techniques. They built up with communal labour a system of massive dykes and embankments. Lands were improved and ahu (upland) and bao (broadcast rice) lands were transformed into lands suitable for the cultivation of the sali crops in upper Assam, the cradle of Ahom culture. They introduced a variety of 'high-yielding' Ahom seed, one of the dozens of sali varieties. The Gond Rajas in middle India reclaimed and peopled their wild forests and dotted their kingdoms with embankments and other irrigation schemes, which were 'admirable works of engineering skill'. The chiefs of all the Dravidian tribes, the Gonds, Nagbansi and Chero encouraged settlement of non-tribal peasant communities such as the Kurmi, Koeri and Kumbi, who alone, with their superior agricultural technology, could generate the agricultural surpluses that the new states needed. ... As surpluses emerged economic differentiation and social stratification developed in tribal society. (Singh, 1982: viii–ix)

The notion of 'peasant' does not fascinate F.G. Bailey (1961). Bailey differentiates 'tribes' from 'castes'. He characterizes caste society as predominantly hierarchical and organic and tribal society as basically segmentary. Bailey (1960) suggests that tribe and caste constitute a continuum, with individual groups' positions determined by the proportion of the population with direct (tribe) rather than mediated (caste) access to land.

In more recent times, data generated though People of India project (ASI: 1985–1995) reveals that a large number of tribes identify themselves as Hindus, and place themselves within local Varna-Jati order. While a majority accepted the Shudra and Vaishya categories, a few claimed even the Brahmin status. Thus, the Gaddi, Pangwal, and Kagati among the Jaunsari claimed Brahmin status. The tribes settled in multi-caste villages locate their status within the local (ritual) hierarchy differently. Thus, PoI project data revealed that 171 tribes (26.9%) regard themselves at a higher status; 298 tribes (46.9%) belonged to middle position; and 161 tribes (25.3%) categorized themselves as being of low status. Many tribes follow one religion. However, in many instances they followed more than one religion, such as Hinduism and tribal religion (90 tribes, 21%) and Christianity and tribal religion (55 tribes, 13%). Christianity is indeed widespread in northeast India (Manipur, 94.55 per cent; Nagaland, 93.09 per cent; Mizoram, 88.46 per cent and Meghalaya, 66.32%). Data gathered through PoI project and other studies on tribal religion reveals that the tribespeople were never swallowed up through any cultural or religious adoption/incorporation/conversion (Das, 2003; Singh, 2003). Indeed several reformist Bhagat movements were also launched but they could not erode the native religious beliefs of the tribes. Tribal priesthood also survives all over India (Das, 2006). K.S. Singh has observed tribal presence even in established hubs of major religions. He says while the spread and influence of Vaishnav ideas upon the tribal societies is better known, the roles of tribes in major shrines of India are less known (Singh, 2003).

III

The British incorporated tribes into the state structure through enforcement of alien civil laws, land taxes and administrative structures in tribal areas. The British colonial rulers demarcated new boundaries in tribal areas and introduced new institutions. They also introduced the notion of private property, and the records of rights in land, and state control over forests, which resulted in the curtailment of rights and privileges of the tribes. All these played havoc with tribal society. The opening up of the tribal areas under the British rule led to a steady immigration of land hungry non-tribal populations into tribal areas resulting in unprecedented land alienation from tribes to non-tribes. The process continued all through the British period and it continued steadily even after independence. Since the advent of colonial rule and through unrestricted movement of plainsmen into the tribal areas, the tribes had been subjected to constant economic exploitation. Massive alienation of tribal lands by moneylenders and superior cultivating castes left the majority of tribespeople steeped in poverty and debt (Sachchidananda, 1990). Landlords, contractors and moneylenders were alien to the tribal society. Colonial rulers encouraged the immigration of 'outsiders' (traders, moneylenders, contractors as also peasant-castes and artisans) into tribal areas and thereby enforced a new system of social stratification. Land came to be categorized as property in tribal areas, mainly through the launch of the Permanent Settlement Regulation (1793) which introduced the 'Zamindari' system (of feudal lords) for the purpose of revenue collection, and thereby drastically restructured the relationship of Adivasis with their territories as well as their affiliation with physical resources. The 1874 'Scheduled District Act', the 1919 'Government of India Act' and later the 'Government of India Act' of 1935 classified the hill areas (northeast India) as excluded and partially excluded areas where the provincial legislature had no jurisdiction. This last Act was found suitable by the postcolonial state which led to enactment of V Schedule and the VI Schedule to provide certain degree of self-governance in designated tribal areas. These regulations failed completely and as a result the government came forward with new regulations, such as the Panchayat Raj (Extension to the Scheduled Areas) Act, 1996 and Forest Rights Act, 2006. They have raised hope and one may anticipate a drastic overhauling of the mechanisms of the self-governance and economic empowerment in near future.

From various accounts, it is evident that during the British period class-based distinctions were swapping the traditional status system among the tribes, particularly in eastern India, mainly Jharkhand. It also led to alienation of land, control of forest economy by the state, emergence of moneylenders and traders, exploitation of the tribal people. This section of moneylenders – traders and non-tribal agriculturists were superior in skills and resources even before they landed on the tribal soil. This implanted a hiatus between them and the tribals. Hence the non-tribals came to be called as Diku (exploiters). The tribals, in general, faced acute pauperization and were forced to migrate in search of employment to far off places. It appears that a good number of studies on tribal social stratification that were conducted by Indian scholars mostly confined to two regions such as Jharkhand and Gujarat. K.L. Sharma has reviewed some of these studies critically (Sharma, 1986; Bose, 1981; Pathy, 1984; Shah, 1979, 1986;

Thapar and Siddiqui, 1991; Badgaiyan, 1986; Doshi, 1990; Singh, 1985; Sachchidananda, 1990). Sharma also referred to some studies which dealt with intra-tribal and inter-tribal status distinctions (Vidyarthi, 1974) and class-oriented stratification (Sachchidananda, 1990; Badgaiyan, 1986). It is seen that scholars have been generally obsessed with ethnic and the class perspectives (Badgaiyan, 1986; Doshi, 1990). Some scholars have dealt with inter-tribal distinctions in terms of historicity, land relations, colonial impact, and contact with non-tribal people, economic development and impact of socio-political awakening. In a couple of studies convergence between the ethnic and the class perspectives has been greatly emphasized (Badgaiyan, 1986; Doshi, 1990). Sachchidananda wrote that social stratification in the states of Jharkhand (then Bihar), West Bengal, Chhattisgarh (then Madhya Pradesh) and Odisha in the pre-colonial period could be observed through the ranks such as the khutkattidars, the village headmen and their subordinate functionaries. The British encouraged these village functionaries for collecting revenue. Munda-Manki and Majhi in parts of Jharkhand thus became colonial agents. These functionaries were influenced by the traders and moneylenders who cheated the native Adivasis through land alienation, moneylenders' usurious practices, and influx of non-tribal traders, contractors and petite administrative officials (Sachchidananda, 1990). This development seriously harmed the pre-colonial tribal kinship system and polity. Forced labour was almost a routine activity. Thekedars as collectors of revenue were new agents of exploitation. This arrangement accentuated class-like stratification between the tribes themselves and between the tribes and non-tribes.

The colonial era also witnessed the penetration of peasant castes and artisan castes such as blacksmiths, potters and weavers, who also further differentiated the tribal society from class point of view; the village society was divided into the khutkattidars and the paria horoko (commoners). The khutkattidars were the real owners of the village land. The khutkatti system was mainly confined to the Munda tribe. Thapar and Siddiqui (1991) also found that the khutkatti system was the basis of the Munda society. The Mundas, Pahans and Mahatos were heads of their clans. Besides these heads of the clans/lineages, the khutkattidars were powerful as they collected tributes from the praja living in the villages. Thapar and Siddiqui write: 'Thus, the tendency towards social stratification which had already begun with the khutkatti system was not only intensified and accelerated under the state, but was also made more complex with the interpolation of various levels of intermediaries'. The tribal mode of production broke down and gave a way to the emergence of a new correlation of social status with landholding and power. The lineage rights over land became weak, and a feudal state on tribal society was superimposed. K.S. Singh (1978) has also highlighted the dysfunctional consequences of the British colonialism. The agency system established by the British was used for ruthless suppression of the tribal uprisings. This also strengthened the feudal elements in tribal society as it encouraged the chiefs and landlords to extract surplus from the tribals as much as possible for the well-being of the Raj in India. The moneylenders had their heyday as no one was there to check the usurious activities perpetrated by them.

Since independence, the factor of ethnicity is being viewed as a means of mobilizing the tribespeople with a view to gain access to economic and political opportunities. Detribalization and ethnicization coexist. In numerous studies, as also in our own case studies, in this volume, we find emergence of a nascent middle class within the tribes, which has been assertive. This class has been less self-assured in greater parts of peninsular India but it has been more forceful in northeast India. Northeast indeed witnessed numerous autonomy movements launched by younger tribal student leaders. Some of them have related the issue of self-determination, identity, autonomy and development with the larger 'tribal question' (Das, 1989, 2007, 2011).

There are several studies of social stratification which bring out the convergence of ethnicity and class, particularly in eastern-central India. The scholars argue that the phenomenon of power and dominance is increasingly dependent upon the questions of ethnicity and class. Writing about Jharkhand, K.S. Singh (1985) observed that the emergence of social stratification as a historical reality was created by colonialism as also the processes of sanskritization and conversion to Christianity. Badgaiyan (1986) wrote that the class and ethnicity were inextricably intermixed in Chotanagpur (Jharkhand) in the nineteenth century. Earlier Hinduism and later on Christianity proved to be an assault on coherent character of the Mundas as a community. The Birsa movement was a direct reaction to the onslaught committed on the Mundas by the British administration and Christianity. Scholars have studied the multiple dimensions of stratification in postcolonial era. They have generally focused on the tribal proprietary tenants, tenants-at-will, and sharecroppers besides landless agricultural and manual workers. It is seen that tribespeople have been attracted towards attaining education and thereby many tribespeople are procuring government employment. Many among them have become senior bureaucrats and professionals like doctors, lawyers, university professors and merchants and traders. The post-independence period, we may say, witnessed strengthening of the class structure in some areas. A study of the Chaudhari tribe in Surat district of Gujarat by Shah (1979) shows the emergence of four economic strata on the basis of occupation and ownership of land. These strata are formed by the agricultural labourers/poor cultivators, middle cultivators, rich cultivators and white-collar employees. The first three categories are constituted by the huge 92 per cent of the working population and only 3 per cent people of the Chaudharis are white-collar employees. In his study of stratification among the Scheduled Tribes in the Bharuch and Panch Mahals districts of Gujarat, Shah (1986) observed that status distinction based on achievements in terms of wealth, property, income, occupation, education and power is emerging. There are differences of status based on education and lifestyle. P.K. Bose (1981) also identifies four classes among tribes of Gujarat, though mainly based on landholdings. These are: rich peasants, middle peasants, poor peasants, and agricultural labourers. Bose reports that the tribes in Gujarat today are equally affected by the processes of planned and unplanned change and by the continuous structural and institutional shifts in rural India. Pathy's study (1984) of five tribal villages in Gujarat reveals five economic categories: landlords, rich peasants, middle peasants, small peasants and farm workers. The distribution and characteristic features of these classes are the same as we find in the study conducted by Shah and Bose. It seems that in a broad sense, the studies of class stratification among the tribes of Gujarat reinforce each other.

IV

The repression and exploitation of the tribespeople in contemporary era have been enduring, as in colonial era. Over 95 per cent of tribes live in rural areas and economic exploitation remains their most acute problem. Less than 10 per cent are shifting hunter-gatherers and many among them depend on forest produce for their livelihood. As India progressed in terms of growth and poverty reduction, the poverty headcount index for the tribes also fell by 31 per cent between 1983 and 2004–05. The relatively slower decline in poverty among Adivasis means that they are increasingly concentrated in the rural areas (http://siteresources.worldbank.org/Resource/244362-1265299949041/India-PSE-Adivasis-Brief.pdf). In states where the tribes are in majority (such as in the north-east) and where they have gained from education, their status is different from the status of tribes living as marginalized groups in the interiors of the central, eastern and western states. NGOs and tribal leaders have taken up the issue of child death in tribal areas. In most states of India, tribespeople live in remote regions where services of public health centres are inadequate. Studies of anthropological survey of India have shown that tribes all over India pursue traditional medicine considerably. Availability of health centres in rural areas differs from state to state. Whether it is maternal and child mortality, size of agricultural holdings or access to drinking water and electricity, tribal communities lag far behind the general population. About 52 per cent of tribal population is below poverty line and 54 per cent tribes have no access to economic assets. These indicators underline the importance of the need of livelihood generating activities based on locally available resources so that gainful employment opportunities could be created at the doorstep of tribal people. Recognizing this need for initiating such livelihood generating activities, the union tribal ministry established an organization to take up marketing development activities for non-Timber Forest Produce (NTFP). In 1987, the Tribal Cooperative Marketing Development Federation of India Limited (TRIFED) was set up with an aim to serve the interest of the tribal community (http://tribesindia.com).

Displacement and uprooting of the tribes have been going on for centuries. Other processes at work today are indebtedness and landlessness. Since 1990 tribespeople have been mainly displaced in such states as Andhra Pradesh, Jharkhand, Gujarat, Maharashtra, Chhattisgarh/Madhya Pradesh, Rajasthan and Odisha. Of this, 8.54 million, that is, 40 per cent have been tribals. However, only 2.12 million (24.8%) have been resettled so far (Planning Commission, 2001: 39). Thus, a vast majority of them have been pushed into the vortex of increasing disadvantage, unemployment, debt bondage, and destitution. This has resulted in inflating the size of the tribal population living below the poverty line. In 1993–94, the tribal population living below the poverty line was as high as 51.14 per cent as compared to 35.97 per cent of the general population (Planning Commission, 2001: 43, Quoted in Xaxa, V., Dialogue with Marginalized Tribes, www.ishvanikendra.com). The British colonialists were the first to see profits in the hinterland inhabited by the Adivasis in terms of rich mineral and forest resources. They undertook mining exploration, set up plantations and constructed railways on a war footing to plunder the vast natural wealth. In contemporary era, new laws, national parks, urbanization, industrialization, including the huge irrigation, hydro-electric and multipurpose projects, thermal plants, steel plants, bauxite and alumina plants, led to the displacement of tribes from their traditional habitats. According to the estimates of the Planning Commission, 21.3 million people were displaced by development projects between 1951 and 1990 alone. Of these, 8.54 million (40%) belonged to Scheduled Tribes that constitute less than 8 per cent of the total population. Only 2.1 million (25%) of them are reported to have been rehabilitated (Planning Commission, 2001: 43, Quoted in Xaxa, V., 'Dialogue with Marginalized Tribes', www.ishvanikendra.com). B.D. Sharma says that the dominant perception of the present administration seems to be that 'a good tribal is a displaced tribal'.

In contemporary era, the contractors, traders and forest officials continue to exploit the tribespeople. The tribespeople are prevented from enjoying their traditional rights of collecting forest produce and they are punished and tortured even for collecting wood for the construction of their huts. On the other hand, the contractor-smuggler-in nexus with corrupt officials of the State, take away the forest wealth without paying tax. The story of exploitation of the Adivasis and the snatching away of their traditional rights over the forests is same all over India. The Adivasis sell the forest produce in the *haat* (the weekly bazaar) at nominal prices. The traders dupe them regularly. The traders also offer loans at an exorbitant rate of 120 per cent per annum to the Adivasis. The unscrupulous traders cheat the innocent Adivasis in every sphere – in pricing, grading, weighing and counting of the forest produce. While the traders and contractors are looting the Adivasis at the micro level, the large industrial houses are also carrying out large-scale exploitation by draining the region of its minerals and natural wealth. Iron ore is sold at a nominal price from Bailadilla mines to the imperialists and the CBB (www.bannedthought.net/India/PeoplesMarch/ 2006/archives/2006).

Even though laws aimed at restoration of land exist, yet, the percentage of tribal cultivators has decreased from 68.15 in 1961 to 54.5 in 1991. Conversely, the percentage of agricultural labourers has increased from 19.71 in 1961 to 32.69 in 1991 (Planning Commission, 2001: 91). A greater threat to the tribes is large-scale dam building for irrigation and hydro-electricity. A number of such schemes have been carried out since independence but the largest is the giant World Bank-financed Narmada Valley project which involves 30 major, 135 medium and 3,000 minor dams, which will flood 350,000 hectares of land, including 11 per cent of the forests of the Narmada Valley. Up to 300,000 people, the majority of them being tribals are forced to relocate to make way for the dam. Furthermore, compensation is limited to landowners (which is difficult for many Adivasis to prove) and is normally given in the form of money rather than land. There have been campaigns by organizations within India and internationally to at least give compensation in the form of an equal amount of land to the displaced but, although these schemes have achieved a limited amount of success in delaying the project and gaining better compensation terms, the dams will still be built. Furthermore, it is doubtful whether sufficient land for resettlement is available in such a densely populated country, where pressures on land are already high. Tribespeople also suffer from increased disease burden because of poverty and consequent malnutrition, poor environmental sanitation, lack of safe drinking water leading to increased morbidity from water borne infections, lack of health care facilities and even social barriers. The malnutrition among tribals, especially women and children, is quite common. In area of education, tribes have made some tangible progress. In many case studies in this volume we note this trend. A review of all India scenario shows that greater educational achievements are confined mainly to the northeastern region and even there, among some of the tribes. As per the 1991 census, the literacy rate among tribes was only 29.6 per cent (The general literacy rate being 52.2%). The female literacy rate stood at 18.2 as against 39.3 per cent for the general population (Xaxa, V., "Dialogue with Marginalized Tribes", www.ishvanikendra.com). Protest movements among tribal groups have a long history. Spontaneous uprisings against the state occurred during the British period, and each such conflagration was an assertion of the cultural and political identity, as well as a claim on natural resources. There is growing recognition among policymakers that increasing militancy in tribal areas is not merely a 'law and order' problem (Singh, 1993). Instead, the causes lie in marginalization – spatial, economic and political – that tribal groups have experienced over years. New laws are in place now. They claim to undo injustices committed earlier. Both the Panchayat Extension to Scheduled Areas Act (PESA) and the Tribal Rights Act, 2006, fundamentally question the power relations between Adivasi and non-Adivasi areas and purport to transfer greater power to the former. Both attempt to give special powers to tribal gram sabhas (village assemblies) to enhance tribal voice on issues related to mining leases and infrastructure development in tribal areas. However, it is widely believed that these legislations have not been implemented in spirit. There are many other initiatives which promise to guarantee tribal empowerment and 'autonomy' for local self-governance. There are numerous measures to establish de facto autonomy and self-rule for tribespeople, but their implementation differs from region to region. In some parts of northeast India, the VI Schedule (Autonomous District Councils) has been successfully implemented.

V

A pervasive cliché conveyed that the anthropologists study the tribes and similar societies which are small in size, 'stateless' and kinship-oriented, where wealth and status are not valued. An evaluation shows that anthropologists have often encountered tribes among whom status and material wealth are cherished, and stratification and competition, though not pronounced, are perceptible. Village studies of 1950s and 1960s, which intermittently continued in 1970s, were influenced by the British social anthropology. Most village studies used the Redfieldian concept of peasant society and studied dimensions of great/little traditions. Some studies also elucidated the congruence between caste, class and power (Beteille, 1965; Chauhan, 1974). Besides sociologists and social anthropologists, historians and economists have studied the issue of stratification mainly from structural-historical perspective, focussing on agrarian and industrial stratification and forms of agrarian production vis-à-vis rural class structure. John Harris has studied the issue of capitalism and peasant farming (Harris, 1982). Many anthropological monographs were brought out in post-independence era. In many cases they were also village studies and they too pursued the structural-functional perspectives. Unfortunately, 'tribal village' studies could not be placed at par with 'caste' village studies. Fact remains that there are village-centred monographs dealing with tribal economic relations and politics at local level (Das, 1993) and there are also village studies which focused on perceptions of the 'lower castes' in local arena of economic relations (Sinha, Bhattacharya and Das, 1993), but such studies have not been adequately accredited. The second mentioned study could be seen as the first anthropological study of the 'lower castes' subalterns in terms of their weak resource base, their low position in social hierarchy, their relative lack of access to facilities provided by developmental programmes and their inadequate participation in institutions.

This volume indisputably deals with village-based tribespeople who live with other tribes as also with caste groups in multi-community villages. The caste groups are economically privileged and they often maltreat the tribespeople who are generally marginal landholders and are often segregated, and discriminated in many ways. The pattern of village life, economic activities and mode of social stratification detectable in predominantly 'tribal villages' indeed differ from caste-villages, where tribes are treated at par with 'low castes' and debarred from many core activities of village life. In view of their diverse social formations, dissimilar historical interactions and uneven economic types, the tribespeople have manifested segmentation, inequality and differentiation in many distinguishing ways, as we will illustrate in this volume.

VI

The tribes are traditionally regarded by the anthropologists as 'stateless' societies or societies with minimal stratification. The anthropologists looked at stratification, till recently, largely in terms of social/political systems (band, tribe, chiefdom, state). They also regarded economies of tribes as fixed types. In reality, today as in past, economies of the tribes are 'mixed' economies. The main subsistence pattern of tribes varied, some tribes indeed pursued multiple economic systems. Tribes living close to forests variously employed food-foraging techniques. Tribes with chieftains (chiefdom) described in this volume, such as the Noctes, Nicobarese, Khasis, Riang have revealed pronounced pattern of stratification, but these are ultimately guided by kinship/clanship principles. As our case studies show, modern conditions have rather favoured the 'chieftains' who tend to preserve their 'privileged status' within the tribe. Ideally, tribes did not have any concept of property. Indeed, among some tribes there existed some families with some wealth created through their hard efforts, but the additional food articles were distributed through 'feasts', such as among the Nagas (Das, 1993). However, differences in terms of wealth leading to economic differentiation such as 'stratification' are now emerging among most tribes all over India in recent years. In some cases, as our case studies reveal, pronounced differentiation of statuses have appeared, and tribespeople are categorizing themselves as 'rich' and 'poor'. In the multi-community villages tribespeople are subjugated by dominant communities, as in the past, and excluded from core sphere of the village life, even though certain sections of the tribespeople have improved their economic conditions considerably. In all parts of peninsular India it is the higher caste people who own and control the greater component of economic resources, such as land. The lower caste people and tribespeople living in such villages are invariably landless or else marginal cultivators. In such imbalanced and unequal situation, the low castes and tribespeople, as our reports reveal, are discriminated against variously. Such discrimination promotes social exclusion and inequality, which are closely linked. Our case studies have revealed these processes in great details.

The twenty-four tribes portrayed in this volume inhabit diverse ecological and cultural – linguistic regions of India. They represent divergent economies. We have located and studied the tribes who are still dependent on hunting and gathering and collection of minor food produce to a considerable extent (Chenchus), shifting cultivation along with hunting, gathering and fishing (Lanjia Saora, Koyas), shifting cultivation with terrace cultivation (Riangs), wet plough cultivation (Lepcha), terrace cultivation (Noctes) and settled agriculture (Lalung, Santal, Bedia). There are pastoral (Gujjars, Todas) and artisan tribes also (Mahali). The tribes we discuss embody diverse social structures/descent systems, such as polyandry (Todas, Lepchas, Jaunsaris), matriliny (Khasi, Lalung) and patriliny (Santal). The Lalung tribe living in Assam plains has adopted patriliny. Some Kinnauris, among whom fieldwork was conducted, claim to be the descendants of the Pandavas and thus they justified the practice of polyandry. We observed that polyandry is still practiced in Jaunsar –Bawar though it is least preferred now. The Todas practice fraternal polyandry, a practice in which a woman marries all the brothers of a family (www.indianmirror.com). We have observed the decline of polyandry among the Todas now. The Lepchas practice monogamy, polygyny, and polyandry forms of marriage and patrilocal residence (Bhasin, 2011). Northeast tribes indeed retain strong kinship based-polities and clanship (Das, 1987, 2009a). Our scholar however observed the decline of polyandry and polygyny among the Lepchas, though the patrilocal residence pattern is prevalent. Our observers found that polyandry is now fast disappearing from tribal societies. The scholars observed that the institution of polyandry will die its natural death with increasing growth and spread of formal education, migration, social mobility, women's awareness of their rights, etc. Further, a reappraisal of the interaction pattern shows that the tribes we studied in the islands, hills and plains regions had variously come in contact with the neighbouring communities in terms of diverse social – cultural and economic relationships and reacted to them variously. Living in physically high altitude rugged areas, the Jaunsaris and the Gujjars of the western Himalaya and the Noctes of the eastern Himalaya established different levels of contact with their immediate and distant neighbours. The tribes of India have a long tradition of 'adoption' and 'conversion' to major religious faiths such as Vaishnavism (Nocte, Riangs), Tibetan Buddhism (Lepchas, Mans), the Bhagat cult (Kokna, Warlis) and Christianity.

In the first case study in this volume, Austin Justin, who is himself an indigenous Nicobarese anthropologist, discusses traditional authority pattern (chieftainship), culture change and hybridization process as also emerging inequality among people of different Nicobar Islands. While focusing on the inhabitants of Car Nicobar Island, new developments taking place in central and southern Nicobar Islands are also discussed. Fieldworks were conducted by author in phases during 1992–93 but afterwards he updated the data for this article by obtaining additional data in 2006. Justin studied mainly in the Seti and Sapëha or Lapati and Kakana villages. The Nicobar Archipelago is inhabited by two distinct indigenous tribes, Nicobarese and Shompen, belonging to the Mongoloid ethnic ancestry. Author considers the Shompen as 'shy' people who lead a nomadic life of forager-hunter and food-gatherer. The Shompen maintain a symbiotic relationship with the Nicobarese of Great Nicobar Island. It may be stated that each Nicobarese tribe inhabiting an island possesses a native name, which shows territorial affiliation. The Nicobarese are mainly horticulturists and herders and pursue other economic pursuits like hunting and fishing. The tuhçts, lineages, have large assets in Car Nicobar. Access to a tuhçt's property is generally open to all but under the direction of the tuhçt Chief. All Nicobarese live in settled villages tending herds of domestic pigs, raising coconut plantations, areca nut (betel nut) and are engaged in other horticultural activities while a sizeable number work in various government and private organizations. Author has used for the convenience sake terms 'Car Nicobarese', 'Central Nicobarese' and 'Southern Nicobarese' for the inhabitants of various islands. The inter-island relations were not very congenial and harmonious, though some economic exchanges occurred and the Chowrayites (native of Chowra) depended on exchange under the barter system. New administrative measures and spread of Christianity led to some changes in the inter-island relations. Despite spread of Christianity, the indigenous tribal religious beliefs and practices are pursued and thus the native shaman, witch doctors, and sorcerers are often engaged to perform rituals. The inter-island social stratification is prominently present in Nicobar Island and it is gradually solidifying the Car Nicobarese who now play a dominant role as agents of change. They have 'a civilizing influence' on the central and southern Nicobarese, as Justin puts it. Prior to the advent of Christianity, the Nicobar islanders according to the author were 'animists'. The Nicobarese of different islands speak different dialects, though most of them can understand and converse in the Car Nicobarese language, which has now become the lingua franca of all the Nicobarese. The Car Nicobarese were the first to modernize themselves by adopting formal education through the Raman script. The Nicobarese tuhçt (maximal lineage) plays a crucial role in society. Certain intra-lineage stratification manifests itself in terms of distribution of economic resources, allotment of duties and specific duties of the head that manages and controls both administrative and economic resources of the tuhçt (lineage) at the village level. All families are bound by norms of lineage principle, and rules of customary law are respected. Head of lineage, knoen-makuo tuhct or maaooto is regarded in high esteem as distinct privileges are accorded to his status. The position of chieftain or senior lineage head is hereditary. After the death of a chief, the next chief is selected from the same lineage, but often knowledgeable persons are not available so a chief from other lineage is accepted. The institution of chieftainship survives at various levels. Island administration is managed by the Island Council in association with village councils. The chief is the head of the Island Council, and he is assisted by vice chief captain and deputy vice chief captain. They do not enjoy special rights, but they play crucial roles in the power structure.

In the next chapter, some aspects of changing economic relations and inequality among the matrilineal Khasi tribe are described by Bibhash Dhar. He provides a broad perspective of the tribe which still boasts of a vibrant chieftainship, supported by elders. In order to access the present rural scene, he conducted a brief study in a Khynriam Khasi village called Mawpat, not far from Shillong. In village Mawpat, the Khasis are mostly cultivators; however, many of them do not have their own land. The landless individuals have taken plots of farmland on lease from rich families. Thus, there is distinct existence of a category of landless people. There are three types of agricultural lands in village, the clan land, individual land and leasehold lands. Analysis of data suggests that there is increase in land possession from community to individual holdings, which is an indicator of economic change. At present the family units have become smaller and individual-oriented. Earlier, the families never participated in any of the tribal durbar meetings but at present they are free to take part in it. In the olden days, the Khasi marriages took place through courtship and also by arrangements. At present, most of the marriages at Mowpat are courtship marriages. Slowly, the parental consent for marriage is losing importance. Divorce rate has considerably increased. The Khasis are of Mon Khmer origin. Tribes of northeast in general and the Khasis in particular have the unique distinction of retaining customary laws and traditional institutions. Dorbar Shnong, the grass-roots administrative unit in a Khasi village/locality, and the District Council assume the rank of the Statutory Panchayati Raj. The Khasi chieftainship survives. However, the Syiems (chieftains) and Syiem Raij (chieftains over Raij lands) as also Ri Raij (Raij land or community-owned land) are converting into Ri Kynti (land owned by individuals). Once a plot becomes Ri Kynti it is easy to sell it off to anyone who has money. Poor villagers are thus increasingly discriminated and exploited by the richer sections. Poverty and relative deprivation have given rise to unrest and violence. Meghalaya state witnessed the growth of two militant tribal groups – Hynniewtrep National Liberation Council (HNLC) and the Achik National Volunteer Council (ANVC). The Khasi Hills Autonomous District Council (KHADC) came into existence in 1952 as per provision of the Sixth Schedule. ADC is empowered to make laws of land, management of forests (except reserved forests), regulation of trade, appointment of traditional chiefs and headmen, inheritance of property, marriage, divorce, social customs, education, markets, taxation, lease for extraction of minerals, etc.

The contemporary economic status of the Lalung tribe in multi-ethnic rural set-up of Assam plains is studied by Ganesh Chandra Ojha. For comparative purpose he has chosen two villages where the Lalung, a former matrilineal tribe, is surviving in the midst of caste groups and competing in economic sphere. A section of rich Lalungs has emerged but majority of Lalungs are landless villagers. He has studied the aspects of landlessness and economic deprivation among them. There are some Lalung families who have prospered through occupational innovation.

The contemporary Lalungs are divided into three sections. The hills Lalungs, called Hazowali, still retain the matrilineal social structure. The Lalungs living in the foothills are called Daliwali. This section has some elements of traditional matriliny. Those who are living in the plains of Assam are called Tholowali. The Tholowali Lalungs have totally changed their way of living – culturally, socially and economically. They have adopted norms of patrilineal descent and are engaged in settled wet cultivation, having abandoned the slash-and-burn (Jhum) cultivation. Changes are also noticed in the agricultural implements. The Tholowali Lalungs use nangal (plough), jawali (harrow), spade, fal, moi, jotiari, jabaka, kanchi, biriya, etc., whereas the Lalungs engaged in Jhum cultivation mainly use digging stick and dao. The Lalung tribe living in the plains has adopted the elements of Vaishnav-Hinduism, but many traditional tribal rituals are still performed. The hills Lalungs worship tribal deities. There are still to be found the tribal priests such as Laro, Deori and Changmoji. The Vaishnav Lalungs abstain from drinking Zu (rice beer) or eating pork. They observe several Hindu ceremonies in their Namghar (prayer house). Ganesh Ojha has studied two Lalung villages, Jarabari and Bormanipur, the former being the revenue village where three types of tenancy of land holding operates. The Lalungs have now become conscious about the value of land and associated economic prosperity. To maximize the yield thus they increasingly employ labourers (both Lalungs and non-Lalungs like Koch, Nath, Hira). Three types of labour employment are – daily, yearly and seasonal. There are women labourers too. The working group of young girls (a group of six girls) called Hadarikhel takes up agricultural works like sowing, harvesting, etc. Following the tribal ethos, cooperation in terms of free labour is provided by kinsmen during agricultural operations. The land owner offers them Zu (rice beer) and chicken. The use of fertilizers and pesticides has helped the Lalungs in raising food production and checking diseases. The Lalung farmers are getting loan from various agencies like district agricultural department, block office, co-operative societies including assistance for procuring good hybrid seeds which are high yielding and disease resistant.

The Lalung society is traditionally a stratified society. In the past, the tribe witnessed state formation. The current village polity has the Gaonbura (headman) assisted by Barika. Deori is the tribal priest who conducts worship at the, sacred centre. An age-set system, which is common among the Nagas (Das, 1993, 2009a), is observable in Lalung tribe. In the past, the plains Laungs followed the path of Sanskritization and adopted some Hindu norms but tribal religious practices were not given up. The three geographical segments of the Lalungs are culturally dissimilar but there is no restriction to take food and water from each other. Marital relations are often established too. The Hinduized Lalungs consider themselves superior from the ritual angle mainly. They have given up drinking Zu (rice beer), and consumption of pork and fowl. The Lalungs of village Bormanipur are prosperous agriculturists, who grow two types of paddy, Ahu and Sali. The Lalungs here have adopted mechanized farming and some families use tractors for ploughing. These economic innovations have created a class of rich Lalungs.

Chieftainship is an important feature of many tribes in northeast India. Most of these chiefs represent their privileged clans and they continue to remain part of the village administration, which is based on kinship/clanship norms and customary laws. Rajendra Athparia has studied the institution of chieftainship among the Noctes of Tirap district in Arunachal Pradesh. Despite introduction of the democratic Statutory Panchayats in villages the chiefs are given privileged status. Rajendra Athparia has studied the current status of the chiefs in the Nocte villages as also the impact of new developments on the tribespeople including the influence of Hinduism/Vaishnavism among them. The village studied is called Soha. Fieldworks were conducted during late 1990s and in 2002 in same areas. The revisits helped update the village data. The boundaries of villages are well defined by streams and hillocks. Each village has a number of territorial sub-divisions, called Chum or Raden. Each Chum has its own Morung or bachelor's dormitory where the youths of the Chum sleep at night. Morung institution is declining in many areas. In Lazu village, there are 24 Morungs. Historically the village of Lazu is an important centre of pottery making. Tattooing was done here in the past. Till 1983–84, tattooing of women was very common in Lazu village. It was stopped by the All Lazu Youth Association. The Nocte chieftainship is not as strong as the chieftaincy among the Wanchos of Tirap and Nagas such as Konyak. The Nocte chief and his descendants form a separate class called Lowangjat (chief is known as Lowang). The commoners are called Sanajat. The Lowangjat are the ruling class who, in the past, received some 'free services' from the Sanajat. In the Lazu area, the commoner class Pansajat, provides the ritual specialists. These classes consist of a number of clans and lineages. In Lazu area, clan-cluster of Kepi provides the chief and the other cluster Tangmo includes the commoner's clan. The chief has the privilege of taking the second wife from the commoner's clan. This is the practice among the Konyak Nagas. The social stratification is clear cut in the Nocte tribe on account of the chieftainship. The ancestors and descendents of the chief family constitute a distinct continuity which defines the supremacy of the Chiefly class, whose members enjoy special statuses and privileges. This social stratification of the tribe is well developed which survives through adhering to traditional norms in respect of marriage and social behaviour. In the contemporary political life of the village the chief continues to play an important role in the council. At present the Lazu Village Council consists of seven members besides the chief who is the ex-officio head. The Noctes from villages like Soha and Namsang, adjacent to the plains of Assam, had historically maintained trade and other economic linkages for procuring commodities like salt, match boxes, iron tools, bell metal dishes, bowls, beads and bangles. The Noctes often visited Brahmaputra Valley, where the Vaishnavism has been widespread. One Nocte chief Khunbao (Lotha Khunbao) was the first to adopt Vaishnavism. Gradually many Noctes adopted the Hindu cult but the Vaishnavism of the tribespeople is of rudimentary form. The Vaishnavite Nocte villages have Namghars (prayer hall) that serve as place of congregational worship. Modern education was introduced among the

Noctes after 1947, unlike other hills areas where Christian missionaries had opened schools and propagated Christianity right from colonial era. The villages near urban centres are in a more advantageous position in terms of availing the facilities of education. The Noctes continue with the traditional method of jhum cultivation but they have also adopted permanent cultivation along with new tools and technology. More and more hills areas are now being brought under modern terrace cultivation, mainly since 1992–93. The principle objective of the agriculture department is to increase food production to solve the problem of scarcity. The Noctes from many villages have joined in road construction programmes and earned good wages. Chieftainship, chiefs, royal clans and many of the privileges of the chiefs have survived and they continue to govern in some villages with help of village elders. Such village councils headed by chiefs coexist with modern wider administrative mechanisms. The village elders indeed are important in the sphere of social control throughout the Northeast hills areas (Das 1993) even though advocates of Zomia Model regard the hills people otherwise.

Reang or Riang of Tripura call themselves as Bru. They are also found in Assam, Mizoram, Manipur and Bangladesh. They speak the Reang dialect locally referred to as Kau Bru/Kak Borok. In the past, they mostly practised the Huk or Jhum cultivation like most other Tripuri tribes. However today, they have adopted modern agricultural practices. Goutam Kumar Bera in his article in this book discusses the issues of 'Primitive' economy, politicization process and emerging stratification pattern among the Riangs of Tripura. Tripura had a tribal state in the past where Riangs were employed by the kings as army personnel. Bera has gathered data from two villages, namely, Krishnamanipara and Maudabari, where bulk of the Riangs are poor tribespeople depending primarily on shifting cultivation. The Riangs were declared as a 'primitive tribe'. Hence, several developmental schemes were launched for them. While in village Krishnamanipara, the Riangs and the Tripuri tribespeople pursue shifting cultivation; in second village called Maudabari, the Riangs practice both jhum and kheto (settled cultivation), as they have some lunga (valley) land. The Riangs call themselves Bru, which means 'man'. Many Riangs continue to speak Kok Borok language, which has a script. After a prolonged agitation Tripura state ultimately introduced Kok Borok language as the medium of instruction at the primary school stage. The government has imposed the Bangla script while the Tripura Upajati Juba Samity (TUJS), TNV and the Tribal National Conference have opted in favour of the Roman script. The Riangs, whose economy depended on food-gathering, hill-food-production, domestication of animals, basketry and mat-weaving, have been among the poorest of the tribes of the state. Our study shows that bulk of these tribespeople remain in apt poverty and excluded from the mainstream. Though officially the village chieftainship was abolished in 1955 after the enactment of Acquisition of Chiefs Rights Act 1954, yet in practice the chief of a village is recognized and respected among the Riangs, and such a chief still heads the assembly of elders (Kami fang-Kerpang). It is mainly since 1962 that the tribal assemblies have been replaced by a statutory council at village level, a democratic institution formed through adult franchise, following the principle of the Panchayati Raj. After prolonged agitation, ultimately the Autonomous

District Council (ADC) was formed in 1985 under the Sixth Schedule of the Indian Constitution. ADC has autonomy in all matters of tribal development and administration. Majority of Riangs are followers of tribal religion, though the elements of Hinduism have been assimilated. The Riang religious order includes the fertility cult, magic, totemic beliefs and witchcraft. The Riangs believe in fala (soul) and in its existence. The Rehabilitation scheme was launched in 1983, to attract the poorest section among the Riang 'primitive tribe' living within the forest areas of the state, by diverting the Riangs from jhum cultivation and to resettle them by providing facilities close to forest areas. But, only a small number of such families could be brought under the scheme ultimately.

Sarit Kumar Chaudhury has studied the issues of landlessness, inter-ethnic competition and increasing deprivation among the Manns of West Garo Hills, Meghalaya. Chaudhury conducted fieldwork in two villages, namely, Daldela and Haldibari. Originally of Burmese origin, the Manns came to Assam as soldiers and after the war took shelter in Lushai, Naga and Garo Hills. Present Manns of Meghalaya are the descendants of those soldiers. Having settled there, they took their wives from neighbouring Rabha, Koch, Garo, Hajong, and Kachari tribes. Being Buddhist the Manns came to interact with Buddhist tribes of upper Assam and Arunachal Pradesh. Buddhist monks also came to Buddha Vihar of Haldibari area to preach Buddhism among the Manns. Due to extensive intermixture with the neighbouring communities the Manns have lost their original Burmese language and now they speak a broken form of Assamese and use Assamese script. They live in Haldibari, Sankarpar villages which are multi-ethnic villages, with Mann, Koch and Garo inhabitants. The Manns are marginal landholders in these villages and in Daldela out of 31 families 29 are engaged in agriculture. Two families are artisans. The Manns are generally poor and 8 families who are small and medium size landholders are engaged in service and 4 landless families are engaged in business. In fact in both the villages the majority of the Manns are landless agricultural/day labourers. Only a few among them are service holders. Comparatively the males are more literates than the females. Education has very little impact on the Manns of Meghalaya. The Manns had a close economic interaction with the Bengali Muslims through Rajabala weekly market in that area. The Manns used to sell their surplus produce to the Muslims at Rajabala, and take cash loans from Muslims in the past. Those who were unable to pay the loan amount transferred their cultivable land to Muslims. During that time transfer of tribal land to non-tribal was not prohibited. In Haldibari most of the lands were transferred to the Muslims of Rajabala and Silkata. Almost similar incidents happened to the people of Deldela village. Economic deficit and resultant land abandonment thus led to deprivation and poverty among the Manns.

The Lepchas of Sikkim present one of the worst examples of discrimination and exclusion on account of their dislodgement in their own homeland, through gradual encroachments, and ultimate domination by outsiders. Lepchas, the indigenous people of Sikkim–Darjeeling region encountered two invasions by two different people, at first by the Bhutias and then by the Nepalis, a larger ethnic conglomeration. At the end the indigenous Lepchas found themselves excluded and pushed to margin. Jyotirmoy Chakraborty has discussed the persistent economic dispossession of the Lepchas in two locations of Sikkim and Darjeeling, in the backdrop of their historicity and indigeneity. He concentrates more on the Lepchas of Sikkim, but he also explains the changing economic scenarios of the two locations and the reactions of the Lepchas thereby. Jyotirmoy Chakraborty argues that the current Nepali numerical dominance in Sikkim has led to linguistic and cultural squeezing of native language and culture. He has studied the changing social-economic scenarios in terms of the historical transformation of the state and gradual immigration of Tibetan-Bhutias and the Nepalis. The Nepalis came to Sikkim by the middle of the eighteenth century. The Lepchas of Sikkim refer to themselves as Rong. While they prevailed in the entire zone in the past, today their main concentration is in the north-central zone, especially in the Dzongu valley. The Nepalis consist of several Hindu castes and Mongoloid tribes. Nowadays the Nepalis are the numerically dominant population of Sikkim and in the political sphere they play the most dominant role today. The economy of the Lepchas in Sikkim as also in Darjeeling (in two villages called Singhik and Nagasay) is primarily based on agriculture. Wet plough cultivation in the terrace is very common in both the areas. The Lepchas themselves cultivate their land. In Sikkim, the Lepchas possess comparatively larger portions of agricultural land and they depend on the Nepali labourers. Sharecropping is very popular in Sikkim, locally called adheya. Kuth is another type of tenancy available in Sikkim. History has it that the hard-working Nepalis came to occupy gradually more and more lands and changed huge mountain tracts into terraces and introduced wet–terrace plough cultivation in Sikkim. Namgyal dynasty followed the theocratic model of Tibet and the lamas instigated a process of Tibetization. They bifurcated the Lepchas into two segments, the aristocrats and the commoners and converted the Lepchas into Buddhists. The Lepchas embraced Buddhism, which was propagated under the royal patronage. However, the Lepchas have retained their mun-bongthing tradition even after their conversion. Thus, we find the co-existence of the two religious traditions like the indigenous mun-bongthing tradition and a comparatively higher faith like the Lamaism of Tibet. The mane (prayer wheel) of the Bhutias, the bamfok (special knife) of the Lepchas and the kukri of the Nepalis – all exist in Sikkim. The Lepchas live with the Bhutias and the Nepali caste groups in rural areas of both locations. Hence, relative statuses are maintained between them. The Nepali Brahmins and the Chhetris are at the top of the social hierarchy, the Pradhans, Mangars, Gurungs, Limbus and Rais belong to the middle order. The Kamis (metal worker), Damais (tailor) and Sarkis (leather worker) are treated as 'lower' groups. Generally, Lepchas and the Bhutias are free from caste-based stratification but due to long and continuous association with the Nepali and the Hindu social system, they consider themselves higher than the Hindu Nepali 'low castes'. Marriage relations among the Lepchas, Bhutais, Sherpas and Nepali Hindu upper and middle castes are allowed and they frequently take place.

Some scholars have argued that calling Himalayan pastoral communities as 'tribes' is incorrect as they have since long absorbed caste norms and are regarded as a part of caste system of the region. The Bhotia of Uttarakhand located in central Himalaya – region is one such example, that Mukul Hazra has studied to ascertain the level and character of stratification and social change. The Bhotia pastoralist economy had traditionally depended on trade with Tibet, woolen handicrafts and terraced cultivation. The Bhotias in Uttarakhand are mainly found in the Garhwal and Kumaon Divisions. In lower valleys they are called Tolcha and those living in the upper valleys close to snowbound Indo-Tibet border district of Chamoli are called Marchha. The Bhotias were declared the Scheduled Tribe in view of their precarious economic condition following the seizer of Indo-Tibetan border trade. This helped them to reorient their economy and obtain new political status too. Scheduled tribal status also provided with the opportunity to get their children better education. There are thus many Bhotia families who have members engaged in government services. Indeed, wealth and political power now determine the higher status, but in the past ritual status was important. Among the Bhotias there are groups such as Tolchas, Marchhas and Jaads. The Tolchas claim the highest rank followed by Marchhas and Jaads. Among the three, the Jaads are considered to be the lowest in social position. Other Bhotias avoid having marital or commensal relations with them. The Jaads follow Lamaistic Buddhism whereas the Tolchas and Marchhas are Hindus. But, all the three groups now claim to be 'Rajputs'. In fact, it was the rich Bhotia families who adopted Hindu norms and declared themselves as 'Rajput'. This label of 'Rajput' was, however, not recognized by the local Hindu Rajputs of the area.

Stratification among Bhotias nowadays depends mainly on economic prosperity and literacy. Those having better economic resources and better education are considered higher in social strata. Serving to these Bhotias are the artisans called as Shilpkars. Thus, in local stratification order we have top two sections of Bhotias (Rajputs as they claim) and the Shilpkars. Four categories of Shilpkars were found in the village such as Lohars, Darji/Auji, Koli and Dholi. Of these four groups, Lohar, Darji and Dholi were found in all the villages. The Shilpkars are not allowed by the Bhotias to enter their houses. The Shilpkars also maintain certain stratification among themselves. Thus, the Lohars claim the highest status among the Shilpkars, followed by the Darji and the Dholis occupy the bottom rung. Among the Dholis, there are two groups the Badi and the Hurkiyas. The Badis are village musicians. The Hurkiyas play on Hurk, a sort of drum. According to another study, the Bhotias in Kumaon region mostly live in and around Dharchula area of Pithoragarh region, and have a distinct identity. Here the tribe of Bhotia is derived from the 'Shauka' tribe and is referred to as 'Shauka'. The other two tribes of Bhotias (Jadhs and Marchhas/Tolchas) have been living mostly in the Garhwal region of Himalayas. The Jadhs are mostly in Uttarkashi region and the Marchhas (traders) and Tolchas (farmers) belong to Chamoli region. The Shaukas follow their own version of Hindu-Buddhist religious traditions and mostly rely on Lamas to conduct their ceremonies and rituals. Bhotias also have elements of the caste system as prevalent among the Kumaoni Hindus (www. kumaoni.org). The Kinnaura tribe is unique in the sense that within this tribe, groups have their caste-like identities like clean and unclean castes, following the norms of pollution and purity. The tribe is also divided into the Hindu and Buddhist sections, though the native religious customs survive.

Pranab Jyoti De has studied the unique tribe-caste cluster, status ranking and social exclusion among the Kinnaura tribespeople in the frontier villages of Himachal Pradesh. The indigenous Kinnaura live in rugged and mountainous terrain of north-eastern border district of Himachal Pradesh. The Kinnauras are classified as a Scheduled Tribe category in the entire region of Kinnaur. Some segments have undergone cultural mobilization through contact with Hindu caste people and adopted the caste appellations such as Rajput etcetera. The Kinnaura consists of five endogamous communities having variant social status as well as different traditional callings and religion. The Kinnauras are divided into two broad categories, namely, the Khosia (Kanet-Rajput) and the Beru. Within the Beru, we find Domang, Chamang and Chanala castes. The Domang category includes Lohar (blacksmiths) and Badhi (carpenters). The Chamang includes the Koli who are weavers. The Chanala includes the Nagalu who are traditionally the basket-makers. About six villages were selected which are located in varying altitudes and are variously affected by modernization. These are Khowangi, Telingi, Kothi, Nigani, Wini and Sungra. In these villages, the tribespeople are found living with other communities. The Rajput Kinnauras form the largest segment followed by the Koli, Badhi and Lohar. Kinnaura Kanets are mostly agriculturists, horticulturists, orchard growers and service-holders. The Nepalis are identified as the Gorkha. The Kinnaura 'tribe' shows unique social formations, which are affected by the factors of terrain, ecology, ethnicity, language, religion, social mobility and stratification. One section of the tribe in historical course acquired the Rajput status and came to be disassociated from native status. What is remarkable is that the growth of a so-called 'clean caste' (the Rajput) originally grew from the tribal stratum. Likewise, some other functional segments gradually acquired the Hindu artisan group identity such as Lohar, Badhi, Koli and Nagaluare. These diverse factors of the social mobility, religious changes and inter-segment hierarchy based on religious considerations have posed a problem in terms of perceiving the tribal integration. The Kinnaura tribal formation defies the very concept of the tribe.

The Gujjar tribespeople have a rich folk tradition of the nomadic pastoral social formation and migration. Being semi-nomadic people they used to migrate to upper parts of Himalayas along with their cattle during the summer season and returned to the plains with the onset of chilly winters. The Gujjars living in Himachal Pradesh are focus of the study conducted by R. Haider. He has chosen to discuss the themes of ritual hierarchy, class formation and social exclusion to situate the predicaments of the contemporary Gujjars, who are learning to settle down in the multi-caste milieu. In addition to village Sahu of Chamba district, additional data are collected from the Bamta village of Bilaspur district by Haider. The Gujjars are distributed over different sub-cultural regions mainly in Bilaspur, Mandi, Chambe and Sirmaur districts of Himachal Pradesh. The Gujjar tribespeople are a poor tribe and considerably excluded from the mainstream, even in villages where they have settled down almost permanently. In such settled locations the economy of these people is dependent on labour works, limited agriculture, service and business to some extent mainly through selling milk and milk products, mutton and woollen products. The Gujjars were variously influenced by cultural beliefs of the Hindus and Muslims. Some states such as Himachal have accorded the status of Scheduled Tribe to the Gujjars, but in many other parts of India such recognition is not accorded. The Gujjar village, Sahu is situated in a hilly terrain. Out of 71 households in the village, the Gujjars (Hindu section) have twenty families, besides four Muslim Gujjar families. Among the dominant Hindu castes are the Brahmin, Rajput, Jat, and several artisan castes. The Rajputs occupy the higher rank in the village on account of their prosperous agricultural occupation. Next come the Jats, ranked below the Rajputs. The castes that stand below the Jats are Mahajan, Jeer/Jheer, Sippi, Arya. The Jeer and Sippi stand below the Mahajan. The lower middle group that consists of Jheer, Sippi, Nai, Dhobi and Kumhar stand below the Jat, Mahajan and Arya. The Dhobi stands below the Nai in the village hierarchy because of his occupation of washing the clothes of the higher communities. At the lower level are included scheduled castes and scheduled tribes such as Hindu and Muslim Gujjar, Gaddi and Mochi. The Gujjars are divided into various clan groups such as Paswan, Khatana, Chauhan, Bainaya, Finda, Gorsi, Kalas and Kasana. The Gujjars take up labour work during the harvest of crop. Ritually they are considered 'impure' and they are thus told to maintain a distance in rural setup. Poverty and social exclusion define their status. The Hindu Gujjars are fast adapting to the settled life and they are learning the technique of agriculture, in order to make agriculture their main occupation. Among them there are only seven families who are still continuing their traditional occupation of pastoralism. The tribal council, Gujjar Biradari, is still active and the Hindu and Muslim Gujjars obey the regulations of the Biradari. It is headed by an elderly person called Numberdar. The Government has introduced the statutory Panchayats since 1956. The Panchayat acts as an executive committee and is headed by the Sarpanch.

The Gujjar are divided into the Hindu and Muslim sections, but they have many common religious beliefs. Both sections continue to venerate many tribal deities. It is observed that both categories of Gujjars believe in hell and heaven. The Gujjars are very liberal and broad minded in their attitude towards religion and traditional deities which are commonly revered by them. At the same time the Hindu Gujjars hold Muslim saints in great reverence and worship Muslim pirs and saints. The Gujjars of Sahu village are not able to provide education to their children on account of the remoteness of the village from the main town of Chamba. The inhospitable terrain further aggravates the situation. The second reason is the poor infrastructure in the region. Owing to these reasons, teachers are unwilling to come to this place as they find it difficult to maintain a decent life. After second or third standard (classes) the dropout rate is very high. This is because children have to go to the field or jungle along with their parents and help them in their work. Socially and economically the communities of village Sahu belong to three classes, upper, middle and lower. The Gujjar, Mochi, Gaddi and Muslims belong to lower classes. Even though the Gujjars in present era have been facilitated with special economic packages and they have been granted lands and are encouraged to adopt agriculture to settle down permanently, yet the Gujjars have found it difficult to adjust in the caste dominated village. The Gujjars in the village are variously subjected to several types of discrimination and social exclusion.

The Mech belong to Bodo-Kachari group of the larger Mongoloid Bodo tribe. They speak the Tibeto-Burman language. They live mostly in Assam and Dooars region of North Bengal. Krishna Mandal has studied changing village economy, religious conversion and social exclusion experienced in the two villages of Jalpaiguri district, close to the western Dooars in North Bengal, by the Mech-Bodos. Villages like Madhya Nararthali and Nararthali are specially described in the present study. The villages are inhabited by Mech people mostly though the Rajbanshi, Rabha, and Oraon tribes are their neighbours. There are some Hindu castes and Muslim families too. In fact, the area has witnessed the entry of the Bangladeshis who live in villages – Madhya Nararthali and Nararthali. They are expert in agricultural operations and the Mech people take the help of Bangladeshi labourers for better cultivation. The majority of the Mechs have adopted Hinduism and some of them have converted to Christianity but the clan groupings remain undisturbed. In the past, the statuses of different clans were hierarchically arranged wherein the top positions were enjoyed by the Mochari, Karji, Champramary and Narginary. The Hindu Mechs are regarded as a part of the caste system and are given lower rank. In the two villages, jajmani system like economic relationship existed between the Mech and potters (Kumar), brass worker, weaver, etc. The Mech also interacted with the Tantis and Jolhas from distant villages on the weekly market days. There are some cases of inter-community marriages reported between Hindu Mech and Rajbanshi, and the Nepalis. Among the Mechs certain hierarchy exists in terms of religious observances. Difference is maintained between those who offer sacrifice and others who do not offer sacrifices. The latter are followers of Ramakrishna Paramhansa. In village Madhya Nararthali among the Hindu Mech landowners 14 adhiars (burgadar or bhagchasis) were found engaged. All the adhiars hailed from the Mech community only. The Jotedar (landowner) leases out a part of his land to the Adhiar with required seeds and manure for cultivation, and in exchange the Adhiar gives back to the landowner 52 per cent of that produce. If the landowner does not give seed, manure, etc., the share comes to a ratio of 40:60. The Mech people engage labourers from their own tribe as also from Oraon, Rabha, Rajbanshi, and the Muslim Bangladeshi settlers.

Living in multi-caste village and through prolonged social and economic interactions, the Mahalis of Medinipur district of West Bengal had gradually adopted the cultural elements of Hindu castes and started worshipping Hindu deities by employing Brahmin priests. In his article S. Chanda has studied the common absorption process of the tribespeople in the rural caste system and also the issues of economic deprivation and social exclusion. Chanda has studied the Mahalis, who are artisans and mainly the basket makers/bamboo workers and partly agriculturists. The Mahalis of Medinipur district of West Bengal have a strong Odia heritage. Chanda says that in the past they spoke Odia and even today many among them speak Odia along with Bengali, and the latter is the official language of the state. Odia is also one of the official languages (minority) of Bengal now. At home however, the Mahalis of Medinipur speak in

Mahali language which they describe as 'Thare', which is more or less similar to the Santali language. Since the tribal Mahali students are taught in state language using the Bangla script, the survival of tribal language in future remains threatened. The Mahalis are poor artisans with very small amount of land which is inadequate for their subsistence. Thus, most families are forced to stick to their original vocation. Even those who have some land find it difficult to carry out agriculture as the capital needed and also the knowledge (technology) to produce the paddy are lacking among them. Thus, the majority of the Mahalis resort to labour works. A labourer is called majdoor and there are labourers such as khot majdoor (they get two meals and tiffin every day) and contract majdoor (working at a fixed rate for a specified period). Chanda has studied the Mahalis in two villages, where the communities are economically divided into poor agricultural labourers, poor cultivators, middle rank cultivators, high ranking rich cultivators and lastly the white-collar employees. The Mahalis of both the villages belong to the stratum of the poor cultivator as also agricultural labourers. Poor Mahalis engaged in basketry partly also belong to this stratum. The poor Mahalis lived in small thatched huts, having a rectangular ground plan, the four walls of which are constructed with bamboo splinters and poles placed vertically. Most of the huts consisted of one room each. Further, the settlement of the Mahalis is physically segregated in the fringe of the village territory. Till recently there were certain restrictions imposed on the Mahalis regarding use of certain facilities of the village including water sources. The Mahalis were placed at par with the 'low castes', and thus they were subjected to the 'ritual exclusion'. It seems the Mahalis were highly influenced by the Santals in the past. As a result out of the thirteen Mahali clans, ten clan names are identical with clan names of the Santal. The Mahalis follow an animist religion and they have tribal religious specialists and also shaman-diviners, witch doctors such as Ojhas and Gunnis who are able to exorcise these spirits and ghosts. Some deities are known as Bongas. Naeke is a village priest who performs all religious performances; Paranik assists the village priest. It shows that living in Hindu caste village, the Mahalis have not abandoned their traditional religious practices, though they have been Hinduized to some extent. The Mahalis live in Changoal and Sarisa villages with Brahmin, Kayastha, Sadgope, Tanti, Napit, Kamar, Dhopa, Hari, Dom, Bagdi, Santal, Munda, Mahali, and Kaibarttas. Living in a multi-caste village for a long time the Mahalis have come to realize that the power and prestige are related to economic prosperity, derived through land ownership, education, social honour, money lending, white-collar jobs, panchayat membership, income and style of life. The Mahali interaction with Hindu landlords is still guided by norms of caste system, as Mahalis are treated as a lower caste. Village relations are now secular in nature such as landowner-farmer, master-servant and the creditor-debtor. The Mahalis now do not bother about any mobility in ritual sphere; rather many among them have opted to gain economic political power. Economic aspirations and innovations have led to rise of some rich Mahali families, but since majority are poor in caste milieu the rise of some received little leverage over village social political space. Thus, living under the shadow of rich peasants and Hindu landlords they find themselves socially excluded.

The Santals identify themselves as Hor. Since the Santals are a highly dispersed tribe, spread in the whole of eastern-central India (with significant presence in neighbouring countries), undertaking any generalization about them will be illusory. Kanchan Mukhopadhyay has studied the Santals living in village Datarampur of Bankura district (West Bengal) in order to understand the dimensions of economic change among them. The village has many castes and two large communities, the Santal and Mahato, who occupy different patterns of settlement (the Santal occupied a linear settlement pattern and the Mahatos a dispersed pattern). Kanchan found the Santals divided into those pursuing traditional religious faith and those following Christianity. Some hierarchy is maintained between Santal patrilineal clans, called as paris. The Hansda clansmen belong to the top, and the Murmu clan enjoys the second place. The Marandi are considered to be wealthy, and Soren are the traditional 'soldiers'. Tudu are good musicians and the Besra are expert dancers. In their daily life the Santals interact with the caste people, who dominate the local milieu. In the local hierarchy the top rung is occupied by the Brahmins, both the Rarhi and the Utkal. There are some castes in middle position (Benias, Goalas and Sunris). In the next stratum are Telis, Kurmi-Mahatos, Karmakars, and others. Further below are placed the Bagdis, the Bauris, and the Muchis. Even within one strata cluster, castes are not equal and distances are asserted primarily through commensal norms. In this scheme the Santals belong to the lowest rung. The Santals experience segregation in many ways in village domain even though being the Hors they have self-esteem and consider themselves as outside any clustering. They retain much of the tribal characteristics and in their religious and social control sphere the traditional headmen play crucial roles. At the same time they participate in activities of the Statutory Panchayat. In economic sphere, the Santals have shifted from the traditional patterns of collective ownership to individual ownership of land. Certain changes in agricultural technology have taken place. It is observed that they have changed the technology minimally to suit their minimum needs. The Santals undoubtedly attach much value to the land they possess, but they are not clever enough like the 'peasant' castes who ridicule them. Aversion of the Santals towards entrepreneurship is also noted. In cultural sphere, it is observed that they accommodate the Hindu religious beliefs but assert the uniqueness of their own belief system. The traditional religious belief system of the Santals is known as sari dharma. It has its own body of mythologies, benevolent and malevolent deities, ways of worshipping and appeasing them. The naeke is the village priest, who is assisted by the kudam naeke. The other specialists related to their religious belief system are the gurus. They are the narrators of the myths.

In a study of Santals of Shikaripara block of Jharkhand, N.K. Das and Santanu Mitra found the prevalence of the Safa Hor sect among a good number of Santal families. The native Santal or the Bonga Hors follow old Santal religion, though they have internalized and worshipped some deities of Hindu origin as local Bonga. In this part of the state, notion of Diku survives. The Diku Bongas (Hindu deities) are Manasha and Kali. The Sindur, an important icon of a married Hindu woman is used by as many as 57 per cent Safa Hor Santal married women. About 26 per cent Bonga Hor married women were also reported as having used Sindur. Tulsi plant or Tulsi pind is available in 57 per cent Safa Hor houses and 4 per cent Bonga Hor houses. Photos of Hindu deities (including calendars) adorn the walls of 62 per cent Safa Hors and only 7 per cent Bonga Hors. Duriyo is a typical tribal straw used to ward off evil influences of witches and the effects of evil eye. It is common sight in the houses of Safa Hors (76%), Bonga Hors (67%) and even Esai Hors (Christian Santals, 83%). Our quantified data and our own observations convinced us that the Santal religious life is syncretistic wherein tribal and Hindu deities are simultaneously worshipped. Our data further reveal that while rice beer has been abandoned by Safa Hors, still a good number of them (38%) consume it on regular basis. The Hindu funeral rites demand cremation of the dead body but a large number of Safa Hors go for burial. Almost all Safa Hors regularly go to Azamganj for holy dip. Interestingly even 25 per cent Bonga Hors also do so. While Bada Chapudia (Shiva Shrine) is visited by 95 per cent Safa Hors, some 7 per cent Bonga Hors have also done so in order to worship Shiva which is claimed to be a Bonga Hor deity. Thus, even though the Santals are among the most 'traditionalist' among the Adivasis they exhibit a unique example of religious syncretism. At the end we found that the concept of 'Sanskitization' and 'spread in Hinduism' models of Srinivas and 'acculturation' theory failed to grasp the religious universe of the Santals (Das and Mitra, ASI report, 2009; Das, 2003).

The tribes of Jharkhand have been the focus of numerous anthropological and historical analyses. Yet, there are some 'minority tribes' in Jharkhand about whom we know little. The Bedias are one such tribe, who have been subjected to severe maltreatment, discrimination and social exclusion historically. Tilak Bagchi has studied the issues of inequality, poverty, social exclusion and culture change among the Bedias of Jharkhand. The Bedia tribe is divided into two segments, native Bedia and Majhi Bedia, the latter segment being the Hinduized section. They are further divided into several clans. Some scholars regard the Bedias as the twelfth clan of the Santals. There are many similarities between the Santals and Bedias and hence they are regarded as an offshoot of the Santals, which is not acceptable to the Bedias. Tilak Bagchi has studied the Bedias of Hesla village located in Hazaribagh region, where the deep caste-tribe interactions led the Bedias to become a part of the local caste system. About a century ago the search for higher status had prompted a section of tribe to follow path of sanskritization like the neighbouring tribes. Regional Hinduized tribal chieftains also encouraged them to do so and to adopt a new name Majhi. The tribe imbibed many Hindu norms and thereby they were accorded a 'low caste' status. The Bedias are the Chhoto (shana) Kurami according to Pashupati Mahato. Despite being part of the village social structure the Bedias feel segregated and excluded from core social-economic sphere of the village as they belong to a much lower strata. Generally, each Bedia village has a pahan, a tribal priest who hails either from the Bedia or Munda community. Beside pahan, Brahmin pandit also solemnises some rituals. Often both are employed in the same family. The sakha or bhagat is their native medicine man, sorcerer, gunin and witch doctor. His status is however low in the Bedia society. The Vaishnav babaji also performs certain rituals and often gives guru mantra to the Majhi Bedias. The Majhi Bedias became Hinduized by discarding many tribal habits.

However, as in most parts of tribal India where we witness multi-faith coexistence and religious syncretism (Singh, 2003; Das, 2003), the Hindu Bedias did not give up tribal religious traits including belief in supernatural powers. The Bedias in Hazaribagh region pursue agriculture as well as collection of produce from forest for selling, besides limited hunting and fishing. Big land owning households enjoy more power and prestige in the society in comparison to the small and marginal landholders. In the Hesla village, the Bedias who are educated and involved in white-collar jobs, teaching, bank, railway, are treated as elites of Bedia society. The Bedias are generally small landholders and in village Hesla they are either landless or small landholders with less than 0.25 acres of land. In the absence of effective poverty alleviation programmes in the region, the tribespeople have been lured to industrial areas in the vicinity where operations of Eastern Coalfields Limited, India Firebricks and such industries are in full sway. Sanskritization did not result in raising the status of the Majhi Bedias since the 'indigenous' Bedias claimed their own status as superior. In the meantime, secular factors have become crucial in determining the status and stratification. Educated affluent and white-collar job holders and their family members often enjoy higher status and privilege in the village. This emerging middle class is not concerned with ritual identity of the people. They believe in achievements in economic sphere and for this they prefer to follow the secular path. In fact, most of the office bearers of Bedia Bikash Samity, Bedia Samaj Unayan Parishad, Bedia Jati Sudar Samity, Gram Vikash Samity, and Adivasi Harijan Committee have drawn members from the educated or affluent Bedias, belonging to both sections.

Verrier Elwin's book *Religion of an Indian Tribe* (1955) had made the Saora tribespeople famous. The tribal religion of the Saora survives between two sections of the tribe even today. Thakurani mata or Budima is their Kuldevi (chief devi). They place a big stone on the ground on a platform, and worship it as deity Thakurani mata. Sometimes, a wooden beam is also used instead of the stone. The Hinduized Saoras celebrate Holi, Deepavali, Navratri, and Shivaratri. The Lanjia Saoras live in hill slopes and forest belts of Gajapati, Ganjam and Koraput districts. The Suddho Saora live in the plains of Odisha. The Lanjia group is the most backward section of the 'primitive' Saora tribe. In order to prepare this article, D.P. Biswas has conducted fieldworks in both the interior/backward section of the tribe and the advanced section. Biswas has compared the diverse economic pursuits and impact of new development programmes on two sections of the Saora tribespeople of Odisha, living in hills and plains. Lanjia Saora and Suddho Saora exhibit the typical characters of the hills and plains people. The former prefer to remain in isolation but the Suddho Saora broadly tend to imitate the norms of the Odia culture, even though they are unable to compete with the Khandayat, Goala, Pano and Keota castes in social and economic spheres. Habitually, the Lanjia Saoras adhere to shifting-cultivation and occasional hunting and gathering of forest products. However, some families among them have developed terrace fields and ventured to adopt cultivation of cash crops such as cashew nut, banana, lemon and poppy. This provided them with substantial profits. The Saoras in plains pursue settled agriculture. The main crops which are cultivated by the Saoras in their terrace land and shifting lands are paddy, maize or jowar and pulses. The tribal council among the Lanjia Saora is called as Sabha Madala. It is headed by the Gomango, who is a non-religious chief. Among the Suddho Saora the traditional political council is called as Sabha Panch, headed by Behera (mukhia) or Dalbera. Office bearers are Gomango, Behera, Kargi and Naik. Baik or Paik, is a messenger. In the past, the Birinda jurisdiction headed by the tribal 'chief' Gomango settled disputes. But, now the area is witnessing the penetration of democratization through establishment of the Statutory Panchayats. The Panchayat members (ward Panch or Sarpanch or Gram Sabha member) are emerging as more powerful. This process has created a rift to some extent, as the ward members and Panch-members assume formal authority and settle inter-tribe disputes and supervise the economic and political matters. A special economic package is provided to this tribe through Saora Development Agency (SDA) and Lanjia Saora Development Agency (LSDA). The Saoras now get free seeds of paddy, ginger, papaya, cashew nut, banana plant and lemon along with supply of manure to cultivate cash crops in their Bagodajami (for shifting cultivation). A carpet weaving training centre has been established through which the Saora women are given training to make carpets and mats with a stipend per month in addition to the earnings from their agricultural work. Under infrastructural development schemes, establishment of community halls for the community to assemble in a particular village once in a week to bring more awareness in them have been undertaken. Under individual benefit schemes, patta land, bullocks, buffaloes, agricultural implements and related items (free of cost) have been provided to improve their economic condition. Some families have indeed benefited and have become somewhat self-sufficient economically, but in the areas of health, education and political participation they are trouncing.

The Rajuars tribespeople of Mayurbhanj district, Odisha, are a fully Hinduized tribe as per existing literature on the tribe. The Rajuar live in multi-community villages and hence are a part of the rural tribe-caste network involving social and economic relations on regular basis. D.B. Mondal has discussed the changing dimensions of social and economic relations of the tribe as observed in two villages, Kamli and Savrangapur. Through prolonged contacts, the Rajuars have come to adopt certain caste norms. They do not accept food and water mainly from the 'lower' castes like Dhoba, Hadi, Dom, Teli, Patro, and Tanti. They also avoid taking food from tribes such as the Mahali, Kotha and Santal, as also the Musalman. Out of 66 households of the Rajuars in Kamli village, 35 families have land and 31 families are landless. In fact, 83 per cent Rajuar families belong to marginal economic category as they have less than 3 acres land per household. The middle class Rajuars possess on an average 4.74 acres of land and only one family belongs to the higher class with more than 8 acres of land. Mondal found that 54 per cent of the families of Kamli village belong to lower income group. The landless Rajuars are mostly engaged as wage labourers in agricultural fields and the construction sites. Constant poverty and helplessness has led many Rajuar people to migrate to nearby urban areas for better economic pursuits. There are instances where after accumulation of earnings in urban areas, some Rajuars have invested money in the village and procured some land. Thereby they have tried to improve their economic status.

An interesting study is made by Kamal. K. Misra (1991) among the Juang tribespeople of Odisha, in terms of inequality (in an unstratified society).

Tribes of India had variously resisted the British colonization and opposed occasionally the imposition of colonial oppressive taxes. The Bhumia tribespeople under the Gandhian ideology had offered *Satyagraha* in 1939–40 under the leadership of Laxman Naik. They had also a launched movement to oppose the land taxes (Singh, 1994: 166). Indeed, the Bhumia tribespeople are aware of the valiant contribution of their tribe in the past. In his article, R.K. Sinha discusses some aspects of historical development of Adivasi solidarity, social movement and a long drawn process of empowerment involving the Bhumia tribe of Madhya Pradesh, who are also called as Bhuiyan-Baiga. Sinha chose village Burdagar for intensive study, which is a multi-ethnic village. The village is divided by 10 Mahallas (wards) and higher castes are located in the middle of the village, and the houses of Yadav, Chourasia, Lakhera, Rana, Kol, Sahu, and Kumbhar (Potter) are located a little away. The Basor and Kumbhar are segregated on the roadside, since they rear pigs. The central part of the village was owned by the tribespeople originally but they have been pushed to Banjar locality where Bhumia, Chourasia, Kori and Kurmi live. The Bhumias were the original inhabitants followed by the peasant caste Barai or Chourasia who settled here due to favourable land condition for betel cultivation. As forest regions were made restricted areas the deprived and landless tribespeople came to work in fields of this peasant caste. In the regional/village social-ritual hierarchy, the Basor, Chamar, Dumar, Kumbhar and tribespeople are placed at the lowest rank by the villagers.

The original name of the tribe is Bharia; hence they were often called as Bharia-Bhumia. To get rid of their low status position they followed the path of sanskritization and accepted Janeu (the sacred thread) and thus adopted the title Thakur. After Sanskritization, they called themselves as Rajbanshi Gond and also as Raghubanshi Gond, having acquired higher status. However, the exigency to retain status of the Scheduled Tribe and to get reservation benefits they reverted back to their original Bhumia identity. They now have a secular approach towards their status and hence formed a larger Adivasi organization called as 'Bhombanshi Bhumia Samaj' which protects the tribal identity and preserves the indigenous folklore of the people. The Bhumias are divided into two strata such as Uttam-Shreni and Nimana-Shreni. In the former strata only 'pure' Bhumias are included. By pure they mean those Bhumias who never established inter-community marriage alliances. The descendants of those who married the non-Bhumia in their lifetime are ascribed as the Bhumias of Nimana–Shreni or 'lower strata'. Further, the Bhumia clans are also arranged hierarchically. Thus, they regard Rathor, Bade-Rathor, Chote-Rathor, and Mahobia clans to be of higher rank. In the past, the Bhumias grew Lac. They also collected minor forest produce and practised shifting cultivation. The changing forest laws gradually alienated them from forest and they adopted bidi-making as their main occupation. Although some of them possess some patches of cultivable land, but the yield received is very scanty. Some Bhumias have acquired some government lands in the village for cultivation. Again, about five Bhumias of the village have been given about two and half acres of land in Bhoodan which is located in the neighbouring villages. In all there are about 60 acres of cultivable lands in the possession of 40 Bhumia families. The Bhumias are marginal cultivators. There are three Bhumia innovators who have undertaken betel cultivation on their own on the basis of lease and share cropping. They made good profits. Majority of the Bhumias are poor and they work as labourers in the betel cultivation grown by the Chourasia caste of the village and earn their livelihood. Some of them are also employed in some permanent jobs as teachers, clerks and peons in Jabalpur. Around 15 Bhumia families of Burdagar regularly migrate for working in brick-making. It is a seasonal migration of Bhumias in which they migrate after the sowing and the harvesting season, to some nearby villages. The overall condition of the tribe ultimately is distressful, even though they had fought for the liberation of the nation. Tamal Maity has studied some aspects of economic scarcity, emerging Adivasi solidarity and dimension of syncretic religion among the Mawasis of Madhya Pradesh. The Mawasis show the typical character of the central Indian Adivasi people who live in the midst of the Hindu castes in villages and gradually adopt many elements of culture and religion of the dominant communities. Like elsewhere in mixed villages the Mawasis are accorded a low position in village hierarchy. Through prolonged culture contact they have adopted many elements of Hinduism, but they have blended them with tribal religion in syncretic manner. Some sections of the Mawasis used modern methods of agriculture in exposed village and improved their economic status to some extent. The Mawasi case study shows that they too suffer from the common economic disadvantages and deprivation, on account of non-implementation of active developmental programmes in the area. The tribespeople have shown inclination to educate their children. This is indeed a positive indication.

In many of our chapters, we have discussed the rising tide of secularization and politicization of the Indian tribes, who have resolutely discarded the ritual values, which previously characterized the ethos of Indian villages. Debesh Roy has studied the changing tribe-caste stratification and secularization process in an Adivasi dominated multi-community village of Nasik district in Maharashtra, where the Kokan tribe forms a sizeable population. Since the village studied is a composite village, Roy describes the stratification at three levels, intra-tribe, inter-tribe and tribe versus caste. Among the tribes and castes are included Kokna, Mahadev Koli, Teli, Vaishya Vani, Mahar and Marwari. The Kokna and the Mahadev Koli are tribes while the Teli and Vaishya Vani form the OBC category, the Mahars are Scheduled Caste and the Marwaris come in the general category. The Koknas are numerically, largest community in the village followed by the Mahars. There is no particular settlement area for any tribe or caste except the Mahars, who live in the southern most part of the village, in Khalchawadi hamlet. The economy of the village is mainly based on agriculture. Almost all the Koknas are agriculturists by occupation and they are generally owner-cultivators. Unlike other village studies of this project, it is seen that the Kokna tribespeople have a rather comfortable social-economic status within the village set-up, in the midst of Hindu castes. The village has only two tribes, the Kokna and the Mahadev Koli. The Koknas (146 households) and the Mahadev Kolis (15 households) are culturally similar to each other and they have some common Deos (deities) and rituals. Earlier they maintained some cultural distinctions but now religious matters are not important. Actually with the influence of modernization and education many differentiations are gradually diminishing not only between the Kokna and the Mahadev Koli, but at the larger village level. The Koknas of Karanjkhed are primarily agriculturists. Out of total 146 Kokna households in the village, sixteen households are landless. Those with good agricultural lands are popularly known as Shrimonth (rich person). There are many such rich families among the Koknas. The rich Koknas encourage their children to get educated and seek better jobs in cities. Since the village was originally a tribal village it had the tribal council called Panch, headed by Police Patil. It had several functionaries, some from neighbouring communities/tribes. Following this model, the present statutory council, also called Panch, is headed by the Panch (Police Patil) and is recommended by the district collector now. The tribal Police Patil is assisted by a Kotwal or Naik. The post of Kotwal is selected from the Mahadev Koli tribe, who also acts as a messenger for all the villagers. It was reported that the Kokna, Mahadev Koli and the Warli are three major tribes of the region who maintained some political relations. It was also a fact that in their traditional political system, recognized at regional level between these three tribes, the head of the Panch (village council) was the Patil who was always from the Kokna tribe. It was so because of the established sense of superiority of the Kokna over the Mahadev Koli and Warli. On account of the new administrative measures, present post of Police Patil is more powerful than the Patil of the traditional Kokna society. There are also elected members in the village council now. The Sarpanch and eight other elected members of the Gram Panchayat have some special social position in the village. In view of the numerical and economic dominance of the Kokna tribespeople in Karanjkhed village, the post of Police Patil and three other elected members of the Gram Panchayat are all from the Kokna tribe, while the post of the Sarpanch is from the Mahadev Koli, who lives in Sarsale village. In this village one also notices the emergence of Adivasi women empowerment. In Karanjkhed, it is an Adivasi Kokna woman who occupies the post of Police Patil, the most powerful and prestigious status at the village level. There are two Mahadev Koli Adivasi women, who have been elected as executive members of the Karanjkhed Gram Panchayat. In the religious sphere, the status of the tribal priest, Bhagat, is supreme, as he is simultaneously the sacred specialist and also a medicine man. The Bhagat also specialises in worshipping Dongrideo and Wagdeo, the two very important deities among the Koknas. The Bhagat gives medicines. With exposure to urban areas and frequent migrations, and particularly with greater impact of the Hinduism, the relevance of the Bhagat has declined. The richer Koknas of Karanjkhed now employ the local Brahmin priests during marriage and for other religious purposes. However, the tribespeople in this village seem least concerned about the religious observances. Rather they prefer to achieve modern economic statuses, through hard work and by educating the children.

Bhakti movements and sectarian religious reformist movements have been very popular in Adivasi areas of western India. The Warlis of Gujarat have witnessed a long tradition of culture change and sectarian movements, though certain sections among them strictly adhere to the original religious beliefs.

Rajendra Sarkar has studied these issues by conducting a village study, whereby he also observed the emerging processes of economic inequality and social stratification. The Warlis, organized around 144 exogamous kuls (clans), are divided into two segments, Dungris and Talatis. Further, the tribe is also categorized into sectarian and religious divisions. There is also a small section of the Christians called as Is-wale Warlis. The Christian section has no Roti-Beti, that is, commensal and matrimonial linkage with the original section of tribe. The Is-Wales are regarded as 'excommunicated stock'. The major sects which are adopted by the Warlis are the Tulsipuala sect, Dandavat or Mahanubhav sect and Sanatan Dharmi panth. The adherents of these sects regard themselves superior to the non-adherents on account of vegetarianism, hygiene and cleanliness in daily life. After the enactment of Bombay Tenancy and Agricultural Land Act, 1948, some portions of land came to be possessed by the Warlis. About 25.45 per cent of the Warli households possess village land, and out of these 75 per cent families own land in between 1–10 acres. Thus, a large number of Warlis are landless, though they are entitled to occupy some sir-pattar (fallow land) on lease from the forest department during a particular agricultural season. The yields procured through several methods are not enough. Hence, most of the poor Warlis work as sharecropper-tenants of rich landlords, belonging to another tribe called Kokna. Such sharecropper-tenants are known as 'bathe', and ordinarily half the yield of the crop is to be paid to the landowner as lease rent. Then there are many Warlis, who depend on agricultural labour available in adjoining regions of Maharashtra and Gujarat. There are several cases wherein agricultural land stands as a surety and which is mortgaged to a tribal relative to get loan. On account of poverty, most Warlis resort to concealed transfer of agricultural land to 'affluent people' also. Then there are benami transactions of land, whereby the land continues in the name of the 'tribal' but it remains in actual possession of the moneylender (non-tribal). Often the tribal works in his own land as agricultural labour. Thus, we notice a camouflaged misuse of tenancy laws in this Adivasi area.

The Koyas form a large tribe of Andhra Pradesh. They are divided into several sub-tribes and are distributed throughout the state and beyond. The Gonds of central India and the Koyas call themselves Koitor. Like the Gonds, the Koyas too have mythical affinity with characters of Mahabharata. Most popular myth surrounds the marriage between Bhima and Vanakanya (forest tribal girl). Their progeny were later known as the Koyas. M. Rajendra Prasad has studied the issues of status ranking, economic deprivation and inter-tribal competition among the Koyas and Lambadis of Andhra Pradesh. The Racha Koya, Gutta Koya, and Gumma Koya living in different ecological set-up are regarded as the original Koyas. Sub-tribes like Kammara Koya, Musuru Koya and Gampa Koya are occupational groups. Then we have the hybrids such as the Doli Koya, Kaka Koya, Matwa Koya and Lingadhari Koya, who are not real Koyas, but are alleged to be plainsmen admitted into Koya tribe. This course of 'tribal absorption' is rather an uncommon phenomenon in Adivasi India. The Lingadhari Koyas (who seem to have been influenced by the Lingayats) are Shaivites. They wear 'lingam' around their neck. The main occupations of the Gumma Koyas are agriculture and fishing. The Koyas are divided into five gattu/gotram/clans.

Diverse Koya sub-tribes are differently placed and they maintain different lifestyles. In some locations they are highly Hinduized but in some other places they retain tribal religious beliefs. Those who have become Hinduized pursue the concept of purity and pollution and consequent commensal norms. At inter-community level, the Koyas and Lambadis, regard themselves as high-ranking tribes and they maintain distance from the Konda Kammara, Konda Kapu and Valmiki. The Koyas occupy the highest place in social scale because of their rapport with Zamindars, the feudal chiefs of Rakhalli, Polavaram and Chodavaram, from whom they received land and settled in plain areas. The Lambadis are placed second, followed by Konda Dora, Konda Kapu, Konda Kammari, Hill Reddies and Konda Jangama. These rankings are relative and disputed and thus we see competition amongst the local tribes. By and large all tribespeople, whether Hinduized or not, continue to venerate tribal deities. The Koya belief system and religious order is syncretic. Rajendra Prasad calls it 'a mixture of Tribal Animism and Hinduism'. Simultaneously, the Koyas depend on magical-ritual performances to get rid of their sickness. The present study reveals that the Banjaras (also called Lambadis), have been craftily purchasing most of the fertile lands of Koyas in recent decades (particularly after 1977 when Banjaras were declared the Scheduled Tribe). This has resulted in the Koyas losing their valuable fertile lands and becoming landless and destitute to some extent. Several development programmes are theoretically launched but the natives do not uncover any result. Most sufferers are the poor Koyas in interior regions. The rich Koyas could approach administration and avail opportunities of grants and loans. Those in better position send their children to schools.

Many tribes in Andhra Pradesh lead a very insecure economic life such as the Chenchus, Kolam, Kondareddy, Konda Savaras and Thotis. These backward tribes are identified as 'primitive tribal groups' (PTGs) because they are at the pre-agricultural stage of economy characterized by low level of literacy and who largely depend on food gathering for their subsistence. Now, the former Primitive Tribal Groups such as the Chenchus have been categorized as 'Particularly Vulnerable Tribal Groups' by the government. Among several earlier works on the Chenchus, mention may be made of the studies by Furer-Haimendorf (1943) and P.K. Bhowmik (1989). Md. Azeez Mohidden and G.V. Ramana have studied the transformation of the Chenchus of Andhra Pradesh from the 'foraging stage' to agriculture. They observed that considerable changes have taken place in recent times in the life of the Chenchus and they noticed the growth of a nascent class formation among them. Mohidden and Ramana have conducted the fieldworks among the Chenchus spread in several settlements (villages) of Kurnool, Prakasam and Mahaboobnagar districts. The Chenchus are divided into Konda Chenchus, Uru (village) Chenchus, Bonta Chenchus, Chenchu Dasaris, Koya Chenchus and Krishna Chenchus. The Krishna Chenchus are the most 'primitive'. Traditionally some hierarchy is maintained between these sub-tribes. Thus, though the Dasari Chenchus claim a status equal to the Konda Chenchus the latter deny such a claim. The Konda Chenchus strongly feel that they are the real Chenchus and are superior to all other sub-tribes that claim to be Chenchus. Furer-Haimendorf

(1943: 287) has mentioned that the Chenchus living in the districts of Kurnool, Prakasham and Mahaboobnagar have adopted the term intiperlu (lineages) from the neighbouring Telugu castes. Each of the endogamous divisions of the Chenchus worships their own deities. The Chenchus who are assigned the duty of cleaning the temple enjoy the community feast and receive the sarees offered to the deities. Census records show that many Chenchus are Hinduized but in reality many tribespeople pursue tribal religious traditions. The Chenchus are typically hedonistic in the sense that they think for the present only and have no concern for their future. So they work for immediate return through the labour work temporarily. That is the reason why instead of adopting the agriculture they continue to pursue collection of the forest produces. Majority of the Chenchus in Marripalem village possess less than two acres of land and thus depend on Minor Forest Produce and on agricultural labour. Agriculture however is emerging as the alternative source of livelihood. Educated and employed Chenchus are economically better off and even enjoy respect among the Chenchus. Although the incipient class consciousness on the basis of wealth is observed among the Chenchus, no clear-cut economic class formation has yet emerged.

According to People of India study of ASI, the Soliga of Karnataka is a forest tribe who have been shifting cultivators and foragers. Now, they have taken to agricultural labour. Some among them are landowning cultivators (Singh, 1994: 1084). S.N. Mahato discusses the themes of pre-agricultural economy, discrimination and impact of rehabilitation programme on the Soliga of Karnataka. S.G. Morab (1977) had earlier studied the economic life of the Soligas in the 1960s when they were exclusively hunter-gatherers and shifting cultivators. These economic pursuits are still observable in interior areas. The government agencies compelled the Soligas to discard shifting-cultivation and shift to rehabilitation centres in the B.R. Hills, and accept the economic assistance. As often happens many of those who resettled really could not avail the proper support. Hence, majority of them became labourers. Denial of the minimum wages and non-availability of works perpetuated poverty among the Soligas. However, there was a small number of fortunate Soligas who procured land grants with patta. The patta landholders gradually enlarged their economic activities and formed a stratum of rich peasants. Gradually the area witnessed the slow growth of obvious stratification within the tribe in terms of landed settled agriculturists (rich peasants) and shifting cultivators/wage earners and labourers. During the last four or five decades, the B.R. Hill areas have witnessed the growth of NGOs and voluntary organizations such as VGKK which is working among the poor Soligas. VGKK along with government agencies introduced many schemes of economic development which had a positive impact. At the same time, the introduction of the Statutory Panchayat institutions and tribal council helped in maintaining social control.

The Todas have been made famous in anthropological discipline through works of Rivers (1906). In recent years, some restudies have been attempted (Walker, 1986). Earlier Todas were polyandrous. The Toda religion is a highly ritualized buffalo-cult (Menon 2003). Madhav Menon has refuted the conclusions drawn by Walker that the Todas are part of 'the Hindu world of south India' because he sees in their social organization existence of hierarchy in the shape of a 'superior' section – Torthoral and an 'inferior' section – Teivaliol. Due to the fact that the inferior section supplies the 'professional' priestly practitioners to the tribe, Menon (2003) calls it the 'reverse of Brahminical Hinduism'. The Todas have two endogamous subdivisions – Tordas and Teivelly and each division is further divided into a number of exogamous clans. Walker refers to Tordas and Teivelly as sub-castes, which may not be a proper inference. Sibir Ranjan Das has studied the pastoral clanship and regional hierarchy among the Todas of the Nilgiris (Tamil Nadu), who live in the vicinity of Kurumbas, Kota, Iruvar and Badagas. In the past, Kota used to play music at the Todas funerals. Todas, have a very close relation with the Badagas. There are some occasions when the Badagas gift the Toda a basketful of grain known as Gudlu. Among the Todas land as a property is a new concept. It has been mentioned earlier that in the past Toda economy was totally dependent on their buffalo and milk. It is no longer their main source of income, yet many of them still make profit from their buffaloes. The Dairy Temples are also disappearing from their life due to paucity of the raw materials which they used to collect from their surrounding forest, which is not accessible now.

VII

In this volume, we have focused attention on issues of social exclusion, discrimination, occupational differentiation as also emerging inequality among the tribes living in rural set-up. Our narratives of tribes in different parts of contemporary India demonstrate that the tribespeople have remained poor and are largely subjected to repression and exploitation. The twenty-four tribes portrayed in this volume represent divergent economies. In most cases, they are motivated to improve their statuses variously. There are thus some positive achievements made by the tribes in various states, by availing the provisions of affirmative action. Such success stories nonetheless are not many. In most cases, all over India the bulk of tribal families, living segregated in the periphery of the village settlements, away from settlements of caste people; remain discriminated as landless agricultural labourers. The bulk of tribal families who own some land often are just the marginal and small farmers. In terms of livelihood and employment, the tribespeople are broadly differentiated as cultivators, agricultural labourers, white-collar/salaried workers and even shopkeepers/traders. In some parts of India they are also industrial workers. The various provisions of affirmative action and reservation could not be enjoyed universally by all the tribes. Thus, we find differentiation in terms of access to education, income/wealth and political power and so on. Tribes of India have been subjected to multiple processes of discrimination and social exclusion, which are embedded in economic, social and ritual spheres (Das, 2009b, 2009c). Even though there are provisions of affirmative action in place and several reservations are provided to minimize discrimination and deprivation, our accounts reveal that the tribespeople in general and the 'weakest' among them, in particular, could not avail the benefits, meant for them. In more recent years, through greater secularization of village society and as a result of democratization processes, the tribespeople have shown determination and made efforts to fight for their rights and identity. As our village studies show there is a rising trend of awakening in tribal areas now. Manoranjan Mohanty rightly says that the rising trend of Adivasi awakening is a defining characteristic of contemporary India. He says, there is an unprecedented scale of assertion of not only the right to livelihood, but also the right to dignity and the right to selfhood among the Adivasis of India. The political upsurge in tribal India in defense of right to land and forest reflects this new awakening which is a positive sign of democratic transformation of modern India (Mohanty, 2011). Ramachandra Guha argues that, over the past four decades, the Adivasis of central India have often expressed their public and collective discontent with the policies and programmes of the state. The Adivasi disaffection has been largely expressed under the leadership of armed Maoist revolutionaries (Guha, 2007). He aptly says that the increasing presence of Naxalites in areas dominated by Adivasis has a historical reason: the Adivasis have gained least and lost the most from sixty years of political independence (Guha, 2007). Guha says that the policies being followed by the Government of India are the antithesis of what one would prescribe. Instead of making tribals partners in economic development, they marginalize them further. Nandini Sundar, who has extensively written on subject matter of Maoism-Naxalism in Adivasi areas, has discussed the repression of Bastar Adivasi Subalterns (1854–1996), from anthropological-historical perspectives. She has since updated the contents of her earlier work (Sundar, 2007).

The Constitution of India provides an array of affirmative action programmes for the tribes, including reservation in the legislature, education, and employment, but these programmes could not reduce the miseries of tribespeople. Rampant corruption and faulty implementation of the development projects are among the major causes of all miseries. India has been successfully experimenting with federalism and Indian Constitution does provide for necessary safeguards for the rights of tribal peoples (Articles 15, 16, 17 and 23). One of the most important acts of legislation in recent decades has been PESA. It is unique as it does not clash with customary laws, focusing more on the smallest settlements. Unfortunately, PESA has not been implemented in spirit. Most recently, the Scheduled Tribes and Other Traditional Forest Dwellers (Recognition of Forest Rights) Act, 2006 (also known as Tribal Rights Act) is enacted which recognizes the preeminent rights of tribals on forest land and which aims at undoing 'historical injustices' committed earlier. Both PESA and the Tribal Rights Act fundamentally confront the old power relations and claim to shift greater power to the tribespeople. Regrettably there is serious lack of positive implementation of the Act in several states, even though, on a positive side, as many as 31,68,478 claims received across the country till 31 January 2012, have been disposed of, in favour of the tribespeople. Deplorably, the Forest Rights Committees have not been constituted at the Gram Sabha level in several states as provided in the Act which seriously hampers verification of the tribal claims. There is interference of 'forest officials' which hampers the process of verification and decision-making at various levels (AITPN, April 2012, www.aitpn.org). Authoritative reports suggest that the human rights situation in areas inhabited by tribespeople in India remains grim. Felix Padel and Samarendra Das (2009) have closely watched the adverse impact of industrialization in south Odisha. They say:

> The mining industry has been intrinsically destructive to human life (if not life on earth) at both ends of the production line: the invasion of Greenfield mines and factories onto indigenous communities and some of the world's last pristine environments that these communities have preserved; and the end result of metal consumed in weapons, systems and wars, at exorbitant economic as well as human costs.

These activist-scholars have rightly placed the miseries of tribes of eastern India in a global frame, putting their predicaments at par with plights of indigenous people elsewhere. Despite negation of Indian state to call the Indian tribes/Adivasis as 'indigenous people', this term is gaining popularity among Indian activists, who have demonstrated their perspectives forcefully and convincingly at global platforms. What is pertinent is that several international agencies have accepted the problems of the Indian tribes/Adivasis as the concern of the indigenous people, who are variously engaged in diverse struggles for autonomy and human rights.

References

Badgaiyan, S.D. 1986, "Class and Ethnicity: Chhotanagpur in the Nineteenth Century", in *Social Stratification in India*. K.L. Sharma (ed.), Delhi: Manohar.

Bailey F.G. 1960, *Tribe, Caste and Nation: A Study in Political Activity and Political Change in Highland Orissa*. Manchester: Manchester University Press.

Bailey, F.G. 1961, "'Tribe' and 'Caste' in India", *Contributions to Indian Sociology*. V: 7–19.

Bhasin, Veena 2011, "Settlements and Land-Use Patterns in the Lepcha Reserve-Dzongu Zone in the Sikkim Himalaya, India", *Journal of Biodiversity*, 2(1): 41–66 (2011).

Bhattacharyya, Harihar, Partha Sarkar, Angshuman Kar (eds). 2009. *The Politics of Social Exclusion in India: Democracy at the Crossroads*. London: Routledge.

Beteille, Andre 1965, *Caste, Class and Power: Changing Patterns of Stratification in a Tanjore Village*. Berkeley: University of California Press (Second edition, 1996. Delhi: Oxford University Press).

Bhowmik, P.K. 1989, *The Chenchus of the Forests and Plateau: A Hunting–Gathering Tribe in Transition*. Calcutta: Institute of Social Research and Applied Anthropology.

Bose, N.K. 1941, "The Hindu Method of Tribal Absorption", *Science and Culture* (7).

Bose, N.K. 1975, *The Structure of Hindu Society*. Delhi: Orient Longman.

Bose, P.K. 1981, "Stratification Among Tribals in Gujarat", *EPW*, Vol. XVI, No. 6, February 7, 1981, pp. 191–196.

Buxton, L.H.D. 1925, *The Peoples of Asia*, London: Kegan Paul, Trench, Trubner & Co.

Cann R.L. 2001, "Genetic Clues to Dispersal of Human Populations: Retracing the Past from the Present", *Science*, 291: 1742–1748.

Chauhan, B.R. 1974, "Rural Studies" in *A Survey of Sociology and Social Anthropology*, Delhi: ICSSR.

Das, N.K. 1987, *Ethnic Identity, Ethnicity and Social Stratification in Northeast India*, New Delhi: Inter-India Publications.

Das, N.K. 1989, "Tribe-Peasant Question in North-East India" in *Peasant and Peasant Protests in India*, M.N. Karna (ed.), New Delhi: Intellectual Publishing House, pp. 33–46.

Das, N.K. 1993, *Kinship, Politics and Law in Naga Society*. Calcutta: Anthropological Survey of India.

Das, N.K. 1994, "Pochury Naga", in *People of India – Nagaland*, N.K. Das and C. Lima Imchen (eds). K.S. Singh: General Editor. Calcutta: ASI and Seagull Books

Das, N.K. 2003, "An Outline of Syncretism", in *Culture, Religion and Philosophy: Critical Studies in Syncretism and Inter-Faith Harmony*, N.K. Das (ed.), Jaipur: Rawat Publications.

Das, N.K. 2006, "People of India and Indian Anthropology", *Economic and Political Weekly*. Vol. 41, No. 29, July 22–July 28, 2006.

Das, N.K. 2007, "Ethnicity, Nationalism & Regionalism in North-East India", in *Ethnicity, Movement and Social Structure: Contested Cultural Identity*, R.K. Bhadra and Mita Bhadra (eds), Jaipur: Rawat Publications, pp. 133–169.

Das N.K. 2009a, "The Naga Segmentary Social System", in *Structure and Exchange in Tribal India and Beyond*, Georg Pfeffer and D.K. Behera (eds), New Delhi: Concept Publications.

Das, N.K. 2009b, "Identity Politics and Social Exclusion in India's North East: The Case for Redistributive Justice", in *Politics of Social Exclusion*, H. Bhattacharyya, P. Sarkar and A. Kar (eds), London: Routledge.

Das, N.K. 2009c, "Identity Politics and Social Exclusion in India's Northeast: A Critique of Nation-Building", *Anthropos*, 104. 2009.

Das, N.K. 2011, "Naga Peace Parleys: Sociological Reflections and a Plea for Pragmatism", *Economic and Political Weekly*. June, 18, 2011, Vol. xlvi, No. 25.

Das, N.K. and Shantanu Mitra 2009, "Syncretism Among the Santal of Jharkhand", ASI Report.

Doshi, S.L. 1990, *Tribal Ethnicity, Class and Integration*, Jaipur: Rawat Publications.

Elwin, Verrier 1955, *The Religion of an Indian Tribe*, Mumbai: Oxford University Press.

Furer-Haimendorf, C. von 1943, *The Chenchus: Jungle Folk of the Deccan*. London: Macmillan & Company.

Ghurye, G.S. 1963, *The Scheduled Tribe*. Bombay: Popular Prakashan.

Government of India, 2001, Planning Commission Report of the Steering Committee on Empowering the Scheduled Tribes, New Delhi: Planning Commission.

Guha, Ramachandra 2007, "Adivasis, Naxalites and Indian Democracy", *Economic and Political Weekly*, 11 August 2007.

Harris, 1982, *Capitalism and Peasant Farming: Agrarian Change and Ideology in Northern Tamil Nadu*, Bombay: Oxford University Press.

Hofer, A. 1979, *The Caste Hierarchy and the State in Nepal: A Study of the Muluki Ain of 1854*, Innsbruck: Universitätsverlag Wagner.

Kosambi, D.D. 1956, *An Introduction to the Study of Indian History*, Bombay: Popular Prakashan.

Kulke, Hermann 1993, *Kings and Cults: State Formation and Legitimation in India and Southeast Asia*, Delhi: Manohar Books.

Lyall, A.C. 1882, *Asiatic Studies: Religious and Social*. London: John Murray.

Menon, T. Madhava 2003, "Tribal Religion and Hindu Cults: Studies from South India", in *Culture, Religion and Philosophy: Critical Studies in Syncretism and Inter-Faith Harmony*. N.K. Das (ed.), Jaipur: Rawat Publications.

Mohanty, Manoranjan 2011, "Adivasi Awakening and Emergence of New Politics", *Frontier*. Vol. 44, Nos. 11–14, September 25–October 22, 2011.

Misra, Kamal K. 1991, "Dynamics of inequality in an Unstratified Society: The Juang", *The Eastern Anthropologist*. 44(3): 213–224.

Morab, S.G. 1977, *The Soliga of Biligiri Ranagana Hills*, Mysore. Calcutta: ASI.

Padel, Felix and Samarendra Das 2009, "Keep the Bauxite in the Mountains", *The Broken Rifle*, September 2009, No. 83.

Pattanayak, D.P. 1998, "The Language Heritage of India", in *The Indian Human Heritage*, D. Balasubramanian and N. Appaji Rao (eds.), Hyderabad: University Press.

Pathy, Jagannatha 1984, *Tribal Peasantry*. New Delhi: Inter-India Publications.

Risley, H.H. 1915, *The People of India*, Calcutta: Thacker Spink.

Ray, Nihar Ranjan 1972, "Presidential Address", in *Tribal Situation in India*, K.S. Singh (ed.). Simla: IIAS.

Rivers, W.H.R. 1906, *The Todas*, London: Mcmillan and Company.

Sachchidananda, 1990, "Patterns of Politico-Economic Change Among Tribals in Middle India", in *Dominance and State Power in Modern India: Decline of a Social Order*, Francine R. Frankel and M.S.A. Rao (eds), Delhi: Oxford University Press.

Sarkar, S.S. 1958, "Race and Race Movements in India", in *The Cultural Heritage of India*, S.K. Chatterjee (ed.), Calcutta: Ramakrishna Mission Institute of Culture.

Shah, Ghanshyam 1979, "Tribal Identity and Class Differentiation: Case Study of the Chaudhary Tribe", *Economic and Political Weekly*, Vol. XIV, Nos 7 & 8.

Shah, Ghanshyam 1986, "Stratification Among the Scheduled Tribes in the Bharuch and Panch Mahal Districts of Gujarat", in *Determinants of Social Status in India*. S.C. Malik (ed.), Delhi: Motilal Benarasi Das.

Sharma, B.D. Press release, Mysore, 22 February 2006, forestrights@yahoogroups.com.

Sharma, K.L. (ed.), 1986, *Social Stratification in India*. Delhi: Manohar.

Singh, K.S. 1978, "Colonial Transformation of Tribal Society in Middle India", *Economic and Political Weekly*, Vol. XIII, No. 30, pp. 1221–32.

Singh, K.S. (ed.), 1982, "Introduction" in *Economies of the Tribes and their Transformation*, K.S. Singh (ed.) New Delhi: Concept.

Singh, K.S. 1985, *Tribal Society in India: An Anthropo-Historical Perspective*, Delhi: Manohar Publications.

Singh, K.S. 1993, "The Problem", *Seminar*, No. 412, pp. 12–18.

Singh, K.S. 1994, *People of India – The Scheduled Tribe*, National Vol. III. Delhi: ASI and Oxford University Press.

Singh, K.S. 2003, "Hinduism and Tribal Religion: An Anthropological Perspective on Interaction", in *Culture, Religion and Philosophy: Critical Studies in Syncretism and Inter-Faith Harmony*, N.K. Das (ed.), Jaipur: Rawat Publications.

Sinha, Surajit 1958, "Tribal Cultures of Peninsular India as a Dimension of Little Tradition in the Study of Indian Civilisation", *Journal of American Folklore*, Vol. 71, July–September.

Sinha, Surajit 1962, "Status Formation and Rajput Myth in Tribal Central India", *Man in India*, 42: 35–80.

Sinha, Surajit, R. Bhattacharya and N.K. Das (eds), 1993, *Anthropology of Weaker Sections.* Delhi: ASI and Concept.

Srinivas, M.N. 1952, *Religion and Society among the Coorgs of South India.* Oxford: Clarendon Press.

Srivastava, Vinay Kumar 2010, "Socio-economic Characteristics of Tribal Communities that Call Themselves Hindu", Religious and Development Research Programme Working Paper Series, New Delhi: Indian Institute of Dalit Studies.

Sundar, Nandini 2007, *Subalterns and Sovereigns: An Anthropological History of Bastar 1854–2006,* Delhi: Oxford University Press.

Thapar, R. 1966, *A History of India,* Vol. I, Middlesex: Penguin.

Thapar, Romila and Siddiqui, Majid Hayat 1991, "Tribals in History: The Case of Chhotanagpur", in *Social Stratification,* Dipankar Gupta (ed.), Delhi: Oxford University Press, pp. 419–430.

Vidyarthi, L.P. 1974, "Tribal Ethnography in India", *A Survey of Research in Sociology and Social Anthropology,* Vol. Ill, ICSSR, Bombay: Popular Prakashan, pp. 31–133.

Walker, Anthony R. 1986, *The Toda of South India: A New Look.* London: Macmillan (Delhi: Hindustan Publishing Corporation).

Weber, Max 1958 (1920), *The Religion of India. Sociology of Hinduism and Buddhism,* Translated by H. Gerth and Don Martindale. Glencoe 1958 (Translation of Max Weber, Gesammelte Aufsatze zur Religionssoziologie, Vol. II, Hinduismus and Buddhismus, Tiibingen

Xaxa, V. 1999, "Transformation of Tribes in India: Terms of Discourse", *Economic and Political Weekly,* 34, 24, June, 12–18, pp. 1519–1524.

Website Sources

www.wikipedia.com

www.tribesindia.com

www-ishvanikendra.com - Xaxa, V. Dialogue with marginalized tribes

http://planningcommission.gov.in/reports/publications/rep_dce.pdf, Planning Commission Report, April, Planning Commission, New Delhi.

www.bannedthought.net/India/PeoplesMarch/2006/archives/2006).

www.indianmirror.com

www.aitpn.org- AITPN, April 2012, The State of the Forest Rights Act: Undoing of historical injustice withered, Asian Indigenous & Tribal Peoples Network

1 Authority Pattern, Hybridization Process and Emerging Inequality in Nicobar Islands

A. Justin

This paper deals with the issues of authority structure, social change and social stratification among the Nicobarese of the Car Nicobar Islands. In doing so however, the situation prevailing among the Nicobarese inhabiting the central and southern groups of Nicobar Islands is elucidated in wider context of inter-faith exchange, syncretism and hybridity. The Nicobar Archipelago, which lies south of the Andaman Islands, is separated by the Ten Degree Channel and consists of 22 large and small islands; out of which only 12 are inhabited. The most northerly archipelago of the group is Car Nicobar, roughly 90 and 150 nautical miles away at the southern tip of little Andaman Island and Port Blair, which is the capital of Andaman & Nicobar Islands. Chowra, Teressa, Bompuka, Katchal, Kamorta, Nancowry and Trinket form the central group of the Nicobar Archipelago. The extreme southern group consists of Pulo Milo, Little Nicobar, Kondul and Great Nicobar. Nicobar Archipelago is the homeland of the Nicobarese and Shompen. However, there are non-Nicobarese populations too, such as the repatriated Tamils from Sri Lanka, ex-servicemen, traders and other heterogeneous people from various corners of the Indian subcontinent. The fieldwork was conducted in two villages of Car Nicobar Islands in 1991 but additional information was also collected in the year 2000–2001 and again in 2006 and incorporated suitably. Seti and Saphea are native names of Big Lapati and Kakana villages respectively, where the original work was done. The former village is located on the east coast between Tapoiming and Kinmai villages, whose traditional native names are Hongehx and Totchak respectively. The latter village is located at the south-east coastal area of Car Nicobar. Seti is said to be the parent village from where the entire population dispersed to different parts of Car Nicobar Island.

Tribes and their Territories

The Nicobarese and Shompen, with common Mongoloid ethnic ancestry, live in Nicobar Archipelago. These are the "indigenous people" of Nicobar Islands. Unlike the Nicobarese who are spread over 12 different islands, the Shompen are found in the interior areas of Great Nicobar Island only. The Shompen are 'very introvert' and lead a semi-nomadic life based on foraging-hunting and food gathering. They continue to live in relative isolation, though they have a sort of symbiotic relationship with the Nicobarese of Great Nicobar Island, who are mainly concentrated in the western coast of this island, as well as Nicobarese of other islands such as Kondul, Little Nicobar and Pulo Milo.

The present population of the Nicobarese is 26,565 with literacy rate of 40 per cent (Census, 2001). The generic term 'Nicobarese' refers to the tribal people of Nicobar Archipelago in general. However, each island community possesses a native name, which has a territorial affiliation. So it is pertinent to distinguish the Nicobarese of dissimilar islands as far as their appropriate identities are concerned. The twelve islands communities inhabiting different groups of the Nicobar Islands call themselves by distinctive terms such as Tarik (native of Car Nicobar), Som Pai (inhabitant of Chowra), Som Luroo (Belonging to Teressa), Som I-ta (natives of Katchal, Kamorta, Nancowry and Trinket), Sop Piheuñ (belonging to Pulo Milo), Sop Panjang (belonging to Little Nicobar), Sap Lamongshe (native of Kondul) and Sap Kanalo (people belonging to Pulo Bhabi of Long that is Great Nicobar). All live in settled villages tending herds of domestic pigs, raising coconut plantations, areca nut (betel nut) and other horticultural activities while a sizeable number work in various government and private organizations in various capacities ranging from the higher and responsible positions to lower echelons as wage labourers.

For convenience sake here "Car Nicobarese", "Central Nicobarese" and "Southern Nicobarese" are used as synonym for the inhabitants of the most northerly islands. The tribal people of Nicobar Islands have for long been in contact with outsiders and have consequently been exposed to various forces of change. The single most important influence on the socio-economic, and religious life of the people is attributed to Christianity. Prior to the advent of Christianity the Nicobar islanders were animists. The striking features prevalent among the Nicobarese of different islands is the variation of the spoken dialects, though most of them can understand and converse in the Car Nicobarese language. It is the lingua franca of the entire Nicobarese in general. Also, there are noteworthy variations in their cultural and social practices; but nonetheless, they share a basic cultural tradition, with slight variations in their social-cultural matrix, belief and practice as well. But it is all the more important to fathom the inter-island relations, stratification, status as well intra-island relations, inter- and intra-village relations and the process of homogenization.

Competition at Inter-island Level and Inter-village Differentiation

Traditionally, each islander was self-contained. Certain rituals were observed in the past to inflict injury to the people of other islands as discussed below. Historical evidence during pre-Christian era shows that the central Nicobarese have a custom of setting a small model of ship or raft and *ap* (canoe) in the sea when the prevailing winds are suitable. The model of ship or raft and canoe is equipped with sails of dried coconut leaves. A *kareava* (fetish) is placed on the canoe and model of ship or raft with all the essential ingredients of an offering, is fixed to expel disease or the evil spirit into a known or an unknown land. The canoe or raft is carried off by the wind, especially north-easterly and south-westerly winds. At the time of sailing, the canoe is set afloat with the

A small model of ship called *hanto* to expel disease and the evil powers.

intention of creating havoc on other islands through the evil spirit that, according to their belief and practices, can spread disease and epidemic. In this manner the tribal people of Nicobar Islands in the past punished each other by sending malevolent spirits to each other. This is a testimony that they have been at enmity with one another in the distant past. Reportedly, the above-mentioned ritual was quite common amongst the Car Nicobarese earlier. A folktale says how the Car Nicobarese had once swindled of the people of Chowra. The two used to barter with articles likes knives, axes, chisels and so on. Once, the Car Nicobarese had cheated the Chowrayite (Nicobarese of Chowra Island) with fake iron implements, which were all made of soft wood but beautifully designed and coloured to look authentic. The latter retaliated by sending *kuseu* (concoction of yam and banana mixed with grated coconut wrapped in the young spathe of areca nut), set adrift on the sea in a small canoe. The canoe was equipped with sails, which were fastened together on a framework. It was carried away by the wind and landed ashore at Kimios village (its name Otrahoon) of Car Nicobar.

There is historical evidence that a team of about 40 *Tarik* (Car Nicobarese or Nicobarese of Car Nicobar Island) paid a periodical visit to Chowra Island way back in the year 1900. On reaching Chowra Island their canoes were cut into pieces. Some of the Car Nicobarese climbed atop the coconut trees. The Chowrayites (Nicobarese of Chowra Island) then cut down the coconut trees and killed the sailors from Car Nicobar Island. Gabriel, the second village headman of Chowra Island corroborated this incident when the author did fieldwork on Chowra Island intermittently during 1986, 1987, 1997 and 2000. This is a clear instance of the Chowrayites' varied attitudes of not allowing strangers to land ashore on their homeland.

There are prominent patterns of cultural differentiation, which show that the central and southern Nicobarese are stratified, belonging to the diverse rungs of the Nicobarese society. Even the Car Nicobarese had openly propounded this thought and they admit the dominant functional roles of sorcerers, shamans and witch doctors of the central and southern Nicobarese for which they are noted. Chowrayites knew the art of pottery whereas Car Nicobarese specialized in basketry and in weaving mats from pandanus leaves. In terms of complexion the people of Nancowry and Katchal especially females, are the fairest. Thus we see there are various ways to perceive the dissimilarities, often from historical perspective.

The Car Nicobarese tribal people were the first to become 'modernized' than others by adopting a form of the Roman script, and accepting the value of education. Of late, the Car Nicobarese script (a variant form of Roman script) is in vogue.

The entire Nicobarese population considers the Chowrayites as their best seafarers and sailors. However, their annual outward and inward voyages to different Nicobar Islands are attributable to many a factor such as the prevalence of winds, weather conditions, and the condition of the sea. They define their life through the notion 'scarcity and survival'. The difficult situation in Chowra Island, which they have to cope with, has shaped their survival strategy to maintain relationships with other islands through barter system, and also with other villages in the same island. Knowledge of sorcery is another feather in the Chowrayites' cap, because this knowledge is often required by all and which influenced the other Nicobarese.

Historically speaking the inter-island relations was not very congenial and harmonious. The drastic change occurred in the inter-island relations generally after Christianity established its firm hold on the native life of central and southern Nicobarese. Beyond doubt, the Chowrayites (the native of Chowra) depend on 'reciprocities' and 'exchange' under the barter system.

There is no denying the fact that inter-island social stratification is prominently present in Nicobar Island. For instance, the Car Nicobarese have played a dominant role as agents of change. They have a 'direct influence' on the central and southern Nicobarese. Older modes of ranking and stratification are not uncommon, mainly through presence of the shamans, witch doctors, sorcerers, etc., and thereby inter-village supremacy is also expressed often. Thus, the Tokirong Seti village (Big Lapati) of Car Nicobar Island has tried hard to maintain its hierarchical supremacy, being the parent settlement and village and the original administrative centre of the Island Council. Not only this, evidence also shows that the first Chief Captain of the island was a resident of Seti.

The Nicobarese are now embarking on the road to modernization. The so-called "An ma-an-lo" (people of Seti, Small Lapati, Kinmai and especially people of Mus village) refer to themselves as the 'cultured people' of Car Nicobar. The headquarters of the traditional council has now shifted from Seti to Pumpai village, also known as Chukcheucha. The people also stressed that they are the people who taught the other Nicobarese the three Rs. During the British period, Mus village was the seat of the Government administrator, however, this was shifted to Elminkuon, a particular place at Ke-e-ro or Perka village during the post independence era. John Richardson Hachevka was the person who converted the Nicobarese language into Roman script, which gained wide popularity among the Nicobar islanders.

In spite of ranking and stratification the inter-village relations are based on mutual cooperation, help and social obligation. Traditionally, each lineage of a particular village had a social tie with a lineage of another village. Following is the chart of such linkages:

1.	Hecho, Kakana	Yin-i, Perka
2.	Rotoh, Kakana	Fanlalo, Perka
3.	Hongsata-oo, Kakana	Tomuluk, Perka
4.	Hapung-ngo, Kakana	Rum, Perka
5.	Kok aich re, Kakana	Otvani, Perka

These linkages are typical of the tribal linkages, observed all over the globe. Strategically, the socio-economic conditions of the Car Nicobarese are comparatively moving upward compared to the central and southern Nicobarese. The tribal people of Katchal and Nancowry, (especially a few families for instance those of Mark Paul, Ayesha, Abu Soul and Harry Saul) are well to do with sound resources and income. It is true that the Car Nicobarese are more exposed to modern amenities of life than those in the central and southern group of Nicobar islands. There is clear emergence of stratification among them. However, there is a wide disparity of living standards also among the Nicobarese of Chowra Island, Teressa, Pulo, Meroe and Kondul. Hence, they are stratified based on their economic standing, status and prestige.

Intra-lineage stratification has traditionally manifested itself in distribution of economic resources, allotment of duties as shared by all lineage members including its head who manages and controls both administrative and economic resources of the tuhet (lineage) and other public affairs at the village level. According to customary law an individual or a family has to fulfil the obligations, duties and other practical needs of the tuhet (maximal lineage) first and his own day-to-day requirement thereafter. But it is customarily compulsory for lineage members to concede to the demands of the tuhet, in principle, whenever such occasions come up. The traditional law of the tuhet is hard work. In a well-organized tuhet whenever a member is in distress, sick or needing treatment outside the island, all lineage members financially assist a family or an individual. Even physical help is extended to the needy lineage members. The entire village, at times, also extends cooperation and all possible help when such occasions arise. Head of lineage, known as makuo tuhet or maàooto is viewed as a person with high status politically, economically and socially. Within a tuhet, the remaining families' are under the control of the lineage head and form a secondary place. The former being the head forms a dominant status, while the latter are known as 'tanoolo' or 'anh-kuo tuhet' in native tongue, and are the actual pillars of the tuhet. They raise garden, plantations, herds of pigs, fowl and so on for the tuhet. Surprisingly, they are identified as subordinates as they are manual working group, but by dint of hard work, seniority in age, knowledge and experience of customary law, and leadership qualities any one could become the head of the lineage. For instance, Gabriel is an adopted son of a parent hailing from Small Lapati (known as Ponchoh village). His predecessor named Meong died in 1985. After his death Gabriel became the lineage head of otoh, Kakana village. Recently he has also been elected as the first village headman of Kakana.

According to household census conducted in 1991, there are ten lineages at Kakana village. Name of lineage heads are mentioned against concerned lineages below:

S. No.	*Lineage (tuhet)*	*Name of lineage head*
1.	Hong kamri	Jonathan
2.	Kuring-ngo	Peter Ye-e
3.	Kok aichre	Lionel Jerome
4.	Sakin	S. Samson
5.	El honghavial	Reuben
6.	Hecho	Edward Kuchat
7.	El otlen	Samson
8.	Hongsata-oo	Joseph
9.	Rotoh	Gabriel
10.	Hapung-ngo	Johnson Reka

Traditional hierarchy exists at inter-lineage level, as lineages are differentiated based on land, wealth, property, prestige and status as well as numerical strength of its members. Hierarchically, Hongsata-oo was placed above otoh. Even these days, the former tuhet is recognized as such. However, its prestige and status is now decreasing, which is attributed to non-unity among lineage members in raising arecanut, coconut plantation and horticultural gardens. Analysing the inter-island status levels, inter-community relationships and intra-village social differentiation and also inter- and intra-lineage social differentiation, it appears that the Nicobarese society is stratified in nature.

Power and Authority of Village Council

The Nicobarese have well organized villages and island councils to regulate their social and political life. Customary laws, norms and practices are in operation. In Car Nicobar there are 15 villages. Several tuhets (lineages) have heads known as makuo tuhet or marooto, who organize all important political, economic and other activities. The village captains (i.e., 1st, 2nd, 3rd headmen) and all the heads of the tuhet, taken together constitute the village council. Traditionally the village captaincy is a hereditary post. The tenure of office is for life time. Succession to the office of the village headman is based on descent, and rights and powers are inherited through descent. The selection for the post of village headman is limited to members of same lineage group.

S.No.	*Village & Island*	*Name of Lineage*	*Name of 1st Headman*	*Name of Successor*
1.	Kakana, Car Nicobar	Hecho	Edward Kuchat	Samuel Kurata
2.	Perka, Car Nicobar	Yin-I	Reuben Hanong	James Reuben
3.	West Bay, Katchal	Hitlaat	Janga	Abu Saul
4.	Champin, Nancowry	M.champin	Islon	Ayesha

The powers of the village council are diffused but are recognized. Traditionally, the word of the village council was regarded as law and the council members themselves were the kamhonka (judges), comprising all the tuhet heads and recognized elderly persons. The role of the village church presbyter also became important in guiding and influencing the village council. The village council performs the three main functions (legislative, judicial and executive) of the traditional form of government in the Nicobarese society. The traditional administrative structure usually concerns itself with the protection of the society from external threats and challenge; the maintenance of internal order, the organization of various activities affecting the welfare of the society and the validation and maintenance of the structure of authority in the society. The village council, as judiciary body, is in charge of general affairs such as settling disputes and correcting wrongs like adultery, abusive language, theft, quarrels, conflicts and other offences connected with the breach of norm and custom. By implication it has the power of framing norms, laws and imposing penalties on disobedience among the people and tuhets, at the intra-village and inter-villages level as well. For all external and internal purposes the village captain is the head of the village council, both at official and non-official level.

Island Council and Hierarchy of Authority

The Island Council, which originally emerged as an authority in the Nicobarese society soon after World War II now provides the Chief Captain or Chieftain and the Vice Chief Captain and Deputy Vice Chief Captain, who assist the former in all relevant issues at village, island and district level too. The introduction of Deputy Vice Chief Captain has emerged recently in mid–2002, to assist the former two office bearers. The Island Council has unanimously nominated Cephas Jack and thus a change has occurred in the authority structure of the Nicobarese community at Island Council level. The Secretary, Tribal Council, has emerged in recent years to assist the Chief Captain or Chieftain and Vice Chief Captain and Deputy Vice Chief Captain at official level. The secretary presents demands for development or grievances if any, that require to be dealt by the administrator at three tiers, namely Village Council, Island Council and District Council respectively. The Island Council consists of the Island Chief Captain or Chieftain, Vice Chief Captain and Deputy Vice Chief Captain, the first, second and third headmen of various villages, a few selected presbyters and also the Bishop, who acts as an adviser and religious head. Of late, the Secretary, Tribal Council has simultaneously been playing parallel roles deemed to have been exercised only by the Chieftain at the official level. Thereby, instances of conflicts have occurred of late; wherein the Secretary has unmindfully violated and ignored the recognized traditional customary norm of taking into confidence the Chief Captain or Chieftain and Vice-chief Captain and Deputy Vice Chief Captain in various issues. Cases in point are cited here. The first such instance is of Thomas Philip. According to tradition Secretary cannot hold the position of village headman, this was the reason why Thomas Philip has been dethroned from the position of Secretary in October 2006. He was holding two posts (being first elected as village headman) simultaneously, which traditional customary norms objected to stringently. This paved the way for engagement of Henry Samuel the same year; after complying with all formalities of nomination for the purpose. On assuming charge Samuel made intermittent dubious trips to Port Blair and New Delhi, besides other unwarranted meetings and activities, without prior approval the Island Council. In view of this, the Island Council has given ample opportunities to the Secretary to mend himself and he has been stringently warned neither to violate nor defy the tradition. Actually, the Bishop of the Andaman and Nicobar Diocese, Andaman and Nicobar Islands, Church of North India, Rt. Rev. Christopher along with other major components of the Island Council has orally warned the concerned individual to curb his activities and mend himself. In brief, the hierarchy of authority as prevalent in Car Nicobar is the Chief Captain, Vice-Chief Captain, Deputy Vice-Chief Captain, the first, second and third captain, and the heads of tuhets. As a supplement to this hierarchy are the functionaries of the Church like the village presbyter, recognized elderly persons, pastorates, mother's union and the Bishop at the top, as well as political functionaries like the councillors of the territorial councils.

Traditionally the office of Chieftaincy is hereditary. Economic status, necessary charismatic qualities to command, controlling authority on relevant matters, seniority in age, proper knowledge of customary law and qualities of administrative leadership are particularly taken into account as criteria for Chieftainship. After the death of a chief, the next chief had to be selected from among the same lineage. Unfortunately there is often no suitable person capable of holding the post. Thereby, the succession goes to another lineage of a different village. The hereditary nature of the offices are not prevailing any more.

Table of Chief Captain at a Glance

S. No.	*Name*	*Sex*	*Post held*	*Tenure*	*Village*	*Island*
1.	Thomas Hala-ainjpa	M	Chief Captain	1950–1963 (till death)	Seti (Big Lapati)	Car Nicobar
2.	Fred Tun	M	Chief Captain	1963–1970 (till death)	Ha-nyoinny (Mus)	Car Nicobar
3.	Edward Kuchat	M	Chief Captain	1970–1992 (till death)	Sapeha (Kakana)	Car Nicobar
4.	Harry Lawrence	M	Chief Captain	1992–2001 (till death)	Ha-nyoinny (Mus)	Car Nicobar
5.	Aberdeen Blair	M	Chief Captain	2001–till date	Otkasip (Sawai)	Car Nicobar

Table of Vice Chief Captain at a Glance

S. No.	*Name*	*Sex*	*Post held*	*Tenure*	*Village*	*Island*
1.	Edwin	M	Vice Chief Captain	1970–1992 (till death)	Mus	Car Nicobar
2.	Harry Lawrence	M	Vice Chief Captain	1992–2001	Mus	Car Nicobar
3.	HIA Hussain	M	Vice Chief Captain	2001–May 5, 2007 (till death)	Chucheucha	Car Nicobar
4.	KvChamberlain Paul	M	Vice Chief Captain	May 31, 2007 Till date	Big Lapati	Car Nicobar

Table of Deputy Vice Chief Captain at a Glance

Name	*Sex*	*Post held*	*Tenure*	*Village*	*Island*
Cephas Jack	M	Deputy Vice Chief Captain	2002–till date	Chucheucha	Car Nicobar

Power and Function of Island Council

The Island Council has the power to enforce order, law and to dispense justice on matters which the village headmen cannot settle at village council level. The members of the former and the latter together form the Island Council. Their executive and legislative powers are not well defined as they ought to be but they are valued within the authority structure. The Island Council head, the Chief and his assistants, Vice Chief Captain and Deputy Vice Chief Captain have no special rights, but they occupy the most prominent position in the power structure. They receive no remuneration or wealth for their position. Their economic privileges and status are drawn entirely from their respective tuhet's resources. Also the village headmen do not derive any wealth from office. Even as arbiters in settling disputes they do not receive any remuneration. All the expenditure of the village headmen is borne by their respective tuhets according to available resources. The extra responsibility of the Village Council head or Island Council chief is to give a decision after consulting the tuhet heads or village headmen as the case may be, which is binding on others. This power is viewed as a kind of status, prestige and position.

The function of the Island Council is to safeguard the interest of the Nicobarese community as a whole, besides upholding the established norms, and simultaneously placing their grievances at the official level. Physical development of the village and island is another area where they have to interact with the official administrator. Organizing economic activities according to the calendar are also under their jurisdiction. Like many other tribal communities elsewhere in the country the legislative powers rest with the Island Council. Though the norms they framed are all unwritten yet, they are imparted to all through the mechanism of power structures at three tier levels – island, village and tuhet. Implementation of all punishments are taken serious note of. For example, for committing adultery, slaughtering of pigs and hosting feast are imposed on the culprit. The special privilege that the Island Council members enjoy is seen in the total support of Village and Island Council, for instance when they fall sick and are referred to Port Blair and beyond, the entire cost of treatment is raised from all members of the stated councils.

Territorial Council

The Andaman and Nicobar administration in 1979 introduced the Territorial Council. Prior to the introduction of this Council one Nicobarese was inducted as member of the Home Ministry Advisory Committee (HMAC). Interestingly, though the Territorial Council has been formed, the Advisory Committee is still functioning and its member is a female Nicobarese. Under the able guidance of the councillor at the top, four other Pradesh Council members were appointed, two from Car Nicobar and one each from Katchal and Nancowry island, to represent the communities of different islands. The councillor and Pradesh Council members were selected from among the village headmen by consensus. In the Village Council, which is more informal than formal, the role and function of the councillor amounts to little, but equivalent to the role of village first headman. Yet as spokesman for the community in all external matters, both to the government and non-official agencies, he holds an important position, playing a vital role. He receives remuneration, and enjoys privileges like official car and bungalow and other benefits according to government rules. His headquarter is located centrally in Port Blair, which is the capital of Andaman and Nicobar Islands. The term of office is five years. According to a policy decision taken by the Andaman and Nicobar administration, the Territorial (Pradesh) Council was abolished in 1996. Following is a list of councillors (Nicobarese) who had been elected by consensus:

S. No	*Name*	*Sex*	*Post held*	*Tenure*	*Village*	*Island*
1.	William Cyril	M	Councillor	1979–1983	S. Lapati	Car Nicobar
2.	Aberdeen Blair	M	Councillor	1983–1995	Sawai	Car Nicobar

In view of streamlining various developmental programmes, the Deputy Commissioner of Nicobars district formed Tribal Councils one each at Car Nicobar and Nancowry Island. Following are the Secretaries of Tribal Council of Car Nicobar Island:

S. No.	*Name*	*Sex*	*Post held*	*Period of serving*	*Village*	*Island*
1.	J.B. Daniel	M	Secretary	1995–December 12, 2000 (Till date)	Kinyuka	Car Nicobar
2.	Thomas Philip	M	Secretary	December 19, 2000–October 19, 2006	Mus	Car Nicobar
3.	Henry Samuel	M	Secretary	Oct 20, 2006-till date	Kakana	Car Nicobar

The position of Joint Secretary has been created for the first time in October 20, 2006 with the unanimous decision of Tribal Council. Martin Luther has been nominated for the position, and a post of spokesperson has been created for the Nicobarese in Andaman Islands. Details of such nominated personnel are furnished in the table below:

S. No.	*Name*	*Sex*	*Post held*	*Period of serving*	*Village*	*Island*
1.	Martin Luther	M	Joint Secretary	October 20, 2006–till date	Kakana	Car Nicobar
2.	OK Thomas	M	Spokesperson	October 20, 2006–till date	Kimios	Car Nicobar

The Tribal Council came into existence in the early 1990s. Unlike the Village and Island Council, the Tribal Council has no recognized legislative, executive and judicial powers. However, it is quite interesting to note that the Secretary is playing a parallel role at par with that of the Chief and Village headmen in his official dealings and interaction with government and non-government officials. Basically, the formulation of Tribal Council was aimed at utilizing the fund allotted for various purposes appropriately and to supervise various developmental programmes under different heads as introduced by the Andaman and Nicobar administration from time to time. Analysing the roles of the Tribal Council it can be stated here that this caused serious threat to the traditional council with its overshadowing power and authority structure, which is more of innovations in nature.

The Nicobarese Association

In the year 1983, young educated Nicobarese who are residing in Port Blair, formed a registered association called Manulo Inkuoken Nicobarese (Nicobarese Employees Welfare Association). The traditional council at Car Nicobar fears the exodus of this Association. A meeting was convened in 1982 at Seti (Big Lapati) village, Car Nicobar. All official members of Village and Island Council and other elderly people took part in the meeting. The meeting was convened to dissuade the Association from being formed. Young and educated people made an appeal to the traditional Island Council at the district level. Their appeal was turned down yet they went ahead and formed the Association. Any Nicobarese who is over 18 years of age can become a member, upon payment of one rupee as admission fee and one rupee as monthly subscription. The Central Executive Committee of the Association consists of a President, Vice President, General Secretary, three Organization Secretaries, one Joint Secretary and Treasurer and four other members. The term of the Central Executive Committee is for a period of three years. The primary objective of the Association is to present relevant problems before the administration. The Association also helps to develop harmony with other communities through sports and other cultural activities. Although the Association has no concern with political issues, however, the traditional council and its elderly leaders feared its political implications.

Political Change and Emergence of Educated Elite

The change in various aspects of the power and authority structure in Nicobarese society is directly and indirectly attributed to Christianity and education. Young educated people gain better opportunities, and prestige and have better access to various sources both at official and non-official levels. The modernization is actually a threat to the elderly people in general and the power structures in particular. Change is also being experienced in all the authority structures, as mentioned earlier. As a result, the election of first, second and third village-wise captains through secret ballot papers were conducted for the first time in 1978. There is a change in the order of captainship, which is now a combination of elderly, recognized and young educated persons. Unlike the past, the current term of captainship is five years. Also the traditional political organization has been greatly influenced by the Andaman and Nicobar administration, through opening two registered Central Cooperative Societies: Ellon Hinengo Limited (EHL) and Manulo Matai Limited (MML). The growth of young individuals (which consists of the educated elite), their ideals, enhanced interaction with officials and other such activities pose new kinds of threat to the traditional council. According to Pandit, the trend towards higher education is increasing, with better facilities and opportunities being provided by the government. These will, in due course, give rise to an educated elite that would in proper time become the political elite and may supplant the traditional leadership (Pandit, 1976: 5).

A conscious effort is being made to give a new shape to the power structures, to influence the election of various village Captains, Island Chief, Vice Chief Captain and Deputy Vice Captain too. It is observed that at present, people opt for those who can speak for and represent the community both at micro and macro level by raising relevant issues that are the demand of the present hour.

Both EHL and MML operate at Car Nicobar, Central and extreme southern Nicobar. They function as guiding factors in the authority structure and thus play a decisive role in political activities. A few educated Nicobarese are trying hard to curb the political power of these cooperative societies, but sadly enough, it is of no avail. The head of Village Council and Island Council should also exercise serious thought on these issues since the future of Nicobar Islands lies in the quality and ability of its leadership to steer the Nicobarese society into modernization.

Of late, the authority structure of the Nicobarese society is going through a crucial phase, whereby both conservative and progressive practices are being followed in parallel. Actually they are very selective in areas of accepting any new changes. Historically, a few educated Nicobarese were keen to contest for the position of the Member of Parliament in the election. There was a clear indication with regard to this in 1984, but for some reasons the candidate withdrew himself. The Village and Island Council expressed concern but when it comes to external matters and problems of serious nature, the Island Council and Tribal Council have sometimes miserably failed to live up to the expectation of the people. This seems to be a drawback of the inbuilt democratic nature of the authority structure among the Nicobarese. But the serious danger that lurks in prosperity is likely to disintegrate the unity among lineage members, Village and Island Council as well as the integrity of the Nicobarese society as a whole. The overall impact of this on the power structure of the Nicobarese community cannot be neglected and need a closer look.

Inequality and Culture Change

Nicobarese are more or less egalitarian people. Nonetheless, certain power and authority are enjoyed by those people who possess wealth, mainly landed property. Social stratification and inequality are witnessed in lifestyles, levels of living, economic pursuits or occupational patterns, material culture acquired and so on. Many Nicobarese now possess modern utensils such as plates, cups, saucers, buckets and other such domestic items. The earthen pot is being replaced by aluminum vessel. Use of steel utensils, plates, crockery and glass is increasingly seen these days. Forks and spoons are commonly used by well-off families and educated people. Some of them invest their savings in valuable objects such as silver spoon and Chinese plates and other household articles, which have status and antique value among the Nicobarese.

Quite a few, but not all can afford light four-wheeler vehicles, scooter, motorcycle, television set, video cassette recorder and player, camera, tape recorder and so on. The new concrete houses are a recent innovation. They now know the concept of privacy, especially the new generation of people who have built their own individual houses. Modern furniture has been introduced. Dress-styles and food habits of the Nicobar Island communities have undergone a tremendous change. New dietary habits and ornamentations are not uncommon among affluent families, especially salaried people. Empirical findings show that there is a wide disparity between the salaried people in service and those who still pursue a traditional economic life. Salaried groups of people are financially secure, whereas the incomes of the traditionalists are irregular and come from various sources.

These days a sizeable member of Nicobarese are in service and are holding responsible positions in different government offices and private organizations. Present percentage of the Nicobarese who are in services shows sharp upward trends. The ever-increasing population of the Nicobarese in and around Port Blair speaks volumes about the mobility of better opportunity seekers for generating better source of income. However, this does not mean that they have actually completely departed from their traditional economic pursuits.

Individual as Tuhet's Assets

The Nicobarese are mainly horticulturists and herders and pursue other economic pursuits like hunting and fishing. The tuhet has a large asset in Car Nicobar. Access to a tuhet's property is generally open to all but under the guidance of the tuhet head. Traditionally an individual or a family residing within the tuhet has to rear pigs and poultry, raise a plantation, etc. Such economic activities determine individual or family status, position and access to resources of the tuhet. An individual or a family has to fulfil the obligation, duties and needs of the tuhet first and his own day-to-day requirements second. These are the criteria which determine an individual's access to property and resources.

The Islands and Ecological Settings

Ecologically, the island-wise territory comprises mainly forest and sea. The intimate relationship of the Nicobarese with their ecological surroundings namely forest and sea, and their horticultural activities are expressed in various festivals, which are semi-religious in nature. Rituals are organized and offerings are offered to appease the benevolent deities for favours.

Rule of Inheritance and Matrilocal Residence

Concerning the inheritance of property, all members of a tuhet and family carry usufruct rights in a viable form. Traditionally, the tuhet's property and wealth could not be alienated or disposed of. As a rule the tuhet and family are the heirs of land and property, coconut and arecanut plantation, herds of pigs and so on. The traditional norms and rules governing relationship is stringently binding on all the lineage members. Rules of inheritance are egalitarian in nature. According to traditional norms, property is inherited equally by all lineage members in a tuhet and family. Both the sexes have equal rights. Lineage is exogamous in nature. Bi-local rules of residence, both patrilocal and matrilocal, are prevalent. The tuhet and family property is not transferable at the time of marriage, but the bride or groom who enters a new tuhet or social abode gains rights spontaneously. The matrilocal rule of residence predominates in the central and southern islands. Dowry is unknown to them, but bride-price in kind is prevalent among the people of Chowra and Teressa Island, though not among the other Nicobarese. Gift articles for example clothes, pigs, fowls and coconuts are treated as bride-price now. The impact of Christianity and education has influenced the practice of the bride price.

The Car Nicobarese family is patrilineal. Lineage is formed through the male members of the tuhet. Interestingly, the residence patterns are bi-local as pointed out before. Ownership of movable and personal property, such as household articles and other equipments, is individual. This includes utensils, crockery, clothing, currency, ornaments, outboard engine, small fishing canoe, fishing nets, harpoons, diving-masks, scooters, bicycles, motorcycles, dah (choppers), huts and houses, radios, tape recorders and other amenities of life. After birth, a child acquires membership in its father's group. Jural inheritance of property is through both the male and female. Male primogeniture is the rule pertaining to social position in a tuhet and family. The central and southern Nicobarese give more importance to women; there are instances of women exercising some authority over men.

Among the central and southern Nicobarese, the rules of inheritance pertaining to land, coconut and arecanut plantation and so on are deeply interwoven with the funeral customs, which show an extravagant display of grief. At the time of and after the funeral ceremonies the offerings, sacrifices and feast should continue, partly to appease the spirit of the deceased and partly to pay homage that the tradition demands. The sibling who performs the funeral service according to traditional practice gains rights to the property of the deceased. If the deceased has no children; some of his kinsmen or even an unrelated individual can perform the last rites and thereby claim property rights. This age-old practice is undergoing change. Christianity and education are largely responsible for this drastic change.

Landowners and Land Tenure System

In each island, there are a number of landowners, known as yom-chun-vîào in the Car Nicobarese language. For instance, Kirut of Tokirong Seti (Big Lapati) is

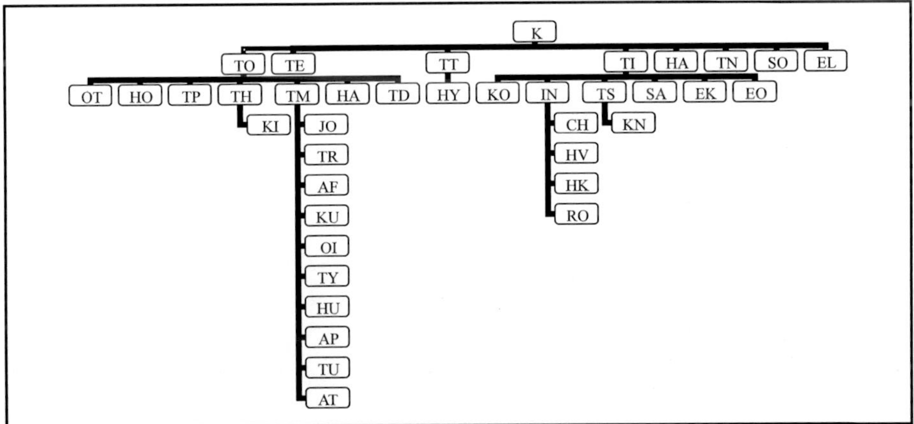

a traditional lineage which had original landowners. Now it is christened with a new name Tilaichmat. The founding father or lineage head of this tuhet had distributed and allotted some acres of land to his kinsmen and traditional friends settled in different villages of the island. There is no such thing as rent or tax or leasing the land, so possession of land had no economic advantage or municipal value. In view of the above fact the original landowner was not necessarily from a prosperous tuhet and family. As a rule no individual person of such tuhet has the right to alienate any portion of it.

Traditionally if a tuhet is rich it generally means that the founding ancestor and household occupants had been industrious in raising horticultural garden, planting coconuts and plantain and the plantations and they are now bearing fruit because its lineage members took great trouble. That is how the socio-economic condition of an individual, a family and a tuhet is measured. Simultaneously, the efforts of the individual members may also be judged.

The original land owning system in Car Nicobar can be understood from the diagram below:

TUHET-KIRUT (TILAICHMAT), TOKIRONG SETI (BIG LAPATI)

Abbreviation

K: Kirut, Big Lapati vill (BLV)	
TT: Tuhet Thomas, Tapoiminj vill.	TO: Tuhet Ol- op, BLV.
TI: Tuhet Innapto, Tapoiminj vill.	TE: Tuhet Evan, Tapoiminj vill.
HA: Hareh (Pinchem), BLV	TN: Tuhet Totan
SO: Sotol, Kinmai vill.	EL: Eltikoso, BLV.
HY: Hayiolngo, Kinmai vill.	IN: Tuhet In-nyatlo, BLV
KO: Kiseutngo Si-o, BLV	SA: Sakin, Kakana vill.
TS: Sachuok, Kakana vill.	EO: Elnganro, Tapoiminj vill.
EK: Eklam, Kimios vill.	HV: Hongchev, Mus vill.
KN: Kicheang, Small Lapati Village (SLV)	RO: Roonto chaf, Mus vill.
CH: Chong-i, Mus vill.	Ho: Tuhet Hongsitioi, Chukchucha vill.
HK: Hook, Mus vill.	TH: Tuhet Elheuh, SLV
OT: Otkikan, Kimios vill.	HA: Hokka, Mus vill.
TP: Tuhet Pirat, Tapoiminj vill.	KI: Kicheang, SLV
TM: Talmak, Mus vill.	TR: Tuhet Rooichka, Mus vill.
TD: Tuhet Dance, Tapoiminj vill.	KU: Kurime, Mus vill.
JO: Job, Mus vill.	TY: Yahe, Mus vill.
AF: Afe, Mus vill.	AP: Aparaa, Mus vill.
OI: Oifi, Mus vill.	AT: Afat, Mus vill.
HU: Hutrav, Mus vill.	TU: Tuhet Tun, Mus vill.

Tuhet Kirut (Tilaichmat), Tokirong Seti (Big Lapati)

As pointed out earlier Kirut is an ancient name of a tuhet at Tokirong Seti (Big Lapati) village of Car Nicobar Island. It is a group of landowners who distributed land to the traditional tuhet's friends and kinsmen in different villages, as is evident from the above illustration.

Land was allotted to various kinsmen and families (and even outsiders in Car Nicobar Island) in a somewhat different manner among the Central and extreme Southern Nicobarese. Of the landowners in Central and extreme Southern Nicobar Islands, Looklo, Umrooi, Lemure, Rani Chong-oo, Rani Laxmi, Watchful Hugh, Sakeo Kahinp, Eura Toviolo, Tang-ngeunh and so on are worth mentioning here. Among these people land is held on individual basis as well as by communal ownership, since a vast spread of land is available and the population is comparatively thin in some of the islands. This is unlike the Car Nicobarese, who are thickly populated and are experiencing pressure of inadequate lands. Owing to the pressure of population on Car Nicobar about 100 and odd Nicobarese families were brought to Little Andaman Island in the early 1970s under the rehabilitation programme of the Andaman & Nicobar administration.

Among the Nicobarese land ownership is based upon the kinship ties. Mann (1984) observed that their system is more or less a "communitarian-cum-feudal social system". The current practice in Car Nicobar, Chowra, Teressa and other islands, where pressure of population is being experienced, is that the land tenure system is based on the principle of allowing a tuhet, family or an individual to carry on horticultural activities by requesting landowners for the cultivation of seasonal or short-term crops like Yam and Taro plantation, as also for long-term crops of coconut and arecanut plantation. Land is allotted for this purpose to a tuhet, family or individual without charging tax or even collecting horticultural produce from them.

Land and Land based Stratification

As long as landowners spare or allot land on request of some tuhets or even to friends for the short-term crops, the relations among tuhet and families are not affected through such mutual economic aid. Nevertheless, the increasing demand for land is putting pressure on the tuhet's capacity to enhance or stretch its land, which of course is limited to meet the needs of its occupants. For instance, in a homestead or lineage named Meuktoheuch, a large maximal lineage in Tokiroong Seti village, whose population is 129 in Car Nicobar is unable to share or set right the production every year. On an average ten persons depend on one coconut tree. Therefore, such usufruct relationships are likely to decline with the pressure of population within the tuhet. So long as a sense of community endures and the customary norm is formally acknowledged within a tuhet, inconsistencies and contradictions in the actual relations among a large lineage group, become ineffective as they still consider themselves to be a united group and an integral part of the tuhet. This is despite the inequality in sharing and exploiting the limited resources within a tuhet. As regards ranking of elites in hierarchical order or class line, the traditional landowners are treated with respect and they form a class by themselves occupying the highest rung of stratification.

The traditional subsistence economy of the Nicobarese is no longer self-sufficient. Moreover, this cannot cope with the increase of their population, a fact which cannot be ignored altogether. Actually, there have been no improved techniques incorporated in the horticultural activities of these people. The use of modern implements, seeds, manure or chemical fertilizers can give an impetus to their horticultural activities. The Nicobarese community does not carry on any trade relationship apart from the barter system, which is prevalent among the people of Car Nicobar and Chowra Island. No labour class is in existence, though the men of Chowra make periodic voyages to Teressa, Katchal, Kamorta, Nancowry and Trinket Island in search of livelihood. They render many kind of labour and in return get some wages in kinds such as coconuts, axes, knives, large logs of wood for making canoe and so on. They work as labourers but they are not treated as labourers. In the wake of modern education and other external factors change is bound to disturb the usufruct rights over land, property, and plantation and so on among Nicobar islanders.

Coexistence of animism and Christianity displayed at the entrance of the Nicobarese dwellings at Rumyaav village, Kamorta Island and other places in Nancowry, Trinket, and Katchal, etc.

Religious Stratification

Theologically, the Nicobarese are divided into three different religious groups. The three religious groups are:

1. Tribal-Animism
2. Christians
3. Muslims

However, there is harmonious coexistence of these groups and certain confluence of practices is discernible. The traditional Nicobarese tribal religion is based on worship and propitiation of benevolent spirits in general. Fear of malevolent spirits is the basis of their belief and practices. Basically, there is tradition of shamanistic exorcising and scaring off spirits, and these are part of he tribal animism. This was the main theological belief and practices of the Nicobarese during the pre-Christianity era. Majority of them embraced Christianity, but there is perpetuation and continuation of tribal shamanistic religion in the Central and extreme southern Nicobar Islands. There is only a handful of Muslim Nicobarese; most of them are concentrated in Car Nicobar, with a lesser number in Nancowry, Katchal, Kamorta and Trinket respectively.

Nicobarese of different islands have varying terms for the traditional priests, shamans and witch doctors. In Car Nicobar they are referred to as totaràong, tomiluono and saàen. The people of Chowra call them kamasun. They are treated as sacred specialists and enjoy great respect among the people. As sacred specialists they perform even today important rituals at time of burial,

Kuimitilo (Memorial Post) used for 'Food offering ritual' to benevolent deities and a modified version of Memorial Post displayed at Car Nicobar Island.

sickness, accident and the like. They can communicate with the spirits and deities and are credited with supernatural powers to chase away spirits, calm storms, change the direction of winds, and bring rain and so on. They opposed Christianity, however, of late some of them have slowly been showing signs of respect and adjustment with this faith; indeed a few witch doctors have been converted to Christianity and in fact baptized with new Christian names such as Mantoov to Marcus, Yangon to Yacob, Rometh to Robert, Roya to Rafael, Hussana to Herbert so on and so forth. The photos show the icons of the tribal religion of the Nicobarese.

The saren (malevolent deity) is much feared. He is even equated with the ferocious totaràong or tomilnono (shaman). At one time the saren was identified as a witch doctor himself; who later took on different roles of harming people in general, even to the extent of causing a person to die. Hence the sarens' actions are treated as being anti-community, unlike the actions of shaman or witch doctor.

The notions of impurity and pollution are visible in various cultural activities of the people. Among the Car Nicobarese quite a few people suffer from an unhealthy feeling or dislike for food, meat and other things. Such urges and habits cannot be equated with allergy. This is known as sin-ok-kuo or so-ov-kuo in the native language of Car Nicobarese. Actually, it is attributed to their belief and practices. The concept of purity and impurity or pollution is attributed to the condition of the mind. Haneto or lanooko (purity) is maintained in their religious practices so that they are clean and sinless before the invisible mighty benevolent deities.

Icons of Tribal Religion

Social Change and Christianity

Conversion to the new faith gained momentum after World War II. At first the tribal people of Nicobar thought that on embracing Christianity they would not be able to pursue traditional economic activities. But now, most of the Nicobarese have accepted Christianity even though old tribal beliefs and practices too survive. Actually, the dawn of Christianity among the Nicobarese is viewed as a landmark in the sphere of social change as the people come to be influenced by the values and benefits of education.

The Christianity network in the entire group of Nicobar Islands is directly under the Church of North India, whose headquarters is located in New Delhi. Every village has a church where prayers are conducted. The Presbyter is the Parish in-charge at the village level. Each village church has a Mothers' Union and

Pastorate Committee consisting of four members, which form an important structural unit at the village level. Strategically, Bishop occupies the top slot in all religious as well as political affairs of the Island Council and at the district level also. The village presbyter and his assistants are equally gaining a place for themselves somewhat on par with the three headmen at the Village Council. However, this happens more when they are influential characters who can mould and shape decision-making by assisting the recognized headmen at village level. The prestige, status and the amount of reverence accorded to the Bishop is tremendous and discernible both at official and non-official level. His subordinates too enjoy such hospitalities and other privileges extended to such revered characters.

The Muslims

Nicobarese Muslims follow the Hanafi and Shafei schools of jurisprudence, and are part of the Sunni sect. Long before the British government established their agency in the Nicobar Archipelago many Muslim traders, for instance, Minicoyans and Indian Muslims originally from Gujarat and Surat visited Car Nicobar, Katchal, Nancowry, Kamorta and Trinket Islands. At that time some Nicobarese showed interest in embracing Islam, partly because they were eager to adopt outside cultural traits. There are only a few Muslims in the central islands of Nicobar Archipelago. They are concentrated in Car Nicobar, Katchal, Nancowry, Kamorta and Trinket. The role of Moulvi (priest) is limited to conduct namaaz (prayer), nikah (marriage), aqiqa (naming ceremony) and burial ceremony. Unlike the church presbyters and deacons the Moulvi does not interfere in any political and administrative issues. However, some Maulvis of different mosques in different villages and islands are making efforts to enter into village affairs both at the level of village and island Council.

On scrutiny of the findings of the present study we see that more than two thirds of the Nicobarese are Christians. The rest are all Tribal-animists and some Muslim. The inter-religious relation is governed by the tribal ethic and is marked by fraternity and mutual cooperation. The tribal people invite each other cordially, not only in religious functions, festivals, and marriages but also in other semi-religious festivals. They respect each other's sentiments and maintain decorum at all levels in terms of religious, cultural, and food habits.

Inter-Ethnic Contact, Hybridization and Change

As pointed out earlier Christianity is largely responsible for the spread of education among the tribal people of Nicobar Archipelago. Educationally, politically and administratively, the Car Nicobarese are a conscious people and are making concerted efforts at all levels to revive their traditional norms and values. They are rather selective in assimilating new ideas, which help them to develop their island territories and its inhabitants. At the same time they are enhancing their affiliation politically and administratively in order to gain an appropriate representation, so that they can project the interests of the community when suitable occasion comes up. The Nicobarese are now beginning to accept and avail of developmental programmes unlike yesteryears, when they expressed mixed reactions vis-à-vis developmental programmes or welfare measures. Some of them have of late taken loans from the bank in order

Nicobarese Inter-island Marriages

S. No.	*Island*	*Religion*	*Sex*	*Name of Bride/Bridegroom*	*Name of Bride/Bridegroom*	*Sex*	*Religion*	*Island*
1.	Car Nicobar	Christian	M	F Richardson +	T. Iris	F	Christian	Nan cowry
2.	Car Nicobar	Christian	M	Bryan +	Barbara	F	Christian	Nan cowry
3.	Car Nicobar	Christian	M	Nicholas +	Nangku	F	Animist	Nan cowry
4.	Car Nicobar	Christian	M	Bendinus +	Martha	F	Christian	Katchal
5.	Car Nicobar	Christian	M	Reginald +	Blendina	F	Christian	Katchal
6.	Car Nicobar	Christian	M	Hatuli +	Yoseere	F	Animist	Nan cowry
7.	Car Nicobar	Christian	M	Aron +	Eunicy	F	Christian	Katchal
8.	Car Nicobar	Christian	F	S. Penina +	Rev. Henry	M	Christian	Chowra
9.	Chowra	Christian	F	K. Penina Henry	K. Miriam	M	Animist	Katchal
10.	Car Nicobar	Christian	M	M. Cheerful +	K. Lalo	F	Animist	Chowra
11.	Car Nicobar	Christian	M	Samson Haran +	S. Molloi	F	Animist	Teressa
12.	Car Nicobar	Christian	M	Thomas Son +	K. Mayo	F	Animist	Teressa
13.	Car Nicobar	Christian	F	K. Thomas +	Harry	M	Christian	Katchal
14.	Car Nicobar	Muslim	F	Samsaath +	L. Justin	M	Christian	Teressa

to establish tea-shop, paan-shop and general shops too. Others have taken advantage of the incentive to keep poultry or rear pigs of new varieties. Other development programmes introduced by the Andaman and Nicobar administration are also being availed of.

The Nicobarese people of Nicobar Archipelago are endogamous in character. Monogamy is the social norm among the people. Lineage is exogamous in nature, and patrilocal and matrilocal rules of residence are prevalent in Car Nicobar. Matrilocal rules are more prominent in Central and extreme Southern Nicobar Islands. In this study, the focus is on the inter-island and inter-community marriages which have taken place in the Nicobarese society and which have led to greater hybridity. A chart showing inter-island marriages among the Nicobarese themselves belonging to different islands and religious groups are presented.

These days inter-island marriages are discernibly increasing. Leave alone marriage alliances, some Car Nicobarese have adopted children of families of Pulo Bhabi village of Great Nicobar. Rev. Matthew adopted a son and a daughter of Samuel; their names are Justin and Hope respectively.

According to our findings the Burmese were the first to intermarry with the native girls of Car Nicobar. Later on Minicoyans and Indian Muslims, originally from Gujarat and Surat followed suit. Nicobarese Muslims are the descendants of the Muslim traders who intermarried with the Nicobarese people of Car Nicobar, Katchal, Nancowry and others. At the beginning, the Muslim traders looked down on the Nicobarese, treating them as uncultured, unclean and unenlightened people, but gradually developed a liking for them. Some of them sought alliance with the native people. They quite often divorced their so-called local 'wives' whenever they were fed up of them. It is also reported that some of the Nicobarese were kept as concubines. They were left uncared for when the traders went back to their respective birth places and lived with their real wives in their respective hometowns. In this way, they left a legacy of half-breeds and miscegenation on these islands. Quite a few of the Muslim traders however, retained their relationships with the Nicobarese women, and converted their wives and children and subsequently settled on the Nicobar Islands.

The Nicobarese of the Central and extreme Southern island have experienced miscegenation with outsiders. The Nicobar islanders have experienced all kinds of external influences for centuries, because their islands are geographically located along an ancient international trade sea route, for example, the sea route from Colombo to Malaysia, Indonesia, Sumatra and vice versa. Actually, the Andaman and Nicobar islands are the gateway to the Bay of Bengal. The era from 15th century onwards experienced tremendous impact of various European missionaries, e.g., Portuguese, French, Jesuit, Danes, Italian, the British and so on. In 1756, the Danes took possession of the Nicobars for the purpose of colonization. They established their headquarters on Kamorta Island; however they could not convert the people and abandoned sovereignty over the island in 1848. Some Italian missionaries also made a futile attempt to spread Christianity in the early nineteenth century. In 1869 the British formally took occupation of the Nicobar Islands after negotiation with the Danes. In the following year the British established a penal settlement at Kamorta Island, which was closed in 1888. Although the possession of the Nicobar Islands was given up they were, however, administratively linked up with the Andaman Islands and this state of affairs continued till the pre-independence period. So from time immemorial the Nicobarese have had regular outside contact.

The tribal people of Nicobar Archipelago continue to be in touch with the outsiders, which is being steadily increased. Incidences of marriages with Bengali, Karen, local born, Madrasi (Tamil), Nepalis and others are also increasing despite the social prohibition imposed by the traditional council. Following tables show cases of inter-community marriages.

Pattern of Inter-Community Marriages

S. No.	*Wife = Husband*	*Communities*	*Remarks*
1.	Mathan = Maunaung (MLE)	NIC = Burmese	W. deserted
2.	Ahas = Olive (MLE)	NIC = Burmese	Till death do apart
3.	Sophia = Shabir (MLE)	NIC = Gujarati	As concubine
4.	Helena = Hussain (MLE)	NIC = Minicoyan	Till death do apart
5.	Kunanu = Tatsiunz (ML)	NIC = Ranchi	W. deserted
6.	N.Alice* = Gopal (MLE)	NIC = Madrasi/Tamil	As concubine
7.	Norah = Kheduram (MLE)	NIC = Ranchi	W deserted
8.	N.Alice* = Raghu (MLE)	NIC = Ranchi	H disappeared
9.	N.ALICE* = Hassan (MLE)	NIC = Nicobarese	W remarried
10.	Johanna = Liquat (MLE)	NIC = Local Born	H died
11.	Peter* = D.Tham (MLE)	NIC = Nepalis	W died
12.	Peter* = Roshini (MLE)	NIC = Nepalis	H remarried
13.	Eutichus = Kisangmu	NIC = Nepalis	H deserted
14.	Eutichus = Priya (MLE)	NIC = Beng. Settler	Continuing
15.	T.Alice = Sethu (MLE)	NIC = Local Born	H died
16.	Sockthit = Joseph (MLE)	NIC = Madrasi/Tamil	Till death do apart
17.	Christina = Karpan (MLE)	NIC = Madrasi/Tamil	Continuing
18.	Meshack = Seema+	NIC = Local Born	Continuing
19.	Lucas = Farida+	NIC = Local Born	Continuing
20.	Standly = K.Khalkho+	NIC = Ranchi	Continuing
21.	Leslie = Anima (MLE)	NIC = Beng. Settler	Continuing
22.	Morison = Beena+	NIC = Beng. Settler	Continuing
23.	Martin Fred = Sheting+	NIC = Ranchi	Continuing
24.	Omega = Shivangki (MLE)	NIC = Telegu	Continuing
25.	Linda = Alexander+	NIC = Ranchi	Continuing
26.	Andrew = L.Seema (MLE)	NIC = Madrasi/Tamil	Continuing
27.	Nahimiah = Iris (MLE)	NIC = Karen	Continuing
28.	Johnitai = Sweta (MLE)	NIC = Local Born	Continuing
29	Omega = Priya (MLE)*	NIC = Telegu	Continuing
30.	Wellington = M.Iamma (MLE)	NIC = Malayali	Continuing
31.	Florita = M.Habib (MLE&CM)	NIC = Mopla	Continuing
32.	Dominic = Susmita+	NIC = Tamil	Continuing
33.	Samuel M = Meena+	NIC = Telegu	Continuing
34.	Pauline = Ranjit M (MLE)	NIC = Beng. Settler	Continuing
35.	Salomie = B. Kumar+	NIC = Tamil	Continuing

Cont'd...

...Cont'd

36.	Susana = S. Majhi+	NIC = Tamil	Continuing
37.	Wellington = Regina O+	NIC = Ranchi	Continuing
38.	Kurehead A = Sandra+	NIC = Nepalis	Continuing
39.	Lali Oomar = S Hussain+	NIC = Local Born	Continuing
40.	Sale-A M = Shemary+	NIC = Karen	Continuing
41.	Flowrence = K Raj+	NIC = Tamil	Continuing
42.	M P Sale-A = Shemary	NIC = Karen	Continuing

* Nic, Beng, W and H as used in the table stand for the Nicobarese, Bengali settlers, wife and husband respectively.

S. No.	*Religion*	*Name*	*Non-Nicobarese*	*NN origin*	*Remark*
1.	Christian	O. Matan	NN	Burmese	Buddhist
2.	Christian	Helena	NN	Tamil	Hindu
3.	Christian	Concissa	NN	Ranchi	Christian
4.	Christian	Nora	NN	Ranchi	Hindu
5.	Christian	Soktit	NN	Malayali	Hindu
6.	Christian	Alice (remarried)	NN	Malayali	Hindu
7.	Christian	Kunangu	NN	Ranchi	Hindu
8.	Christian	Kanano Lelehe	NN	Local born	Hindu
9.	Christian	Christina	NN	Tamil	Hindu
10.	Muslim	S. Kunchang	NN	Local born	Hindu
11.	Christian	M. Augustine	NN	Bengali	Hindu
12.	Christian	Florence	NN	Tamil	Hindu

Thus, it is clear from the above data that hybridization is now entering into the core culture of the Nicobarese people. The Central and extreme southern Nicobarese have also reported interference of non-Nicobarese in horticultural activities and plantation as well. Influx of non-Nicobarese is reportedly increasing in the Nicobar Islands. For instance, Tamils from Sri Lanka have been rehabilitated at Mildera of Katchal Island and ex-servicemen in Great Nicobar Island. Influx of labourers is not uncommon. The floating petty traders have also economically exploited the Nicobarese. They brought materials from outside the islands and overcharged the community.

Significantly, the impact of cultural contact with the non-Nicobarese has resulted both in evil as well as favourable consequences. Accepting Christianity and education have by and large benefited the Nicobarese. However, the number of premarital and extra marital sexual relationships is on the increase. The floating non-Nicobarese and the employed population have implanted some immorality in the Nicobarese girls, who are sexually exploited. In the wake of modernization and awareness of the importance of cash-money, prostitution is viewed as a real fear and menace for the Nicobarese community. The Nicobarese of today are exposed to the external world and have absorbed its values consciously, and sub-consciously with the hope of making a better tomorrow, and they have gone into it without thinking deeply or constructively.

In fact, despite regular culture contacts the Nicobarese have retained native cultural traits, including religious and linguistic identity. It has been pointed out before that the Car Nicobarese language is the lingua franca among the entire

Nicobarese of different islands. As a supplement to this process of integration, presbyters are posted in different islands, not only to preach and propagate the gospel of Christianity, but to teach them the three Rs in Car Nicobarese language. Of late, the Car Nicobarese script is being developed and accepted by most Nicobarese of different islands and thus, the lingua franca and the scripts of Car Nicobarese are gaining popularity in other Nicobar islands. Nicobarese language programmes were launched from All India Radio Station, Port Blair on August 1, 1976. Since then the All-India Radio Station of Port Blair broadcasts a Nicobarese programme for 30 minutes every evening. The programmes in the Nicobarese language cover not only talks on various topics and development programmes in general, besides other important issues, they also accommodate individual talents by providing slots for poetry readings, story telling, riddles and other cultural programmes that enhance awareness. The All India Radio Station, Port Blair has organized literacy programmes in 1994 and 1995 in different Nicobar Islands in collaboration with the Deputy Commissioner, Nicobars District. The entire coverage of the programmes were broadcast for half an hour every evening and the response from the different islands in Nicobar was quite encouraging. This is one of the positive outcomes of the homogenization process.

At last, it may be restated that distinct social and economic differentiation had existed between various islands. Kinship norms and leadership rules also shaped inequality. The advent of Christianity and impact of education also created class-like segments. The impact of hybridization is definitely offering a serious challenge to the kinship oriented and lineage based socio-cultural life of the Nicobarese. More importantly, there is an identity crisis among the hybrids and the indigenous segment of people. Those who have improved their economic level and also those who have adopted new religions realize that they can not do away with tribal values and native culture. This dilemma in Nicobarese society as a whole is attributed to this hybridization process. The openness towards syncretism and other processes of amalgamation of tradition and modernization are all parts of hybridization (Justin, 2003).

References

Justin, A. 1990, *The Nicobarese,* Calcutta: Seagull Books.

Justin, A. 1993, "The Necobarese Herders and Horticulturists: Problems of Cultural Contact", in T.N. Pandit and N.K. Das (eds.), *The Pre-Agricultural Communities of India,* Calcutta: Anthropological Survey of India.

Justin, A. 2003, "The Coexistence of the Tribal Religion and Christianity among the Nicobarese", in N.K. Das (ed.), *Culture, Religion and Philosophy: Studies in Syncretism and Inter-Faith Harmony,* Jaipur: Rawat Publications.

Mann, R.S. 1984, "Social Stratification and Tribal Structure", in *Anthropological and Sociological Theory,* Jaipur: Rawat Publications.

Pandit, T.N. 1976, "Socio-Political Trends in Nicobar Islands", Port Blair: Anthropological Survey of India, Mimeographed.

Pandit, T.N. and A. Justin 1993, "The Authority Structure in the Nicobarese Society", in M.K. Raha (ed.) *Polity Political Process and Social Control in South Asia: The Tribal and Rural Perspective,* New Delhi: Publishing Home.

2 Economic Deprivation, Occupational Innovations and Growing Social Stratification among the Lalungs of Assam

G.C. Ojha

This paper discusses the varied dimensions of economic deprivation, occupational differentiation and emerging patterns of social stratification among the Lalung tribe, who had the matrilineal social structure in the past, before their contact with the dominant Hindu patrilineal communities, who influenced them immensely. In doing so, we will first discuss the identity issues pertaining to this tribe. The present study is based on the data collected through participant observation method. Data are collected from two Lalung villages, Jarabari and Barmanipur, located in Marigaon and Nagaon Districts of middle Assam during 1992 though data were updated later. Of these villages Jarabari is more exposed to social change and Barmanipur is less exposed to social change. We find that in both villages the Lalung have a sizeable population, but in village Jarabari a greater economic differentiation and upward social economic mobility is observed due to greater interaction with Hindu caste groups, particularly the Nath, and by adoption of the facility of education.

The Lalung Identity: Matriliny to Patriliny

The Lalung are one of the major tribes of Assam. The original name of the Lalung is *Tiwa*. *Ti* means water and *wa* means great. From their origin myth and their religious practices, it is observed that the Lalung were originally living close to some water source. Tiwa is also associated with the term 'Tibbatia', meaning people hailing from Tibet. Lalung is a Karbi word, *Lang* and *Lung*, meaning 'water' and 'to get resource' (or 'to get emancipated') respectively. Hence, the stream of water from which one can obtain emancipation is called Lalung and the people residing on the bank of that source of water are *Lang Lung*, later called Lalung. They trace their origin in Tibet region, from where they migrated and lastly arrived at Pragjyotisha and established a principality. Then they moved towards Kapili Valley and established Tribeg, a princely state. They ruled Tribeg for about sixteen generations. After the Ahoms victory over the Kacharis, Chiefs of Lalung in the Nagaon district were retained as subordinate chiefs. One legend describes that they originally inhabited in the Jantia Hills of Meghalaya and moved into plains of the Nagaon district because of economic considerations.

At present, the Lalung are divided into three sections. The Lalung living in the hills are called *Hazowali* (living in the hills of Assam and hills of Meghalaya). They are still retaining their traditional matrilineal culture. Secondly, the Lalung living in the foothills are called *Daliwali* (living in places like Sildhang, Neli, Digaru, Ulukundhi, Rongdoloi, etc.). In this area some of them follow their traditional matrilineal way of life but majority of them have changed into patrilineal culture. Thus, they are placed in a transitional stage in the changing scenario. On the other hand those who are living in the plains of Assam are called *Tholowali*. Here they have totally changed their way of living, culturally, socially and economically. They are now maintaining the patrilineal descent, at the same time most of them are now engaged in the settled wet cultivation, having abandoned the slash and burn cultivation practice of the earlier days.

Das (1982; 1985; 1987: 53–62) has critically discussed the issue of transformation among the tribes such as Lalung, Koch, Rabha, Garo and Khasi, using comparative perspective. Das found that while shifting from tribe/matriliny sphere to Hindu/patrilineal fold, several tribes exhibited varied degrees of sanskritization. He also reported formation of multi-clan mahari amongst the Lalung of Meghalaya. Besides culture change, changes had taken place in the material culture of the community. The houses of the hills were dwelling type, constructed mainly with the help of bamboo and thatch. On the other hand the houses in the foothills and plains are mainly built with bamboo and mud. Many changes are also noticed in the agricultural implements. The Lalungs living in the plains generally use *Nangal* (plough) *Jawali* (harrow), spade, *Fal, moi, Jotiari, Jabaka, Kanchi, Biriya,* whereas in the hills areas for Jhum cultivation the Lalung mainly use digging stick and *Dao*.

The Lalungs are found in considerable strength in the south-western tract of Nagaon and Marigaon district, particularly in the areas of Jamumamikh, Raha Marigaon and Jagiroad, across the Kamrup district, finally terminating at the confines of the Khasi hills (Ri-Bhoi district) of Meghalaya. Beyond this area concentration of the Lalung decreases. They are fairly found to the mouth of river Brahmaputra and to the east of Nagao.

The homeland of Lalungs, which can be geographically defined over contiguous parts of Nagaon (undivided) and Kamrup districts and the hills to the south of them, is not homogenous in ethnic composition and ecology. In Nagaon the Lalungs form about 12 per cent of the total population, are not numerically significant compared to other communities such as the Koch, Kaibarta, Kachari, Nath and Muslims. But they are the most predominant among the tribal groups. In Marigaon district, villages are under the *ryotwari* system, which means that each individual holder of land in made responsible for the payment of land revenue direct to the Mauzadar engaged by the government. There are three types of tenancy under which land is held for cultivation. These are Lakheraj, Kisfkheraj and Kheraj.

The Lalung have their own dialect, belonging to the Tibeto-Burman group of language: According to Grierson's classification their dialect is known as *Dowan*, considered to be one of the sub-groups of the main Bodo group of languages. According to B.K. Barua, B. Narjaree and Bishnu Rabha, the Lalung belong to Tibeto-Burman Mongoloid segment, who arrived here through the river course of Lohit (Brahmaputra) doing silkworm trading activities (Gogoi, 1986; 1987).

Majority of the Lalungs in the plains cannot speak their own mother tongue in general. Lalungs living in the hills still retain their own dialect. Though most of the plain Lalung adopted the Assamese language in general, but now-a-days they have tried to revive their dialect and tried to introduce the dialect in the primary level of school education. As they have no original script of their own, they adopted both the Roman and Assamese scripts side by side. The Assam Government in pursuance of their demand recognized the Lalung language in the primary level of school education in the Lalung dominated areas. They have also tried to revive their own cultural activities particularly in the field of dance, music and literature. A good number of songs and rhymes have already been revived and published in their own dialect using the Assamese script.

Social Structure: Life Cycle Rituals

The impurity arising out of birth is known as *kachasua*. The period extends from the date of birth till the date of *Aausgara* ceremony. During this period clan members observe certain taboos. They do not take out paddy from the granary. No ceremony can be observe during this period nor any member of the clan can enter the *Borghar* of another clan. Among the Lalungs marriage is the accepted form of union between a man and a woman. Illegal union especially in incestuous relations are very much hated and in no circumstances social recognition is given to such unions. Monogamy is the socially recognized type of marriage. Broadly the Lalungs have four forms of marriage, viz., *Borbiya, Joronbiva, Poluaiana* and *Gobbia rakha*. The well-to-do and educated Lalungs prefer Borbiya. This type of marriage has long drawn formalities and huge expenditure is required. In this type of marriage the guardians of the prospective couple take the initiative. *Zelas* or go betweens who are experts in the historical and legendary background of the community play important roles in such marriage. Marriage rituals are observed at the house of bride. *Zu* and pork are essential items in the marriage feast for traditional Lalungs. The *Jororn biya* is an arranged marriage. Generally, persons of low income group take resort to this type of marriage. On the appointed date the boy's party consisting of the elderly relatives proceeds to the girls house with ornaments, dresses and three *bhars* (baskets full of eatables including *Zu*) the elderly people of girls village bless the couple for happy conjugal life.

Poluai Ana (marriage by elopement) is widely prevalent among the Lalungs. Traditionally, the Lalung marriages are held under this system and no social stigma is attached to it. Less expenditure is involved in this type of marriage. At present the Lalungs, particularly of the plains, are patrilineal people but a very thin link with old matrilineal system is traced which is reflected in the *Gobhia rakha* (son-in-law living in wife's house) type of marriage. Generally parents having lone daughter without any male issue prefer to have *Gobhia*. Not much ritual formalities are observed in such type of marriage. Among the hill Lalungs of Karbianglong district is *Gobhia* is the most popular form of marriage. The rule of clan exogamy is strictly followed even in this type of marriage.

Among the Lalungs the marriage rules are governed by the *Borjela*. The *Borjela* is a specialist, selected by the Khel members. He is expert in tribal folklore and religious activities of the Lalung. He is considered to be the religious head of *Bongsha* or *Khuta*. He is also addressed as *Zelagabi*. His part is hereditary. After the death of the *Borjela* his son becomes the *Borjela*. If there is no son his post goes to the brother of *Borjela*. He is formally accepted by the village elders in the courtyard of the *Borghar*. He has certain restrictions in his diet and movement. Ele and carb are prohibited items for him. He can go to the cremation ground but cannot play active role in the cremation. *Borjelas* are generally appointed to solemnize religious activities concerning to marriage in the residence of bride. His main activities includes examining whether the number of agreements and betels given by the groom's family is correct or not. This indicates the clan (*paneh bhoni, set bhoni and na bhoni*) of which the groom is affiliated to; if he finds it correct he puts them on a bananas leaf in the middle of the room. He then pours over them a few drops of the *Zu* (rice beer) as oblation to the originated sisters.

The Lalungs pursue both cremation and burial system. Previously, dead bodies of wealthy and respectable persons only were cremated, but now a day cremation is the general rule. Each clan is supposed to have its own space allotted to it in the *hatham* (burial ground) which is known as *maker*. They cremate the dead bodies in their respective *maker*. The hill Lalung prefer burial which they call *sapat thowa*. Death causes pollution. The house has to be purified by those who belong to a clan different from that of the dead person. The inmates of the house shed their clothes and on that day do not take rice, fish and meat and do not take out paddy from the granary. All the clan followers also abstain from taking fish and meat till the 7th day after cremation. Karam is a community purification ceremony after death in which the pending death ceremonies of a few families of a *bongsha* are solemnized jointly in the *Borghar* on the day of Karam. The *gayety* shaves the heads of the sons of the deceased. All the families of a *bangsha* have to contribute to the common fund of the Karam. Formerly, Karam was seven days function but nowadays it is a one-day affairs. In the feast the Karam is observed with a pig and fowls. Every *bangsha* (lineage) has to bring one *bhar* which contains one basketful of rice, one pot of *zu* (rice beer) one-bunch nuts and five bundles of betels. Karams ends the death purification ceremony. After the *Borjela* has finished his oblatory rites the groom and the bride pays their respect to him and to the kinsmen present there by bowing down before them.

The Lalung khel selects a *giyati* (priest) to preside over the socio-religious occasions like Karam and allied ceremonies. It may be noted that the *giyati* must not belong to the Khuta in which the ceremonies are observed. The *giyati* takes all responsibilities of the cremation rites. Every Khuta select on *giyati* for performing the cremation rites and at the time of need he has to be formally invited. The *Giyati Mel* entrust the giyati to perform the rites in connection with the death. The *giyati* informs the villagers to bring the dead body to the *Maker*. In some villages the female *giyati* spread some *Akhoi* (fried rice) on the way to the cremation ground with the belief that the soul of the dead will get all pomp and pleasure in the next life if it walks over the *Akhoi* (fried rice). The *giyati* first applies fire over the face of the dead body. Later on *giyati* recites the *mantras* for the eternal peace of the soul.

Religion and Religious Transformation

The Lalung being a tribe have their own religious order. The *Boriela, Gharbuta* and *Harikunwari* are the three religious heads without whom there cannot be any religious ceremonies at the *Borghar* or *Bongsha*. The *Harikunwari* may be married or unmarried. A girl from the age of 8/9 can become *Harikunwari*. She must remain in the *Bongsha* (lineage) even after the marriage. In other words her husband must be a *Gobhia*. In general, Lalung society is going through changes in the religious sphere. Majority of them, are still maintaining their traditional way of religious activities. Their traditional religion is based on belief in some tribal deities. They are the followers of Sakta religion but the images of the deity is in the *thong* and puja paraphernalia are not the same used by the other non-Lalung Saktas. The hill Lalung worship stone images of deities, while their plains counterpart do not install any image in their altar. Of course the *Zela* or *Tripod* is found in their altars which is a symbol of Lord Shiva. The officials who are entrusted to perform the religious ceremonies are *Laro, Deori* and *Changmoji*. The *Laro* is the village priest, he generally performs religious ceremonies. He is not a preceptor but a specialists in the traditional priestly functions. The office is not hereditary. The main function of the *Deori* is to serve ceremonial meal to the deities, on the other hand the *Changmaji* deputy chief of the *Samadi* (bachelor dormitory) is to perform as assistant to the priest, during the religious functions. The *Gharbura* or *Zelagabi* is the religious head of a Bongsha or Khuta. His post is hereditary. After his death one of his son becomes *Gharbura*. He is formally accepted by the village elders in the *Borghar*. All the religious functionaries are considered to be of the superior status than that of the general people. At the time of any kind of feast, the food is offered to them in the household plate instead of plate made of banana leaves. They are also given *Zu* (rice beer) from the bell-metal pot whereas the general Lalung takes *Zu* from banana leaves.

Lord Mahadeo is their supreme God. All worships begin with a prayer to Lord Mahadeo. He is the protector of crops and human beings. The conception about Lord Mahadeva is still prevalent among all sections of Lalung. Among the Lalungs the benevolent male deities are Mahadeo, Ganesh, Parameshwar, Badarmaji, Buolakong and Kuber and the female benevolent deities are Aigosari, Lakshimi, Padumi, Kalika, Kamakhya, Saru Ai, Bor Ai. The *Gharbura* utters mantras, which differ from clan to clan. The Lalungs call the mantras as *bedang*. The *Than* is a religious place established in a village or in a cluster of villages. Formerly *Jongkong* (God of agriculture) was also worshipped in the Thans. But nowadays this puja is not performed in all Lalung villages. Sacrifices form essential part of the puja.

A good number of plains Lalung have gradually come to adopt some traits of the Hindu religion, particularly its form of Vaishnavism. The Hinduized Lalung do not maintain *Borghar* nor do they consume *Zu* (rice beer) or pork. They observe the caste Hindu religious ceremonies in their *Nama-Ghar* (prayer house). Nowadays two broad religious divisions are found among the Lalung – one maintaining their traditional religious belief and practices and the other section following the Hindu-centric *Vaishnavism*. The Hinduized Lalung establish *Nama-Ghar* where they perform the different Hindu religious ceremonies. A section of Lalung has come under the influence of Christians and converted into Christianity. These influences are found in the areas like Monaa and Haribari village.

Village One: Jarabari

Jarabari village consists mainly of the Lalungs and just one Brahmin family and one Koch family. There are three hamlets, viz., Alakapur, Milanpur, and Janabari proper. The name Jarabari is understood to have been derived from a lemon knows as *Jaranemu* in Assamese. *Jaranemus* are still grown in the village in almost each and every household, and this is a source of cash income. The Lalung community of village Jarabari consists of a number of *Kuls* (clan). Earlier, the village Jarabari had a dense cover of forest and the trees of *Jeranemu* in particular. As far the history of migration is concerned, it is understood that the different clans of the Lalung community migrated to this village at different times. The village Jarabari has 103 Lalung households and one Brahmin and one Koch household. The total population of Lalungs at village Jarabari is 621 of which male population is 392 (51.85%) and female (48.15%). The total area of village is 687 acre.

Myth prevalent reveals that the Lalungs once happened to live in the Jaintia kingdom and it is believed that the people adopted *jhum* cultivation from their contact with the Jaintias. However, after the Lalung came down to the plains areas of Assam they took up the plough cultivation. At present the Lalungs practice the winter paddy crop known as *Sali* and it is now the major crop produced by the Plains Lalung. The Lalung tribespeople living in the high altitudes practice even to-day *jhum* cultivation.

Agriculture and Land Management

Agricultural land in the village, Jarabari may be classified into four types, *Kathu amti* (land block soil), *Maubalia mati* (soft soil), *Bali sahia* (almost sandy), and *Dhumbali* (sandy soil). *Kathua mati* is best suited for the cultivation of both the varieties of winter paddy know as *Sali* and *Bao* and also for the summer paddy known as *Ahu*. Wheat and some vegetables also grow well in *Kathua mati*. Sugar cane grows best in *Maubalia mati*. Mustard, castor, tomato, cabbage, etc., are much suited in the *Bali sahia* type of soil while *Dhumbali* is good for potato, chilli, brinjal, etc. The village Jarabari is a revenue village. Such villages are known as Kisam. In Assam, record of land settlement was done in 1960 only although they came here long back. After 1960 the villagers were provided with permanent land records, locally known as *Miyadi Patta*. Agriculture is the principal means of the livelihood for the Lalung but they did not procure official documents. Initially the ownership of land was directly under the *Raja* (king). Hence, there was no individual ownership. However, there was an unwritten rule that ownership of land could be obtained by paying a share of the produce to the Raja.

The estates in village Jarabari belongs to the category called *Kheraj*. In the periodic *Kheraj* the landholder is given settlement rights for a specific period at a time. Locally it is known as *miyadi* land. In the annual *Kheraj*, the settlement rights are on a year-to-year basis and it is known as *touji* land. *Kheraj* land under periodic lease carries with it heritable and transferable rights subject to payment of land revenue. Thus for all intent and purposes, this is a piece of permanent property. On the other hand in the yearly lease, the landholder has a right of use for the year only, though the lease is normally renewed, except in those cases where land is required for some public purpose. As per the tenancy rules the owner of the holding paid annual revenues at the office of the Mauzadar. The Lalung settlement in the village Jarabari, as mentioned earlier took place some hundred years ago. They own land without any record. The people cleared the jungle and started settled paddy cultivation.

Table 1

Classification of Land Owning Household : Village Jarabari

S. No.	*Category of land bighas*	*Land owning household*	*Total land owned (in bighas)*	*Land owned/household (in bighas)*
1.	Only homestead	23	8 bighas 2 kathas	0.35 bighas
2.	1–3	32	71 bighas	2.22 bighas
3.	4–6	25	126 bighas	5.04 bighas
4.	7–9	10	74.5 bighas	7.45 bighas
5.	10–12	8	87.5 bighas	10.94 bighas
6.	13+	5	77 bighas	15.4 bighas
	Total	103	444 bighas, 2 kathas	4.31 bighas

The total land of all 103 households is 444 bighas and 2 kathas. 23 households possess only homestead land with average of 0.35 bighas. The average land per household is 4.31 bighas. The agricultural land of the Lalung are of three classes namely, high land or *bam-mati*, low land or *da-mati* and garden land or *bari-mati*. Garden lands of the people of Jarabari are situated in the village. The *bam-mati* or high lands of the people of Jarabari are located in the neighbouring villages namely Satabar, Majgaon, Chabukdhara of Charaibahi mauza, more or less within a radius of 10 km. The *da-mati* or low lands are situated adjacent to the *kasadhara beel* (marshy land). These lands are about 5 km away from the village Jarabari. The immovable property of the Lalungs of Jarabari includes both agriculture and basti (homestead). After the death of the father or even before his death the land is divided equally among his sons. The father may keep one share for his use, which after his death goes to that son who lives with him and *takes* care of him till his death. The house goes to that son who lives with his father till his death. Among the Lalungs of Jarabari, daughters do not inherit property.

The Lalungs of Jarabari are agricultural people. Table 2 shows that cultivation is the main occupation of the people. Altogether in 40 families primary occupation is agriculture and secondary is service. A combination of service as primary and agriculture as secondary pursuit is the most respected way of life in the village. It is clear that agriculture is the most important pursuit of the people.

The agricultural land, of the Lalungs of Jarabari is situated near their village. The *bam-mati* (high land) are situated at the east and north side of the

Table 2

Occupation with Household Type and Size: Village Jarabari

Type of occupation	*Nuclear*					*Extended*					*Others*					*Total*				
	1–3	*4–6*	*7–9*	*10+*	*T*	*1–3*	*4–6*	*7–9*	*10+*	*T*	*1–3*	*4–6*	*7–9*	*10+*	*T*	*1–3*	*4–6*	*7–9*	*10+*	*T*
Agri	9	19	3	—	31	1	2	3	3	9	—	—	—	—	—	10	21	6	3	40
Service	2	4	—	—	6	—	1	1	—	2	—	—	1	—	1	2	5	2	—	9
Labour	1	4	1	—	6	—	1	1	—	2	—	—	—	—	—	1	5	2	—	8
Teacher	1	1	1	—	3	—	—	—	—	—	—	—	—	—	—	1	1	1	—	3
Business	1	—	2	—	3	—	—	—	—	—	—	—	—	—	—	1	—	2	—	3
Blacksmith, Carpentry	—	—	—	—	—	—		—	—	1	—	—	—	—	—	—	1	—	—	1
Fishing	—	1	—	—	1	—	—	—	—	—	—	—	—	—	—	—	1	—	—	1
Agri, Carpentry	1	2	—	—	3	—	—	1	—	1	—	—	—	—	—	1	2	1	—	4
Service, Agri	1	8	1	—	10	—	2	7	6	15	—	—	—	1	1	1	10	8	7	26
Agri, Teacher	—	1	—	—	1	—	—	1	—	1	—	—	—	—	—	—	1	1	—	2
Agri cum business	—	—	—	—	—	—	2	1	2	5	—	—	1	—	1	—	2	2	2	6

village namely Bampathar and Galbhag (kuch para) respectively. The *da-mati* (low land) are situated adjacent to the kasadhara beel which is about 5 km away from the village. The *basti-mati* (homestead land) of the people of Jarabari are situated adjacent to their homestead.

The Lalungs of Jarabari depend mostly on the monsoon. Generally, rainfall is quite sufficient for cultivation so they need not depend upon irrigation for supply of water in the fields. There are only two diesel pumps in the village. These two are owned by the Lalungs of Jarabari. So these two families who have got diesel pumps for irrigation in the high land mostly grow double and triple crops in a year. However, the other villagers take them on hire for irrigating their own cultivable land. They pay some amount of money to the pump owner.

After harvesting *Sali* paddy in Kati-Aghon (November–January) land is left fallow for four months and Ahu paddy is sown in the month of April. Paddy is heaped in bundles. These bundles are carried from the field with the help of *banka* or carried by the bullock cart. Though in the Lalung society no occupational grouping is found, yet there is a division of labour. Heavy labour is done by men such as to prepare and repair the plots, ploughing, transporting, manuring, threshing grains, etc. The women perform jobs like weeding, harvesting, transplanting, etc., in the agricultural field. As the Lalung are becoming conscious about the value of land, its produce, etc., they have started employing labourers either Lalung or non-Lalung like Koch, Nath, Hira, etc.

Three types of labour employment are noticed, namely daily, yearly and seasonal. In case of daily employment, a male or a female receives payment either in cash or in kind. In case of yearly wage, a person receives cash varying from ₹ 300 to 400 per year and two meals a day and clothes. This type of labour is locally known as *borcher morogia*. The third category of labour is employed during Sali and Ahu paddy operations. The duration of such employment is about 3 to 4 months. The land owner supplies the bull and plough to the labourer, the labourer tilling the soil of landlord for two days. In lieu of this he will get the chance to till the soil of his own land for one day with that bull and plough. This system is known as *Melamorogia*. Moreover there is another seasonal labourer engaged for 2–3 months known as *bondha morogia*, who performs the duty of tilling soil in the agricultural field of the land-owner. The *bondha morogia* gets only ₹ 300 per month including meals and clothes. During the harvesting seasons both men and women go to the field and reaping is done by the women folk and males carry the bundles of paddy to their houses. Threshing is done by the males. The working groups of young girls (a group of six girls) in the village is called *hadarikhel*. When a family is facing trouble during the time of transplantation, harvesting, etc., the neighbours assist the family. The landowner offers them *Zu* (rice beer) and chicken. This type of mutual cooperation is known as *chenehuwa* (helping with love). And when a family calls some people to help them in the agricultural field for harvesting, etc., it is known as *manuh mata* (calling men). The landlord offers *Zu* (rice beer) and chicken to such people with a meal. There is another kind of helper for the agricultural field who is known as *muniboa*. The *muniboa* (a kind of daily wage labourer) receives one *don* (about 5 kg) paddy per day from the landlord.

Both bullocks and buffalo are used for cultivation. There are seven pairs of buffaloes in the village. The households that own more cultivable land possess one or more pair of bullocks. The bullocks are used for ploughing, and transporting paddy from agricultural field to home. The buffaloes are used for the cultivation of sugar cane. The *Nangal* (plough) is most widely used agricultural implement of the Lalung of Jarabari. It consists of a beam, a yoke and the body. The yoke rests on the neck of the two bullocks. They use *Juwali* (harrow) in their fields, which looks like a ladder. The length of a *Juwali* is about 1.5 metre and the breadth is about 30 centimetres. A beam is tied to the centre of the yoke. The man behind the plough stands on the ladder which is pulled by the bullock. Other agricultural implements are *kor* (spade) *Fal, Moi, Jot jari, Salmari, Dilabari, Jabaka, Dalimari, Kanchi* (sickle), *Biria Okhoni, Bindha, Khanti* (garden spade), and *Chelan.*

Fertilizer and pesticides have helped the agriculturists in raising food production and checking diseases. Only 15 families of Jarabari informed that they are familiar with fertilizers like Urea, D.A.P. and pesticides like BAC for paddy, metacide (for Jute) and aldrex. The farmers are getting loan from various agencies like district agricultural department, block office, cooperative societies. Only limited number of farmers use the hybrid seeds. Often the farmers fail to gather requisite capital for cultivation from the production of the previous year. The farmers borrow money from the local moneylenders on interest. In lieu of money the farmers have to give a portion of their land to landlords until the money is repaid. This system is known as *mati bondhoki diya* (land mortgage). Poor people from Jarabari are often engaged as labourer by the neighbouring villages. Moreover, the agencies like DRDA, District agricultural office, nationalized banks extend loan for specific agricultural purposes like installation of pump sets, purchase of bullocks, etc., with 50 per cent subsidy.

The Lalung have indigenous method of protecting the crops. They also offer a *puja* to Goddess Lakchhmi before starting the cultivation to protect the crops. They construct scarecrows on the paddy field by using the branch of *pachpafia, Akenda tree,* and *kekora* (crab) to scare the birds. All the farmers of village Jarabari use the traditional plough for cultivation. At that time the rate of hiring a tractor was ₹ 80 per bigha, which was expensive for the Lalung of Jarabari. There are only two diesel pumps in the village for irrigation purposes. These two sets were individually procured from the DRDA for ₹ 14,000 per set (50% subsidy).

Marketing facilities are available in the local markets known as *hats*. These *hats* are connected with the PWD road. There is a daily bazaar at Barapujia. The Lalungs visit this bazaar for their daily needs. Moreover they regularly visit nearby weekly markets for selling paddy. They visit weekly Jaluguti bazaar for cow, bull, goat, duck, hens, etc., and for selling jute. Those who grow other crops in larger quantities, sell their products to the non-Lalung middlemen like Bihari, Marwari inside the village itself although the villagers know that the lion's share of the profits will be taken by these traders. Small growers carry their produce either as shoulder loads or on bicycle to the market.

We notice in the area the *adhi* system, an old system, wherein the landowner gives only land and the *adhiar* (who cultivates the land) bears all expenses and the produce is divided into two parts. They also lease the land for cultivation of the crops like *Sali* and *Ahu* or *bao*. This system is socially practiced by the Lalungs of Jarabari. Land is normally leased to those who are labourious. Good output of crop can only be ensured from the labourious *adhiar*. Another system is known as *sa-adhia*. In this system the farmer takes the land on lease from the landowner, and both cultivate two equal portions. The landowner supplies seeds for his portion, and at the time of harvesting the landowner collects the paddy from his portion. In *chukti* system the land is given on lease for two or three years for a fixed amount of money.

The tribal people have indeed come to realize the value of the money; hence, above share-cropping methods have become popular and thus tribal families have improved their economic statuses. Some families are more prosperous than others. We may say that these developments have led to the birth of the rudimentary classes. More than twenty families are enjoying the *adhi* (share cropping system) in the village. They receive the land from the Lalung tribal people as also from the Brahmin, Kalita, Kaibarta, Hira, and Nath to cultivate *Sali* and *Ahu paddy* or *Bao paddy*. About 142 bighas of *adhi*-land is distributed among the 25 Lalung *adhiars*. Out of 25 *adhiar* families some 5 are landless families, depending solely on the *adhi* land.

Table 3

Land Holding with Household (Type and Size): Village Jarabari

Type of land-holding in bighas	*Nuclear*					*Extended*					*Other*					*Total*				
	1–3	*4–6*	*7–9*	*10+*	*T*	*1–3*	*4–6*	*7–9*	*10+*	*T*	*1–3*	*4–6*	*7–9*	*10+*	*T*	*1–3*	*4–6*	*7–9*	*10+*	*T*
Only home-stead	4	11	2	—	17	1	2	1	2	6	—	—	—	—	—	5	13	3	2	23
1–3	9	15	2	—	26	—	2	2	1	5	—	—	1	—	1	9	17	5	1	32
4–6	9	7	2	—	12	—	2	5	5	12	—	—	1	—	1	3	9	8	5	25
7–9	—	6	—	—	6	—	1	3	—	4	—	—	—	—	—	—	7	3	—	10
10–12	1	1	—	—	2	—	1	4	—	5	—	—	—	1	1	1	2	4	1	8
13+	—	—	1	—	1	—	—	1	—	4	—	—	—	—	—	—	—	2	3	5

Table 4

Village Jarabari: Landholding with Occupation

Type of land-holding in bighas	*Varieties of occupation*								
	Agri	*Service*	*Agri labour*	*Business*	*Teacher*	*Artisan*	*Fishing*	*Nursery*	*Total*
Landless	11	—	20	—	1	2	1	1	36
1–3	27	12	2	4	2	1	—	—	48
4–6	22	13	2	1	4	3	—	—	45
7–9	8	7	—	—	3	—	—	—	18
10–12	7	9	—	—	—	—	—	—	16
13+	6	6	—	1	1	—	—	—	14
Total	81	47	24	6	11	6	1	1	177

It is seen that 23 families (22.33%) are landless (they only have homestead land) and 32(31.07%) families have 1 to 3 bighas of land, and 25(24.97%) families have 4 to 6 bighas of land respectively. As per the peoples perceptions these little quantities of lands are not sufficient for them to fulfil their daily consumption throughout the year. Hence a good member of families depend on share-cropping, as we discussed. In most of the cases these tenants have invested money both in cash or kind for acquiring bulls and plough and in some cases seeds also. Another point is the presence of tribal clan land. Every *kul* (clan) has own fund from where the *kul* (clan) members of the particular clan can get certain amount of cash by paying nominal interest.

Eleven landless families are sharecroppers hence they are involved in agriculture. The service families who are holding more than 10 bighas of land are upper class people of the village and 22 families heaving 4 to 6 bighas of land form middle economic class and the remaining form lower class.

Table 5

Village Jarabari: Literacy with Occupation

Literate level of households	*Occupation of the member*									
	No.	*Agri*	*Service*	*Labour*	*Business*	*Teacher*	*Artisan*	*Fishing*	*Nursery*	*Total*
Illiterate	42	38	1	19	3	—	2	1	—	64
Primary I–IV	19	17	4	—	—	—	1	—	1	23
Secondary V–X	33	25	32	5	3	2	3	—	—	70
X+	9	1	9	—	—	9	—	—	—	19

The Lalungs of Jarabari indeed considerably depend on agriculture. Literacy level is low and educational achievements are miserable.

Second Village: Barmanipur

The Lalung village Barmanipur is located on Marigaon–Bhuragaon road. The village is at a distance of 7 km from the Marigaon state highway. Communication to and from the village is not difficult. In neighbouring villages different ethnic groups, viz., Chutia, Koch, Jugi, Hira, Kaibarta, Kalita, are inhabited. The Lalung community has a marriage relationship with Karbi, Bodo, Chutia, Koch and Jugi, though the instances are less. In village Barmanipur all landholdings belong to the *kheraj* system. In *kheraj* the landholder is given settlement rights for a specific period at a time: in the annual *kheraj* the settlement rights are given on a year-to-year basis. Cultivation and service are the main occupation of the villagers of Barmanipur and rice is their staple food. All the families grow paddy in their fields. The distance of most of these fields from their home is within three kilometres.

Table 6

Village Barmanipur: Population According to Household Census

No. of household	*Male*		*Female*		*Total*	
	No.	*%*	*No.*	*%*	*No.*	*%*
102	302	47.2	338	52.8	640	100.0

The household and population analysis shows that the total number of household at Barmanipur is 102. Table 6 shows that the total population of the village was 640 out of which 302 were males and 330 females. The percentage of male and female was 47.2 and 52.8 respectively. It is thus seen that the number of females is higher than that of males.

On the basis of linguistic evidence, the Lalungs have been classified with the Bodos or the Kacharis of Assam. In fact, their language is more closely connected with the Dimasa branch of the Bodo people. Edward A. Gait in his *History of Assam* says that the Kacharies are believed to be very closely allied to the Koches and also, to the Chutiyas, Lalungs and Marans of the valley and the Garos and Tipperas of hills (Gait, 1963: 248). Dr Grierson in his Linguistic Survey of India states that in 1891 there were forty thousand Lalung speakers in Nowgong, Kamrup and Khasi and Jaintia Hills. In Nowgong, they have a tradition that their ancestors came from the Jaintia Hills, in the reign of the Jaintia Raja, U-Mon Gohain. Another account also says that the Lalungs were the autochthones of the Jaintia Hills (Grierson, 1903: 49). The figure came down to 10,576 in 1961 census. Again the figure further came down to 9,954 as per 1971 census. The reason for this variation in the decade is probably conversion of Lalungs into Koch. Though they are maintaining their distinctive tribal culture the Lalungs are influenced by the dominant Assamese language and culture.

In the village Barmanipur only 5 per cent people can speak their own Lalung Language. Assamese being the dominant language the people of these villages have acquired a natural proficiency in it. Not only the villagers speak Assamese language among themselves but even in dealing with any outsider they use Assamese language as the medium of communication. The educated persons know English and Hindi as they learn it in schools and colleges. Around Barmanipur there are villages inhabited by Assamese people like Brahmin, Kalita, Keot, Koch, Kaibarta, Nath, Hira, etc.

Table 7

Village Barmanipur: Distribution of Population in Different Types of Household

Type of household	*Total*	*Total*	*Population*	*Total*	*Male*	*Total*	*Female*
	Household	*No.*	*%*	*No.*	*%*	*No.*	*%*
Nuclear	62	319	49.84	150	23.43	169	26.41
Extended	40	321	50.16	152	23.75	169	26.41

The family-type of the village Barmanipur is found to be both nuclear and extended type. There are 62 nuclear families against 40 extended families in the village; their percentage being 60.8 and 39.2 respectively. The percentage of nuclear family is higher than that of extended family. Out of total population, 640,319(49.84%) individuals are from nuclear families and 312(50.16%) individuals are from extended families.

Table 8

Village Barmanipur: Number of Family Members, Household-wise

No. of family members	*No. of household*		*Male*		*Female*		*Total*	
	No.	*%*	*No.*	*%*	*No.*	*%*	*No.*	*%*
2–3	11	10.77	12	1.88	15	2.35	27	4.23
4–5	31	30.38	70	10.94	71	11.09	141	22.03
6–7	39	38.28	113	17.65	135	21.09	248	38.75
8–9	11	10.77	44	6.87	47	7.34	91	14.11
10–11	4	3.92	18	2.82	25	3.90	43	6.72
12+	6	5.88	45	7.03	45	7.03	90	14.06

At Barmanipur village there are 102 families. The families are classified into 6 grades depending upon the number of individuals in the family. Table 8 shows that 6 to 7 members holding family are the most prominent in the village. Their percentage is 38.28 in 39 households, 4–5 members family in 31 house holds has a percentage of 30.38, which is the second highest percentage.

Education

Formal education has played a vital role in all aspects of the community life. The percentage of literacy among the Lalungs as per 1971 census was 21.5 (male 31.47% and female 11.14%) (Census of India, 1971). Following are the finding of our present study in Barmaniur village. In Table 9 the literacy rate has been counted from the age of 6 (six). Out of total population 640 the illiterate male population is 90(14.06%) and female is 169(26.40); in primary standard (Class I to IV) male 76(11.87%) and female 54(8.44%). In middle school (Class V to VII) the number of males are 40(6.26%) and females are 26(4.06%). In the literacy standard of high school (VIII to X) males are 43(6.72%) and females are 32(5%) and in higher education (above HSLC) only 9(1.41%) males and only one female (0.16%) have been found in the village Barmanipur. From the above discussion we see that the illiterate persons of village Barmanipur are 259(40.46%) while the literate persons are 281(43.91%) hence the literacy rate of the Barmanipur village is much higher than that of the general literary rate of the Assam.

Table 9

Village Barmanipur: Level-wise Literacy Distribution

Literacy Level	*Male*		*Female*		*Total*	
	No.	*%*	*No.*	*%*	*No.*	*%*
Illiterate 0–5 years	44	6.87	56	8.75	100	15.62
6+	90	14.06	169	26.40	259	40.46
Primary I–IV	76	11.87	54	8.44	130	20.31
Middle School V–VII	40	6.26	26	4.06	66	10.32
High School VIII–X	43	6.72	32	5	75	11.72
College	9	1.41	1	0.16	10	1.57

In case of secondary classes (from the age 11 onward) out of 114 only 86 students are going to school (Table 9).

Almost every Lalung village has lower primary school, where the medium of education is Assamese. Student aspiring for High School education have to go to nearest High school which is situated within easy reach of the villagers. The High School students of Barmanipur have to go to Bishnurabha High School, Manipur which is at a distance of 2 km, since there is no High School in the village. The colleges are established at district headquarters Marigaon. From primary to college level the medium of education is Assamese. Now-a-days in all the Lalung villages, formal education is imparted to the children.

Before independence, there were very few L.P. Schools and the Lalung did not have much of formal education. In those days the *Samadis* (bachelors' dormitory) played the role of training. To-day, however, there are *Samadis* in a few Lalung villages but no training of the youths is provided (Sharma Thakur, 1985: 20). Though the *Samadis* are noticed in the Barmanipur village nowadays they are completely inactive to train up the children. This is happening due to the introduction of formal education.

Table 10

Village Barmanipur: Distribution of Household by Occupation

Name of occupation	*No. of household*		*Population engaged*	
	Nuclear No.	*Extended No.*	*Nuclear No.*	*Extended No.*
Agriculture	48	33	63	73
Service	3	2	6	7
Labour	6	2	16	8
Teacher	1	1	1	1
Business	2	1	2	2
Artisan	1	1	1	1
Fishing	1	—	1	—

Table 10 shows that cultivation is the main occupation of the people. Altogether seven families depend solely on agriculture. It is clear that agriculture is the most important economic pursuit of the people of Barmanipur. There are 8 families in the village whose primary occupation is labour (including agricultural labour). There are 7 families whose primary occupation is service and secondary occupation is agriculture. Also there are two families who took business (shop keeping) as their occupation. There is only one family who is engaged in fishing as its primary occupation. It is seen that next to agriculture the service is the most prized occupation of the people. A combination of service as primary and agriculture as secondary pursuits is the most respected way of life in the village. There are only two artisan families in the village.

Land Management

The Table 11 shows that all the villagers have some amount of land- holding of their own. At the category No. 7 (landholding of 16 bighas and above) 25 households are found. Each family occupies 24.39 bighas of land per household. It is the highest frequency for per household. The highest land-holding households are at the category No. 3. It occupies 130 bighas of land. It shows that landholding per household is 5 bighas.

Table 11

Village: Barmanipur Distribution of Land Owning Households

S. No.	Category of land in bighas	Land owning household	Total land owned in bighas	Land owned per house-hold (in bighas)
1.	Only Basti (homestead)	8	9	1.12
2.	1–3	4	12.5	3.12
3.	4–6	26	130	5.00
4.	7–9	21	174	8.28
5.	10–12	12	134	11.16
6.	13–15	8	112.5	14.06
7.	16+	25	561	24.39
	Total	102	1,138	—

At the category No. 4 are 21 households and their total land in bighas is 174. The average land for household is 8.28 bighas. The 8 families with 13–15 bighas of land from the upper class. There are 47 landholding families with 4–9 bighas (Category No. 3 and 4) and they belong to middle economic class. The rest from the lower class.

Table 12

Village Barmanipur: Landholding with Household Type and Size

Type of land-holding (in bighas)	Nuclear					Extended					Total				
	1–3	4–6	7–9	10+	Total	1–3	4–6	7–9	10+	Total	1 3	4–6	7–9	10+	Total
Landless (only home-stead)	—	—	—	—	—	—	—	—	—	—	—	—	—	—	—
1–3	4	5	3	—	12	—	1	1	—	2	4	6	4	—	14
4–6	5	13	5	—	22	—	3	1	—	4	5	16	6	—	27
7–9	3	4	1	—	8	—	6	5	2	13	3	10	6	2	21
10–12	—	5	—	—	5	—	2	3	1	6	—	7	3	1	11
13–15	—	1	—	—	—	—	1	2	2	5	—	2	2	2	6
16+	—	11	2	—	13	—	3	2	5	10	—	14	4	5	23

Table 13

Village Barmanipur: Occupation with Household Type and Size

Type of occupation	Nuclear					Extended					Total				
	1–3	4–6	7–9	10+	T	1–3	4–6	7–9	10+	T	1–3	4–6	7–9	10+	T
Agricul-ure	8	33	8	—	49	—	12	9	9	30	8	45	17	9	79
Service	—	2	1	—	3	—	2	1	1	4	—	4	2	1	7

Cont'd...

...Cont'd

Labour	2	3	—	—	5	—	2	1	—	3	2	5	1	—	8
Teacher	—	1	—	—	1	—	—	1	—	1	—	1	1	—	2
Business	1	1	—	—	2	—	—	1	—	1	1	1	1	—	3
Artisan	—	1	—	—	1	—	—	1	—	1	—	1	1	—	2
Fishing	—	—	1	—	1	—	—	—	—	—	—	—	1	—	1

Table 14

Village-Barmanipur: Literacy with Occupation

Literacy of household	*Occupation of the members*							
	No.	*Agri*	*Labour*	*Business*	*Teacher*	*Service*	*Artisan*	*Fishing*
Illiterate	67	77	22	1	—	1	—	1
Primary I–IV	14	28	—	1	—	—	2	—
Middle V–VII	7	12	1	1	—	5	—	—
High school VIII–X	12	22	—	1	—	6	—	—
College	2	—	—	—	2	1	—	—

Table 15

Village-Barmunipur: Landholding with Occupation

Type of land-holding (in bighas)	*Varieties of occupation*							
	Agri	*Service*	*Labour*	*Business*	*Teacher*	*Artisan*	*Fishing*	*Total*
1–3	11	1	14	—	—	—	1	27
4–6	29	4	5	1	—	1	—	40
7–9	34	1	—	2	1	—	—	38
10–12	17	—	—	1	—	1	—	19
13–15	16	3	—	—	—	—	—	19
16+	37	5	—	—	1	—	—	43

Table 16

Village-Barnanipur: Landholding with Household Type and Size

Land-holding (in bighas)	*Household type and size*														
	Nuclear					*Extended*					*Total*				
	1–3	*4–6*	*7–9*	*10+*	*T*	*1–3*	*4–6*	*7–9*	*10+*	*T*	*1–3*	*4–6*	*7–9*	*10+*	*T*
1–3	2	6	3	—	11	—	1	1	—	2	2	7	4	—	13
4–6	6	12	4	—	22	—	3	1	—	4	6	15	5	—	26
7–9	3	5	1	—	9	—	6	5	2	13	3	11	6	2	22
10–12	—	4	—	—	4	—	2	4	1	7	—	6	4	1	11
13–15	—	1	2	—	3	—	2	1	2	5	—	3	3	2	8
16+	—	12	1	—	13	—	2	2	5	9	—	14	3	5	22

The Tables 12, 13, 14, 15 and 16 provide basic economic and literacy data, pertaining to second village. The Lalungs are almost exclusively agriculturists. At Barmanipur almost all the householders are agriculturists of which some of the households have an additional occupation besides agriculture. Agricultural methods practiced in this village are similar to those of the neighbouring villages. The plough is the main agricultural implement, which is drawn by a pair of bullocks. The Lalungs of Barmanipur also practise mechanized farming. Some families use tractors for ploughing.

The most important crop is paddy and its cultivation is predominantly more than all the other crops put together. The villagers generally grow two types of paddy, *Ahu* and *Sali*. The soil of the village is very suitable for the production of *Sali*. The *Ahu* cultivation is practiced at the *da-mati* (lowland). It is found that some households who have suitable lands for cultivation of *Ahu* paddy do cultivate the same. The average yield per bigha of *Ahu* pady is reported to be lower than the average yield per bigha of *Sali*. It is also reported that after harvesting *Ahu* the villagers cultivate *Sali* on the same plot of land. The *Bao* paddy is also grown in a limited scale. Along with *Sali, Ahu* and *Bao* paddy the Lalungs of Barmanipur grow some quantities of mustard, arum, turmeric, ginger, brinjal and chillies, etc.

Those who grow paddy and other crops in larger quantities, sell their products to the non-Lalung middlemen inside the village itself, although the villagers know that the lion's share of the profits is taken by these traders. Small growers carry their produce either on shoulder or on bicycles to the market. There are village-shops in the Barmanipur. Generally these shops are owned by the local Lalung villagers.

Village Stratification

The Lalung society is a stratified society. In the past the people had their chiefs. There was also a Lalung kingdom. The Lalung *Raja* was called *Deo Raja*. Tribal polity is now seen only at village level. Now there are tribal clan elders in village having different socio-religious assignments. Barmanipur is still a tribal village and hence besides the 'gaon bura' there are *Pathak, Medhi, Gayanu* and *Barali* who have been assigned different roles in the socio-religious ceremonies. These office bearers are also found in nearby Vaishnavite Assamese villages and the Hinduized Lalungs have introduced the same in their own tribal village structure.

The properties of the Lalungs of Barmanipur village can be divided into movable and immovable categories. After the death of the father or even before his death the land is divided equally among his sons. The father may keep one share for his use, which after his death goes to that son who lives with him and takes care of him till his death. The house goes to that son who lives with his father till his death. In the village Barmanipur it is noted that daughter does not inherit property.

Altogether, 124 married couples live in the Barmanipur village. Out of 124, majority of the couples (90) have solemnized their marriage according to the *Poluai Ana* (marriage by elopement) system. Fifteen marriages have been solemnized according to the *Joron Biya* system; 10 couples performed their marriage by

Boraiya system and 8 couples followed the *Gobhia Rakha* system. Only one couple accomplished marriage at the civil court. Intercommunity marriage is also allowed. Collected data reveal that in the Barmanipur village, out of 124 married individuals, 9 have solemnized their marriage with the Koch and 4 individuals, have performed their marriage with the Karbi tribe and only one case of marriage is found with the Bodo tribe.

Tribal Legal System – Leadership

Among the Lalung villagers the *Borkhel Bichar* is the most popular and predominant rural judicial institution. Thus, if anybody is found to have committed wrong the villagers submit a complaint narrating the history of the activities of the wrong-doer before the villagers. Then the elderly *jelas* of the village gather and hear the dispute and decide penalty. The elderly people of different *khels* compose the *Borkhel bichar*.

The council of elders is the highest judicial body in the village. The headman of statutory village council may not be its member but he acts in strict collaboration with it.

There is another important body in Barmanipur known as *Gaon Unnayan* Committee (village development board). The committee directs all the development activities like construction of roads, school buildings, and other welfare works in village. This is besides the Gaon Panchayat. The head of the Statutory Gaon Panchayat is known as *Sabhapati* (president). Ten members are selected, but strength of Panchayat can, however, vary with the size of the population. Every adult member (above 18 years) of the village is entitled to vote. The *gaon panchayat*, being the statutory body, is supposed to perform many functions such as development of agriculture and forest, development of communication, development of animal husbandry, cottage industries and fisheries, digging of wells and tanks, and other matters as may be assigned from time to time. At the apex level, the councillor and chief councillor of Zilla Parishad maintain links with the village-councils.

Social Structure, Pattern of Stratification and Political System

In a Lalung village there are a number of *khutas* of different clans. The *khutas* of different clans in due course form a *khel*. The number of *khutas* varies at different places. But at least two *khutas* are needed to form a khel. The members of *khutas* may intermarry. The members of same clan may have membership in separate *khutas*. The *khuta* social grouping may be regarded as the extension of a family. A *khel* in a true sense is a broader territorial devise within the village. Every *khel* has a *Namghar* (prayer house). Though it is primarily a place of religious service, the elders can meet there to discuss any matter or to settle dispute between the members of the *khels*.

The Lalung society is a stratified society and there are different office bearers in a village having different socio-religious assignments. Among the Lalungs a village does not form the lowest administrative unit. In a village there are so many *khels*. Every *khel* has its own priest. A full-fledged *khel* generally consists of two age-sets, namely *Bura-khel* and *Deka-khel*. The *Bura-khel* consists of the members of older persons. On the other hand the younger members of the community form *Deka-khel*. The chief office bearers of the *Bura-khel* are known as *Doloi, Loro, Pator, Changmaji, Deori,* etc.

Among the Lalungs the *borkhel bichar* is the most effective rural political institution. The elderly people of different *khels* compose the *borkhel bichar*. After the declaration of the judgment of *borkhel* if the wrongdoer opposes the decision he may be excommunicated from the village social life. With a fear of excommunication nobody is found violating the rules of the *borkhel bichar*.

Kinship System and Clan Stratification

The Lalungs have a lot of fables and legends. One of the legends says that in ancient period twelve sisters were living in the Rangamati hills. As they could not get proper husbands, they decided to commit suicide by plunging into the river. At that moment the God appeared before them and provided them twelve persons to marry. Their children grew in numbers. These twelve groups formed twelve clans. Among these twelve clans Macharang, Machereng and Mabo Magor came to occupy the highest statuses in the social hierarchy. Kings and princes belonged to these three *clans*. From all these clans grew surnames, which were associated with their respective assignments in the kingdom. The assignments of the state were to rule (Deo Raja, Deka Raja), to collect revenue from the landowners (Deka Doloi, Bor Doloi) and to settle the disputes with the help of royal officials (Pator). The Lalung used a number of titles, which indicated social and political renks such as Deo Raja, Deka Raja, Pator, Senapati, Knowor, Bordolo, Doloi, Deori, etc. Most of the titles were originally given by the king, according to nature of work for the smooth running of the administration. The Lalungs also have another set of hierarchical clusters of clans such as *Nababahuni* (nine sisters), *Satbahuni* (seven sisters) and *Panchbahuni* (five sisters). Inter-cluster marriages are allowed. The clans belonging to *Nababahuni* cluster are considered as superior clans. It may, be noted that this clan superiority does not create any social imbalance.

Agriculture Economy and Economic Deprivation

Our two village studies have shown that the land is the main resource of the Lalung, because they are predominantly agriculturists. Initially in all Lalung villages, the resources and land were directly under the *Raja*. Hence, there was no individual ownership apart from the *Raja*. This type of ownership of land persisted among the Lalung inhabiting the hills till recently. Generally, the hills Lalungs practise slash and burn cultivation. But those who are settled in the plains of Assam share a common pattern of agricultural economy with other communities such as Kacharis, Nath and Kaibartas. The main produce of the Lalung villages was paddy but now horticultural crops are also grown and sold for cash. However, large number of Lalung families in these villages are economically deprived, as they have no land.

Weaving, spinning and rearing of cocoons are part of the economy. Knowledge of weaving is considered as a special qualification of the bride. In the hill villages weaving of both *eri* (thread of cocoon) and cotton is an essential part of the craft to be done by the housewives. They are also experts in other traits of art and craft. Both floral and geometrical designs are popular among them in textile designs. The Lalungs of the hills are experts in bamboo and caneworks, carving of animals 'and birds' figure are seen in the entrance beam of the house among the Lalung living in the hills.

Emerging Aspirations, Culture Contact and Social Change

Today no tribal economy in Assam is wholly and fully self-contained. A good number of tribes are now shifting towards the money economy, with the help of market and Banking facility. This is not always a collective effort of the community, but only the ventures undertaken by the individuals. Individuals are showing new aspirations to maximize the economic resources. Among the plains Lalungs crucial social changes have taken place. The tribe in general has shifted from matrilineal to patrilineal system of social structure. In the matrilineal set-up, still existing in hills areas the *Borjela* represented in every generation a particular line of male descent. Thus, *Borjela* means the person who is the eldest male in the family of birth. Every family and clan had *Borjela* of their own. The *Borjela* of any family bears domestic responsibilities towards his sisters, for solving disputes or directing the divisions of land or management of the property in general. Further, *Borjela* of the clan bears the ceremonial and social responsibilities as the male head of the clan for all its members. In plains villages the role of Borjela is not crucial. It is male head of family who is supreme. It is observed that gradually most of the Hinduized Lalungs gave up *Zu* (rice beer), pig and fowl. On the other hand the hilly sections of the Lalungs still maintain their traditional food habits. Among the educated Lalungs we notice acceptance of western dress and modern life style. But the same people have not given up their family obligations and kinship usages.

Adoption of patriliny corresponded with a process of local Sanskritization. The urban influence and culture contact have also led to a reasonable sense of hygiene. Sufficient stress is given on cleanliness of surroundings of the house as well as body and clothing. Changes are also noticed in connection with traditional marriage custom and inter-ethnic marriages are common. Nowadays a good number of intermixing is found with the different communities like Brahmin, Kalita, Kaibarta, Hira, Nath, Jain, and Bengali. It is also found that the intermixing with the lower Hindu groups like Nath, Kaibarta and Hira caste are also prevalent. In case of marriage with girls of 'low caste' like Nath, Hira, Kaibarta they realize penalty in cash and kind from concerned individuals, failing which the person may be excommunicated from the village society. In case of inter-caste marriage involving Lalung and upper castes the Lalung accept it.

Nowadays almost every Lalung family is showing interest in education. Generally, each Lalung village has one L.P. School where the medium of education is Assamese. Students aspiring for high school education go to nearest High School, situated within easy reach. Colleges are established at district or sub-divisional headquarters and willing students also avail the hostels. The institution of Lalung bachelor dormitory or *Samadi* (deka sang) has completely disappeared among the plains Lalung. This institution is found in a few villages in the hills with some modification. In the plains the bachelor's dormitories in most of the cases have been converted into library and clubhouse. In some cases, particularly amongst the Vaishnavite Lalung, such dormitories have been converted into *Namghar* (prayer house). The Lalung have shown great interests in rural developmental activities. Different welfare programmes are going on in most of the plains Lalung villages, where people are actively participating in the schemes pertaining to education, enhancement of capabilities in the field of economy and daily ways of life.

Acknowledgement

Author is grateful to Dr N.K. Das for his constant guidance, comments and editorial assistance.

References

Baruah, A.K. 1989, *The Lalung (Tiwas),* Tribal Research Institute, Assam, Guwahati.

Bordoloi, B.N. 1987, *Tribes of Assam* (Part II), Tribal Research Institute, Assam, Guwahati.

Das, N.K. 1982, Review of Works on Social Structures of Matrilineal Tribes of North East India and Observations thereon. *J. Indian Anthropological Society.*

Das, N.K. 1985, 'Descent, Filiation and Affinity among the Matrilineal Tribes of Khasi and Garo Hills of North East India' in *Tribal Institutions of Meghalaya.* Ed. S.K. Chattopadhyay. Gauhati: Spectrum Publications.

Das, N.K. 1987, *Ethnic Identity, Ethnicity and Social Stratification in Northeast India,* New Delhi: Inter-India Publishers.

Deori, M. 1988, *Tiwa Janjati Ary Bhaser Itihas,* Tribal Research Institute, Assam, Guwahati.

Gogoi, L. 1986, *Tiwa Sanskritir Ruprekha* (Part I), Hariharmandir, Dewaguri, Raha, Nagaon.

Gogoi, L. 1987, *Tiwa Sanskritir Ruprekha* (Part II), President Tiwa Mathonlai Tokhra, Silsang, Nagaon.

Pator, G. 1987, *Tiwa Siwantha Lai,* Rangmilee Manta, Marigaon, Assam.

Senapati, G.C. 1974, *Tiwa Jatir Mangkhapsthapan Aru Sadal Dratha,* Ringsang, Second Year, Vol. II.

Sharma Thakur, G.C. 1972, *The Plain Tribes of Lakhimpur,* Sibsagar and Nagaon, Tribal Research Institute, Shillong.

Sharma Thakur, G.C. and M.C. Saikia 1982, "Review of Works on Social Structures of Some Matrilineal Tribes of Northeast India and Observations Thereon", *Journal of Indian Anthropological Society* 17, pp. 199–214.

Shyam Choudhury, N.K. and M.M. Das 1973, *The Lalung Society,* Calcutta: Anthropological Survey of India.

3 Inter-Ethnic Competition, Deprivation and Changing Power Configurations

The Maans of Garo Hills

Sarit Kumar Chaudhury

Identity and Ethno-history

The present study intends to elucidate the outline of social stratification and emerging patterns of social change and deprivation amongst the Maan tribespeople of Meghalaya. For this study fieldwork was carried out for two and a half months during January to March in the year 1995 in the two villages, namely, Daldela and Haldibari. Secondary source data of later period are incorporated in this article. The Maan, a little-known Scheduled Tribe of Meghalaya, is located in West Garo Hills. The entire population of the tribe is scattered over six villages, namely, Haldibari, Sankarpar, Rajangola, Deldela, Bongal Khata and Shyam Nargar under Selsela Block. The district of Goalpara of Assam bounds the tribe on the east, Khasi Hills district of Meghalaya on the West and the Mymensing district of Bangladesh on the south. It is noteworthy to mention here that Selsela Block, as a whole, is identified as a backward Block and all the six villages, where the Maans are living are also officially considered backward villages. All these villages where the Maans are living are divided into two clusters, which may be termed cluster A and cluster B. The natural set-up of these villages shows that the first three villages can be put under 'A' cluster while latter three villages shape cluster 'B'. These clusters 'A' and 'B' work as two separate corporate functional units though these are linked together by a central authority which in turn helps to maintain the wider Maan social solidarity.

Before discussing the social structure of the Maans it is better to have a look into the history of Assam. The history reveals that two kings of Assam Purnananda Buragohain and Bodan Chandra Borphukan, fought with each other to settle internal problems. In order to win the battle, Bodan Chandra tried to get help from the Maan king of Burma. In response to his request the Maan soldiers entered Assam for the first time in the history of Assam. Following that, during other two successive periods they invaded Assam. During their invasion they entered Goalpara, Sylhet and Chittagong. Later they tried to invade areas under the control of the British and proceeded towards Cachar where they were confronted with British soldiers in 1824. But unfortunately the Maan soldiers were severely defeated and consequently fled away to different areas. In 1825 their main concentration in Assam, came under the control of the British. The then chiefs of the Maan soldiers, Champhukan and Bagali Phukan sent one Buddhist monk as a middleman to the British Colonel for a treaty. That treaty finally took place and accordingly Maans agreed to leave Assam and return to their homeland in Burma. But some other Maan soldiers took shelter in Lusai, Naga and Garo Hills. The British captured Lusai, Naga and Garo Hills with the help of those Maan soldiers. Naturally, British authority was pleased with the efficiency of the Maan and gladly rehabilitated those Maan-soldiers in Masakpara, situated at the border of Goalpara and Garo Hills. Later on, some of the Maans migrated from this area to Bongal-khata and Ronkhula (Deldea) villages. To encourage the spirit of those great warriors the then British administrator offered them some tax-free areas (Nakrach) in 1895. At the same time, the British administrator requested the Maans to help them in their administration. The present Maans of Meghalaya are the descendants of those soldiers. The most significant fact is that no female counterpart came along with them. Naturally, those soldiers, who settled down in the Garo Hills after relinquishing their duty as hired soldiers, took their wives from different neighbouring communities such as the Rabha, the Koch, the Garo, the Hajong, the Kachari and various Assamese caste groups in order to maintain their family life which in turn helped them to form Maan ethnic community. Their Mongoloid features are to some extent obliterated by the admixture with the neighbouring non-Mongoloid caste-Hindus, Bengalis or Assamese. Due to such close biological and cultural intermixture their physical features as well as cultural traits emerged as a unique.

It is a well-known fact that long back, since the formation of Haldibari village, the Maans were a very good landholding community. But later on, they became landless. Being Buddhist the Maans had religious affiliation with the other Buddhist communities who lived in upper Assam and Arunachal Pradesh. As a result of that some of them used to visit these places and in turn some Buddhist monks also came to reside in their Buddha Vihar to preach Buddhism among them. As a result of such close interaction they learnt that in some parts of Arunachal Pradesh and upper Assam, cultivable lands are very easily available at a very low price. That provoked many Maan families to sell their land situated at Haldibari area and proceeded towards Arunachal and upper Assam. But finally, they became very much frustrated seeing that cultivable lands are not easily available and moreover those lands are not much suitable for cultivation. Then finding no alternative way a large number of families returned back to Garo hills and became landless. Some of the Maans tried to survive or settle there by marrying girls from various Buddhist communities. A few Maans died during this transition phase. Some of the Maans procured cultivable land but those lands were turned into wasteland due to the excessive sand of small tributaries.

Language and Religion

Due to extensive intermixture with the neighbouring communities the Maans lost their original Burmese language. Now they speak a mixed language of Assamese among themselves. But this also varies from one village to the other on account of the influences of neighbouring communities. A few Maans who have a good outside exposure in relation to the business or services, especially those who are better educated, can speak English and Hindi also. Naturally, their language differs whenever they interact with outsiders. They have completely forgotten their original Mon script (Burmese script) and now they have accepted Assamese script. But most of them proudly refer to two important kinship terminologies, *Amei* and *Aphou* by which they call their mother and father respectively. Undoubtedly, these two terms are Burmese in origin and transcended from their forefathers. Barua (1994) writes that after the formation of Meghalaya in 1972, the Maan and the other Hindu communities like the Rabha, the Hajong, the Koch and the Rajbanshi became minorities in the state, which directly or indirectly developed within them a sense of insecurity and feeling of discrimination. They felt threatened by the numerically dominant Christian tribes like the Garo, the Khasi and the Jaintia. Naturally, the Maan along with their neighbouring communities like the Hajong, the Koch and the Rabha have formed a "composite group" based on certain common features. Religion plays a central role in the formation of Maan ethnic identity. Despite high intermixture, the religious thread still holds the key to their social solidarity. They are Buddhist by religion and belong to the Hinayana sect of Buddhism. A small section continued to pursue tribal religion among them.

Marital Relations with Neighbours

As regards marriage alliance the Maans maintain some restrictions. As per their social norms they have marriage restriction with non-Maan. At the same time their society has made a provision to accept outsiders by converting their religion to Buddhism. They do not have any restriction regarding marriage with Buddhist communities. But as a whole they have expressed strong reservation about the marriage with Muslim boys or girls though they have a close economic interaction with them. The case of ceremonial kinship with the Muslim is common and is seen in Deldela. One reason of dissent among Maan is that Muslims have procured some of their lands.

The Studied Villages

The village Haldibari situated within the 'A' cluster of villages is a roadside village, whereas, both the Haldibari and Sankarpar are more than a kilometre away from Holdibari bus stand. As Haldibari is situated in a lowland area surrounded by a small rivulet during rainy season the villagers of Haldibari have to come to bus stand by small boats. All these villages are multi-ethnic villages. The Maan, the Koch and the Garos inhabit in these villages. The villages, namely, Bongal khata and Shyam Nagar situated within Cluster 'B' villages are roadside villages, whereas, Deldela is comparatively an interior village. It is situated about 4 km away from the Chibinang bus stop and is connected by unmetaled road. The village Deldela is a part of Ronkhula village which is again a multi-ethnic village like Shyamnagar and Bongal khata. However, in Ronkhula the Maans and the Rabhas live separately and the habitation of the Maans is locally recognized in Deldela village. Two villages, namely, Haldibari and Deldela from the two clusters, 'A' and 'B' have been selected for intensive fieldwork for the present study. However, some basic information are collected from the villages, Rajongola and Sankarpara. It may be mentioned that the present study does not intend to present a comparative account because of the fact that the studied villages represent almost similar socio-economic structure, as well as, these are located in the similar ecological set-up with a slight degree of variation in terms of resource utilization and mode of interaction and intermixture with neighbouring communities. To have a clear idea about the demography of the above mentioned two villages, data are presented in the table given below.

Table 1

Family Size and Population

Family Size	*Daldela*			*Haldibari*		
	Total family	*Total population*	*Average size of family*	*Total family*	*Total population*	*Average size of family*
1–3 (small)	6	18	3	11	38	3
4–6 (medium)	16	94	6	21	104	5
7–9 (large)	8	64	8	8	63	8
10+ (very large)	1	8	8	3	33	11
Total	31	184	6	43	238	6

Table 1 shows that village Haldibari is bigger than village Daldela. In both the villages the number of medium size families is more than the number of very large and small size families. Very large families are least in number. This indicates that a process of change in observable in family typology. The trend shows that the very large families are breaking down.

Table 2 presents the family and their landholdings. This table shows that no family in the village Haldibari holds big landholding which ranges from more than nine acres to 23 acres. The families having medium size holding is more in number than that of the other size of holdings. The extended (large and very large) families of Daldela village possess big size landholdings. This data corroborates the same findings as is evident from the data of Table 1. It is proved that as the big size families are breaking down, lands are also divided among the members of the families. As a result, big holdings are reduced to small holdings. This fact is ascertained from the data presented in the Table 2. It shows that nuclear families of smaller sizes possess small holdings. Landholdings of families and occupation of the head of the family is presented in Table 3. It shows that majority of those who possess land are cultivators. On the other hand majority of the landless people are engaged as labourers. The data of the village Daldela show that out of 31 head of families only two are engaged in occupation other than agriculture. They are artisans. The data of Haldibari village show that 8 families who are small and medium size landholders are in service and four landless families are engaged in business.

Table 2
Family Type and Landholding

Land-holding (size in acre)	*Land owning family type and size*															
	Daldela								*Haldibari*							
	Nuclear Family				*Extended Family*				*Nuclear Family*				*Extended Family*			
	1–3	*4–6*	*7–9*	*10+*	*1–3*	*4–6*	*7–9*	*10+*	*1–3*	*4–6*	*7–9*	*10+*	*1–3*	*4–6*	*7–9*	*10+*
Marginal (up to 1)	1	1	—	—	—	—	—	—	—	—	—	—	—	—	1	—
Small (1+ –2)	—	1	1	—	—	—	—	—	—	—	—	—	—	—	1	1
Medium (2+ –9)	—	2	2	—	—	—	—	—	1	3	1	—	—	—	—	1
Big (9+ –23)	—	—	—	—	—	—	1	1	—	—	—	—	—	—	—	—
Landless	5	13	1	—	—	1	1	—	10	13	4	—	—	5	1	1
Total	6	17	4	—	—	1	2	1	11	16	5	—	—	5	3	3

Table 3
Landholding and Occupation

Village	*Land-holding (size in acre)*	*Primary Occupation of the head of the family*						*Total*
		Cultivators	*Landless Share Cropper*	*Agricultu re/Day Labourers*	*Artisan*	*Business*	*Service*	
Daldela	Up to 1	2	—	—	—	—	—	2
	1+ –2	3	—	—	—	—	—	3
	2+ –9	2	—	—	—	—	—	2
	9+ –23	1	2	—	—	—	—	3
	23+	2	—	—	—	—	—	2
	Landless	—	2	15	2	—	—	19
	Total	10	4	15	2			31
Haldibari	Up to 1	1	—	—	—	—	1	2
	1+ –2	—	—	—	—	—	2	2
	2+ –9	—	—	—	—	—	5	5
	9+ –23	—	—	—	—	—	—	—
	23+	—	—	—	—	—	—	—
	Landless	5	2	22	1	4		34
	Total	6	2	22	1	4	8	43

The data on occupation and literacy of the head of the families are presented in Table 4. These data also corroborate the findings of the Table 3. The majority of the people are engaged in agriculture and some as agricultural/day labourers. The data also reveal that majority of the non-literate work as labourer. Two non-literates of the Haldibari village are the employees of such non-government establishment that does not require a literate person. People of the village

Haldibari who have read up to Class X are in service. The table also shows that education has very little impact on the Maans of Meghalaya. Still some people have come out of their stage of non-literate and are finding avenues of modern occupation like service. Besides the occupation of the head of the families, the data on the occupation of the workers of both the villages are presented in Table 5. In both the villages the majority of the workers are landless agricultural/day labourers. Only a few people are service holders. Table 6 shows that literate of both the villages have read up to class X only. Comparatively the males are more literates than the females. The data also supports the same fact that majority of them are non-literates and some of them got school education only.

Table 4

Literacy and Occupation

Village	*Educational standard of head of family*	*Occupation of the head of the family*						
		Cultivation	*Landless Share Cropping*	*Agricul-ture/Day Labourers*	*Artisan*	*Business*	*Service*	*Total*
Daldela	Non-literate	10	2	13	2	—	—	27
	I–IV	—	—	—	—	—	—	—
	V–VI	—	—	1	—	—	—	1
	VII–X	—	2	1	—	—	—	3
	P.U.	—	—	—	—	—	—	—
	Graduation	—	—	—	—	—	—	—
	Total	10	4	15	2			31
Haldibari village	Non-literate	1	—	20	—	3	2	26
	I–IV	2	2	1	1	—	—	6
	V–VI	2	—	—	—	—	—	2
	VII–X	1	—	1	—	1	6	9
	P.U.	—	—	—	—	—	—	—
	Graduation	—	—	—	—	—	—	—
	Total	6	2	22	1	4	8	43

Table 5

Distribution of Workers in Different Occupations

S. No.	*Occupations*	*Daldela*			*Haldibari*		
		Male	*Female*	*Total worker*	*Male*	*Female*	*Total worker*
1.	Cultivation	—	1	1	3	—	3
2.	Landless Share Cropping	12		12	2	—	2
3.	Landless Agricultural/ Day labour	26	29	55	20	30	50
4.	Business	2	—	2	6	—	6
5.	Service	—	—	—	6	1	7
6.	Artisans	—	—	—	1	—	1
7.	Teaching	—	—	—	—	1	1
	Total	40	30	70	38	32	70

Table 6
Literacy

Literacy Standard	*Literacy Achievement*					
	Daldela			*Haldibari*		
	Male	*Female*	*Total*	*Male*	*Female*	*Total*
Non-literate	82	79	161	84	85	169
Primary	5	4	9	20	19	39
Middle	3	4	7	5	9	14
High	7	—	7	13	3	16
P.U.	—	—	—	—	—	—
Graduation	—	—	—	—	—	—
Total	97	87	184	122	116	—

The literacy of the family head is presented in the Table 7 and 8. Table 7 shows that none of the family head of the village Daldela is a female whereas there are two female heads in the village Haldibari (Table 8). Only four heads of the village Daldela are literates. It is observed that none of the male head of the family is below the age group 16–30 with the exception that one female head of the village Haldibari belongs to the age group 0–15. The non-literates belong to different age groups. However, most of the aged people are non-literates. Majority of the middle aged people are also non-literates.

Table 7
Village Daldela: Age, Sex, and Literacy of the Head of the Family

Literacy Level	*Male Head*						*Female Head*					
	0–15	16–30	31–45	46–60	60+	Total	0–15	16–30	31–45	46–60	60+	Total
Non-literate	—	2	8	14	4	28	—	—	—	—	—	—
Primary	—	—	1	—	—	1	—	—	—	—	—	—
Medium	—	—	1	—	—	1	—	—	—	—	—	—
High	—	—	1	—	—	1	—	—	—	—	—	—
P.U.	—	—	—	—	—	—	—	—	—	—	—	—
Total	—	2	11	14	4	31	—	—	—	—	—	—

Table 8
Village Haldibari: Age, Sex, and Literacy of the Head of the Family

Literacy Level	*Male Head*						*Female Head*					
	0–15	16–30	31–45	46–60	60+	Total	0–15	16–30	31–45	46–60	60+	Total
Non-Literate	—	8	9	3	5	25	1	1	—	—	—	2
Primary	—	2	2	2	—	6	—	—	—	—	—	—
Medium	—	—	1	—	—	1	—	—	—	—	—	—
High	—	3	5	1	—	9	—	—	—	—	—	—
P.U.	—	—	—	—	—	—	—	—	—	—	—	—
Total	—	13	17	6	5	41	1	1	—	—	—	2

Interaction with Outsiders

Economic Interaction

The Maans maintain a very close interaction for a long time with the Bengali Muslims through Rajabala, one of the biggest and oldest weekly markets in that area. They used to sell their surplus production to the Muslims at Rajabala. Naturally in case of any urgency or to meet the expenses on marriage or on their significant rituals the Maans used to take cash loan from Muslims. Those who were unable to pay back the loan amount with interest often transferred their cultivable land to them. During that time transfer of tribal land to non tribal was not prohibited. A section of the Maans who were landholders but not hardworking people also sold their land to their neighbouring communities and earned money to run their families. In Haldibari most of the lands were transferred to the Muslims of Rajabala and Silkata. Almost similar incidents took place in Deldela village. These transfers of land led to agrarian stratification gradually. In general, land is individually owned. However, in Deldela the Maan have a common grazing ground for the community as a whole. Individual land is transferred from fathers to sons. Of late, some of them have started to give their daughters a portion of agrarian land.

Political Interaction

It is observed that there is a close connection between the economy and power. In fact, some of the Maans who are economically sound control the political power. Like many other tribes the Maans have their own traditional village political organization. It can be mentioned here that in case of cluster 'A' villages, namely, Haldibari, Rajangola and Sankarpara, they have a common headman called *Gaon Bura*. Village male elders generally assist him. *Dukra*, a messenger also assists the *Gaon Bura*. *Dakra* is paid for his service. The post of village headman is not hereditary. However, if we look into the list of the previous village headman some sort of kinship bond is traced between earlier headmen. The power, kinship and economy are thus linked up. In case of a selection of new village headman, his knowledge, age, experience and respectability for his social connection as well as economic status are taken into consideration. Females are not allowed to interfere in their traditional political structure. Now, new authority structure in the form of statutory village council and district Council are very much active. Statutory village council is formed to look after the common interests of the various groups of people living in the village. Such council consists of a president, a secretary and several other members. Each community irrespective of caste or creed has a chance to send a representative who is incorporated in the structure of village council. In fact, this emerging power structure has reduced the importance of tribal *Gaon Bura* to a great extent. However, such democratic institutions have not eroded internal structure of Maan society. The Maan interact with all communities and during the annual general Buddhist conference all six villages belonging to the Garos, the migrant Bengali Hindus and the Muslims meet together and discuss various problems and prospects as a whole and try to find out means to meet the common interests of all the communities.

Religious Interaction

The Maan took shelter with help of the then British authorities and settled in West Garo Hills. Then they started marrying women from different communities in order to form a Maan society. During those days they were not Buddhist and used to worship local tribal god and goddesses and had a habit of drinking and dancing. They had their own religious specialist, viz., Deosi (priest) and Thanqdhara (assistant priest). In course of time some of the Buddhists of Burma came to know about their existence in west Garo Hills. Thus, at first Urimala and later Unandra and Uchandra, all Buddhist monks, came from Burma and preached Buddhism among the Maans by establishing Vihar (Buddhist temple) for each Maan village. At present there is one Vihar for the Maans of Haldibari, Rajangola and Sankarpara. The remaining three villages have a separate Vihar (Buddhist temple).

As far the religious functionaries are concerned for each Vihar they have one Chang Deka/Sang Deka and one Pathek. Chang Deka is responsible for the maintenance of Vihar and for conducting daily activities, viz., lighting candle to Lord Buddha and so on. It is his responsibility to make proper arrangement for the Bhante or Sraman (both Buddhist monks) whenever they pay a visit to the Vihar or stay back in relation to various Buddhist rituals and also on the invitation of the villagers. Pathek is considered as Buddhist village priest higher in status to Changdeka. In the absence of Bhante or Sraman or other higher Buddhist monks, he has to perform all necessary rituals as per Buddhist tradition. These posts of Changdeka and Pathek are not hereditary. These posts are considered very sacred and especially Pathek must follow the Panchashil or five principles of Buddhism, i.e., to abstain from drinking wine and luxurious way of life, to abstain from killing animals both for consumption and ritual purposes, to follow righteous thought and righteous deeds. After the death of such religious functionaries it is the responsibility of the villagers including village headman to find out a person who can take the responsibility of such a sacred rites and duties in relation to the thoughts of Buddhism. The post of Bhante or Sraman is not hereditary. They are trained in Buddhist thought written in Pali or Sanskrit language by staying in a Buddha Vihar for a considerable period of time. Their duty is to preach to the people Buddhism as well as train them on how to take part properly in various rituals. Most of the Bhantes are staying in the Buddha Vihar of Upper Assam, Arunachal Pradesh and in Shillong. Most of them belong to the Khampti, the Singpho and the Assamese community. Some of such monks also belong to the Maan community itself. Most of them also stay in the Buddha Vihar of Upper Assam. Generally, these Maan monks now take leading role in various festivals as well as rituals. Earlier, they had a good contact with the Buddhist monks of Burma but with the drawing of international political boundary such contacts have been stopped completely.

Stratification, Deprivation and Social Change

We have discussed above how the Maans were deprived of their land and became poor. However some families had courage to struggle and improve their status. Many shifted to non-agricultural occupations. If we consider the economic structure of the Maans we find that certain inequality existed and accordingly their lifestyles also varied. In each studied village a few families were economically well placed in comparison to the rest of their population. Undoubtedly their whole economic structure survived through agriculture. Basically they are settled agriculturists though some of them started shifting to some other occupations, viz., business, government service, school teacher, etc. Educational status of the Maan is not encouraging at all. But those who are educated are adopting new occupations. In fact, except a few families, most of the Maan families do not have any land. Naturally this leads to two broad classes; one is landholding class and the other landless class. All sorts of agrarian categories, viz., tenants, share cropper, absentee landlord, agricultural labourer, etc., are existing in the Maan society. We have seen various patterns of constraints and deprivation involved in leading agricultural life, mainly where dominant groups are procuring lands from Maan tribespeople.

Among Mann the upper strata could utilize their resources in a best possible way, which in turn helped them to make their economic base more strong. But unfortunately none of them tried to introduce improved agricultural technology to make the overall situation much better. Of course, those who have substantial amount of land are now trying to get another crop (Rabi) during a year. But such attempt is not very much successful due to the lack of irrigational facilities.

There are three types of agricultural labourers. They are:

(i) Agricultural daily labourers locally called as Kamla. During agricultural season they are in great demand.

(ii) Masra Chakar labourers who are engaged on contract basis for agricultural season. Generally this category includes male members only who work for their community members and for the affluent neighbouring communities. During agricultural season they stay in the house of land owners and they got then ₹ 250 to 300 per month with food and shelter. Generally female members are not taken for such contract.

(iii) Bacharia Chakar (labourer on yearly contract). Usually a Maan who is quite well off and having large landholdings keeps such male or female labourers for the whole year. They work not only during agricultural season but also for the whole year to assist the landowner in other domestic work. They are paid in kind in a fixed quantity.

Above discussion indicates that the Maan tribe has a large number of families who are landless and who depend on daily labour work for survival. Many of them had landed property but gradually they had to sale their land to neighbouring communities, in order to meet their immediate needs. This section of the landless Maans has emerged as the most deprived section.

Reference

Barua, S. 1994, "Mann", in *People of India: Meghalaya,* Vol. XXXII, (ed.) K.S. Singh, Anthropological Survey of India, Calcutta.

4 Chieftainship, Vaishnavism and New Political System among the Noctes of Arunachal Pradesh

R.P. Athparia

The purpose of this article is to describe the system of traditional stratification among the Noctes by discussing the chieftainship, clan ranking and economic domain. Issue of social change is discussed mainly in the context of adoption of Vaishnavism. Kinship based polity is still relevant hence the clan based class like inter-group interactions are crucial. Chiefly clans still enjoy higher strata and greater privileges. The fieldwork for this study was done for three months from December 1995 to February 1996 in three villages namely, Lapnan, Lazu and Soha of Tirap district, Arunachal Pradesh. Data collected later through re-visit were incorporated. The Tirap district is adjoining Myanmar, and it is the only district of the state, which lies entirely to the south of the Brahmaputra river. The district is bounded on the north by the Dibrugarh district, Assam, on the south by Myanmar, on the east by the Changeling district and on the west by the Sivasagar district of Assam and Mon district of Nagaland.

The literal meaning of the term Nocte is people living in a planned community (Dutta, 1978). The Noctes inhabit the south-western and central parts of the district. The habitat is most undulating with hills ranging from 2,500 ft to 6,000 ft. Towards the Burmese (Myanmar) border, it is a country full of luxuriant, evergreen commercially important vegetation. A rich variety of wild and domestic animals and birds comprise the fauna of the area. The Noctes of the lower region bordering the plains are known as *Hawa* and those living in the upper region are known as *Koute*. *Hawa* means peoples of the plains land or people living towards the plains. *Koute* means hills or hill people. Within these two broad divisions of *Koute* and *Hawa,* there are four main groups. These are *Tuti* Nocte, *Lawa* Nocte (more accurately called Barap Nocte as they live mainly on both sides of the Barap river), *Hakhun* Nocte and *Hawa* Nocte. There are social differences among these four main groups. Dialect-wise, the Noctes are divided into nine groups, namely, Pthung, Domlak, Hakhun, Hawa, Jope, Lazu, Khapa, Dedem and Sangniyak. Of these Sangniyak and Dadom dialects are akin to *Hawa* group. Grierson (1909) has placed the Nocte language in the Naga-Kuki-Chin group of the Tibeto-Burman family of languages. The Noctes in general call their dialect as *Jap,* while the Lazu Noctes call their dialect as *Ret*. Jope dialect is spoken by most of the Nocte villages, namely Tut, Nokna, Thungja, Panlam,

Kolam, Kothung, Linwang, Katang, Jankang, Watlom, Thumjang, Phungs, Sangra, Lamsai, Lamlo and Bunting.

Nocte Villages and Territorial Divisions

There are 58 Nocte villages in Tirap district. Nocte villages are situated on hilltops and also on the slopes of the hills. The villages are thickly populated with clusters of houses. The people of the Lapnan village originally spoke Wancho dialect of the Wakka area, but after their settlement along with the Noctes they adopted the Nocte dialect of the neighbouring villages, though the original Wancho dialect is also used. Thus, the dialect of Lapnan village has become a mixed one. Their original dialect is called *Tang Jap*.

The Nocte villages are generally situated at a distance of about 4–5 km. In only a few cases villages are found farther. A village is locally known as *Nok, Thin* or *Ha*. Each village name has a particular meaning. The name of the Soha village is derived from two words *so* means back side, and *ha* means land. So, Soha means land in the back side. However, the Soha people say that Soha means to search for land and *so* means to search and *ha* means land. Likewise, Lazu is also derived from two words, *la* means kite and *zu* means water. The name Lazu is given because a kite fell into the water there.

Lazu is the largest village in the whole area with 381 households. The total population of Lazu village according to the household survey carried out by the researcher was 1,811 persons with 878(48.48%) males and 933(51.52%) females. Due to increase of population, a number of smaller villages have sprung up from the Lazu village. These villages are Sinhan, Rahu, Kuthung, Noklo, Lungliang, Sanyu, Ponkong, Longho and Sanlam. These villages pay annual tribute called *khe* to the Lazu chief. For our study the parent village Lazu and one of the subordinate villages namely Rahu were studied. The total number of households in Rahu village was 45 with a population of 108 persons. Out of this 50(50%) were males and 56(49.24%) females. The village name Rahu has been derived from a big thorny tree. Under this tree, the village is situated. Soha village is situated in the foothills. The Lapnan village, which is located near the district headquarters of Khonsa, is also a big village. According to the survey conducted by the researcher, the total number of households in the village was 119. The total population of the village was 714 persons. Out of this 363(50.84%) were males and 351(49.16%) females.

The boundaries of villages are well defined by streams and hillocks. The roads maintained by the villages connect one village with another. These roads are the main routes of communication. Regular buses ply from Khonsa to Lazu and from Deomati to Soha villages. Each village has a number of territorial sub-divisions, called *Chum* or *Raden,* the number varies according to the number of households in the village. Sometimes on the basis of migrants to the village the *Chum* may be formed. In Lazu, there are nine *chums,* namely Relom, Sonds, Thamkho, Chonu, Hope, Rukhiyek, Tangnu, Tangsa and Thamlong. In Soha, there are four *chums,* namely, Palong, Hada, Longmaktong and Pondap. The Lapnan village has four *chums,* namely Thamneusong, Khuneu, Khamsa and Khangong.

The *chums* have their own meaning. They are named after the type of land, position ecological and so on. The social and ecological meanings of the *chums* are as follows:

(a) Relom – towards the jungle
(b) Sonsa – under the citrus tree
(c) Thamkho – near the water
(d) Chonu – abundance of citrus tree
(e) Hope – come here
(f) Rukhiyek – near the main part
(g) Tangnu – migrants of Tangnu
(h) Tangsa – descendants of Tang
(i) Thamlong – stony hot land
(j) Pondap – chief's *chum*
(k) Sumdamdap – middle of the village
(l) Hada – lower village, and so on.

Each *chum* has its own Morung or bachelor's dormitory where the youths of the *chum* sleep at night. In Lazu village, there are 24 Morungs. Out of twelve *chums,* Rilom *chum* has two Morungs, Sonsa–four, Thamko–two chonu, and Themlong–two. On the other hand, Loha village has only two Morungs. Palong and Hade *Chums* jointly have one Morung and the other three *chums* jointly have one Morung. In Lapnan village, three *chums* have only one Morung. This Morung is situated in the Chief's *chum*. A *chum* is the basis for division of community work, which is generally performed by the *chums*. The respective *chums* organize their own annual festivals in the place called Chatam. Each *chum* also performs festival dances separately although on the concluding day of all the festivals like Loku all *chum* members join together in merry making and dance.

In Lapnan village, there is one primary school and the higher secondary school is located within a radius of 100 yards from the village. The total number of matriculates and graduates is very less in the village. Out of the total population of 714 persons, only 156(21.85%) have passed VI standard and above. The literacy among the Lazu is high in comparison to other villages. The total literacy is 43.28 per cent which is higher than the literacy of the district which is 22.55 per cent according to the 1991 census. There are altogether 12.01 per cent individuals who have obtained the higher degree of engineering and pharmacy. In Soha, there is one High School. In the school, there are altogether five teachers from the village. Comparatively, Soha people are better in education. In Lazu there is one High School. The literacy of the village is 7.34 per cent. It can be said that the people are interested in sending their children to school. There is one masters degree holder in the village. He has obtained M.A. in history from Arunachal University. It is said that due to non-availability of college facility in the district the boys and the girls have to stop their education after matriculation.

The House Type and Status Articulation

A house is called Hum, Hem, Kim, Nok and so on by the Noctes of different areas. There is no universal pattern of construction of the house in the village (Dutta, 1978: 46). They are clustered and wherever the land is available a house is built. However, hill slopes are preferred.

The house type is not similar in all the Nocte villages. In Lazu village, thatch is used for roofing while palm leaf (*Tokpat*) is used in Lapnan and Soha villages. In all the three villages, the main structure of the house, that is posts and beams are made of wood and walls, floors, and roof are made of split bamboo. Building materials are available in the locality and the villagers are not required to go to distant places to collect the building materials. It is seen that palm leaf and thatch are grown by the individual families in their own cultivated plots.

The houses are raised on bamboo piles and are rectangular in shape. There are three sloped roofs, two at the sides and the third covering the front side of the house.

An open bamboo platform in the front side of the house is invariably found. This platform is the most essential part of the house, as it serves the purpose of porch and is used for drying food stuff, paddy, rice and other articles and also for husking. The main house consists of a long room which is divided by partitions into different compartments. Usually, a house has two main sections, the front room, and the main room. In the main room, the women sleep, cook food and keep all the household articles. In the front room, the head of the household sleeps. This room is decorated with skulls and bones of animals, beaks of birds and various other articles such as gun, bows and arrows and so on, hung on the walls and pots. One side of this room contains a hearth, locally known as *Tap,* around which the guests sit.

The Noctes of Lapnan village can be differentiated into two strata in terms of house type and possession of the household articles. One stratum does not have a single piece of furniture like chair, table or bench while the other stratum has cane furniture like chair, *Mura,* wooden cot and so on. Out of 119 households, 40(34%) households have television sets.

At Lazu and Raho villages, television is not available in any house. Data on the household articles are not available for Soha village but it can safely be said that the lifestyle of the villagers of Lapnan village is better than Soha and Lazu villages.

House construction is considered as community work. Even the building materials are collected jointly. On completion of the construction, the owner of the house has to feed the people with rice, rice-beer and if possible with meat, preferably pork. The whole village takes part in the construction. At the completion of the house, they dance, eat and drink. The dance is called *Humhonbunong.* Generally, the construction is completed in one day. Only in the case of a chief's house and a *Morung* the work continues for two to three days. Earlier, the persons from subordinate villages also used to take part in the construction of the chief's houses. They had to bring materials like cane, bamboo and palm leaves. This was obligatory. But now this practice is slowly disappearing from the society. Chiefs have no authority now but privileges are still enjoyed by men of dominant royal clans

At Lazu, each stage of construction is followed by a ritual. After erection of the main post, a ritual called *Ha-tap* is performed. In such ritual, a buffalo is killed and an old man of the *Morung* performs the ritual by pouring rice beer near a side of the post called *Khamnu. Waku* is the next ritual performed on completion of the platform. A grand feast is arranged with rice, rice-beer and meat of buffalo or pig. In the *Humlong* ceremony, new fire (*Wan Hiyan*) is lighted in the house by the process of friction. No fire from another house is used. The fire lighted on the day of *Humlong* ceremony is never allowed to be put off. The ceremony performed on completion of a *Morung* construction is called *Punlong.* It is similar to *Humlong*.

The ceremony connected with the house construction is different from village to village. At Soha and Lapnan villages, no ceremony is performed before construction of a house though divinations are observed to select the site. If the omens are found to be correct they try to confirm it by seeing the omen on an egg. If both the divinations are favourable then only the site is finally selected for construction of the house. On completion of the house construction, a *Neom* (ritual) called *Hajun* is performed. At Kolagaon, a dog is sacrificed. The sacrifice is done when construction starts in a newly selected site and not for construction at the old site.

Occupational Differentiation and Stratification

Occupational differentiation existed always in the society. Even today it is exhibited in occupational specialization of villages. Lazu is an important centre of pottery making. The old women of the village are engaged in pottery (*Ha tit*) which they sell or exchange for foodstuff in other villages. The pottery is hand-made and the clay is brought from the nearby river bank. The potters mostly make pitchers of various sizes with broad mouths and narrow necks. The finished products are carefully kept in one corner of the house. The Nocte pitchers are very heavy due to thickness. Pottery making is done in the winter season. The other Nocte villages have no knowledge of pottery industry.

Like pottery, blacksmithy, locally known as *Teppa*, is carried on mainly in the Lazu area. Dutta (1978: 58) has mentioned that there are more than a dozen blacksmiths in the area. But in the present investigation only two blacksmiths could be traced, they are Nopong Wangsa and Nangpha Khomkhu. Both are holding key position in the village council. They make daos, small spades, knives, scrapers and spear heads and repair the old iron implements of the village. Those involved in pottery, blacksmithy are economically advanced.

In any tribal society there are local standards which characterize the norms of strata. In this society for example even items of personal decoration spell out the value of status. Thus, hair style and personal adornment also matter. In studying the dress and personal adornment of the Noctes one cannot ignore the characteristic styles of holding the hair and here we may consider the contribution of Assam. The typical hairstyle of a Nocte man in which the hair is shaved all round the head leaving the rest to grow long, intended to be tied in a bun, indeed, bears a strong resemblance to the *Satriya* style (characteristic hairstyle of the Vaishnava devotees) of Assam. In fact, it has been claimed by some that this style came into fashion during the time of Lotha Khunbao, the ancestor chief of Borduria, Laptang and Namsag villages, who was the first Nocte to initiate and adopt Vaishnavism. Neog (1976: 24) states that the chief Lotha Khunbao was initiated into Vaishnavism by Sri Ram Dev who was the abbot of the Chaliha Bareghar *Satra* (Vaishnavite monastery) near Naharkatiya, sometime in the 17th century. As regards the wearing of the hair in *Satriya* style, Neog (1976: 13) comments that the attribute of not taking beef and allowing the hair to grow long in the middle of the head were probably the influence of Vaishnavism. This fashion is seen among the contemporary Noctes of Lapnan and Soha villages.

Noctes of Lazu area however, do not practise such hairstyle. But in contrast to the women of lower regions, the Lazu women crop the hair very closely. The reason for this is to distinguish them from men and also to make them less attractive. The way Lazu women crop their hair they are known as *Khosu* by other Noctes.

It is found that the Lazu women are tattooed on the face and chest. There is one straight horizontal line from the forehead to the tip of the nose. Seven vertical lines in each check meet at both the ends of the mouth, making two angles at both the sides. Tattooing of women has died out in the lower region. The traditional tattoo patterns for women in lower regions were 'v' shaped design with circular ends on the face, a feather design on the chest and stomach and zigzag patterns on the neck.

Men generally do not tattoo their face or bodies, though in some villages like Lazu, tattooing done at various levels and in phases was common till recently. At Lazu, tattooed persons were locally known as *Kahang,* meaning brave men. It was a sign of bravery. It was performed after the harvest, specially on the occasion of *Khotang* festival. First tattoo mark was done on the face. Second and third were done at the thigh, nose *(Ngon wi),* forehead (*Khang wi), chee (Man Wi),* chin (*Ka Wi)* and neck *(Bo wi)*. It was done by male members only and the performer was known as *Wi Pa.* He received remuneration for his service in kind and cash. Tattooing was practised in order to gain more and more land. The head hunter, *Kahangs,* invited all the *Kalangs,* that is elders for the celebration by sacrificing a pig for the *Khotong* festival. All the old *Kahangs,* that is chief and elders of the village used to go together to a place near Lazu village called *Kholum.* The different clan *Kahangs* sat clanwise for dinner. There was restriction for preparation of certain food. Only local salt and local rice were used. After the feast, all *Kahangs* raised slogans and sang war songs. Neog (1976: 15) has opined that the practice of head hunting is gone. Today, there are no head hunters and the art of male tattooing too is not in practice among them.

Till 1983–84, tattooing of women was very common in Lazu village. It was stopped by the All Lazu Youth Association. The association fines ₹ 500 to the persons who indulge in tattooing. Locally, the ban for tattooing is known as *Manvi phak.*

Cultural Impact of Assam

Both tangible and intangible cultural heritages of Assam had impact over Noctes. The indigenous textile industry never existed among the Noctes, and as such, they used to bring the necessary clothing from Assam in exchange of locally extracted salt. No weaving in traditional loom is found among the Noctes. Whatever they have come to know about weaving is through the influence of the craft centre. During the era of the Ahom kings, the Namsangias paid tributes with articles such as elephant tusks, spears, salt and cotton (Dutta, 1978: 59–60).

In general, a loin cloth for a man and a skirt hanging from the waist to the knee for a woman were the usual dress of the Noctes. Girls in the Lazu area formerly wore a narrow black skirt purchased from beyond the Patkai (Dutta, 1978: 60). At present, this has been replaced by mill-made cloth. Over the skirt, a red cloth locally known as *Khat Change,* about two yards in length, is worn as a shawl, to cover the body.

In contrast to the upper Noctes, among the lower Noctes of Soha area, the clothing is thoroughly patterned after the Assamese. Sometimes, it is very difficult to distinguish a Nocte girl from that of an Assamese girl in the manner of dress. Dutta also says that "In the lower Nocte areas especially in the villages near the Assam border, the young girls wear Mekhala and Chadar like Assamese girls, it becomes difficult to distinguish them."

In this connection, mention may be made of the two popular dress items of Assam which have acquired distinct places in the lower Nocte cultural practices because of long established relation between the two. These are Assamese *Gamusa* (towel) and Phulam Japi (decorated bamboo umbrella). It is not unusual to find Soha Nocte men tying round the head an Assamese *Gamusa* which is an indigenous craft product of Assam, which plays a significant role in ceremonial costume. Curiously enough, the offerings made to the spirits during a curative rite in the lower Nocte society very often includes an Assamese *Gamusa.* It is also needed on many other ceremonial occasions. The place occupied by the *Phulam Japi,* locally called *Hup-Moktap* or *Hup-Puckak,* is also no less important. It is a common practice with the Nocte women of lower areas to hold a *Phulam Japi* in hand while carrying a new born baby to the *jhum* field for Nabamba (ceremony relating to name giving). It is, however, very difficult to say exactly at what time these two elements reached the Nocte area, but these were adopted from Assam.

Both men and women wear ornaments. The Nocte hat is decorated with tusks of wild boars, feathers of hornbills and often flowers. Flowers are worn in the holes of the ear lobes which also serve as ear ring. Nocte ornaments are chains of coloured beads. Nocte chiefs wear bead necklaces which cannot be worn by others. A coiled cane belt is worn during work in the field or when the men go out for hunting. Ivory armlets, wrist bands of plaited basketry work decorated with cowri shells and head dresses of conch shells are in daily use.

In the Lazu area, the women wear large earrings made of brass or silver wire. The head gear, locally known as Rongchang is made of locally available rope called Pong Pong Bee, cane (Ra), boar's teeth (Wakneba) and enemy's hair (Ean khocho).

As compared to lower Noctes, the upper Noctes have little ornaments. Women of Lazu usually wear bead necklace and coin necklace. They normally do not purchase or use the ornaments purchased from the local markets.

Economic Diversification and Economic Ranking

The basic means of livelihood of the Noctes is shifting cultivation or *jhuming*. It is the primary occupation of all the studied villages, namely, Lazu, Lapnan and Soha. In addition, people of the Lapnan and Soha villages do contract work for government roads and are also engaged in timber works to earn cash money. However, all the villages have joined in road construction programmes and so increased their incomes. In addition, many villagers go down to the plains after completing their agricultural work to do contract work, in the tea gardens of the neighbouring plains.

Table 1 shows that the cultivators are the maximum, that is 67.50 per cent in Lapnan and 94.90 per cent in Lazu village. Next to agriculture, government jobs were the most common employment, engaging 26.25 per cent of the people of Lapnan village and 4.85 per cent in Lazu village. Labourers in PWD (Public

Works Department) – road construction and other formed are 4.05 per cent in Lapnan and there is no worker in this category in Lazu village. Business and contractor works are 1.25 per cent and 0 per cent in Lapnan while it is only 0.24 per cent in Lazu village.

Table 1

Village	*Total population*	*Total workers*	%	*Culti-vator*	%	*Govern ment service*	%	*Labour in PWD*	%	*Bus-ness*	%	*cont-actor*	%
Lapnan	714	320	44.81	216	67.50	84	26.25	13	4.06	4	1.25	3	0.9
Lazu	1811	824	45.44	782	94.90	40	4.85	—	—	2	0.24	—	—

As the Lapnan village is situated close to the district headquarters, the white-collar jobs are availed by many here in comparison to Lazu village. Likewise, business and contractor works are also procured. The Soha people earn cash money from the trading in betel leaf. They depend on this article for their livelihood. They purchase rice when their own stock is exhausted with the cash they get from selling betel leaf.

Dutta (1978: 67) has written that the inter-village trade of their local products also helped in the livelihood of the villages. They traded in baskets, bamboo mats, rain-shields, decorated spears, sticks, hats and salts. Another item of their inter-village trade is opium which in the past was an important source of income. The Lazu people grow opium on a large scale and sell this to the neighbouring villages at a high price. Opium is the source of income on which many villagers of the Lazu village depend for their livelihood. They purchase rice regularly from the fair price shops located in the circle headquarters, with the cash they get from the opium.

The Noctes of all the three villages own cultivable land between 3 to 10 acres. In Lapnan village the rich section owns more than 10 acres of land and they are at the top of the economic ladder. The richer section also does the business and contractor works and they constitute 2.19 per cent of the total worker's population. Next to the rich, the middle rank people who are cultivators as well as government employees constitute 27.50 per cent. The remaining section constitutes 67.50 per cent and is solely dependent on cultivation. The rich and middle groups engage labourers during the harvest season. The members of their families work at their own farms but they rarely work as wage earners on other's farms. The few rich cultivators possess fisheries also. They also grow cash crops like arum, potato, sweet potato, etc. The members of their families, particularly the educated boys and girls, do not work even in their own farms. They employ Wanchoo labourers in their fields.

Stratified Clans and Chieftaincy

The Nocte society is based on patrilineal descent and it has a surviving chieftainship. There are royal or chiefly clans and clans of commoners. The chieftainship has greatly affected their social life, leading to two distinct classes. However, the classes are not so conspicuous as found among the neighbouring Wanchoos of Longding sub-division of Tirap. The chief and his descendants among the Noctes form separate class called *Lowangjat*, and the chief is known as *Lowang*. The commoners are called *Sanajat*. The *Lowangjat* are the ruling class who extracted work from the *Sanaja*t. In the Lazu area, the commoner class is known as *Pansajat*. The Handigui and other ritual officials are selected from this class. Each of these two classes consists of a number of clans called Cu or Ru with various names and unequal numbers in each class. The exogamous character of the clan regulates the marriage system of the tribe. A striking feature of the Nocte society is that the *chums* are also exogamous. Marriage between members of different clans within a *Chum* is prohibited, unless it happens under some exceptional circumstances. Marriage is not possible between members of all *chums* as it is believed that certain clans constituting different *chums* have had a common ancestry. All clans within a particular *chum* have a common name.

In Lazu area, there are two distinct groups of clans. One group Kepi, constitutes chief's clan and the other Tangmo, the commoner's clan. Marriage within Kepi or Tangmo is prohibited, but it can take place between the two. The chief has the privilege of taking the second wife from the commoner's group. Both the groups have eight clans each. Dutta (1978: 115) has shown the clans of the Lazu Noctes as follows:

Table 2

Tribe: Laju Nocte, Village: Laju – Clan Stratification

Moiety	A	B
	Kepi	Tangmo
	Wang Dung	Hodung
Clans	Wangsa	Rumsa
	Ootai Wangsa	Kong kang
	Nyamtai Wangsa	Nok Pa
	Janpi	Moniyak
	Ransong	Juja
Clans	Sapong	Khosa
	Mophuk	Kempa

The author regards the *Kepi* and the *Tangmo* as two moieties with a number of clans. Dutta states that the social structure of the Lazu Noctes represents dual organization. However, in our study we have found that there are twelve clans each in *Kepi* and *Tangmo* group. These are as follows:

Kepi Moetiy Clans	*Tangmo Moiety Clans*
Wangdong	Hadong
Wangsa	Rumsu
Nymte	Kompa
Oote	Nokpa
Rongsong	Namphu
Zenpi/Jenpi	Khotom
Khisum	Zemson/Jemson
Mophu	Manna
Longse	Kongkang
Sapong	Khusan
Pantok	Zuzha
Rangwong	Moinak

These clans are further distributed in different Morungs, dormitories which are shown in the Table 3.

Table 3

Morung	*Clans*	Allied Clans with Morung links	
Ralom	Clans		
Morung	Nyamte		
	Wangsa		
	Rangwang		
	Pantok		
	Rangkong		
	Sapong		
	Matshu		
	Matey		
	Jotan		
	Zenkhee		
Tangsa and			
Thalom Morungs	Runchu	Oote	Maiyk
	Nokpa	Thambah	Jinpi
	Sapong	Tangsa	Khambay
	Zenchen	Koilang	Thaktey
	Nyamte	Hoto	Khimshin
	Ranto	Thakte	Longsay
	Pangkhu	Rangto	Tagin
	Yakyak	Khosum	
Tangnyu	Hadong	Rongsang	
Dannyu	Rumchu	Namphu Chausa	
Morungs	Jenpi	Jenpi Chansa	
	Resom	Jenpi Rosom	
	Kompa	Jenpi Pulong	
	Nampha Tangsa	Namphu Pulung	
Tangnyu Dangsa	Jenpi		
	Jenpi Khowna		
	Kompa Tekpa		
	Habia		
Tangnyu Toknyu	Hadong		
	Nokpa Tangnyu		
	Nokpa		
	Nokphu		
	Sapong		
Tangnyu Toksa	Rangson	Namphu	Tangsa
	Nokpa	Jenpi	Pulung
	Kholam	Jenpi	Rosem
	Rosem	Namphu	Longbo
Hopa (Panu)	Haniqul	Sennu	
	Ngonpa	Kongnok	
	Hopu	Khocha	

Cont'd...

...Cont'd

	Nymte	Dealoo
	Ponkha	Wangsa
	Hokhu	Henmo
Hopa (Panyu)	Nagongpa	Nyamte
	Pagkhu	Hekhu
	Hopa	Kangnong
	Wangcha	Sannu
	Dialo	Hondiqui
	Hommong	
Hopa (Danchal)	Habia	Kampa
	Khocha	Hangchan
	Woyak	Ninniak
	Mophuk	Nahang
	Khosiang	Matey
Shumnang	Komkhu	Holo
	Nksok	Motook (Motsok)
	Lamkhu	Wakok
	Kokoki	
Chincha Moneng	Sanhu	Waltham
	Choncha	Lowang
	Jolam	Thaktey
	Sopong	Khomjo
	Homtak	Tincha
	Chatey	Rangnyu
	Kong Kang	Phakan
	Moiyak	Chatey
	Khomjo	Phankar
	Roho	Sanlam
	Noklo	Chanyu
	Walkrop	Rangwong
		Sannyu
Thamkho Dannyu Morung	Nyamte	Panchun
	Mophuk	Thumkho
	Hadong	Sumlum
	Thamlong	Dancha
	Jeya	Channyu
	Hamrong	Nlkpa
	Khokam	Kongkang
	Mannow	Pandit
Channyu Dansa Morung	Lowang	Panjen
	Yum Lowang	Noknyu
	Rangsong	Homkha
	Kholia	Channyu
	Jeya	Monyuk
	Thamkho	
	Wangdong	

Cont'd...

...Cont'd

Rukhiyet	Kothung
Morung	Joren
	Ransong
	Hasen
	Rumsu
	Tiat pa
	Thiaktey
	Changmyu
	Khislum
	Kangnyu

From Table 3, it is found that the clans are distributed in different Morungs. However, the Channyu Dansa Morung has the Lowang clan. In other Morungs, all the clans have been mixed up and some new clan members have joined the village from other village. Therefore, the Kepi and the Tangmo groups cannot be classified as moiety as referred by Dutta (1978). In Raho village, a subordinate village under the Lazu chief has twelve clans, namely Langsey, Rangmey, Nokpa, Wangsa, Kongkang, Sapong, Lowang, Sokto, Hodong, Namphu, Phamlon and Oote.

From Table 4 it is found that the Langsey clan has the population of 42(21.32%), out of which 24 are males and 18 females. The Phamlon clan has the population of 3 out of which two are males and one female. Next to Langsey, Kong Kong clan occupies the highest number (20.81%) which is followed by Sapong (10.67%), Nokpa (10.15%), Hadong (8.64%), Rangmey (8.12%), Lowang (5.58%), Wangsa (4.06%) and so on.

Like Raho, in other two studied villages, Lapnan and Soha grouping of the clans is somewhat different. In these villages, each clan is an exogamous unit for regulation of marriage. Soha village has seven clans namely Lowang, Moidam, Ramba, Ngongba, Sabin, Songthin and Chin. These clans are independent. They marry among themselves but not within the same clan. Like Soha, Lapnan village has six clans, namely Lowang, Chimyeng, Bongyang, Suiyang, Tesia and Khoiyang out of which Chimyang has the maximum population (25.63%), while Lowang constitute only 1.12 per cent.

Besides regulating marriage, the distinction of clans is manifested itself in various social behaviours. At Lazu, when the Kepi group kills a buffalo, the meat from the head is not eaten by the Tangmos. Likewise, the Kepis do not eat meat received from the two classes and Kepi and Tangmo do not sit together in community feast. In some villages, the Lowang group occupies a prestigious position in all social and religious functions. The chief of the Lowang is honoured in all spheres.

Table 4

Clans	*Male*	*Female*	*Total*	*Percentage*
Langsey	24	18	42	21.32
Rangmey	10	6	16	8.12
Nokpa	9	11	20	10.15
Wangsa	3	5	8	4.06
Kong Kong	19	22	41	20.81
Sapong	12	9	21	10.67
Lownag	5	6	11	5.58
Sok To	2	2	4	2.03
Hadong	6	11	17	8.64
Namphu	4	3	7	3.55
Phamlon	2	1	3	1.52
Oote	4	3	7	3.55
Total	100	97	197	100.00

Family

The elementary unit of the Nocte society is the family, consisting of the parents and their unmarried children, or sometimes a newly married couple without an issue. Children are often adopted. Adoption of children of the same clan is also prevalent. There are different terms for adopted children. A male adopted child is called *chancimiya* in Lapnon village. The family structure of the Noctes of Raho village is shown below:

Table 5

Family Structure Showing Members in Different Categories.

Type of family	*Total households*	*Total population*	*Percentage*
Hu, Wi and unmarried son and daughter	18	89	45.19
Widower, married sons, their unmarried children	2	11	5.58
Unmarried male	2	2	1.01
Husband and wife without any issue	5	10	5.08
Hu Wi, children and widow mother	2	10	5.08
Widow, unmarried son/daughter	4	12	6.09
Hu Wi, married son, son's wife, and children	4	23	11.68
Hu, Wi married sons, son's wife, grand children unmarried son/daughter	4	28	14.22
Widow	1	1	0.50
Widow, married sons, son's wife, unmarried daughter and grand children	1	6	3.04
Unmarried brothers	1	4	2.03
Divorced male	1	1	0.50
Total	45	197	100.00

Normally, the sons live with the father till their marriage. But as soon as the sons marry, they establish independent households, with the exception of the eldest one who continues to live with the parents. The Nocte family may be termed as nuclear and extended type. The extended type is always horizontal. Vertical extended type of family is not in vogue.

The members of the family work jointly for each other. They take meal from a common hearth served by the eldest female member of the family. Each member has his allotted duties and responsibilities, which he should strictly adhere to. The kinship tie is very rigid which binds all the members of the family in a bond of unity.

The family property, both movable and immovable, is regarded as common and all male members enjoy equal right over the property so long as they live together. But when a younger brother separates and establishes his new house, he cannot claim any property except those which are given to him by his father or eldest brother. Some household articles and a portion of cultivable land are normally lent to the younger brother for a period of two to three years so that he may be able to maintain his new household.

The women do not inherit any parental property.

Marriage Types and Formalities

The term for marriage varies from village to village. At Soha, it is called *Zad-a-sang*. At Lazu village, it is known as *Moinulet* or *Madat,* and *Lammin* at Lapnan village.

Monogamy is the ideal and general practice but there is no restriction against polygyny. The majority of the people, however have one wife. The chief only enjoys the privilege of polygyny. Rather it is the custom with the chiefs to marry two wives and among them elder one is *Wangsa dong* and the younger *Wangsa nadii. Wangsa dong's* eldest son can inherit the chieftainship. *Wangsa dong* is the daughter of a chief from another village. *Wangsa nadii* is from the commoner's class and from the village of the chief. There are instances of a chief's marrying more than two wives. The chief of Lapnan village has three wives, the eldest one *Wangnu* is from the clan of the commoner's class.

At Soha, the first wife is called *Nukho* and the second wife *Nuza*. *Nan Nu* are those families with whom marriage negotiation can take place. Usually, mother's brother 's daughter is called *Nam Nu*. Widow marriage is known as Za To Nu We Pang Me Lap. In such case, a fine is imposed on the husband. It includes a pig, one bell-metal plate, etc. *Ma-mat Lap* is the marriage of a widow with her deceased husband's brother. In this type of marriage, no fine is imposed. The Soha people believe that if the widow or widower remarries, then they suffer from incurable diseases. It is called *Ba-a-lap.* To avoid such cases, they perform *Wo Shi Dong Khan* ritual. In such ritual the man sacrifices a cock and sprinkles its blood in front of his house. The invitees touch the blood and come inside the house.

The marriage of the widower with his deceased wife's sister is known as *Ma Mat Lap.* In such case also, the widower sacrifices a cock and performs the *We Shi Dong Khan* ritual.

In the ritual of *Wa Shi Dong Khan* a portion of the chicken is kept fixed on a bamboo pole in front of the house to signify inheritance of the widow. The feathers of the chicken is taken by each man of the village to his respective house. It is said that those who cannot take the feather cannot eat in the house of the person when the marriage has taken place. If anybody violates the rule, then he/she is sure to suffer from some disease.

The junior levirate is the commonest type. Cases of senior levirate is restricted in the villages like Soha, Lapnan and Lazu. At Lazu, levirate marriage is locally known *as Thempnu melet. Thempun* means widow and *Melet* means marriage. Normally, the widow stays at least two years in her deceased husband's house. After two years, she is free to marry any man but outside her deceased husband's clan. Junior sororate is known as *Melet,* meaning marriage.

Cross-cousin marriage is the preferred form of mating among the Noctes. Marriage with the daughter of the mother's brother is their most favoured one, and the mother's brother's daughter is considered as the potential wife of the father's sister's son. At Lapnan village, this type of marriage is called *Hu-Cha-Ni-Cha* while at Soha, it is called *Nam nu*. This term is used to refer to all marriageable girls of mother's brother. This is shown in the following genealogical chart:

Genealogical Chart of Cross-cousin Marriage

Village: Soha

Wamgsam Lowang-Wangsadong

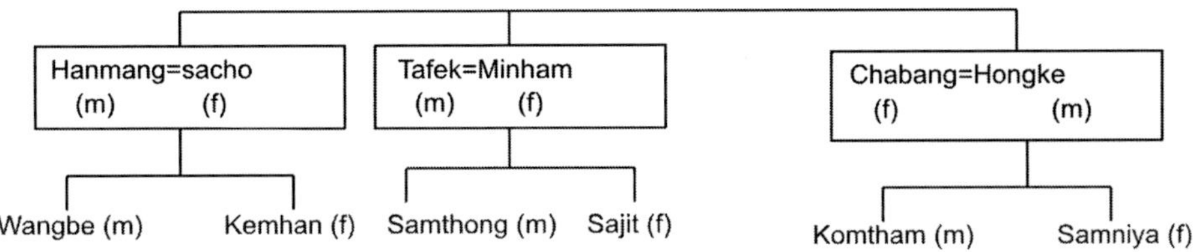

From this genealogical chart, it is clear that Samthong has married his mother's daughter and Komtham has married her father's sister daughter.

At Lazu, the mother's brother's daughter is called *Anu*, a term applied to describe one's wife. Sometimes, the father's sister's son refers to the mother's daughter as *Nga Moinu Le* meaning she is my wife.

The father's sister's daughter type of cross-cousin marriage is, however, not favoured. In cross-cousin marriage considerable socio-economic significance is attached. The prime considerations for such marriage are mutual help and cooperation, and adjustment of temperament. There is freedom in the choice of a mate other than the cross-cousin and this freedom offers an ample opportunity to consider such factors as beauty, age, character, capability to work and adjustment in the family. It is probably because of this freedom that divorce cases are very less in Nocte society.

In general, marriage takes place after negotiations between the parents of both the boy and the girl. Negotiation marriage is called by various terms like *Kakhat, Achiyen, Sad-s-sang*. At Lazu, the negotiation is preceded by betrothal in case of early age of the boy and the girl. It is called *Seng Kakhat*. Negotiation is initiated by the boy's parents through the exchange of rice-beer (*Kham*), and *Sali* (a kind of creeper chewed along with betel leaf and betel nut).

At Soha there are three forms of marriages such as marriage by negotiation, through love and elopement which are called *Chumrek, Huset* and *Chonest* respectively and each form is performed in different ways.

In *Chumrek*, negotiation (also called *zad-a-sang*) between the parents of the boy and the girl takes place when they attain adulthood. On the following day of negotiation, the boy along with some young boys of his clan goes to work in the *jhum* field of the girl. This is called *Pokat Bonbe*. The boy alone will stay for the night at the girl's house and the other boys return to their houses. At the girl's house, the boy is treated as an honourable guest. He returns to his house the next day. In the girl's house, he is, however, not allowed to talk to the girl or even see her. This is called *Rong Fak Sa*. After the negotiation, the parents of the boy distribute tobacco (Wekhu), odd number betel leaf and areca-nut, lime (*Tokban*) and tea leaf (*Falap*) to the elderly persons in the clan. It is called *Wekhu Fafak*. After that both the parties agree for *Pokat Bonbe*. One day after *Pokat Bonbe* the boy again visits the girl's house and works in the *jhum* field specially for cultivating the millet. It is called *Lam Lang Nat*.

On the marriage day, locally known as *Chumrek Sa*, the boy's family sends two pigs to the girl's house. It is called *Kam Suk.* In the boy's house a feast is arranged. After sending the *Kam Suk*, the bridegroom dresses in the groom dress called *Sangta Ba* and goes to the bride's (Sangata-nu) house. The groom is accompanied by a clan boy (*Roba*) and an old man (*Kampa*). In the bride's house, the bride, the groom, the *Roba*, the *Kampa* and one girl of the bride's clan called *Ronu* eat their meal together from the same plate. This ritual is called *Sam-rom-sa*. The meal is served by an old woman called *Ran nu*. The bride then proceeds to the groom's house, accompanied by her friend, relatives and fellow villagers. The *Sam-rom-sa* is also performed at the groom's house. It is followed by feasting and drinking. The bride stays at the groom's house.

On the second day, relatives are entertained at the groom's house. On the third day, the bride prepares rice-beer and entertains the relatives of the groom. On the fourth day, the bride and the groom, accompanied by the *Ro ba* go to the field and work there. *Sam-rom-sa* is performed there. After that, the newly married couple accompanied by the *Ro ba* and *Ro nu* go to the girl's maternal uncle to give him rice-beer and one cloth.

This form of marriage is a lengthy one and involves heavy expenditure. The present economic condition does not permit the people to perform the marriage with the old formalities. So, they have resorted to less expensive forms of marriage such as elopement *(Huset)* and love marriage (*Khaphak*).

Beside, they spend on feasting and drinking. The girl's side has to offer the articles such as one bell metal plate, one bell metal *(Warm)* bowl, one hen with chickens, one basket (*Hura*), one dao and one spade. The groom has to give bride price locally known as *Thang da.* It includes one pig, and one cow. It is called *Cho wang wak-a-man.* For the bride's mother, the groom has to give one cloth called *Nunam.* The ritual is called *Nusa.* After performing *Nusa,* the groom has to give one pig. It is called K*haphak.*

In case of *Huset* form of marriage, the boy elopes with the girl to his house and his parents inform the girl's parents through someone of the village. After that, exchange of rice-beer takes place. In case of *Khakhap* marriage, the marriage ceremony is preceded by negotiation. The girl is brought to the boy's house on the day following negotiation. A pig is killed and all people assembled there take the meat with rice beer. Pre-marital sex relation is not tolerated by Soha Noctes. If the girl becomes pregnant, the boy responsible for the pregnancy must marry her.

The performance of the marriage ceremony varies among lower Noctes and upper Noctes. Among the Lazu Noctes, a system of *Yawn-Pangmi* is prevalent. It was a practice where the bride for a boy is selected by his parents when the boy is in his infancy. Once the match is selected, a public announcement is made to bring it to the notice of the villagers, when the boy becomes adult and is able to pay the bride price then only the marriage ceremony takes place. The bride price in Lazu is still higher in comparison to other Nocte areas. There is the gap between onset of puberty and actual time of marriage. In the past there was a system whereby a boy will go in front of a house and will call *Mainu Tungala,* means, is a girl available. If he gets a favourable reply, then he will enter the house and spend the night with the girl who has welcomed him. After one or two visits they develop a fancy and such a boy is called the *Pangmi* of the girl and the girl is called *Yawn* of the boy. The parents of the girl and all the villagers including her future husband (with whom she has been engaged) will come to acknowledge their *Yawn-Pangmi*. The Yawn-Pangami is now discouraged, mainly after 1993.

Death and Disposal of Dead

Death is locally known as *Mangrit* in Lazu area. When a man dies due to old age it is considered as natural death, and the cause is attributed to the will of almighty God (*Jaubani*). Death due to prolonged illness, though equally natural is considered to be due to the action of the evil spirits (jok). Natural deaths are called *Lummi* at Soha while unnatural deaths due to reasons such as fall from tree, drowning, death while pregnant or death on delivery are unnatural and called *Sami*. Such unnatural deaths are also called *Chalem*.

Three different methods of disposal – cremation, burial and exposure on platform are found among the Noctes.

In lower region like Soha and other villages a dead is cremated. At Soha it is called *Mangcho*. Cremation is done near the house. After the cremation two pieces of ginger are thrown to the pyre. It is called *Sang Khothok*. On this day, the gingers (Sengnu) are cut in three pieces and offered to the dead.

In case of cremation, the pyre has to be prepared by the clan members and relatives. The charred bones of the skull and legs are collected and wrapped in a leaf. An effigy called *Rang Sang* depicting the dead is made and the bones are put inside it. It is then placed in a small hut constructed near the dwelling house and kept there till *Sang Khothok* is performed. After this, it is brought to the main house and kept till the *Pongtu* festival is performed after the sowing of millet in April–May. Following this, all connection with the dead is severed and no offering is made again. As this practice is a lengthy one, the Soha Noctes have changed over to burial. Cremation is, however, obligatory in accidental deaths.

Disposal of dead by burial is practised by Lazu and Soha Noctes. At Soha, natural deaths are buried. The pit for burial is dug by the clan members. In the bottom and at the two sides, wooden planks are fixed to form a framework inside which the corpse is laid, wrapped in a piece of new cloth and mat. At Lazu, the burial ground is called *Yet*. The cloth for wrapping is usually red, called *Khat Chang*. Here at Lazu the pit is dug slightly slanting and the head is placed on the higher side. At Soha, the head is placed on the wooden planks. At Lazu, an effigy (*Tangmi*) made on the first day, is fixed near the head and enclosed in a bamboo fence. Personal belongings are hung on the effigy.

At Soha, before the burial, a lock of hair is removed from the dead, and placed in a bamboo tube near the grave. At the time of annual festival called *Rang Sang*, the lock of hair is taken out and the relatives express sorrow and grief. The maternal uncle fixes the spear near the grave. It is called *Wolumlamchoi*. It is not done in case of female dead. It is done to show the path of the dead to the other world. On the day of *Rang Sang* old ladies of the dead express sorrow and a feast is arranged by sacrificing a hen.

At Lazu, the first day of the death is accompanied by feasting. It is called *Mangpo*. Second day is the *Mangrum*. On this day, the dead is buried. The third and the last day is the *Yut Khang*. On this day, all the clan members and relatives of the dead assemble at the dead's house and express sorrow.

This is another method of disposal of dead. This method is found in Lapnan village. The dead body is exposed on a bamboo platform over which a piece of cloth is spread. The body is first lifted by four old men called *Ramba* or four old women called *Ramnyu* and then carried by other clan members. Personal belongings and articles of food and drink are hung from a crossed bamboo pole near the platform. These grave goods are called *Mong sathiyok*.

Origin and Mythology: Tradition of Chieftainship

The Noctes have legends about their origin. They believe that supreme God called *Jauban* had created all human beings. The Nocte believe how the first woman and a man met and produced many children. It is said, originally marriage took place between the daughter of the sky and the spirit on earth. These first men were the Noctes and their descendants were the Ahoms.

The Noctes believe that their original homeland was in Myanmar (Burma). Legends of migrations describe the journey from Myanmar beyond Patkoi hills to the locations of their present villages. The district of Tirap being situated between the plains of the Brahmaputra on the west and the valley of the Irrawady on the east, has seen the movement of people from various places from time immemorial. The Noctes have also come, through such movement and settled in the various villages of the district.

The Soha people say that originally they were the inhabitants of Nzeimung beyond the Patkoi range. When the population increased, cultivation became a problem in the hills as there was shortage of salt and clothing also. So many people decided to leave the place and after crossing the Patkoi hills came to a place called Thungjang where they did not stay long. From Thungjang they came to Phungsa near Lazu. Both these villages are still in existence on the bank of the Barap river and are inhabited by the Noctes. From Phungsa they came to Longcho after crossing a hill called Langtok. Longcho is the place where the present Phunthing village is situated. From Longcho they came to Moinak, the site of the present Turet village. From Moinak they came to Soha where they finally settled. When they settled at Soha, there were three villages in that area. These villages were Doidam, Kenon and Mapoiya. The present inhabitants of Mapoiya village are people from Soha who occupied the village after driving out the original inhabitants.

The Lazu Noctes originally migrated from a place called Sansit at Myanmar. From there they came to a place called Chunu near Patkoi hills. Staying for a short period at Chunu they migrated to the present habitat. The first chief who established the village at Lazu was Dinbang.

Apparently, the lower Noctes have migrated from the upper regions of the Patkoi ranges. However, some Nocte villages have been established by people migrating from other Nocte villages. There are also some villages which were established by the people from the Wancho and Tangsa areas. Lapnan, one of the villages under study, situated near the district headquarters Khonsa, was established by the Wancho of the Wakka village of Longding sub-division of the district. These people migrated originally from *Ofana Nu* near the

Indo-Myanmar border. Due to increase of population they have abandoned their original village and settled in the present habitat. At the time of settlement at this village, they agreed to pay tribute to the Borduria chief who permitted them to settle in Lapnan village. The tributes included rice-beer locally known as *Ucha* and elephant tusk. Originally, eighty families first came from Wakka and stayed at a place *Kam Sin Jong* near present Kheti village. There they were frequently disturbed by the Kheti villagers and so they migrated to Lothungi near their present village. At Lothung, they stayed for about thirty years before they finally shifted to present Lapnan site. The first chief who came with the party was Naisan. After Naisan sixteen chiefs have passed away in the present habitat.

History and Affiliation with the Nagas

During the British period, the Noctes and the Wanchos were referred to as Eastern Nagas (Dutta, 1978: 20). Dutta states that in 1871 there were 14,383 Nagas of different clans namely Namsangia, Borduria, Dodum, Joboka, Banfers, Toopigonya and Sologria. Of these, Namsangia, Dadum, Borduria and Toopigonya are the present Noctes. In 1884, there were 6,000 Namsangias and 3,000 Bordurias.

The earlier administration reports mainly dealt with the problems of administration of the area, which remained unexplored for a long time. Some detailed account of Lazu Noctes is available in the old *Gazetteer* of the Sadiya and Bliparai Frontier Tracts where they have been mentioned as Nagas of Sadiya Frontier Tract.

By an agreement in 1975–76, the Namsong chief transferred the land to two tea gardens, namely Namsong and Hukanjuri, on an annual compensation of ₹ 475. This payment was once withheld for one year owing to the chief's failure to obey the orders of the government. This chief of Borduria was allowed by the same agreement to hold 200 bighas of land near Jaipur, free of cost. Both Borduria and Namsang chiefs had to send annual reports to the Deputy Commissioner, Dibrugarh and to pay tributes to the British government. In return, they received gifts from the British administration.

When the administrative headquarters were shifted from Dibrugarh to Sadiya and the power of the Deputy Commissioners were transferred to the political officers in September 1942, the chiefs of Namsang and Borduria opposed it. In 1942, the Nocte area was declared partially administered.

Though the area was not wholly administered yet it is not that the Noctes were opposed to the government at that time. Instead, they were helping the government whenever required. In 1874–75, the chief of Namsang helped the British administration by providing labour required for the survey party engaged in exploring railway line. The Nocte labourers were also engaged in cleaning the railway line between Makum and Dumduma. They also came down during the cold season for tea plantation work and other types of labour. The British government did not interfere in the internal affairs of the Noctes, but they were not allowed to carry their quarrels into the British territory. For violating this order, they were punished by courts.

There were hostilities for about fifty years between the chiefs of Namsang and Borduria. However, this fighting ceased for sometime in 1882–83 when the

Gosain of Bareghar Satra of Naharkatia made the Noctes his disciples. Reviewing the book entitled *Sri Ram Dev Charit,* Maheswar Neog writes that the chiefs of Namsang and Borduria were initiated into Vaishnavism by Sri Ram Dev, who was the head of the Chalish Bareghar Satra. According to the report of the British government in 1884–85, the Namsang chief had 27 villages with a population of 6,150 in 1,230 houses. The Borduria chief on the other hand had 19 villages with a population of 9,325 in 1,865 houses.

As evident from records and traditions, the Noctes came in close contact with the people of Assam during the Ahom days (1228–1826 AD). The relation between the two were mostly of a commercial nature, which afterwards turned into a cultural relationship through preaching of religion.

Political System and Chieftainship

In the bygone days, the Noctes were frequently engaged in inter-village fights, raids and head-hunting expeditions. The political life within the village was maintained by the chief with the help of elders council. Each village has such a council of elders which maintains law and order, takes decisions on intra-and inter-village disputes and also organizes the developmental works in the village.

The Lazu Village Council consists of seven members besides the chief who is the head. The other members are *Nhopa, Wangsa, Otai, Nyamtai* and two old members called *Kampa.* The members of the Soha Village Council are *Lowang, Ngongba, Moidom, Ramba, Totba, Reba* and few elderly persons called *Noktang.* The composition of the village council in Lapnan village is similar to the other villages with variations in the number of members and their designation. Whatever may be the pattern of composition, the active members always come from the clans of the chief. The chief is called *Lowang.* He is the final decision-making authority of the society. His decision is finally arrived at after consulting with the other members of the council.

The office of the *Lowang* is hereditary and the eldest son from the chief's first wife called *Wongstadong* is the heir. The *Wongstadong* has to be the daughter of a chief of another village. The social stratification of the Noctes is based on the chiefs, their ancestors and descendents who constitute a distinct class and enjoy special social position and privileges. This social stratification of the community is well marked and is reflected in respect of marriage and social behaviour. The chief's class is called *Lowangjat* (*Kepi* in Lazu). A chief may take wives from the commoner class, but the commoners cannot take wives from the *Lowangjat.* In social gatherings like community feasts, the two classes take different seats. Though the difference in not visible in daily life but in social life a chief enjoys many privileges. It is observed that the chief gets the largest share of the community hunting and fishing. The cultivation of the chief's fields is done by assistance of the commoners. The death of the chief is a matter of concern for the entire village community. The villagers paid in the past annual tribute to the chiefs in kind. Rice- beer for any festival in the chief's house is prepared by the village. The chiefs of Namsang and Borduria are considered to be of divine origin and hence the special privileges. Some of the privileges are shared by the family and the lineal relatives of chief.

A chief is not supposed to do any manual work. There was a system of compulsory labour called *Pokat* involving the subordinate villages. All subordinate villages are, however, not required to work under this system. Only those villages which had been subjugated by a powerful chief were required to give their compulsory labour. The villages which assisted the Namsang chief under *Pokat* system are Doidam, Soha, Turet, Mapoya, Dongron, Kenon and Longkhaw. These villages also paid separate tributes to the chief. The chief of Borduria also enjoyed such free labour from Lapnan village. The Lazu chief received service and tributes called *Se* or *Soksa* from the villages like Kothung, Kolam, Chinhanm Longliang, Pongkong, Nogto (Noklo), Sanyu (Seniew) and Rahu.

A chief's name is not uttered by a commoner in his presence or absence. He is referred to as *Lowangdong*. He enjoys precedence on all matters. Even in walking or marching he must lead. All powers whether administrative, executive or judiciary were concentrated in the person of the chief who used to organize head hunting after discussions and deliberations in the meeting of the council of elders. In addition to the judicial powers, the chief played an active role in some developmental activities also. The chief kept the village well-fortified from outside attack since some inter-village raids occurred in the past. In social activities like marriage, religious functions, natural calamities, etc., the chief extended help to the villagers.

The chieftainship and powers of chiefs still survive despite introduction of Panchayati Raj system. This new democratic council has not taken away all the powers of the chief. This council has been empowered to formulate and to execute the developmental plans in addition to the implementation of various welfare activities. However, the traditional functions and powers in relation with the customary laws and religious spheres are still in the hands of the chief.

Religious Attributes

The Nocte's conceptualization concerning the existence of the high god and the tutelary supernatural beings is a highly variable one. No two Nocte villages manifest identical ideology in respect of the nature and attribute of the high god or the supernatural beings. Nevertheless, the Noctes in general believe in the existence of high god whom they call *Jauban, Jongban or Tesongi* in Doidam village. He dwells on the earth, being the cause and effect of all happenings in the life of an individual. He manifests a duality of character–both good and evil. His benevolent temperament brings in happiness and prosperity and his evil disposition is accompanied with miseries and misfortunes. These two aspects are referred to as *Kat Jauban* and *Wongi Jauban* respectively. In lower Nocte villages, the two aspects are manifested by *Rang Jauban* and *He Jongban,* the former dwells in the sky and the latter on the earth, looking after and protecting the village.

The Noctes believe in the existence of a number of spiritual beings dwelling in the jungles, ditches and rivers and streams and causing various ailments like fever, cough, dysentery, etc. The Noctes of Soha village also identify the deities who cause various diseases. These are *Hakho* (village spirit), *Jok* (water spirit), Bodap (jungle spirit), *Pongaba, Phin-thang, Kangsak, Chimthang, Dasi, Sima, Mlapi,*

Tatongi, Tulamjon, Lamchom, Hakhochom, Ha Jongban (protector of the village who lives in the jungle) and *Hom jonban* (household deity).

Apart from the belief in an array of deities and demons, the Noctes perform a variety of rituals that are believed to be efficacious for the welfare and well-being in the life of man. The Noctes believe that proper performance of rituals can bring about economic betterment and prosperity in the life of an individual. Further, performance of certain rituals whenever the need arises can avert the incidents of death, disease and misfortune.

The ritual performed for *Jauban* and other benevolent spirits are called *Chuam* and those performed for malevolent spirits, particularly for the curing of diseases are called Tingtoi or *Satjop*. The ritual performance in Soha area to propitiate the high god, *Tesong* is called *Hasom*. It is performed once in the month of *Namsa* (June–July) for the welfare of the village and for protection against diseases. *Lamrit* ritual is performed at Soha village in the month of *Datu* (April) to appease *Wang Janban*. All ritualistic performances are done by the experts. While the diviner prescribes ways and means, the priest performs the ritual. The divining is called *Taba* in Soha. At Lazu, the diviner is done by the officials of the village council, namely *Nyamtai, Otai* and *Ngopai*.

Vaishnavism: Impact of Assamese Culture

The Noctes are a lone tribe who adopted Vaishnavism nearly two and a half centuries back, amidst a large number of tribal groups inhabiting the sprawling mountainous territory to the north and east of the Brahmaputra valley. By the time, the Noctes came to practise Vaishnavism, it underwent a good deal of modification, especially after the demise of the prime abbot Sankar Deva and his close associate and follower, Madhav Deva.

Besides following their tribal beliefs and practices, the Noctes have adopted Vaishnavism, though in a rudimentary form till now, and are affiliated to the Shree Shree Chaliha Bareghar Satra (Vaishnavite monastery) of Nazira, in the Sibsagar district of Assam. The Nocte chief Khunbao, who is also called Lotha Khunbao, the ancestor of the present chief of the lower region, was the first to embrace this sect, when Shree Ram Dev Ata was the Adhikar (abbot) of the *Satra*. The *Satra* at that time was at a place called Merbil some eight miles east of Naharkati in the Dibrugarh district of Assam. After adoption of this sect, Khunbao came to be known as Nagai Noruttam, which means best among men. Khunbao was followed by all the people of lower Nocte region in adopting this religious sect. Gradually, the Noctes of the other villages also became disciples of the Satra. But the Noctes of the upper region of Lazu area were not affiliated to this religious sect.

The Vaishnavite Nocte villages have Namghars (prayer hall) that serve as a place of congregational worship at the time of the Satradhikar's (chief of the Satra) visit. It is an occasion for novices to become Saran (disciple) by accepting religious codes of conduct from the Satradhikar, sidha-bhojani (food) and paying Guru-kar (tribute), and observing annual ritual liabilities, which they believed brought virtue and earned dharma.

The Nocte Vaishnavite faith is conspicuous by the absence of any devotional song, dance and staging of any religious drama, called Bhavana, the cardinal features of the Vaishnavism. However, the typical hairstyle of the Noctes in Lapnan village bears a strong resemblance with the Satrirya style (characteristic hairstyle of the Vaishnava devotees).

The Noctes are a turbulent tribe who had frequently been at war. The history of almost all villages in the Nocte country is replete with treacherous headhunting raids. Hence, apparently the tenets of Vaishnavism with its serene sublime philosophy of surrender to one God, *Eka Saran,* in the person of Sri Krishna, could hardly fit with the socio-cultural ethos of the Noctes. Vaishnavism could make headway among the Noctes on account of two inherent factors of the new faith. One, the people are impressed not by the concept of surrender to one supreme Almighty God in the person of Sri Krishna, but by the egalitarian spirit of the *dharma* or faith. Second, the people developed a fascination, or rather an inclination, for undergoing *saran* under a protector in order to earn what the Noctes call *dharma,* that is, religious merit. The people treat *dharma* as immensely valuable; it can avert misfortunes. Whenever there arises an individual or collective sense of crises or untoward happening, the Noctes make it a point to visit the Satras, especially the Chaliha Bareghar Satra of Nazira, for the purpose of acquiring *dharma.* It was learnt from the Noctes themselves that their guru or Chaliha Bareghar Satra also used to visit the Nocte village quite regularly till the fifties of the twentieth century. In the second half of century the visits of the *guru* had become few and far between. Yet the people have never parted with the faith. They are seen to aspire for merit or *dharma* which they believe gives them healthy life, good harvest, plenty of wealth and abundance of game and forests and many children.

As in Assam, the Nocte villages also have miniature Mamghars that serve as a place of congregation worship at the time of the Satradhikar's visit. The religious activity is accompanied with great merriment and rejoicing.

In Assam, all extra-religious devices to popularize the Vaishnavite faith among the Assamese masses include devotional song, dance and staging religious drama locally known as Bhaona. In accordance with Assam's puritanical Vaishnavite observances, recital of scriptures and staging of religious hymns called Nam Kirtan by congregation of devotees is held at the Namghar on every *gurubar* or Thursday. The Noctes who lead a very hard and arduous life are very much preoccupied with procuring day-to-day food from morning till evening. Concern for sheer survival hampers congregational assemblage and prayer. It is through choice that the Noctes have since adopted and practised certain select traits of the *Eka Sarana Bhagavati Dharma.* And these traits are those that serve the people's immediate purpose most.

In recent years, the Noctes evinced interest in adopting some new features like holding and practising of Nam-Kirtan, Bhaona, etc. Dutta (1978: 253) reports that since 1966 Nocte disciples were imparted training in performing Nam-Kirtan for running Namghars and that Sri Gopal Krishna Dev Goswami, the Satradhikar of Chaliha Bareghar Stara, performed Bhaona of Ram Bijoy, etc., in the Namghars at Namsang, Borduria and Khonsa. Traditional aspirations for material prosperity and individual and group well-being have since kept the people attached to some features of *Eka Sarana Bhagavati Dharma* in conjunction with the traditional animistic beliefs. In view of the acceptance of some new feature of Vaishnavite faith in recent years, as noted above, it could well be anticipated that the Noctes may develop pristine form of Vaishnavism in the foreseeable future.

Interaction with the Brahmaputra Valley

The Noctes, particularly the lower Noctes, had close relationship with the Assamese of the Brahmaputra valley. The Noctes who were called the Nagas by the Assamese used to come down to the plains for barter and trade.

There are many Nocte villages like Soha, Namsang and others adjacent to the plains of Assam. The people of these villages have long been visiting the plains for trade and seasonal work in the tea gardens of Namsang and Hukarjuri. They also visited a number of towns of Dibrugharh and Tinsukia districts of Assam like Naharkatia, Joypur, Margherita etc., especially in the winter months of December to February. These visits were undertaken for procuring certain essential commodities like salt, match boxes, iron tools, bell metal dishes, bowls, buckets, beads and bangles from the plains. Such visits by Noctes to the plains has reduced since the onset of the 1980s as Khonsa, the district headquarters town, and other townships like Deomali and Lazu developed by leaps and bounds over the years. Prior to the development of vehicular surface traffic to the Nocte country till late fifties of the twentieth century, the river Burdihing, which has its source from the Tirap mountains, flowing northward to join the Brahmaputra, served as a waterway to take the Nocte entrepreneurs to the areas in the lower reaches of the river. It can well be perceived that free intercourse and movement of men and materials, long before the British period, actually laid the foundations of socio-cultural relationship between the Noctes and the people of Brahmaputra valley in the past.

Education

Modern education was introduced among the Nocte after 1947, after the establishment of the education department in the North-East Frontier Agency. In the initial stage of the spread of education, a few primary schools were opened in the whole of the Nocte area. But in course of time, the people became conscious of the benefits of education and demanded opening of more and more schools in the area. Today, there are higher secondary schools, five high schools, 16 middle schools, 110 primary schools and 21 pre-primary schools in the whole area. As per 1991 census, total number of students in the schools are 12,873 out of which, 8,307 are boys and 4,566 females. Total number of teachers in these schools are 472. Beside these, there are schools run by the Rama Krishna Mission at Deomali and the Sarada Mission at Khonsa. The Sarada mission has opened a new horizon in the field of women's education among the Noctes.

It is observed that Nocte girls are now coming forward more and more for higher education. It is clearly visible from the household data of Lapnan village where the education is nearly 50 per cent. Comparatively, the urban based villages are in a more advantageous position in education than the rural village like Lazu.

Dutta (1978: 255) states that earlier the bachelor's dormitory or Morung served as the only institution for transmission of cultural heritage from generation to generation. The author says that in the Morung, the youth were taught certain civic duties such as the safety and welfare of the village. Now the Morung, serves as the centre for the annual festival rather than anything else. The Noctes are now interested in modern education.

Agriculture Development and Social Change

In the field of agriculture some changes have taken place among the Noctes. It is found that besides the traditional method of jhum cultivation they have adopted permanent cultivation along with the new tools and technology. They have now realized the value of improved method of cultivation. Many of them have come forward to reclaim more of the cultivable wasteland and thus brought about self-sufficiency in food. The area brought under modern cultivation in 1992–93 was 175 hectares. The significant change was that improved seed was sown in about 1,325 hectares of land in 1992–93.

Since the inception of modern administration in the Nocte area, rapid changes have taken place. It is thus found that in Lapnan village television, tape recorder and modern musical instruments are increasing at a faster rate compared to Lazu. The villages of upper region have not yet been able to access the modern amenities like the lower region. The lower Nocte region has progressed in the production of more vegetable and fruits. Even in *jhuming,* the lower Noctes have improved with regard to timely sowing, making contour logging, providing strip cropping, etc. However, the people of the whole area depend mostly on the fair price shops for some food grains. There are altogether 52 fair price shops in the Nocte area and 15 cooperative stores located at various places in the area. The principle objective of the agriculture department has been to assist villagers to increase food production to solve the problem of scarcity. For this purpose, several schemes such as land reforms, irrigation, supply of improved variety of seeds and plants, plant protection, livestock upgradation have been taken up by the agriculture department.

All the developmental activities have brought about a change in the outlook of the people. The government staff posted at different places are not looked down upon as a group of foreigners. There are no inter-village feuds now and the people can move freely and there is no fear of attacks by the enemies. The bitter taste of the 'Police State' of the British administration has been replaced by the idea of welfare state where government and people are equal partners in nation building.

Along with the development of the area, changes have also taken place in the social-cultural life of the people. The rule of tribe endogamy in marriage has gradually weakened in the society. There are instances of marriage of Nocte girls with persons outside the community. There are greater interactions between Lewangjat (the chief's class) and the Sanajat (commoner's class). Now, the privileges of the chief's are diminishing in the face of the modern social and administrative set-up.

Chieftainship and Panchayati Raj

Chieftainship, chiefs, 'royal' clans of chiefs and many of their privileges have survived and people still recognize them. Chiefs had earlier governed the villages with the help of village elders council. Such village council still survives, but modern administrative arrangements are being superimposed over clan based councils. Once the Noctes were a warrior tribe and headhunters who involved themselves frequently in the inter-village disputes and raids. The political life of the people was maintained by the chief and elders, through village council which was called Ngothum or Ngonthit. This council maintained law and order, decided disputes within the village and with other villages. Now a days, the Nocte village councils function almost in accordance with Statutory Panchayats and undertake all sorts of activities for the development and welfare of the people, besides deciding their disputes.

The chief, or the Lowang is the head of the council, but he depends on other members. As per new provisions the council deals with both civil and criminal cases. However, in case of heinous offence, the council informs the police and forwards the case before the court of law. But generally the council tries to settle the case in the village council itself as far as possible. Nobody in the village can overrule the decision of the council.

The introduction of Panchayati Raj System thus has not affected the function of the village council, rather it has strengthened the functioning of the village council, where chief is nominal head. The Gaon Panchayat members, the Anchal Samity members and Zila Parishad members may also be the members of the village council since the provision for dual membership is in practice. The Gaon Panchayat members or the Anchal Samity members, being the members of the same village community, show respect to their traditional village institution including the chief. The council members and the Gaon Panchayat members sit together to take a decision on any matter. The village council members cannot overrule the arguments of the Gaon Panchayat members, Anchal Samity members and Zila Parishad members. The North-East Frontier Agency Panchayat Raj Regulation (Regulation 3 of 1967) as amended by the NEFA (Administration) supplementary Regulation, 1972 defines that Gram Panchayat is a body of persons elected according to the tribal customary methods by the residents of any village or a group of villages. The Regulation 3 of 1967 had earlier provided for a three tier structure of self- governing bodies namely, Gram Panchayat, Anchal Samity and Zila Parishad.

The Statutory Panchayat is an important unit of planning and development. It is the modern political authority through which various developmental and welfare activities are channelized at the inter-village level. It has an effective part to play for promotion of education, improvement of agricultural crops and increased production and also in the sphere of administration.

The Zila Parishad is the highest unit of self-government at the district level and it consists of Vice-President, one representative of every Anchal Samity in the district who is elected by the members from amongst themselves, and six members nominated by the Governor from the community. It advises the Governor on all matters concerning the activities of the Gaon Panchayat and Anchal Samity situated within the district. Zila Parishad has functions like doing budget estimates of the Anchal Samity, distribution and allocation of funds and grants to the Anchal Samity, the coordination and consolidation of the plan proposed by the Anchal Samity and drawing up the district plan. Land settlements and raising of revenues are the main functions of the Zila Parishad. There are seven Anchal Samities and one Zila Parishad functioning in the district.

Conclusion

In this article we have discussed the themes of social stratification, social-cultural change and impact of modern democratic polity over a tribe where chiefs ruled till recently. The Nocte tribe is characterized by chiefs, chiefly and commoner clans, Morung (dormitories) and village council of elders. Like other parts of North East there is smooth transition of administration at village level, because the tribal rights over land and water are recognized and customary laws are used in settling disputes. The tribe has long tradition of conversion to Vaishnavism, a Hindu sect of Assam. Culture contact is reflected in adoption of Vaishnavism, which allows tribespeople to consume meat and also to pursue tribal religion. Assamese dress pattern is adopted by Nocte girls. The Noctes are now aware of value of education as it has helped them get better jobs.

Acknowledgement

Author thanks the project coordinator Dr N.K. Das for his critical comments and editorial assistance.

References

Dutta, P. 1978, *The Noctes,* Shillong: Directorate of Research, Government of Arunachal Pradesh.

Dutta, Parul 1975, "Beliefs and Rituals of the Noctes of the Arunachal Pradesh", *Arunachal News* 4:10.

Grierson, G.A. 1909, *Linguistic Survey of India,* Vol. III, Part I, Calcutta Kolkata: Government Press.

Neog, M. 1976, *Snehari Arunachal: My Hill So Strong,* Jorhat: Assam Sahitya Sabhai.

5 Immigrant Encroachment, Economic Deprivation and Cultural Squeezing

The Lepchas of Sikkim-Darjeeling

J. Chakraborty

In this article our objective is to discuss the current predicaments of the Lepchas in two locations of Sikkim and Darjeeling. Our focus is more on Lepchas of Sikkim who experienced the onslaught of heavy encroachments by immigrants who squeezed them culturally and also deprived them economically. Further, it also intends to understand the traditional system of stratification and impact of cultural contact and economic development on the growth of modern social stratification. This study was conducted in two locations, Kalimpong in hilly Darjeeling district and Sikkim, the hilly state where the Lepchas are autochthones. The study covers not only the dimensions of stratification among the Lepchas but also stratified relationships between the Lepchas and the other tribespeople as well as between the Lepchas and non-tribespeople. The fieldwork was done in two villages called Singhik, situated in Sikkim, and Nagsay, situated in Kalimpong sub-division of Darjeeling district. Both the villages were selected on the basis of numerical dominance of the Lepcha population as well as cultural factors. The fieldwork was carried out in two phases, November–December 1992 and December 1994 to February 1995, and further visits. The data were collected by conventional anthropological techniques, census survey, case studies and participant observation. Both the qualitative and quantitative primary data have been collected from the above mentioned two villages. To enrich the primary data gathered from these villages and also for proper interpretation, data have also been collected from the other locations. Available literatures from different sources have also been consulted for comparison and suitable interpretation. These secondary data have been utilized to understand the ethno-history and the traditional mode of stratification of the Lepchas as well as of the region they live in.

An attempt has been made here to understand the emerging pattern of inequality among the Lepchas of Darjeeling and of Sikkim Himalayas in the backdrop of traditional social structure of the Sikkimese society. Three important aspects like education, landholding and occupation have been examined with a view to understand the different perspectives of inequality among the Lepchas and their neighbours in both these locations. General data on the traditional system have been presented pertaining to the Sikkimese society as a whole, while specific data on stratification and change have been presented with reference to the Lepchas and their contact with neighbouring tribes and non-tribes.

The Lepchas of Eastern Himalayas: Identity of Tribe

The eastern Himalaya region is unique for its geo-physical condition as well as for its varied ethnic groups. The principal rivers of Sikkim, Teesta and Rangit pass through different routes of Sikkim and meet at Peshoke near Darjeeling. They divide the whole tract of land into three broad divisions. The Lapchas are the earliest settlers of Sikkim. They regard themselves the autochthones of Sikkim. The Bhutias came to this land from Tibet in the early 15th century and the Nepalis migrated to this land in the 18th century. Lastly, the British came to this land of Sikkim in the 19th century. This land is a confluence of four traditional monarchies – Sikkim, Bhutia, Nepal and Tibet. The peoples of these four monarchies have been in contact with Sikkim. The plainsmen too have been in the area for a considerable long time and thus have formed polyethnic cultural situation in Sikkim. Tibetan Buddhism became the state religion because of its affiliation with the ruling families (Chougal). However; Nepali language emerged as lingua franca in the state of Sikkim in due course.

The Lepchas, as a nature worshippers, are locally called Juktenmoo. They believe that they are the children of holy Kanchenjunga. As a first settler they occupied the most suitable land of Sikkim. But with the passage of time and large scale immigration of the Nepalis they dispersed from their original homeland into surrounding regions. The Lepchas who resettled in the three regions, Rejong, Tamsang, and Ilam, were known as Rejong Moo, Tamsang Moo and Ilam Moo respectively. These became their ethnic names. The word Moo, in Lepcha language, means inhabitants. Initially all these three Lepcha inhabitants, Rejong, Tamsang, and Ilam used these ethnic names as their surname. However, at present, only Tamsang surname is used in the Kalimpong sub-division. The members of each of these regional groups had more or less separate social entity (Bagchi, 1997: 364). Bagchi wrote that this horizontal segmentation was gradually transformed into some form of vertical status ranks, associated with prestige on the basis of purity of their blood. According to Das and Banerjee (1962) the Rejong are said to occupy the upper most position, the Tamsang are assigned the lower most position and the Ilam are given an intermediate position in the social hierarchy. The Tamsang are assigned the lower status on the ground that they were subjugated by the Bhutias as well as they were influenced by the Bhutanese culture.

Constant pressure of immigrants like the Bhutias and the Nepalis on this land of the Lepcha has brought many significant changes in the social structure and economy of the Lepcha. The Bhutias who came from Tibet as early as seventeenth century not only brought their own Buddhist religion but also turned the land of the Lepchas to a Buddhist theocratic state in the form of Mouggal dynasty. The Mouggal ruler ruled over Sikkim for more than 332 years or so. Hence Tibetan Buddhism became the state religion because of its affiliation with the royal families. Although the Nepali immigration to this land of Sikkim started early they immigrated in bulk during the middle of nineteenth century

(Subba, 1989: 1). The large scale immigration of Nepali population to Sikkim changed the ethnic character of the region. The Nepalis gradually settled and introduced innovations by procuring lands of native Lepchas and changed low yielding simple slash and burn type of cultivation into high yielding settled terrace cultivation. Through adoption of new agriculture method, the Lepcha subsistence economy changed into surplus economy in some places. Gradually barter system of transaction turned into market economy. Within a short period of time the Nepalis encroached into Lepcha areas and became numerically dominant and the indigenous Lepchas and the Bhutias became numerically insignificant. This process led to economic deprivation and cultural squeezing of Lepchas. Nepali language became the lingua franca of the state. Bagchi (1997: 365) wrote, "This crisis in the history of the Lepcha and the fear of their total annihilation, curiously enough supplied the necessary enzyme which de-stratified the so called trifurcated Lepcha society in the present century". However, this hierarchical ranking was followed, more or less up to first quarter of the preceding century. Different scholars have studied the Lepchas in different perspectives and at different time and space. Das and Banerjee (1962) pointed out that growth of individualism has developed in contemporary situation. Deb Burman is of the opinion that there is a trend of inequality among the Lepchas of Kalimpong. G. Bagchi has also pointed out that stratification has emerged among the Lepchas on the basis of territorial differentiation among them. The present study will emphasize on these changes that took place in the social structure of the Lepcha society.

It has already been mentioned that the Lepchas are the earliest settlers of Sikkim. They claim to be the autochthons of this land. No definite history is available as to when the Lepchas came to settle in this area. Beauveir Stocks, a pioneer anthropologist is of opinion that they immigrated to this land from an ancient colony of Southern Tibet. However, some scholars believe that the Lepachas came from Assam and they belong to a Tibeto-Burman tribal group. The Lepchas believe that they are the children of holy Kanchanjunga. They prefer to be called or refer to themselves as Mulanchi Rongkup. However, the word Lepcha appears to be of Nepali origin, which refers to a people of submissive nature.

In Sikkim the Lepchas are mostly found in the North district especially in Dzongu valley (Lepcha reserve) although they, at present, are sporadically distributed in other districts too. In fact, the Lepchas and the Bhutias are settled in central and northern Sikkim especially on hill slopes in humid climate and comparatively less productive zone. The Lepchas have their own language called ring or 'rong-ring'. They are amiable, always cheerful and peace loving people of Himalayas. They have converted to Buddhism. Their matrimonial alliances beyond ethnic boundaries have led to an erosion of Lepcha traditional culture.

Review of Literature on the Lepchas

A good number of scholars had done some significant works on the Lepchas of which *Notes on the Lepchas of Sikkim with Vocabulary of their Language* was published in 1840 by A. Rchibold Camphill. In 1854 Sir J.D. Hooker, the first European physiologist surveyed Sikkim and its neighbouring areas and published the survey results in *Himalayan Journals*. German philologist, G.B.

Mainwaring who passed a considerable long time with the Lepchas had published his book entitled, *A Grammar of the Rong (Lepcha) Language* in 1976. Another significant work, *Folklore and Customs of the Lepchas of Sikkim* was published in 1927 by Beauvein Stocks which contained myths and legends related to life and culture of the Lepchas. An important publication, Gover's *Himalayan Village* appeared in 1937. This was based on Lingthem, a village in Dzongu, the Lepcha reserve. This was more descriptive than analytical. The book, *Living with Lepchas: A Book about the Sikkim Himalayas* was published by John Morris in 1938. It is an ethnographical study of the Lepchas of Dzongu. The book entitled, *The Lepcha of Darjeeling and Kalimpong* was published by A.K. Das and S.K. Banerjee in 1962. This was based on anthropological research on socio-economic life of the Lepchas of Kalimpong. Foning who belongs to the Lepcha tribe has written a book entitled, *My Vanishing Tribe*. This book contains some ethnic views about his community. However, his experiences are mostly based on Darjeeling district. The book, *Himalayan Lepcha* by R.N. Thakur was published in 1988. Here the author has tried to systematize the earlier facts within his own experience.

The above authors have presented the picture of the Lepcha life and culture to some extent. However, most of the writings are not based on anthropological methods and thereby lack empirical facts. The object of this study is to bring into focus some aspects of stratification of the Lepcha in the backdrop of larger Himalayan society where the Lepchas are a part. A.C. Sinha's two books, *Politics of Sikkim: A Sociological Study* and *Politics of Sikkim* has been based on the studies of the Himalayan people. He has described the changing politics and the role of Kazis in Sikkim politics. He has further emphasized the aspect of ethnicity and resource distribution in Sikkim.

Ethno-History

As per prevalent oral tradition the Tibetan king who professed Buddhism invited Padmasambhava from Nalanda. He was a teacher of Tantric Buddhism and was popularly known as Guru Rimpochi. The great Guru also visited Sikkim and Bhutan for the dissemination of Buddhism. It is probable that large scale immigration of Bhutias to this land of the Lepchas took place after arrival of Buddhism. It may be mentioned here that Sikkim had developed trade relations with Tibet long since, even before the advent of Lamaism. The Tibetans used to export salt to Sikkim and import rice from Sikkim. There are folk tales on the relation between the Lepchas and the Tibetan Buddhists too. One such story narrates that a Lepcha chief who had no son became father of a son with the blessings of a Buddhist monastery. This incident had a good impact on the Lepchas and they welcomed the new religion, Buddhism. A reverse story is also prevalent among the Lepchas. The story narrates that Khye Bhumsa, a Tibetan noble was advised by his Lama to seek the blessing of the Lepcha hero Thekong Tek. Under his blessing he ultimately became father of a son. The Lepcha hero also predicted that the descendant of Khye Bumsa will be the ruler of Sikkim in future. Incidentally, Phuntsog Namgyal, the king of Chogyal dynasty was from that family. Such relations between the Lepchas and the Tibetans intensified friendship between them. Later, the Tibetans became popular as Bhutias. A brotherhood relationship was also established between Khye Bumsa and the Kong Tek at 'Kabhilongtore' or in short 'Kovi', 21 km away from Gangtok towards north district (Kotturan, 1982: 31). It may be stated that those above mentioned stories helped to establish some linkage between the Buddhist tradition and the Lepcha animistic tradition.

In the middle of seventeenth century, three veteran Lamas of Red Hut sect assembled at the Yaksam (a place in west Sikkim) in 1642 and decided to establish a kingdom for the growth of Buddhism in Sikkim. They felicitated Phuntsog Namgyal as first ruler of Sikkim with the title Chogyal or Dharmaraja. Sikkim is popularly believed to be the home of the Kirati tribes which include the Lepchas, the Limbus or Yakthamba, Mangar, etc., since prehistoric times (Sinha, 1983: 64). To check the alliance of the Kirati tribes, the foresighted ruler divided Sikkim into twelve *dzongs* or districts namely Lamu, Dallon, Yangthanog, Song, Libing, Maling, Simik, Poudon, etc., under the advice of Lamas. The ruler appointed twelve Lepcha chiefs as Dozongpon or governor, one for each district. It may be mentioned here that Sikkim was ruled by the different tribal chiefs. Under the influence of these chiefs Sikkim was segmented in different territories. Further, the king formed a council of twelve ministers mostly taken from the leading Bhutia warrior families. Sinha wrote that there were two dozen families of nobles who were considered the pillars of the Lamaist church for the sustenance of the Namgyal dynasty as the rulers (Sinha, 1983: 10). Hence, the Lepchas came under the control of the Bhutias. The Limbu and Mangar chiefs initially resisted to their best but they also recognized the Chogyal as their king though they were free to rule as they liked (Kotturan, 1983: 32–33).

Another important measure taken by the first ruler to be closer to the Kirati tribes was that he invited all the Kirati chiefs to a meeting. In that meeting the king proclaimed that the Bhutia or the Lhapas (Tibetan term for Sonthers), the Lepchas or the Monpas (the indigenous Lepchas) and the Tsongs (Limbu) are considered to be father, mother and son of the same family. The new council was called 'Lhomontsong' (Sinha, 1975: 4; Kotturan, 1983). The Lamas had an upper hand in the state affair, from the very beginning when Phutsog Namgyal became ruler of Sikkim. During the reign of the fourth king, a group of Lepcha and Bhutia courtiers were proclaimed to constitute the institution of aristocracy popularly known as 'Kazis' The third Namgyal ordained that the second of every three sons of the noble Bhutia family must be a monk of the sacred Pemiorgchi monastery (Sikkim a Concise Chronicle, 1963: 9). Thus only the royal Bhutia children were privileged to be the monks of this monastery. It may be mentioned here that the coronation ceremony of all the Namgyal kings were conducted by the Lamas of this sacred monastery. Sinha mentions that during the period from 1642 to 1874 out of total eight Namgyal rulers only the first two and the last one came in power in their maturity and the rest of the kings were enthroned at their early age. As a result during this period, the Kazis had a strong hold in the state affairs by variously acting as pro- Tibetan and anti-Tibetan as well as pro- British and anti British (Sinha, 1983: 5).

In the middle of nineteenth century an influential section of the Kazis favoured the Nepali settlement in Sikkim (Sinha, 1983: 65). In course of time some of them emerged as leasehold landlords or Thikadhars attached to Sikkim Durbar. They became rich and occupied various positions in Sikkim administration. Some of them were Buddhist and some Hindus (Kotturan, 1982: 19).

Basnet mentions that the Lepchas had some form of organization before the Tibetan overshadowed them. The Rongs or the Lepchas were organized by one Turve, who was eventually given the title 'Punu' 'Pano' or king. With the death of the last king Tubh Athau Punu, the Lepcha kingship came to an end. Gradually the tribe began to elect an old man as teacher, guide as well as tribal priest (Basnet, 1974: 9).

The Lepcha Clan/Putro/Agit/Thar

Most important unit of social organization is a clan. In Sikkim it is locally called Putro and in Kalinpong it is called Thar or Agit. These are all patrilineal exogamous units. During our survey good number of Putro such as Lukseun, Aram, Sanbha, Eden, Bokolinge, Karthan Youmling, etc., have been found. However, none can put light on the meaning and history of these Putros. Members of all these groups enjoy equal status. In Kalimpong more than seventy Agit of the Lepchas such as Olengmoo, Barlomoo, Brimoo, etc., have been found. One story regarding the origin of the Agit is available in their oral tradition. It says that once upon a time there was a demon in the forest where the Lepchas also lived. The demon used to harass unnecessarily the Lepchas from time to time. Hence the Lepchas became afraid of him. There was an old hunter in the forest. He planned to kill the demon. He called in ten well bodied Lepchas and told them his plan on how to kill the demon. He also showed them the cave of the demon where the demon used to sleep. The Lepcha youth attacked the demon and were successful in the operation. The first hero who cut the head of the demon was called Sada, the second hero who goggled the eyes of the demon was called Simik. Similarly, the person who cut the intestine was called Kali Krishna and the one who cut the limbs of the demon was called Sangden, etc. Hence, the story reveals that at first there were only ten Agit but it grew up to seventy or more. Both in Sikkim and in Kalimpong the function of the Agit or Putro is restricted to matrimonial alliances only. Beside marriage regulation, Agit has another function, i.e., ancestor worship. There is no hierarchy among the members of the Agit or Putro. Members of all the Agits enjoy equal status.

Lepcha Family

Family is the smallest unit of Lepcha society. Both nuclear and extended families are found among the Lepchas. Family size varies from small to medium. However, a few large extended families are also found. Father or the eldest male member of the family acts as head of the family. Residence after marriage is patrilocal. However, two cases of matrilocal residence through resident son-in-law are found. A limited number of polygamous families are also found among he Lepchas. The Lepchas society is patrilineal both in succession and in inheritance. There is no differentiation in the structure and function of the family in between the Lepchas of Sikkim and Kalimpong. Property is equally distributed among the male members of the family.

Lepcha Marriage

Monogamous marriage is the most popular form of marriage among the Lepchas. However, in a few cases they enter into polygamous wed lock through plural marriages. Marriage mostly takes place at the age of eighteen either by negotiation or by courtship. Bride price prevails in the society and it is mostly practised by the Buddhist Lepchas. It may be mentioned that a few Lepchas still retain Buddhist tradition even after conversion to Christianity. In negotiating a marriage the Lepchas follow clan exogamy. Both cross cousin and parallel cousin marriages are practised. Both forms of sororate marriages are practised by the Lepchas

The Lepchas are divided into two religious groups: (a) Buddhist and (b) Christian. Generally a Buddhist marries a Buddhist and a Christian marries a Christian. Both the groups practise marriage by engagement. As an effect of modernization inter-group marriages are also introduced among the Lepchas. In our studied area we found nineteen inter-ethnic marriages among the Lepchas. However, marriage between the Lepchas of Sikkim and the Lepchas of Darjeeling is a rare thing though they belong to the same stock.

The Bhutias

It has already been mentioned that the Bhutias or the Bhotia who were originally Tibetans immigrated to Sikkim as early as 15th Century. But it is difficult to ascertain their actual time of arrival. Their political control of Sikkim started with the coronation of the first Chogyal in 1642 as the king. The Bhutias were mostly traders and herdsmen but later on they learnt the art of cultivation. Patriarchal polyandry was originally the common practice among the Bhutias. Even today the Bhutias of Lachung and Lachen valley of North Sikkim practise polyandry. With the spread of education such practice is losing its importance. The Bhutia live in a joint family set-up. They prefer marriages to be arranged and settled by their respective parents. Both man and woman are permitted to divorce.

The Bhutias are mostly Buddhist. However, a few of them embraced Christianity. It was the practice of the Bhutias that they used to send one child into the monastery to become a Lama, the religious priest. This was prescribed by the ruler too. In Sikkim, a good number of Bhutia Lamas, are holding the post of head Lama in the famous monastery. It may also be mentioned here that during the time of Choygal dynasty the Lamas used to exert tremendous influence on the rulers of Sikkim.

The Nepalis

The Nepali is a blanket term which consists of Hindu castes like Brahmin, Chhetri, Thakur and the low castes like Kami Damani and Sarci. The other groups, Rai, Gurung,Magyar, Tamang are also covered by the term Nepali. The Nepali immigration started long after Bhutia settlement in Sikkim. Large scale immigration of the Nepalis took place during British era. The Nepalis are spread throughout east, south and west. However, they were kept away from North Sikkim. They are mostly Hindus although the Tamang, Rai are Buddhists.

The large scale immigration of the Nepalis in Lepcha land has created a serious problem for the original inhabitants. They outnumbered the Lepchas and the Bhutias. The Lepchas and the Bhutias were more interested in traditional education at the monastery as well as religious works, whereas the Nepalis were interested to send their children to schools. Further the Nepalis were hardworking people whereas the Lepchas and the Bhutias were less active in agriculture especially in the wasteland area. The lifestyle of the Nepalis especially in respect of food and dress are simple than that of the Lepchas and the Bhutias. Comparatively the marriage ceremonies among the Lepchas and the Bhutias are elaborate and expensive than that of the Nepalis. Again the Lepchas and the Bhutias spend a lot of time in their religious performances, whereas the Nepali religious performances are very short.

Inter-ethnic Relation in Sikkim: Darjeeling Himalaya

In Sikkim we find mainly three ethnic groups the Lepchas, Bhutia and the Nepalis. The Lepchas are said to be the original inhabitants of Sikkim. The Bhutias had migrated to Sikkim from Tibet in the middle of seventeenth century. The Nepalis' immigrants came to Sikkim later on as labourers. The other early inhabitants of Sikkim are the Limbus and the Tamangs. However, now-a-days they have assimilated with the Nepalis, as a major ethnic group (Dhamla, 1991: 244). Before presenting the socio-religious and socio-cultural relationship among the three groups, namely, the Lepchas, the Bhutias and the Nepalis it is better to have an idea about the religious affiliation and spoken language of each of these groups. Table 1 shows that 12.8 per cent population belong to the Lepchas, who profess either Buddhism or Christianity. They speak language called Rong/Lepcha. Nearly 14.1 per cent population belonging to the Bhutia professes Buddhism and speaks Bhutia language. Out of the 81 per cent Nepali people 9 per cent population are Hindus and 72 per cent population are Buddhist. 3.7 per cent of them speak Sherpa, 5 per cent speak Tamang and the rest 72 per cent speak Nepali. Only 2 per cent of the trading community profess Hinduism and speak Nepali. It may be noted that Hindu Nepali groups of people speak Nepali while Buddhist speak their own mother tongue.

Table 1

Distribution of Ethnic Groups by Religion and Language

S. No.	*Ethnic Group*	*Religion*	*Language Spoken*	*Percentage of Population*
1.	Lepcha	Buddhism/Christianity	Rong/Lepcha	12.8
2.	Bhutia	Buddhism	Bhutia	14.1
3.	Sherpa	Buddhism	Sherpa	3.7
4.	Tamang	Buddhism	Tamang	5.0
5.	Brahmin	Hinduism	Nepali	8.4
6.	Chhetri	Hinduism	Nepali	11.6
7.	Pradhan	Hinduism	Nepali	3.5
8.	Rai	Hinduism	Nepali/Rai	14.6
9.	Limboo (subba)	Hinduism	Nepali/Limbu	9.4
10.	Mangar	Hinduism	Nepali/Mangar	2.6
11.	Gurung	Hinduism	Nepali/Gurung	6.1
12.	Scheduled Caste	Hinduism	Nepali	5.9
13.	Trading community	Hinduism	Nepali	2.2

Source: Ecology, Culture and Change

Chart 1 shows that the indigenous communities like the Lepchas and the Bhutias are not Hindus whereas the later migrants like the Nepalis and the trading community profess Hinduism. The Bhutia were originally the trading community whereas the Nepalis were trader as well as good agriculturist. The Tibetan Bhutias imposed Buddhism on the animistic Lepchas. After the

Chart 1

Communitywise Affiliation to Religion

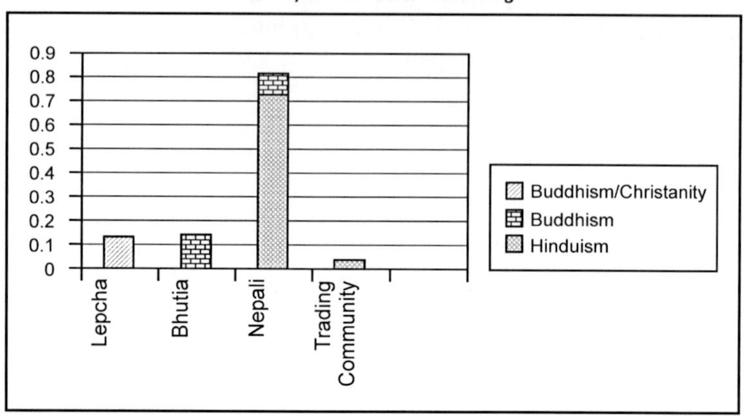

immigration, the Bhutias, as economically advanced group, implanted the religious and political authority in the minds of the Lepchas. It was easy for them because the Lepchas were docile and submissive by nature, and were living with their subsistence economy. Afterwards the Nepali immigrants outnumbered the Lepcha-Bhutia population. As a result the control of resources changed from the control between the Lepacha and the Bhutia to the control between the Nepali and the combined force of Lepcha-Bhutia. The Nepali, as a dominant population, had spread their culture and language among the Lepchas and the Bhutias. All the three ethnic groups of people had a long contact among themselves and hence they developed a socio-religious as well as cultural relationship. The monastery, the church, the market, the school are the main platforms where they interact with each other. The Bhutias converted the Lepchas from animism to Buddhism and they always enjoyed a superior position both politically as well as spiritually. The Bhutias were a advanced trading class. Being enthusiastic they also acquired the knowledge of agriculture. On the other hand the Lepchas were carefree, docile and in fact backward in all walks of life than that of their Bhutia counterpart. Hence, Bhutia came to occupy some special position in the social, political and religious spheres.

The Lepchas refer to the Nepali as "loom-kunchu" that means "unkind people". The Nepalis immigrated to Lepchas land as labourers. Afterwards they became share croppers. A few of them emerged as Thikadar or leasehold landlords. Here it may be mentioned that with the British intervention in Sikkim a new economic class called Thikadar emerged out of the Nepali people. The Nepalis gradually imposed their language on the indigenous people. In course of time the Lepchas were pushed back to remote areas of hilly tracts. Of course, the British government imposed ban on the transfer of tribal lands. However, the economically conscious Nepalis, utilized the loopholes of this law. The hard working Nepalis transferred hilly land of Sikkim into terraces and introduced settled plough cultivation. Hence, in the economic sphere the Lepchas and the Bhutias together interacted more frequently with the Nepalis because of required labour force. However, in the religious sphere the Lepchas and the Bhutias are closer to each other and they differ from the Nepalis because of their religious separation from the Nepalis. In the monastery they sit together, pray together, enjoy feast together and even exchange their views freely. But after the ceremony they maintain their respective identity. A Bhutia or a Nepali can easily enter inner part of the Lepcha house but the Bhutias maintain a distance from the Lepchas and also from the Nepalis in this respect. They hardly allow Lepchas and the Bhutias into the inner apartment of their house. Hence, in this respect, they maintain some sort of superiority. In marriage negotiation though they allow a Lepcha bride but they hardly allow any of their daughters to marry a Lepcha boy. During our survey in Singhik village only one case was reported where a Bhutia girl came as a bride in a Lepcha house. Obviously it was a case of love affair. There are, however, a number of cases where Lepcha brides were accepted in the Bhutia and Nepali societies although the Nepali maintained distance from the Lepchas being beef eaters.

The Nepalis, as a dominant population, have retained their language, social customs, dress and religious performances in Sikkim. On the other hand, they have implanted their language, Nepali in Sikkim and as such Nepali became the lingua franca for the people in Sikkim. It was easy for them because the Nepali immigrants numerically surpassed the Lepchas-Bhutia population of Sikkim within a decade. The British used the Nepalis for various purposes such as to encounter the Bhutias who had a stronghold in Sikkim, to open up and to construct roadways in the hilly tracts and to open the Tibet road. Here we can visualize the Nepalis as a sort of buffer group used by the British for geo-political purposes.

Preview of Traditional Stratification

From the ethno-historical facts of feudal Sikkim it is evident that the traditional Tibetan social hierarchy existed in Sikkim. The highest position in the social hierarchy was assigned to the monks or Lamas, the middle position to the aristocrats or the Lepcha-Bhutia nobles and the lowest position to the commoners (both the non-official Lepcha, Bhutia and other Kirati tribes). It is thus seen that Sikkimese social structure was a three-tier social hierarchy. It may be mentioned that the Kazi or the aristocrat had matrimonial alliances with the members of the Tibetan, the Lepcha, the Limbu and the Bhutanese nobel families as well as with the members of the Namgyal family of Sikkim. Further, though the Kazihood was very much hereditary, even a commoner could be a 'Kazi', for example Rai Bahadur Lobzang Chhoden (Sinha, 1975: 8–9).

Since the Sikkimese economy is primarily based on agriculture and the monarchial system is mainly based on the control of the landed estate, the Lamas induced the Dzongpon to symbolically surrender their land to the ruler. After some initial hesitations and suspicions this was done (Basnet, 1973: 15). The aristocrats enjoyed those landed estates. The early inhabitants, the Lepchas and other Kirati tribes were made tenant cultivators and they emerged as the commoners in Sikkimese social structure. The commoner had no title of land and all the lands were under the possession of royal families, and the Kazi families. The officials like Thikadars and Mondals collected revenue or tax from the tenant cultivators. This revenue system created a sharp division among the people of Sikkim. It divided the people of Sikkim into two broad categories (a) landlords and (b) actual cultivators. The common Bhutias were mostly herdsmen or traders and the Lepchas were mostly cultivators along with other Kirati groups. Of course,

Kotturan wrote that there were no such class or caste distinctions, which normally inhibit the social interaction among the people in the society based on unequal terms. However, forced labour and slavery were prevalent in the society. The Bhutia used to engage the Lepcha children as slaves (Kottruran, 1983: 54–55).

Further, if we examine we will find that the social structure of Sikkimese tribal society is very much unequal in respect of duties and privileges. The institution of Kazihood acted as authority group in the society. Their principal interest was to enjoy land revenue. There was a clear demarcation between the rich and the poor. By virtue of their power, the Kazis or the nobles had two establishments – one of them in the rural set-up, which they maintain as their natal attachment; and the other nearer to the kingdom, which help them to maintain their official dignity. Some of the Kazis used to marry and maintain families to retain their considerable rural estates in the form of paddy, cardamom field, and orchards even after the abolition of the special privilege of the aristocracy. Their social status, economic pursuits and educational advancement (because their children were mostly educated in Gangtok, Darjeeling or even outside the country) were achieved through some sort of feudal patronage as revealed in dealing with the non-elite commoners.

Basnet mentioned that the Bhutia element predominated both as feudal and leasehold landlords in Sikkimese polity. Since inter-community marriage between the high status Bhutias and the Lepchas of the upper strata (Lepcha nobles) were frequent, the common Lepchas of the society developed some sort of inferiority and were separated from the nobles. On the other hand the Lepcha aristocrats began to identify themselves with the Bhutia aristocrats (Kaziz) and lastly the Lepcha Kazis chose to forget their Lepcha ancestors (Basnet, 1974: 67). During my fieldwork when I asked a Bhutia Kazi of Maling estate in North Sikkim, where are the twelve Lepcha Kazis families of Namgyal dynasty, the Bhutia Kazi replied with a smile "Sir who wants to be a Lepcha when the king himself is a Bhutia?" In this connection, I asked the then chief minister of Sikkim, Kazi Lendup Dorji Kangsorpa that being a Lepcha Kazi why he was writing Dorji Kangsarpa along with his name. He replied with a smile, "all are mixed". Sinha mentioned that during post 1950s period there was a polarization between the king and the Kazi on the one hand and the commoner on the other. The Kazis found berth in the new bureaucratic system. They were nominated for the higher post as they were sent abroad for higher studies. He further mentioned that 32 per cent higher bureaucrats in Sikkim belonged to the Kazi families (Sinha, 1975: 58). Sikkim became the part of India in 1975 and thus the Namgyal dynasty came to an end.

Traditional Landholding and Contemporary Inequality

Sikkim had feudal pattern of landholding in the past. In contemporary social situation, the possession of agriculture land by the Lepchas of Sikkim reveals significant facts. The rate of diversification of occupation is greater in Darjeeling because the possession of land in Darjeeling is comparatively less and the adoption of Christianity among the Lepchas is comparatively more in Darjeeling than that of Sikkim. The non-traditional occupations like teaching, private and government services, and other technical jobs have given Lepchas a new economic identity. But still the rural inhabitants are mostly dependent on agriculture. According to 1971 census 48.69 per cent Lepchas substantiated their livelihood from agriculture.

Land is the main resource in rural areas of Darjeeling and Sikkim Himalayas. Hence, the economy of the Lepchas is primarily based on agriculture. It is evident from the surveyed village that on an average a Lepcha household owns 3.71 acres of terrace land in Singhik. The average landholding in Nagsay is less than that of the Singhik. The average landholding in Nagsay is only 1.93 acres. The possession of agriculture land by different households reveals an interesting pattern for understanding economic differentiation in both the areas. The distribution of land among the Lepchas of Singhik and Nagsay are presented in Table 2. Present Sikkim is characterized by contemporary high degree of urbanization as well as widespread literacy, which have generated high per capita income especially in urban centres. After decades of merger with Indian Union Sikkim has undergone dramatic changes both in economy and culture, development of roads, health centres, power supply and free education, which have brought enormous changes. All such changes have tremendously affected the social structure of Sikkim. Education and economic wealth, however, are neither acquired evenly nor distributed uniformly among the different ethnic groups.

The state of Sikkim which was formed with the theocratic structure of Chogyal and the social structure of early Sikkimese society, witnessed inherited feudalism and gradual abolition of landlordism and lastly the change from monarchism to democracy.

Social Stratification

Changing Pattern

There was simple stratification in traditional Sikkimese society. One clan used to dominate the entire society. There were two classes of people (1) the Kazi who used to rule in the name of Chogyal or the king and (2) the commoners who were governed. Elders say the society was simply divided into oppressors and the oppressed. The traditional stratification, however, has already been changed as Sikkim has transformed from monarchy to democracy. In Sikkim, land played a prime role from the very beginning. Land was the pillar of feudal Sikkim. Even at present land is one of the important criteria in consideration of one's position in the Sikkimese society because land is still the only resource in non-industrial Sikkimese society. On the basis of landholding, the present Lepcha society may be divided into four conventional economic categories such as: (a) rich peasants (b) middle peasant (c) poor peasant and (d) landless agricultural labourers.

Rich Peasants

The rich peasants belong to the highest economic strata. Table 2 shows that Lepcha families holding more than 5 acres of agricultural land are 23.33 per cent and 2.86 per cent at Singhik and at Nagsay respectively. The average size of land holding in this group is 8 at Singhik and 6 at Nagsay. The interesting feature is that the percentage of total land in the holding of more than 5 acres is more at Singhik (50.27%) and less at Nagsay (8.85%). The reverse picture is observed in case of small landholding, i.e., holding up to 2 acres of land. The percentage of total land in this holding is higher at Nagsay (56.46%) than that of the Singhik (18.31%). Most of the people of Singhik who have bigger holdings, i.e., holding of more than 5 acres of land live in brick built own houses situated on the roadside. The children belonging to these families are studying in Gangtok or in any other town (Table 5). Possession of livestock is also comparatively high among this group (Table 3). Most of them are employed in white-collar jobs (Table 4). They have emerged as affluent class. They enjoy the highest status in the society.

Middle Peasant

This group belongs to next higher economic order. The people of this group have landholdings that ranges from 2 acres to 5 acres. Table 2 shows that people belonging to this group constitute 33.34 per cent and 20 per cent of families at Singhik and Nagsay respectively. The average size of land-holding of this group is 3.36 acres of land at Nagsay and 3.50 acres of land at Singhik (Table 2). This category of peasant holds 34.69 per cent of total land at Singhik and 31.42 per cent of land at Nagsay. The people of this category live in comparatively good houses. A few of them also have brick-built houses. The livestock data also supports this view of middle position (Table 3). Education achievements of this group is less than that of the rich (Table 5). They have accepted service or white-collar jobs as new avenues (Table 4). They enjoy the status in the society at par with the rich peasants.

Poor Peasant

This is the third category in the economic order where land-holding per family is limited to two acres. Nearly 40 per cent of families at Singhik and 68.57 per cent of families at Nagsay belong to this economic category. The average land-holding per family, in this category is only 1.70 acres and 1.59 acres at Singhik and Nagsay respectively. The significant point is that the people of this category occupy 56.46 per cent of land at Nagsay and 18.31 per cent of land at Singhik (Table 2). Hence it is clear that the poor peasants at Nagsay are

Table 2

Size of Lepcha Land-holding

Name of village	*Size of land-holding*	*No. of families*	*%age of total families*	*Average size of holding in acre*	*Total land (in acre) occupied*	*%age of total land in the village*
Singhik	Landless	1	3.33	—	—	—
	Up to 2 acres of land	12	40.00	1.70	20.4	18.31
	2 + to 5 acres of land	10	33.34	3.50	35.0	31.42
	5 + acres above	7	23.33	8.00	56.0	50.27
	Total	30	100.00	—	111.4	100.00
Nagsay	Landless	3	8.57	—	—	—
	Up to 2 acre of land	24	68.57	1.59	38.16	56.46
	2+to 5 acre of land	7	20.00	3.36	23.52	34.69
	5+ and above	1	2.86	6.00	6.00	8.85
	Total	35	100.00	—	67.68	100.00
	Grand Total	65	100.00	—	179.08	100.00

Table 3

Possession of Livestock Related to Landholding

Name of village	Landholding in acres	Cow		Bullock		Goat		Pig		Poultry birds	
		No.	%	No.	%	No.	%	No.	%	No.	%
Singhik	Up to 2 acre of land	26	37.14	11	43.31	20	38.46	11	45.84	56	33.14
	2 + to 5 acre	25	35.71	7	26.92	16	20.77	5	20.83	41	24.26
	5 + and above	19	27.14	8	30.77	13	25.00	6	25.00	60	35.50
	Landless	—	—	—	—	3	5.77	2	8.33	12	7.10
	Total	70	100.00	26	100.00	52	100.00	24	100.00	169	100.00
Nagsay	Up to 2 acre of land	28	71.79	10	41.67	12	63.17	14	66.67	128	69.57
	2 + to 5 acre	10	25.65	14	58.33	3	15.79	5	23.81	40	21.74
	5 + and above	1	2.56	—	—	2	10.52	1	4.76	4	2.17
	Landless	—	—	—	—	2	10.52	1	4.76	12	6.52
	Total	39	100	24	100.00	19	100.00	21	100.00	184	100.00

Table 4

Occupation of the Lepchas Related to Landholding

Name of the village	Landholding in acres	Agriculture				Teaching				Service				Other jobs			
		M		F		M		F		M		F		M		F	
		No.	%	No.	%	No.	%	No.	%	No.	%	No.	%	No.	%	No.	%
Singhik	Up to 2 acres	12	30.77	5	41.67	—	—	—		1	20.00	1	100	—	—	—	—
	2 + to 5 acres	15	38.46	5	41.67	—	—	1	100	1	20.00	—	—	—	—	—	—
	5 + and above	12	30.77	2	16.66	—	—	—	—	3	60.00	—	—	—	—	—	—
	Landless	—	—	—	—	—	—	—	—	—	—	—	—	1	100	1	100
	Total	39	100	12	100	—	—	1	100	5	100	1	100	—		1	100
Nagsay	Up to 2 acres	19	65.52	12	100	1	50	2	66.67	9	64.28	3	33.34	3	75	—	—
	2 + to 5 acres	9	31.03	—	—	—	—	—	—	3	21.43	4	44.44	—	—	—	—
	5 + and above	1	3.45	—	—	1	50	1	33.33	—	—	—	—	—	—	—	—
	Land less	—	—	—	—	—	—	—	—	2	14.29	2	22.22	1	25	—	—
	Total	29	100	12	100	2	100	3	100	14	100	9	100	4	100	—	

Table 5

Standard of Education Related to Landholding

Name of the village	*Landholding in acres*	*Primary Std.*				*Secondary Std.*				*Graduate level*				*Other Training*			
		M		*F*		*M*		*F*		*M*		*F*		*M*		*F*	
		No.	*%*	*No.*	*%*	*No.*	*%*	*No.*	*%*	*No.*	*%*	*No.*	*%*	*No.*	*%*	*No.*	*%*
Singhik	Up to 2 acres	16	69.56	13	52.00	46	66.82	25	59.52	7	100	2	66.67	—	—	—	—
	2 + to 5 acres	5	21.74	7	28.00	17	24.64	11	26.19	—	—	1	33.33	—	—	—	—
	5 + above	1	4.35	—	—	1	1.44	—		—	—	—	—	—	—	—	—
	Landless	1	4.35	5	20.00	5	7.25	2	4.76	—	—	—	—	—	—	—	—
	Total	23	—	25	—	69	—	42	—	7	—	3	—	—	—	—	—
Nagsay	Up to 2 acres	18	41.86	10	38.46	17	43.59	7	31.82	—	—	—	—	—	—	—	—
	2 + to 5 acres	10	23.26	11	42.31	14	35.90	8	36.36	2	66.67	—	—	—	—	—	—
	5 + and above	15	34.88	5	19.23	8	20.51	7	31.82	1	33.33	1	100	—	—	—	—
4.	Landless	—	—	—	—	—	—	—	—	—	—	—	—	—	—	—	—
	Total	43	—	26	—	39	—	22	—	3	—	1	—	—	—	—	—

gradually trying to come out of their poorest condition. In this category, people are living in small Nepali type hut. They have a good number of livestock (Table 3) which substantiate their family income. Education level of these people is comparatively high (Table 5). They are in search of opportunities occupation like service (Table 4).

Landless Labourer

This is the lowest category. The people belonging to this category are the poorest of the poor. Only 3.33 and 8.57 per cent of families of the Lepchas at Singhik and at Nagsay respectively (Table 2) belong to this category. Obviously, this category has emerged in Lepcha society as an effect of changed situation. In fact, landlessness in Lepcha society was absent even in the near past. People try to substantiate family income from the livestock as well as agricultural labour work. People at Nagsay prefer service as an occupation.

Table 6

Economic Divisions

Village	*Economic Division*	*Possessions and Engagements*			
		Land (in %)	*Bullock (in %)*	*Graduate (in %)*	*Service (in %)*
Singhik	Rich peasant	23.33	30.77	–	60.00
	Middle peasant	33.34	26.92	–	20.00
	Poor peasant	40.00	43.31	100	20
	Landless labourers	3.33	–	–	–
Nagsay	Rich peasant	2.86	–	–	33.33
	Middle peasant	20.00	58.33	21.43	36.67
	Poor peasant	68.57	41.67	64.28	–
	Landless labourers	8.57		14.29	–

Chart 2

Economic Divisions

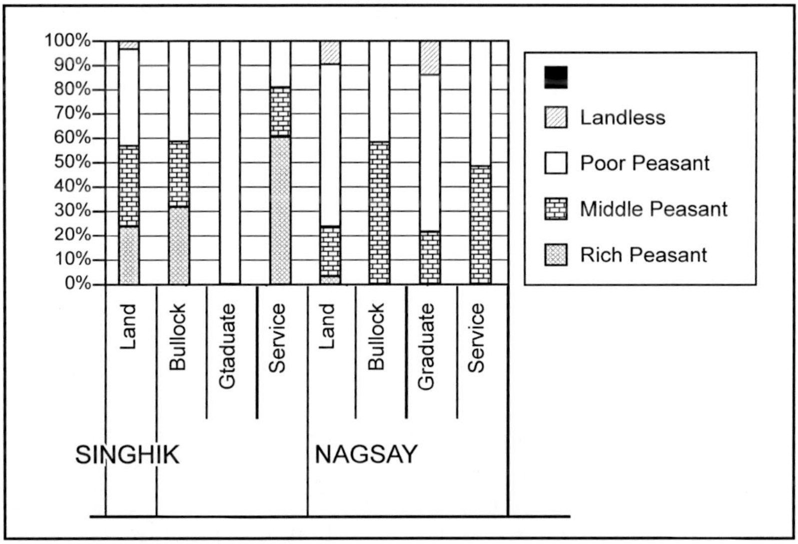

Table shows that the rich and the middle peasants of both the villages (also engaged) are in service. Landless are not in service. The difference between the two villages lies in the fact that the rich and middle peasants of Singhik possess much land while those group of people of Nagsay do not possess so much of land and, graduates of Singhik village belong to the poor peasants while the graduates of Nagsay village belong to the groups from middle peasant to the landless labourers.

Chart 2 shows the differences of the four groups of people as the Rich peasant, middle peasant, poor peasant and the landless labourers in two villages called Singhik and Nagsay in terms of their possession of land and bullock and their educational attainment up to graduate level and also in their engagement in service.

Occupational Diversification

Agriculture is the traditional occupation of the Lepchas and still a major section of the rural inhabitants is associated with this age-old occupation. However, with the growth of education and modernization, a section of the Lepchas especially those who are nearer to the town or are educated in towns like Gangtok and Kalinpong, because of their good economic background, have emerged as service holders. Different occupational categories related to people have been presented in Table 4. It reveals that the rich peasants of Singhik and also of Nagsay prefer service as their occupation. The significant aspect is that the people of this category have fascination for teaching profession. It is quite significant that the middle peasants of both the areas of Singhik and Nagsay also prefer service and teaching as their profession. It is also very interesting that a large number of the poor peasants of Nagsay are engaged in teaching and in other jobs like printing, carpentry, etc., in addition to their normal agricultural activities. However, more numbers of people of this category at Singhik are involved in agriculture rather than in service. It may be noted that the attraction towards service is aggravated due to impact of Christianity and the impact of Christian missionaries in Darjeeling and Kalimpong. The people of Singhik are still more dependent on agriculture, and the influences of Christianity in this village are almost negligible. However, a good number of Christian Lepchas are living for a considerable long time in Mangan, the district headquarters and its surrounding areas.

Level of Education

According to census reports the Lepchas show a steady growth in education. In 1971 the Lepchas of West Bengal occupied the topmost position in education among the ten major Scheduled Tribes of West Bengal. It is an obvious fact that like other tribal groups the Lepcha males are more advanced than that of their female counterpart. Similar trend is also observed in Sikkim.

The level of education of the Lepchas of both the settlements, Singhik and Nagsay, presents an interesting pattern. Economic condition of the people is the controlling factor of their education. Level of education related to possession of land for both the locations of Singhik and Nagsay is presented in Table 5. It reveals that there is steady growth of education in the families of rich peasants both in Singhik and Nagsay though the number of families in this category is very limited. The middle peasant families also show their favour for education on the whole. However, both the sexes of the poor peasants show some significant preferences for modern education. The achievement of the female education is up to graduate level. There is a tendency among the landless labourers to be least educated. This is clearly reflected in both the villages. It is clear that the poor and the middle peasants cannot achieve higher education because of their limited agricultural income resources and more inclination towards religion.

Religious Differentiation

Spread of Buddhism

Animism was the earliest form of Lepcha religion. When they came in contact with the Tibetans they were converted to Lamaistic Buddhism, which is embedded in pre-Buddhist faith of Tibet (Bell, 1928: 297). In addition to their performance of Buddhistic rituals, the Buddhist Lepchas now observe their traditional animistic rituals conducted by Mum and Bothing. The service of Mum and Bothing are essential in all of their life crisis rituals. Hence, Das and Banerjee have termed the Buddhist Lepchas as animistic Buddhist.

Lama is the priest of the Buddhist Lepcha. The Lepcha priest is very similar to that of the Tibetan priest. The performance of religious duties of Lama in Sikkim is more orthodox than that of the Lama in Kalimpong. During our survey at the village Singhik I found that one or two boys from almost each house were sent either to Gangtok or to Namchi for the purpose of becoming Lama. It may be mentioned that Lepcha religious text is written in Tibetan. Since the religious texts are written in Tibetan script and the common people are ignorant of it, there remains a big gap between the Lama and the laity and also between the religious language and the daily communication language. So a Lama needs proper training to learn how to read religious texts written in Tibetan and how to conduct the religious performances. A Lama is allowed to marry and perform his normal social duties in addition to the performances of religious rites at the monastery during festive days. A Lama is paid a nominal remuneration for his service. However, the post of Head Lama is purely honorary. He looks after the monastery. The position of Head Lama is hereditary. However, the hereditary position of the Head Lama in almost all monasteries is not maintained now (Thakur, 1988: 93).

Spread of Christianity

The spread of Christianity in Darjeeling dates back to the middle of nineteenth century. The Lepchas say that poverty has paved the way for their conversion to Christianity. Das and Banerjee have rightly pointed out that the British Missionaries could secure easy access among the Lepchas and smoothly convert them to Christianity mainly due to the backwardness of the people. During British period Protestant mission flourished and did much work among them. The Roman Catholic missionaries came to this land of the Lepchas later and established the church. They opened schools and provided different health services. Christianity spread among the Lepchas slowly and gradually. Conversion to Christianity brought prosperity. It may be mentioned that some other non-Lepchas like the Nepalis and the Bhutias were also converted to Christianity. Thakur wrote "The Christianity being the religion of the masters Lepchas no more were looked down upon by the Bhutias and the Nepalis, they felt more at home with the missionaries by identifying themselves with the white people at least religiously". Christian Lepchas mostly belong to two sects – Roman Catholic and Protestant. The number of Lepcha converts in each of these sects is almost equal, though the exact number of Christian Lepcha is not available.

Religious Affiliation

On the basis of religious affiliation the Lepchas are divided into two broad divisions: (a) The animistic Buddhist and (b) the Christian. The animistic Buddhist group or the Buddhist group largely follow Buddhism as a whole but retain certain practices of their pre-conversion religion, based on Mum-Bothing tradition. There are two controversial opinions on the figure of Christian population in Kalimpong area. The non-Christians think that the Christian population in Kalimpong region is less than 50 per cent of total Lepcha population. However, the Christian claim their figure in this region to be about 60 per cent of the total Lepcha population. In the village Nagsay the non-Christians are dominant. Out of 35 families in Nagsay only 7 families belong to Christians. Similarly in Singhik most of the Lepchas are non-Christians. However, in the Kalimpong town especially in Mission compound, the Lepchas are mostly Christians. It has already been mentioned that literacy level among the Christian Lepchas is comparatively higher than that of their Buddhist counterpart. The nature of interaction among these two groups of Lepchas is very restricted. In the village level normally a Buddhist Lepcha hardly visits a house of a Christian Lepcha or vice versa. Even if they meet on the way they normally avoid any dialogue. On enquiry it was known that a Buddhist Lepcha did not visit even his brother's house after his death because he belonged to the Christian group. In the village Singhik there was a incident. A Lepcha was converted to Christianity a few months before to our visit to that village. Instantly, the converted was isolated from the other villagers. It was decided by the villagers that whoever will visit the Christian house will be punished by a cash fine of ₹ 1,000. During my survey the Buddhist interpreter very clearly refused to go to that house and narrated the fact. From the above fact it is clear that the Buddhist have higher status than that of their Christian counterpart. But the Christian Lepchas notionally do not feel any such differences.

During my field visit I also observed a quite opposite scene. I took part in the Lepcha New Year festival, Namboon or Namsoon held at Bon where a good number of Lepchas assembled to grace the occasion. Suddenly I observed that at least five reputed Christian Lepchas came to take part in the occasion. They also took meals there and did not feel uncomfortable. It is clear that ethnically the Lepchas are not hierarchically arranged and they do not observe purity and pollution among them as that of the Hindus. Further it may also be noted that Christianity was comparatively less effective among the Lepchas of Sikkim, especially those who live in North Sikkim. Only in Maling and Singhik there are

17 Christian Lepcha families. However, religious differentiation among the Lepchas has more or less segmented the society into two broad divisions each of which maintains some sort of solidarity among themselves. Marriage, however, takes place across the religious groups.

Stratification in the Region

Sikkim is at present inhabited by different ethnic groups like the Lepchas, the Bhutias, and the Nepalis. These ethnic groups have enriched the cultural heritage of Sikkim. Of these three ethnic groups, Nepali is a blanket term which covers both tribal and non-tribal people such as Brahmin, Chhetri, Pradhan, Rai, Limboo, Mangar, Gurung, Sherpa, Tamang, Kami, Damai, Sarki, etc. All of them speak Nepali language (Table 1). The Lepchas, the Bhutias, the Sherpas and the Tamangs are primarily Buddhist. Among the Hindu ethnic groups the Brahmins and the Chhetris are at the top of the social order, the Pradhans, the Mangars, the Gurungs, the Limboos and the Rais belong to the middle order. The rest of the Nepali Hindu groups like the Kamis (metal worker), the Damais (tailor) and the Sarkis (leather worker) are treated as comparatively lower.

Generally the Lepchas and the Bhutias are free from caste based stratification but due to long and continuous association with the Nepali and the Hindu social system, a section of them consider themselves higher than some Hindu groups. The Lepchas feel that they are superior to the Kamis, the Damais and the Soonkis who are considered 'lower-castes' by the Hindu Nepalis. The Brahmins and the Chhetris accept both raw and cooked food prepared in oil and ghee from all castes and also from the Lepchas, the Bhutias, the Sherpas and the Tamangs. However, the low castes are not allowed to enter the Lepcha and the Bhutia houses. They make separate sitting arrangements in case they invite these castes. Normally they avoid social interaction with these people.

A few years back, one Lepcha girl fell in love with a boy of lower caste of Kalimpong and married him. This incident was condemned by the Lepchas and they raised a hue and cry for this act of forbidden marriage. However, marriages among the Lepchas, the Bhutais, the Sherpas and the Nepali Hindu upper and middle castes are allowed and they frequently take place. Further, the middle order Nepali Hindus retain their middle position in the social order, by not accepting water from the so-called 'untouchable-castes'. They accept water from the Lepchas in brass pot *(pital ki bartan)* which is never polluted. This is acceptable to all. Let us now consider the position of the Bhutias, a segment of Sikkimese society. The Bhutias are mostly of Tibetan origin and as such they emphasize their link with the rulers of Sikkim. The Bhutias who came from Bhutan are popularly known as Drukpa. However, the Tibetans who migrated later on are known as Khanpa on the grounds that they came from Khanpa Province of Tibet. In the Sikkimese social structure, the Bhutias of Tibetan origin ascertain higher rank because of their link with the aristocrats. Under this feeling perhaps the Lepcha Kazis were wholly absorbed in the Bhutia Kazi class and they chose to forget their Lepcha ancestors (Basnet, 1974: 67). Sherpas maintain a strong association with the Bhutias and they also prefer to visit a monastery of Bhutia dominance. Thus they consider them to be a sub section of the Bhutias.

Conclusion

The foregoing discussion and analysis clearly indicate that the present Lepcha society is very much stratified. The whole group is segmented internally, though apparently looks like harmonized. This is reflected in their socio-economic practices, social statuses of members within the group and in their lifestyle patterns. Since land is the main resource to survive, the possession of land is very significant in the life of the Lepchas. On account of their feudal heritage, land played a very important role in shaping their political and cultural ethos. The traditional Lepcha society is survived with its limited technology and resource utilization. The population pressure on the land of the Lepchas and the long intervention of exogenous forces into the life and society of the Lepchas has brought changes in their religion, language, and in the political authority structure. The authority structure of chieftaincy was changed to monarchy at an early stage. The Lepcha chiefs surrendered their land to the aristocracy of the Chougyal. The hilly lands were gradually transformed into fine terraces and the plough cultivation was introduced, mainly with arrival of the Nepali immigrants.

As a cumulative effect of various changes the Lepcha society get divided into four broad classes on the basis of land possession, namely, the rich peasant, the middle peasant, the poor peasant and the landless. The rich and middle Lepcha peasants who are more conscious about the market economy now produce surplus products. They also enjoy the maximum benefits such as the supply of looms, fertilizer, subsidies offered, educational opportunities and job facilities. As a consequence, their purchasing power has greatly increased even some of them have purchased land from their fellow members. On the other hand the conditions of the poor Lepcha peasants have degenerated, even a few of them have become landless labourers during the last three decades. The social and economic gap between these groups have increased because of their different life styles. The poor peasants are becoming isolated from their rich counterparts. The situation in Sikkim varies from that of the Darjeeling. The village Singhik is comparatively more backward than Nagsay and as such stratification is more prominent in Nagsay than Singhik. The percentage of landless labour as well as poor peasant is more in Nagsay than Singhik. Such differences are mainly because of uneven development of the two areas and effect of Christianity, which is more in Nagsay than in Singhik. Further, communication system has helped the urban dwellers to keep close ties with the rural counterparts as observed at Nagsay. It is generally agreed that implementation of development in tribal areas has faded the traditional institution. The economic and educational advancement mostly cut across the ethnic boundary. The children of the rich and the middle Lepcha peasants are becoming friends of educated middle class Nepali boys and girls, which leads to even matrimonial alliances.

The Lepcha society has undergone changes gradually after they have come in contact with various exogenous ethnic groups. When the Lepchas came in contact with the Bhutias they were converted to Buddhism. As a result of their interaction with the Buddhist Bhutias they were segmented on the basis of religion and experienced monarchical control. However, the Lamaistic Buddhist differentiate themselves from the animistic Buddhist. The animistic Buddhists regard themselves to be purer than that of the Lamaistic Buddhist and they try to revive their traditional form of religion and culture. Gradually when they came in contact with the Nepalis they became aware of Hindu Varna system as practised by the Nepalis. Thus, in interaction they maintain a distance from the 'low rank' Nepali castes. The Nepali and other ethnic groups also recognise this stand of the Lepchas. Then, after the Lepchas came in contact with the Christian missionaries they became Christians and some among them were educated and absorbed in white-collar jobs.

Fact remains that the Lepchas in general have been influenced by immigrant Nepalis in Sikkim-Darjeeling regions. However, it is the indigenous Lepchas of Sikkim, the oldest settlers, who came to be drastically affected by huge immigration of outsiders (at first Bhutias and then Napalis), who gradually encroached lands-forests of natives and made the native Lepchas economically deprived. Gradual Nepali numerical dominance also led to linguistic and cultural squeezing of native culture and language.

Acknowledgement

Author is grateful to the project coordinator Dr N.K. Das for his constant guidance, his comments and editorial suggestions in finalizing this article.

References

Bagchi, G. 1997, "The Problems of Lepchas in Darjeeling Himalayas", *Man in India*, Vol. 57.

Basnet, L.B. 1974, *Sikkim: A Short Political History*, New Delhi: S. Chand and Co.

Das, A.K. and S.K. Banerjee 1962, *The Lepchas of Darjeeling District*, Tribal Welfare Dept., Government of W.B.

Foning, A.R. 1987, *Lepcha: My Vanishing Tribe*, New Delhi: Sterling.

Morrist, J. 1983, *Living with Lepchas*, London: William Heineman Ltd.

Sinha, A.C. 1975, *Politics of Sikkim: A Sociological Study*, New Delhi: Thomson Press Ltd.

Sinha, A.C. 1983, *Studies in Himalayan Communities (Text and Context)*, New Delhi: Books Today.

Subba, T.B. 1989, *Dynamics of Hill Societies*, Delhi: Mittal Publication.

Thakur, R.N. 1988, *Himalayan Lepchas*, New Delhi: Archives Publishers Distribution.

6 Matriliny, Christianity and Economic Inequality

The Khasis of Meghalaya

Bibhash Dhar

In this paper the issues of identity, matrilineal social structure and emerging economic inequality are discussed from the anthropological perspective. Of the four groups among the Khasis, the Khynriam Khasi has been selected for the present study. This paper is based on data collected from the village Mawpat, situated at five kilometres to the north of Shillong. The matrilineal tribespeople called the Khasis are the old inhabitants of Meghalaya. The name of this tribe is, however, variously spelt by earlier authors. In this regard, Choudhury (1978: 1) has observed, "the confusion, it appears, started with Rennell who about 1980 AD in his pioneer map gave the term 'Cussy' for the land of the Khasis. Dr Buchanan-Hamilton in his account of the tribe written about 1810, came nearest to the present form of the spelling with his '*Kasia*' and Dalton followed Dr Buchanan-Hamilton in the use of the same term ..." The land of the Khasis presents a picturesque plateau, ravine, brooks, waterfalls, innumerable number of sierra and magnificent gorges. The climate of Meghalaya, especially the East Khasi Hills district, is remarkable for the excessive rainfall. The present name of the state is much befitting as the rain-bearing clouds and fog always hover around the hills of Meghalaya. This state was earlier a part of the state of Assam and in 1971 it was carved out as a full-fledged state.

Linguistically, culturally and ethnically, the Khasis is a distinct group having minimum affinity with the other tribal groups. The Khasis speak Mon-Khmer language of the Austric family and exist as an island in an area where all other tribes speak the Tibeto-Burman languages. During the course of field investigation among the Khasis, it could be ascertained that the original name of the tribe was *Ri-Lum* and the word 'Khasi' has been subsequently coined by the interest developed in course of their indigenous trade transactions. In this context, Shadap Sen (1981: 14) has mentioned, "Broadly speaking, this community can be divided into three groups, the Khasis, the Syntengs and the Wars. The Khasis live in the highest parts of the mountains, in the Khasi Hills around Shillong ...". It is broadly agreed that the Khasis belong to the matrilineal group of Mon-Khmer speaking people who claim the present Khasi Hills as their ancestral homeland. This group also includes the Lyngams in the west, which according to Ehronfels is the 'culturally intermediate' group between the Khasis and the Garos. The broad Khasi tribe traditionally includes the territorial groups like the Bhoi, the War and the upland Khasi.

The Khasi origin myth has it that the family of the Syiem (the Khasi chief) of the State of Shillong sprang up from the goddess called Ka pa Syntiew ('she who was hired by a flower'). She was the daughter of the god of the Shillong peak, which is still held sacred by many Khasis. This goddess took the form of a young maiden and lived in a cave called Marai which is near the village of Pomlakrai, near Shillong. People could not reach her as the entrance of the cave was narrow. A person from the Bhoi region (now the Ri-Bhoi district) belonging to the Mylliem clan chalked out a noble plan to bring her out of the cave. He held out a flower, locally known as U 'tiw-ja-lynteng, towards her at the entrance of the cave and she responded immediately. As she was attracted towards the flower she stretched out her hands towards the flower. The man slowly started to walk back with the flower held in hand until she was well out of the cave. He brought her home, took a lot of care of her and ultimately married her. Slowly she gave birth to a few sons and daughters. The people loved her children because of their pleasing look and good manners and everybody wanted those children to rule over them. As they were the children of a goddess they were known as Ki Syiem Blei and Ki Syiem Shillong, the divine chiefs of Shillong.

Keeping in view the basic objectives of the paper we will now discuss the issues of social structure, economic activities at village level, the literacy status and patterns of traditional and contemporary social stratification.

Level of Village Education

The Khasis were introduced to formal education system by the Christian missionaries who started working in the region in colonial era. After independence the government authorities opened schools and colleges for the spread of education among the Khasis. It is observed that the teachers in the schools are from the same village Mawpat and all of them belong to the same community, the Khasis.

Total literacy level of the Khasis of the village Mawpat is shown in Table 1. It is observed that the highest percentage of literacy achievement (i.e., 41.38%) is in the Standard, VI–X. In this literacy level the male have the higher percentage of literacy achievement than that of the female. The next higher percentage (i.e., 28.28%) is in the Standard I–V. In this literacy level also the male have the higher percentage than that of the females in literacy achievement. The lowest percentage of literacy achievement (i.e., 13.79%) is in the literacy standard from Matric to XII. In this category also the level of educational achievement of the female is less than that of the male. A small percentage of 16.55 in literacy achievement are observed in the literacy level of above XII. A close observation of Table 1 shows that although the main feature of the Khasi society is matrilineal, the literacy achievement of the Khasi female is comparatively low in all the four levels of education.

Table 1
Literacy Standard

Literacy standard	*Male*		*Female*		*Total*	
	No.	*%*	*No.*	*%*	*No.*	*%*
Class I – V	21	14.48	20	13.79	41	28.28
Class VI – X	35	24.13	25	17.24	60	41.38
Matric – XII	11	7.58	9	6.20	20	13.79
Above XII	15	10.34	9	6.20	24	16.55
Total	82	56.53	63	43.43	145	100.00

Chart 1
Literacy Standard

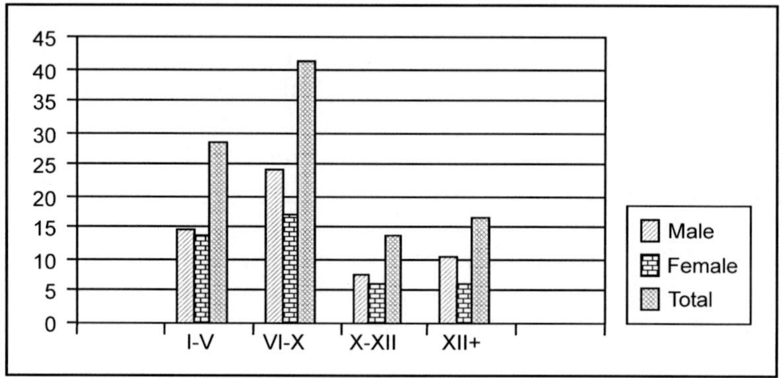

The above histogram on literacy achievement of the Khasis of the studied village shows that the achievement standard of the male is higher than that of the female at all levels. This finding does not corroborate with the fact that the Khasis are matrilineal; and in many places girls are encouraged for getting educated. This is an indication of change.

Economic Parameter and Diversification

The colonial ethnographers observed that the Khasis were known to be agriculturists since ages. Their main crop was a local variety of red paddy known as *Kbasaw*. As they cultivated on hills they never used to plough the soil but used digging stick for the purpose of Jhum or shifting cultivation. Gurdon observed that the Khasis subsisted mainly on: (i) highland or dry cultivation and (ii) lowland or wet cultivation. It is worth mentioning that even in old days the Khasis were well aware of cash crop cultivation and with this intention the people used to grow potatoes in large quantity, orange, betel nut and betel. In the pre-colonial period, the Khasi availed such opportunities to earn their livelihood. Some of them were engaged as porters, carrying potatoes to the markets in Sylhet district (in present Bangladesh). Way back in 1901, the Census Report of 1901 showed that there were 14,000 "general labourers" in the hills. They included both the Khasi male and female. A good number of Khasis, both male and female, also worked as construction labourers employed on road works and on building construction. A few Khasis even ventured for white-collar jobs in the various government offices and printing press in Shillong. There was also a fair demand for the Khasi domestic servants, both among the Europeans and the Bengali-Assamese clerks who were employed at the Shillong administrative headquarters. A considerable number of females were also employed in the manufacture of country spirit. The probable distillers were approximately not less than two thousand. The spirit was distilled both for the domestic consumption and also for commercial purpose. Some of them were also engaged in cattle breeding. There were a few carpenters around Shillong and its neighbourhood. The Bhoi Khasis of the low country, however, knew how to weave cotton cloth. Mostly the females were the weavers. The above accounts of the Khasis evidently support the fact that the Khasis had diversified their economy in the various ways since past. They were also engaged in indigenous trans-hill trade on their surplus native-grown items. This trans-hill trade provided the Khasis an opportunity of interacting with the plains people to a considerable extent. Gurdon (1977: 87) observed that the land in the upland region is classified into two categories, namely, (a) public lands and (b) private lands. Again public lands are divided into four categories. They are: (i) Ka Ri Raj or Ka Ri Siem – These lands are intended to support the Syiem family, which cannot be alienated; (ii) Ka Ri Lyngdoh – These lands are for the support of the Lyngdohs or the priests of the state; (iii) Riushnona or village land – These lands are set apart to provide a supply of firewood, thatching grass, etc., these are the property of the village. The individual inhabitants of the village are not allowed to collect the produce of such lands; (iv) Ki Lawkyntang – These are sacred groves, situated near the summit of hills composed of oak and rhododendron trees which are held sacred. Private lands are sub-divided into *ri-kur* or lands which are the property of the clan and *ri kynti*, family or acquired landed property.

Diversification of occupation is also noticed in the studied village Mawpat. The people mostly are cultivators; however, many of them do not have their own land. The landless have taken plots of farmland on lease at the rate of ₹ 5 per clan plot. At present there are two types of lands in the study area. They are the individual land i.e., private land and clan lands. Most of the cultivable lands are on the brae region hence they practice Jhum cultivation in those lands. Only a small plot of land is available in the whole village for wet paddy cultivation. Some of the landless Khasis of Mawpat village have taken land on lease. The Table 2 shows the diversification of occupation in the village. It may be mentioned here that those families that are engaged in different modern occupations like the government jobs and the miscellaneous occupations are basically agriculturists. They engage agricultural labourers called Mongrels to till their agricultural lands. The Khasi males and females at present are seen to be involved in all types of jobs right from the work in the kitchen, baby-caring, cultivation, daily labour to white-collar jobs. However, carpentry, lumberjacks and other hard works are exclusively done by the males. The women inherit the landed property, hence their economic solvency is observable.

Table 2

Occupations of the Village Mowpat

Occupation	*No. of families*	*Male*	*Female*	*Total*	*Per cent*
Agricultures	35	26	41	67	53.85
Agricultural labourers, landless and daily wage earners	20	12	29	41	30.77
Government jobs	6	11	13	24	9.23
Miscellaneous occupations (taxi driving, carpenters, domestic maids, etc.)	4	3	9	12	6.15
Total	65	52	92	144	100.00

Table 2 shows that majority of the people (53.85%) are engaged in agriculture. In every field of occupation the females are more in number than the males. This supports the matrilineal nature of the society.

Chart 2

Occupations

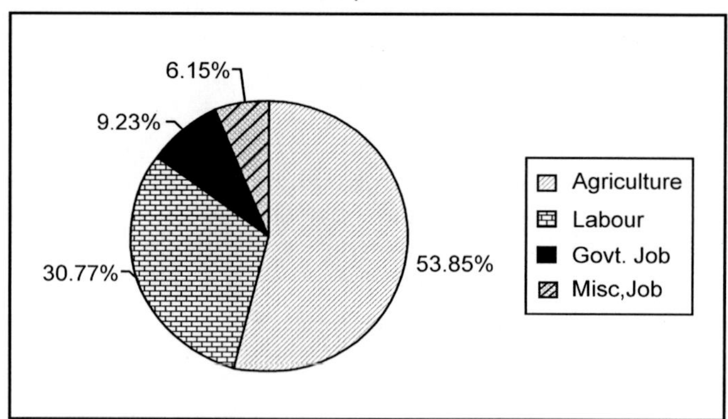

The above histogram (Chart 2) portrays that majority of the people are engaged in agricultural activities. Very few people are engaged in government jobs.

Table 3

Familywise Possession of Land

Quantity of land in acres	*No. of families possessing land (in acres)*						
	Only Clan land	*Only individual land*	*Only leasehold land*	*Clan and individual land*	*Individual and leasehold land*	*Clan and leasehold land*	*Total families*
2–3	3	2	4	—	—	—	9
4–6	—	8	7	1	—	—	16
7–8	—	1	0	—	—	—	1
8+	—	6	1	—	1	1	9
Total	3(8.6%)	17(48.6%)	12(34.3%)	1(2.8%)	1(2.8%)	1(2.8%)	35(100%)

Table 4

Types of Land in Quantity

Clan land (in acres)	%	*Individual land (in acres)*	%	*Leasehold land (in acres)*	%	*Total land (in acres)*	%
10	5	122	61	68	34	200	100

As revealed in Table 3 there are three types of agricultural land in Mawpat. They are the clan land, individual land and leasehold land. Out of 35 landholder's families the possessors of individual land is highest in number, i.e., 17(48.6%). The next higher position pertains to possession of leasehold land (34.3%). The possessors of clan land are not much (8.6%). Land possession in combination, i.e., Clan land and individual land, clan land and leasehold land, and individual and leasehold land is very negligible. Table 4 shows that out of the total land of 200 acres, 122 acres (61%) land exist as individual land. The next higher position goes to leasehold land (34%). The possession of clan land is least (5%). Chart 3 also proves this fact that the individual land is highest in quantity and clan land is least in quantity. This is an indicator of economic change, i.e., the change in land possession from community to individual holdings, which is a modern trend.

Chart 3

Types of Land in Quantity

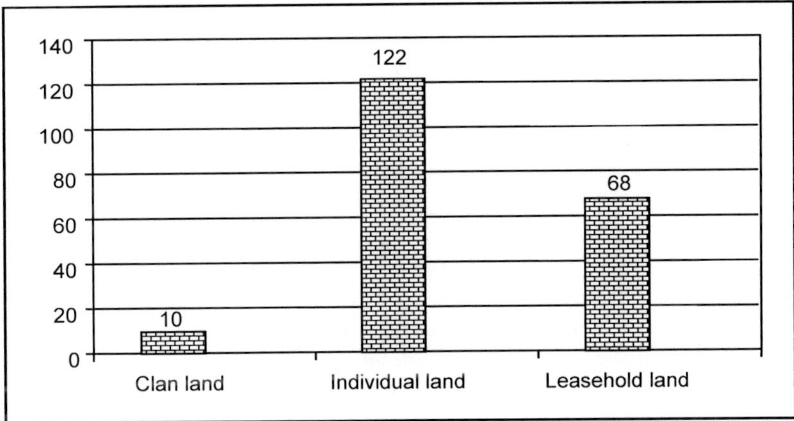

It is ascertained from Table 3, that the possessors of higher quantity of land are very few. Only 17.14 per cent families possess individual land that falls in the category of 8+ acres.

The field observations help us conclude that there has developed clear-cut stratification among the land possessors. The families that possess much quantity of land are assigned a higher status than those families that possess less quantity of land. This is also an indicator of change, which shows a change from kin based hierarchy to economic inequality.

Indigenous Trade Relations

It is seen that in the colonial era the Khasis had a well-developed indigenous trade relations with the plains district of Sylhet in the erstwhile undivided

Bengal now Bangladesh. Through this trade contact the Khasis borrowed a number of cultural traits. However, the caste structure of the plains people and their patrilineal norms could not influence the Khasis as observed among other matrilineal tribes of the region (Das, 1985). Though the people developed a close contact with the people of Sylhet much before they came in contact with the British, still they had not adopted the concept of purity and pollution. They even did not learn any rite related to puberty. However, on the death of a family member or a relative they turn all the calendars and wall hangings for three days, do not play any music and do not watch any entertainment show on the television or on other media. They also pass these nights sleeplessly. They even had not learnt the plains-people's plough cultivation technology, as they did not intend to practise it in their fields. After they came in contact with the British they were converted to Christianity and they adopted the western way of life. They came in contact with modernization and they learnt how to use power tiller and even tractors to till their land. At present they make use of this technology in their fields.

Social Structure

The Khasi term for matrilineal clan is Kur. The Khasi society is divided into many Kurs. Many of such Kurs are again subdivided into sub-clans known, as Kpoh. It is, however, difficult to produce a list of the total number of clans of the Khynriams. Clan division is the chief indicator of social differentiation found among the Khynriam Khasis of Mawpat village. A list of the clans as found in the village Mawpat is given in the Table 5. It is believed that most of the clans have originated in the traditional kingdom of Shillong and later on, they spread in different directions. The clans are strictly exogamous divisions. There is no greater sin in the society than to commit the sin of having sexual relations with the member of the same clan. This is considered incest. For obvious reasons marrying within the clan is a taboo. In the olden days, as per the customary law, such offenders were excommunicated. All the members of the Kurs trace their descent from the mythical ancestress. These ancestresses are also sometimes referred to as the grandmothers of the individual clans. There are 65 families in the village belonging to 42 clans. The names of the clans along with the number of members are presented in Table 5. Residence after marriage is matrilocal or nuoloal as the case might be.

Table 5 shows the distribution of the clan members of the village Mawpat. It is difficult to ascertain whether all the names mentioned in the table are full-fledged clans or some of them are sub-clans. This is because there is no special function of sub-clans. Sub-clans are also exogamous as that of the clans. However, the Khasi informants of each clan have narrated a story about the origin and ancestress of their respective clan. It is seen in the Table 5 that Pyngrope clan has the highest number of members (19.93%) and thus numerically dominant over other clan members. The next, higher numerical dominance (14.92%) is enjoyed by the Kharkongor clan. The third highest numerical dominance is accorded to the Wahlangs (10.49%). All these clans are exogamous and at the same time there is no preference given by any clan for matrimonial alliances. No clan hierarchy among the clan members is observed during the study. In the pre-Christian era, the Lyngdohs were revered by others but with the introduction of Christianity and the subsequent conversion of the people to the faith, the Lyngdohs have almost lost their earlier ritual position.

Table 5

Mawpat Village: Distribution of Clan Members

S. No.	*Clan name*	*Male*	*Female*	*Total (%)*
1.	Baire	1	—	1(0.27)
2.	Bamon	1	5	6(1.65)
3.	Duia	5	3	8(2.2)
4.	Jahrin	2	—	2(0.55)
5.	Kharkongor	21	33	54(14.92)
6.	Kharsawian	1	—	1(0.27)
7.	Kharnaior	1	—	1(0.27)
8.	Kharbuki	2	3	5(1.38)
9.	Kharir	4	5	9(2.48)
10.	Kharsohtun	7	6	13(3.59)
11.	Kharmawphlang	5	3	8(2.22)
12.	Kharmalki	2	4	6(1.65)
13.	Kharmuid	1	2	3(0.82)
14.	Kharmuti	—	1	1(0.27)
15.	Khaongwar	2	3	5(1.38)
16.	Kurkalang	7	4	11(3.03)
17.	Lyngdoh	3	2	5(1.38)
18.	Myrboh	1	2	3(0.82)
19.	Mawrie	2	2	4(1.1)
20.	Marbaniang	9	8	17(4.69)
21.	Myrshing	4	1	5(1.38)
22.	Myasong	1	—	1(0.27)
23.	Myrshian	5	2	7(1.93)
24.	Mukhim	3	4	7(1.93)
25.	Nongkhlaw	—	1	1(0.27)
26.	Nongkhlaw	3	1	4(1.1)
27.	Nongkynrih	1	—	1(0.27)
28.	Nongum	6	5	11(3.03)
29.	Nongspung	4	5	9(2.48)
30.	Nongseij	1	—	1(0.27)
31	Nongpiur	1	—	1(0.27)
32.	Nongbet	6	2	1(0.27)
33.	Pdah	1	1	2(0.55)
34.	Pyngrope	33	37	70(19.93)
35.	Ryntathiang	3	—	3(0.82)
36.	Sankly	1	—	1(0.27)
37.	Sohtun	6	5	11(3.03)
38.	Syiem	4	6	10(2.76)
39.	Shylla	1	—	1(0.27)
40.	Suting	—	1	1(0.27)
41.	Wahlang	20	18	38(10.49)
42.	Warjri	4	2	6(1.65)
	Total	185	177	362

Matrilineal Inheritance

Following the rigid matriliny as practised by the Khasis, the property items of the mother, both movable and immovable, are divided among the daughters and the youngest daughter, *Ka Khadduh,* gets a lion's share that includes the ancestral house. *Ka Khadduh* is supposed to observe all the family rites and rituals and she is not allowed to dispose of the property without the consent of the other sisters and the maternal uncle (Das, 1985).

State Formation and Traditional Ranked Clans

Stratification in Khasi society is clearly discernible in their traditional political organization. Gait (1926) has observed that there was a tendency among the Khasis to split up into a number of petty communes each under a head. From time to time ambitious chiefs conquered them and formed a large territorial chieftainship. Subsequently, Khasi 'state' came into being. The chief of a Khasi state is known as Syiem. This Syiem is succeeded, not by his own, but by his sister's son. Gurdon (1914) has remarked that the Khasi state is a limited monarchy. Indeed in state affairs, the council of ministers, known as Durbar, remained crucial. The *Syiem* presides over the Durbar, the executive council. The village Sirdars, (the village headmen) were entrusted with the job of settling petty disputes and other petty matters. Within Durbar there is one Lyngdoh (priest) and four Mantris (Ministers) in every Raid, or commune. The Lyngdoh exercises both secular and religious powers. Apart from these portfolio holders there are clans in the Khasi society, which are ranked into high and low on the basis of reverence they are shown. Thus, the Khasis have four ranks in their society. They are the *Syiems,* the chiefs; the *Lyngdohs,* the priests; the *Bakhraws,* the nobles and the common people, which included the cultivators, the black-smiths, the traders and other laity. Then there are clans with minor powers. This 'clan stratification' of the Khasi clans was not at all a rigid one. Intermarriage was always allowed between these clans. A person belonging to the clan of *Syiem* or *Lyngdoh* could marry girl from any clan.

Social Hierarchy among the Khasis

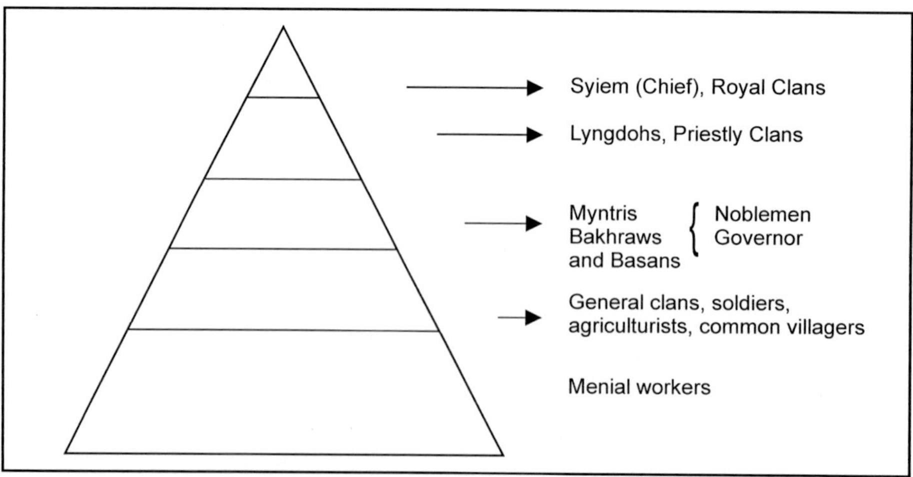

Process of Culture Change

The Serampore Baptist Mission, a branch of the London Baptist Society was the earliest Christian mission to arrive in the Khasi Hills. Krishna Chandra Pal, a Bengali disciple of William Carey of the Serampore Mission, was the first to arrive in this land of Khasi. Pal concentrated in the district of Sylhet, now in Bangladesh and converted a number of Khasis. William Carey continued to take interest in the conversion of the Khasis with the help of Bengalis from Sylhet. Using the Bengali alphabets he translated the Bible into Khasi. After a gap of 10 years, in 1829, James Roe, a young man from Scotland gave up his military job after arriving in the land of Khasis, devoted himself to preaching Christianity in the region. Later on, he along with others opened three schools at Sawrai, Mawsmai and Mawmluh.

Later, the Welsh Calvinistic Methodist Mission through its Welsh Presbyterian Foreign Mission established a firm base for Christianity in the Khasi Hills. The Roman Catholics started work at Laitkynsew in Shella by about 1890. Soon Roman Catholics spread over other parts of Khasi Hills. The other Christian sects also followed in no time. The arrival of the British and missionaries to this land in the early nineteenth century led to culture change.

Mathur (1979) observed that the Khynriam Khasis living in the central belt of Khasi Hills had opportunities to have contacts with the Hindus on account of the proximity of their territory with the plains. The Syiems, for running the administration thus appointed the Hindu and the Muslim officials. The Syiems of Khynriam, Mylliem and Cherra states used to visit the plains from their territory to collect the various dues from their subjects. It is known from the writings of some non-Christian Khasis, particularly those of Babu Jeebon Roy, Sib Charan Roy, Mahon Singh and others that the Khasis were influenced by the Hindu literary traditions to a certain extent. The Brahmos and the Rama Krishna Mission converted about a thousand of the Khasis. And only a handful of Khasis, mostly their females, had embraced Islam by marrying the Muslims. However, there are no Muslim or Hindu families in the studied village. After the Khasis have been converted to Christianity the Khasis attend the churches of different denominations. Limited contact with the non-Christians made some Khasis to adopt to the Hindu faith while others to Islamic faith. The non-converted Khasis belong to their traditional faith. Thus, culture contact has created divisions within the society on the basis of religious faith. With the growth of Christianity, educational developments, occupational mobility and coming of the outsiders into the hills, Khasi people did not object to free mixing of their boys and girls with those of other communities. This had resulted in several inter-ethnic marriages. Indeed there are some Khasi clans formed exclusively by the children of the 'outsiders'.

The Khasi revivalist movement has its roots in pre-Independence era, when the Khasi elders put up a strong resistance to the growing Christianity. The leaders emphasized that the Khasi solidarity can be achieved by creating awareness, as well as by adopting common social, cultural and political goals. Keeping this objective in their mind, the Khasis established the Seng Khasi organization as early as during 1899. The aim of the organization was to safeguard the doctrine of truth and the essence of Khasi culture and religion and to discard western and Christian influences. It intended to revitalize the Khasi ways, manners, folk songs and finally, folk dance. The aim was to inculcate in the youth the value of Khasi culture.

Stratification and Change in the Village

The Khasis prefer not to move out of their traditional habitat in order to take up some job elsewhere although the younger generation of Mowpat, prefer to go out of the hill habitat in connection with higher studies. A Khasi is deeply attached to his land and kin mostly. It is observed at Mowpat that on seeing a stranger in the village a Khasi may hardly come forward to enquire about the stranger's purpose for coming, but once he/she becomes sure that the person has not come with any bad intention, he/she will respond warmly with smiles, friendly and hospitable attitude. The missionaries have largely initiated the change which has taken place in the present Khasi society of Mowpat. Those who were converted to Christianity received the enlightenment of the world through education. The missionaries opened most of the educational institutions at Mowpat. The educated Khasis are now able to sit for examinations for better jobs. The unlettered are still handicapped due to lack of education, hygiene and the like. The differences between the educated and the non-educated have created inequality within the Khasi society. Further, the educated are comparatively more rich than the non-educated. The economic differences have thus strengthened the inequality among them. A non-Khasi is allowed to marry a Khasi woman by adopting the Khasi ways of life. Acceptance of such inter-ethnic marriages in the Khasi society also leads to a sort of differences particularly among their children.

It is revealed from the present study that in the recent time there developed three sharp classes in the Khasi society. They are the rich, the educated urban inhabitants and the non-literate rural people. The inequality in Khasi society mainly exists at the economic level. There is the gulf of differences between the rich and the poor Khasis, the educated and uneducated, urbanites and villagers, though it is not as wide as felt elsewhere in the country. On the basis of inequality the Khasis are divided into three sections: the educated doing government jobs, the peasants and the landless. In the studied village, it is observed that there are sections of the educated engaged in the government jobs, the landholders and the landless. It is also observed that the educated aspire for white-collar jobs and especially medical profession, engineering, independent trade and business and of late to be politicians. Among the uneducated section of the people there is worry that their children are yet to receive the benefits of education. It is also a fact that though the percentage of education is high in Khasi Hills, yet the light of education is yet to reach all sections.

In some families the parental authority over the children has declined. Since parents are bound to keep themselves busy for the day-to-day work in office, trade and business, and in the evenings they need some time to relax and some prefer a drink or so, the children are left to themselves. They may pay attention to their studies or roam about as they wish. Earlier, the Khasi families were large and kin-oriented and thus there were many grown-up members to take care of the children in the family. At present the family units have become smaller and individual-oriented. As a result, a vacuum is created whereby the care of the children in the family is adversely affected. The young boys and girls are freer and the society is also more permissive and hence there is free mixing of boys and girls in the studied village in particular, and the upland region in general. However, younger generation allow neither their women to marry a non-tribal nor to accord tribal status to those born out of such inter-community marriages. Earlier, the village families never participated in any of the *durbar* meetings but at present they are free to take part in it. However no women of the study unit have yet taken part in the *durbar* meetings.

At present, most of the marriages at Mowpat are courtship marriages. Slowly, the parental consent for marriage is losing importance. Divorce rate however has considerably increased. Earlier, in case of marriage between an orthodox Khasi and a Christian Khasi, the church debarred the Christian from entering the church for six months but at present such punishment is not very common practice. A couple violating the norm of clan-exogamy is punished of course, but it is not that cruel as practiced earlier. The study unit is a uni-ethnic village and there are several clans in the village and as such there are no cases of violating the norm of clan exogamy at the village. Changes are noticed in the aspects of property. At present household rights are allotted to the individual. This is in sharp contrast to the practice of pre-Independence period. Changes are also there in other aspects of the Khasis society. The Khasi girls now use tailored dresses like frocks and skirts. Male dress is totally westernized. The food of the Khasi of this study unit has remained largely the same as before but egg, bread, milk, cakes, etc., are added to their diet. The structure of the Khasi house has also changed. Modern houses are distinctly similar to that of the non-Khasis. Most of the houses are of reinforced cement concrete instead of the traditional Khasi houses built of timber, and CGI sheets. Some of the houses even possess the house-warming systems of the western style.

Conclusion

In order to conclude it may be stated that the Khasis are much concerned towards preserving their identity. Prior to the advent of Christianity into the Khasi Hills the Khasis did not feel that their culture and religion were in danger of being wiped out by alien culture. With the arrival of Christianity, which was not a peaceful process, the Khasis became aware regarding the loss of identity. The advent of Christianity made them conscious of their tribal identity, which was at stake. The advent of Christianity was not a peaceful process. In the beginning there were conflicts between the converts to Christianity on the one side, and the upholders of Khasi traditions, on the other.

The Khasis living in Mowpat have undergone a spectacular transformation during the last fifty years or so. They have risen from a superstition-ridden primitive economy and have come a long way and now stand at the threshold of the modern economic era. They have acquired education and new skills and mobilized variously their resources. The matrilineal clan-based society however survives intact to a great extent, despite western influence on the Khasi society of Mowpat brought about through imposition of the Christianity. Occupational mobility and success of democratic political institutions have led to emergence of some individual leaders, modern in all respects. There is little role played by the ranked clans and their elders in the village today. Villagers are more concerned with economic pursuits now. This has led to economic inequality in society.

References

Choudhury, J.N. 1978, *The Khasi,* Shillong: Canvas.

Dalton, E.T. 1872, *Descriptive Ethnology of Bengal,* Calcutta: Government Printing.

Das, N.K. 1985, 'Descent, Filiation and Affinity among the matrilineal Tribes of Khasi and Garo Hills' In *Tribal Institutions of Meghalaya.* Ed. S.K. Chattopadhyay. Gauhati: Spectrum Publications.

Gait, E.A. 1926, *A History of Assam,* Calcutta: Thacker Spink and Co.

Gurdon, P.R.T. 1914, *The Khasis,* London: Macmillan.

Mathur, P.R.G. 1979, *Khasi of Meghalaya,* Delhi: Cosmo Publications.

Shadap Sen, C.N. 1981, *The Origin and the Early History of the Khasi Synteng People,* Calcutta: Firma KLM.

7 Changing Village Economy, Religious Conversion and Social Exclusion

The Mech-Bodo of North Bengal

Krishna Mandal

The objective of the present work is to discuss the stratification pattern and social change among the Mech and their interactions with neighbouring communities. The Mech are the segment of the Bodo ancestry. The Meches are concentrated mostly in the foothills regions of the district of Jalpaiguri. Some of them are also found in the districts of Cooch Bihar and Darjeeling. They speak Mech dialect, which is part of the Bodo language. More than two months of fieldwork was conducted amongst the Mech. Standard anthropological methods and techniques were used in the collection of first hand data among the Mech tribe of Jalpaiguri district. In this paper, data collected from the Hindu Meches and Christian Meches are elucidated in order to portray the social stratification and social change.

The Mech Bodo Identity

Although there are some studies on the Meches, but no exhaustive ethnographic account on them is available. Gait (1926) has described their migration and calls them as an 'aboriginal tribe'. Dalton (1872) in the book, *Descriptive Ethnology of Bengal* describes their distribution, migration and similarities with other tribes. Risley (1891: 86–91) says that the Meches of Darjeeling and Jalpaiguri district are divided into two sub-tribes, Agnia Mech and Jati Mech and they practise sub-tribe endogamy. The Meches in general identify themselves as the Bodo, which means a great people. In West Bengal they are known as Mech only. Gait (1891) describes that the Bodos entered from Patkoi hills into Assam in 1228 AD. They then spread to Goalpara, Jalpaiguri and Cooch Bihar using different ethnic names including Mech or Mesh. When Bhutan was in possession of western Duars of Jalpaiguri, the Mech migrated there, had matrimonial bonds and took office under that government. According to Grierson, Mech dialect belongs to the Tibeto-Burman sub-group of Assam-Burmese. The Mech do not have any script. They use Roman script only. In West Bengal their script is Bengali.

Distribution of the Meches in Jalpaiguri District

Police Station	*Rivers*
Jalpaiguri Sadar including Rajganj	Between River Mahananda and the Tista
Mal, Nagrakata	Between River Tista and Jaldhaka.
Madarihat, Alipurduar, Kalchini	Between River Toorsa and River Raidak.
Kalchini, Kumargram	Between River Raidak and River Sankosh

Source: Handbook of Scheduled Castes and Scheduled Tribes C.R.I.W.B.

Economy, Kinship and Family

Rice (*mai*) is the staple food of the Meches. In bygone days the Meches were mostly engaged in shifting cultivation, called Hadong. They are now settled agriculturists. They practise plough cultivation, locally called *'hal-oai-nai'*. The land possessed by the Meches is classified into three categories, namely: (1) High land or *danga* where vegetables such as potato, brinjal, cabbage, barbati, etc., are grown; (2) Medium type of land or *Saharia*, where paddy, jute, etc., are grown; and (3) Low type of land or *Dahal*, where paddy, jute, etc., are grown. They consider medium type of land as the best because it fulfils all purposes of farm production. Low type of land is best for paddy cultivation only. They are also specialized in areca nut (*guai*) cultivation and jute (*patto*) cultivation. They rear domestic animals and birds like pig, goat, cock, hen, cow, bullock, pigeon, etc. Generally the Non-Christian Meches rear pigs, especially by the women. They are economically benefited through selling the pigs in the market. The Christian Meches eat pork but they avoid rearing pigs on the ground that pigs are dirty animal and it is not good to rear pigs in their house premises. However, their women rear goats, cocks, hens and other such animals. Poor Meches take loan from the Gram Panchayat for buying pigs, goats, cows, etc. They repay the loan in suitable monthly instalments. Domestic animal like pig has a good economic and socio-religious value in their society.

There are good numbers of the people who continue to pursue the old tribal religion. However, from the perspective of the religion the Meches are divided into two main sections, namely, the Hindu Meches and the Christian Meches. Cock and hen are sacrificed in religious ceremonies like Bathou worship, whose Hindu version is Shiv Puja. The Christian Meches eat beef.

The Meches are again divided into several clans such as Basumata, Mochari, Iswarary, Narginary, Hajari, Champramary. Each clan has certain significant characteristic. The members of Basumata clan are the receivers of the land (Basumata) offered by the deceased family after the death of a person in that family. The members of Mochari clan are very courageous. Nargi means one who treats the mourners with dry jute leaves. The members of a clan who perform such duty are assigned the name Narginary. Rice is called as Champram by the Meches. During cooking of rice those Meches who ran away for fear of the Asura were known as Champramary. Now on the occasion of wedding ceremony Champramary clan members are assigned the duty of cooking food. With the passage of time the Meches forgot diverse roles of the clan members. Both the Christian and the Hindu Meches follow clan exogamy.

The Meches are patrilineal and they follow the rule of the patrilocality. After the death of the father the property of the deceased person is divided among sons only, the female members are given the rights over cattle only, such as pig, fowls of the family. If there is a single female child the entire property is owned by her after the death of the father. There are three types of families among the Meches. They are nuclear, extended and single families. In the family, the husband is the head and he takes decisions on behalf of the family members. The wife shoulders all the family responsibilities. She cooks for the family, takes care of the children and helps during the agricultural operations. In addition to their duty of cooking and rearing of their children, the female do transplantation of paddy and reaping of paddy. Females are also engaged in spinning and weaving. Avoidance relationship is observed between elder brothers *(bey-oai-howa)* and younger brothers' wife *(bey-oai-hinjau).*

The Area of Study and the Studied Villages

The present district of Jalpaiguri is bounded by the district of Darjeeling and Bhutan on the east, the Sankos river marking the boundary line between the eastern and western Duars, Cooch Bihar and district of Rangpur on the south, and the district of Dinajpur, Purnia and Darjeeling, on the west. There are two Sub-divisions, 13 Development Blocks, 122 Gram Panchayats, 774 Mouzas and 315 ITDP Mouzas in the district of Jalpaiguri.

Two villages, namely, Madhya Nararthali and Nararthali under Kumar Gam Block and Police station, in the district of Jalpaiguri are selected for the present study. Both the villages are multi-ethnic villages, where live the Rajbanshis, Meches, Rabhas, Santals, Oraons, Brahmins, Kayasthas, Namasudras, and Muslims. There is a large concentration of Hindu Meches in the village Madhya Nararthali. The Christian Meches are numerically dominant in Nararthali village. There are four primary schools and one high school within the vicinity of the villages. The tribal people are also numerically dominant in the adjacent villages.

The settlement pattern of the two villages is linear, having two parallel rows of huts. The Mech, the Rabha and the Oraon houses are built on wooden poles. The roof of the room is generally thatched with straw by the poor people and covered with the tin sheet by the economically sound people. There are two ration shops in the two villages. There is no electricity in any of these villages. One High School up to Class X standard is situated in the village Nararthali. In every village, two to three Anganwadi centres are there for the all-round development of the children below 5 years of age. Two Panchayat offices are situated in the village Nararthali, by the side of the Marakata – Tiamari metal road. In every village one Shiva Temple is situated where the villagers from the respective villages worship Lord Shiva.

The Hindus dominate in the village Madhya Nararthali. In this village, there are 75 Hindu Mech households and 19 Christian Mech households. The Christians dominate in the village Naralthali. In this village there are 24 Hindu households and 79 Christian households. Among the Christian population 50 per cent of them are females while among the Hindu population less than 50 per cent are females. In the two villages there are 335 Hindu males and 289 Hindu females, while there are 299 Christian males and 297 Christian females. There are altogether 197 families and 1,220 total population (Table 1).

Table 1
Village-wise Population

	Hindu Population				*Christian Population*			
Name of the village	*No. of households*	*Male*	*Female*	*Total*	*No. of households*	*Male*	*Female*	*Total*
Madhya Nararthali	75	250	217	467	19	60	61	121
(%)		(53.53)%	(46.47)	(100.00)		(49.59)	(50.41)	(100.00)
Nararthali	24	85	72	157	79	239	236	475
(%)		(54.14)%	(45.86)	(100.00)		(50.32)	(49.68)	(100.00)
Total	99	335	289	624	98	299	297	596
%		(53.69)%	(46.31)	(100.00)		(50.17)	(49.83)	(100.00)

The Hindu Mech of Madhya Nararthali comprises of 250 male and 217 female. Out of 250 male, 16.06 and 37.26 per cent are married and unmarried respectively. Out of 217 female, 16.49 per cent are married and 25.48 per cent are unmarried. Out of 61 Christian males, 19.01 per cent are married and 30.58 per cent are unmarried. Out of 60 Christian females, 19.83 per cent are married and 29.75 per cent unmarried (Table 2).

The Hindu Mech of Nararthali village comprises 85 males and 72 females. Among the males 17.20 per cent are married and 36.30 per cent are unmarried, while among the female 18.47 per cent are married and 24.84 per cent are unmarried. There are 239 Christian males and 236 Christian females in the same village. Among the Christian males, 18.32 per cent are married and 30.32 per cent are unmarried while among the female 19.58 per cent are married and 28.42 per cent are unmarried (Table 2).

It is clear from Table 3 that family comprising 5 No. of members is highest (i.e., 16 families) among the Hindu Mech of Madhya Nararthali village while lowest no. of family (i.e., 1) comprises one member only. The highest frequency among the Christian Meches of the Madhya Nararthali village is 6; each of these families comprises 5 members, while lowest frequency is one family which comprises 14 members. In the Nararthali village, the highest frequency among the Hindu Meches is 7; each of these families comprises 5 members, while the lowest frequency is one. In this village the highest frequency among the Christian Meches is 18, each of these families comprises 4 members.

Table 2

Village-wise Hindu and Christian Population

Name of the Village	Total no. of families		Hindu Mech										Christian Mech									
			Married		Unmarried		Wido-wer	Wido-w	Divorcee		Total Hindu		Married		Unmarried		Wido-wer	Wido-w	Divorcee		Total Christian	
	Hindu	Christian	M	F	M	F			M	F	M	F	M	F	M	F			M	F	M	F
Madhya-Nararthali	75	19	75 (16.06)	77 (16.49)	174 (37.26)	119 (25.48)	1 (0.21)	21 (4.50)	–	–	250 (100)	217 (100)	23 (19.01)	24 (19.83)	37 (30.58)	36 (29.75)	1 (0.83)	–	–	–	61 (100)	60 (100)
Nararthali	24	79	27 (17.20)	29 (18.47)	57 (36.30)	39 (24.84)	1 (0.64)	4 (2.55)	–	–	85 (100)	72 (100)	87 (18.32)	93 (19.58)	144 (30.32)	135 (28.42)	8 1.68	7 (1.47)	–	1 (0.21)	239 (100)	236 (100)
	99	98	102 (16.35)	106 (16.98)	231 (37.02)	158 (25.32)	2 (0.32)	25 (4.01)	–	–	335 (100)	289 (100)	110 (18.46)	117 (19.63)	181 (30.37)	171 (28.69)	9 (1.51)	7 1.17	–	1 (0.17)	300 (100)	296 (100)

Figures in parentheses are percentages.

Table 3
Family Size

Number of members in the family	Madhya Nararthali No. of families and percentage Hindu (%)	 Christian (%)	Nararthali No. of families and percentage Hindu (%)	 Christian (%)	Total families percentage (%)
1	1 (1.33)	–	2 (8.33)	–	3 (1.52)
2	2 (2.67)	–	–	1 (1.26)	3 (1.52)
3	4 (5.33)	–	1 (4.16)	10 (12.66)	15 (7.61)
4	7 (9.33)	2 (10.53)	1 (4.16)	18 (22.78)	28 (14.21)
5	16 (21.33)	6 (31.58)	7 (29.17)	8 (10.13)	37 (18.78)
6	15 (20.00)	4 (21.05)	2 (8.33)	16 (20.25)	37 (18.78)
7	12 (16.00)	3 (15.79)	3 (12.50)	7 (8.86)	25 (12.69)
8	7 (9.33)	3 (15.79)	1 (4.17)	5 (6.33)	16 (8.12)
9	5 (6.67)	–	3 (12.50)	6 (7.59)	14 (7.11)
10	2 (2.67)	–	1 (4.17)	3 (3.80)	6 (3.05)
11	2 (2.67)	–	1 (4.17)	2 (2.53)	5 (2.54)
12	–	–	2 (8.33)	1 (1.26)	3 (1.52)
13	–	–	–	–	–
14	–	1 (5.26)	–	2 (2.55)	3 (1.52)
15	2 (2.67)	–	–	–	2 (1.02)
Total (%)	75 (38.07)	19 (9.64)	24 (12.18)	79 (40.10)	197 (99.99)

Table 4
Family Types of Two Villages

Type of family	No. of families in Madhya Nararthali and (%) Hindu (%)	 Christian (%)	No. of families in Nararthali and (%) Hindu (%)	 Christian (%)	Total families percentage (%)
1. Nuclear	47 (62.67)	14 (73.68)	11 (45.83)	44 (55.69)	116 (58.88)
2. Nuclear (incomplete)	6 (8.00)	–	–	8 (10.13)	14 (7.11)
3. Extended	21 (28.00)	5 (26.32)	11 (45.83)	27 (34.18)	64 (32.49)
4. Single	1 (1.33)	–	2 (8.34)	–	3 (1.52)
Total (%)	75 (100.00)	19 (100.00)	24 (100.00)	79 (100.00)	197 (100.00)

Table 4 shows that there are 61 nuclear families in Madhya Nararthali village and 55 nuclear families in Nararthali village. There are 26 extended families in Madhya Nararthali village and 38 nos. of extended families in Nararthali village. Comparatively, the incomplete families and single families are negligible. Nuclear families are more in number both among the Christians and the Hindus.

Table 5

Landholding of the Meches of Two Villages

Name of the Village	*Hindu Mech*						*Christian Mech*					
	Type of cultivable land in Bighas						*Type of cultivable land in Bighas*					
	Dahal (low)	*Saharia (medium)*	*Danga (high)*	*Homes in Bighas*	*Other type of land in Bighas*	*Total land in Bighas*	*Dahal (low)*	*Saharia (medium)*	*Danga (high)*	*Homes in Bighas*	*Other type of land in Bighas*	*Total land in Bighas*
Madhya-Nararthali (%)	362.75 (41.49)	310.75 (35.54)	78.00 (8.92)	97.50 (11.15)	25.25 (2.89)	874.25 79.41% 99.99%	55.25 (39.75)	54.75 (39.39)	12.75 (9.17)	14.75 (10.61)	1.5 (1.08)	139.00 17.28% 100.00%
Nararthali (%)	60.00 (26.46)	129.00 (56.89)	14.50 (6.39)	22.25 (9.82)	1.00 (0.44)	226.75 20.59% 100.00%	101.50 (15.25)	352.00 (52.89)	104.50 (15.70)	94.00 (14.12)	13.5 (2.04)	665.5 82.72% 100.00%
Total (%)	422.75 (38.40)%	439.75 (39.94)	92.50 (8.40)	119.75 (10.88)	26.25 (2.38)	1101.00 100.00 100.00	156.75 (19.48)	406.75 (50.56)	117.25 (14.57)	108.75 (13.52)	15.0 (1.86)	804.50 100.00% 99.99%

Landholding Pattern and Economic Differentiation

Total land possessed by the Hindu Meches of both the villages is 1101.00 Bighas, of which 874.25 bighas of land are held by the Hindu Meches of Madhya Nararthali village and 226.75 bighas of land is held by the Hindu Meches of Nararthali village. So the per family landholding (i.e., total land/total family: 874.25/75) of the Hindu Meches of Madhya Nararthali is 11.65 bighas, whereas per family landholding of the Hindu Meches of Nararthali village is 9.45 bighas 226.75/24. So comparatively landholdings of the Hindu Meches of Madhya Nararthali is higher than that of the Nararthali village (Tables 4, 5). It is also clear from the Tables 4 and 5 that possession of the total land by the Christian Meches of both the villages is 804.50 bighas. Per family landholding (total land/total family, i.e., 139/19) of the Christian Meches of Madhya Nararthali is 7.32 bighas, while per family land holding of the Christian Meches of Nararthali village is 8.42 bighas 655.5/79. Per family land holding of the Christian Meches of both the villages is 8.21 bighas, i.e., 804.50/98 and per family landholding of the Hindu Meches of both the villages is 11.12 bighas, i.e., 1101.00/99. This shows that per family landholding of the Hindu Meches is higher than that of the Christian Meches. It is significant that low land held by the Hindu Meches is higher than that of any other category of land, while medium type of land, which is the best land, held by the Christian Meches, is higher than that of any other category land held by them (Table 5).

Table 6(A)

Family-wise Landholding of the Hindu Meches (Madhya Nararthali Village)

Type of land	*Families having quantity of land in Bighas*				*Landless Families (%)*	*Total number of families (%)*
	0–4.5	*4.5–9.5*	*9.5–14.5*	*14.5 & above*		
Cultivable (%)	20 (26.67)	13 (17.33)	11 (14.67)	12 (16.00)	19 (25.33)	75 (100.00)
Homestead (%)	69 (92.00)	—	—	—	6 (8.00)	75 (100.00)
Other (%)*	19 (25.33)	—	—	—	56 (74.67)	75 (100.00)

* Other type of land consists of betel nut garden and bamboo garden.

Table 6(A) shows that 25.33 per cent of the Hindu Meches of Madhya Nararthali village do not posses any cultivable land and 8 per cent of them do not possess homestead land even. Highest number of families (i.e., 20) possesses land below 4.5 bighas and the lowest number of families (i.e., 11) possesses land ranging from 9.5–14.5 bighas.

Table 6(B)

Family-wise Landholding of the Christian Meches (Madhya Nararthali Village)

Type of land	*Families having quantity of land in Bighas*				*Landless Families (%)*	*Total number of families (%)*
	0–4.5	*4.5–9.5*	*9.5–14.5*	*14.5 & above*		
Cultivable (%)	4 (21.05)	10 (52.63)	2 (10.53)	1 (5.26)	2 (10.53)	19 (100.00)
Homestead (%)	16 (84.21)	—	—	—	3 (15.79)	19 (100.00)
Other (%) *	2 (10.53)	—	—	—	17 (89.47)	19 (100.00)

* Other type of land consists of betel nut garden and bamboo garden.

Table 6(B) shows that 10.53 per cent of the Christian Meches of Madhya Nararthali village do not possess any cultivable land and 15.79 per cent of them do not possess homestead land even. Highest number of families (i.e., 10) possess land ranging from 4.5–9.5 bighas and the lowest number of families (i.e., 1) possess land 14.5 and above bighas.

Table 6(C)

Family-wise Landholding of the Hindu Meches (Nararthali Village)

Type of land	*Families having quantity of land in Bighas*				*Landless Families (%)*	*Total number of families (%)*
	0–4.5	*4.5–9.5*	*9.5–14.5*	*14.5 & above*		
Cultivable (%)	5 (20.83)	6 (25.00)	3 (12.50)	6 (25.00)	4 (16.67)	24 (100.00)
Homestead (%)	21 (87.50)	—	—	—	3 (12.50)	24 (100.00)
Other (%)*	1 (4.17)	—	—	—	23 (95.83)	24 (100.00)

* Other type of land consists of betel nut garden and bamboo garden.

Table 6(C) shows that 16.67 per cent of the Hindu Meches of Nararthali village does not possess any cultivable land and 12.50 per cent of them do not possess homestead land even. Highest number of families (i.e., 6) possess land ranging from 4.5–9.5 bighas and also quantity of land ranges 14.5 and above bighas and the lowest number of families (i.e., 3) possess land ranging from 9.5–14.5 bighas.

Table 6(D)

Family-wise Landholding of the Hindu Christian (Nararthali Village)

Type of land	*Families having quantity of land in Bighas*				*Landless families (%)*	*Total number of families (%)*
	0–4.5	*4.5–9.5*	*9.5–14.5*	*14.5 & above*		
Cultivable (%)	14 (17.72)	13 (16.45)	10 (12.67)	13 (16.45)	29 (36.71)	79 (100.00)
Homestead (%)	67 (84.81)	—	—	—	12 (15.79)	79 (100.00)
Other (%) *	12 (15.19)	—	—	—	67 (84.81)	79 (100.00)

* Other type of land consists of betel nut garden and bamboo garden.

Table 6(D) shows that 36.71 per cent of the Christian Meches of Nararthali village do not possess any cultivable land and 15.79 per cent of them do not possess homestead land even. Highest number of families (i.e., 14) possess land below 4.5 bighas and the lowest number of families (i.e., 10) possess land ranging from 9.5–14.5 bighas.

In the village Madhya Nararthali among the Hindu Meches, 55 families practise agriculture and 16 families earn their livelihood as labourers, while among the Christian Meches, 13 families practise agriculture and 5 families work as labourers. In Nararthali village, among the Hindu Meches, 16 families practice agriculture, 4 families earn their livelihood by labour work, while among the Christian Meches, 44 families practise agriculture and 25 families wholly depend on labour work. The 'Bangladeshis' who have immigrated to the villages of Madhya Nararthali and Nararthali are experts in various types of cultivation and the Meches take the help of Bangladeshi labourers for better cultivation of their lands. When suitable Bangladeshi labourers are not available they take the help of the labourers belonging to their own community. Besides daily labourers, they engage labourers on annual contract basis from different communities like the Rajbanshis, the Oraons, the Rabhas, and the Muslims. Out of the total Hindu Meches of both the villages 8 families engage 17 labourers on annual contract basis from the communities mentioned above. As many as 15 Christian Meches belonging to both the villages engage 20 labourers on annual contract basis.

In the Madhya Nararthali village there are two non-recorded adhiars among the Christian Meches, while among the Hindu Meches there are four recorded adhiars and two non-recorded adhiars. In Nararthali village there are 6 adhiars among the Hindus. Adhiars are contract-sharecroppers in many parts of this region. Among the Christian Meaches of Madhya Nararthali village there are two primary school teachers, one Home Guard and one Police constable, while among the Hindu Meches of Madhya Nararthali there is only one chowkidar. In the village Nararthali there are one chowkidar, one Assistant teacher, one clerk, one Police constable among the Hindu Meches, while there are two Primary school teachers, one soldier, one tea stall owner, one Assistant teacher, one truck driver, and one bamboo dealer among the Christian Meches. It is thus observed that Christian Meches are comparatively more employed in the field other than agriculture than that of the Hindu Meches.

Table 7(A) shows that among the Hindu Meches of Madhya Nararthali village the highest percentage of cultivable land (28.01%) is possessed by the Basumata clan and the lowest percentage (1.06%) of cultivable land is possessed by Saibya clan. On the other hand among the Christian Meches of this village the highest percentage of land (80.04%) is possessed by the Narginary clan. Table 7(B) shows the distribution of land of Nararthali village. The highest percentage of cultivable land (54.55%) is possessed by Hindu Karji clan members, while the lowest percentage of cultivable land (1.47%) is possessed by the Hindu Thakur clan members. Among the Christian Meches the highest percentage of cultivable land (57.53%) is possessed by the Narginary clan members.

Menial work plays an important part in the lives of the Meches. Some of them are engaged as handcart pullers, carpenters, masons and labourers of one kind or another within or outside the village. Thus we observe that the Mech tribe has multiple relations of economic nature with different communities, who are generally dependent on them. Sharp economic differences are seen among Christian and traditional Meches also. Clanwise economic ranking is also witnessed

In the village Nararthali among the Hindu Meches, the highest percentage of male literates, i.e., 44.18 per cent are found in the Narginary clan and lowest number of literates, i.e., 2.33 per cent are found in Thakur clan. In case of female, the highest literacy rate, i.e., 43.75 per cent are found in Karji clan and lowest percentage of literates, i.e., 6.25 per cent are present in Thakur and Saibya clan simultaneously. The maximum percentage of illiteracy rate, i.e., 42.86 per cent are found among the Basumata male clan members, while the lowest illiteracy rate, i.e., 11.91 per cent are found among the males of Thakur clans. In case of female, the highest rate of non-literate, i.e., 37.5 per cent is found among the Basumata and Narginary clan members, while and lowest rate of non-literate, i.e., 7.14 per cent are found in Saibya clan members (Table 8A). The highest percentage of education, i.e., 55.0 per cent and 33.33 per cent in I–IV standard is found among male in Narginary clan and among females, in both the Basumata and Narginary clans (Table 8A). There is no graduate among the Hindu Meches of this village. They have gained maximum achievement in education up to Class VIII only. Among all the clans (including male and female) the highest educational achievement rate (i.e., 39.79%) is found in Basumata clan and lowest educational achievement rate (i.e., 4.08%) is found in Saibya clan.

Among Christian Meches of Nararthali village, the highest literacy rate (55.26%) is found among the male members of Narginary clan and among female the highest literacy rate (i.e., 54.88%) is observed in the Narginary clan (Table 8B). The highest male non-literates (i.e., 52.87%) are found in the Nargianry clan, while the highest female non-literates (i.e., 54.37%) belong to the same clan (Table 8B). There are four graduates; two of them belong to the Narginary clan.

In the village Madhya Nararthali among the Hindus, the highest male non-literates (i.e., 44.25%) belong to the Narginary clan while the highest female non-literates (i.e., 45.78%) also belong to the same clan. The highest male literates (i.e., 29.20%) belong to the Basumata clan and the highest female literates (i.e., 37.34%) also belong to the same clan. The highest educational achievement of the Hindu male (i.e., 45.09%) is found in the Narginary clan and the highest female educational achievement (i.e., 32.07%) belongs to the Basumata clan (Table 8B). There is one male graduate who belongs to the Saibya clan. In the village Madhya Nararthali, among the Christian Meches, the highest male literacy rate (i.e., 88.09%) is achieved by the Narginary clan and the highest female literacy rate (i.e., 87.88%) is also achieved by the Narginary clan. There is one male graduate who belongs to the Narginary clan (Table 8B). Thus, considerable educational differences exist among the Christian and 'Hindu' Mech segments. Use of term 'Hindu Mech' is meant to specify the non-Christian traditional Meches, most of whom have adopted Hindu norms and beliefs, even though they pursue tribal religion to a great extent.

Culture Contact

After the independence of India, and particularly with the introduction of modern transport system, the Meches have come in close contact with the caste Hindus. Development work, administrative activities and the new credit system in the form of banking have entered the tribal villages. Again political parties, coupled with new institutions with decentralization of power have helped them to come in close contact with the administrative agents, and people from neighbouring areas. Several new economic schemes and development programmes are being implemented among them by the Gram Panchayat. The contact situations are indeed multiplied in this manner. The Meches are in contact with the potters (Khumars), brass workers, and weavers through weekly market where they sell their ware in exchange for money.

The Meches have come in contact with the other communities like the Rabhas, the Sanatals, the Oraons, the Rajbanshis, the Namasudras, the Kayasthas and the Brahmins, in various social and cultural fields. The Meches have economic contact with the Rajbanshis, the Sanatals, the 'Bangladeshis', the

Oraons, the Muslims and the Rabhas. The Meches employ them as labourers in their farms as daily labourers and sometimes on annual contract basis. Further, they have monetary transaction (as loans) with these people. The Meches employ the Bangladeshi-Rajbanshi carpenters for making windows, doors, etc. Through these contacts they exchange various cultural norms. The Rajbanshis procure liquor *(Jou)* from the Meches, the Rabhas, the Sanatals, the Oraons and also drink liquor in the company of Meches.

Social Stratification, Social Change and Social Exclusion

The Meches are divided into the Hindu Meches and the Christian Meches. The 'Hindu Meches' are further subdivided into three sections, those who believe in performance of *pujas* on the basis of sacrifices pigeon, hen, etc., and those who believe in the performance of *pujas* without sacrifices. Further, there are Meches who are followers of Sri Sri Ramakrishna Paramahanshadev. However, the followers of Ramakrishna Paramahanshadev are not found in the village of Madhya Nararthali and Nararthali. They are found in neighbouring villages.

The Christians are subdivided into Protestants and Catholics. The Protestants and the Catholics are further subdivided on the basis or their affiliated churches, such as Churches of Northern India (CNI), (Headquarters is situated in Darjeeling district), North East Lutheran Church (NELC), (Headquarters is situated in Cooch Bihar district), Free Church (independent Church), (Headquarters is situated in Dakshin Nararthali), Kamakhyaguri and Roman Catholic (Headquarters is situated in Jalpaiguri district).

As we observed in two villages the Meches are divided into diverse strata of the land owners, tenants and labourers. Each of these strata is assigned its respective status in the society. Land owners enjoy the highest status in the society. The tenants have the higher status than that of the labourers. Labourers and share-croppers normally belong to several non-Mech tribes of the area.

Social change in Mech society is observed in various fields. Enormous changes have taken place in their economic system. Their subsistence economy has changed into profit-based economy, both rural based and urban-market economy. Previously, they used to cultivate according to their needs and never went to the market for selling their products. Now they are cultivating cash crops. They learnt the improved method of cultivation from their neighbours. The development schemes too have helped the people to mobilize themselves economically. A few of them are in various services like Defense service and teaching profession and are involved in business like selling of vegetables, grocery, stationery, and liquor business. They send their children to school. The youth prefer to be engaged in service and to be involved in business and in other petty jobs. Girls also attend school along with the boys. There are important changes observed also in their food habit. Previously, they used to take half boiled/roasted non-vegetarian food with less oil and without spices. Now they consume pulses more than that of the previous days. They have now adopted cooking process of their Hindu neighbours. They now take sufficient oil and spices.

The Meches have considerably adapted to new patterns of dress. Changes in the dress are observable amongst the young urban Meches. Unmarried girls wear midis, long skirts, frocks, etc. Unmarried boys wear full pants, half pant, shirt, trousers, etc. Urban influence and the hostel environment have brought these changes. However, in dress pattern, comparatively the Christian Meches are more adaptive than the Hindu Meches. Previously, the Meches used to go only to the local medicine-man (*baidya*) for treatment of any sorts of ailment. But now they go not only to the medicine-man but also to the modern physician for treating their patients. There is one medical sub-centre in the village Madhya Nararthali. Mech females consult the attending practitioner for any maternity problem. They even take their patients to the hospital situated 15 km away from the villages for consultation with the physicians. Change has taken place in the marital relations of the Meches. Previously, no inter-community marriages took place among the Meches and other communities. Now inter-ethnic marriage takes place across their tribal boundaries with the Rajbanshis, the Nepalis, and the Jogis and even with the Brahmins. Previously the Meches were not allowed to enter into the courtyard of the Rajbanshis. In case they had to enter into the courtyard of the Rajbanshis for some work they used to clean the courtyard with cow-dung. They had no commensal relations with the non-Meches generally. Now they exchange bride and exchange food with the Rajbanshis, the Oraons, Nepalis and other Hindu castes. These are drastic changes observed amongst these tribespeople. Fact remains that while tribal communities (with or without Hinduization) are uniting through marital and economic relations, clear-cut social exclusion and segregation is maintained between these and Christian tribespeople. Due to influences of the electoral politics and functioning of democratic institutions, tremendous changes have occurred in their political life. They are now covered by the Statutory Panchayat system. They send their representatives to Gram Panchayat, Panchayat Samiti and to Zilla Parishad. Two Meches belonging to these two villages are elected as Pradhans and another two of them are elected as executive members. One Mech from Madhya Nararthali village is elected as Sabhadhipati in the Zilla Parishad. The Panchayat System is slowly curtailing the significance of tribal political systems and also the role of traditional Gaonbura, the village headman.

References

Dalton, E.T. 1872, *Descriptive Ethnology of Bengal*, Calcutta: Government Printing.

Das, A.K. and M.K. Raha 1966, Handbook of SC and ST Special Series, No. 8 CRI Government of West Bengal.

Gait, E.A. 1926, *A History of Assam*, Calcutta: Thacker, Spink and Co.

Grierson, G.A. 1926, *Linguistic Survey of India*, Calcutta: Government of India.

Hunter, W.W. 1976, *A Statistical Account of Bengal*, Vol. X, "Districts of Darjeeling and Jalpaiguri and State of Kuch Behar", London: Trubner.

Risley, H.H. 1891, *The Tribes and Castes of Bengal*, Reprint 1998, Calcutta: Firma KLM Pvt. Ltd.

Table 7(A)

Clan-wise Distribution of Land (Madhya –Nararthali village)

Hindu Mech									Christian Mech								
Name of clan	*Cultivable (bigha)*	%	*House site (bigha)*	%	*Other (bigha)*	%	*Total (bigha)*	%	*Name of clan*	*Cultivable (bigha)*	%	*House site (bigha)*	%	*Other (bigha)*	%	*Total (bigha)*	%
Narginary	187.00	23.69	29.00	29.74	4.25	16.83	211.25	24.16	Narginary	98.25	80.04	12.75	86.44	1.5	100.00	112.50	80.94
Basumata	210.50	28.01	33.50	34.36	14.00	55.45	258.00	29.51	Basumata	—	—	—	—	—	—	—	—
Mochari	100.00	13.31	9.75	10.00	4.00	15.84	113.75	13.01	Mochari	—	—	—	—	—	—	15.5	—
Iswarary	174.00	23.15	13.25	13.59	3.00	11.88	190.25	21.76	Iswarary	—	—	—	—	—	—	—	—
Thakur	72.50	9.65	5.50	5.64	—	—	78.00	8.92	Thakur	14.50	11.81	1.00	6.78	—	—	—	11.15
Champramary	8.50	1.13	4.50	4.62	—	—	13.00	1.49	Champra-mary	—	—	—	—	—	—	—	—
Saibya	8.00	1.06	2.00	2.05	—	—	10.00	1.14	Saibya	—	—	—	—	—	—	—	—
Boragaon	—	—	—	—	—	—	—	—	Boragaon	10.00	8.15	1.00	6.78	—	—	11.0	7.19
TOTAL	751.50	100.00	97.50	100.00	25.25	100.00	874.25	99.99	TOTAL	122.75	100.00	14.75	100.00	1.5	100.00	139.00	100.00

Table 7(B)

Clan-wise Distribution of Land (Nararthali village)

Hindu Mech									Christian Mech								
Name of clan	*Cultiv able (bigha)*	%	*House site (bigha)*	%	*Other (bigha)*	%	*Total (bigha)*	%	*Name of clan*	*Cultiv able (bigha)*	%	*House site (bigha)*	%	*Other (bigha)*	%	*Total (bigha)*	%
Narginary	51.0	25.06	3.75	16.85	–	–	54.75	24.15	Narginary	321.00	57.53	56.75	60.37	4.5	33.33	382.25	57.44
Basumata	32.5	15.97	7.5	33.71	–	–	40.00	17.64	Basumata	53.50	9.59	13.25	14.09	2.5	18.52	69.25	10.41
Karji	11.0	54.55	9.0	40.45	1.0	100.00	121.00	53.36	Karji	–	–	–	–	–	–	–	–
Saibya	6.0	2.95	2.0	8.99	–	–	8.00	3.53	Saibya	–	–	–	–	–	–	–	–
Thakur	3.0	1.47	–	–	–	–	3.00	1.32	Thakur	51.00	9.14	3.00	3.19	1.0	7.41	55.00	8.26
Iswarary	–	–	–	–	–	–	–	–	Iswarary	15.50	2.77	3.50	3.72	–	–	19.00	2.85
Mochari	–	–	–	–	–	–	–	–	Mochari	58.00	10.39	4.00	4.26	1.5	11.11	63.50	9.54
Borogaon	–	–	–	–	–	–	–	–	Borogaon	54.00	9.68	9.50	10.11	4.0	29.63	67.50	10.14
Bazari	–	–	–	–	–	–	–	–	Bazari	5.00	0.98	2.00	2.13	–	–	7.00	1.05
Champramary	–	–	–	–	–	–	–	–	Champramary	–	–	2.00	2.13	–	–	2.00	0.03
TOTAL	230.5	100.00	22.25	100.00	1.0	100.00	226.75	100.00	TOTAL	558.00	100.00	94.0	100.00	13.50	100.00	665.50	99.99

Table: 8A

Clan-wise Education of Mech (Nararthali village)

Name of Clan	Total Population		Illiterate		Literate		Class-wise Educational Standard Educational Standard								Total Illiterate	Total Literate
							I–IV		V–VIII		IX–XII		BA/BSc/B.Com			
	M	F	M	F	M	F	M	F	M	F	M	F	M	F		
Hindu Mech																
Basumata	23	23	18	21	4	2	1	2	3	–	–	–	–	–	39	6
(%)			(42.86)	(37.5)	(9.31)	(12.5)	(5.0)	(33.33)	(21.43)						(39.79)	10.17
Karji	20	12	6	5	14	7	6	1	3	3	5	3			11	21
(%)			(14.28)	(8.93)	(32.55)	(43.75)	(30.0)	(16.66)	(21.43)	(50.0)	(55.55)	(75.0)			(11.23)	(35.59)
Thakur	6	6	5	5	1	1	1	–	–	1	–	–			10	2
(%)			(11.91)	(8.93)	(2.33)	(6.25)	(5.0)			(16.66)					(10.21)	(3.39)
Saibya	5	5	–	4	5	1	1	1	2	–	2	–			4	6
(%)				(7.14)	(11.63)	(6.25)	(5.0)	(16.66)	(14.28)		(22.22)				(4.08)	(10.17)
Narginary	32	26	13	21	19	5	11	2	6	2	2	1			34	24
			(30.95)	(37.5)	(44.18)	(31.25)	(55.0)	(33.33)	(42.86)	(33.33)	(22.22)	(25.0)			(34.69)	(40.67)
Total	85	72	42	56	43	16	20	6	14	6	9	4			98	59
(%)			(100.00)	(100.00)	(100.00)	(100.00)	(100.00)	(99.98)	(100.00)	(99.99)	(99.99)	(100.00)			(100.00)	(99.99)
Christian Mech																
Narginary	130	129	46	56	84	73	24	30	27	29	31	14	2		102	157
(%)			(52.87)	(54.37)	(55.26)	(54.88)	(52.17)	(61.23)	(50.94)	(50.0)	(63.26)	(53.85)	(50.00)		(53.68)	(55.08)
Basumata	34	34	21	14	13	20	4	9	8	7	1	4	–		35	33
(%)			(24.14)	(13.59)	(8.55)	(15.14)	(8.69)	(18.37)	(15.09)	(12.07)	(2.04)	(15.38)			(18.42)	(11.58)
Borogaon	32	24	10	9	22	15	7	3	7	8	7	4	1		19	37
(%)			(11.49)	(8.74)	(14.47)	(11.28)	(15.22)	(6.12)	(13.21)	(13.79)	(14.28)	(15.38)	(25.00)		(10.00)	(12.98)

Cont'd...

...Cont'd

Champramary	3	6	3	4	—	2	—	—	—	2	—	—	—		7	2
(%)			(3.45)	(3.88)		(1.50)				(3.45)					(3.68)	(0.70)
Hazari	4	10	1	6	3	4	1	2	2	2	—	—	—		7	7
(%)			(1.15)	(5.83)	(1.97)	(3.01)	(2.17)	(4.08)	(3.77)	(3.45)					(3.68)	(2.46)
Iswarary	9	9	3	7	6	2	1	—	4	1	1	1	—		10	8
(%)			(3.45)	(6.79)	(3.95)	(1.50)	(2.17)		(7.55)	(1.73)	(2.04)	(3.85)			(5.26)	(2.80)
Mochari	17	12	—	1	17	11	7	5	3	4	6	2	1		1	28
(%)				(0.97)	(11.18)	(8.27)	(15.22)	(10.20)	(5.66)	(6.89)	(12.25)	(7.69)	(25.0)		(0.53)	(9.83)
Thakur	10	12	3	6	7	6	2	—	2	5	3	1	—		9	13
(%)			(3.45)	(5.83)	(4.61)	(4.51)	(4.35)		(3.77)	(8.62)	(6.12)	(3.85)			(4.74)	(4.56)
Total	239	236	87	103	152	133	46	49	53	58	49	26	4		190	285
(%)			(100.00)	(100.0)	(99.99)	(99.99)	(99.99)	(100.0)	(100.0)	(100.00)	(99.99)	(100.00)	(100.0)		(99.99)	(99.99)

Table: 8B

Clan-wise Education of Mech (Madhya Nararthali village)

Hindu Mech

Name of Clan	*Total Population*		*Illiterate*		*Literate*		*Class-wise Educational Standard Educational Standard*								*Total Illiterate*	*Total Literate*
	M	*F*	*M*	*F*	*M*	*F*	*I–IV*		*V–VIII*		*IX–XII*		*BA/BSc/B.Com*			
							M	*F*	*M*	*F*	*M*	*F*	*M*	*F*		
Narginary	79	75	50	65	29	10	21	6	7	2	1	2			115	39
(%)			(44.25)	(45.78)	(21.17)	(13.34)	(31.34)	(18.75)	(23.34)	(7.41)	(2.56)	(12.5)			(45.09)	(18.39)

Cont'd...

...Cont'd

Basumata	72	59	32	31	40	28	20	9	8	14	12	5			63	68
(%)			(28.32)	(21.83)	(29.20)	(37.34)	(29.85)	(28.13)	(26.66)	(51.85)	(30.77)	(31.25)			(24.71)	(32.07)
Mochari	38	33	9	15	29	18	11	6	8	8	10	4			24	47
(%)			(7.96)	(10.56)	(21.16)	(24.00)	(16.42)	(18.75)	(26.66)	(29.63)	(25.64)	(25.00)			(9.41)	(22.17)
Thakur	13	12	5	10	8	2	6	2	1	—	1	—			15	10
(%)			(4.42)	(7.04)	(5.84)	(2.66)	(8.95)	(6.25)	(3.34)		(2.56)				(5.88)	(4.72)
Iswarary	34	26	10	13	24	13	4	6	6	3	14	4			23	37
(%)			(8.85)	(9.15)	(17.52)	(17.34)	(5.97)	(18.75)	(20.00)	(11.11)	(35.90)	(25.00)			(9.02)	(17.45)
Champramary	12	9	7	7	5	2	5	2	2	—	—	—			14	7
(%)			(6.19)	(4.93)	(3.65)	(2.66)	(7.46)	(6.25)							(5.49)	(3.31)
Saibya	2	3	—	1	2	2	—	1	—	—	1	1	1		1	4
(%)				(0.7)	(1.46)	(2.66)		(3.12)			(2.56)	(6.25)			(0.39)	(1.88)
	250	217	113	142	137	75	67	32	30	27	39	16	1		255	212
			(99.99)	(99.99)	(100.00)	(100.00)	(99.99)	(100.00)	(100.00)	(100.00)	(99.99)	(100.00)	(100.00)		(99.99)	(99.99)
Christian Mech																
Narginary	51	54	14	25	37	29	15	7	11	16	10	6	1	—	39	66
(%)			(77.77)	(89.28)	(88.09)	(87.88)	(100.00)	(70.00)	(91.66)	(94.12)	(71.43)	(100.00)	(100.00)		(84.78)	(88.00)
Thakur	7	5	4	3	3	2	—	2	—	—	3	—	—	—	7	5
(%)			(22.22)	(10.72)	(7.14)	(6.06)		(20.00)			(21.43)				(15.22)	(6.66)
Borogaon	2	2	—	—	2	2	—	1	1	1	1	—	—	—	—	4
(%)					(4.76)	(6.06)		(10.00)	(8.33)	(5.88)	(7.14)					(5.33)
Total	60	61	18	28	42	33	15	10	12	17	14	6	1	—	46	75
(%)			(99.99)	(100.00)	(99.99)	(100.00)	(100.00)	(100.00)	(99.99)	(100.00)	(100.00)	(100.00)	(100.00)		(100.00)	(99.99)

8 'Primitive' Economy, Politicization Process and Emerging Stratification among the Riangs of Tripura

Goutam Kumar Bera

This paper deals with the issues of indigenous economic pursuit, politicization process and emerging stratification amongst the Riang of Tripura. The primary data have been collected from two villages, namely, Krishnamanipara and Maudabari by using normal anthropological methods and techniques like the interview and the observation techniques. Tripura, a small hilly state, having an area of 10,477 sq. km is situated in the north-eastern part of India. During the British colonial rule the area was known as Hill Tipperah. Assam and Mizoram bound it on the east, west, and Bangladesh on south. It is believed that the erstwhile state of Tripura has derived its name from Tripur, a king of the state. Hunter (1876: 357) opines that the name of the state was given in honour of the Tripureshwari temple located at Udaipur, which was built around 1501 A.D.

Identity of Communities

Tripura originally comprised only the tribes like the Riangs, and Tripuri. According to 1981 Census the total population of Tripura was 20, 53,058, which consisted of indigenous tribal people and large immigrant communities from erstwhile East Pakistan (present Bangladesh). Among the indigenous tribes, the Tripuri has the highest percentage of population (55.61%) followed by the Riang (14.37%), the Jamatia (7.59%), the Chakma (6.36%), the Halam (4.23%) and the Mag (2.95%). Other tribal groups like the Garo, Munda, Lushai, Oraon and the Santal have a negligible population. Among the Scheduled Castes, the highest percentage of population is that of the Namasudra (38.88%) followed by the Jalia Kaibarta (15.50%), Mahishya (14.90%), Mali (10.9%), Dhoba (10.35%) and the Chamar (2.19%).

The Tripuri, who are believed to be the descendants of the Royal family fall under Indo-Mongoloid linguistic family. The Tripuri speak Kak Barak language, which is a Tibeto-Burman language of Sino-Tibetan speech family. The Halam speak Halam and the Mag speak Burmese language while Chakma language bears Bengali influence. Bengali, spoken by the immigrants, has now become the leading language of the state. Each community has a specific pattern of settlement.

Agriculture is the economic mainstay of the people living in this state and the tribes still resort to shifting *Jhum* cultivation with the help of *takkal,* a kind of indigenous chopper. *Jhum* cultivation is a form of primitive pre-agricultural activity. Economic activities of the communities are described below.

Table 1

Occupational Pattern of the People of Tripura

S. No.	*Occupations*	*N. Tripura*	*W. Tripura*	*S. Tripura*
1.	Food gathering and hunting	25%	5%	7%
2.	Shifting cultivation	45%	30%	15%
3.	Secondary cultivation	15%	40%	55%
4.	Other occupations	25%	25%	23%

Source: Census of India Report of 1991.

Table 1 shows that majority of the tribal people of Tripura are engaged in shifting cultivation in North Tripura while majority of them are in secondary cultivation in West and South Tripura. The other occupations include daily labour, business and service (Chart 1).

Chart 1

Other Occupations

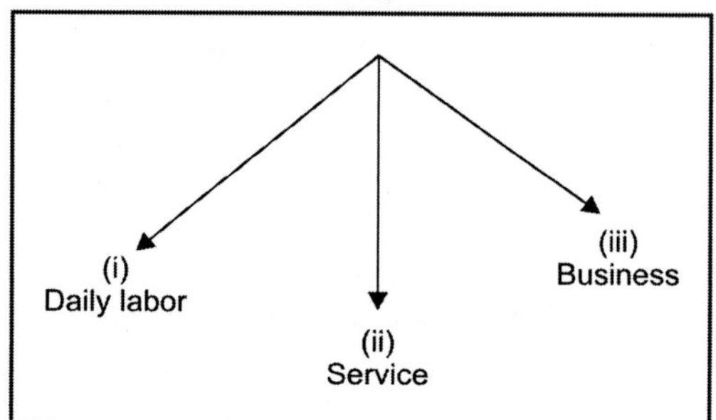

Rice is the staple food of most of the communities. Tribals are very fond of bamboo shoot. Earlier, the tribals used to rear milk cows, but they never consumed milk or milk products. Now, this practice is on the wane. The tribal communities prefer to wear self-made clothes. Males wear turban and a narrow piece of cloth as lower garment. Females wear a long piece of cloth called *pachchra* and they cover their breasts by a small piece of cloth called *risha,* which is embroidered with various designs. The Riang women adorn themselves with various ornaments. The necklace of the Riang is called *rangbatang.*

The political systems of the tribes survive. Tribes in Tripura have retained the customary laws till date. They maintain their two-tier system of authority both at village level and at the inter-village level. All the communities are patrilineal by authority and descent except the Garo and the Khasi who are matrilineal. Most of the communities are united through common village organization which reflects remarkable social solidarity in tribal community. Both bride price and dowry and also *jamaikhata* (marriage by service) are practised by tribals. Though the tribals have great faith in 'animism' some of the Magh have absorbed Hindu way of life, while some Chakma are converted to Christianity, and the Murasing and the Majipure profess Vaishnavism. Some people of this state also profess Islam and Buddhism. Tribes have sacred specialists and as such they do not obtain service of the Brahmin priests.

The Riang Identity

Table 2

Comparative Literacy

District	Census (1981)	Census (1991)
North Tripura	18.7%	17.06%
West Tripura	8%	23.2%
South Tripura	11.6%	13.5%

The term Riang is widely used appellation of a tribe, who prefer to call themselves as Bru, which, in their language means 'man'. Early reference of the Riang (as Reyangas) is available in the accounts of Dalton (1872), Lewin (1869), and Scott (1900). The language spoken by them is radically the same as that of the speakers of the southern Shan state. They profess Buddhism. In the fifteenth century, Maharaja Dhanyak Manikya defeated the Pathan with the help of two Riang army generals. Mukherjee (1959) has presented a legendary account on the relationship of the Riang with the king of Tripura. Singh (1994) has also presented a mythical account on the origin of the Riang tribe. The rate of literacy among the Riang is very low. According to 1981 census Report, only 19.68 per cent Riang are literates of which 20.63 per cent are males and 4.34 per cent are female.

Table 2 shows the comparative picture of literacy rate in different districts of Tripura. It is observed that in 1991, there is an increase of 16.8 per cent literacy rate among the Riang over a decade.

Table 3

Literacy Rate During 1961–1991, Tripura

Year	Total percentage	Male percentage (N=8,21,403)	Female percentage N=(5,47,164)
1961	24.34	35.31	12.36
1971	36.19	46.84	27.84
1981	50.10	61.49	38.01
1991	60.39	70.08	50.01

Note: (1) Literacy rate for 1961 & 1971 relate to population aged 5 and above, the rate for the years 1981 & 1991 relate to population aged 7 and above.

The Table 3 shows the literacy rate in Tripura during 1961–1991. It may be mentioned that in 1981 and in 1991 census children of age group 0–6 have been treated as illiterate.

Table 4

District-wise Literacy Rate

State District	Total population 1991			Literate Population		
	Total	Male	Female	Total	Male	Female
West Tripura District	2,744,287	1,410,545	1,334,282	1,368,567	821,403	547,169
North Tripura District	1,289,086	662,408	626,678	703,211	416,118	287,093
South Tripura District	690,565	356,002	334,563	341,540	203,757	137,965
Tripura	765,176	392,135	373,041	323,816	201,710	122,106

Source: Census of India 1991, Series-24, Tripura, paper-1 of 1991, Provisional Population Total, Director of Census Operation, Tripura.

The Table 4 shows the district-wise literacy rate of the state of Tripura as per Census Report of 1991.

Table 5

Area-wise Population Distribution and Occupation (1991 Census)

District	*Total population*	*Male*	*Female*	*Occupation*
N. Tripura	61,144	31,368	29,776	A=15% B=45% C=15% D=25%
W. Tripura	3,124	1,623	1,501	A=5% B=30% C=5% D=25%
S. Tripura	44,475	22,634	21,841	A=7% B=15% C=55% D=23
State	1,08,743	55,625	53,118	

Source: Census of India 1991.

Note: A = Food gathering and hunting, B = Shifting cultivation, C = Secondary cultivation, D = Other occupation= (1) Daily Labour, (2) Service, (3) Business

Table 5 shows that the total population of the Riang in the state is 1,08,743. They are distributed unevenly in three districts, namely, North Tripura, West Tripura and South Tripura. Majority of them in the two districts, namely, North Tripura and West Tripura practise shifting cultivation whereas majority of them in South Tripura practice secondary cultivation.

The Studied Villages

The present study was carried out in two villages, namely Krishnamanipara and Maudabari. The former village, i.e., Krishanamani- para is situated under the jurisdiction of Teliamura Block in West Tripura district and is located at a distance of 31 km north of Chakmaghat near Chamalchhara bridge. The other village, Maudabari is located 22 km, south of Udaipur under the jurisdiction of Matari Bari Block in south Tripura district. Maidabari is a uni-ethnic village. This village is bigger in size than that of Krishnamanipara. There are 36 Riang families in this village, located on undulated plains having patches of forest infested with wildly grown vegetation in between houses.

Table 6 reflects that the Riang prefer to live in uni-ethnic villages. Table 7 shows the population of the Riang in the village Krishnamani- para is 10 per cent of the total village population, which comprises 50 males and 54 females. The total Riang population of the village Maidabari is 206 comprising 98 males and 108 females.

Table 6

Ethnic Composition

S. No.	*Village*	*Ethnic Group*	*No. of families*	*Percentage*
1.	Krishnamanipara	Riang	15	83.33
		Tripuri	3	16.66
2.	Maidabari	Riang	36	100

Table 7

Sex-wise Riang Population

S. No.	*Village*	*Population*				
		Male		*Female*		*Total*
		No.	*%*	*No.*	*%*	
1.	Krishnamanipara	50	48.07	54	51.92	104
2.	Maidabari	98	47.57	108	51.92	206

Table 8
Age-wise Population

Age Group	Village Population					
	Village Krishnamanipara			Village Maidabari		
	Male	Female	Total	Male	Female	Total
0–5	6	11	17	13	17	30
6–10	3	11	14	15	22	37
11–15	9	4	13	7	13	20
16–20	5	7	12	7	5	12
21–25	4	3	7	4	10	14
26–30	5	6	11	10	13	23
31–35	6	4	10	8	7	15
36–40	4	1	5	14	10	24
41–45	2	3	5	9	2	11
46–50	1	—	1	1	1	2
51–55	1	2	3	1	3	4
56–60	1	2	3	4	2	6
61–65	2	—	2	1	3	4
66 and above	1	—	1	4	—	4
Total	50	54	104	98	108	206

Table 8 shows that highest number of people in the village Maidabari, is in the age group 6–10 and the next higher population is in the age group 0–5. In the village Krishnamanipara the highest number of people is in the age group 0–5 and the next higher population is in the age group 6–10. The lowest population in both the villages is in the age group 46–50.

Literacy of the Studied Village

There is no primary school in the village Krishanamanipara. The nearest primary school is located at Jibalchhare, 4 km to the north of the village. The middle school is located at Chakmaghat 31 km to south of the village, and the secondary school is located at Teliamura, 39 km to south of the village. None of the literates in this village is a matriculate. The nearest primary school of the village Maidabari is located at Dataram Jolahibari, 2 km to north of the village. The middle school is situated at Maidabari Bari 12 km to north of the village, and the secondary school is located at Udaipur 22 km to north of the village. None of the literates in this village is a matriculate.

Table 9 shows that there are 38 literates in the village Krishanamanipara of which 24 are males and the rest 14 are females, and 57 literates in the village Maidabari of which 28 are males and 29 are females. These literates include both students and drop-outs and also adult literates. The maximum aged male literate in this village Krishanamanipara is only 31 and the maximum aged female literates are two, one is 27 and the other is 29. The maximum frequency of literates in both the villages is in the age-group 11 to 15 years who are all students studying in both primary and middles schools. It is followed by 11 people in the village Krishanamanipara and 12 in the village Maidabari who belong to the age group 16 to 20 years. These people comprise both students and persons who are drop-outs. Education is not encouraged by the guardians because of the distance of the location of schools and also for their preoccupation in household activities.

Table 9

Age and Sex-wise Literacy of the Two Villages

Age group (in years)	Krishanamanipara Village			Maidabari Village		
	Male	Female	Total	Male	Female	Total
6–10	3	1	4	1	4	5
11–15	9	4	13	7	12	19
16–20	5	6	11	7	5	12
21–25	4	2	6	4	7	11
26–31	3	1	4	9	1	10
Total	24	14	38	28	29	57

The Riang prefer to live in uniethnic settlement. However, in case of multi-ethnic settlement they exclusively form a hamlet of their own, which is called Kami in their own language. However, nowadays while naming a settlement they make use of Bengali words like *Pada, Bari* and *Para*. A village is generally named after any of the related facts like the founder of the settlement, the headman of the settlement, the nearby river or the topographical feature of the area.

While selecting a site the Riang prefer the flat top of a hill of moderate height. As their economic activities are based on hills, they consider hilltops as the convenient sites of settlement. The Riang do not live in a village for a long time. Each village is abandoned periodically and jhum fields are abandoned every year. The youth dormitory among the Riang is called Sikakatangmanitak. Usually, the Riang use the north-west corner of their house for cooking and eating purposes. They do not lie down keeping their head in the west direction because they believe that the sun dies in the direction of the west.

The Family

Table 10 shows that there are 15 Riang families in the village Krishnamanipara. They have formed a Kami (hamlet) on the forest-clad hilltop. Out of these 15 families, 9 are nuclear in size and the rest 6 are extended type of families. The village Maidabari, being uni-ethnic in nature, accommodates 36 families of Riangs of which 27 are nuclear type of families and the rest 9 are of extended type. This also shows that nuclear type of family predominates the extended type of family.

Table 10

Types of Riang Families

S. No.	Village	Families						Total Families
		Nuclear			Extended			
		No.	%	Average Size	No.	%	Average Size	
1.	Krishnamanipara	9	60	4.7	6	40	4.37	15
2.	Maidabari	27	75	10.16	9	25	9.77	36

The Riang families (*nok-khung*) prefer the extended type of family because of the fact that they prefer patrilocal residence. The family usually comprises a man, his wife, unmarried children, married sons and their wives. The head of the family, both in principle and in practice, ensures cooperation among the members of the family, job distribution, and maintenance of social relations with agnates and cognates and performances of rituals. The family property passes through the males and the remains, if any, are confined to the Sandai, agnates, sons and brothers, father's brother's sons and their grandsons and so on, but exclusively to the exclusion of the women. In the event of a man having no male child, the Sandai can bequeath a share to a married daughter living permanently in that family. The rest of the property passes on to the deceased man's brothers and their children. A widow is entitled to a very small share of her deceased husband's family under the care of the Sandai so long as she does not remarry. Only one such case is found in the village Krishanamanipura.

The Riang practise the adoption of any child from any clan through the performance of Sandaiharimi rite and worship of a female deity Songruma. This shows the flexibility of family and kinship structure. In the event of adoption, the adopted son loses all socio-ceremonial ties with his biological parents, his natal Sandai and his own kin group and is assimilated to the kinship group of the new family and the new Sandai. After adoption, the adopted boy takes the clan name of the man who adopts him. In case the boy is the member of the same clan, no ritual performances are observed, otherwise Sandaiharimi is observed in the presence of an assembly of the elderly members of all the clans and the village headman where the biological father of the boy ceremonially hands over his son to the man who adopts him. Thus, the boy is absorbed in the new family and becomes the legitimate heir of the man who adopts him. The Sandai members in Kau Bru are called *buithithahani erungtungha bududuhaphasimi*, i.e., they are of same blood and *houchuthaha kailaimi*, i.e., those who can be married. The Sandai members are the persons of the father's agnatic lineage comprising primarily two ascending and two descending generations from ego.

The Marriage

The Riang follow two principles in marriage, viz: *Halakcham* and *Halakchaya* and two concepts, namely, Sandai and Houchu in the alignment of relatives. *Halakcham* envisages the proper relationship and *Halakchaya* is the forbidden relationship in marriage. *Halakcham* is the children of two male siblings. They are the marriageable partners. *Halakchaya* is the children of two female siblings. They are not marriageable partners. These principles indicate that they practise parallel cousin and not the cross cousin marriages. Of late, flexibility in marriage rules is observed and hence cousin marriage of all types is taking place. The marital status of the two villages is presented in the Table 11. It shows that half of the population in both the sexes of the two villages is married. Only one case of widow has been found in the village Krishnamanipra

While analysing the above principles of marriage Mukherjee (1960) attests that all types of cousin marriage show that there is no incest feeling in the society. The frequency of these marriages also establishes that marriage with one's father's brother's daughter is the predominant form of cousin marriage.

Table 11

Marital Status

Village	Married		Widow	Total Population		
	Male	Female		Married + widow	Unmarried	Total
Krishnamanipara	25	25	1	51	53	104
Maidabari	53	53	—	106	100	206

The low frequency of cross-cousin marriage, their absence in grandfather's generation and the non-alignment of paternal and maternal uncles and aunts with parents-in-law possibly suggest that cross-cousin marriage was introduced later. The frequency of parallel cousin marriages is declining. But it is a fact that parallel cousins are socially very important and significant in the traditional Riang family. However, it is on the wane. The causes of the breakdown of joint households and the feeling of Sandai bond are assumed to be due to the economic reasons, i.e., possession of farm land and trade in cash crops. Marriage among the Riang is known as Kailaimi. Monogamy is the most prevalent type of marriage though polygamy, sororate and levirate marriages are permitted in the society. Remarriage of divorced and widow is practised. Marriage between a bachelor and a divorcee or between a spinster and a divorcee is called *kalai kalaimi* and that between a divorcee and a divorcee is called *kaklai lalaimi*. Widow remarriage is called *Randiranda Lalaimi*. Marriage of a widower with a spinster is called *Sockchok-basiskik*. A man can marry his elder brother's widow but not his younger brother's widow *(Waiyro)*. He can marry his wife's younger sister but not his wife's elder sister *(Waiyrao)*. Marriage by capture (*Toikhaitlamo*), intrusion *(Haiuhphaimi)* and elopement *(Broitomkhailaimi)* were practised in the past. Divorce *(kaklaimi)* is allowed.

Kinship System: The Clan and Lineage

The Riang clan (*panji*) follows the rule of patrilineal descent. The clan structure (*panji-haro*) divides the community into two segments called Molsoi and Meska clans (Mukherjee, 1959).

Gan Chaudhuri (1983), suggests the existence of twelve clans. The present study finds the existence of fourteen clans, namely: (1) Meska, (2) Msha, (3) Apeto, (4) Riang (clan of the Kash Kau kings, now negligible), (5) Raikchauk, (6) Tuimui Yaphaoh, (7) Tauma Yakcho, (8) Raiksom (negligible), (9) Molosi, (10) Chorkhi, (11) Chongpreng, (12) Nouhkham, (13) Uairem and (14) Yakstam (on the wane). However, the interesting feature of the clan is that it is not the social unit, which regulates marriage; neither does it play any role in the spheres of land-ownership, chieftainship and priesthood.

Sandai, a social unit, may be broadly classified as lineage, and it plays a vital role in the kinship behaviour of the Riang. It is a homogeneous, patrilineal group.

Table 12

Clans and Sub Clans

Clans	Molsoi	Meska
Sub clans	Dalbong	Raikchak
	Sagarai	Charkhi
	Nowkham	Musa
	Apeta	Tuimuiafs
	Changpreng	Wairem
	Iakstam	Tamyakcha

Chart 2
Genealogy

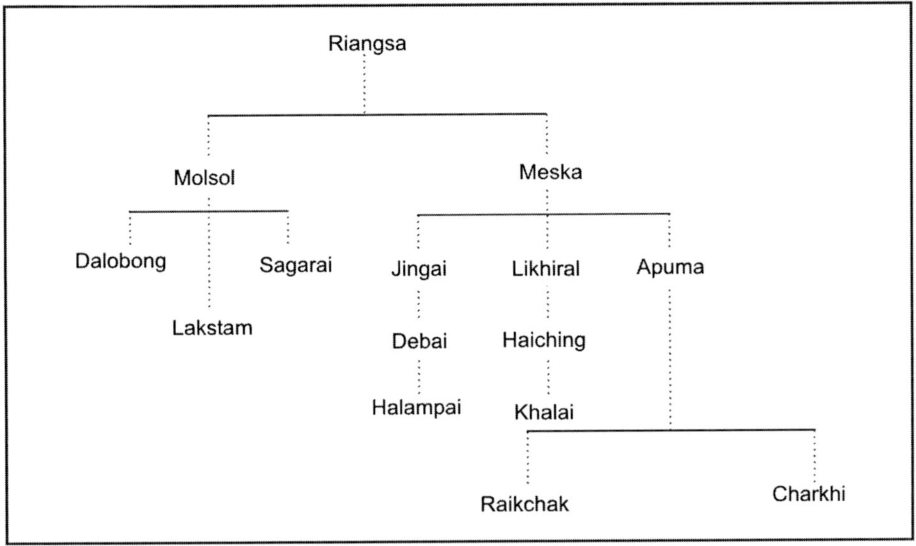

Chart 3
The Riang Kinship System

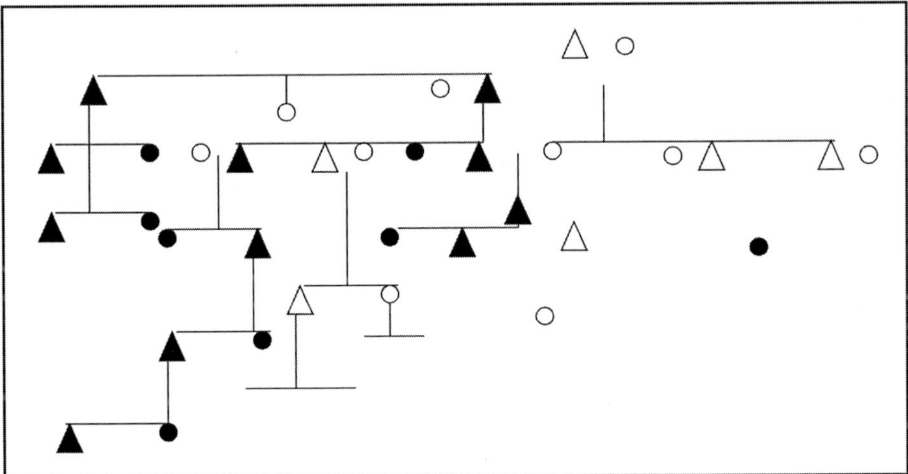

The Riang kinship is based on Sandai (Agnates) and Houchu (Affines) (Chart 3). It may also be mentioned here that all consanguine relatives include collaterals like a man's father's father and his brothers' children, his father and father's father's brothers' children, his brothers, his own and brothers' children and their grandchildren. Houchu members include most of the relatives on the mother's side who are affinal kin-people in the general sense. The difference between these two is that the Sandai members must be of the same clan, whereas the Houchu members may be of the same or a different clan.

Table 13

Riang Kinship Terms

English	*Riang*	*English*	*Riang*
FFF	Aiung	WeBW	Uaiuk
FFM,MFM	Aiung broi	WyB	Prangrobg
FF,MF	Achu	WyBW	prangink
FM MM	Achoi	WeS	Uaiuh
Father	Apa	WeSH	Sarutha
Mother	Among	WyS	Prangrongyuhma
FeB	Aiung	WYSH	Saru
MeB	Aiung	Husband	Nouhbrouh
FesH	Aiung	Heb	UAI
Mesh	Aiung	HeBW	Uaiuk
MeBW	Aiung burai	HyB	Prangrong
FeBW	Aiung burai	HyBW	Prangrongiuk
FeS	Aiung burai	HeS	Uaiuh Didi
MeS	Aiung burai	HeSH	Uaiuh Didi
FyS	Atai	HyS	Prangrong
MyS	Atai	HySH	Prangrongiuk
FyBW	Atai	Son	Sajla
FyB	Mama	Brother's son	Baigna
MyB	Mama	Elder sister's son	Baigna
FySH	Mama	Younger sister's son	Yongha
MySH	Mama	Elder brother's daughter	Baigni
Father-in-law	mkra	Elder sister's daughter	Baigni
Mother-in-law	Kraiuk	Daughter	Sayouh
Step-mother	Amaktai	Younger brother's daughter	Yong
Brother (e)	Ata	Child's father-in-law	Chamai
Brother (y)	Phayong	Child's mother-in-law	Chamaiyouh
Sister (e)	Bi	Son's wife	Haingyouh
Sister (y)	Hanao	Daughter's husband	Chamaroi
eBW	Bachoi	Grand child	Souh
YBW	Waiyouh	GGC	Bora
esh	kumoi	GGGC	Rasi
YSH	Buai	GGGCC	Rafe
Wife	Hin	GGGCCC	Rakoi
WeB	Uai		

It is evident from Table 13 that there are several kinspeople in the Riang terminological system. These are mostly terms of reference but also a common term of address. Broadly speaking, the kinship system can be classified as 'Classificatory system' (Murdock, 1949) of kinship. The salient features of this system are:

1. Kin terms are organized on the principle of generation,
2. Identical terminology is used for elderly relatives in the parents' generation irrespective of their sex,
3. Emphasis on the relative age of the kin.
4. Does not envisage different terminologies according to the sex of the ego.

The Economy: Primitive *Jhum* and Other Occupations

The economic activities of the Riang mainly comprise food-gathering, food-producing, domestication of animals, basketry and mat weaving. They collect *muia* (bamboo shoot), *muikutu* (arum), *khangka* (wild brinjal), *raicak* (soft top of cane), *thalik thampai* (wild banana), *mai khoni* (mushroom), etc., from the forest. However, with the continuous receding of forests, dependence on forest for gathering food is decreasing. They catch fish in streams, rivers, marshy lands and lakes for self-consumption. The usual method employed are trapping, catching by hand, and killing by poisoning. They use the juice of ruo (a creeper) as poison. Hunting of wild games and animals is done individually, and annually in a small group of persons. Only males go out for hunting and females are tabooed. The most common domesticated animals are pig, fowl, cat and dog. Of late, though rare, they have started keeping cow and buffalo in some areas where the villages are situated at comparatively lower elevations and where plough cultivation is in practice. The Riang are apt in making baskets of various types in checker and twill patterns. Weaving of baskets is done mostly by men and women are prohibited. The knowledge of basket making is an important criterion in marriage. The Riangs are also traditionally engaged in weaving and wood-work. Both men and women communally take part in the major activities like cutting and clearing of forest patch, selection of exact site, firing of woods, clearing the debris, sowing, weeding, and so on. The selection of site for *jhum* is done in the months of November–December and harvesting of paddy begins about ten months later, i.e., August–October (Table 14). As all varieties of crops and vegetables do not grow at one point of time, harvesting is done from *ashada* (June–July) to *ashwina* (September–October).

Table 14

Work-cycle in the Huk (Jhum) Field

Time	*Local Name*	*Jhum operation*
Kartik to Paush (November–December)	Huk-howmi	Clearing of forest patch with help of Dao (chopper) by menfolk only
Chaira (March–April)	Huk-showmi	Firing of dried braches, bamboos, etc., by menfolk only
Baisakh (April–May)	Huk-maikheimi	Planting of seeds by menfolk.
Jaisthe to Sravan (June–July–August)	Huk-taimi	Weeding is done by both men and women
Bhadra to Asuin (August to October)	Mairami	Harvesting of paddy/crops done by men and women

The Riang who are settled on plains have started cultivation of paddy (Kherib and Rabieropo). It is contemplated here that the frequency of settled cultivators is very less not because of the fact that the villages are located mostly on hills but also because of the fact that they are ignorant of the technology of plough cultivation. Of late, it is argued that *Jhum* cultivation is not ecologically viable and hence the government agencies attempt to foster the production of cash crops. Sporadic attempts are made to grow teak, orange and pineapple in North Tripura District. Tripura Rubber Plantation Corporation (TRPC) has initiated attempts to plant rubber trees in South Tripura District. However, the

Riang who are traditionally *Jhum* cultivators cling to it, although they are learning now many other vocational expertise.

Table 15

The Chief Crops of Various Seasons

Type of Land	*Kharif Crops (rainy season crop)*	*Rabi Crops (summer season crop)*
Wet lowland	The Aus and the Pos variety of paddy	—
Dry upland	Jute, sugarcane, sesame or a Aus varieties of paddy	Mustard, tobacco, pulses like the masur, moong, kalai, vegetable like, potato, brinjal, chili, groun, karols, radisa, kochu, bean, tomato, onion, etc.

Table 15 shows that while the Riang practise plough cultivation they produce varieties of crops in the rainy season and in the summer season on the lowland as well as dry land.

Table 16

Sex-wise Main Economic and Other Activities of the Riang

S. No.	*Activities*	*Main Economic Activities*		
		Men	*Women*	*Both*
1.	Agriculture	(i) Clearing, cutting and burning of forest patch for Huk *(Jhum)* (ii) Planting of seed in Huk *(Jhum)* (iii) Ploughing and leveling of tilled soil in settled plough cultivation	Husking of Paddy	(i) Transplantation of the seeding (ii) Weeding (iii) Harvesting
2.	Hunting	Hunting of wild games and animals	Taboo	—
3.	Fishing	—	—	Buying traps, etc.
4.	Animal husbandry	Pasturing, taking care of pigs, fowls and cattle.	Feeding of pigs, fowls and cattle	—
5.	Basketry	Basket making	Taboo	—
6.	Weaving	Weaving and spinning	Weaving	Dyeing
7.	Marketing	carrying paddy and vegetable on shoulder, selling and buying in market	—	Buying in market
		Other Activities		
8.	House building	(i) Felling trees and bamboo for posts. (ii) Thatching the roof	—	Help in thatching
9.	Load carrying	Carrying heavy load on shoulders	Carrying light loads.	—
10.	Collection of fuel wood	Cutting of tree	—	Carrying in bundles on head and shoulders

Table 16 shows that although the Riang women are hard working, the Riang men take the major load of their economy. The Riang manage labour in Huk land on the basis of mutual cooperation and hence no cash payment is made for this labour. Each man works in a particular field by rotation and on any day a man may employ another man who himself may be owner in a different land. Hence, the deployment of labour force is an internal arrangement of the Riang, possibly because of strong mutual ties and common interest in the traditional mode of occupation.

On comparing the two contrasting types of shifting and plough cultivation it is found that while cotton, maize, sesame are exclusively grown in their Huk land, though in less quantity; paddy is the main crop in Kheto or Luangs land. They only consume the paddy grown in Huk land. On the contrary, the paddy grown by settled cultivation is both exchanged and sold in the market. Only planting method is followed in *Jhum* land whereas broadcasting or transplanting method is followed in plough cultivation. It is to be noted that the *Jhum* land area of Tripura is yet to receive its due recognition in the land tenure system of Tripura as there is no Jhum Land Regulation Act.

The Religion: Coexistence of Multiple Beliefs

The Census of India 1981 enumerates that 94 per cent of the Riangs are Hindus, 5.92 per cent Christians and the rest 0.08 per cent are Buddhists. In both the studied villages, the Riang have adopted the religious traits of the Hindus but they keep pursuing tribal religion. The religion of the Riang, both in principle and practice, thus contains elements of animism, dream revelation, fertility cult, magic, polytheism, taboo, totemic belief and witchcraft. The continuation of animistic beliefs and acceptance of Hindu religious beliefs constitute the core of their religion. Hinduism has left an impact on their indigenous beliefs and practices. The Riang believe in *fala* (soul) and assume that while a person is asleep, his or her soul can leave the body, take the form of a *leincha* (grasshopper) and roam about here and there and again come back, and re-enter the body. The sacred specialist or priest among the Riang is called Aukchai. One can only become an Aukchai if he is a married man and has only one wife, i.e., a man who practises monogamy. Belief in dream and divination also occupies a major place. The Riang sorcerers practise both imitative and contagious magic. The magicians prescribe amulets and talisman to ward off evil spirits, cure disease, befriend a person, cause divorce or unite a person. The names of deities are given in Table 17. As a result of close contact with the neighbouring Hindu communities; different Hindu deities and the cult of Vaishnavism have found place in the religious axis of the Riang. Of late, the Riang have also accepted vegetarianism in principle.

Table 17

Gods and Goddesses (Tribal Religion)

Names of Gods/Goddesses	*Power, Role and Status*
Buraha	A male God dreaded for this power of destruction.
Haicukma	Wife of Buraha
Jampira & Kalpira	Sons of Buraha.
Thuinairao	The king of Riang deities, God of death.
Soinairo	Recorder of virtue and vice equated with Chitragupta who writes the destiny according to Hindu concept.
Sibrai	A male God
Taocing	Chaungama, wife of Sibrai
Toibuma	Goddess of water.

The Political Organization

Some Chiefs of the Riangs namely, Lngsika, Paisika, Taileongha and Tolikluha submitted themselves to the king of Tripura, Ratna Manikya who was also tribal. The king honoured them and nominated one of the leaders as the chief of the Riang conferring on the title, Rai. Traditionally the Riang had four-tier political organization. The first one was known as Ata, which was composed of thirteen attendants and functioned under the king Kaskau. The second one was known as Saia, which was composed of twelve officials known as councillors who worked as messengers, store-keepers, rent collectors, drum beaters, flutists, and generals and it functioned under Rai. These two units existed till the third decade of last century. The third unit, which had executive and judicial functions, comprised of three administrative chiefs, called Chowdhury Sardars spread in three administrative divisions, Belonia (Madhuripur) Udaipur and Amarpur, the three major areas of past concentration of the Riang. The fourth unit consisted of Holui Chowdhury of each village and the Sardar of each hamlet. They were assisted by Karbari (messenger) and the council of elders of each hamlet. It is apparent that in the past, the Riang had institution of self-government. But it was radically changed during the princely period and especially after India achieved independence. Statutory council system now shapes the political organization. Though the village chieftainship was abolished in principle in 1955, yet in practice the chief of a village unofficially existed and maintained a council of his own. The tribal village council is not a relic of the past. Since 1962, a uniform pattern of Statutory Panchayati Raj has been introduced. Tripura Tribal Area Autonomous District Council (ADC) was formed in 1985 under the Sixth Schedule of the Indian Constitution. Except the maintenance of law and order, the ADC has autonomy in all matters of tribal customary laws and administration. ADC is basically an institution of self-governance.

Inter-Ethnic Relations and Inter-Community Hierarchy

The Riang have been in contact with the ruling community of Tripura, the migrant Hindu caste groups and other tribes, namely the Mag, the Noatia, the Halam and the Tripuri for a long time. Among the Hindu caste people, the Brahmin astrologers have the access to almost all the Riang households to perform the worship of Hindu deities and planets, namely, Sani, Nabagraha, Satyanarayan and so on and to prepare the horoscopes. Some of the Riangs have also accepted the doctrine of Vaishnavism from Vaishanava preceptors. The Riang employ Muslim agricultural labourers to work in their agricultural field when necessary. They also employ the Mag and the Noatia in case they need additional labour.

Of late, the Riang have recognized the concept of hierarchy and have placed themselves in a ladder of social hierarchy. They consider the Hindus especially the Brahmins and the Tripuria as their superiors in rank and place the Mag, the Noatia and the Halam as their inferior in rank. They consider the Mag and the Muslim as lowly placed group. However, they maintain cordial relationship with other ethnic groups while interacting in the weekly markets and in economic transactions.

Impact of the Development Programme

In view of their pre-agricultural technology and low level of literacy the government of India at one time declared the Riang as 'Primitive Tribal Group'. In the year 1983, the Government of Tripura initiated a project to rehabilitate the Riang families living within the Reserve forest area of the state and the Forest Department implemented the project in 1985–86. The main objective of the project was to divert the Riang from *jhum* cultivation and to resettle those in Reserve forest areas, by providing them necessary assistance to resettle. Nearly 5,485 Jhumia (the families who practice *jhum*) were covered in the first phase of the project from 1985–90 and in the second phase, i.e., within the time period from 1990–91 to 1996–97, about 3,500 Riang families were rehabilitated. The TRP and PGP provided them two and a half hectare of land for teak plantation, one and a half hectare of land for fruit plantation, five hectare of land for cashew nut production and a half hectare of land for fuel wood. Certain land was proposed for constructing Longa (mini barrage) in between two *tilla* (hillock) where water would be logged for pisciculture. In order to enhance economic profits the waist loom was also provided. Six *mutha* (bundle) of thread was provided for the preparation of Pachara (waist cloth). In 1985, the Tripura Tribal Area Autonomous District Council (TTAADC) was formed under the Sixth Schedule of Indian Constitution, which aimed at autonomy in all matters of tribal development and administration. Riang became part of autonomous council and hence governed by the rules of TTAADDC.

Culture-Contact, Stratification and Social Change

Culture and language, though often affected after culture-contact, provide basic identity. The language of the tribespeople of Tripura is known as Kak-Barak, the literal meaning of which is the language of men. The language belongs to the Tibeto-Burman group of languages and its root can be traced to Sino-Tibetan speech family. The ethnographic universe of the Riang is shaped through the cognition of Riang worldview in terms of its myth of creation and its mechanism of the maintenance of Riang ethnic boundary. The identity of 'Barak' language as Kak-Barak and the social organization comprising the social units and institutions like clan, lineage, family, kinship, marriage, village, religion, economic organization, political organization and inter-ethnic relationships shape the identities of allied tribes, who maintain some distinctions based on economic pursuits and culture-contact. From the origin, mythology and history of the Riang, it is apparent that the Riang society comprised of a traditional system of stratification, which was articulated through unequal clans occupied by the chiefs and their associates. This process of stratification developed a sense of hierarchy of ranks in the society, which continued over centuries. A modern pattern of stratification also grew slowly. Traditional and modern stratification often co-existed and complemented each other. This sort of stratification was based on social considerations, i.e., the ascribed and achieved status of an individual, prestige and power and also the economic considerations, i.e., ownership and control over resources and so on. The traditional village council under the rule of Holui Chowdhury brought in the essence of stratification in the political axis where the chief enjoyed the authority and power of administration.

The inclusion of Aukchai in the village council attributed more power to the council and its members in terms of religious beliefs as the Aukchai is believed to possess supernatural powers.

As a result of close contact with the neighbouring Hindu communities, different Hindu traits and the cult of Vaishnavism found place in the religious world of the Riang. Of late, Vaishnavism has made an enormous influence among the Riang, which has also encouraged them to resort to vegetarianism in principle.

The Riang clan structure is stratified. Primarily the clan structure assumes the form of bisection of the community having two segments of Meska and Molsoi. Secondly, the Riang clan names have historical association with mythical kingdom. Thus, one clan is believed to be the clan of the Kaskau king and the clan names Raikchauk and Raiksom are believed to have originated from the names of two army generals of the bygone day. It is therefore we notice that clans are hierarchically arranged. As we discussed clear-cut distinctions are maintained between two categories called Sandai (agnates) and Houchu (affines). These categories differentiate an individual from the point of view of marriageable and non-marriageable kinsmen. Apart from the relationship of marriageable and non-marriageable kins, these concepts also indicate the pattern of inheritance and succession in a family. Following two major principles of marriage, i.e., Halakcham and Halakchaya, the Riang maintain a stratified alignment of relatives in the lines of Sandai and Houchu. This pattern of stratification reflects the principles of cousin marriage among the Riang. Traditionally the Riang had an in-built system of stratified political organization which operated at the village level, zonal level and at the state level. The abolition of chieftainship and introduction of Panchayati Raj have withered away the stratified rigidity of Riang authority structure. Social change in Riang society is traceable right from foundation in the history of the Riang in Tripura. The Riang came in contact with the ruling community of the state of Tripura around the fifteenth century. In the last decade of the nineteenth century they came in contact with the Magh, the Tripuri, the Halam, the Noatia and others. Right from 1940s they came in contact with the Bengali Hindus who started pouring in by this time. Around 1935, the Riang came in contact with a member of the Noatia tribe, who introduced Vaishnavism and made attempts to proselytize the Riang. This was followed by pouring in of the Hindu Vaishnavites and regular contact with the Hindus by 1944 due to steady inroad of Hindu refugees from the neighbouring districts of erstwhile East Pakistan.

It is apparent that the first contact with the larger ruling community was self-initiated and friendly, which resulted in the voluntary political submission to the king. The next contact during 1980s with the Mag resulted in a shift in their traditional practice of Jhum economy. They learnt the technology of plough cultivation from the Magh. Their settlement pattern also started changing due to the transformation of forest lands. The third impact was Vaishnavism which discouraged the tribal theology based on sacrifice of animals and it also led to acceptance of vegetarianism. The removal of the tribal chief marked another footstep towards social change. The establishment of Bengali refugee settlements was another landmark which opened the channels of close and regular contact with alien culture. Another landmark that brought transformation in Riang society was the Riang protests of 1942–43 led by Ratannumi Noatia in defense of rights of natives of Tripura. There are other processes of change witnessed at kinship and the family level. The extended family structure has been almost broken down resulting in formation of smaller nuclear family. The link between the clans and political organization has also been affected owing to the discontinuation of the council of the chief. The clan rituals which could consolidate the members of respective clans are performed. At the level of kinship behaviour, the intensity of the Sandai bond has been maintained and ritual for unity among the agnates is often performed now. Important changes are reported in marriage field. The marriage by intrusion and elopement are obsolete now. Moreover, there is decline in the frequency of parallel cousin marriage which has resulted in weakening the Sandai bond of kinship.

The council of the chief has been disorganized and the chief is no longer a leader. However, the disputes over ownership of land, etc. are now settled by the clan elders. The bachelor and youth dormitory system, as an institution, are almost extinct. The Riang have shown considerable change in terms of economic mobility. Many have taken to plough cultivation. The exchange of service in agricultural activity through cooperation has declined. They have also started growing new varieties of paddy and going for wage earning as labourer. the Riang people have experienced some empowerment after introduction of Autonomous District Council.

Table 18

Organizations and their Affiliation

S. No.	*Name of the Organizations*	*Affiliation*
1.	All Tripura Tribe Force (ATTF)	Leftist supported
2.	National Liberation Front of Tripura (NLFT)	Mainly headed by Riang activists Dhananjay Riang in South Tripura District and Dhaniram Riang in North Tripura District were leaders
3.	Tripura Tribal youth Force (TTYF)	—
4.	Tripura Reserve force (TRF)	—
5.	All Tripura Tiger Force (ATTF)	Leftist supported
6.	Peoples Liberation Organization (PLO)	North-east Indian insurgent group
7.	Commando Force (CF)	Rightist supported
8.	Tripura National Volunteer Force (TNVF)	Rightist supported
9.	Sengkrak	Rightist supported
10.	Seven Star (north zone)	NE Indian group
11.	People Liberation Army (PLA)	Rightist supported
12.	Tripura Tribal Volunteer force (TTVF)	—
13.	Tripura Tribal Activists (TTA)	—
14.	All Tripura National Forces (ATNF)	An offshoot of the Sengkrak group.
15.	Army of Tripura People's Liberation Organization	—
16.	Tripura Hill Peoples Party (1983)	—

Like other hill area, Tripura also has a long history of tribal movements (Mukherjee and Singh, 1982). At one stage sixteen insurgent groups operating in different regions of Tripura covered forest-clad hilly ranges and the interior regions where tribal villages are situated. The present author could collect the names of several organizations and their affiliation to the respective political parties (Table 18). All these sixteen groups have self-claimed chiefs and forces that resort to armed struggle. It is reported that the National Liberation Front of Tripura (NLFT) led by Dhanajoy Riang had a considerable influence on the Riang.

Tripura was originally a tribal state. Its kings belonged to Bodo segment. There were many tribes is Tripura, such as the Riang, who depended on hunting and shifting cultivation. In view of their backwardness the government declared them as 'Primitive Tribal Group'. However they had organized themselves under their chief who had some linkage with the state authority in past. Arrival of refugees and other immigrants and land alienation forced them to resort to armed struggle.

At the same time democratic institutions have been introduced. Sixth schedule, special development package, adoption of settled cultivation, Hinduization and educational achievements have created a new social order. A new middle class has emerged which is concerned about plight of the people. The native tribes are worst sufferers in Tripura. Dul to encroachment of their land they opted for armed struggle but they failed. They were provided with Autonomous Councils but they state authorities never financed development programmes, which resulted in continuous deprivation of tribespeople.

References

Davis, K. and E.T. Dalton 1872, *Descriptive Ethnology of Bengal,* Calcutta Kolkata: Indian Studies, Past and Present (Reprinted in 1973).

Davis, K. and W.E. Moore 1945, "Some Principles of Stratification", *American Sociological Review* 7.

Fallers, L.A.1977, "Equality and Inequality in Human Societies", in S. Tax and L.G. Freeman (eds.), *Horizons of Anthropology* (2nd ed.), Chicago: Aldine.

Fried, M.H. 1967, *The Evolution of Political Society: An Essay in Political Anthropology,* New York: Ransom House.

Gan Chaudhuri 1983, *The Riangs of Tripura,* Tripura, Directorate of Research.

Grierson, G.A. 1928, *Linguistic Survey India,* Vol. I, Part II, Calcutta Kolkata: The Bengali Secretariat Press.

Hunter, D.E. and P. Whitten 1976, *Encyclopaedia of Anthropology,* New York: Harper & Row.

Hunter, W.W. 1876, *The Statistical Account of Bengal,* Vol. VI, London: Routledge.

Lewin, T.H. 1869, *The Hill Tracts of Chittagong and the Dwellers Therein,* Calcutta Kolkata: Bengal Printing.

Marx, Karl 1934, *The Class Struggles in France,* New York: International Publishers.

Mukherjee, B. 1959, "The Riang", in *Bulletin of the Department of Anthropology,* Vol. VIII, No. 1, p. 107.

Mukherjee, B. 1960, "Cousin Marriage among the Riang", *Anthropos,* Vol. 55, Face 5–6. pp. 734–738.

Mukherjee, B. and K.S. Singh 1982. Tribal Movements in Tripura in K.S. Singh (Ed.) Tribal Movements in India. Delhi: Manohar.

Mudock, G.P. 1949, *Social Structure,* New York: Macmillan.

Parsons, Talcott 1954, "An Analytical Approach to the Theory of Social Stratification", in *Essays in Sociological Theory,* Rev. ed., New York: Free Press.

Scott, George J. 1900, *Gazetteer of Upper Burma and the Shan State,* Rangoon: Government Printers, Vol. I, Part I.

Sen, Kaliprasanna (ed.) 1337, T.D., *Srea Rajmala,* Agartala: Vol. I.

Singh, K.S. (ed.) 1994, *The Scheduled Tribes,* Calcutta Kolkata: An S.I. and Oxford Univ. Press.

Singh, Kailash Chandrai 1896, *Rajmala,* Agartala.

Smith, M.G. 1966, "Pre-industrial Stratification System", in N.J. Smelser and S.M. Lipset (eds.), *Social Structure and Mobility in Economic Development,* Chicago: Aldine.

Weber, Max 1946, *Essays in Sociology,* New York: Oxford University Press.

Weber, Max 1947, *The Theory of Social and Economic Organization,* New York: Oxford University Press.

9 Culture-Contact and Emerging Middle Class among the Santals

K. Mukhopadhyay

This paper intends to understand the process of social change and new patterns of stratification as emerging amongst the Santals. If we consider the Santals and try to demarcate their position, we would find them to be socially more heterogenous and having more internal stratification compared to tribes of the Andamans. However, we would not find all the Santals in the same social, economic or political stratum. The situation would be further complex if we consider the social, economic or political position of the Santal vis-à-vis their non-tribal neighbours. We would see various forms of inequalities; depending on various factors responsible for creation of inequality operative in society. The present exercise is not an analytical study to understand the above mentioned factors or to delve into the underlying principles of inequality. It is rather a descriptive account of the phenotypes – of what are manifested at the surface. The study has a further limitation. It studies one tribe and that also in one village. Like other village studies our effort would be to understand the macrocosm in the microcosm.

The present work has been conducted among the Santal inhabitants of a multi-ethnic village, called Datarampur, in the district of Bankura, West Bengal. Datarampur is situated in Khatra sub-division of the above district. The village can be reached from the sub-divisional town following either a 6 km long dirt road or an 8 km long alternative road. The whole area is undulated, and rocky. In comparison to the silty plains lying east, the soil here is low in fertility. About twenty-five years back, canal irrigation reached these parts. Prior to that many persons from Datarampur and adjacent villages, particularly those with little or no cultivable land, had to migrate eastward in search of jobs. Canal irrigation has given a boost to the agrarian economy by turning the previously single crop into multi-crop ones and by raising the yield to some extent. As a result there was some income generation in the area. Khatra became a centre for trade in agricultural produces and in those consumer goods which the local population can now afford to buy. This one-time village of Khatra has taken the shape of a small township, and it is still growing. Trade and construction works have generated some employment. Coupled with round the year agricultural work, such employment generation had effectively checked the eastward migration of people in search of jobs.

Bankura including Rarh area is home to several caste groups and some tribes. The Rarhi Brahmins settled down in the area long ago and they are known after this western most part of Bengal known as Rarh. They are supervisor cultivators, traders, teachers, and white-collar job holders at government offices and banks. Utkal Brahmins are Brahmins from Odisha, who settled down in this area during the last one century or a little more. They are primarily supervisor cultivators. Many of them are engaged in different white-collar trades. Poddar or Bania are a caste of traders. They have sizeable amount of agricultural land also. These three groups are the wealthiest social groups of the area. They enjoy high social status also.

The Bhumij, who once were the 'jamindars' of the area, are now clearly divided into two types. The once jamindars have lost most of their land at throwaway prices; sometimes they have gifted the land away. Now they have little property to subsist on, but refuse to do almost any work for earning their livelihood. Then there are Bhumij who do not have any such glorious past. These people do almost any work for a living, including menial work, excepting for a few aristocratic families. The Bhumij have fallen from the socio-economic status they once enjoyed.

There are several caste groups, who are primarily engaged in agriculture as land owner cultivators. Some of these castes are Goala, Sunri and Mahato. They are locally considered as expert cultivators and vegetable growers. Some villages of this area, which are mostly inhabited by the Goalas, meet almost the entire demand of vegetables in the local market. These caste group enjoy a middle position in the local social hierarchy.

The artisan and servicing castes are the Napit (barber), Lohar (blacksmith), Khumar (potter), Gorai (oil press), Mochi (cobbler). They are not treated at par, but are ranked on the basis of their trade. Napit or Khumar are given a much higher position than the Mochi. But each group is indispensable for the local society as well as the local economy. However, the entire group is placed below the agriculturists.

The lowest rung is occupied by the Bauri or the Bagdi, who are either landless or own very little land. They are the people who work as wage labourers for the agriculture sector. The Santals and some of the artisans like the Mochi are also placed in this rung by their neighbours.

The Tribe

The Santals are one of the large tribes of the country. They are distributed over five states, namely Jharkhand, West Bengal, Odisha, Assam and Tripura. In Assam they are not a Scheduled Tribe. In 1981, they numbered more than four million and a quarter excluding the state of Assam. Numerically, only the Gond and the Bhil are larger than the Santal. The Santal speak a language known as Santali. They call themselves Har, meaning men, and refer to their language as Har Rar or speech of the Har. This language belongs to the Munda branch of the Austro-Asiatic family. In all the eastern states the Santal are primarily engaged in agriculture, as landowning cultivators and as agricultural wage labourers also. There are quite a number of Santals engaged in salaried jobs in public as well as in private sectors. Though they are yet to catch up with their educationally advanced neighbours, Santal men have joined white-collar jobs in various organizations in a wide range of capacities. The Santals were taken to the northeastern states of Assam and Tripura by the tea-planters as 'coolies'. Even now many of them work for the tea-gardens, while some of them have taken up other vocations including agriculture. "The traditions and origins of the Santals would make us believe", noted Mallick (1993), "that they were nomads and were essentially a hunting and food gathering tribe". Their initial method of producing food was shifting cultivation *(dahi)*. Later they learnt cultivation and irrigation. Eventually, they came to be adjudged as skilled and efficient cultivators of land. Their skill was utilized by the jamindars, who invited the Santals to settle in their territories for reclaiming forest land and turning the same into agricultural land

Very often these jamindars either evicted the Santals from the reclaimed land or tried to extract as much revenue from them as possible. Such treatment from the jamindars and the limitless exploitation of the people by money lenders and traders compelled the Santals to stand up in rebellion several times during the nineteenth century. The rebellion that took place during 1855–56 surpassed all previous tribal uprising in scale and intensity. They took up arms against the jamindars and mahajans, the state power protecting the interests of the latter. Regular British army declared war on these tribals armed with bows, arrows and battle axes and perpetrated such brutality which made even some British army officers feel ashamed.

The Santal people have shown remarkable knack for dance and music. The folklore of the Santal is rich and a thorough study of the same is yet to be accomplished. The Santal devote quite some time to making and playing musical instruments. On special occasions, and sometimes without any such occasion, they spend long hours in singing and dancing. *Raska*, the Santal word for pleasure, is essential for them. It has been observed by Culshaw (1949: 39) that these people "turn from their difficulties and sorrows to find solace in one or other of the many ways in which they can experience raska"

Social Differentiation and Clan Ranking

The tribe, the Har can be divided into two broad groups on the basis of religious faith. One section has taken up Christianity as its religion, while the other part still practises traditional religious faith, known as *sari sarna*. The people are almost unanimous in saying that a Christian is equally a Har and a follower of *sari sarna*. This sense of oneness, however, is not always very strong in practice. Some Santal persons of the area told the author that they would never allow any breach of rule of endogamy by any Santal. Any instance of extra-marital relation between a Santal and a non-Santal would call for similar punishment, which any breach of rule of endogamy would invite. The men here reported one instance that took place in the area in recent times. It was suspected that a Santal lady, a teacher of one high school, was having some extra-marital relation with one of her male colleagues. This man belonged to a Hindu caste, was a married person with some children. The two went away to some other place on some pretext and spent some days together. On their return, both of them were suspended from their jobs. To the question why this lady was punished; there was some hesitation among the informants. Then one of them muttered "she is a Christian after all. Our Christian brothers should do something about it."

The Santal are divided into several exogamous clan groups, known as Paris. According to the Santal myth of genesis, the original human couple had twelve sons and twelve daughters. These sibs violated the laws of incest and formed twelve families, which gave birth to twelve clan groups. Consequently some of the clans got lost or were ex-communicated and cannot be traced anymore. Nine of these clans could be traced in the studied village and its adjacent villages. These are; Hansda, Murmu, Kisku, Hembrom, Marandi, Soren, Besra, Tudu and Core. These clans are supposed to enjoy equal social position. Each of these clans are further divided into sub-clans, each one having a specific name, certain taboos and rites to observe and some specified deities to propitiate. The clan groups are functionally of equal status barring a few exceptions. Any clan can intermarry with any other clan, but normally a Kisku family would not negotiate a marriage with the Marandi and vice versa. Similarly, marriage between a Tudu and a Besra are avoided as far as possible. In both the cases, there are tales in support of such practice. In essence the tales are alike in narrating how, long back, a person from one clan betrayed a person from another clan, committed treachery, and enmity grew among the clans.

The above mentioned instance of avoidance may appear like hierarchy among the clans. In fact, there is no such hierarchy in practice. But notionally the people often arrange the clans vertically. The model of arrangement is undoubtedly borrowed from the Hindu Varna model, and often parallels are drawn to that model. The original couple, Pinchu Handom and Pilchu Budi, came out of eggs laid by one divine goose. The Hansda clan is known after that goose, so they are given the highest position. Murmus, who are known for their meticulous ways of observing religious rites, are also given an esteemed position. Both these groups are equated with the Brahmins, though they do not serve others as priests. Kiskus were the kings and they were brave, courageous people. The Sorens were the soldiers, so, these two clans are the Kshatriyas in the tribe. The Marandi were wealthy traders, and they were very miserly people also. So, they possess both the goodness and the bad quality of the Vaishya. Though it is not clearly said who the Sudras are and what are their attributes, certain specializations are imagined in the rest of the clans also. The Besra and the Tudu are considered to be good entertainers, experts in dance and music. Notably, the Santal who are so fond of *raska*, put the entertainers at a low social position, even if it has nothing to do with everyday life. This reflects the Varna model which ascribes the musicians and dancers a lowly social existence. Culshaw (1949: 70) noted that such notion of hierarchy is probably of recent origin and was fabricated by the tribe or certain parts of it to compensate the low social status ascribed by their caste Hindu neighbours. It should be noted that this scheme of hierarchical arrangement damages the notion of solidarity of the tribe.

One significant inequality in the Santal society is the inequality between the sexes. It is a male dominated society, where descent, inheritance and succession follows male line. It is only recently that right of women in property has been accepted, though in a limited way. Sons share the ancestral property among themselves without giving any part of it to their sisters. Only in absence of sons, daughter inherits fathers property. Even few decades back, members of the same lineage used to divide among themselves the property of those who died without leaving a male child. Any position of power within the society is inaccessible for the women. Even the membership to the village council is denied to them. The custom of polygyny adds to their misery. It is not that all the males go for multiple wives, but in almost every village one would come across one or two families, where there are co-wives. Sometimes the first wife deserts the household when husband marries for the second time. If the first wife is issueless, that is often cited as the reason for second marriage.

The Santal males can also be seen to live together with their paramours, without marrying them. Such concubinage, if we can use the term, further jeopardizes the status of the concerned women. Not only the wife suffers due to such relationship; the other lady is also not given any social recognition. She is not allowed to take part in any social or religious rites. Her children also cannot marry, unless she gets married herself and thus legitimizes her children. This social recognition is necessary for another purpose. If a man dies without marrying his paramour, she would not be allowed to enjoy any part of his property. In fact, after death of her lover she becomes a solitary woman without a family and without any property to support her.

The Santal youth of the area often compose and perform one act plays. Sometimes a night long performance is organized, where young boys from different villages assemble and perform several plays throughout the night. These boys attempt a sort of awareness campaign through their performance. They take up subjects for their plays, which they feel to be socially relevant. One such subject is witch hunting, the superstitious beliefs related with this and the harm such beliefs related with this can cause. In the studied village and in its adjacent area some people believe in the efficacy of witchcraft and sorcery, but no incident of witch hunting has taken place in several years. Other subjects depicted in the plays are necessity of universal literacy or necessity of protection of forests. Some informed young boys were asked, if polygyny or concubinage have been dealt with as a social problem in any of these plays. It was revealed that they never thought about this issue seriously.

Economic Differentiation

In terms of social differentiation, we observed some notions of hierarchy. Economic differences on the other hand are much more concrete and can be measured with relative ease. But there is a tendency among the people to gloss over such differences and give the outsider some idea of tribal solidarity.

The village Datarampur has a population of 463 souls. Ethnic group-wise break-up of this population gives the following view:

Table 1

	Population and Households Size					*Avg Household Size*
	Ethnic Groups	*Population*			*No. of Households*	
		Male	*Female*	*Total*		
1.	Santal	121	130	251	47	5.34
2.	Mahato	80	78	158	28	5.64
3.	Tantubay	18	13	31	6	5.17
4.	Pramanik	9	8	17	3	5.67
5.	Bhumij	9	7	16	3	5.33
	Total	237	226	463	87	5.32

The above table shows that the Santals are the largest group in the village. If we consider the total population or number of the households, they constitute more than half of the village population.

Almost the entire population of the village depends on agriculture for their livelihood. Sometimes they do so as landowning cultivators, at other times as agricultural wage labourers. There are some non-agricultural sectors where employment as wage labourer is available. The major area of non-agricultural employment is construction of house in and around Khatra town. The boom in construction works in the area has largely been caused by the boom in agricultural economy. Canal irrigation has changed the scenario of agriculture and had helped to generate the wealth, which is being invested in construction works. Some of the villagers are engaged in trade. Many of them deal in agricultural produce like paddy or rice. A good number of them are engaged in trade of livestock.

Before we discuss the occupational categories, let us consider the pattern of landholding, since land is the primary resource utilized for living. The unit of measurement, bigha, is one-third of an acre.

Table 2

Landholding Pattern

	Landless	*Up to Five Bigha*	*5 to 9 Bigha*	*10 to 14 Bigha*	*15+ Bigha*	*Total No. of households*
1. Santal	2 (4.26)	22 (46.81)	18 (38.30)	3 (6.38)	2 (4.26)	47
2. Mahato	1 (3.57)	6 (21.43)	13 (46.43)	5 (17.86)	3 (10.71)	28
3. Tantubay		5 (83.33)	1 (16.66)			6
4. Pramanik		3 (100.00)				3
5. Bhumij	1 (33.33)	2 (66.66)				3

Figures in parenthesis denote percentages of households.

Table 2 shows that landless households are few in the village. While households possessing less than five bighas of agricultural land are majority among the Santals, the Mahatos are more prosperous as nearly half of them possess land between five to ten bighas. However, there is no 'very rich' household in the village. Largest holding among the Mahatos is 25 bighas, while it is around 20 bighas among Santals.

The pattern of landholding and types of occupations are shown in Table 3.

Table 3

Occupational Categories

	Agriculturist	*Agriculturist + wage labourer*	*Wage Labourer*	*Agriculturist + Trader*	*Service Hoder + Agriculturist*
Santal	8 (17.02)	30 (63.83)	2 (4.26)	1 (2.13)	6 (12.77)
Mahato	15 (53.57)	5 (17.86)	1 (3.57)	7 (25.00)	
Tantubay	1 (16.66)	4 (66.66)		1 (16.66)	
Pramanik				3 (100.00)	
Bhumij		2 (66.66)	1 (33.33)		

Figures in parentheses denote percentages of households.

Table 3 shows that very few Santal households depend on agriculture only. A clear majority of them work as wage labourers along with doing agriculture. Mahatos on the other hand are primarily agriculturists. While some Mahato households go for wage earning, almost equal numbers of them carry on some sort of trade. The Santals show some aversion to trade. Only household in that category runs a tailoring shop at Khatra market. The Santals compensate the aversion by doing salaried jobs as teachers, bank personnel, policemen or railway employees. All these jobs are in the government sector. The benefit of job reservation for Scheduled Tribes has given rise to such economic achievements.

Intra-tribe economic differentiation exists among the Santals. Economically the Santals divide people into two groups, *kishar* or wealthy and *rangech* or poor.

A group of senior male Santals of the village were asked to categorize all the Santal households. They came up with three categories, the *kishar* and the *rangech*, and then a group of *madhyabitta*, the Bengali term for middle class. They revealed that they do not have a Santal equivalent for the term, as such a way of categorizing such people is rather recent. However, the emergence of a middle class is a reality and the categorization is a necessity, they feel. After few days of discussion, a person from another village came up with a Santali term, which everybody felt to be appropriate to describe the middle class group. The term is *soharae sambharam*. *Soharae* is the major festival of the Santals and it takes place in autumn. This is a tough time for the poor people. The winter crop is yet to be *harvested* and after a prolonged lean season the autumn crop of coarse paddy, if there was any, provides some food for the family. The *Rangech* people find it very difficult to observe *soharae* with their almost empty coffer. The *kishar* only can celebrate *soharae* luxuriously with their savings. The *soharac sambharom*, a traditional usage in Santali, is used to denote people who can somehow manage to celebrate *soharae* in a modest scale. They define *kishar* as such people, who can very well subsist on the earning they get from their agricultural land. Still they have some surplus, which they used to give others as loan. Nowadays they sell the surplus away. The Rangech are people who have little or no income from land and depend largely on wage labour.

They kept five households in the *kishar* category, eleven in the category of Rangech and the rest were put into the middle class group. Per capita land holding in the first group is 2.81 bigha, among the poor households it is 0.61 bigha while the middle class have 0.97 or about one bigha of arable land per person. It should be noted that amount of landholding is not the only criterion for such categorization. Among the two landless households, one has been kept in the category of Rangech, while the other one bas been considered to be a middle class one. Other factors like livestock, to some extent quality of land are taken into consideration. But a very important factor is human resource. If there are a few able bodied persons in a family who can regularly go for wage earning, they can compensate for small holding of land. In case a person of the household employed in some salaried job in some organized sector, the household would experience some affluence in comparison to other households with similar resource base.

The Santal villagers rarely count their income and expenditure. Book keeping is done by one household only, where the head of the household is a school teacher. So for purpose of categorizing households economically, measurement in terms of income expenditure is not attempted by them. They count accumulation of wealth with help of certain manifestations. Thatching of roof by burnt clay tiles instead of straw is one such marker. When tiles are replaced with corrugated galvanized iron sheet, a household can definitely be considered *kishar*. When a single storeyed mud house becomes *kotha bari* or two storeyed, it definitely speaks of some affluence.

The wealthiest households command some respect from their co-villagers. The major motive behind showing such respect is that, these households, with their surplus income, can come to help the neighbours in hours of distress. In traditional village council of the Santals, no berth was kept for the wealthy ones. In recent years, we can see that berth has been created in the village council in recognition of their economic status. However, dependence on wealthy people for procuring loan has become less after introduction of irrigation and generation of employment almost round the year.

Political Differentiation

The most important person in a Santal village is the Majhi Haram, the village headman. Whenever a village was established, the senior-most member of the pioneer family becomes the first incumbent of the post. This post is hereditary, ensuring a special status for the family in the village. This headman heads the village council also. He is assisted by several other office bearers, who are; *Jog majhi*, one who is the moral guardian of the village youth, the *godet* or the messenger, who is on employment of the village council and is paid his salary in kind once in a year by the villagers; the *naeke* or the village priest, he is chosen by the gods for the post through a session of trance; *kudam naeke* is the assistant priest. The full body of village council is known as *sholo ana*, and is consisted of all adult Santal males of the village.

It has been noted that areas, where there is a sizeable Santal population and there are a number of mono-ethnic Santal villages, village councils still exist. Datarampur, the village under study, is situated in such an area where the Santals live in multi-ethnic villages, in close proximity with many other ethnic groups. In such villages the village councils often take a different shape.

The Datarampur village council is headed by the majhi, who also acts as naeke. There is no kudam naeke in this village. There are incumbents to the other two posts of Jog majhi and godet. There is one more post in the council, that of the *bhaddo*. Nobody could state clearly the specific function of bhaddo. He has certain roles to play when there is a marriage or some other social function in the village. The bhaddo then receives important guests on behalf of the villagers. The first bhaddo of Datarampur was a person who was the wealthiest among the Santals in his times. He had enough surplus cereals, which he gave others on loan and earned interest. He had clients among Santals as well as among Mahatos and other non-Santals in the vicinity and was addressed as Mahajan. Afterwards, bhaddo became a hereditary post, male primogeniture being the rule of succession. It can be conjectured that the post came into existence to recognize the economic status of the mahajan socially. The probable root of the term bhaddo is bhadra, meaning gentleman.

The majhi of a Santal village commands respect from his co-villagers almost unconditionally. Whatever be his personal attributes, he is the most respected person of the village by virtue of his post. However, leadership quality is counted. One particular majhi of a certain village in the area was found to be young, without much experience and lacking in jural acumen. However, he is never shown any disrespect in the village council meetings for his observations. Fact remains that in meetings the sholo ana gets the view of the majority approved. On the other hand one majhi of another village, who is endowed with many leadership qualities and finer judicial senses, has the advantage that he can get the sholo ana to support his views with less persuasion.

The Santals had elaborate system of social control beyond the village level. A cluster of villages formed a territorial unit of 'pargana' with one Parganait to look after the temporal affairs of its residents. The supreme authority used to be the hunting council, consisting of all Santal adult males assembled at Ajodhya hills in Purulia district on the occasion of the annual hunting festival. No effective office of Parganait is in existence in the area under study. If there is any inter-village dispute, the majhi of concerned villages confer. If the dispute concerns the whole tribe, an assembly of as many majhis as possible discuss the matter. These days the term Parganait is often used to designate people well conversant in customary law. Such persons, even if they are not holding any official post, are consulted by the majhis. Such persons are considered to be among the most respected ones.

Another group of persons are honoured for their expertise. They are the narrators of mythological tales, known as gurus. A guru and his companions are invited to narrate mythologies on occasions of Karam puja or funeral rites. Culshaw studied the Santals of southern part of Bankura district about half a century ago. He reported that it was the job of the village headman to memorize the tales and narrate the same on appropriate occasions. Culshaw could find very few headmen apt in performing the role and he apprehended that both the tales and the art of narration would die out (1949). It seems the emergence of these gurus, the expert narrators, is rather recent. It has helped to revive and reinstate the Santal oral tradition.

Nascent Stratification Caused by Culture Contact

The Santals have come into contact with many communities for long and have exchanged many items of culture with them. However, they guarded certain cultural items very cautiously and kept them as intact as possible. These were such items which served as identity markers for them. This attitude gave rise to an image of the Santal as a conservative in matters of culture. The Santals almost never accepted any alien element into their culture unconditionally and en masse. Often, new elements were accepted, if those were at all accepted, by a few persons amongst them. Thus, partial acceptance and assimilation of such elements gave rise to some internal differentiation amongst them in terms of such culture change. We have discussed how the social divisions of the Santal have been affected by the Hindu Varna system and how this has triggered a sense of stratification among the people. In fact, certain elements of Hinduism have affected individuals or family units and these have influenced the statuses of the concerned persons. The neighbouring ethnic groups of the areas treat the Santals in the same bracket with the 'lowly castes', the Jal-achal ones. In retaliation, in general, the Santals avoid inter-dining with any of them. Violation of the taboo could degrade a person ritually. Nowadays this rule has been relaxed. The Santal males accept cooked food from almost anybody. The females are however somewhat traditionalist. They accept only uncooked food from other castes and still feel inter-dining with others should be avoided. In the studied village however, the Santal women have broken the rule in relation to the Mahatos, with whom they have stayed for long as good neighbours. There are some Santal folk performances which may appear degrading from the Hindu perspective. The Santals kill cow for beef by the hitting on its head.

The Santal have responded positively towards the facilities of formal education, though in a limited way. There are some Santal men and women who have passed high school examination or are graduates. A section of them reside in their native village and often teach at school. Then there are some who have salaried jobs and stay at their respective working place, towns or cities away from home. Such educated persons, it was felt from the opinion of the elderly villagers do not command any additional respect for the fact that they are educated. In comparison, a person who is well versed in customary laws but cannot read a letter is more respected. The educated ones get alienated from the people as they think of their own betterment only. One elder commented that the educated persons are like burnt clay pots. They have come from the earth but now they are different and cannot go back to earth easily.

References

Culshaw, W.J. 1949, *Tribal Heritage: A Study of the Santals,* London: Butterworth Press.

Mallick, S.K. 1993, *Transformation of Tribal Society: Prelude to Jharkhand,* Calcutta: Minaria Associates.

10 Economic Discrimination, Social Exclusion and Caste Hierarchy

The Mahalis of West Bengal

S. Chanda

This paper provides the analysis of village based caste system and place of Mahali tribe in it. The Mahalis are traditional bamboo workers. They are an endogamous tribe, but they share common surnames with the Santals and even their languages have a great affinity. The Mahalis are scattered unevenly in West Bengal in the districts of Jalpaiguri (13,098), Medinipur (5,538), West Dinajpur (2,103), 24-Parganas (1,575), Malda (1,327) and Burdwan (1,100). The bulk of the population is concentrated in Jalpaiguri and Medinipur. Dalton (1972, 1978), Russel and Hiralal (1916) and Grierson (1904) considered the Mahalis as one of the derivates of mixed origin. Risley (1891, 1915) regards the Mahalis as a Dravidian people and also a branch of the Santals separated comparatively at a recent date from the original stock. It is possibly based on the fact that both these communities have got a few common totemistic clans. Risley however, assumes that the Mahalis are excluded for the adoption of bamboo work as a new occupation, which the Santals consider as degrading. Even today, the Santals never consider the Mahalis as equal and treat them as 'socially low-grade' group in day-to-day interactions. The Mahalis have been divided into five sub-groups namely: (1) Bansphor Mahali who make baskets and do all kinds of bamboo work; (2) Pator Mahali who are basket makers and labourers; (3) Sulunkhi Mahali who are cultivators and labourers; (4) Tanti Mahali who carried palanquins and (5) Mahali Munda.

The Mahalis of West Bengal are mainly concentrated in Medinipur district of West Bengal. This district has an area of 3,208.5 square miles. The name Medinipur was given by Meddini Kar, a chieftain of the thirteenth century and author of a Sanskrit text called Medinikosh. In the east and north of Medinipur district the dialect commonly spoken is Bengali. In central Medinipur the dialect is the variety classified by Grierson as south-western Bengali, which in the southwestern part shades off into Odia. A form of Odia is spoken in the south of the district,. It is also spoken in the west of the district. In 1891, the number of persons speaking Odia returned as 5,72,796 and in 1901 as 2,70,495.

Ethnic and Linguistic Classification of Region

Apart from Brahmins, Kayasthas, Bagdis, Bauris, there are few other castes whose predominance in the district is seen. A brief ethnographic account of the communities follows. Local tradition states that the Kaibarttas or fisherman originally settled on the banks of the river Sarju or Gogri in Oudh, and that they came to Medinipur, led by five chiefs and conquered it. The Kaibarttas of Medinipur are subdivided into two sub-castes, the Uttar Rarhi and the Dakshin Rarhi, the latter being again subdivided into four classes, called Lalchatai, Ekside, Doside and Makunda. The Lalchatai, the highest of the clans, appears to be of hypergamous origin. It is explained that they used to have a red mat to sit on, as a mark of social distinction, at the meetings of the Kaibartta caste. The next two names are of middle strata. The Tuntias or Tutias are a Muslim caste whose traditional occupation is the cultivation of the mulberry tree (tunt) for feeding silk worms. Now they have taken to ordinary cultivation and field labour, while some do rope making. Males of the ordinary Ajlaf class will usually eat with Tuntias (Mitra, 1952).

The Mahalis speak their own language, which is akin to Santali. But they are now adapting the languages of the areas inhabited by them. In 1931 Census Report of West Bengal, it is mentioned that the Mahalis are almost completely a Bengalized people, retaining some of their original dialect terms. Gait notes that the Mahalis are mainly found in Chotanagpur, Santal Pargana and Odisha state and their language is 'Mahli' but many also speak Hindi. He also stated that 'Mahali' appears to be a dying language. Grierson opined that 'Mahli' and 'Karmali' are almost identical to the Santali language.

Among themselves, the Mahalis of Midinipur speak in Mahali language which they term as 'Thare', which is more or less similar to the Santali language. They know Bengali, Odia and to some extent Santali language. They are found to communicate with their own people as well as with other castes and tribes in Mahali, Santali, Bengali and Odia.

Village-Study

Two villages, which were taken up for study, are Changoal of Kharagpur Police Station and Sarisa of Narayangarh Police Station of Medinipur district. The Mahalis live in multi-ethnic villages where several communities live together. Some of the villages are also entirely inhabited by the Mahalis. In every village, there are a few public or sacred places like the Jaherthan (sacred grove) of the Bongas and deities like Dharam (God of righteousness), Garam (village tutelary deity) etc., and generally a virgin grove or a big tree in the village is kept reserved as the sanctuary of the deities, Dharam and Garam. The Mahalis live in separate hamlets. There are a few privately owned ponds used for domestic purposes by some well-to-do Mahalis. The villages awfully lack even the most minimum sanitary arrangements. The paddy fields, or any open space thickly covered with bamboo groves are used for morning evacuation by males and females of the village.

As regards, modern resources, mention may be made of the rural health and midwifery centres located in the villages. The midwife occasionally visits the houses of the Mahalis when called during childbirth and often the Mahalis get medicine free of cost from the local health centre. The Block Development Department near the villages helps the Mahalis in various ways, offering doles, industrial loans and loans for cattle.

Demographic Aspect

Table 1

Village, Castes and Tribes Family Number and Population

Name of caste/ community	*No. of family*	*Total population*	*Land quantity (acres)*	*Per family landholding*	*Ritual Status*
Village: Changoal	*(a)*	*(b)*	*(c)*	*(d)*	*(e)*
Mahali	31	132	19.00	0.62	Adi*
Brahmin	10	105	103.50	10.35	CL**
Kayastha	36	216	96.00	2.66	CL
Sadgop	56	410	126.00	2.25	CL
Tanti	12	58	82.00	6.83	CL
Santal	70	340	24.00	3.43	Adi
Total	215	1261	450.50	2.09	

* Adi – Adivasi, CL** – clean caste

Table 2

Pattern of Land Ownership

Name of caste/ community	*No. of family*	*Total population*	*Land quantity (acres)*	*Per family landholding*	*Ritual Status*
Village: Sarisa	*(a)*	*(b)*	*(c)*	*(d)*	*(e)*
Mahali	37	140	7.50	0.20	Adi*
Napit	4	16	4.50	0.28	CL**
Kamar	14	56	16.00	1.14	CL
Hari	36	89	18.00	0.50	UCL***
Dom	26	107	17.00	0.65	UCL
Munda	55	139	32.00	0.58	Adi
Dhopa	7	40	8.00	1.14	UCL
Bagdi	42	180	31.00	0.76	UCL
Total	221	767	135.00	0.61	

*Adi – Adivasi; CL** – clean caste; UCL*** – unclean caste

The total population of the Mahalis in West Bengal, according to Census of 1971 was 47,247 among whom 23, 928 are males and 23,319 females; and in 1981 Census it is 50,288 of whom 25,474 are males and 24,814 females. The total population of two villages is 2,028 and 436 families having land 585.50 acres, which gives us a picture of per capita land holding with 1.30 acres. The total families of Mahalis are 272 distributed in 68 families having total land of 26.50 acres only.

The following Table shows the total strength according to sex and age group wise population of the Mahalis in the villages that were studied.

Table 3

Sex and Age Group-wise Population of the Mahalis of Changoal and Sarisa Villages

Age group	Male	Percentage	Female	Percentage	Total	Percentage
0–4	17	6.25	14	5.15	31	11.40
5–9	17	6.25	24	8.82	41	15.07
10–14	9	3.31	15	5.51	24	8.82
15–19	7	2.57	10	3.68	17	6.25
20–24	13	4.78	18	6.62	31	11.40
26–29	13	4.78	18	6.62	31	11.40
30–34	16	5.88	15	5.51	31	11.40
35–39	13	4.78	7	2.57	20	7.35
40–44	5	1.84	6	2.21	11	4.04
45–49	4	1.47	4	1.47	8	2.94
50+	16	5.88	11	4.04	27	9.93
Total	130	47.79	142	52.20	272	

From the Table 3 it is revealed that out of 272 total populations of two villages the percentage of female is higher (52.20%) than male (47.79%). Traditionally people in between the age 15–50 years 89 (32.7%) females and 87 (31.9%) males respectively are regarded as main working force of the village.

Education and Social Change

Education is an important factor inducing change in society. The Mahalis in the studied villages are found to be educated to a certain extent. A very few of them have completed secondary school education. Some of them have read upto Class VIII. Previously, the Mahalis did not encourage their children to have education, and now they send their children irrespective of their sex to primary and secondary schools. There are only three boys of Changoal village studying in Secondary school. Except a few, all the Mahali children above the age of five are regularly attending the village primary school. No Mahali boy or girl is found to study in college. In every Mahali village there is one primary school and in some villages there are middle schools also which impart education upto Class IV and Class VIII respectively. Children of all castes and communities study in these schools . There is no college in the village itself.

The villagers are imparted with adult education in the village itself, where classes are held in the evening. In Changoal village primary school, the teachers from Changoal village are A. Ray of Sadgope caste and Raitan Singh of Munda community. No Mahali teacher is found in the village. The other teachers in the village primary and middle schools are from surrounding villages and from other places. They come from different communities. The Mahalis are found to maintain interaction with the teachers of different castes and communities outside school hours. In general, they discuss the developmental activities, political as well as educational matters. There is a 'Nirakshar Durikarau School' held at the community hall where the Mahali teachers teach caste members in the morning as well as in the evening. The teachers are Gita Rani Mahali, Sandha Rani Mahali and Tarapada Mahali from Changoal village. In Changoal Anchal there are fourteen primary schools of standard IV and two middle schools of standard VIII. The high schools are outside the village and there are three such schools in the Anchal. Colleges are at Kharagpur and Midinipur town. It is interesting to note that in the two villages out of a total of 130 males, only 42 males (15.4%) in the age group 15–25 have attended the local schools. Among females in the same age group 15 (5.5%) have attended the school in the village.

Other Factors of Social Change

The transport facilities, though not sufficient, cannot be said to be inadequate in all the villages. The nearest market where the villagers can sell their local produce is held within the radius of 3 to 11 km. It is sometimes held weekly and some times bi-weekly. The Mahalis attend this market every week to sell their commodities and also to purchase their requirements. The villagers, who have bullock-carts, prefer to use these for carrying their produce in large quantities. For small quantities they carry the loads on head or a long elastic bamboo stave exclusively used for carrying load – the stave is carried on the shoulder, as it is convenient for them. Apart from these markets the villagers have to depend upon the village shops and peddlers who occasionally visit the villages for selling utensils, cloths, shoes and other necessities of life. The barter system is also prevalent and is often practised by the Mahalis.

The villages have Panchayats consisting of village people represented through caste members and tribal members, and the Mahalis are also represented in the Panchayats.

The Mahalis are non-vegetarian but they do not kill baraha (pig) and do not take its flesh. They do not eat fish like Boal and Guzar. They take locally available vegetables and pulses along with rice. Rice is their staple food. They take fruits on festive occasions. Milk is beyond their reach. They do not take sim (flat beans) in the month of Chaitra (March–April), mulo (radish) in the month of Magh (January–February), pumpkin in the months of Jaishtha (May–June) and Bhadra (August–September) and bel (wood fruit) in the month of Jaishtha. They chew *paan* (betel leaf), smoke mainly bidi and occasionally a cigarette, and take snuff. No change has as yet occurred in their food habit.

The Mahalis have small thatched huts straggling here and there. The huts have a rectangular groundplan, the four walls of which are constructed with bamboo splinters and poles placed vertically. Later these are plastered over with mud and cowdung. The framework of the roof is made of bamboo having two slopes. A special type of rope prepared from Sabai grass ties these. The straw bundles are placed on the framework all along the slopes for thatching. The majority of the huts have no windows, but a few holes nearly one foot in diameter on the walls of the hut serve the purpose of windows. These huts have generally one door with shutter. Most of the huts consist of one room each of which is used by them for all domestic purposes, right from childbirth to propitiation of ancestral spirits. They have no definite choice for orientation of the huts which are constructed in a sprawling fashion facing all sides and huddled together. A few comparatively better-off Mahali families have mud-built, straw thatched huts with more than one room. Their plinths are sufficiently raised from the ground and these are provided with a little window and a door with shutter. A few families have small kitchen gardens attached to the huts, including a small courtyard. In such cases, these courtyards are fenced with thorny bamboos to prevent intrusion of man or animal from outside, and it was found in the huts of a number of families in many villages. In most of the huts, the Mahalis do not make any separate arrangement for keeping cattle or goats. These animals are generally kept on one side of the verandah attached to the hut. Only in a few families there are separate cowsheds. Those who possess agricultural implements keep them in a covered place in the rear of the hut, but these are brought out to the front verandah and kept there as soon as the agricultural operations start.

Discussion

The Mahalis of Midinipur district live in multi-ethnic villages and they are in close contact with various Hindu castes in their day-to-day interactions. As a result of close contact, the Mahalis have accepted certain elements of Hindu caste culture like worshipping Hindu gods and goddesses, employing Hindu priest for their ritual activities. Despite such interactions with the caste Hindus in various activities, the Mahalis are conscious about their ethnicity.

The Mahalis who are economically somewhat well off and have some educational background and modern outlook, are hesitant to interdine and intermarry with others of their tribe. Here we see growth of specific economic classes among the people. This class consciousness is revealed in various spheres of life including marital relations. However, they may take daughters from lower strata but never give their daughters to families of lower strata.

In most of the villages, the Mahalis live in separate hamlet or in a separate 'Para' or lane, thus maintaining a distance from other castes and communities of the village. However, certain restrictions are imposed on the Mahalis in using the private water resources owned by high castes, sacred places belonging to higher castes and for using 'common' cremation/burial ground. Thus a distinction is made between high and low castes/communities in terms of pure and impure statuses and which is visualized in the utilization of certain amenities of the village. The Mahalis are regarded as a sort of 'lower caste' in the sphere of village-stratification.

Economic Structure

The Mahalis are bamboo workers and cultivators of paddy. However, they own small land plots. Paddy is the main crop. In the village ownership of land is taken as a measure of social status, which can be earned by wealth. Whenever a Mahali gets surplus finance he tries to invest in land. Majority of Mahalis are principally dependent on basketry, and cultivation is only a secondary occupation.

There are two factors, which force Mahalis to be dependent more on bamboo-work rather than agriculture. Firstly, they own very small amount of land which is unsuitable for their subsistence: indeed the production is not up to their minimum satisfaction. Further, agriculture requires not only capital but also concerted labour, for its development which is lacking among them.

Secondly, the Mahalis have not mastered the agricultural and technological knowledge for the cultivation of improved paddy seeds. Nevertheless, the Mahalis participate in agriculture in all possible ways as owner-cultivator, share-cropper, contract-cultivator and agricultural labourers of every kind. In return they receive good amount of paddy, which substantiates their lower income from basketry. The joint efforts of men and women of the family is used to cultivate paddy fields, when owned or taken in share basis. Women try to perform lighter work. Women perform the jobs of transplanting, weeding, harvesting, threshing, winnowing, together with men. They carefully transplant the young rice-shoots, spurn the shoots, pick the weeds. Women in groups are seen to reciprocate the work of one another in the fields. The most important operation is harvesting when men, women and children work together to complete the operation as early as possible.

Fowls, pigs, chickens, ducks and goats are important, primarily for religious sacrifices and secondarily as food items and mainly for entertainment of guests during feasts. Sacrifice plays a very important role in Mahali life. It is required for appeasement of deities and Bongas who occasionally send diseases in the form of epidemic when they are hurt by the offending acts of believers. The Mahalis keep good numbers of fowls and goats. Besides, livestock is also used as money. The diviners and the medicine men are paid through livestock. Sometimes commodities from the potter, weaver and articles of consumer's goods are purchased by selling livestock. In the elaborate system of lending, borrowing and sale, the animals are used by the Mahalis and other tribal and non-tribal lower castes as a chief negotiable property.

After harvesting and threshing which ends in January–February, the Mahalis again resort to bamboo work and invest the whole time for the production of baskets. Occasionally young adults go for hunting in groups. The game is scarce in the alluvial tract and in jungle areas. It is scarce as the forests of the region are reserved and all kinds of trespassing is penalized. As a result small birds and games of native varieties such as dove, wild goose, crane, squirrels, rabbits, and several other varieties are the main kill. The games are distributed among the participants. There are individualistic ways of catching games. Nets are spread across the trees to ensnare the bait.

Fish are abundant in the local ponds and streams and in the flooded paddy fields, during rainy season. Fish are caught both individually and collectively. In collective fishing, shares are distributed on the basis of number of participants. Men, women and children catch fish in small hand nets and traps. Anyone may go to any paddy field and pick as many as he can. The wealthy and poor equally catch fish from the paddy fields. Catches are mainly for family consumption and are scarcely sold.

Barter continues to have an important place in the economic system. Paddy or rice is paid for by labour in the agricultural fields. Baskets are sold to the villagers in exchange for salt, pulses, sugar, wheat, etc. Under the broad category of management and labour, two groups of people are mainly involved in the management of land and organization of production namely: (1) cultivating and new cultivating owners of land and (2) sharecroppers and agricultural labourers. The cultivating owners work directly on the land. In addition to their family labour, they also hire labourers depending on the intensity of their agricultural operations. The new cultivating owners cultivate their land by hiring plough and labourers.

The tenant cultivators or the sharecroppers are usually landless tenants who take others' land on sharecropping basis. Agricultural labourers work on others' land for wages. The wage may be daily, seasonal or annual contract. In few cases, the non-cultivation landowning castes have gradually started cultivating land by hiring plough. In such cases the owners keep some landless tenants and agricultural labourers on regular basis. The Mahali families who have some land, cultivate a part or entire holding under their direct control. In such cases they keep plough and other agricultural implements. They sometime even employ some agricultural labourers. In two villages we got only 56 males who were the agricultural labourers as well as non-agricultural labourers. Only seven families are cultivating owners of the fields, but all the families are also involved in basket making.

The share-croppers are locally known as *jotedaars*. However, land is generally given out to share-croppers on purely verbal contract. A share-cropper might take land from more than one owner and an owner may give his land to more than one sharecropper. The annual contract between a landowner and a sharecropper is sometimes for successive years. It all depend on the relations between the two. It is interesting to note that one can raise his status as a sharecropper from agricultural labourer by owning a plough and a pair of bullocks. If requires considerable efforts on his part to accumulate some money for acquiring plough and bullock, and for pursuing cultivation. In some cases, the landowners help the sharecroppers in acquiring plough and bullocks by giving them loan or by purchasing the same for them. The sharecroppers in return have to work for the land-owner in ploughing the latter's land. The situation is reversed when a sharecropper fails to perform his duties. He has no option but to leave the cultivation and to become an agricultural labour again.

The sharecropper sometimes ploughs other's land against cash payment. A plough operator on an average requires about six hours to plough per bigha of land. This is an extra source of income for the sharecroppers. During cultivation season there is a demand for this kind employment. The terms and conditions of agreements between the landowners and sharecroppers varies according to the condition of soil to be ploughed, paddy to be cultivated, area to be covered in cultivation, etc. Due to various psychological constraints and in view of greater demands between two partners, this system of sharecropping is not encouraged.

Agricultural labourers as a whole are called *majdoor* and there are three types of agricultural labourers found. These are: (1) Khot majdoor who are employed for the period of cultivation at rate of ₹ 30 to 40 per bigha of land. This apart, they get two meals and tiffin every day . About a bigha of land is given to each one of them for cultivation. The landowners supply them necessary inputs for cultivation. (2) Contract labourer/*tivla* majdoors are those who work under employers at a fixed rate for a specified period. They are not paid if works remain incomplete in the employer's field. The wages vary from ₹ 120 to 160 per work for cultivation of paddy over one bigha of land. (3) Day-time *labourer/din* majdoor is one who works on daily wage basis. The rate of wage varies according to the intensity of the agricultural operation. During fieldworks the wage rate is ₹ 30 to 40 per labourer per working day. Besides, cash labourers get food two times. They are supposed to work for 9 to 10 hours with a break for an hour for lunch. Though there is a locally standardized wage rate for the agricultural labourers, yet individual cases vary according to the personal negotiation as well as manipulation of the situation. The minimum wage for the agricultural labourers fixed by the government, i.e., Panchayat is about ₹ 40 per day.

Normally an agricultural labourer can get employment for field operations at the most for 7 to 8 months a year. The demand for labourers is not uniform throughout the year. Some men and women among the families of the agricultural labourers have other casual sources of income. For example, making of *morai/* for storing grain, stacking hay and thatching the roofs are some of the casual works from which the male labourers earn their livelihood for some days. Likewise female labourers can earn some paddy from their employer's house by winnowing the already thrashed out straw.

Table 4

Extended Grades of Occupation

Village	*Caste/ communities*	*Occupation*
Changoal	Mahali	Basketry, cultivation
	Brahmin	Priesthood
	Kayastha	Scribing, land- holding
	Sadgope	Landholder
	Tanti	Business
	Santal	Cultivator
Sarisa	Mahali	Basketry
	Napit	Barber
	Kamar	Blacksmith
	Hari	Sweeper
	Dom	Sweeper, basketry
	Munda	Cultivator
	Dhopa	Washerman
	Bagdi	Agricultural labour

Table 4A

Local Stratification of Occupations

Occupation	*Grade of occupation*
Priesthood	Highest
Scribing, landholding	Very high
Religious mendication	High
Business, trading	High
Barbering, blacksmithy	Low
Cultivation, basketry	Low
Washing of clothes	Low
Sweeping, midwifery	Lowest
Leather working	Lowest

Improved methods in cultivation and the other expenses have generated a sense of helplessness among a large number of small cultivators. They regard cultivation by improved methods being huge investment of money. In the past they used to depend mainly on their labour and bullocks and plough, indigenous technology and self chosen seeds. There are two major heads for which hard cash is required during cultivation – one is for payment of wage to the labourers and the other is for purchasing fertilizers, insecticides, improved variety of seed, hiring tractor, using tubewell, cooler and so on.

The channels of finance and temporary loans are threefold in the village, that is: (1) Agricultural co-operative society; (2) Private moneylenders; and (3) Local businessmen. Individual cultivators are more or less tied up with the local traders. They can get loans at any time from these people. Though they know that these traders or moneylenders

Table 4B

Comparative Status /Social Position of Communities: Villagers' Notion

Caste/communities (in 2 villages)	*Social position/status**	*Caste/communities (in 2 villages)*	*Social position/status**
Brahmin	1	Hari	4
Kayastha	2	Dom	4
Sadgope	2	Bagdi	4
Tanti	2	Santal	4
Napit	3	Munda	4
Kamar	3	Mahali	4
Dhopa	3		

1 – denotes highest; 2 – medium to high;
3 – low; 4 – lowest.
*(it is from Mahali point of view)

make heavy profits, yet they feel that this is the only assured source available to them from whom they can borrow money at any time without undergoing many formalities. For borrowing money from the co-operative bank /society, apart from the formal and legal procedures, the cultivators also have to clear their earlier dues which at times is not easy for them. But they can take loans any time from the private moneylenders with or without payment of the previous dues, knowing it fully that the moneylenders take full advantage of this situation.

Economic Differentiation

Considering all castes and communities in the two villages it is found that from the economics point of view, the villagers can be divided into following categories, namely: (1) Agricultural labourers; (2) Poor cultivators; (3) Middle

Table 5

Economic Differentiation among Villagers

Village	*No. of Families*	*Agriculture & poor cultivators*	*Middle cultivators*	*Rich cultivators*	*White-colla r jobs*	*Others*
Changoal	Mahali (31)	31	—	—	—	—
	Brahmin (10)		4	2	3	1
	Kayastha (36)	4	12	6	10	4
	Sadgope (56)	12	16	7	16	5
	Tanti (12)	4	3	—	5	—
	Santal (70)	36	14	4	10	6
Sarisa	Mahali (37)	37	—	—	—	—
	Napit (4)	1	—	—	—	3
	Kamar (14)	7	—	—	—	7
	Hari (36)	8	—	—	—	28
	Dom (26)	6	—	—	—	20
	Munda (55)	15	—	—	—	40
	Dhopa(7)	2	—	—	—	5
	Bagdi(42)	22	—	—	—	20
	Total	185	49	19	44	139

cultivators; (4) Rich cultivators; and (5) white-collar employees. The Mahalis of both the villages, belong to the poor cultivators category but by combining basketry with cultivation they are aspiring and claiming the middle economic group. Table 5 shows Mahali families as poor cultivators but many among them had emerged as middle cultivators. In some villages in the vicinity the Mahalis had emerged as rich cultivators.

Thus, we see that out of 436 families 185 belong to agricultural labourers and poor cultivators category; 49 belong to middle cultivators and 44 have white-collar jobs, 139 are engaged in other economic pursuits and only 19 are rich cultivators having 5 acres of own land.

In Mahali society family groups compete among themselves for maximization of productive ends. Interfamilial cooperation occurs when necessity demands. Despite a limited range of co-operation the behavioural characteristic of Mahali economic relations may be called competitive. Each family competes with one another in processing the basketry, for greater participation in agriculture and the like.

The Mahali economic system is influenced by environmental as well as cultural factors. Land is limited. Those who possess land scarcely have enough finance to adopt new technologies to increase yield. Hence, they are forced to borrow from the local landowners, moneylenders, and basket-traders at exorbitant interest-rate. The rate of interest varies form 10 to 50 per cent. The amount of loan goes on mounting every year. Hence most of the families are indebted. Besides, there are many other causes, which lead to economic crisis. Apart from small holding and landlessness, crop failure affects most badly those who cultivate on contract basis (Sanja). The lack of sensible use of paddy and overexpenses during feast and festivities, illness, marriage ceremony and such other expenses also forces them below the level of subsistence.

Most of the families are nuclear in size with two to three working individuals. Bamboo work has three steps: (a) procuring of bamboo and its sizing and splitting; (b) scraping and weaving of the baskets; and (c) disposal of the products. All families are engaged in bamboo works. As such interfamilial amity turns into interfamilial rivalry and antagonism.

Discussion

The Mahalis are traditionally bamboo basket makers but also practise agriculture to some extent. It is seen that their little possession of cultivable land as well as landlessness force them to cultivate land either as tenants or as sharecroppers as also as agricultural labourers, though each family is involved in basket making as a major occupation. Their basket making technology is simple and marketing of their products is normally linked with middlemen known as Diku and who take away portion of income belonging to Mahalis.

Social Structure

Clan System and Clan Ranking

The Mahali clan is patrilineal. The Mahalis call it 'Jati' which means a closed group, the membership of which can be attained only by birth. The Mahali clan names conform to some local varieties of plants and animals. The special relations to totems shows the identity and the unity of the clan. Each clan has a totem and certain strict taboos are observed with regard to chosen animal. Marriage within the same clan is strictly prohibited. After marriage girls are initiated into the respective clans of their husbands. Some clans have several sub divisions, which are marked by differences in their behavioural patterns. It is to be noted here that the Mahalis share ten clan names with the Santals, the dominant tribal group of the area. Three clans are of separate origin. The 13 clans of Mahalis are: Baske/Kanti (vegetable), Besra (hawk), Hansda (wild goose), Hembrem (arecanut), Kisku (kingfisher), Mandi (blue bird), Murmu (an animal), Soren (a constellation), Todu (ground rat), Chori (lizard), Samah (a kind of grass), Pirhi (round pumpkin), and Khangar (jackdaw). In the studied villages we came across, some clans which are uniformly distributed among 68 families of both the villages such as Baske (5), Besra (8), Kisku (8), Soren (8), Todu (8), Mandi (9), Hembrem (7), Murmu (5), Khangar (8).

Table 6
Subdivisions of Clans

Clans	*Subdivision*
Mandi	(a) Sada Mandi
	(b) Mur
Kisku	(a) Sada Kisku
	(b) Kisku
Soren	(a) Sak
	(b) Sadup
Besra	(a) Sada
	(b) Besra
	(c) Bital
Hembrem	(a) Gua
	(b) Sada
	(c) Bital

It is reported that certain clans have sub divisions as mentioned in Table 6, whereby certain stratification is maintained and observed while negotiating marriage alliances. The concept of high and low is distinguished on the basis of ritual purity criterion. However, at the operational level stratification is not maintained so strictly.

In reality it is very difficult to differentiate between higher and lower sub divisions and higher and lower clans, except 'Sada' subdivision, which is treated as a 'higher one'. But in respect of other subdivisions, the Mahalis find it difficult to make differentiation. Stratification on the basis of clan is not prominent among the Mahalis but it is notional. Instances, however, are noted where people are ranked socially higher and lower on the basis of their clan affiliations. For example, clans like Samah, Pirhi and Khangar, which do not have similarities with the clans of Santals, are considered as low. We may say that a general distinction is made among certain clans of Mahalis in terms of higher and lower. The officials of Mahali tribal council and religious officials are always elected from certain higher tribal clans. For example, the village headman is selected from the Mandi clan. The deputy headman is always selected from Baske clan while the assistant headman is mostly selected from Besra clan. These preferences are generally common everywhere.

Family

Family Size

Family among the Mahalis is a residential unit having communal relations and common economic resources, the members of which take food in common.

Family size is often variable. The size of family shrinks when children grow up and break away from their parents to establish their own conjugal units. There are other factors that expand or limit family size, by birth and death. Some families having no children, resort to adoption of children from outside the family. Cases of polygamy, incorporation of Ghar Jawai, splitting of couple due to quarrel, adoption of children and death affect the size of family. Among Mahalis out of 68 families 37 are nuclear 17 are extended and 12 are joint families. The smallest family consists of two persons and the largest of 13 individuals. Hence, the family size here ranges from 2 to 13 persons.

Family Types

Among the Mahalis the average family size is approximately 5.4 persons per family. Hence, it can be concluded that families are mostly medium-sized. Generally, there are four types of families. Frequency of elementary or simple family is highest among the Mahalis, nearly 64.60 per cent. Intermediate family is found in appreciable number (20.05%) and joint or extended family is small in number (9.90%). The polygamous family is exceedingly small in percentage (5.45%). The process of nuclearization starts when sons leave their father or brothers separate after the death of the father.

Birth

The Mahalis believe without any hesitation that cohabitation between men and women results in conception, and sterility is attributed to some supernatural agencies. In Mahali perception the Bongas are also responsible for the conception. Women only become fertile after they reach maturity. Their husbands sometimes consult the Ojhas or medicinemen to find out the causes of barrenness. When the Ojha fails to determine the cause, he simply ascribes it to the will of the Bongas.

Old Mahalis consider that barrenness has increased appreciably compared with earlier days. They attribute this partly to the widespread practice of adultery. Their contention is that adulterous intercourse with many men spoils a woman's capacity for bearing child, and the wrath of the Bongas intermingle with this. There are various other supernatural influences which prevent conception, according to Mahali belief. These are witchcraft, curses of relatives and influences of dissatisfied Bongas and ancestors.

At the time of delivery, generally a Hadi (Scheduled Caste) woman, is asked to render her service as the midwife. In case of delayed birth or difficult birth, a Gunni or Ojha, spirit-finder or a local doctor is called by the Mahalis. There is practically no scope for setting apart a confinement-room because the majority of the Mahalis possess a small hut of a single room, without any additional space to allot for this purpose.

Marriage

"A wife is a necessity", goes a Mahali saying. She bears children, takes care of the household, cooks food, prepares baskets and helps her husband in agricultural operations. The bride and the groom in many cases remain quite unknown to each other before their marriage. When marriages are arranged by the parents and close relatives, they prefer possession of a few good qualities among the boy and the girl. The girl should be hardworking, expert in cooking, a willing housekeeper and a helper in economic activities, restrained in behaviour, chaste, obedient, amiable and further, a bit attractive and her parents should be of good ancestry and good character.

Marriage Prohibitions and Payments

The Mahalis prohibit marriage among certain categories of relatives. Marriage within the same clan groups and immediate kin groups is strictly prohibited. There is also prohibition on marriage with blood-kins and with close classificatory relations, even between the children of two ceremonial friends (Fuloin) who call and consider themselves as brothers (Bokoin Kora) and sisters (Bokoin Kuni). A man may marry one of his wife's relations of the same generation . He may also marry the widow or divorced wife of any of his elder male consanguine relatives of the same generation.

Tribal endogamy is strictly maintained by the Mahali. In certain cases, union between cross-cousins takes place incidentally, though it is not considered as an offence. Marriage of this type is exceedingly rare amongst the Mahalis. Such marriage is never arranged by the family members, but takes place as a result of 'Aur-apar' or 'Tena', that is application of vermilion on the forehead of the girl by force, or by 'Angir', that is elopement.

Marriage generally takes place when boys and girls are comparatively adult. Girls marry at the age between 16 and 20 years and boys between 20 and 25.

Payment of bride price in cash and presentation of sarees (women's clothes) are important aspect of Mahali marriage. The transaction of bride price confirms the marriage contract; though the boy and the girl are recognized as husband and wife with the solemnization of marriage. The bride price is called 'Bapla gonong', which literally means' marriage money.

The amount of bride price varies according to the economic condition of the groom's father. The bride price in the Mahali society generally varies from ₹ 250 to 500, which is settled during the negotiation and paid in cash, along with three pieces of clothes (female wear) for Yo (mother), Dai (bride's elder sister) and Bahu (bride). The amount of bride price is mutually settled by the groom's father and bride's father

The boy's father kills a goat during the first visit of the bride's party for negotiation and offers them a feast. The girl's father also kills a goat for the entertainment of his guests when the groom's party visits his house.

Half of the bride price is handed over to the bride's father when the bride's party visits the groom's house for fixing the date of marriage. This is the bride price agreement. The contractual obligations begin with the first payment of the bride price. In certain cases of betrothal, the payment of bride price may be made in instalments to be paid within a period of one to three years, in accordance with the economic condition of the bridegroom, and the relative age of the bride.

It was observed that sometimes the wives desert their husbands and temporarily live with their lovers. In such cases, the deserted husbands try to get back the bride price they already paid. In Mahali marriage, payment of bride price entitles the husband to some rights, e.g., an exclusive right of sexual relationship with his wife, certain powers for controlling her activities, rights to employ her for economic services, matched by his own economic obligation to her, and the right of fatherhood of her children. The extent and duration of these rights depends largely on the stability of marriage. The husband, in turn is obliged to provide the wife and the children with food, clothing and housing. He must give her sexual satisfaction and take care of her during illness. He must obtain her consent if he wishes to take an additional wife. If a Mahali is asked to explain the significance of this custom of paying bride price, he says that it enables men to obtain wives.

The custom of paying bride price prevalent amongst the Mahalis has both economic and non economic elements as stated above. The payment of bride price serves the important social functions such as the fostering alliance between the respective kinship groups of the husband's and wife's families and legalizes and stabilizes marriage.

Marriage Types

There are at least seven types of marriage or method to get a wife. The most popular type is the marriage arranged or negotiated by the families concerned, which is known as 'Bapla'.

The initiative for negotiation may be taken by either of the families concerned, but usually the boy's parents make the first approach. A boy may express his choice to his parents. Sometimes, the relatives (father's brothers, mother's brothers, elder sister's husband) act as a 'go between' (Raibar). The girl's elder brother (Marang boyha) has some authority over her with regard to her marriage, and so his consent is usually necessary before a marriage. Before the marriage the groom's relatives go in a small group to the girl's parents for fixation of the bride price (Bapla gonong). A feast is held by killing a goat or a fowl to entertain the guests during this visit, which makes the proposal for the marriage valid. The girl's relatives are invited to pay a return visit after the bride price has been settled. They go to the groom's house to finalize the negotiation and on that day, half of the bride price is handed over to the bride's father. A similar feast is arranged to entertain the bride's party. Another feast is held on the marriage day to entertain the invitees. Though the Mahalis have no fixed convention for offering or receiving presents, the bride's relatives usually present household equipments to her, and the groom's relatives present the bride's clothing, garments, etc. These customs are recently adopted by Mahalis from Hindu neighbours.

Another practice in vogue amongst the Mahalis is called 'digosha' or 'Duar Lebet'. In this case, the parents of the groom take the bride to their house promising to pay the bride price, in due course, at the time of celebration of the marriage. A feast is held by killing a goat or fowl in the house of the bridegroom's parents, in which relatives and villagers of both the parties join as witness to the marriage. Sometimes the bride becomes pregnant before the actual marriage ceremony, but this does not stand in the way of her getting married.

The third type of marriage is called 'Ghar mechrano' or marriage by intrusion. The bride forcibly stays in the groom's house, where she is generally ill-treated by groom's parents and relatives. If she can still remain firm in her desire and tolerate such ill-behaviour calmly and with patience, she is finally accepted as wife of the groom.

The fourth means of getting mates is marriage by elopement or 'Angir' or marriage by force that is 'Aurapar' or 'Tana'. The boy and the girl run away to the house of one of their relatives or friends, where the boy puts on vermilion mark on the forehead of the girl. When this occurs the girl's parents go to the boy's parents and disclose the incident. Later on, the marriage is solemnized with the payment of the bride price. Marriage 'Aur-apar' or 'Tana' also takes place when the boy forcibly rubs vermilion on the girl's forehead and the parting of the hair, either in paddy field or in any solitary place.

The fifth type of securing mates is known as 'Sanga' or remarriage of a widow or divorced woman. Sanga is less costly and the usual marriage rites are not observed. Only the permission of the village elders and neighbours of the families involved and the consent of the bride are necessary. The bride price is less than the price paid in other types of marriages. Sometimes when the parents or brothers of the widowed or divorced girl cannot find her any suitable bride-groom for remarriage, she is given to a selected man by the father or brother as a gift or 'Dan'. In such case, the groom is exempted from paying the bride price.

Courtship or mutual consent 'Raji Khusi' or 'Nirboloona' is another way of getting a wife. Here the young people often choose their own mates and inform their parents at a future date. The procedures of marriage in this type are similar to Bapla.

The seventh type of marriage involves making the groom 'Ghar Jawie' or resident son-in-law. The bridegroom thus remains in the house of the bride's parents after marriage, and is called 'Ghar Jawie'. The parents of the groom in such cases do not expect any support from their married son, whose primary obligations are shifted to his parents-in-law. In this case, the bridegroom's father is exempted from paying the bride price. The bride's father usually keeps a 'Ghar Jawie' if he has no male heir, or the male heir is a child. Although the 'Ghar Jawie' leaves his parents after his marriage, his relation with the members of his family and right of inheritance of his father's property do not come to an end. He gets an inferior status in the Mahali society, but can lawfully inherit the parental property.

Temporary unions, of course, occur in the Mahali society, but Mahalis do not recognize these as conventional marriages, as mentioned earlier. Illicit and casual unions are becoming serious problems in recent times in Mahali society. Divorce is quite easy in Mahali society. Any one of the partners may bring a complaint and after hearing in the Bichar Sava, divorce is permitted on sufficient grounds. Major causes of divorce are adultery, barrenness or sterility and incompatibility.

Death

The bodies of the dead are both buried and burnt. Children below five years of age, death due to epidemic diseases and dead body of leper are usually buried. The Mahalis have their separate burial or cremation ground known as Sasan. During cremation or burial all the belongings of the deceased are cremated or buried. The utensils of brass or any other objects of high price are auctioned in the cremation ground. Excepting the relatives and clan members of the deceased, anybody can purchase these things. Purificatory ritual is observed after ten days when the relatives of the deceased shave and take purificatory bath.

After death they observe a pollution period of 13 days. They go to a nearby river bank (ghat) for shaving and giving pinda to the deceased with the help of a Brahmin priest. This is called 'ghat sraddha'. On the fourteenth day they arrange a feast for the relatives and friends and this ceremony is called Aushumukti (coming out from the vegetarian food taking). During the pollution period the sons take only hobissy (rice along with some vegetables boiled in an earthenware pot). They also perform the 'sradh'. They have to do annual 'sradh' which is called 'bachharki'.

Discussion

Hinduization process has affected the Mahalis to a great extent. The Mahalis of the present day do not consider themselves socially inferior like Muchi, Hari, Dom, though in reality, they have no position in the social hierarchy. It is interesting to note that many Mahalis have developed a tendency to discard their clan names and changed their surnames akin to local Hindu castes. For example, members of clan Hansda use surname Hanti, members of clan Mandi use surname as Mondal, clan Besra has become Bera. All these surnames are the adoptions from the local Hindu cultivator castes like Mahishya. It may be noted here that the Mahalis in the past used their clan names as their surnames. Due to contact with neighbouring Hindu castes, and through sanskritization a tendency of adopting Hindu caste surnames is noticed among the present day Mahalis of some areas of Midinipur.

Despite Hindu contacts no specific ritual status is enjoyed by Mahalis. Mahalis however make distance from most Scheduled Castes. Thus certain stratification is maintained in respect of castes and communities who are considered lower in social position to Mahalis. Certain food habits like eating of beef as well as certain types of job and customs like stripping off the skin of animals, carrying of night soil and so on were then taken into consideration by the Mahalis as the basis of stratification. Thus, Mahalis do not maintain any social or other sorts of interaction with the communities like Gorai, Hari, Dom, Methor, etc.

When a Mahali gets married outside his own community he is usually excommunicated by the members of the community and is socially boycotted for all purposes. Social exclusion is maintained here on the basis of notion of pure and impure. Those who marry outside the community are considered as 'impure' and inferior in social position. Among Mahalis as in other tribal communities, inter-community marriage is strictly prohibited and any sort of breach of social norms is great offence. A sharp line of distinction is made between offenders and non-offenders and as such social behaviours are also manifested accordingly.

The members of various tribes and castes have their scale of placement in respect of neighbouring communities. The Mahalis regard Ho, Munda, Kharia, Bedya and so on as socially inferior. But Santal enjoy superior position and status. On the other hand, Santals do not consider Mahalis 'equal', though the Mahalis share their clan names. Because of their food habits and customs, the Bagdi, Dom, Hari, Muchi and so on are not permitted to interact with the

Mahalis in any form as they are treated as socially low class of people. Conversely, the above referred communities consider Mahalis as 'tribe', having low status – so they do not maintain any sort of interaction with Mahalis since they consider themselves as 'superior'.

It is interesting to note that whatever may be differences all these communities interact with each other in normal way in rural transactions, in the field or in village social/cultural gatherings and even in crisis situation, without considering any social stigma attached.

Political Organization

The Mahali political organization at village level is facing disintegration due to modern forces of change, mainly because the political parties are now trying to control the members of statutory village council. However, the Mahalis have not changed completely in political-village-administrative matters. Hence traditional headmen are still respected. These tribal officials are:

(a) Manjhi Haram (headman)
(b) Paranik
(c) Gorait

The officials of Mahali tribal council are always selected from certain higher order clans. For example, the village headman is mostly selected from the Mandi clan. The deputy headman is selected from the Baske clan while assistant headman is selected from Besra clan.

It is seen that most villagers, the Mahali, prefer to approach traditional headmen for dispute settlement. One way of settling disputes is to lodge a complaint to the headman (Manjhi Haram), who settles the dispute after consultation with other Mahali council office bearers and the village elders. The elders sit with the office bearers and discuss about the matter of dispute. Both the persons involved in the dispute state their own versions of the case which is probed by the council members by questioning them to ascertain the facts and thereafter they declare their verdict on the dispute. The litigants accept the verdict of the council officials and the village elders. If there is any doubt about the facts, certain oaths are taken by the complainant and the defendant during their disposition. A decision cannot be taken unless there is unanimity of opinion amongst the council members. Disputes between members of nearby villages, among whom there are good social contacts and ties, can also be settled mutually by involving members of the Mahali council of each village, which often becomes difficult to do. Disputes are often settled by imposing fines, which may also include payment towards damages. Occasionally, the payment for damage is not collected easily from an offender hence sometimes there is use of physical force. At present there is a growing tendency to seek justice through the intervention of the police, by discarding tribal-council.

Religion

The Mahalis believe in mysterious powers possessed by certain objects, persons, spirits and deities. There are spirit doctors, witch finders called Ojhas or Gunnis who are able to exorcise these spirits and ghosts. Spirits or Bongas are differentiated or classified according to their attributes. Some of them thus are benevolent in nature such as Basumata (mother earth). Dharam (god of righteousness), Garam (the tutelary deity of the village), Sitla (goddess of epidemic diseases), Chandi (female forest deity), Mansa (goddess of snakes) and Haramko (ancestor spirit). The goddesses Sitla and Chandi are held in awe and respect because of their hot temper. They easily become angry even on account of minor negligence during their propitiation and they become beneficent, when appeased with the proper prayer, offerings and sacrifices. The malevolent spirits are Yugini or Sim Bonga who reside at the outskirts of the village and ghosts of lower order like Chirghuni, Baghot, Gomua, etc. There are experts who display both sacred and profane occult arts. They are known variously in Mahali society. The sacred specialists mainly exert their influence for the betterment of the Mahalis. Naoke, that is village priest performs all religious performances; Paranik assists the village priest; Rum, Gunni or Ojha perform functions of diviner, medicine man, soothsayer, spirit-harbourist, witch finder, etc. The sorcerer or the black magician practice black magic which is known as Ban or Singer. It causes illness or harm. The Dain or witch practises occult art.

There are a number of festivals prevalent in Mahali society. Festivals include the worship of their deities and spirits who are supposed to protect them from natural calamities. Magh Sim is a communal festival performed in the month of Magh (January–February). This is the festival of certain new fruit offerings. They believe that the observance of this festival protects them from epidemic diseases like small pox, cholera, etc. Fowl sacrifice is made to the deity named Dharam, Garam, Marangburu (hill god), Haramko and Yugini (goddess of epidemic diseases) as a token of respect. Baha festival is observed on the full moon day in the month of Phalgun (February–March). Offerings of flowers like Sal *(Shorea robusta)*, Polash *(Butea frondosa)*, and Mahua *(Madhuka latifolia)* are made to the deities. Likewise Asaria is performed in the month of Ashar (June–July) before the paddy seeds are sown. Dasai festival is observed in the month of Aswin (September–October) on the 8th day of the brighter half of the moon to avoid attack of evil eyes and evil spirits . This is held in honour of Goddess Durga. 'Nal Sakrat' is held in the month of Aswin (September–October) to feed 'sad' (the desired food) to Goddess Laxmi (goddess of wealth). Akhan festival is observed on the first day of the month of Magh (January–February) to express gratitude to God Dharam for good harvest. Sakrat is held in the month of Paus (December–January) and involves individual worship of Goddess Laxmi. The Mahalis like their caste neighbours also perform Tusu festival. Karam festival is performed on a new moon day in the month of Bhadra (August–September). Besides, the Mahalis also worship Lord Hari, Lord Satyanarayan (the truth incarnate) Viswakarma (the deity of technology) and Goddess Kali (goddess of strength). All of them belong to the Hindu religious pantheon.

Rituals of Cultivation

Unlike different upper castes who observe a number of rituals associated with agriculture, the Mahalis observe only a few rituals and ceremonies which have certain relevance to agricultural production. While the upper castes villagers perform rituals according to the lunar position in the Bengali calendar, the Mahali rituals do not always correspond with the Bengali calendar.

Table 7
Calendar of Village Festivals and Rituals

Month	*Festivals and Rituals observed by caste Hindus*	*Festivals and Rituals observed by Mahalis*
Baishak (April–May)	Naba Barsha	—
	Sasan Kali puja	Sasan Kali puja
	Ambubachi	—
	Manasa	Manasa
Asad (June–July)	Manasa/Dashaharan	Asaria
Sravana (July–August)	Manasa/Nag Panchami	—
	Aranna	Aranna
Bhadra (August–September)	Janmashtami	Karam
	Gomba Purnima Manasa/Satpuri	Tusu
Aswin (September–October)		Dosai
Katrik (October–November)	Kojagori Laxmi puja	Kali puja
	Nalmara, Durga, Kali	
Agrahayan (November–December)	Nabanna	—
Paus (December–January)	Laxmi puja	Sakrat/Laxmi
	Pous Sankranti	
Magh (January–February)	Mahri Saptami	Magh-Sim/Maghi
	Goranga	
Falgun (February–March)	Shiva Ratri	Baha
Chaitra (March–April)	Shive Gajan	Charak/Gajan
	Raksha Kali	

It is observed that the Mahalis are influenced by Hindu castes and they adopted several Hindu rituals. They also participate in village festivals of Hindus.

It is observed that some rituals are performed in the house, while others, are performed either in the temple or in a particular village site including agricultural fields. It is observed that propitiation occurs every year. While Manasa is worshipped generally during cultivation season, Laxmi is worshipped during pre-harvest/post-harvest period. The upper caste cultivators observe the auspicious days for initiating the first ploughing, sowing and harvesting operations. The Mahalis as well as lower caste cultivators do not have such obligations.

Discussion

Among the Mahalis, the specialists who practise both sacred and profane occult arts, such as Neoke (the village priest), Paranik (assistant to priest), Rum (Shaman) who ascertains the ensuing misfortune; Gunni/Ojha who functions as medicine man/woman, diviner, occupy special status in their society. These specialized persons consider themselves superior in rank in the local caste milieu because of their functional specialization. Even in day-to-day interactions with these specialists, certain prestige and status are shown to them by the Mahalis in general and their advice is still sought in any crisis situation.

Changing Inter-Ethnic Relations and Developmental Activities

The Mahalis have dual identity. They still identify themselves as Adivasi and follow the customs of the tribe. However, the villagers, the caste Hindus, regard them as a 'low caste'. Village level inter-ethnic relations are influenced by this perception. In day to day life however relations are influenced only by economic-political consideration. Mahalis are an artisan community but they depend on other artisans as well. The Mahalis have intercommunity linkages with many Hindu castes and they are served by the Brahmin priest in their religious ceremonies. They exchange or accept kachcha, pucca and siddha food from all communities except the Muslim and Dom. They do not exchange kachcha food with the Brahmin and Kayastha. Intercommunity marriage has also taken place with the Kayastha and Paramanik. The Mahalis share the wells, temples, crematorium, roads, schools and other public utilities with caste Hindus. There is socio-economic interdependence between the Brahmin and Mahalis, the Mahali and Baishnabs, barber and Mahali, but these relationships are not bound by actual jajmani relationship. The Mahali villagers are now linked with Panchayat office and local political leaders, but they are not getting enough supports from these sources to escape their severe poverty stricken condition. Literary level is very low among the Mahalis. For health and medical care they go to local dispensary or hospital. Their drinking water is procured from tube-wells. Sometimes they receive the facility of Integrated Rural Development Project (IRDP) or District Rural Development Agency (DRDA) programme. Sometimes they are self-employed and engaged in paper packet making. Their residential area has not been electrified. They use coal, wood, cowdung and kerosene as energy resources.

The main development programmes are initiated in the villages, mainly through the Block Development office in the area. The village Panchayats consisting of village people have members from the castes and communities. The Mahalis are also represented in the Panchayats. Hence they are able to state their misery to local authorities and they also receive some relief from time to time.

The Mahalis received homestead land as 'patta' in some of the areas like at Chotomatkatpur under Narayangarh Police Station and also in Ramnagar Adibasi Palli under Ramnagar Police Station when they had to shift to those places due to natural calamities. Besides, at the time of acute distress, government distributes dry doles or provides relief work to the affected people and provides some sort of employment also.

The villagers used to get the cash loan under the schemes of Integrated Rural Development Project and District Rural Development Agency, Shilpa Loan, and other from the Block Development Office. Besides, there are some Co-operative banks also who help and provide different types of loans. The Rural Agricultural Development Society also renders help to the villagers in terms of loan for agricultural development. Shilpa Loan is obtained for industries like basketry, from the District Rural Development Agency. Besides, government has also taken up a number of other development programmes through Block office.

Conclusion

The Mahalis normally live in multi-ethnic villages. They live in separate hamlet settlement, thus maintaining a distance from other castes and communities of the village. At present no distinction/restriction is maintained in using the public roads or tracks by any caste or community. However, certain restrictions are imposed on the Mahalis for using the private water resources owned by 'high castes' or in the use of sacred places belonging to higher castes or in using cremation/burial ground meant for higher castes. In fact in whole rural area broad distinction is made between high and low castes/communities in terms of 'pure' and 'impure'. However, notion of pollution is no more stronger now. Pollution factor is changing also due also to urban contact and introduced development activities, including safe drinking water facilities.

The Mahalis are traditionally bamboo basket makers but they also practise agriculture to some extent. It is stated that their little possession of cultivable land as well as being landless forces them to cultivate lands either as tenants (which is not practised regularly) or agricultural labourers, though each family pursues basket making as a major occupation. Their basket making technology is simple and marketing of their products is linked up through middlemen known as 'huri mahajan' who often exploit them. Nowadays a few Mahali families have become owner cultivators of small plots of land. Those Mahalis depending on agriculture now have become economically well off. However, Mahalis who have landed property apparently do not make any distinction in day-to-day interaction with those Mahalis who do not have land.

Stratification observed in Mahali society is now visualized in terms of modern economic ranking as also in terms of clan based functional specialization. Thus, Naeke (the village priest), Paranik (assistant to priest), Rum (Shaman who ascertains the ensuing misfortune), Gunni/Ojha (who functions as medicine man, diviner, etc.) occupy special status in their society. These specialized men consider themselves superior in rank in the local social system because of their functional specialization. Many lower caste Hindus also regard them as superior.

Among the Mahalis stratification based on clan status is still recognized. The clans which have relation with the santal clans are regarded as superior clans. Thus, clans like Samah, Pirhi and Khangar, which do not have similarities with the clans of Santals are considered as low. Certain stratification is maintained among ten clans of Mahalis in terms of higher and lower. The officials of Mahali tribal council and religious officials are always selected from certain higher order clans. For example, the village headman is mostly selected from the Mandi clan. The deputy headman is always selected from Baske clan while the assistant headman is mostly selected from Besra clan.

Living in a multi-ethnic village, the Mahali maintain various statuses. Thus, present day Mahalis do not consider themselves socially inferior to the Mochi, Hari, Dom and other castes of the Hindus, though in reality they have no comfortable position in the social hierarchy. They are lower to Brahmin and middle rank castes. It is interesting to note that many Mahalis have developed a tendency to rename their clan names akin to surnames of local Hindu castes. The new adopted surnames are often the surnames of the local dominant cultivator castes like Mahisya etc.

How far the Mahalis have attained a 'status' in local Hindu society and hierarchy is a matter of dispute. The insiders' and outsiders' perspectives seem to significantly vary in most cases. The Mahalis however maintain some distance from the neighbouring tribes such as Ho, Munda, Kharia, and Bedia whom they consider as socially inferior. But no such distinction is maintained with Santals because of their identical origin. Though the Mahalis share their clan names with several Santal clans but the Santals consider Mahalis as lower in social rank.

Among the Mahalis clan ranking, clan-based headmanship, joint family and basketry as primary occupation survive. Major changes are observed in terms of economic diversion and seeking democratic status and power. Nevertheless, the Mahali interactions with Hindu landlords are still guided by norms of caste system, as Mahalis are treated as a lower caste. The Mahalis are not seeking any ritual status, rather some families have opted to gain economic and political power. Economic innovations led to rise of some rich Mahali families, but since majority of Mahalis remain historically poor in a caste milieu they exercise little leverage over the village social-political space. Land is important as basis of status and power. Hence many Mahalis are trying to gain access to land as owners or share croppers. However, living under the shadow of rich peasants and Hindu landlords they find themselves socially excluded and economically discriminated.

Acknowledgement

Author thanks the coordinator, Dr N.K. Das, for critical comments and editorial modifications.

References

Dalton, E.T. 1872, Descriptive Ethnology of Bengal, Calcutta: Government Printing Press.

Dalton, E.T. 1978, Tribal History of Eastern India. New Delhi: Cosmo Publications.

Grierson, G.A. 1904, *Linguistic Survey of India*, Government of India, Calcutta Government Press.

Mitra, A. 1952, *Census of India, 1951, District Census Hand Book, Midnapur,* Government Publications, New Delhi.

Risley, H.H. 1891, *The Tribes and Castes of Bengal,* Calcutta: Secretariat Press.

Risley, H.H. 1915, *The People of India,* Calcutta Kolkata: Secretariat Press.

Russel, R.V. and R.B. Hiralal 1916, *Tribes and Castes of the Central Provinces of India,* Vol. IV, London: Macmillan Co.

11 Adivasi Economy, Slow Impact of Development and Discrimination

The Saora of Odisha

D.P. Biswas

The present paper describes the economic discrimination, stratification and social change among the Saora tribe of Odisha. The study examines the major features of social stratification, the nature of social segments in existence, and the economic system as also the criteria of deprivation. The Saora is one of the oldest known tribes, living in the hilly forest belt in Odisha with little communication and lesser economic and educational facilities. Two major groups constitute the Saora. The first one is the Lanjia Saora – the traditional group living in isolation, who maintain some contact with the neighbouring Telugu and Dom communities in market places. The Telugu people migrated from Andhra Pradesh to Serango of Odisha and are involved in trading and other businesses; and the Doms migrated here for trading purposes from other parts of Odisha. The second group *Suddho Saora* is an advanced group with some economic and educational achievements. They interact with other communities namely Odia Brahmin, Khandayat (cultivator group), Keota (Scheduled Caste fisherman community) and Dhoba (washerman), who also have migrated, from different parts of Odisha.

All the neighbouring groups refer to the Saora as backward and place them at the lowest rank in caste society. Over a longer period of time some Saoras had come in contact with neighbouring communities through communication, inter-personal relations and common welfare measures and schemes of government. Such contact over a prolonged period of time has brought about changes in the Saora's social and cultural life.

The Identity of the Tribe

The Saora are one of the major tribes in Odisha, Many scholars have studied the Saora in different territorial zones on the basis of various parameters including habitation, social groups, customary law, and divided them into many categories. Verrier Elwin (1955) in his classic book *'Religion of an Indian Tribe'*, had differentiated the Saora and their ancestors primarily on the basis of social customs. B. Singh (1987) in his work describes the pattern of leadership among the Saora, their decision making process and way of functioning. The Harijan and Tribal Welfare Department, Government of Odisha published a book edited by U.N. Patnaik (1989).

The Saora live in inaccessible areas. They are categorized under primitive tribal groups. They are also called by several names like Saura, Saro, Saur and Adivasi. The phonetic expressions of the community however show a wide range of variations. Elwin in his classic book, *Religion of an Indian Tribe* used the spelling of the tribe as Saora. He also gave many reasons about their 'primitive-ness' and customs. Elwin (1955: 7) has claimed the correct pronunciation of the tribe Saora, but in Andhra-Odisha border area, the Telugu people call them as Savara or Sahara, whereas the Odias call them Saura.

The Saora belong to the Proto-Australoid racial group (Patnaik, 1989), and derive, their name from Sagories. The implication was that the traditional Saora was always seen to carry an axe on his shoulder, while going about in his economic pursuit of hunting-gathering. But the present Saora people do not have any idea about this, they believe that they are the descendants of the King Savar, a tribal ruler during the time of Lord Shiva. Many scholars have divided the Saora into many categories according to their food habits, economy, social and religious position. But while collecting information in different Saora inhabited areas in Odisha, it is actually found that the tribe has two main divisions, hill Saora and plain Saora. The hill Saora are referred to as *Lanjia Saora.* They are the traditional group that strictly remains in the hill slopes and forest belt of Gajapati, Ganjam and Koraput districts of Odisha. The plain Saora are referred to as *Suddho Saora* or the reformed group. They remain adjacent to urban people in Khurda, Mayurbhanj, Cuttack, Bolangir and in some pockets of Kalahandi and Ganjam districts of Odisha.

The Saora settlements are close to mountain ranges flanked by fertile bushes, valley and hilly lands, surrounded by medium to deep jungles; but there is some definite pattern of Saora settlement, their huts seem to be placed in two parallel rows or cross-rows facing in the same or opposite directions. The huts are mostly rectangular in shape, made up of mud, bamboo-strips, thread, straws, thatches and leaves.

Table 1

Tribal Population and their Distribution in Different Districts of Odisha

Name of the district	*Male*	*Female*	*Total*
Sambalpur	53,105	54,592	1,07,697
Sundargarh	683	705	1,388
Keonjhar	3,989	3,940	7,929
Mayurbhanj	1,440	1,469	2,909
Balasore	818	804	1,622
Cuttack	11,029	10,990	22,019
Dhenkanal	10,112	10,186	20,298
Phulbani	1,662	1,698	3,360
Bolangir	22,929	23,657	46,586
Kalahandi	2,875	2,820	5,695
Koraput	22,584	23,356	45,940
Ganjam (including Gajapati)	33,632	35,569	69,201
Puri (including Khurda)	17,483	17,936	35,419
Total	1,82341	1,87,722	3,70,063

One of the suggestions about the origin of 'Saora' is from 'Saba Roya' – 'Saba' means dead body and 'Roya' means to carry; in the earlier days the Saora used to carry the dead bodies. But at present the Saora have no idea about this and traditional Saora groups are unable to trace the myth. In appearance the Saora are a pre-Dravidian tribe; long head, flat nose with depression at the roof, eye-brow ridge prominent, and facial features well-marked. Saora is their dialect belonging to Mundari branch of Austric language group, mostly used by the Lanjia Saora group. Most of them can speak in Odia to communicate with others. The Suddho Saora have forgotten the Saora dialect; they use Odia for reading and writing and communicating with others.

The traditional Saora male still use Lonjha, a short piece of loin cloth around their waist and a portion of which hangs down on the back side and looks like a tail. As a result of this habit they are called Lanjia Saora, or long-tailed Saora. Their upper portion remains undressed. The traditional Saora women use *Gatunkab,* a short waistcloth with border and also a short skirt; they now use short blouse. Occasionally they use single-bead necklaces. Now the *Suddho Saora* males use short dhoti, shirt and banyan; their females use single piece of sari and often sari with blouse. Some converted Lanjia Saora now wear pants, shirt and such modern clothes.

Their principal food is a gruel prepared using rice, ragi or ghatia boiled with water and salt. Besides, they also consume fruits, roots, tubars, vegetables, and flesh of fowls and goats. They also consume honey and milk. They like to eat non-vegetarian food more than the vegetarian dishes, but such food is irregular. In the morning some of them take *Chada-chaha* (breakfast) which consists of tea and fried maize.

Family is the most basic social unit, and it plays a dominant and significant role to maintain social control over the family members and to organize economic pursuits. The Saora mostly have a nuclear family system but about 40 per cent have joint family. They have an institution called *Birinda* which consists of 20–30 close relatives living in a compound, which regulates the norms and customs of their families. The status and role of Birinda according to their social and economic set-up will be described afterwards. Marriage is permitted between the members of same Birinda of other villages. Monogamy is the usual practice but polygamy is also permitted, and a man can be permitted to have two to three wives according to his capacity. This is especially true of the Raita families who are the big landholders having big house, good amount of land and manpower. They can have more than one wife, some of them even have four wives. Junior levirate and junior sororate type marriages are allowed in the Saora society.

The religious ceremonies among the Saora is very simple. During birth, no pre-delivery ceremony is observed, delivery takes place at the corner of their own house with the help of an elderly woman (*Dien*) of their village belonging to the same community. After seven days, purificatory bath is given by the Dien to the mother and newborn baby. On the same day *Jonam patrer* or 'namkaran' is performed by the *Bhuyya* (sacred head). For marriage there is no hard and fast rule; marriage is mostly performed by negotiation, but marriage by capture and marriage by service in the past was also permitted. *Panshal* or *damda* (bride price) is given in both cash and kind; ₹ 60–100 or a maximum of ₹ 1000 cash as well as 10–15 bottles of country liquor is given to the bride's father. Marriage function is performed at the bride's place and a feast is given by the bride's father. In death ritual, the dead body is mostly cremated; in case of death by cholera, smallpox or by snakebite, their dead are buried. *Gaur* (communal feast) is offered to the relatives after cremation of dead body on the same day.

Both the Lanjia Saora and Suddho Saora follow Hindu religion but a section of Lanjia Saora in Serango area have become Christianized. They received some economic support and relief and other forms of help from the Christian Missionaries established in that region. *Thakurani mata* or *Budima* is their Kuldevi (chief devi), there is no particular shrine of the Goddess. They place a big stone at the corner of their villages slightly high on the ground on a platform, this remains open under shade. The Saora put oil and vermilion on the stone which they believe as Thakurani mata. Sometimes, a wooden beam is also used instead of stone. They offer puja regularly, but special puja is observed for Thakurani mata or Budima after harvesting of a crop once in a year during Magh, with *Udbathi* (incense sticks), *Mabatee* (candle), *Kadali* (banana), *Pijuli* (guava) offered during the puja. They also sacrifice fowls and goats in honour of the devi for plentiful agricultural produce. Holi, Deepavali, Navratri, Shivaratri, Kartick-unam are the major festivals observe by the Saora. The Christianized group observe Good Friday, New Year's day and Christmas day, in addition to observance of Hindu festivals.

The Saora are famous for wall paintings which they call Iron or Itlain. The inside of traditional Saora huts mostly consist of sketches of human beings, hunting games, horse, aeroplanes, elephants, gunmen, moon, stars, sun, cycle and others and some sketches do not have any definite figures. Folk songs and folk dances are popular and mostly performed during marriage ceremony.

The Saora tribe is divided into following divisions:

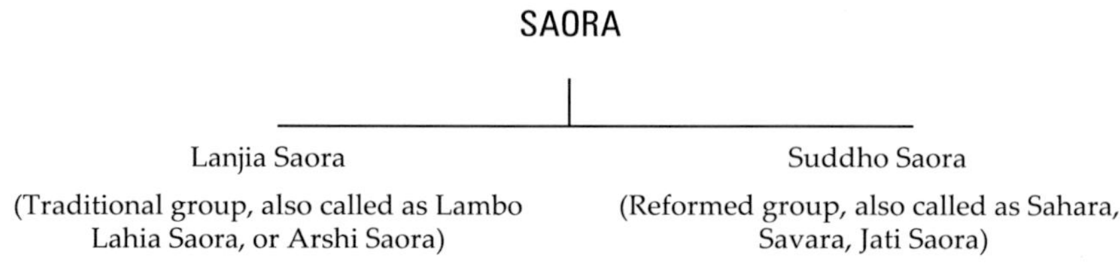

In the present study, the author has studied two villages. These villages represented the tribe pursuing customary norms of behaviour, intra-group relations, internal social hierarchy and customary laws to maintain the society. The first village where work has been carried out is Bhoboni village, under Serango Gram Panchayat of Parliakhemundi Sub-division of Gajapati district (earlier in Ganjam district), situated about 400 km away from Bhubaneshwar (the capital of Odisha). Lanjia Saora live in the forest. In the past they had to lead a nomadic life and were fully dependent on hunting/gathering, moving around the jungle from one place to another. Most of the Lanjia Saora villages are found to be in deep inaccessible areas; in most cases hidden under the forest clad hills, making it very difficult to reach the village through stiff, zig zag hilly paths. The Lanjia Saora built their houses following a definite pattern, facing towards each other.

The second village studied is Radhacharanpur, situated at about 100 km away from Bhubaneshwar main road, under the block and district of Khurda in Odisha. The village is largely inhabited by the Suddho Saora and consists of 80 households, two Keota (SC) families and one Dhoba family. The Suddho Saora also referred to as Sahara are reformed group. They have quite clean, serially arranged habitation pattern, living almost in plain areas adjacent to urban people surrounded by plain land. They are mostly engaged in settled agriculture and agricultural labour and also wage labour in construction work.

From forest-village, 55 families of Lanjia Saora were interviewed for understanding traditional life patterns, house-type, dress pattern, food habits and use of Saora dialect. From the other village also 55 families, mainly Suddho Saora were interviewed who have some interaction with neighbouring communities, and who have mostly lost the traditional Saora dialect and customs and adopted Odia customs and habits. The surrounding people regard the Saora as having a lowly status in the social hierarchy.

Table 2

Village-wise Distribution According to Sex

S. No.	*Name of the village*	*No. of families*	*Name of the group*	*Male*	*Female*	*Total*
1.	Bhoboni	55	Lanjia Saora	128	139	267
2.	Radhacharanpur	55	Suddho Saora	131	116	247
	Total	110		259	255	514

From the above table, we learn that a total of 110 families have been covered of which 55 households of Lanjia Saora consist of 128 males and 139 females and the Suddho Saora group consists of 131 males and 116 females, with a total of 247 persons.

Traditional Political System

The Lanjia group is the most discriminated section regarded as the 'primitive' Saora tribe; also known by the others as jungle tribe or jungle Sabaro. They are held as backward in view of their traditional dress pattern, variety of indigenous food habits – mainly gruel and flesh of wild animals, language tone, poor economic condition, isolated settlement and illiteracy. The Lanjias however believe that they are the original Saora and refer to the Suddho Saora group as inferior, who have lost their original identity. On the other hand the Suddho Saora claim that they are the pure and 'civilized' group who have developed their manner and customs living adjacent to plain area people, and they regard Lanjia Saora as inferior to them.

The important feature of social system of Saora is lesser visibility of clan or lineage segments. However, they have an agnatic core based on Birinda system, an institution that consists of a number extended families or close nuclear families. According to Elwin (1955), Birinda is a remarkable feature of Saora social organization consisting of all the descendants from a common male ancestor, whose members (men and women) are of the same blood. This we may call as lineage anthropologically indeed. Birinda works as a democratic force in

Saora society, whose members enjoy equal rights and privileges. It controls the negotiation of marriage, inheritance of property, social functions and also solves the social and economic problems of the Birinda segment people. The term Birinda is used only by the Lanjia Saora, whereas the Suddho Saora use the word Sanghia in place of Birinda. Marriage within the Birinda of same village is strictly prohibited; members stand as brothers and sisters. Violation of Birinda rules can bring hard punishment and exile. Birinda also looks after the succession, authority and inheritance of the property of the deceased. If a person dies as issueless, the Birinda takes the dead person's property and distributes it among the poor Birinda members. In this case the *Karjya (sradh)* ceremony of dead person and the death rituals are performed by Birinda members. The lower Birinda group members also sometimes consult with the seniors with higher position like – Gomango Birinda, Raita Birinda and Bhuyya Birinda regarding the management of economic and ceremonial matters.

The status and position of Birinda groups in Saora political system can be categorized under the following heads:

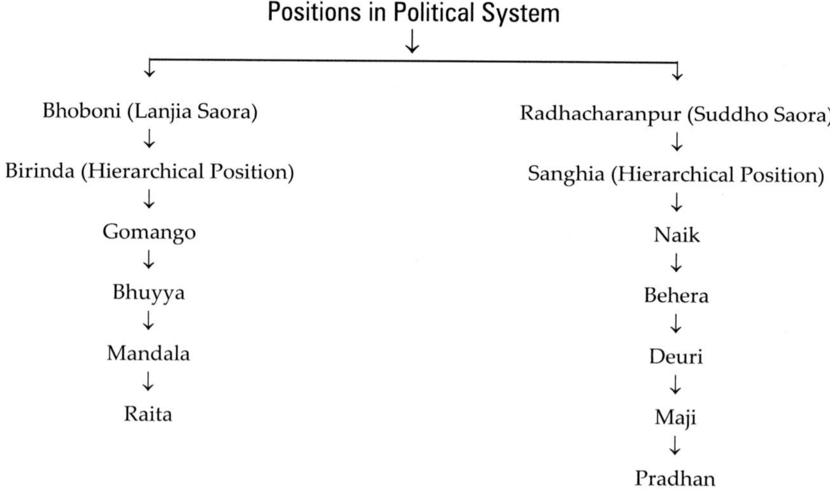

The Birinda group or Sanghia group are formed according to the ancestry of different chiefs with considerable power and position in a Saora village. The positions have different statuses and are distinguished by the Gomango (super head), followed by the Bhuyya (sacred head), then the Mandala (middle manager), the cultivator or caretakers of cultivable lands and lastly the Raita (general people). The management of social rules, the distribution power and social roles among the different positions are specified in different ways validating hierarchical positions. Gomango has been the only important leader or supreme head who enjoys a hereditary post, who has full authority to solve any dispute in social, political and religious matters. But nowadays, authority has been divided among the members of the Birinda or Sanghia according to their performance and abilities.

The village-wise distribution of the Birinda and Sanghia positions are as follows:

Table 3
Village-wise Distribution of Headmen

Village	*Birinda*	*No. families*	*Total*
Bhoboni (Lanjia Saora)	Gomango	21	
	Bhuyya	2	55
	Mandala	2	
	Raita	30	
Radhacharanpur	Sanghia		
(Suddho Saora)	Naik	28	
	Behera	3	
	Deuri	10	55
	Maji	11	
	Pradhan	3	
Total			110

Among the traditional Lanjia Saora out of the 55 families we studied 21 belong to Gomango, two belong to Bhuyya, two belong to Mandala Birinda and maximum 30 members belong Raita. Among the reformed Suddho Sarora group, out of 55 studied families 28 belong to Naik, three belong to Behera, Deuri has 10 members, 11 belong to Majhi and three belong to Pradhan. These are positions of headmen in political system.

Political System: Traditional and Modern

The Saora have an effective political organization. Like in the past intra-tribe and intra-village problems and disputes are settled in a joint meeting consisting of elders and village headmen. The 'primitive' Lanjia Saora live in and around the hill slopes and forest belts and they do not like to mix with the neighbouring communities. Even today they try to maintain their traditional dispute settlement mechanisms. Suddho Saora have come more effectively within modern statutory village councils, but their traditional headmen continue to enjoy authority and power.

'Saora Political System'

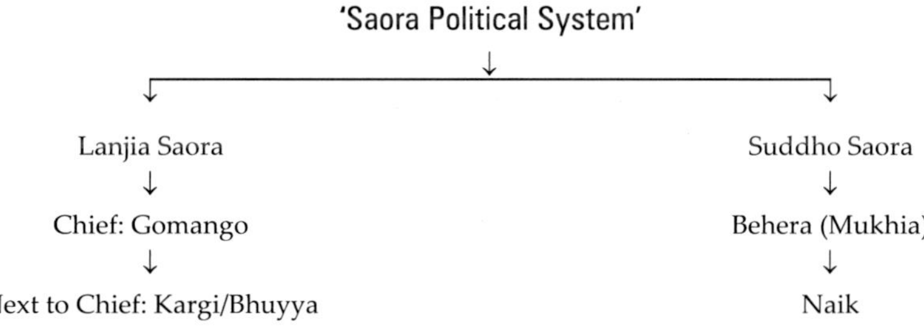

Intra-village political structure of the Lanjia Saora is called *Sabha Madala* (traditional Panch) headed by the Gomango (secular chief). Arrangement of marriages, sale of cultivable lands, inheritance of parental property, cases of divorce, organizing of communal feast in death ceremony and all such issues are dealt with and resolved under the supervision of Gomango. Among the Suddho

Saora their traditional political council is called as *Sabha Panch*, headed by *Behera* (mukhia) or Dalbera. Besides they also follow the Statutory Panchayat rules which cover different social and political affairs.

The role and status of Gomango, Behera, Kargi and Naik are theoretically different but their functions are in the same. The traditional caste council is headed by the Gomango followed by Kargi who solve their problems sitting together with the Sabha Mandala (5/6 elderly persons of the society). Baik or Paik, a messenger of their community is sent to call the Mandala people. Gomango initiates the discussion regarding any social matter after consulting with the Kargi and Mandala members. Punishment is imposed differently for different cases. Thus, the punishment for theft is by cash or by beating; for crop damages by cattle through cash punishment; for divorce – cash fine; for quarrel and violence the fine of 2 to 3 bottles of country liquor is imposed. These are the traditional norms. The Gomango still try to maintain the law and order of the Lanjia Saora in the traditional way. Of course, some changes have been among the Suddho Saora people. Among the Suddho Saora, if Behera is unable to solve the problem the case is referred to the court or police.

Nevertheless, with the introduction of Panchayati Raj, the Panchayat members (Ward Panch or Sarpanch or Gram Sabha members) are asked to settle disputes in some particular matters. Each and every Saora village or two to three small villages have a Ward Panchayat of Saora People, selected by voice vote or by secret ballots. This Panchayat deals with inter-ethnic quarrel like – hijacking of girls from among the Saora by the non-Saoras, distribution of proceeds of wage labour in government construction works, violation of forest rules, crops being harmed by cattle from neighbouring communities and other such issues.

Economic Parameters: Landholding Pattern and Category

The Saora possess two types of landed property – shifting land (locally called as Bagoda or Baru-buro-ai) and terrace land (locally called as Billu or Saroban-Buro-ai) where they produce two different varieties of crops. The categories of land and crops grown are specified below.

In the shifting land (*Bagodajami*) the major crops maize, joar, pulses are sown around the same time in the a same land before the rain starts; these are harvested at different times in the year. In the terrace land (*Billujami*) only after the rain starts the paddy is grown and is harvested in a particular time. The Suddho Saora possess only plain agricultural lands (*Billujami*), where they cultivate only rice (*Runku or dhanna*). Crops are mainly dependent on rain water; very few of them are irrigated from wells and canals.

The land tenure system among the Saora is more or less feudal. Land for shifting cultivation is free, the Saora in their territory occupy cultivable lands within the framework of their customary law. Some families specially the Gomango, occupy more land than their necessity, the rest of the families share comparatively less amount of land. During the British period, and even thereafter the administration recognized the tribal rules and rights of headmen (chiefts) for their land management. The Suddho Saora occupy plain land. After they shifted to the plain area, they restricted their family members and discarded chieftainship.

The traditional Saora practise both shifting cultivation and terrace cultivation. Regarding the control over the cultivable lands and economic resources, there is no restriction over occupying land for shifting cultivation; any family can clean and occupy any amount of jungle land according to their ability to cultivate. But ownership of the main landed property (recorded in name of their individual family) that is the terrace land or *Billujami* or paddy land depends upon the discretion of the village-authorities. Among the Suddho Saora, the *Billujami* or plain agricultural land are recorded in the name of particular families. Of course the Naik families occupy maximum amount of land as they are dominant Sanghia group in Radhacharanpur village. Thus we witness that in the traditional system of village social structure stratification based on possession of land exists. Chiefs and headmen holding higher positions enjoyed greater economic benefits.

The land holding pattern of the two villages is as follows:

Each and every Saora village has a portion of terrace land (*Billujami*) surrounding the foothills, mostly owned by that Saora group. By customary law, Gomango families of Lanjia Saora are entitled to the larger share and the rest are distributed among the others according to their position. Among the Suddho Saora maximum number of plain agricultural lands are owned by the Naik families and the rest are distributed among the other Sanghia groups. Table 4 clearly shows this unequal distribution of land among the villagers.

Table 4

Village-wise Landholding Position

Name of the village	*Name of community*	*Name of the subgroups*	*Landless*	*0–1 acre*	*1–3 acre*	*3–5 acre*	*No. of families*
Bhoboni	Lanjia Saora	Gomango	—	—	—	21	21
		Bhuyya	—	1	1	—	2
		Mandala	—	1	1	—	2
		Raita	5	6	12	7	30
Radhacharanpur	Suddho Saora	Naik	—	10	18	—	28
		Behera	1	2	—	—	3
		Maji	3	8	—	—	11
		Deuri	3	7	—	—	10
		Pradhan	3	—	—	—	3
Total			15	35	32	28	110

Among the Lanjia Saora the Gomango and Raita are in possession of better and greater portion of lands. Raita families were caretakers of lands. So they managed to retain more lands in their names, even after independence, and thus the Bhuyya came to be in third position. But in case of shifting land, there is no definite portion of land recorded in the name of any individual and there is no restriction on how much land a family can clear and utilize for growing crops in any portion of jungle surrounding their area. The *Bagoda* or shifting land is used for 3–4 consecutive years to grow crops, after that the family can leave that portion or it can also retain it under their custody. There is no restriction to cultivate any shifting land under the ownership of any family.

The Tribal Economy: Agricultural Production, Expenditure and Cost

The main crops which are cultivated by the Saora in their terrace land, and shifting lands are paddy, maize or jowar and pulses. The expenses of cultivation to produce any type of crops are quite less, even then the Saora are not able to produce high amount of crops compared to other communities in Odisha. The expenses and output of the cultivated varieties of crops are given below.

Table 5

Expenditure of Production

Land cultivation	*Crops*	*Production per bigha*	*Production cost per quintal*	*Total market value of produce*
Shifting cultivation	Maize, jowar and pulses	2 quintal	₹ 200	₹ 1600
Terrace cultivation	Paddy	2.5 quintal	₹ 500	₹ 2500

Majority of the Saora families are nuclear type consisting of husband, wife and 3–4 children (unmarried). It is a common feature that they have one or two bigha of terrace land and half bigha or more of shifting land. So the production from landed property is not sufficient to maintain their families.

The resulting deficit is managed through working as wage labourers in different areas such as construction work like stone-binding in terrace lands, road and canal construction works initiated by development agencies and also by collection of firewood, honey and such items and selling them to the nearby markets. Of course there are some big landholders having 3–5 acres of land specially the Gomago families who earn more from their cultivable lands and easily manage their annual family expenditure.

Angartang (bullocks) and *Bengtal* or *Podo* (buffaloes) are the prime domestic animals used for ploughing the fields and also for carrying crops from the field after harvesting with the help of bullock carts; *Kisser* (dogs) are simply used for watching and hunting purposes. *Kukra* (hens), *Ghusri* (pigs) and *Chheri* (goats) are domesticated for different purposes. There are a number of agricultural implements used in different stages of agricultural operations.

The important agricultural implements are plough, leveller, bullock cart (corier), Dao (sickle), Kurule (spade) and hoe. These are used differently for all crops.

Types of labourers can be categorized under three main heads. They are mainly engaged as wage labourers in agricultural fields and construction work on daily wage basis, annual basis and seasonal wage basis.

Types of Labourers

In the Saora society the labourers are locally called as *Mulio.* The types of labourers and their working variations are described in details under the following heads:

1. *Mawad Mulio*: These are male members of 16 to 50 years of age, and they mainly do agricultural work such as ploughing, sowing and harvesting. They are also engaged in work under the Public Work Department (PWD) and construction work. They are the prime agricultural labourers and get higher rate of wage, i.e., ₹ 25 in cash or 2 kg of rice, wheat or pulses, bidi as well as tiffin of *jau* (boiled-rice) with salt and vegetables per day.
2. *Maipi Mulio*: They are female members from 15 to 45 years of age. Their work includes repair, cleaning of Bagoda land, weeding, harvesting and winnowing and storing of crops. They do all types of wage labour along with their menfolk, besides household work. Their wages are ₹ 15 cash or 1 kg of rice, wheat or pulses and tiffin of *jau*.
3. *Gauda Mulio*: They are younger labourers between 15 and 20 years of age, and they mainly do *Nigahani* (watching of crops which can be damaged by wild animals, monkeys, cattle and birds); they also do cattle herding. Their wages are ₹ 100 or 20 kg of rice for doing *Nigahani*, and ₹ 200 or 50 kg of rice for *Ferro* or *Chheri char-bako* (cattle herding) for the whole year. A cattle herd consists of 10–15 cows and buffaloes. The wages are paid on seasonal or annual basis.

Besides, there is a special category of labour called *Bhalo Mawad Mulio* (young energetic male persons) between the age of 25 and 45 years, and their wages are quite high than the other *Mulios*; they get ₹ 10 extra compared to *Mawad Mulios* and also bidi, cigarettes and two times tiffin.

They have vast knowledge about the agriculture practised in all seasons, pertaining to any crop in any type of land. They are hard workers and can put extra labour in different agricultural seasons. Some of the *Bhalo Mawad Mulios* take land from the big landholders – Gomango and Raita families – as sharecroppers. They also get wages from those families throughout the year and a kind of patron-client or landlord-labour relationship is observed. The poor Saora families depend on rich families and they often get crops and money on loan if their crops are damaged due to drought.

Religious Specialists

The Saora follow some form of Hinduism and tribal religious beliefs and customs. Their sacred specialists *Bhuyya*/*Janni* or *Pujjak* are hereditary posts, and they mostly look after the religious and ritual matters. The sacred head also acts as a medicine man; sometimes he also gives advice on social matters but his power is less than the Gomango – the supreme political head of the Saora. The activities of sacred specialists can also be categorized under the following heads:

(a) *Bhuyya*: The chief priest, holding a hereditary post, presides over agricultural festivals, name giving ceremony, arrangement of marriages and Gaur ceremony in death rituals.

(b) *Janni* (a priest): The second man who assists the chief priest during ritual performance and also sometimes acts as a chief priest in absence of *Bhuyya*. It is mostly an ascribed post.

(c) *Kundan* (male shaman): A sacred specialist, who acts as a messenger to transmit religious knowledge to the community. He also sometimes acts as a medicine man. *Kundan-boi* (female shaman) also performs the same activities like the *Kundan* but it is restricted only to some families. *Kundan-boi* also performs midwifery duties in their community.

Both the Lanjia Saora and Suddho Saora observe the regional festivals like Deepavali, Holi, Makar Sankranti, Navratri and tribal festivals. Now they have more and more local level contacts with the neighbouring Hindu communities during religious fairs.

Developmental Programmes and their Impact

The areas under study are predominately inhabited by the Lanjia Saora (traditional group) and Suddho Saora (reformed group). The Saoras are the oldest known backward tribe in Odisha, who mostly remain below the poverty line. There are many developmental programmes run by the SDA (Saora Development Agency) and LSDA (Lanjia Saora Development Agency) under the sponsorship of the State Government and Central Government – for the welfare of the Saora people. As a result of the implementation of various developmental programmes, the Saora have been able to raise their economic position.

The Saora have benefitted from schemes run by welfare agencies in a variety of ways. They have had free seeds of paddy, ginger, papaya, cashewnut, banana plant and lemon supplied to them along with supply of manure to cultivate cash crops in their Bagodajami (fields of shifting cultivation).

A carpet weaving training centre has been established, through which the Saora women are given training to make carpets and mats with a stipend of ₹ 300 per month in addition to the earnings from their agricultural work. Under infrastructural development schemes, establishment of community halls for the community to assemble in a particular village once in a week to bring more awareness among them have been undertaken. Under individual benefit schemes supply of patta land, bullocks, buffaloes, agricultural implements and related items (free of cost) have been carried out to improve agricultural production and economic condition.

All these above schemes are mainly provided towards the Lanjia Saora of Ganjam and Gajapati districts of Odisha. But for the Suddho Saora area towards Khurda district, the welfare programmes are very few. For the Suddho Saora, the programmes launched in the studied village are:

> *Kutiro-jyoti project*: run by the Block Development Office, this provides free electricity and establishment of land-based electric pumps to provide irrigation freely for one time per crop.
>
> *Indira Awas Yojona*: establishment of half-pucca cottage with asbestos-roof, provided for 20 poor Suddho Saora families in Radhacharanpur village, with a common well for drinking water, free of cost.

But in the Suddho Saora areas no programme like cottage industry or local crafts training programmes are launched to substantiate the income.

Culture Contact and Trends of Social Change

Though there are many external factors operating like education, adaptation of culture and customs of surrounding communities, impact of development programmes which have influenced them in many ways, even then the Lanjia Saora try to keep themselves in isolation from others towards the forest belt and try to maintain traditional customs and rules, and they are more interested to pursue shifting cultivation. But the Suddho Saora remain very close to 'civilized Odia culture' and Odia customs, even though they are unable to improve their social and economic position to the level as enjoyed by the Khandayat, Goala, Pano and Keota families.

In respect of socio-political affairs, the role of Statutory Panchayat is becoming more powerful than the traditional tribal Panchayat (*Sabha Mandala*) as observed in many cases. For example, the prestige of tribal-headman Gomango is certainly high but nowadays only the cases of arrangement of marriage, divorces, inheritance of parental property, illegal sex relationship and arrangement of annual ritual ceremonies are kept under the jurisdiction of Gomango. On the contrary, under the new 'headman' of Statutory Panchayat, the ward Panch-members in consultation with the Sarpanch, look after the settlement of quarrels pertaining to crop damages by other's cattles, elopement of girls with men from other's community, acquiring of and shifting lands, distribution of relief and wages of government construction works and implementation of forest rules. In the past, these duties remained under the Birinda jurisdiction headed by the tribal 'chief' Gomango; now Statutory Panchayat members and ward Panch members are becoming important, mainly for settling inter-tribe disputes and issues pertaining to economic and political matters.

In spite of economic opportunities, the traditional Lanjia Saora continue shifting cultivation and occasional hunting and gathering of forest products. Of course, innovative new cash crops are being grown on their land that they used for shifting cultivation, such as cashew nut, banana, lemon and poppy. Use of improved seeds, implements, chemical fertilizer, insecticides and improved technical know-how are now part of the innovations all around. These have helped in improvement of the Saora cultivation. The agriculture has also improved with the assistance from the migrant Tibetan Kumbhars and several Odia castes who also practise shifting cultivation as it is less expensive. On the other hand, among the Suddho Saroa, their main economic source, that is, plain agricultural lands are very limited. Due to increase in number of family members, and the formation of nuclear families, which are living separately, ultimately parental property is getting fragmented and distributed among the new families, hence there is tremendous land shortage. No other alternative economy is available, and no development programmes have been launched for them (unlike in case of the Lanjia Saora) – and so the Suddho Saora are becoming economically weaker.

A section of Lanjia Saora, mostly nuclear families have adopted Christianity. Nevertheless the religion change is often resented at certain platforms in the area. Many youngsters are getting married in church. Despite Christian marriage however, these people are obliged to follow the traditional Birinda rule as pursued in 'tribal negotiated-marriage'. Some of the Suddho Saora people, having acquired improved social-economic statuses, often engaged *Bamda* or purohit from Brahmin families of neighbouring villages to perform marriage ceremonies as followed by Odia Hindu castes. As regards the educational facilities, it may be stated that a residential high school has been established – Bhoboni Ashram School at Bhoboni village, run by the State Government. With lot of efforts, now there is enrolment of almost the 50 per cent of Adivasi children, who are now going to school. The Lanjia Saora children, in traditional set-up, in general are mostly engaged as *Nigahani* (for watching of crops) and *Gai-chanai-bako* (cattle herders). These children miss the education. The Saora Development Agency and Lanjia Saora Development Agency are now extending much economic help to the poor Saora people. New habitation pattern, economic improvement through free patta lands, free seeds and manure, regular wages, carpet and mat weaving programmes are some important innovations in the economic sphere of this tradition-bound tribe, which is modernizing the economic life of the tribe. It may be stated at last that the Saora tribe has two sections, located in two geographic locations, but one section has obtained benefits of development programmes and other section has remained discriminated.

References

Das, N. 1965–66, "The Birinda of Lanjia Saora", in *Adivasi,* VII(2), pp. 5 –12.

Elwin, Verrier 1955, *Religion of an Indian Tribe,* London: Oxford University Press.

Kar, R.K. 1981, *The Savaras of Mancotta,* New Delhi: Cosmo Publishers.

Patniak, U.N. 1963–64, "The Saora of Ganjam Hills", in *Adivasi,* VI(1), pp. 6–13.

Singh, B. 1984, *Level of Leadership in Saora Society,* Souvenir of Adivari Exhibition, Bhubaneshwar: THRTI.

12 Social Exclusion, Discrimination and Tribe-Caste Hierarchy

The Rajuars of Odisha

D.B. Mondal

The present study has been carried out among the Rajuars of Mayurbhanj district, Odisha. Though the Rajuars live in separate hamlets, many Hindu castes and tribes surround their habitat. The Rajuars have developed symbiotic relationship in economic and social life with those groups living around them and have absorbed some cultural traits from the Hindu castes. About 34 per cent of the Rajuars live in Khate Block. This area was once covered by thick forest. Now some forest land has been converted to terrace fields for cultivation purposes. The physical feature of Mayurbhanj district is characterized by undulating landscapes with hills which are popularly known as 'Simlipal hill'; and is situated in the central part of Mayurbhanj. Climate of this region is characterized by dry weather during summer and extreme cold weather during winter.

The Identity: The Rajuar

The Rajuars are a lesser known tribe of Odisha. They are one of the numerically small tribes. According to 1981 census, their population was only 2,313, which comprised 1,159 males and 1,154 females. About 80 per cent Rajuars inhabit in the Mayurbhanj district and a small number of their population is scattered over twelve districts of Odisha (Table 1). They mostly reside in rural areas (Table 2) and have been in contact with the Hindu castes. They have developed close interaction with them through the trade of flattened rice. As a result of these factors, the way of life of the Rajuars is changing fast.

They are known by different names as Rajuwar, Rajulas, Bagal, Churakota in different areas. The Rajuars of Kamli village are known as Bagal. Bagal means who graze the cattle. They worked as cattle herder in the houses of Kurmi Mahato for a long time. Since then they were called as 'Bagal'. Now they use the term as their surname. In Balasore area they are called as Churakota. They also use Bagal as their surname. The word Rajuar has been derived from the terms 'Raja' and 'war', it means associate of the king. The Rajuar of Kamli village claim Kshatriya descent and assert that their ancestor was 'Boyan Raja'. They have migrated to Kamli village from Rairongpur areas of Odisha. Before that they were in Midnapur district of West Bengal. They also say that their ancestors had migrated from Nagpur long ago.

Table 1
Population Distribution of the Rajuars in Odisha

District	Male				Female				Total Population	
	1961		1981		1961		1981		1961	1981
	No.	%	No.	%	No.	%	No.	%	No.	No.
Sambalpur	11	1.93	26	2.24	11	2.46	22	1.90	22	48
Sundargarh	4	0.76	28	2.41	—	—	28	2.43	4	56
Keonjhar	—	—	43	3.71	—	—	34	2.55		77
Mayurbhanj	533	93.34	916	79.03	423	94.63	912	79.82	956	1828
Balasore	10	1.75	50	4.31	—	—	54	4.88	10	104
Dhenkanal	—	—	1	0.09	—	—	1	0.09	—	2
Phukbani	—	—	—	—	—	—	1	0.09	—	1
Balangir	—	—	—	—	—	—	1	0.09	—	1
Kalahandi	—	—	1	0.09	—	—	—	—	—	1
Koraput	7	1.23	65	5.81	4	0.89	66	5.72	11	131
Cuttack	6	1.05	28	2.42	9	2.02	35	3.03	15	63
Puri	—	—	1	0.09	—	—	—	—	—	1
Total	571	—	1159	—	447	—	1154	—	1018	2313

Table 2
Distribution of the Rajuar Families

S. No.	Name of the Village	No. of Families	Sub-Division/ block	Distance from Kamli Village
1.	Kamli	66	Khunta	—
2.	Purana Pani	4	Khunta	14
3.	Bansh Khunta	45	Khunta	6
4.	Bhupar	25	Khunta	7
5.	Jalghara	15	Barsahi	5
6.	Tangra	5	Barsahi	8
7.	Jamhat	3	Barsahi	6
8.	Ostia	3	Baripada	20
9.	Budhai kuda	6	Rairangpur	21
10.	Amdia	45	Rairangpur	18
11.	Jharan	4	Rairangpur	19
12.	Asma	20	Rairangpur	20
13.	Kalajhari	15	Rairangpur	21
14.	Jamda	1	Rairangpur	20
15.	Savrangapur	35	Balasore	70
16.	Jalweswar	15	Balasore	80
17.	Hundibanga	20	Suliapada	45
18.	Paik sahi	8	Baisinga	37
19.	Manikpur	7	Basta	42
20.	Panda Chhula	40	—	—
21.	Ektali	13	Baising	37
22.	Totapada	15	Baising	43
	Total	410		

According to Russell (1910), the Bhuiyas of Central Provinces had a sub-caste called Rajuwar. The Rajuars are an offshoot of the Bhuiyas. Dalton (1960) has mentioned that the Rajuars of Surguja area regard them as lower Kshatriyas. According to Risley (1891) the Rajuars of Manbhum have immigrated from Nagpur. Rajbansi is a synonym of the Rajuar. The Rajuars of the village Kamli claim that their social and culture affinity with the Bhuiya is still very close and intimate. They have asserted that they freely exchange food and water with the Bhuiya of this region. Traditionally the Rajuars were herdsmen and were called Bagal. Later on, a section of the Rajuars were engaged in preparing pounded rice (*chura*) by indigenous husking paddle (Dhenki). The Rajuars were then called as Churakota. Gradually, they learnt cultivation from the neighbouring peasant communities. Nowadays, most of them are engaged as cultivators, wage labourers and traders.

The preference of their settlement pattern is a proof of their homogeneous nature. They live in plains and practise cultivation in terrace lands. The Kamli and Savrangapur villages are dominated by Rajuar tribe having 66 and 36 households respectively (Table 3). Besides, a few caste groups like the Brahmin, the Kamar, the Patra, the Tanti, the Karon, and the tribes like the Bhuiya, the Munda, and the Bhumij are residing in different hamlets in the same village. Most of the Rajuars live in one-room hut with two compartments and a small verandah. Joint/extended families, build their houses all around a small courtyard. Huts are made up of mud walls with thatched or tiled roofs.

They speak a dialect, which is close to Odia. Rice is their staple food. They do not take beef and pork. But they consume other non-vegetarian food items. They seldom consume milk, tea, curd, etc. However, they consume alcoholic drinks like *hadia, tari,* etc., during festive days. Both male and female smoke *bidi* and use *guraku*. They take *pakhal* (stale rice) as Tiffin. They take *roti* made of wheat powder especially at dinner. The Rajuars, an endogamous tribe is divided into a limited number of clans, viz., Nag *(snake)*, Singha (lion), Kencho (earth-worm) etc., (Table 6). Though theoretically clans are exogamous they cannot strictly observe clan exogamy due to limited number of clans and small size of population. Marriage within the same clan is thus allowed with gap of certain generations. Clan is again divided into lineages (*bonso*). The people strictly follow lineage exogamy. Thus, marriage within a lineage is not allowed.

The Villages

To understand the changes that have taken place among the Rajuars and the social stratification that determines the level of inequality among them, the fieldwork was carried out in two villages, named Kamli and Savrangapur where the Rajuars are the dominant group. Kamli is a multi-ethnic village located in semi-exposed area and is situated 15 km away from the Baripada town. The other village is Savrangapur, which is also a multi-ethnic village. It is situated in the vicinity of Balasore city. The landless Rajuar from Kamli and Barhkhulie villages have moved to this location in search of livelihood based on urban oriented jobs. These villages are selected with a view to comparing the changing pattern and understanding the extent of stratification that exist among the Rajuars in two contact situations.

Junior sororate marriage is permitted by them. Adult marriage is the rule. But child marriage was once in practice among the Rajuars. They prefer to acquire spouse through negotiation. Marriage by mutual consent and marriage by service are permissible. Monogamy is the rule. Polygamy is practised by them only if the first wife is barren. They use vermilion and shankha (bangle made of shell) as a marriage symbol. Rules of succession are patrilineal and normally eldest son becomes the head of a family (*murubi*). Male equigeniture is the common rule of inheritance. Eldest son gets little more share of his father's property (*jeth bagh*). Daughter may get only the ornaments of her mother. Both joking and avoidance relationship exists between certain members of a family. Joking behaviour exists between grandparents and grandchildren, between a man and his wife's younger sister and between a man and his elder brother's wife. Similarly a man avoids contact with his younger brother's wife or with his wife's elder sister. Remarriage of divorcee, widow and widower is permissible. The kinship terminology of the Rajuars is classificatory and they borrow some terms from the Odia people.

Table 3

Village-wise Ethnic Composition

Ethnic group	*No. of Families*				
	Kamli Village		*Savrangapur Village*		
	No. of Families	*%*	*Ethnic Group*	*No. of Families*	*%*
Rajuar	66	39.53	Rajuar	36	87.80
Bhuiya	60	35.93	Patro Tanti	1	2.44
Patro Tanti	25	14.97	Khandayat	1	2.44
Munda	15	8.98	Santal	3	7.32
Karan	1	0.59			
Total	167		Total	41	

Table 3 shows the distribution of the Rajuar and other communities in these villages. It reveals that the Rajuar is numerically dominant tribe in these villages. The other dominant community, is the Bhuiya. They have separate hamlets. Comparatively caste people are few in number. Table 4 shows the distribution of sex-wise population and average family size in these two villages. It reveals that family size in urban village is a little less because of family planning programs are more implemented in this urban village than that of the other village.

Table 4

Village-wise Population Distribution

Name of the village	*No. of families*	*Population*					*Sex ratio female per 1000 male*	*Average family size*
		Male	*%*	*Female*	*%*	*Total Population*		
Kamli	66	155	51.84	144	48.16	299	929	4.5
Savrangapur	36	78	53.79	67	46.21	145	859	4.0
Total	102	233	211	444		4.35		

Table 5
Clan-wise Distribution of Families

Name of natal clan		*Name of Villages*			
husband	*wife*	*Village Kamli families*		*Village Savrangapur families*	
		No.	*%*	*No.*	*%*
Nag	Nag	43	65.15	21	58.42
Nag	Singha	6	9.09	3	8.33
Nag	Kencho	2	3.02	2	5.56
Nag	Not known	1	1.52	—	—
Singha	Nag	10	15.15		
Kencho	Nag	4	6.06	4	11.11
Nag	Chandi			1	2.78
Singha	Kencho			1	2.78
Singha	Nag			4	11.11
	Total	66		36	

Table 5 shows the distribution of clans and nature of clan endogamy. Although the members of Nag clan select their mates from other clans most of the marriages have taken place within their own clan. The Nag clan of both the villages practise clan endogamy; 65.15 per cent and 58.42 per cent marriages of the village of Kamli and Savrangapur respectively have taken place within the same Nag clan. Other clan members practise clan exogamy.

Table 6
Clan-wise Distribution of Population

Clan name	*Families of Kamli Village*		*Families of Savarang-pur Village*		*Villages*											
					Kamli village population						*Savrangapur village population*					
					Male		*Female*		*Total*		*Male*		*Female*		*Total*	
	No.	*%*	*No.*	*%*	*No.*	*%*	*No.*	*%*	*No.*	*%*	*No.*	*%*	*No.*	*%*	*No.*	*%*
Nag	52	78.79	27	75.00	124	80.00	117	81.25	241	80.00	55	70.51	53	79.10	108	74.48
Singha	10	15.15	4	11.11	20	12.90	17	11.80	37	12.37	11	14.10	8	11.94	19	13.10
Kencho	4	6.00	5	13.89	11	7.09	10	6.94	21	7.02	12	15.39	6	8.95	18	12.41
Total	66		36		155		144		299		78		67		145	

Table 6 shows that the number of persons in Nag clan are more and the number of persons in other clans are very few. As a result the members of the Nag clan do not find their mates in other clans and are forced to marry within their own clan by avoiding certain generations. For other clan members there is no dearth of mates.

Table 7

Age-group-wise Marital Status of Kamli Village

Age-group	Marital status										Total Population	
	Unmarried		Married		Widower		Divorcee		Total			
	M	F	M	F	M	F	M	F	M	F	No.	%
0–4	18	15	—	—	—	—	—	—	18	15	33	11.03
5–9	22	18	—	—	—	—	—	—	22	18	40	13.37
10–14	11	14	—	—	—	—	—	—	11	14	25	8.36
15–19	8	3	—	9	—	—	—	—	8	12	20	6.68
20–24	7	—	8	10	—	—	—	—	15	10	25	8.36
25–29	2	2	11	18	—	—	—	—	13	20	33	11.03
30–34	—	1	12	12	—	—	—	1	12	14	26	8.69
35–39	1	—	11	13	—	—	1	—	13	13	26	8.69
40–44	—	—	12	4	—	—	—	1	12	5	17	5.68
45–49	—	—	9	4	—	—	—	—	9	4	13	4.34
50–54	—	—	10	4	2	2	—	—	12	6	18	6.02
55–59	—	—	4	3	3	5	—	—	7	8	15	5.01
60+	—	—	2	2	1	3	—	—	3	5	8	2.67
Total	69	53	79	79	6	10	1	2	155	144	299	100
%	23.00	17.72	26.42	26.42	2.00	3.34	0.33	0.66	58.84	41.16		
G. Total	122		158		16		3		299			
%	41		53		5		1		100			

Table 8

Age-group-wise Marital Status of Savrangapur Village

Age-group	Marital Status										Total Population	
	Unmarried		Married		Widow		Divorcee		Total			
	M	F	M	F	M	F	M	F	M	F	No	%
0–4	11	9	—	—	—	—	—	—	11	9	20	13.79
5–9	11	3	—	—	—	—	—	—	11	3	14	9.65
10–14	5	7	—	—	—	—	—	—	5	7	12	8.27
15–19	3	5	—	1	—	—	—	—	3	6	9	6.20
20–24	10	1	3	7	—	—	—	—	13	8	21	14.48
25–29	—	3	8	4	—	—	—	—	8	7	15	10.34
30–34	1	—	4	6	—	—	—	—	5	6	11	7.58
35–39	—	—	6	4	—	—	—	—	6	4	10	6.89
40–44	—	—	4	1	—	—	—	—	4	1	5	5.44
45–49	—	—	1	1	—	—	—	—	1	1	2	1.37
50–54	—	—	3	4	—	1	—	—	3	5	8	5.51
55–59	—	—	3	4	1	3	—	—	4	7	11	7.58
60+	—	—	2	2	2	1	—	—	4	3	7	4.82
Total	41	28	34	34	3	5	—	—	78	67	145	100
%	28.27	19.31	23.45	23.45	2.07	3.45	—	—	—	—		
G. Total	69		68		8		—		145			
%	47.59		46.89		5.52		—		100			

Table 9

Population-wise Family Type

Type of Family		No. of Families				Total Population								Average Size of Family	
		Village Kamli		Village Savrangapur		Village Kamli				Village Savrangapur				Village Kamli	Village Savran-apur
		No.	%	No.	%	M	F	Total	%	M	F	Total	%		
Nuclear		43	65.15	27	75.00	90	82	172	57.52	60	52	112	77.24	4.00	4.14
Extended	(a) Vertical	20	30.30	4	11.11	59	57	116	38.80	13	11	24	16.55	5.8	6
	(b) Horizontal	1	1.51	—	—	5	4	9	3.01	—	—	—	—	9	—
Broken		1	1.51	2	5.55	1	1	2	0.67	1	2	3	2.07	2	1.5
Incomplete		1	1.51	3	8.33	—	—	—	—	4	2	6	4.14	2	2
Total		66		36		155	144	299	100	78	67	145	100		

Table 7 and 8 depict the marital status and age-group-wise distribution of Rajuars in two villages. It reveals that married persons are more in Kamli village than in Savrangapur village. Due to influence of urbanization, marriage age has been raised among the Rajuars. To some extent divorcee percentage is also higher among the urban dwellers. Nuclear type of family is common. There are about 32 per cent extended type of families in Kamli village. The percentage of extended families is much less among the Rajuar, who are settled in urban areas.

There are altogether 66 and 36 families in Kamli and Savrangapur villages respectively. Table 9 presents the distribution of different types of families in two villages located in two different ecologies. It reveals that nuclear families are more (75%) among the Rajuars of exposed area, especially among those who are landless and extended families are more, i.e., 32 per cent in Kamli village against 11 per cent in Savrangapur, the more exposed village. This suggests a relationship between nuclear family and landlessness. In Kamli village still some families that live together, have separate kitchen and hold the land jointly. More number of broken and incomplete families is found among the urban Rajuars than that of their rural counterpart. This is also an interesting feature of social change.

Table 10

Family Size in Village Kamli

No. of Individuals		*No. of Families*	*Percentage*
1.	Small	1	1.51
2.		7	10.00
3.	Medium	11	16.66
4.		14	21.21
5.		21	31.81
6.	Extra medium	3	4.54
7.		3	4.54
8.	Large	4	6.06
9.		1	1.51
10.		1	1.51
	Total	66	100%

Table 10 reveals that though there are different sizes of families in Kamli village, the majority of the family (70%) comprises 3–5 members. Only 6 families are large in size, having more than 8 members. Large families are almost absent in urban village.

Table 11

Literacy among the Rajuar in Kamli Village

Educational Standard	*Male (%)*	*Female (%)*	*Total (%)*
Non-literate	78 (50.33%)	131 (91%)	209 (70%)
Literate without any specific standard	23 (14.84%)	8 (5.55%)	31 (10.35%)
Primary (I–V)	40 (25.81%)	5 (3.45%)	45 (15.03%)
Middle (VI–VIII)	5 (3.22%)	—	5 (1.63%)
High school (IX–X)	7 (4.51%)	—	7 (2.33%)
Post Martic XI +	2 (1.29%)	—	2 (0.66%)
Grand total	155	144	299

Table 11 depicts level of literacy among the Rajuars in Kamli village. Of the total Rajuar population 30 per cent are literate. They include school going students or those knowing how to write their names. Literacy among the female (9%) is much lower than the male (49%). Probably due to lack of awareness, shortage of time and unwillingness their females are least educated. Only 13 females are literate. The percentage goes down further when we consider the formal education systems. The Rajuars cannot continue their education beyond the primary standard on account of their pecuniary disadvantage. Only two persons passed matriculation examination in Kamli village and one of them passed B.A. examination.

According to 1961 census 11.8 per cent of the Rajuars were literate. Women among them were further less educated. Literacy among the Rajuars has increased considerably because of the establishment of local schools. There are two schools located in Kamli village. One is residential Seva Ashra School which is up to VIII standard and it is functioning since 1952. Another primary school that has up to V standard has recently been established. For higher education the Rajuars go to neighbouring high school and college at Baripada. The teachers of the village school are mostly non-tribal and are from outside the village. The medium of instruction in formal education is Odia. It is interesting to note that the percentage of literacy among the Rajuars of Savrangapur is less. Probably the school-going students are employed in menial jobs at an early age.

Tribal Economy: Landholding Pattern

Table 12 and 13 present the distribution of lands in Kamli village. The Rajuars have 64.08 acres of cultivable land, that means per family and per head average land is only 0.97 and 0.33 acres respectively. The Table 12 shows that 83 per cent Rajuar family belong to marginal category that has land up to 3 acres and average landholder has 1.83 acres. The middle category Rajuar is represented through a few numbers (5) and each occupies on an average 4.74 acres of land.

Table 12

Landholding Pattern in Kamli Village

Category of farmers	*Amount of land in acre*	*Families*		*Total land in acre*	*Average landholders in acre*
		No.	*%*		
Marginal	0.0–0.50	5	14.28	1.50	0.31
	0.50–1.00	9	25.71	6.01	0.66
	1.00–2.00	11	31.42	14.32	1.30
	2.00–3.00	4	14.42	9.70	2.42
		29	82.85	31.59	1.08
Middle	3.00–5.00	3	8.57	13.14	4.64
	5.00–8.00	2	5.71	10.55	45.27
		5	14.28	23.69	4.74
High	8.00+	1	2.85	8.70	8.70
		1	2.85	8.70	8.70
Total landholders		35	100.00	64.08	1.83
Total landless		31			

Only one family belongs to higher category that has land more than 8 acres. It is clear from the analysis that out of 66 household of the Rajuars in Kamli village 35 families have land and 31 families are landless. Of course a few landless Rajuars have acquired land of the Bhuiya and the Kurmi communities for periodical cultivation. Table 13 shows the pattern of cultivable and homestead landholding in village Kamli. It reveals that per family landholding is below one acre.

Table 13

Average Pattern of Landholding among the Rajuars (in acres)

Cultivable Land	*Amount of Land Per family ***	*Amount of land per head ***
64.08	0.97	0.33
Homestead Land		
13.81	0.20	0.07

**Total No. of family is 66 and individual is 299

Table 14 shows that the total land of the village Kamli is 536.86 acres. Of this total land 376.85 acres is cultivable and the rest of land is uncultivable. The total homestead land is only 8.04 acres.

Table 14

Distribution of Land in Kamli Village

Kind of land	*Quantity of land in acre*
Abadi (cultivable)	376.85
Anabadi (uncultivable)	44.67
Government land	84.48
Gochor (Grazing)	17.43
Basti (homestead)	8.04
Bon (forest)	—
School	5.39
Total	536.86

Other Occupation

Data on income is calculated on the basis of agricultural produce, earning as wage labourers, salary of service people and subsidiary sources of income. It is stated earlier that the Rajuars are mostly marginal cultivators. However, they earn mainly as daily wage labourers and as traders. On an average, a Rajuar family is constituted by two working persons, i.e., husband and wife. There are primary as well as subsidiary economic activities of the Rajurs of both the villages. The Rajuars are mainly agriculturists. Table 15 presents the occupations of the Rajurs in detail. In Kamli village, 62.12 per cent Rajuars who have land are engaged in cultivation. 58.33 per cent of the Rajurs of Savrangapur village who are landless are engaged either as agricultural labourers or as day labourers. Besides being engaged in cultivation and as agricultural / wage labourers, small number of them is engaged in their traditional trade, service and in other jobs. In the village the Rajuars are mostly marginal cultivators and they are to depend on rains for irrigating the fields. Since the produce from agriculture is not enough, people are engaged in other sources of income and hence they try to search jobs in urban centres. Fifty per cent Rajuars of Kamli village are engaged in the business of selling of flattened rice during the festive occasions. They are engaged as wage labourers and in preparation of rope from sabai grass and thus supplement their income by these subsidiary occupations in general. In the village they get only 15–20 days work round the year and at that time labour charge was ₹ 10 to 15 per day. The labour charge in urban area is just the double, and as such the income of the Rajuars in urban centre is better than that of the rural areas.

Table 15

Distribution of Families by Occupation

Name of Occupation	Village Kamli		Village Savrangapur	
	Families		Families	
	No.	%	No.	%
Cultivation	41	62.12	3	8.33
Trade	9	13.63	2	5.55
Agricultural labourer/ wage labourer	15	22.73	21	58.33
Service	1	1.51	6	16.66
Other jobs	—	—	4	11.11
Total	66	100.00	36	100.00

Table 16 shows the annual income of the Rajuar families in Kamli and Savragapur village. About 54 per cent of the families of Kamli village belong to lower income group, i.e., those who earns less than ₹ 5,000 per year. The Table reveals that people belonging to lower income group in urban village is very few. By and large about 75 per cent Rajuar in Savrangapur village belong to middle income group. Most of their average earning is ₹ 8,000 per year. It is interesting to note that people belonging to higher income group are more in number in urbanized village than in rural area.

Table 16

Family-wise Average Annual Income

Income group	Kamli Village		Savrangapur Village	
	No. of household	Percentage	No. of household	Percentage
Lower: below ₹ 5,000	36	54.54	2	5.56
Middle: up to ₹ 10,000	24	36.36	27	75.00
Higher: above ₹ 10,000	6	9.09	7	19.44
Total	66		36	

Table 17

Working Force and Dependants

Village	Working Force			Dependant			Total Population		
	M (%)	F (%)	Total (%)	M (%)	F (%)	Total (%)	M (%)	F (%)	Total
Kamli	94 (31.43)	84 (28.09)	178 (59.53)	61 (20.40)	60 (20.00)	121 (40.47)	155	144	299
Savrangapur	47 (32.41)	45 (31.03)	92 (63.45)	31 (21.38)	22 (15.17)	53 (36.55)	78	67	145
Total	141 (31.77)	129 (29.05)	270 (60.81)	92 (20.72)	82 (18.47)	174 (39.19)	233	211	444

Table 17 presents the working forces and the dependants of the Rajuars in two villages. It is a fact that in tribal society dependants are those who cannot work and are not engaged in any productive activity. Table 17 shows that working force among the urbanized Rajuar is higher (63.45) because in urban areas people get more employment opportunities and as such even minors as well as aged persons are engaged in work. On the other hand dependants are more in rural areas than in urban areas.

Elements of Stratification

Land is one of the factors which shapes social stratification. There are only a few people who have more quantity of land and on the other hand there are more people who have less quantity of land. Thus, the possession of land determines differences among the people. Education is another feature which differentiates the individuals within the society. Among the Rajuars literacy rate is not very high. Only 25 students are studying in local school. Their average education standard is only up to primary stage. Only a few male students have crossed the primary stage. Only one Rajuar has passed B.A. and one is studying at local college. The educated person gets prestige in the society. It is observed that they differentiate educated people from others. Their family members also enjoy a little bit higher status in the society and thus feel proud of being educated.

Income of a person is indeed the main factor of differentiation in the society. Income has direct link with the prosperity of a family. Property in association with educational prestige upgrades their social status. Variation of income reflects on various life styles and creates stratification in the society. Occupation is hallmark by which individuals are distinguished from one another. In Rajuar society a person having good quantity of land or being engaged in service is regarded as wealthy. Some sort of socio-cultural and economic elements also differentiate the individuals in the society. Among the Rajuars possession of material assets like, radio, cycle, tape recorder, T.V. wooden furniture, etc., also differentiate the individuals. Most of the Rajuars though possess a cycle but only a few have radio, tape-recorder, etc. Comparatively, urbanized Rajuars possess more material assets than the rural Rajuars. Possession of valuable assets including gold or silver ornaments brings extra prestige to the women in their society. Income and assets based inequality jointly differentiate the individuals who possess them from those who do not possess them.

The Rajuar society is divided into a number of clans. The majority of the families of Kamli village belong to the Nag clan. In Kamli village out of 66 households, 52 households belong to Nag clan. The village headman, Paramanik, priest of the Rajuar society belong to Nag clan. The Nag clan members have numerical dominance and being the original clan of this village exercise some powers and influence over the Rajuars of other clans. These clan members take the main part in the village festivals and they mainly control the law and order of the Rajuar society. However, in Rajuar society all the clans are regarded equal in status and no distinctions are made between the members of these clans. In the multi-ethnic village set-up, the Rajuar settle in a separate hamlet. They share with other communities village wells, road, pond, common cremation ground and they also visit the village temples freely. Thus, stratification in sharing the village public places is almost nil among the villagers. They are now free to construct their houses at any place in the village, depending on individual choice and capability.

The landless Rajuars are mostly engaged as wage labourers in agricultural activities or in construction of house. In the agricultural season, the Rajuars like other agricultural labourers are employed as wage labourers in the fields of land-holding castes and tribes. Inter-community differentiation is marked by observing commensality and connubial relationships as per traditional norms.

The Rajuars are an endogamous tribe in Odisha. They do not have any territorial, social or linguistic division. The Rajuars of Jharkhand and West Bengal are recognized as Scheduled Caste, whereas they are a Scheduled Tribe in Odisha. The Rajuars of Odisha have, however, connubial relation with the Rajuars of Midnapur. There are some instances where they had brought brides from the Rajuars of Midnapur in Mayurbhanj district. The Rajuars have no commensal as well as connubial relationship with the Bagal caste. The Bagal is recognized as a cattle herder community in this region. The Rajuars live in the midst of 22 caste and tribal groups. They maintain social difference with them by observing different norms in exchange of food and water from them. They do not accept food and water from the SC castes like the Dhoba, the Hadi, the Dom, the Teli, the Patro, the Tanti, etc., and also from tribes like the Mahali, the Kotha, the Santal, etc., as well as from the Musalman. Now of course the males may accept food and water from the Patro, the Tanti, the Munda and the Bhumij. They consider the position of the Bhuiya as little higher because they wear sacred threads and worship the village deities. This is despite the fact that the Rajuar is an offshoot of Bhuiya tribe. However, in the village Rajuars are regarded as superior to others. There are some instances of marriage between Rajuar boys and Munda girls. As they consider the Mundas to be equal with them there is no objection to establish connubial and commensal relationship with them.

The Rajuars accept food and water from the higher caste groups like the Brahmin, the Karan, the Gouda, the Baistom, the Barik, the Kurmi, the Mahato, etc. They have commensal relationship with the tribes like the Bhatudi and the Bhuiya. Usually Rajuar women do not take food in the house of the communities that are considered socially inferior to them. However, the male members have no objection to take ceremonial food from some communities that may be considered lower in local social hierarchical order. The Rajuars have clear cut understanding of the local hierarchy in the local situation. They have confusion to place them in the social hierarchy in relation to the caste groups. The concept of purity and pollution is not very clear to the Rajuars although they have constant contact and exposure with the neighbouring Hindu castes. Thus some sort of stratification does exit between the Hindu and the tribal communities. The idea of social exclusion has grown stronger and apparent under the Hindu caste system. Whatever may be the socio-economic position of the Rajuars, but they maintain patron-client relationship with the Brahmin, the Kamar (blacksmith), Barik (barber), Dhoba (washerman), Khumbhar (potter), etc., which does not lead to any conflict is society.

Inter-Ethnic Stratification

Table 18

Regional Hierarchical Order of Castes and Tribes

Categories of Status	*Communities*
Upper group	1. Brahmin
	2. Vaishnav
	3. Kshatriya
	4. Karan
	5. Khandait
	6. Goura
Middle group	1. Goala
	2. Kurmi
	3. Mahata
	4. Barik
	5. Bhuiya S.T.
	6. Rajuar S.T.
	7. Teli
	8. Kumbhar
	9. Kamar/Bindhani
	10. Munda S. T
Lower group	1. Patro Tanti S.C.
	2. Khobe S.C.
	3. Santal/Majhi S.T.
	4. Mahali S.T.
	5. Pano S.C.
	6. Muchi S.C.
	7. Hadi S.C.

The population of Kamli village can be broadly divided into two groups, the tribal and the non-tribal. The Hindu castes who live around the Rajuar tribe are divided into multiple endogamous castes and they belong to different hierarchical positions as shown in Table 18. Each caste group is more or less a homogeneous group as far as its way of life is concerned. Endogamy and commensality make each of them a separate group. Due to long association with the Hindu castes, the Rajuars have been accorded certain social position in the regional caste hierarchy, but social exclusion of the tribes and their marginalization in caste system is apparent.

Table 18 reveals an approximate social position of different castes and tribes, inhabiting this region. Altogether, 22 ethnic groups are residing in this area, and they can be broadly classified into three categories, namely, upper, middle and lower groups. There are Brahmin, Vaishnav, Kshatriya, Karan, Khandait and the Goura in the upper category. They are considered to have high position in the regional social hierarchy. The Brahmin is in the topmost position amongst them. The position of the Vaishnav is quite high because of the fact that the local communities consider them as 'Guru'. The position of the Kshatriya, Khandait and Karan are similar to each other because they belong to high caste groups. The Goura have a low position amongst the caste group of upper category. They accept water from all the communities irrespective of caste or tribe. The intermediate groups are mainly peasant communities. However, a few tribes like the Bhuiya, Rajuar and Munda occupy a higher position than some other castes in the regional hierarchy. The social position of the Bhuiya is higher than the Rajuars. The Bhuiya wear sacred thread and worship the Lord Siva and for this fact people consider them higher than other castes and tribes. Though the Rajuars consider the Bhuiyas to have equal status with them, some Rajuars place the Bhuiyas at a lower status. The lower strata is formed mostly by the Scheduled Castes. The castes like the Patro, Tanti, Dhoba, Pano, Muchi, Hadi and tribes like the Santal and the Mahali are included in this group. The position of the Hadi amongst these groups is lowest. They are an unclean caste whose traditional occupation was leather work and removal of the dead animal. These social positions of different castes and tribes are based on the concept of purity and pollution as also economic considerations.

Table 19 shows the approximate regional ranking of different castes and tribal communities. This ranking is based on ritual, economic and social factors. It reveals that the Rajuars occupy almost the middle rank in the regional social hierarchy. They consider all the Scheduled Castes inferior to them in ranks and thus they mostly do not take water and food from them. Tribal women are not allowed to take food in the house of any community that is considered lower to them.

Table 19

Regional Hierarchical Order: The Ranks of Castes & Tribes

Ranks	*Name of Caste and Tribe*	*Ranks*	*Name of Caste and Tribe*
1	Brahmin	12	Munda S.T.
2	Vaishnav	13	Kumbhar
3	Kshatriya	14	Kamar/ Bindhani
4	Karan	15	Teli
5	Khandait	16	Patro Tanti S.C.
6	Goura	17	Dhaba S.C.
7	Kurmi Mahhata	18	Santal/ Majhi S.T.
8	Goala	19	Mahali S.T.
9	Barik	20	Pano S.C.
10	Bhuiya S.T.	21	Muchi S.C.
11	Rajuar S.T.	22	Hadi S.C.

The Rajuars live along with tribes like the Bathudi, the Saunti, the Savar, the Bhuiya, the Munda, the Santal, the Mahali, the Kalha and the Lodha. They have developed some sort of social hierarchy amongst them (Table 20). The Bathudi, the Saunti, the Savar and the Bhuiya consider them to have higher rank than the Rajuars and as such they do not accept food and water from them. The Santals and the Mundas occupy the middle rank. The Mahali, the Kalha, and the Lodha occupy the lower rank in the regional social hierarchy because they take beef and pork. The Rajuars do not take food and water in the house of the Santal because they take pork. Besides, the caste groups consider the tribal groups who live in unhygienic condition and do not take the service of Brahmin below to their rank.

Brief Ethnography of the Communities

A brief description of the local ethnic groups with their traditional occupation and interaction are given below.

The Brahmin

Brahmin is a well-known priestly caste that occupies the highest social position in the regional social hierarchy. The Brahmins of this district are mostly of Utkaliya class which is divided into two broad sections, viz., the Dakshinatya and the Jajapuratya. The following groups of Brahmins are also found:

Table 20

Local Hierarchical Order Prevalent Among the Tribe

Status	*Name of Tribes*
Higher	Bathudi Saunti Savar Bhuiya Rajuar
Middle	Munda Santal
Lower	Mahali Kalha Lodha

(i) Jharua – also known as Aranyaka.
(ii) Halua (from Hal, a plough) – who claim to be Balaram Gotri.
(iii) Sarua – those who grow arecas, arum, and coconut besides doing ordinary cultivation.
(iv) Ved Brahmins – who live upon alms.
(v) Pandas – who serve as priests and cooks.
(vi) Bauchaua and jaya – Andhra Brahmins of somewhat lower rank.
(vii) Atharva vedi.
(viii) Baishnab or Vaishnav (Baragi, Baistam).

The Kshatriya

There is no category of Kshtriya in Odisha, but some high castes regard themselves as 'Rajput'.

The Khandait

They are the martial caste of Odisha. The Rajas of Odisha used to retain large armies of Khandaits. There is difference of opinion as to the origin of the word. The general view is that it is derived from words like 'Khanda' (a sword), 'Kanda' (an arrow) and 'Katari' (a dagger). The other explanation is that Odisha was formerly divided into Khanda or groups of villages each in charge of a Khandapati which might have been corrupted to Khandait. Most of them are agriculturists.

The Karan

The origin of the word is said to be from the word 'Karani' which means clerk or writer. This caste has a high social position and the people of this caste are generally engaged either in government and private service or in agriculture.

The Gaura

The Gauras are herdsman in Odisha. Though the traditional occupation of Gauras is cow keeping and dealing in milk and allied products, in Mayurbhanj they appear to have completely forgotten that occupation and are engaged in cultivation and other means of livelihood like selling handia. They occupy a higher position in the society.

The Kurmi

The Kurmis who were formerly a tribe are now one of the castes in the district. They are agriculturists and are chiefly found in Baripada, Panchpir, and Bamanghaty sub-divisions. They are also found in the neighbouring Keonjhar district, in Manbhum and Midnapur district of West Bengal and in Singhbum and Ranchi district of Jharkhand. The Kurmis are conscious of their own status. They do not allow inter-caste marriage. They accept the service of the Brahmin priest. They practice 'bride price'.

The Goala

They are a cultivator caste who grow onion, garlic and vegetables. They are distributed in Baripada and Kaptipada Sub-divisions.

The Barik

This is a barber caste. The Bariks are found in all the districts of Odisha including Mayurbhanj.

The Kumbhar

They are pot-makers. The name of the caste is derived from Kumbha, a water pot.

The Kamar

The occupation of the Kamar is iron smelting and blacksmithy. The Hatua Kamars are the indigenous Kamars of Odisha while Bangala Kamars are immigrants from Bengal. There is no Kamar in Kamli village. However, the Rajuars take the services of the Kamars of the neighbouring village.

The Teli

Oil-pressing and selling are the traditional occupations of this caste. The original low position of the Teli is attributed to their employment of bullocks for pressing oil. The name comes from the Sanskrit word 'Tailika' or 'Taila' (oil). Now they are engaged in business and cultivation.

The Tanti

The name of the caste is derived from 'Tanta' or handloom. They are a Scheduled Caste of Odisha.

The Dhoba

They are washermen and are also called Rajaks. They are distributed almost evenly throughout the district.

The Pano

The Panos are mainly divided into two groups, namely, Jena Pano and Pano Tanti. The Patra Panos are now known as Pano Tantis.

The Dom

They are mainly bamboo workers and drummers. Some of them are cultivators. They beat drums on the occasion of marriage.

The Mochi

The Mochis are cobblers. They are admittedly descended from the Chamars. The Chamars were formerly tanners but they seem to have given up that occupation. The Chamars have given up tanning and the Mochis are now both tanners and cobblers. The Mochis have social rank below the Chamars.

The Hadi

They are usually scavengers, sweepers, basket makers and bamboo workers. A large concentration of this caste is found in Baripada Sub-division.

The Bhuiya

The Bhuiyas are land owning people. They were once zamindars or sub-proprietors in Parganna Uperbhag in Baripada subdivision.

The Bathudi

They enjoy tribal status and they are adopting agriculture as main occupation. The Bathudis are chiefly found in Panchpir Sub-division.

The Saunti

The Sauntis are a less developed community. They call themselves Saunta, meaning, gatherer, which has later been corrupted to Saunti.

The Bhumij

The Bhumij are mainly concentrated in the central part of Baripada Sub-division. In some localities they accept bride from the Mundas and are known as Bhumij Munda. The Bhumijs are cultivators and some are agricultural labourers.

The Munda

The Mundas are not a native tribe of Mayurbhanj district. They are mostly agriculturists.

The Santal

The Santal are native of the region. They have rich folk culture. Santal script originated in this district. The Santals either bury or cremate their dead. The ordinary occupation of this tribe is cultivation and agricultural labour.

The Mahali

Risley conjectured that the Mahalis are a branch of the Santal tribe. The totems of the Mahalis and Santals are generally same. Gait is of opinion that the Mahali language is a variant of Santali.

The Saora (Savar, Saura of Sabara)

The Saora have a rich cultural tradition. The tribe has strong link with Jagannath cult. It was around 1930 during the Gandhi's reform movement; the tribal people like Saora in this region by and large abstained from taking beef and stopped eating pork. They threw away some of their tribal culture and accepted the service of the Brahmin for their life cycle rituals and social ceremony. They are regarded as superior among tribes.

Social Change and Cultural Adaptation

The Rajuars live in multi-ethnic villages. Hence they have been influenced by the dominant Hindus. Certain Hindu dominant communities like the Karans, the Brahmins and so on are the reference groups to the Rajuars. They emulate the cultural norms of these groups. The Rajuars were traditionally non-agricultural community who pursued vocations like making of pounded rice, cattle rearing, etc., and they served the highly skilled settled agriculturists as agricultural labourers or domestic helpers. They have learnt cultivation from the Kurmi

Mahatos. They are now settled agriculturists. This practice of cultivation has made a tremendous impact on the life and culture of the Rajuars. They now accept the ritual services of the Brahmin priest and take part in several Hindu festivals like car festival of Lord Jagannath, Holi, Dewali, Durga Puja, Kali Puja, Siva Ratri and so on. After independence their contacts with the outside world have increased to a great extent. Their traditional culture has undergone several changes. Such changes are observed in their material possession, house pattern, quality of household articles such as furniture, dress, ornaments, cycle, transistors, etc. They try to imitate the culture and way of life of the neighbouring communities. They have stopped taking beef, pork and even liquor. However, on festive occasions they consume liquor.

Changes have occurred in their life cycle rituals and practices. Instead of bride price they accept dowry now. Recently, both courtship marriage and marriage performed in the temple are more frequent. Now marriage takes place at bride's village instead of groom's village and the marriage party does not consist of whole village. Quality of food has also been improved. They now invite the other caste and tribal people in their marriage feast. Previously, marriage rituals were held at day time but now the marriage rituals are performed in the evening or at night similar to those of the caste Hindus. They fix the marriage date according to Hindu auspicious date and month. They employ the service of the Brahmin priest for life cycle rituals and also accept the service of *Jyotish* (astrologers). Tribal dances, song and games which were once associated with their daily life are now changing fast. They now perform dance and sing songs only during marriage or Karma festival. They worship the Hindu gods and goddesses along with their traditional deities. Besides engaging their ritual specialist, they engage the Brahmin priest (*purohit*) for the performance of rituals.

Migration and Economic Change

The shortage of land as well as economic insecurity defined the social status of the tribe. Landlessness and marginal holding of land forced the Rajuars to migrate and to settle in urban-industrial complex in Balasore city, where their economic status improved on account of earning wages as industrial labourers. They also came to be involved in petty trade and business. Some of them were employed in regular service. Women were also absorbed as menial workers easily. All these developments created a rudimentary form of inequality between the rural and the urban Rajuars. In urban sector, job is easily accessible to each and every Rajuar. Impact of urbanization, higher level of aspiration and occupational mobility have led to sort of class formation. The enterprising Rajuars are moving towards the economically sound positions. The urbanization has greatly affected the structure and function of the family. Joint families were predominant in the earlier Rajuar society. The joint/extended families among the migrant Rajuars is much less in number than that of the rural Rajuars.

This stratification between the rich and the poor among the Rajuars has led to social exclusion between them. Ritual standards are not crucial now. Economic considerations are more important now. Differences between rich and poor are manifested in their material life such as possession of modern assets like transistor, cycle, tape recorder, furniture and so on. Now migrant Rajuars also go to the local hospital and dispensary for treatment. The Rajuars are now much interested to take part in Kirtan (holy songs) and Jatra (open theatre) performances. They observe almost all the Hindu festivals. Makar Sankranti is their prime festival. Good number of Rajuars have visited the sacred places like Puri temple. Changes are observed in political sphere also. The Statutory Panchayat system has minimized the power of their traditional tribal council.

Conclusion

The Rajuars of Mayurbhanj retain many tribal characters including clan organization and tribal religious beliefs, but they have been influenced by Hindu culture due to long cultural and economic contacts. Thus, they have been Hindus to some extent. The Hindu groups own major economic resources in village, where the Rajuars also live though segregated from caste localities. Poverty is rampant due to increasing landlessness among the Rajuars who often migrate to urban areas for employment as labour. Migration has led to better economic gains and those with lands and wages through migration have emerged as upper class among the Rajuars. Now all Rajuars aspire to improve their statuses, but local norms and village conditions force the Rajuars to suffer from social exclusion and discrimination.

Acknowledgements

In order to collect data for this report long fieldwork was conducted in Mayurbhanj district. Author is grateful to Director, Anthropological Survey of India, Kolkata for providing opportunity to conduct fieldwork. The author is grateful to the Coordinator of the project, Dr N.K. Das, whose critical comments during the workshop held in Kolkata, helped to organize the data and revise the report in a suitable manner. Editorial assistance provided by Dr Das is also acknowledged.

References

Deb, P.C. 1975, *Social Stratification and Mobility in Rural Setting*, Delhi: Researches Publications.

Mann, R.S. 1984, "Social Stratification and Tribal Social Structure", in *Anthropological and Sociological Theory*, Jaipur: Rawat Publication.

Singh, K.S. 1994, *People of India, Scheduled Tribe*, Delhi: Oxford University Press.

13 Foraging to Agriculture

Nascent Class Formation among the Chenchus of Andhra Pradesh

Md. Azeez Mohidden and G.V. Ramana

This paper discusses the original hunting-gathering economy and social change amongst the Chenchus of Andhra Pradesh. In doing so, an attempt is made to describe the changing patterns of interactions at inter-community level. It also describes the effect of modernization and development programmes. About two months fieldwork was carried out in late 1990s among the Chenchus spread in 28 settlements (villages) of Kurnool, Prakasam and Mahaboobnagar districts. Data have been gathered mainly from the tribal villages like Chintala, Nakkanti, Bavipenta, Marripalam, Chinnarotla Peddarotla, Koraprolu, Peddamantanala, Bheemarayunicheruvu in Prakasham district and Byrluti, Nagluti, and Indereshwaragudem in Kurnool districts. Data are collected from multi-tribal villages like Palutila in Prakasham district and Palemcheruvu in Kurnool district. Data have also been gathered from Srisailam, a multiethnic village that is the pilgrimage centre, where different communities like the Brahmin, the Vaisya, the Reddy, the Balija, the Sale, the Lingayat, and the Muslims reside along with the Chenchus. Data have also been collected from the rehabilitated village called Kollalachervu. Data on multi-ethnic interactions are mainly collected from the villages called Mannanur, Jangamreddivaripalle and Vatvaripalle in the district of Mahaboobnagar; and Srisailam, Sunnipenta, Ahobilam, Panyam, Mahanandi, Kottalacheruvu, Atmakur, Nallakaluva, Pagidyala and Bannur in Kurnool district. Map-1 and Map-2 depict the State of Andhra Pradesh and surveyed villages in Kurnool and Mahboobnagar districts. The main household census survey was carried out in the villages of Marripalem and Bavipaenta in Prakasham district and Byrluti, Nagluti, Srisailam and Kottalecheruvu in Kurnool district.

The Identity of the Chenchu

The Chenchus of Andhra Pradesh are classified as Primitive Tribal Group (PTG). The Chenchus in the past used to live mainly on roots, honey and wild game (*District Gazetteer of Mahaboobnagar*, 1976: 47). They also lived in small settlements called Gudem, which are located adjacent to the plains villages in Kurnool district (*Kurnool District Gazetteer*, 1974: 63). They are also found in small pockets in other districts, namely, East Godavari, Krishna, Ranga Reddy, Warangal,

Map I

Surveyed Area in Andhra Pradesh

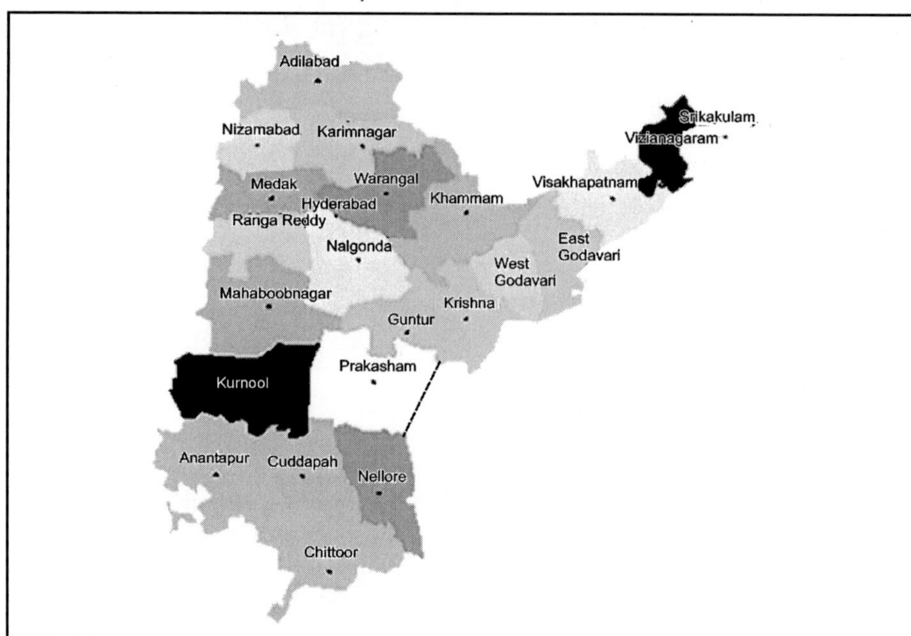

Nalgonda and Khammam. They are located in the Nallamalai forest of Kurnool, Prakashem in Mahaboobnagar district (Table 1) and also in Guntur district.

Table 1

The Chenchu Settlements in Kurnool, Prakasham and Mahaboobnagar Districts of A.P.

Mahaboobnagar District	*Prakasham District*	*Kurnool District*
Mannanur	Maruoaken	Srisailam
Jangamreddipalle	Bavipenta	Byrluti
Vatwaripalle	Chintala	Nagluti
	Nakkanti	Kottalacheruvu
	Palutla	Palemcheruvu
	Peddarotla	Nallakaluva
	Chinnarotla	Mahanandi
	Koraprolu	Pagidala
	Bheemarayunicheruvu	Atmakur
	Peddamantanala	Panyam
		Sivapuram
		Ahobilam
		Sunnipenta
		Hariharanagar
		Indreshwaragudem

The term Chenchu is said to have been derived from the term 'Chettu' (a tree in Telugu language) which in course of time has been distorted. The people who lived under tree thus came to be called Chenchus. As per the old Census reports these people used to eat 'Chunchu' (a type of vegetable). Till recently the chenchus had solely depended on foraging. Very large number of Chenchus living in Bheemarayuni, Cheruvu and Petcheruvu villages still collect tubers, roots and leafy vegetables like 'chechugadda', while some of them are now engaged as wage labourers (Table 2). A majority of them still sustain on honey, tamarind, soap nuts 'sara papu' (cashew nuts), broom sticks, hill mangoes, mushti seeds, etc.

The Chenchus are divided into many segments, with varied occupations now, and spread in many parts of the state. According to Rao (1991), the Chenchus are divided into: (1) Konda Chenchus, (2) Uru (village) Chenchus, (3) Yanadi Chenchus, (4) Bonta Chenchus, (5) Chenchu Dasaris, (6) Koya Chenchus and (7) Krishna Chenchus. The Krishna Chenchus were the mendicants and beggars. They are mainly inhabited in the district of Guntur. Some scholars believed that this community is a conglomeration of the Chenchus and other primitive nomadic tribes like the Dommera and the Nakkala (Bhowmick, 1991: 18–19). According to the Census of India (1961: 8) there are four broad groups, viz., (1) Koya Chenchus inhabiting the region of Bhadrachalam in Khammam district, (2) Konda Chenchus found in the Nallamalai forest of Kurnool and Mahaboobnagar district, (3) Chenchu Dasari of Kurnool district and (4) Ura Chenchus.

Furer-Haimendorf (1943: 299) mentions that besides the Jungle Chenchus, three other endogamous groups namely the Telugu Chenchus, the Krishna Chenchus and the Bontha Chenchus are found in different areas of Andhra Pradesh. The Telugu Chenchus claim that they are the Konda Chenchus but they have become 'Telugu' because the agricultural communities like the Kapus regard them as a Telugu caste and accept food and water from them. The Krishna Chenchus once lived in the town of Nandikotkur of Kurnool district and lived on begging in the town. Presently, they are not found in the area. The Uru Chenchus are originally Konda Chenchus. After having settled down in the plains and foothills of Nallamalai forests in search of livelihood some generations back they have added the term, 'uru' to Chenchu word. They are still maintaining martial relations with the Konda Chenchus as before.

According to informants there are five Chenchu endogamous groups that are broadly based on territory and occupations. They are (1) Bontha Chenchus, (2) Koya Chenchus, (3) Dasari Chenchus, (4) Alike Dasari Chenchus, and (5) Adavi or Konda or Deva Chenchus. The Bontha Chenchus live in Chenchupeta as well as in Guntur. They are nomadic people and they depend on bamboo work. The Koya Chenchus live in Bhadrachalam. The Dasari Chenchus also called "Mundlakarrarvandl" are found in Pagadiyal, Bannur, Pentcheral and in Kurnool districts. Dasari Chenchus have immigrated from Atmakur town and nearby villages about 25 years ago and settled down at Byrluti. They are originally mendicants and have started making mosquito sticks. They purchase raw materials from forest department for preparation of these sticks. They sell these sticks in large scale (i.e., by carrying in trucks) in towns of Kurnool, Prakasham and Gantur districts. They are also called 'Butta Chenchus' and are found in small number in Jangam Reddivaripalle of Mahboonagar district. They earn

Table 2

Distribution of Workers in Different Occupations

Name of Settlement/Village	*Different Occupations of Chenchus*																				
	Agriculture			*Agriculture related wage labour*			*MFP**			*Service*			*Basketry*			*Begging*			*Total*		
	M	*F*	*T*	*M*	*F*	*T*	*M*	*F*	*T*	*M*	*F*	*T*	*M*	*F*	*T*	*M*	*F*	*T*	*M*	*F*	*T*
Srisailam	—	—	—	3	3	6	17	20	37	11	3	14	1	0	1	0	1	1	32	27	59
Bairluti	1	1	2	5	6	11	37	45	82	1	0	1	—	—	—	—	—	—	44	52	96
Nagluti	2	2	4	7	7	14	21	19	40	1	0	1	—	—	—	—	—	—	31	28	59
Kottolacheruve	—	—	—	—	—	—	11	15	26	7	3	10	—	—	—	—	—	—	18	18	36
Bavipenta	—	—	—	—	—	—	34	36	70	—	—	—	—	—	—	—	—	—	34	36	70
Marripalem	17	14	31	26	28	54	13	13	26	1	0	1	—	—	—	—	—	—	57	55	112
Total	20	17	37	41	44	85	133	148	281	21	6	27	1	0	1	0	1	1	216	216	432

*MFP – Minor Forest Products

their livelihood principally by wholesale marketing of mosquito sticks in Kurnool and Guntur cities. They also depend on collection of forest products. The Konda Chenchus feel that they are superior to these two sub-groups although Dasari Chenchus are economically better off in comparison to Konda Chenchus. On the whole, the Konda Chenchus claim superiority over the Dasari Chenchus. Dasari Chenchus are also called Yanadi Chenchus. They have adopted the term 'Yanadi' due to their marital relations with Yanadis of Nellore district. However, some informants have admitted that they are not Yanadi Chenchus but are Adavi Chenchus. The Adavi or Konda or Deva Chenchus strongly feel that they are the real Chenchus who are found in and around Nallamalai forests of Mahaboob Nagar, Kurnool and Prakasam districts.

According to prevailing myth the Konda Chenchus are the descendants of goddess Chenchulaksmi, wife of Lord Mallikarjuna, whereas the Dasari Chenchus claim to have descended from the goddess Adi Lakshmi, sister of Chenchu Lakshmi and wife of Lord Mallikarjuna. However, the Konda Chenchus do not endorse the mythological origin of Dasari Chenchu on the ground that they have no privileges of conducting first religious rituals either at Srisailam or at Ahobilam. This story is in conformation with the account given by census report (1961: 1) as well as Furer-Haimendorf (1943).

The Chenchus who have been living in towns or major multi-ethnic villages (particularly of Mahaboobnagar district) over decades have abandoned the practice of using bow and arrow, yet a majority of the Chenchus have retained the skill of using bow and arrow. In rural milieu even today all male children over 8–10 years learn the skill of using bow and arrow either with their own effort or under the guidance of their elders in uni-tribal or even multi-tribal villages. In these areas all Chenchus including their women and able-bodied children, carry bow and arrow as well as dog for honey collection from the jungles. However, the art of using bow and arrow and the company of dogs is not found among the Dasari Chenchus. Due to the strict enforcement of laws by Tiger Sanctuary (1963) they are hardly allowed to carry out hunting expeditions on large scale, though Adavi Chenchus still hunt small animals like rabbits, parrots, jungle fowls, peacock, etc., in the night without the knowledge of forest department.

Since the settlement areas of the Chenchus fall under Reserve Tiger Forest area they have been rehabilitated in the newly constructed houses provided to them at Kottalcheruvu and also in the nearby non-tribal villages and nearby towns. However, because of their attachment to the forests over centuries, most of the Chenchus are not mentally prepared to leave their original abode and settle in the houses provided to them under various welfare schemes of the Government. Nearly half of the resettled Chenchus have returned to their original settlement in spite of availability of various livelihood opportunities and various schemes like tailoring, bamboo mats, etc. As economic support, goats and cattle are also provided to some families belonging to a few selected villages. However, they are not making use of these benefits. Rather, they are confident of making their livelihood by selling fuel wood as well as M.F.P. collected from forest to the town people during different seasons.

In early days they used to go to forests in groups and used to stay for one week in the forest for the procurement of honey. Because of the restrictions of

Tiger Reserve Project since 1981 and with implementation of Wild Life (protection) Act 1972, the Chenchus are scared of entering the forest. They are also afraid of entering into interior regions because of the fear of falling prey to the wild animals. So, now they go to the forest in the morning and return to their abode in the evening after collecting gumwood and other produce. They make complaints to the forest department that their domestic animals are being killed by the wild animals and hence they demand adequate compensation.

Old records show that before the enactment of Madras Forest Act 1882 the Chenchus of Kurnool district lived on food gathered from the forest. They also collected *muttas* (protection fees) from the pilgrims who passed through their settlement till 1960. The collection of *muttas* was stopped after the construction of all- weather road connecting Atmakur, Domala and Srisaitam in 1957–58. In 1917 the Forest Officer, F.R. Wood pursued the Chenchus to work as labourers in the plantation work. A school was established in 1940. In 1932 an area of 6,141 acres was demarcated for the Chenchus for cultivation. Besides, to protect the Chenchus from exploitation the Forest Department started to purchase the Minor Forest Products compulsorily from the Chenchus. Efforts were also made by the then Nizam Government to assist the Chenchus in changing their economy through lease right of land in 1932. In spite of all these interferences the Chenchus could not take cultivation so successfully. None of the villagers of Kottalacheruvu and Bvipenta are cultivators, although land has been allotted to them.

Social Organization

A majority of the Chenchu clans are associated with totems. They have some idea about the origin of these clans. Some feel that Tokala clan is named after the tail of Lord Anjaneyaswamy. Chevula is named after the ears of Adi Laxmi. Nimmalla clan is associated with Nimma Chettu (lemon tree). Dasari is associated with the Dasari tree (a kind of tree found in the forest). Avula means cow in Telugu language.

Furer-Haimendorf (1943: 287) has mentioned that the Chenchus living in the districts of Kurnool, Prakasham and Mahaboobnagar seems to have adopted *intiperu* (lineages) from the neighbouring Telugu castes like the Kapus, the Besta and the Sale. For example Tokala is the *intiperu* of the Bestha and the Kapu castes. The main function of the clan is to regulate marriage alliances. Only at Mannanur, we have come across the attachment of particular *intiperu* with particular *gotramulu*. For example, Vempalla is the *intiperu* of Kannimoni clan, Pachchipula is the *intiperu* of Kalraju *gotram,* Ratheshella is the *intiperu* of Nallapotula *gotram* and Palendra is the *intiperu* of Dasari clan.

Each of the endogamous divisions of the Chenchus worship their own deities. The deities of the Dasari Chechus are Basamma, Veerabhadramma, Maramma, Sunkamma, Golusamma, Venkateswara, Anjaneyaswamy, Mariamma, Potraju, Jammulamma, Obulesu, Pamuleti, Madduleti, Kammagiraiah, Veeranna, etc. The clans called Tokala, Kudumaula, Chevula, Dhamsali, Dasari, and Arti are associated with the clan deities called Gurappa, Bayanna, Hanumantha, Lingammayya, Gurappa, and Ankalamma respectively.

The principal deity of the Konda Chenchu is Lingamayya while the principal deity of the Yanadi Chenchus is Lord Narasimhaswamy. They also worship female deity to appease her for their protection from communicable diseases like small pox, cholera, or chicken pox, etc., and also from the malevolent effects of evil doers. The Konda Chenchus sacrifice fowl or goat to the deities. They perform *jatra* (fair) in honour of the local male and female deities like Viplakuntla, Bayanna, Peddamma. All the Konda Chenchus, Dasari Chenchus and Yanadi Chechus worship Hindu gods of wider pantheon like Lord Venkateswara, Rama, Anjaneyaswamy, Lord Narasimha, and Lord Shiva, etc. The Chenchus who are assigned the duty of cleaning the temple, enjoy the community feast and receive the sarees offered to the deities.

A few Chenchus also visit local Muslim *Pirs* (saint) for getting relief from their physical or mental strains and take part in *Urs* (anniversary of Muslim Pirs). The Chenchu families of Chintala village visit church every Sunday at Dornala town. Sadarampenta Chenchus (near Palemcheruvu of Kurnool district) also follow Christianity. A Christian Father from nearby Kottalacheruvu visits and preaches the tenets of Christianity every Sunday. According to 1981 census, 99.47 per cent of the Chenchus are Hindus while 0.25 per cent is Christian, 0.01 per cent is Muslim and 0.27 per cent of them profess other religion.

The Chenchus are typically hedonistic in the sense that they think of the present only and have no concern for their future. No concept of economic saving or economic maximization is observed among them. So they work for immediate return through the labour work temporarily. That is the reason they are least interested in adopting to agriculture. Thus they continue to pursue collection of the forest produces. They say they earn instant money by selling the fuel wood and other minor forest resources. So a majority of them depend on forest economy for their livelihood.

The Konda Chenchus earn their livelihood mainly by collecting forest products available in and around their *gudems/pentas* (settlements). Majority of them collect forest products within the specified areas in the jungle which are earmarked for particular clans called Polamu and Puttalolla. If there is any encroachment in collecting forest products the defaulters are punished by the Peddamanishi of Chuchu *gudem*.

Owing to the non-availability of the tubers in recent years, there is a gradual change of their food habits. Instead of consuming wild tubers like Chenchugadda, Mulugadda, Kaluvagada, Dumpagadda, Thungagadda, etc., they now consume leafy vegetables. Now, they also prefer to take rice instead of jowar, ragi, etc. The Konda or Yanadi Chenchus do not eat beef. The school-going children prefer the common morning dishes consisting of idly and dosa. The consumption of self-manufactured liquor made out of Ippapuvvu (mohuwa flower) is their favourite habit. Sometimes they take arrack from government shops whenever they get monetary benefits under various welfare schemes provided through Integrated Tribal Development Agency (ITDA).

There is a change in the dress pattern among the male and female. The young Chenchus have adopted the change although many old men stick to wearing *goochi* (a lion cloth) and women now prefer to wear sarees. Now, a majority of young male Chenchus wear shirts and pants and female wear colourful sarees. The school-going boys wear trousers and shirts while girls wear saree and blouse. There is a change in their hair style also. Instead of having *koppu* (knotting of free grown hair) the young male comb their hair and the young female follow the hair style of the plains women. The young prefer to use cosmetics like toilet powder, coconut oil, etc.

The Studied Villages

The village Marripalem is situated at a distance of 5km to the east of Chintala village, which is located beside the Srisailam-Dornala state highway. It is exclusively a Chenchu inhabited agricultural village. This village is surrounded by Bommalapuram, Chintala, Dornala and Alepalem on the east, west, north and south direction respectively. Bavipenta, an interior village is situated at a distance of 30 km from its Mandalam headquarters of Yerrogond Palem. The village Byrlutigudem is situated at a height of 1,150 feet above sea level on Kurnool-Srisailam bus route and lies between 78°42′50″ east longitude and 150°53′14″ north latitude and is surrounded by Naglutigudem village and Pasurukla and Bhavanji river on the north, Rollapenta village on the east and Siddapuram village and tank in the south-west and Krishnapuram on the west. Kottalacharuvu is a rehabilitated multi-ethnic village situated 15 km away from Almakur town. Srinalilam is a famous pilgrimage centre located at an altitude over 1,500 above the sea level in the most picturesque northern most plateau of the Nallamalai hill. Table 3 shows the distribution of population in the studied villages on the basis of sex.

Dasari, Manla, Udutala, Uttaluri, Gurram, Gulla, Avula, Tokala, Chevula, Jella, Chigurla, Damsani, Nallopotu, Topi are names of clans found in the surveyed villages (Table 5). The Dasari Chenchus have clans like Nallapotula, Gundla, Mandli, Kudumala, Pakkili, Arthi, Chigurla, Dasari, Golusollu, etc. Some clans like Arthi, Chigurla, Pasula, Manla, Dasari, etc., are also found among the Konda Chenchus. Kaki, Savaram, Mokula, Mogili, Puli, Rangollu are some of the clans found among the Yanadi Chenchus of Ahobilam. Lord Narasimhaswamy is their chief god. Kaki members worship Venkateswarlu and Ankalamma deity whereas Indla members worship Muniswamy as clan deities.

Table 3

Sex-wise Distribution of Families and Population

Name of Village	*Total No. of Families*	*Total Population*	*Male*	*%*	*Female*	*%*
Srisailam	36	132	67	—	65	—
Bairlutigudem	50	169	84	—	85	—
Naglutigudem	31	94	50	—	44	—
Kottalacheruvu	19	91	40	—	51	—
Marripalem	44	212	105	—	107	—
Bavipenta	36	139	69	—	70	—
Total	216	837	415	49.6	422	50.4

Table 4
Inter-clan Marriage

	Clan of Husband	Clan of Wife	Total Marriages
1.	Arthi	Chigurala (5), Pulcherla (5), Uttaluri (3), Bhumani (2), Nallapothuala (1), Gulla (4), and Chevalu (1).	21 (8.8)
2.	Avula	Not known	1 (0.4)
3.	Barmala	Manla (2)	2 (0.8)
4.	Bhumani	Kudumala (7) and Gijjanami (1)	8 (3.3)
5.	Chevula	Tokala (2), Damsani (2) and Ujaluri (1)	5 (2.1)
6.	Chigurla	Arthi (1), Bhumani (1), Gulla (2), Kudumala (2), Manla (3), Pulicherla (3), and Udatala (1)	13 (5.4)
7.	Damsani	Chevula (1), Kudumala (3) and Jella (1)	5 (2.1)
8.	Dasari	Arthi (1), Bhumani (5), Chevula (1), Chigurla (2), Gulla (2), Kudumala (7) Manla (2), Pulicherla (1), Thota (1) and Uttaluri (5).	27 (11.3)
9.	Gubula	Nimmala(1)	1 (0.4)
10.	Gulla	Damsani (1), Arthi (3), Bhoomani (1), Chigurla (3), Kudumala (1), Nimmala (1), Pulusala (1), Thota (1), Uttaluri (5) and Pulicherla(5)	22 (9.2)
11.	Gurram	Kudumala(1)	1 (0.4)
12.	Jella	Dasari (1), Gulla (1), Kudumala (5), Manla (1) and Nimmala (1)	9 (3.8)
13.	Kudumala	Bhoomani (27), Chigurla (1), Chevula (1), Damsani (5), Dasari (4) Jella (7), Gollolu (1), Manla (2), Nimmala (2), Pulicherla (10) and Tokala (1)	61 (25.5)
14.	Manla	Pittala (2), Nimmala (2), Chigurla (1), Dasari (3) and Uttaluri (1)	9 (3.8)
15.	Nallapotula	Arthi (1)	1 (0.4)
16	Nimmala	Arthi (2), Pulicherla (2), Kudumala (1) and Tokala (2)	7 (2.9)
17.	Pittala	Manla (1) and Tokala (1)	2 (0.8)
18.	Pulicherla	Arthi (2), Barmala (1), Chigurla (1), Kudumala (5), Nimmala (2), Tokala (1) and Dasari (1)	13 (5.4)
19.	Talari	Pulicherla (1) and Dasari (2)	3 (1.3)
20.	Tokala	Chevula (1), Chigurla (2), Gulla (1), Kudumala (3), Nimmala (4), Pittala (2) and Pittavari (1)	14 (5.9)
21.	Topi	Uttaluri (1)	1 (0.4)
22.	Udutala	Dasari (1)	1 (0.4)
23.	Uttaluri	Dasaari (6), Gulla (1), Manla (1), Nimmala (1), Topi (2) and Udutala (1)	12 (5.0)
	Total		239 (100.0)

Figures in parenthesis indicate percentage.

Table 5
Clan-wise Population Distribution

	Clan name	Male		Female		Total	
		No.	%	No.	%	No.	%
1.	Arthi	40	4.8	43	5.1	83	9.9
2.	Avula	1	0.1	1	0.1	2	0.2
3.	Barmala	2	0.2	5	0.6	7	0.8
4.	Bhumani	16	1.9	18	2.1	34	4.1
5.	Chevula	2	0.2	2	0.2	4	0.5
6.	Chigurla	23	2.7	19	2.3	42	5.0
7.	Damsani	10	1.1	9	1.1	19	2.3
8.	Dasari	51	6.1	50	6.0	101	12.0
9.	Gubula	2	0.2	3	0.4	5	0.8
10.	Gulla	26	3.1	34	4.1	60	7.2
11.	Gurram	4	0.5	3	0.4	7	0.8
12.	Jella	15	1.8	12	1.4	27	3.2
13.	Kudumala	116	13.9	118	14.1	234	28.0
14.	Manla	15	1.8	20	2.4	35	4.2
15.	Nallapothula	2	0.2	3	0.4	5	0.6
16.	Nimmala	9	1.1	9	1.1	18	2.1
17.	Pittala	3	0.4	5	0.6	8	0.9
18.	Pulicherla	21	2.5	20	2.4	41	4.9
19.	Talari	8	1.0	5	0.6	13	1.5
20.	Tokala	28	3.3	28	3.3	56	6.7
21.	Topi	—	—	1	0.1	1	0.1
22.	Udatala	2	0.2	1	0.1	3	0.4
23.	Uttaluri	19	2.3	13	1.5	32	3.8
	Total	415	49.6	422	50.4	837	100.0

Table 6 depicts that a majority of the marriages are negotiated marriages instead of the earlier type marriage by elopement. This is a major change observed in acquiring mates. The people belonging to the old generation say that they practiced marriage by elopement. The common age at marriage is 15–18 year for girls and 18–20 years for boys. Monogamy is the common form of the marriage (Table 7). There are 8 cases of polygamous marriages. The maximum number of polygamous marriages is four and is found in Marripalam which is a typical agricultural village of the Chenchus. Having adopted the agriculture they consider it important that all family members work in fields. In order to get more lands they sometime justify having more than one wife. Neolocal residence is the rule after marriage. Levirate and sororate marriages are allowed. The Konda Chenchus accept the services of the Brahmin priest for conducting marriage rituals. Some of them also consult the Brahmin for *muhurtam* (auspicious time). Educated Chenchus invite guests by sending wedding cards. They also make use of microphone during wedding ceremony.

Table 6

Family Type-wise Marriage Forms

S. No.	Type of Household	Marriage by Negotiation	Love marriage	Marriage by Elopement	Total
1.	Nuclear	68 (28.4)	102 (42.7)	8 (3.3)	178 (74.5)
2.	Extended	3 (1.2)	—	1 (0.4)	4 (1.7)
3.	Others	30 (12.5)	22 (9.2)	5 (2.1)	57 (23.8)
	Total	101 (42.3)	124 (51.9)	14 (5.8)	239 (100.0)

Figures in parenthesis indicate percentage.

Table 7

Distribution of Married Population

S. No.	Village studied	Marriage held in		Total no. of Couples/ Households	Total no. of Marriages
		Same Village	Different Village		
1.	Kottalacheruvu	17	1 (Guntur Dt)	18/18	18 (9.6)
2.	Bairluti	31	Total 10 Peddamantala-3 R.Koduru-3 Kottapalem-1 Nagluty-2 Srisailam-1	40/40	41 (21.8) (One case of sororal polygyny)
3.	Nagluti	19	Total 9 Bairlluti-3 Marripalem-1 Peddamantala-1 Srisailam-1 Chintala-1 Petcheruvu-1 R.Koduru-1	28/28	28 (14.9)
4.	Srisailam	20	Total 13 Palutla-3 Nagluti-2 Mahanandi-3 Petchuruvu-2 Appapur-2 Palemcheruvu-1	31/31	33(17.5) (2 cases of non-sororal polygyny)
5.	Marripalem	24	Total 19 Peddamantanala-4 Nallakaluva-1 Chemikevaram-1 Tummalabailu-1 Billigondipenta-1 Bavipenta-1 Panakamadugu-2 Kotturu-1 Guttachenu-1 Suddagunta-1 Garadipenta-1 Palutla-1 Petcheruvu-2 Srisailam-1	39/37 (Total 37 h.holds, two households are extended families)	43 (22.9) (4 cases of non-sororal polygyny)
	Total	129 (68.6)	59 (31.4)	180/178 (95.7/94.7)	188 (100.0)

Figures in parenthesis indicate percentage.

Table 8

Family Size-wise Distribution of Population

S. No.	No. of Family Members	No. of Household	Male		Female		Total	
			No.	%	No.	%	No.	%
1.	1–3	97	100	12.0	111	13.3	211	25.2
2.	4–6	103	252	30.1	247	29.5	499	59.6
3.	7–9	14	55	6.6	51	6.0	106	12.7
4.	10+	2	8	0.9	13	1.5	21	2.5
	Total	216	415	49.6	422	50.4	837	100.0

Table 9

Family Type-wise Distribution of Population

S. No.	Type of household	Total no of Household	Total Population		Total Male		Total Female	
			No.	%	No.	%	No.	%
1.	Nuclear	165	696	83.1	359	42.9	337	40.2
2.	Extended	2	12	104	6	0.7	6	0.7
3.	Other	49	129	15.4	50	6.0	79	9.4
	Total	216	837	100.0	415	49.6	422	50.4

Table 9 shows that majority of the families are nuclear families. Separation and remarriage is very common in their society. So to avoid this, husbands are always cautious about it. This is the reason that they avoid contact with the non-tribals living around them and even the visiting officials.

Education is very poor among the Chenchus. The literacy rate in the past was 9.71 per cent (1981 Census). There are only 21 male and 2 female who have passed class X in six project districts of ITDA area, viz., Kurnool, Prakasham Guntur, Mahaboobnagar, Nalgonda and Ranga, Reddy districts (Mohan Rao, 1991: 421). There is only one Chenchu MBBS doctor working as Physician in Kurnool district and another from Mahaboobnagar who studied Ayurvedic medicine. Education among the girls is very poor. The literacy rate of the female is 5.92 per cent as against 13.34 per cent among male (1981 Census). Table 10 and 11 depict the literacy level of Chenchus and enrolment of the Chenchu students respectively in the six surveyed villages.

After the declaration of the Chenchus as a primitive tribal group (PTG) in Andhra Pradesh, a number of Ashram schools, hostels and residential schools have been established by ITDA. It also provides 25 kg of rice (through Girijan Co-operation Corporation (GCC) to the parents of each school-going child as an incentive and to motivate the tribal parents to send their wards to schools regularly and to reduce the problem of drop-outs and stagnation. Despite these incentives, it has been observed that the enrolment of girl students is very poor and rate of absenteeism is more both among the Chenchu teachers and the Chenchu students particularly those inhabiting interior villages like Nekkanti and Palutla of Prakasham district.

Table 10
Literacy-wise Distribution

S. No.	Literacy level	Male		Female		Total numbers	
		No.	%	No.	%	No.	%
1.	Primary	156	18.6	123	14.7	279	33.3
2.	Upper Primary	36	4.3	22	58	58	6.9
3.	High school	13	1.5	6	0.7	19	2.2
4.	10+2 (Intermediate)	—	—	1	0.1	1	0.1
5.	Degree (BA)	1	0.1	—	—	1	01
	Total	206	24.6	152	18.1	358	42.7

Table 11
Enrolment of the Chenchu Students

Village studied	Expected no. of student Primary class(5–9)			Actual student in Primary classes (5–9)			Expected no. of student in Secondary class (10–14)			Actual student in Secondary classes (10–14)		
	M	F	T	M	F	T	M	F	T	M	F	T
Kottala cheruvu	7	10	17	7	10	17 (100.00)	6	2	8	5	2	9 (87.5)
Bairluti	12	14	26	12	12	24 (92.3)	14	4	18	13	4	17 (94.4)
Nagluti	14	9	23	14	4	18 (78.3)	4	3	7	4	2	6 (85.7)
Srisailam	15	10	25	15	10	25 (100.00)	11	4	15	9	3	12 (80.0)
Marripalem	17	18	35	13	13	26 (74.3)	10	14	24	1	—	1 (4.2)
Bavipenta	12	12	24	7	6	13 (54.2)	15	6	21	5	2	7 (33.3)
Total	77 (51.3)	73 (48.6) (100.0)	150	68 (45.3)	55 (36.7)	123 (82.0)	60 (64.5)	33 (35.5) (100.0)	93	37 (39.8)	13 (14.0)	50 (53.8)

Figures in parenthesis indicate percentages.

In order to provide quality of education, Andhra Pradesh Residential Schools Society had built four residential schools. The total number of the Chenchu students in the Ashram School is 1,030. Ashram schools as well as residential schools are providing both boarding and lodging facilities, dress material, bedding material, text books, notebooks to the students, free of cost. The total numbers of Ashram schools in the project is 43 and the strength of the Chenchu students is 2,686 (Mohan Rao, 1991: 422). Besides these schools, ITDA established 60 single teacher schools and 9 temporary schools. There are 16 tribal welfare hostels for boys and 3 for girls in the area. There is a pre-examination training centre for the Chenchus at Sunnipenta (run by ITDA) to train them in typewriting, short hand both in Telugu and in English besides extending coaching for competitive examinations conducted by APPSC, UPSC, LIC, Banks, Railway Service Commissions, etc.

ITDA maintains a list of educated unemployed Chenchus and sends details of such candidates to recruitment agency. Thus, some 106 educated Chenchus have been appointed as teachers both in single teacher schools and in Ashram schools. About 20 Chenchus have been appointed as guard and watchmen in forest department (ITDA – PTG Report, 1991: 22).

Table 12

Family-wise Distribution of Cultivable Land

S. No.	Name of the village	No. of families				Total family
		Landowners		Landless		
		No.	%	No.	%	
1.	Srisailam	22	61.1	14	38.9	36
2.	Byrluti	31	62.0	19	38.0	50
3.	Nagluli	27	87.1	4	12.9	31
4.	Marripalem	32	72.7	12	27.3	44
5.	Kottalacheruvu	18	94.7	1	5.2	19
6.	Bavipenta	15	41.7	21	58.3	36
	Total	145	(67.1)	71	(32.9)	216 (100.0)

Figures in parenthesis indicate percentages.

In many cases land for cultivation is provided to Chenchus as economic incentive, but most of them take little interest in agriculture. Table 12 depicts the distribution of landowning households. The Chenchus of the village Kottalacheruvu possess the highest percentage of land while the highest percentage of Chenchu families of Bavipenta is landless.

Table 13 shows the size-wise land owning families. Highest no. of families owning land have holding of 5 acres while lowest no. of families holding land have holding of 14 acres. Table 14 shows that only 112 families out of the total land owning families of 606 are involved in agriculture or agricultural activities. The highest no. of families practising agriculture belongs to the village Marripalem. It is reported that a large number of these families do not consume alcoholic drinks. As a result, all the families are economically better off and enjoy respect among the Chenchus as well as in the Project office (ITDA) and Tribal welfare department. Nobody was

Table 13

Land Ownership

S. No.	Size of land	Land owning Families		Total land owned in acres
		No.	%	
1.	1 acre	4	1.8	4
2.	1½ acre	2	0.9	3
3.	2 acre	20	9.3	40
4.	2½ acre	18	8.3	45
5.	3 acre	19	8.8	57
6.	4 acre	15	7.0	60
7.	5 acre	51	23.6	255
8.	6 acre	3	14	18
9.	8 acre	7	302	56
10.	10 acre	3	1.4	30
11.	12 acre	2	0.9	24
12.	14 acre	1	0.5	14
	Total	145	67.1	606

found doing cultivation in the villages of Kottalacheruvu and Bavipenta although the land was given to Chenchus for cultivation. In Bavipenta, forest land is under cleaning stage. In Kottalacheruva 18 families have been allotted 2.5 acres of land each, but nobody undertook cultivation at the time of fieldwork. So, actually 14 households fully and 98 households partially depend on agriculture.

Table 14

Source of Irrigation and Possession of Oxen

S. No.	*Name of the village*	*Total of families depending upon agriculture/agriculture related activities*	*No. of dug wells*	*Total pairs of oxen*
1.	Srisailam	22	1	6
2.	Nagluti	27	—	2
3.	Byrluti	31	1	1
4.	Marripalem	32	14 (7 families share)	11
5.	Kottalacheruvu *	—	—	—
6.	Bavipenta *	—	—	—
	Total	112	16	20

* The Chenchus do not depend upon agriculture or agricultural related activities even as secondary occupation in Kottalacheruvu and Bavipenta. So the Chenchus in these villages are not treated as agricultural families.

Table 15

Working Upper and Lower Class in Marripalem

Occupation based class	*No. of families*	*No. of workers*		
		Male	*Female*	*Total*
Upper class group (agricultural primary and goverment job	12	18	14	32 U/class
Lower class group (agricultural wage labours and collectors of MFP and land owning household up to 2 acres)	32	39	41	80 L/class
Total	44	57	55	112

It may be possible to place different families in economic classes, based on their occupation and derived income. Thus, Table 15 shows that a large number of the Chenchus in Marripalem village who are in possession of about 2 acres of land and who depend on MFP and on agricultural labour that is resorting to more than one occupation are treated as lower class group. In this lower group there are as many as 80 workers belonging to 32 families. Employed Chenchus are economically better off and they enjoy respect among the Chenchus and other villagers. For example, K. Polaiah as Sarpanch and Kudumala Perumal as local leader, who are also hard working farmers, belong to the upper class and enjoy respect. Even Kundumala Hanumaiah who is working as a watchman is economically better off and hence in local perception of Chenchus he enjoys respect as upper class Chenchu. Table 16 shows that out of the 32 land owning families of Marripalem, 9 families possess highest quantity of land. Each of them possesses five acres of land. These families are regarded as upper class families, who have moved away from past foraging level to agriculture and other occupational level.

Table 16

Land Owning Families in Marripalem

S. No.	*Size of land in acres*	*Land-owning families*	*Total land owned in acres*
1.	One	4	4
2.	Two	3	6
3.	Three	5	15
4.	Four	6	24
5.	Five	9	45
6.	Eight	3	24
7.	Ten	1	10
8.	Fourteen	1	14
	Total	32	142

Although the incipient class formation on the basis of occupation is observed among the Chenchus, no clear-cut economic class formation has yet emerged. Most of the families are still involved in the collection of MFP and belong to economically low-income group. Their possessions are also minimal.

Social Stratification and Regional Hierarchy

There is nascent stratification noted amongst the various segments of the Chenchus. These are based on several traditional and modern factors. As we discussed there are some segments who broadly belong to level of foraging. Some segments are mentally so much attached with gathering that they are not using the land allotted to them for agriculture. The Konda Chenchus strongly feel that they are the real Chenchus and are superior to all other endogamous segments of the Chenchus. However, they accord equal status to Uru Chenchus and maintain marital relations with them. They feel that the Dasari Chenchus are originally Dasari caste who claim to be Dasari Chenchus in order to get benefits under ITDA Schemes. The Dasari Chenchus were traditional mendicants and semi-nomadic people. Now they are engaged in collection and selling bamboo sticks either on wholesale or retail in the fairs of the major villages and towns of Kurnool and Guntur districts. A few educated persons amongst them have secured jobs in A.P. Road Transport Corporation as drivers and conductors. Such achievement of this group is possible because they live amidst plains people and are exposed to modern forces. Although the Konda Chenchus have no direct and continuous contact with the Koya Chenchus and the Botha Chenchus they claim themselves superior to all these and other Chenchu groups on the ground that agricultural communities like Kapus accept food and water from them. But the Konda Chenchus do not accept food and water from the Dasari Chenchus, and the Scheduled Castes and tribes like the Yerukula and the Yanadi. They place the Brahmins followed by the Vaisyas (Komati), the Kapus, the Jangamas, and the Balijas in the upper stratum; the Sugalis and themselves in the middle stratum ; and the Yerukalas, the Dhobis, the Barbers and the Scheduled Castes in the lower stratum in social hierarchy. The educated and economically better Konda Chenchus and the Chenchus resettled in rehabilitated villages like Kottalacheruvu and Koraprolu have started employing the Brahmin priests in marriage rituals. They also have started printing wedding cards since 1980. There are three cases of Chenchu girls married to Sugali males in the rehabilitated villages of Nallakaluva and Kottalacheruvu and in one case a Chenchu woman is married to a Muslim male in Srisailam of Kurnool district. Although the Dasari Chenchus claims that they have marital relations with the Konda Chenchus, there is not a single case of marriage between the Konda Chenchus and the Dasari Chenchus in the studied villages.

Different segments of the Chenchus have as many as 72 Kulamulu (clan). Though, the clan members of Bhumini claim the highest status amongst the clans, there is no hierarchy among the Kulamulus of the Konda Chenchus. There is Annadammula Varusa (phratry-like relation) observed among some pairs of Kulamulu. For instance, the Bhumini and the Pulicherla clans belong to one such cluster and the Arthi, the Kudumula and the Nimmala belong to another such cluster. Marriage within these clusters is forbidden because all the phratry members are considered as brothers having been descended from a common ancestor. Thus we notice among the chenchus a phratry-like formation though this feature is not described as such by the ethnographers. After a gap of several generations marriage may take place among members of phratry. There are two cases of Kudumula males marrying to Nimmala females in our studied area.

As a result of continuous contacts with the Hindu communities the Chenchus have been provided a place in regional caste hierarchy in relation to local communities. The following chart depicts the relative positions of the communities in the regional hierarchy.

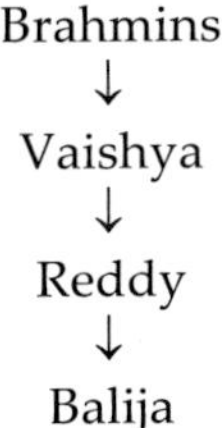

Golla (shepherd), Sale (weaving caste) Kumar (pot maker),
Kummari (blacksmith)

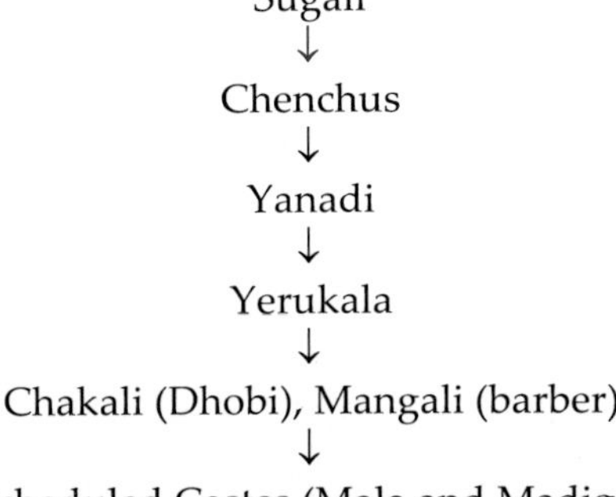

(The Muslims and Christian communities are placed outside caste-hierarchy)

The rural social stratification of the communities in this part of the state is as per expected lines, whereby the Brahmins and the Vyaisyas belong to the higher echelons. The Chenchus regard themselves placed at lower rung but they regard Scheduled Castes as of lowest rank.

Economic Development and Social Change

As a result of the constant contact with the neighbouring Hindu castes and the city dwellers, and as a result of some developmental schemes, several changes have taken place among the Chenchus. Many Chenchus have started possessing cots, chairs, steel utensils, radios and cycles. While several segments of the Chenchus have adopted the changing mode of life, there is still one segment of the traditional Chenchus still living in 'primitive' conditions such as those living in interior villages like Bavipenta where most of male Chenchus wear *Gochi* (loin cloth). Among the advanced segments of the Chenchus urban traits have been increasingly adopted. A majority of Chenchus thus now wear half pant or *Pancha* and sleeveless or full-length kurta or shirt. Females wear saree and blouse. So, one cannot distinguish the Chenchus from others in appearance.

Despite obvious social changes, there is little change seen with regard to size, type of families and forms of marriage among the Chenchu tribe. However, they have stopped the practice of child marriage. It is also remarkable to note that the Chenchus of Palemcheruvu, an agricultural village, now even employ Brahmin priest in the performance of some rituals. There is change in acquiring mates. Instead of their old practice of elopement they now prefer marriage by negotiation. An educated Chenchu male now prefers to marry an educated Chenchu girl. Well established and employed persons among them demand and take dowry. Besides, they also allow inter-community marriages. However, there are a few cases of inter-tribe marriage alliances. Thus, there are Chenchu girls who have married to persons of Sugali tribe.

The Konda Chenchus of Mahaboobnagar district have been engaged in agriculture for long, on account of their continuous interaction with peasant/agriculture communities like the Reddis and the dominant tribe like the Sugalis. Efforts have been made to introduce better agriculture techniques by providing implements like oxen, free land, hybrid seeds, fertilizers, etc., among the Chenchus. It was observed that even the Chenchus living in interior villages like Palutia (24 km from the main road) have started growing cash crop like cotton and they admit that they have acquired this skill from their neighbouring communities. A few Chenchu families of the villages like Marripalem, Korraprolu and Garapenta have taken up agriculture as a principal source of livelihood by increasingly using fertilizers, insecticides, and improved varieties of seeds supplied by ITDA. Some of Chenchus also learnt the skill of rearing cattle and sheep supplied by the ITDA and they have also started drinking milk. Some of them sell MFP and work as labourers. Forest contractors employ some of them as wage labourers.

Under education programmes, ITDA introduced single-teacher schools in Chenchu inhabited Gudems in which only Chenchu teachers are appointed. Chenchu teachers are also appointed in Ashram schools. Chenchu students are provided free notebooks, textbooks and dress material. ITDA used to provide

25 kg of rice and one litre of edible oil to each Chenchu family which sent children to schools.

Under animal husbandry programme, the Chenchus are given sheep, goat, and cows. Under agriculture programmes, ITDA provides fertilizers, insecticides, agricultural implements, improved varieties of seeds and even tractor under cooperative management and pairs of oxen to some families who are involved in cultivation. Some of them are also employed as forest guards, GCC salesmen, peon and cooking assistants in ITDA and in Ashram schools. Some of them are also employed as (part time) salesman's jobs in local branches of GCC (Girijan Co-operative Corporation). It may be stated that till recent past most of Chenchus lived like foragers but new economic opportunities are changing their life. As a result, although no clear-cut economic class formation has emerged, one can identify the high-income group and the low-income group among the Chenchus of Marripalem and Srisalam.

With the establishment of ITDA office at Sunnipenta (Srisailam dam) and MADA office at Mannanur (Amarabad Mandalam of Mahaboobnagar district) awareness of the Chenchus towards development programmes has increased considerably. Some of them visit these offices and get the benefits. It was alleged that the ITDA and MADA offices have been extending welfare programmes mainly to Konda Chenchus inhabiting Nallamalai hill areas and to Yanadi Chenchus of Ahobilam area to some extent.

Conclusion

It is observed that various segments of the Chenchus have made progress in economic field but some sections remain poor, least educated and unaware of several programmes of development. Some sections have now organized themselves politically and started NGOs. Thus the Konda Chenchus living in Srisailam formed an association called Srisailam Anadi Chenchulavari Sangam in 1984. The Dasari Chenchus have established S.T. Chenchu Sangham in 1982, with the objectives of diffusing new information among its members making them aware of various development plans of the Government and to guide them towards the economic, educational and cultural betterment of the tribe in cooperation with the Government and lastly to protect and safeguard the interests of members of the Sangham. All males above 18 years may become members by paying a nominal fee.

Out of the three endogamous groups; the Konda Chenchus occupy the highest status because of their traditional association with the sacred Srisailam temple. As a result of constant interactions, many Chenchu villages have adopted Hindu caste norms, but they are accorded lower rank in caste-hierarchy. Conflict and rivalry is reported among different segments of Chenchus. In comparison to Konda Chenchus, Dasari Chenchus are exposed to modern forces like urbanization. Large number of Chenchus among them have secured jobs in state government. Though Dasari Chenchus claim to have marital relations and commensal norms with Konda Chenchus, but no such instances are observed. Konda Chenchus say that they maintain neither commensal nor marital relations with the Dasari Chenchus and the Yanadi Chenchus. Although no-clear cut economic class formation has emerged, but, one can notice the emergence of a class of middle-income group Chenchus who are involved in agriculture and service particularly among the Chenchus of Marrpalem and Srisailam.

Acknowledgement

The authors are grateful to Dr N.K. Das, Coordinator, for his constant guidance and support during data collection, data analysis and report writing.

References

Bhowmick, P.K. 1991, *The Chenchus of the Forests and Plateau: A Hunting-gathering Tribe in Transition*, Calcutta: Institute of Social Research and Applied Anthropology.

Census of India 1961, *The Chenchus: A Scheduled Tribe of Andhra Pradesh*, Vol. I, Part V-B(IV), Office of the Registrar General, India, Ministry of Home Affairs.

Furer-Haimendorf, C.V. 1943, *The Chenchus: Jungle-folk of the Deccan*, London: Macmillan.

ITDA-PTG. Report 1991, "Chenchu Activities, Srisailam."

Mohan Rao, K. 1991, *Chenchus and their Development in the Forests and Plateau.*

Rajagopal, M.V. 1974, *Gazetteer of India–Andhra Pradesh, Kurnool,* Hyderabad: Government of Andhra Pradesh.

Rajagopal, M.V. 1976, *Gazetteer of India-Andhra Pradesh, District Gazetteers Mahaboobnagar,* Hyderabad: Government of Andhra Pradesh.

Rao, Venkat 2004, *Dimensions of Transformation in Tribal Societies (with reference* to AP), New Delhi: Sarup & Sons.

Sastry, V.N.V.K. 1990, "Chenchu Food-gatherers and Hunters of Nallamalai Forests in South-India: Problems of Transition", 6th International Conference of Hunting and Gathering Societies, University of Alaska, May 28 – June 1.

14 Inter-Tribal Competition and Status Ranking among the Koya and Lambadi of Andhra Pradesh

M. Rajendra Prasad

This article describes economic competition between the Koyas and Lambadi people in the context of land alienation process and various economic activities in two contexts, traditional and modern. The Koya are a major tribe of Andhra Pradesh. A major focus of this article is to describe emerging stratification within sub-tribes of the Koyas. They are distributed throughout the state. But they live predominantly both on the banks of the river Godavari and its tributary, the Sabari in the district of Khammam and West Godavari and East Godavari agency area. According to the 1991 Census there are 41.99 lakh tribal people constituting 6.3 per cent of the total population of the state (92.4% in rural area and 7.6% in urban areas). In Khammam, Adilabad and Visakhapatnam districts the tribal population constitute 25.2 per cent, 17.0 per cent and 14.37 per cent respectively, while in Mahaboobnagar (98.4%) and Vishakapatnam (98.3%) tribal population live in rural areas. Tribes living in urban areas are more in Krishna (22.9%) and Guntur (20.6%). The distribution of total tribal population is furnished in Table 1. According to 1961 Census the population of Koyas was 2,20,146 and their population increased to 2,85,226 during 1961–1971 decade registering a decimal growth rate of 22.8 per cent. The population increased to 3,59,799 during 1981 census registering a growth rate of 20.7 per cent. During the next decade (1991 census) the total Koya population was 4,28,880 with growth rate of 19.2 per cent. The district wise Koya population is given in Table 2.

Identity and Origin Myth

Koi, Koya Dora, Koya, Koya Gond, Koya Vadu, Koya Vandeu (pl) are the synonyms of Koya tribe of Andhra Pradesh. The terminology varies from one place to another. In Adilabad and Warangal districts, they are called Koya Gond, whereas in Khammam they are referred to as Koya and Doralu. In East Godavari and West Godavari districts, they are called Doralu. The name Koi is derived from the root 'Ko' or 'Ku' – meaning mountain, which indicates that they are mountain or hill dwellers. Gustov Oppert says that Telugu 'Kodu', corresponds to the term 'Konda' or Gonda, the word 'Konda' in Telugu signifies only mountain and not mountaineer.

Table 1
Distribution of Population

Country/State A.P Districts Name	Total Population	Total Rural Population	Total Urban Population	Schedules Tribes Population	Percentage of Total Population	Scheduled Tribes Rural Population	%	Scheduled Tribes Urban Population	%
India	84,63,02,683	62,86,91,676	21,76,11,012	6,77,58,380	—	6,27,51,026	92.6	50,07,354	7.4
Andhra Pradesh	6,65,08,008	4,86,20,882	1,78,87,126	41,99,481	6.3	38,80,254	92.3	3,19,227	7.6
East Godavari	45,41,222	34,60,418	10,80,804	1,76,083	3.9	1,68,137	95.5	7,946	4.5
West Godavari	35,17,568	27,89,015	7,28,553	84,648	2.4	77,474	91.5	7,174	8.5
Adila bad	20,82,479	16,00,903	4,61,576	3,54,902	17.0	3,44,013	96.9	10,889	3.1
Karim Nagar	30,37,436	24,13,617	6,24,319	83,017	2.7	76,885	92.6	6,132	7.4
Waran goal	28,18,832	22,72,210	5,46,622	3,85,309	13.7	3,69,655	95.9	15,654	4.1
Khammam	22,15,809	17,67,646	4,48,163	5,58,958	25.2	5,27,089	94.3	31,869	5.7
Nakgonda	28,52,092	24,13,639	3,38,453	2,75,638	10.8	2,66,400	96.6	9,238	3.4
Srikakulam	23,21,126	20,30,888	2,90,238	1,34,067	5.8	1,31,225	97.8	2,842	2.2
Vizianagaram	21,10,943	17,47,443	3,63,500	1,90,185	9.0	1,85,759	97.7	4,426	2.3
Visakhapatnam	32,85,092	19,76,509	13,08,583	4,68,886	14.3	4,60,882	98.3	8,004	1.7
Krishana	36,98,833	23,73,879	13,24,954	91,767	2.5	70,767	77.1	21,000	22.9
Guntur	41,06,999	29,20,299	11,86,700	1,81,588	4.4	1,44,196	79.4	37,392	20.6
Preakasam	27,59,166	23,05,264	4,53,902	98,854	3.6	81,324	82.3	17,530	17.7
Nellore	23,92,260	18,23,198	5,69,062	2,14,062	8.9	1,77,459	82.9	36,603	17.1
Chittor	32,61,118	26,15,286	6,45,832	1,04,938	3.2	93,919	87.5	11,019	10.5
Cuddapak	22,67,769	17,22,796	5,44,973	47,414	2.1	70,761	85.9	6,653	14.1
Anantarur	31,83,814	24,35,761	7,48,053	1,11,207	3.5	99,131	89.1	12,076	10.9
Kurnool	29,73,024	22,04,924	7,68,100	76,455	1.8	45,453	80.5	11,002	19.5
Mahbubnagar	3,07,705	27,34,858	3,42,192	2,27,405	7.3	2,23,671	98.4	3,734	1.6
Raongareddi	25,51,966	13,46,789	12,05,177	1,09,394	4.3	87,517	80.0	21,877	20.0
Hyderabad	31,45,939	—	31,45,939	28,946	0.9	—	—	28,946	—
Medak	22,69,800	19,41,313	3,28,487	95,042	4.1	92,098	96.9	2,944	3.1

Table 2
District-wise Koya Population in Andhra Pradesh

S. No.	*District*	*1981 Census*	*1991 Census*
1.	East Godavari	30,263	37,228
2.	West Godavari	33,336	42,336
3.	Adilabad	18,505	24,056
4.	Karim Nagar	1,917	2,358
5.	Warangal	39,824	52,568
6.	Khammam	230,481	299,625
7.	Srikakulam	46	51
8.	Vizoamagara	349	429
9.	Visakhapatnam	1,238	1,523
10.	Krishna	360	443
11.	Guntur	651	800
12.	Parakasam	279	343
13.	Nellore	138	170
14.	Chitoor	99	122
15.	Cuddapah	124	153
16.	Ananthapurl	319	392
17.	Kurnol	321	394
18.	Mahabubnagar	86	105
19.	Rangareddy	649	798
20.	Hyderabad	151	185
21.	Medak	508	625
22.	Nizanmabad	50	62
23.	Nalgonda	105	129
	Total	3,59,799	4,64,895

The Gond tribe of Chhattisgarh and the Koya of Adilabad district call themselves Koitor. The last syllable 'tor' means Dora' or 'Master' or gentleman or 'Saheb' or 'Lord' and Koyas affix this term to their names. The Koyas of Bhadrachalam and Rakhapathi Taluks in upper Godavari are called 'Doralu' (masters) by their Mala (SC) and Madiga (SC) labourers.

The word Koi lost its original meaning when they moved to the plains and adopted the name Sassi Koya (plain Koya), whereby they came to be distinguished from Gutta Koya (Hill Koya). Reverend J. Cain writes that about two hundred years ago, they were driven from the plateau in the Bastar country by famine and disputes (Thurston, 1909). The Gutta Koya (Hill Koyas) are those who lived in the highlands of Bastar. The Kois who reside near the banks of Godavari are known as 'Gommu Kois' and Mayalotilu. The word *Gommu* refers to the banks of the Godavari. Thus, for instance, all the villages on the banks of the Godavari are called Gommullus.

The Racha Koya claim descent from the legendary king Pagidida Raju, a Koya chieftain during the reign of the Kakatiyas who protested against the misrule of the Kakatiya kings who collected revenue during severe drought conditions. Raju and his wife, son and two daughters fought in the battle and lost their lives. The descendants of the couple – Pagidida Raju and Sammakka call themselves Racha Koya. The current research reveals that the Koyas are called by different names in different regions of their habitation. Whatever may be the name, their cultural – beliefs, marriage rules, surnames and *gotras* (Gattu) are almost the same in entire Andhra Pradesh, as they all come from their original habitation of Bastar Region of Chhattisgarh and settled in border hill areas of Andhra Pradesh and some gradually migrated to plain areas and the river banks of Sabari and Godavari. The different synonyms are derived in accordance with their geographical settlement. There are several legends connected with origin of the Koya. The Koya claim to be the descendants of two sisters of the Pandavas. It is said that the younger sister had cursed the elder one to become a 'Koya' meaning 'like a stick having no sympathy' for the simple reason that the elder sister, had on one day, finding a she-calf in the jungle hid it in her house without informing her sister, leaving the younger sister alone in the jungle, From that day the elder sister's progeny are known as Koyas and younger one's offspring are called Naikpods. According to other legend the second Pandava prince, Bhima during his exile happened to meet the daughter of a Nishad king, while she danced at a tribal festival. Bhima and the Nishad princess known as Vanakanya (forest girl) fell in love with each other and they were married. Their progeny were later known as the Koyas.

The most popular legend shows that several Koya groups of different regions in Andhra Pradesh are the descendants of Bhimadur (Bhima, the second son of king Pandu of Mahabharata epic), and the local tradition has it that when Bhimadur and his brother, Dharma Raju, went for hunting in the jungle, Bhima met a 'wild' woman of the woods, with whom he fell in love and subsequently got married. The result of their union was Koya people.

Stratification and Regional Hierarchy

Social stratification among Koyas may be visualized at two levels: at the regional level between koyas and other communities and at the level of the segments of Koya tribe.

The Koya enjoy a dominant ethnic status among the tribal groups of the region. Their social status is accepted and recognized by all the tribals residing in multi-tribal villages of Koya region. The Koyas occupy the highest place in social scale because of the centuries old cultural contact with feudal chiefs, the Zamindars of Rakhalli, Polavaram and Chodavaram. They established rapport with Zamindars and settled in plains areas and acquired substantial cultivable lands in the agency areas. The Koyas are predominant numerically also in the tribal area of Andhra Pradesh. Due to their population strength and possession of cultivable lands, they occupy the highest place in social hierarchy. The Lambadies are placed second, followed by Konda Dora, Konda Kapu and Konda Kammari then Hill Reddies and Konda Jangama. The bottom place is occupied by Valmiki. The regional hierarchy at inter-tribal level in Adilabad, Warangal, Khammam, East Godavari and West Godavari is as follows:

1. Koyas
2. Lambadies
3. Konda Dora, Konda Kapu, Konda Kammari
4. Hill Reddies, Konda Jangama
5. Valmiki

Stratification at the Level of Sub-tribes

The Koya tribe is divided into several functional endogamous sub-tribes, which are divided into certain exogamous clans similar to Gond clan system. Sub-tribes within Koya have their independent statuses. Their relative statuses are ascertained and determined, following certain notions of purity and pollution, as may be seen in following chart. The chart shows the ranking based on traditional functions and occupations of sub-tribes:

	Sub-group	*Occupation*
1.	Lingadhari Koya	Pujari
2.	Racha Koya/Bhima Koya	Agriculturist
3.	Gumma Koya	Agriculturist
4.	Gutta Koya	Podu Cultivators
5.	Murasa Koya	Brass Worker
6.	Kammara Koya	Carpenter
7.	Gampa Koya	Basketmaker
8.	Matwa/Matta Koya	Toddy trappers
9.	Kaka Koya	
10.	Oddi Koya	Priest
11.	Doli Koya	Story Tellers
12.	Pottadi Koya	Alms dependants

The Doli Koya, Kaka Koya and Matwa Koya are not real Koyas but plains people admitted into Koya tribe. Racha Koya live in agency plains areas while Gutta Koya live in hill tops. The Gumma Koya living on the river banks are the original Koyas. Sub-tribes like Kammara Koya, Musuru Koya and Gampa Koya are still dependant on their occupations.

Lingadhari Koyas

Lingadhari Koyas occupy the highest place among the sub-tribes of Koya. The Lingadharis mainly inhabit in Kunavaram and Chintoor mandals in Khammam district. These people are different from the other Koya groups in many aspects, such as food, dress, performing rituals, etc. Their surnames also differ from the other sub-tribes. Lingadhari Koyas are Shaivites. They worship Lord Shiva. Male members wear *lingam* around their neck. The Lingadhari Koyas do not eat beef and they do not accept cooked food from other sub-tribes, but they marry girls of lower sub-tribes by performing the purification ceremony, wherein a golden ring heated in fire is kept on the tongue of such girl and they ask the girl to take bath in Godavari or any other holy river nearby. Then they admit the girl into their fold. If a girl from Lingadhari Koya marries a Koya boy of another sub-tribe she is ex-communicated. It is seen that Hindu norms have been adopted by this sub-tribe.

Racha Koya

Racha Koya/Koya Doralu occupy the second place among the sub-tribes. Most of the Racha Koyas are agriculturists and distributed in East and West Godavari districts. They accept food from the Lingadhari Koyas but not from the other Koyas.

Gumma Koyas

The Gumma Koyas generally reside on the banks of river Godavari and Sabari and their tributaries. Their main occupation is agriculture and fishing. They eat meat and also accept food from all the other sub-groups of Koyas except from Doli Koya and Pottadi Koyas.

Gutta Koyas

The Gutta Koyas generally live on hill top regions in the border areas of Andhra Pradesh and Chhattisgarh. These people are different from other Koya sub-tribes. The Gutta Koyas are short in stature.

Doli Koya

The Doli Koya are also called Arthivadu. Their population is small in number. They are concentrated in Musalamadugu village of Dummungeradu mandal of Khammam district and sparsely distributed in Bhadrachalam, Palavancha division. These people were regarded as 'untouchable'. They are not allowed generally to enter the house of upper strata Koyas. But they are very important functionaries in Koya community. These people play crucial role at the death of any person and they also conduct death rituals. On these occasions they narrate the history and genealogy of the particular katta (clan) throughout the night. EachKoya sub-tribe has its own Doli Koyas. They treat them as servants. Each household gives ₹, 10 and 10 kg of paddy per year. Aiyappan (1948) reported that the Doli Koya are not real Koyas. The present study also reveals that these Koyas are not real Koyas, because their surnames are different from Koya-surnames such as sakkina, nakka, roti, aanam, pandra, dasi, etc. These surnames do not coincide with other Koya surnames. Their names also have suffixes like yya, murthy, rao (Buchayya, Bandayya, Laxmayya, Nageswara rao, etc.) and culturally also they differ when compared with other Koyas.

Pottadi Koya

Pottadi Koya occupies lowest strata in Koya hierarchy. They consider them selves 'lower' as Doli Koyas. They are small in number. They live in settlement away from the village.

Clan Organization

The Koyas are divided into five gattu/gotram/clans namely, Beram Bai gotram (Yedavagotta), Mudava Gatta, Paradi Gotram (Nalugava gattu), Bandani Gotram (Ideva getta) and Arava gattu. Each *Gatu* (gotram) is further divided into several surnames (inteperlu). It seems that the Koya have borrowed the term gotram from the neighbouring castes and affixed to their clans. But the number of clans is disputed. Aiyappan and Rev.J.Cain reported five clans, namely; Peramboyudu, Mudavagattu (third clan), Pare Gattu, Nute Muppayo Gottu (130 clan) and Vido Gattu (Aiyappan, 1948). Murthy (1991) mentioned five more clans in addition to the above mentioned clans except Nute Muppayo Gattu. These are Okato Gattu (first clan), Rendo Gattu (second clan), Nalugava Gattu and two other. Singh mentions five clans namely Mudava Gattu, Nalugava Gattu (paradu gotram), Idavagattu, Aravagattu and Yedavagattu (Singh, 1993). Affinity between some clans is strong and they regard themselves as brother – clans or phratry, which is common among the Gonds. According to Murthy, Nalugava Gattu and Peramboyana (6th clan) form one phratry, Mudava Gattu and Paradi Gottu (7th clan) form another phratry. Further, Muppayi Mudava Gattu and Aravayi Nalugava Gattu form one phratry and Idava Gattu is an independent phratry. The data analysed by the author reveals that the Koyas have five clans and three phratries.

The above clan divisions are close to description of Mohan Rao's clan division. But it differs from Murthy's classification of clan names as well as phratry formation. The interesting feature in all these studies is that the Bandani gotram (Aidavagattu) emerges as an independent group. This independent Bandani gotram maintains marriage alliances with all the other gotras.

Commensal Relation, Concept of Purity and Pollution and Status Ranking

Living in close proximity of Hindu communities the Koyas and other tribes have adopted certain norms of pollution and purity. Such norms and norm of food exchange have come to characterise the local stratification, which will be discussed below. The Koyas, Lambadies, Konda Dora eat the flesh of goat, sheep, fish, pork and cow including the veal. Konda Kammara and Konda Kapu abstain from eating beef, but they eat meat of wild pig. The hill Reddies and Konda Jangama are strictly vegetarian. Their subsistence is mainly based on minor forest collection, food gathering and Podu cultivation. Though their economy is 'primitive' in nature, they occupy highest place in social scale and regional hierarchy followed by Koya, Lambadi, Konda Kapu and Konda Dora, while the Valmiki occupy the lowest status in social hierarchy.

Commensal relationship exists between Konda Dora and Konda Kapu, Koya and Lambadi. But they do not accept food from the lower caste groups Mala and Madiga and lower tribal groups like, Valmiki, Kammara. The Konda Jangama accepts neither cooked food nor water from the hands of tribes other than Hill Reddies. While on their visit to shandy or attending to any ceremonial function in the locality or in a far away place, they carry their food material and cook their meal, i.e., chodi ammbali prepared out of regi powder. They dine separately at an isolated spot. Socially, the higher ranking tribes like Koya and Lambadi do not share the same platform with Konda Kammara, Konda Kapu and Valmiki in their ceremonial functions. They form separate rows or separate place for dining. The hill Reddies maintain aloofness from all and do not participate in ceremonial functions (Figure 1). Brahmins now attend ceremonies of rich Koya tribal people. They accept raw food from tribes.

Ranking among sub-Tribes of Koya Tribe

The Lingadhari Koya are Saivaites, popularly called *Pujarllr* by other sub-groups of Koya tribe. They are vegetarian. They do not maintain commensal relations with other sub-tribes like Racha Koya, Gumma Koya, Gutta Koya, Murasa Koya, Matta Koya and Kaka Koya. They are much respected people and have higher status among the Koyas. Some people believe that the Lingadhari Koya are not real Koyas, they are the plains people admitted into Koya fold. Some of their surnames are Beraboyana, Gumpanepalli, Darunmuda, Sunammu and Menapa, etc., which are different from Koya surnames.

Figure 1

Status Ranking Based on Commensal Relation

FOOD ACEPTING COMMUNITIES (TRIBES: HILL REDDIES – KONDA KAMMARI; CASTES: VALMIKI – BRAHMIN)

	HILL REDDIES	KONDA JANGAMA	KOYA	LAMBADI	KONDA DORA	KONDA KAMMARI	VALMIKI	MALA	MADIGA	RIDDY	BRAHMIN
HILL REDDIES	Exchange of Cooked Food									Acceptance of Cooked Food	Acceptance of Cooked Food
KONDA JANGAMA	Acceptance of Cooked Food	Exchange of Cooked Food								Acceptance of Cooked Food	Acceptance of Cooked Food
KOYA	Acceptance of Cooked Food	Acceptance of Cooked Food	Exchange of Cooked Food	Exchange of Cooked Food	Exchange of Cooked Food	Acceptance of Raw Material	Acceptance of Raw Material	Acceptance of Raw Material	Acceptance of Raw Material	Acceptance of Cooked Food	Acceptance of Cooked Food
LAMBADI	Acceptance of Cooked Food	Acceptance of Cooked Food	Exchange of Cooked Food	Exchange of Cooked Food	Exchange of Cooked Food	Acceptance of Raw Material	Acceptance of Raw Material	Acceptance of Raw Material	Acceptance of Raw Material	Acceptance of Cooked Food	Acceptance of Cooked Food
KONDA DORA	Acceptance of Cooked Food	Acceptance of Cooked Food	Acceptance of Cooked Food	Exchange of Cooked Food	Exchange of Cooked Food	Acceptance of Raw Material	Acceptance of Raw Material	Acceptance of Raw Material	Acceptance of Raw Material	Acceptance of Cooked Food	Acceptance of Cooked Food
KONDA KAMMARI	Acceptance of Cooked Food	Acceptance of Cooked Food	Acceptance of Cooked Food	Acceptance of Cooked Food	Acceptance of Cooked Food	Exchange of Cooked Food	Acceptance of Raw Material	Acceptance of Raw Material	Acceptance of Raw Material	Acceptance of Cooked Food	Acceptance of Cooked Food
VALMIKI	Acceptance of Cooked Food	Acceptance of Cooked Food	Acceptance of Cooked Food	Acceptance of Cooked Food	Acceptance of Cooked Food	Acceptance of Cooked Food	Exchange of Cooked Food	Exchange of Cooked Food	Acceptance of Raw Material	Acceptance of Cooked Food	Acceptance of Cooked Food
MALA	Acceptance of Cooked Food	Acceptance of Cooked Food	Acceptance of Cooked Food	Acceptance of Cooked Food	Acceptance of Cooked Food	Acceptance of Cooked Food	Exchange of Cooked Food	Exchange of Cooked Food	Acceptance of Raw Material	Acceptance of Cooked Food	Acceptance of Cooked Food
MADIGA	Acceptance of Cooked Food	Acceptance of Cooked Food	Acceptance of Cooked Food	Acceptance of Cooked Food	Acceptance of Cooked Food	Acceptance of Cooked Food	Acceptance of Cooked Food	Acceptance of Cooked Food	Exchange of Cooked Food	Acceptance of Cooked Food	Acceptance of Cooked Food
REDDY	Acceptance of Raw Material	Acceptance of Raw Material	Acceptance of Raw Material	Acceptance of Raw Material	Acceptance of Raw Material	Acceptance of Raw Material	Acceptance of Raw Material	Acceptance of Raw Material	Acceptance of Raw Material	Exchange of Cooked Food	Exchange of Cooked Food
BRAHMIN	Acceptance of Raw Material	Acceptance of Raw Material	Acceptance of Raw Material	Acceptance of Raw Material	Acceptance of Raw Material	Acceptance of Raw Material	Acceptance of Raw Material	Acceptance of Raw Material	Acceptance of Raw Material	Acceptance of Cooked Food	Exchange of Cooked Food

Acceptance of Cooked Food
Exchange of Cooked Food
Acceptance of Raw Material

Commensal relationship exists between the Racha Koya and the Gumma Koya, Murasa Koya and Kamma Koya, Kaka Koya and Matta Koya. But marriage alliances are forbidden between these pair of sub-groups. The Gutta have distinct identity among Koya sub-tribes. They do not intermingle with other groups either in ceremonial functions or in marriage rituals. They occasionally visit Shandy to sell articles such as dry chillies, tobacco, etc.

Pottadi Koya have been poorest among the Koyas. The Pottadi Koyas occupy the lowest rank among all the sub-groups. The Doli Koyas are bards, story tellers and genealogists. On the

Figure 2

Status Ranking Based on Intra-Tribal Commensal Relation

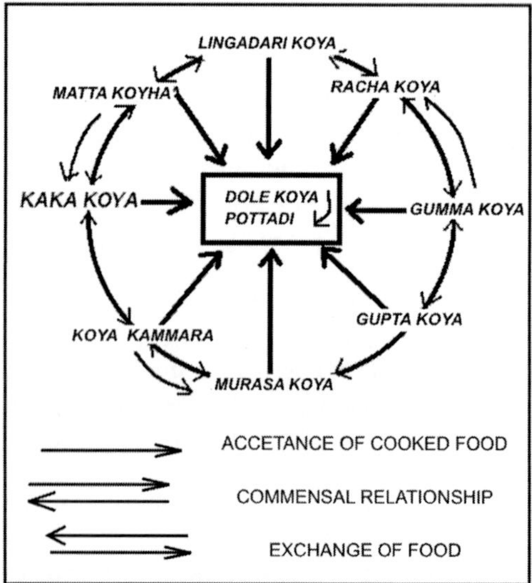

day of death, they recite stories throughout the night and praise the glory of the deceased. Because of their occupation, they occupied in the past the lowest status in social hierarchy They accept food from all the sub-groups (Figure 2). Many of old norms are changing so also economic activities.

The present study was carried out in two villages, Chinna Bheempalli and Vootla from East Godavari agency area and two villages, Venkannapalem and Boiji Kopallu from Khammam agency area. Chinna Bheemapalli is a multi-ethnic village situated at a distance of 5 km from Gokavaram town. Frequently the buses are plying via Peda Bheemapalli and Pasullabad, from where Chinna Bheemapalli is just one km. Hence, the village people are having close interaction with town people since more than eight decades exchanging their agricultural products; for commodities such as cloth and metal implements.

Vootla, is an isolated village and inhabited by the Koya amidst thick forest. The village is surrounded by nine big hills, namely Nalla Konda, Mallikarjuna Konda, Vusirikonda, Sirimanu Konda, Chinta Konda, Addu Konda in the West, Naradu Konda, Seta Metta in the North and Tithiri Konda in the East. The village is located 22 km away from the Gokavaram town. There is no transportation facilities for the village and one has to reach the village by foot passing through thick forest and by crossing several streams. These people are not having much interaction with plains people but they meet their neighbouring brothers at Shandy in Gokavarm town.

Venkannapalem is an isolated village, adjoining V.R. Puram Mandal. The Koyas living in the village are different from E.G. Koyas with regard to dress pattern, hair style. The other village Bojjikopally is situated near the Bhadrachalam town. Under tribal development the Government has implemented certain schemes to provide safe drinking water facilities through bore wells, ring wells and Chernvu, etc. We shall describe below briefly the impact of development schemes and who actually are benefited by these schemes.

The population of the above villages is presented in Table 3.

Table 3

Population of Koya as per Household Census in Selected Villages

Village name	*Type of household*	*No. of households*	*Male*	*Per cent*	*Female*	*Per cent*	*Total*
Chinna Bheempalli	Nuclear	58	131	47.8	143	52.2	274
	Extended	7	22	46.8	25	53.2	47
	Total	65	153	47.7	168	52.3	321
Vootla	Nuclear	50	121	51.9	114	48.5	235
	Extended	25	64	46	75	54	139
	Total	75	185	49.5	189	50.5	374
Yenkannapalem	Nuclear	27	58	51.3	55	48.6	113
	Extended	3	6	50	9	60	15
	Total	30	64	50	64	50	128
Bojji Kopallu	Nuclear	10	44	48.4	47	51.6	91
	Extended	2	4	40	6	60	10
	Total	12	48	47.5	53	52.5	101
	Grand Total	182	450	43.9	574	56.1	924

The village Chinna Bheempalli has a total population of 321 living in 65 households with 153 males (47.7%) and 168 females (52.3%). Of the 65 houses studied there are 7 extended families consisting of 22 males (46.8%) and 25 females (43.2%).

A total of 374 people live in 75 household of Vootla Village. Out of the total population 185(49.5%) are males and 189(50.5%) are females. Out of the 75 household, 25 are extended families which comprise 64(46.0%) males and 75(54%) females, resulting in a total population of 139. One hundred twenty-eight people live in 30 households of Yenkannapalem comprising 64 males (50%) and 64 females (50%) of the 30 households, 3 households are extended families comprising 15 people, of whom 40 per cent are males and 60 per cent females. In the 21 households of Bojji Kopallu the males constitute 48(47.5%) and females number 53(52.5%). A total of 10 persons are living in 2 extended families, out of 12 households with 4 males (40%) and 6 females (60%).

Out of 182 households, spread over 4 villages, the total population (1024) constitute males 450 and females 574. There is a striking variation in extended and nuclear families among the four villages. Vootla has 33.3 per cent of extended families. Vootla shows the traditional characteristics of the tribal village, whereas the other three villages show a tendency of having more nuclear families.

The age and sex composition of the Koyas residing in four villages from whom the census data was collected is presented in the table. Children constitute 30 per cent of the population in three villages except in Vootla in the age group of 0–4 years. The frequency of female children is higher than the male in Chinna Bheempalli, Vootla and Bojji Koppulu, whereas reverse trend is observed in Yenkannapalem. The proportion of males in relation to females is very low in Vootla, while moderate values are reported for Chinna Bheempalli and Bojji Kopplu. The males out member females in Yenkannapalem (Table 4).

The frequency is almost equal in the 5–9 years age group in Chinna Bheempalli, and Bojji Koppalu, where as the proportions are significant in other two villages. The sex ratio is comparable in three villages, but a highly disproportionate value is obtained for the Vootla village. The frequency in 10–14 years age group is almost equal in Cinna Bheemapalli and Yenkkannapalem, while the proportion are dissimilar in Vootla and Bojji Koppalu. The sex ratio is equal in Yenkannapalem and the proportion of males is double to that of females in 10–14 years age group in Bojji Koppal. In Chinna Bheemapalli the frequency of females is slightly higher to that of males. The female outnumber males in the 15–19 years age group in Vootla, Venkannapalem and Bojji Koppalu, while a slightly reversible trend is observed in Chinna Bheemapalli. The per cent frequency is slightly higher in males aged 20 years and above in Vootla and Yenkannapalem while reverse trend is observed in two other villages (Table 4). The child woman ratio is extremely low in Bojji Koppalu (21.2) while the highest value (48.9) is recorded in Chinna Bheemapalli followed by Vootla (41.7) and Yenkannapalem (37.5) which depended on agriculture in all the four villages.

Land-Holding Pattern

The families holding irrigated lands are more in Vootla compared to other villages, however the average wet land- holdings per household is high in

Table 4

Age and Sex Composition of the Koyas Inhabiting the Four Villages

Age group	Chinna Bheemapalli				Vootal				Yenkannapalem				Bojji Koppallu			
	Male	Female	Total	Sex Ratio	Male	Female	Total	Sex Ratio	Male	Female	Total	Sex Ratio	Male	Female	Total	Sex Ratio
0–4	19 (12.4)	25 (14.9)	44 (13.7)	76	17 (9.2)	33 (17.5)	50 (13.4)	51.5	10 (15.6)	5 (7.8)	15 (11.7)	200	3 (6.3)	4 (7.5)	7 (70)	75
5–9	30 (19.6)	34 (20.2)	64 (19.9)	88.2	31 (16.8)	21 (11.1)	52 (13.9)	149.6	12 (18.8)	14 (21.9)	26 (20.3)	85.7	11 (23.4)	13 (24.5)	24 (24.0)	84.6
10–14	17 (11.1)	19 (11.3)	36 (11.2)	89.5	20 (10.8)	15 (7.9)	35 (9.4)	133.3	5 (7.8)	5 (7.8)	10 (7.8)	100	6 (12.8)	39 (5.7)	92 (9.0)	200
15–19	15 (9.8)	14 (8.3)	29 (9.0)	107.1	9 (4.9)	17 (9.0)	26 (7.0)	52.9	5 (7.8)	10 (15.6)	15 (11.7)	50	3 (6.4)	5 (6.4)	8 (8.0)	60
20 & above	72 (47.1)	76 (45.2)	148 (46.1)	94.7	108 (58.4)	103 (44.3)	211 (56.4)	104.9	32 (50.0)	30 (46.9)	62 (42.2)	106.7	25 (51.1)	28 (52.8)	52 (52.0)	85.7
Total	153	168	321	91.1	185	108	374	979	64	64	128	100	47	53	100	88.7

Figures in parenthesis indicate percentage

Chinna Bheemapalli followed by other villages (Table 5) which is nearly 2 acres per household. Comparatively the Koyas own more rainfed lands than irrigated lands. The average dryland holding reported per household is also higher. Though more households own dry lands in Vootla, the average is much less compared to the landholding observed in Vootla and Venkannapalem. Nearly 50 per cent of households in Chinna Bheemapalli and Vootla posses both irrigated and rainfed lands, whereas only 4 households, out of 21 possess this type of agricultural lands in Bojji Koppal. Out of the four villages, Yenkannapalem showed maximum frequency, nearly 75 per cent of the households. In Vootla villages more households are having rainfed lands than in other Koya villages. In Table 6 the non-agricultural occupations and services as pursued by four villages are mentioned.

Table 5

Distribution of Wet and Dry Landholding

Village name	*Th*	*Ll*	*%*	*Lh*	*%*	*Wlh*	*Twl*	*Aw*	*Dlh*	*Td*	*Adl*	*Bd*	*Od*
Chinna Bheemapalli	65	18	(27.7)	42	(64.6)	28	67	2.4	38	263.5	6.9	25	13
Vootla	75	15	(20.0)	58	(77.3)	37	64	1.7	52	189.5	3.6	31	21
Yenkannapalem	30	1	(3.3)	29	(96.6)	26	53.5	2.1	30	91	3	25	5
Bojji Kopalu	21	8	(38.1)	13	(61.9)	4	8	2	13	68	5.2	4	9

Th = Total households
Ll = Landless households
Lh = Landholding households
Wlh = Wet land households
Twl = Total wet land
Aw = Average wet land
Dlh = Dry land households
Td = Total dry land
Adl = Average dry land
Bd = Both wet and dry land
Od = Only dry land households

Table 6

Occupations Pursued in Four Villages

Village →	*Chinna-Bheemapalli*		*Bojji Koppalu*		*Vootla*		*Yenkana palem*	
Occupation	*Male*	*Female*	*Male*	*Female*	*Male*	*Female*	*Male*	*Female*
Kuli	35	41	14	18	36	40	14	17
Agri Primary	26	27	9	6	76	69	17	15
Attender	0	0	1	0	0	0	0	0
Bank employee	1	0	0	0	0	0	0	0
Business	1	0	0	0	1	0	0	0
Cow boy	0	0	0	0	3	0	0	0
Driver	0	0	0	0	1	0	0	0
Excise constable	1	0	0	0	0	0	0	0
Health worker	0	0	0	0	0	1	0	0
Kirana shop	0	0	0	0	0	2	0	0
Police	0	0	0	0	1	0	0	0
Postman	1	0	0	0	0	0	0	0
Washerman	0	0	0	0	0	3	0	0

Economic Deprivation and Owner-Tenant Relations

There are different types of land management practices prevalent in the Agency area. These practices involve owning different types of land, using land as share-cropper, using land on lease. Different types of practices are described below:

Kavulu

This is a kind of agreement for leasing the land between the landowner and the tenant. The landowner gives his land to the tenant on lease, for a fixed period receiving certain amount of money. After the expiry of the term as decided by the party, the tenant returns the land to its owner. The money to be fixed depends on the fertility of the land and lease period.

Vaddi Teermana Kavulu

When a person is in need of money, he borrows certain sum of money by giving his land as collateral to a cultivator or a moneylender. The borrower has to pay a fixed interest for the amount received, every year. The cultivator or money-lender will be in possession of this land until he gets his money back. Generally this agreement is done through written documents by both parties. In this type of agreement the person who has borrowed money has many chances to lose his land. In case of his failure to pay the interest regularly interest accumulates over the years. He often finds it difficult to pay this lump sum amount at a time (Vide Table 8 for various operations of agriculture during a year).

Sama Palu (Equal Share)

This is a contract between a landowner and a landless person. Both the parties cultivate the land, bearing all the expenses equally for manure, seeds etc. If they appoint labour at the time of ploughing or harvesting, they pay wages to the labourers from their share of grains. In this contract the period of tenure is one year. This can be renewed every year. Landowner gets a small portion of crop from the person using his land. In some areas it is found that the landowner gets an extra share called *Bhoomi Vata*. In this case, out of three equal parts the landowner gets two parts and the tenant gets one part of the total yield.

Religious Domain

The Koyas have been very much influenced by Hindu religion from times immemorial. Therefore, we observe that most often they are worshipping Hindu deities. They celebrate Hindu festivals like Sankranti, Dassara, etc. The festivals and ceremonies are performed collectively, which show their solidarity. The Koyas depend on magic and divination also to come out of their sickness. Tribal deities are worshipped for various purposes like curing diseases, good harvest, improvement of cattle wealth and avoidance of natural calamities, etc. The tribals believe that the pujas are performed to avoid evil spirits, for the welfare of an individual as well as the entire community. Table 7 provides the calendar of important village festivals.

Due to conversion to Christianity, lot of changes are taking place in their day-to-day life, food habits and cultural behaviour. As per the present study in Chinna Bheemapalli village, 17 families had converted to Christianity, through

Table 7
Calendar of Festivals

Deity Venerated	*Festival*	*Purpose*	*Month*
Maisamma	Maisamma panduga	To avoid conflict and quarrel	July–August
Pandu raju	Iepp puvvu panduga (Bassia latifoila)	For collecting Ieppa flower/eating purpose/ preparing garden	January–February
Mthyalamma	Mthyalamma panduga	Cholera/smallpox	—
Mthyalamma	Mthyalamma panduga	To eat Indian beans	February–March
Mthyalamma	Kothalapanduga	To eat the new product of any crop	August, September and October
Goramaru	Velpulu panduga (Kolupula panduga)	Clan festival	Yearly once
All Village deities	Peeda ritual		June–July
Grama thalli	Bhumipanduga	Good luck at the time of sowing the seeds	June–July
Panchapandavalu	Kondapanduga (rock festival)	Good luck before going for hunting	April–May
Konda Demudu	Gadela panduga (cattle festival)	For well-being of the cattle	March
Nukalamma	Nukalamma festival	Prevent smallpox	—
Gudi Bapanamma	Godibapanamm festival	Prevent village from ill health	March
Maddi Ramakka	Kothalapanduga	Harvesting	September

Godavari delta mission and Southern mission. These two missions have built permanent churches and conduct regular masses. In Voolta 10 families have embraced Christianity. Prayers are held in a small hut. There are plans to build a permanent church. Yenkanapalem and Bojji Koppalu are gradually showing affinity towards Christianity.

Recapitulation

The Koya have ethnic and linguistic affinity with the Gonds. Like Gonds, they are divided into many sub-tribes. Sub-tribes of Koyas have traditional occupations and those in hills still pursue shifting-cultivation. They remain poor and more excluded from other groups who are gradually advancing in economic field. The Koyas regard Bhima as their apical ancestor. The Koya sub-tribes spread in plains regions have come to be influenced by Hinduism differently. Koya sub-tribes living in multi-ethnic villages are accorded lower positions by the caste-Hindus. Old considerations of pollution are slowly loosing importance in economic affairs. The Koyas living in tribal areas enjoy high status in relation to tribes such as Lambadi, Konda Dora, Konda Kapu, Hill Reddy and Valmiki, mainly because of their numerical and economic dominance. The Koyas now face competition from Lambadis, who claim tribal status and hence try to procure fertile lands of Koyas. Lingadhari, Rocha and Gumma sub-tribes of Koyas enjoy higher ranks compared to Gutta, Murasa, Kammara, Matta, Doli and Pottadi Koya sub-tribes who are socially excluded and economically

Table 8

Economic Activities of the Koya During the Calendar Year

Name of the month in the Koya region	*Approximate month in English calendar*	*Agricultural operation*	*Forest collection and other activities*
Chitra	March	Clearing the jungle on a hill slope for new podu land. Storing of fire wood	Clearing the Beedi bushes. Collection of ieppa flowers, hunting, fishing and casual labour in tobacco field. Casual labour for bamboo cutting.
Jesta	April	Burning the felled forest portion of podu. Making new ploughs and other agricultural implements	Collection of roots and tubers, Ieppa flowers, fishing and manual labour (collection) of price mangoes, jack fruits). Bamboo cutting, collection of beedi leaf (last week).
Kathara	May	Ploughing and digging of Garnvu and podu fields. Sowing sama, chodi ragi, korra, maize, dry paddy kandulu (Red gram), Harvesting Dudamalu	Collection of beedi leaf throughout the month. Collection of ripe mangoes, jack fruits. Collection of Ieppa flower. Hunting, bamboo cutting
Mulagesira	June	Transplantation of wet paddy in the last week. Beginning of weeding of ragi and paddy crop	Collection of ripe mangoes, jack fruits.
Arudhra	July	Agricultural operation like sowing Chikkudu (Indian beans) beans, oliselu, cucumber and transplanting brinjal and paddy. Harvesting of sama, chodi, Korra, and weeding, etc.	
Asalvaru	August	Weeding in paddy fields, harvesting jowar, bajra, harvesting budamalu, aarlu	
Magapuge	September	Weeding in paddy fields, sowing sama, pairu nuvulu (miger crop)	Manual labour
Utara	October	Harvesting sama and dry paddy	
Asthasitha	November	Harvesting chodi (ragi) paddy, Kandhi (red gram)	Selecting the small toddy trees for thati peechu, manual labour.
Santhi	December	Harvesting paddy (ragi) and chodi, Kandhi (red gram), pesaralu, green gram	Preparing the thati fibre, making ropes of 'Mokutallu', manual labour.
Vishanli	January	Harvesting miger seed, beans, ganti	Preparing the thati fiber, making ropes and mokkutallu, collection of toddy (last week).

deprived being shifting-cultivators, brass-workers, and carpenter, toddy trapers, bards and those depending on alms. There are several economic development schemes, but poor Koyas in interior villages could not get adequate support. Those Koyas who depended on agriculture, worked hard to improve their status. Rich Koyas could approach administration and avail opportunities of grants and loans. Such Koyas received better education and joined white-collar jobs. Many rich Koyas now follow marriage rules of Hindus. Brahmins are invited by them to conduct marriage and other rituals.

References

Aiyyappan, A. 1948, *Report on the Socio-Economic Conditions of the Aboriginal Tribal of the Province of Madras*, Madras: Government Press.

Census of India 1981, Series 2, Parts IX and IV, Andhra Pradesh.

Dumont, Louis 1966, *Homo Hierarchicus*, Delhi: Vikas Publications.

Furer-Haimendorf, Christoph von 1945, Aboriginal Rebellions in the Deccan, *Man in India*, Vol. XXV, 4, pp. 208–217.

Mohan Rao, K. and K. Cahandra Raju 1993, Koyas of Andhra Pradesh, *Gririjana Samskriti*, Vol. 1(1), Hyderabad: Tribal Welfare Department.

Murthy, A.S. 1977, Koyas: The Village and its Function in Andhra Pradesh, *Vanyajathi*, Vol. 25 (3), pp. 14–18.

Murthy, A.S. 1981, Koya Dora Society of Andhra Pradesh, *Folklore*, Vol. 22 (10), pp. 214–15.

Murthy, A.S. 1991, *Religion and Society (A Study of Koyas)*, New Delhi: Discovery Publishing House.

Murty, A.S. 1972, Caste Stratification in Tribal Koya Society, *Journal of Indian Anthropological Society*, Vol. 7 (2).

Samanta, R.K. and M. Narasimha Reddy 1983, Farm Leadership among Koya Tribes of Andhra Pradesh, *Man in India*, Vol. 63.

Singh, K.S. 1994, *The Scheduled Tribes People of India, National Series*, Vol. III, Delhi: Oxford University Press.

Staurt, H.A. 1893, Koya in Census of India 1891, Part I, Report, Vol. XIII, E. Thurston, 1909, *Castes and Tribes of South India*, Vol. IV, Madras: Government Press.

Thurston, E. 1906, *Ethnographic Notes on Southern India*, Madras: Government Press.

Tyler, Stephen 1965, Koya Morphology and Patterns of Kinship Behaviors, *American Anthropologist*, Vol. 68(3).

Tyler, Stephen A. 1964, Field are for Planting Swidden Agriculture among the Koyas of South India, *Journal of Indian Anthropological Society*, Vol. 9(1), pp. 17–38.

Tyler, Stephen S. 1964, Former Analysis of Koya Kinship Terminolity in Emenesn Felicitation, Volume ed. by B.H. Drishnamurthy.

Veerraju, P., M.S. Babu, G. Jaikishan, J.M. Naidu and N.M. Blake 1982, Genetic Studies on the Koya Dora and Konda Kammara Tribe of Andhra Pradesh, India, *Human Hereditary* (32), pp. 240–245.

Veerraju, P. 1978, *Consanguinity in Tribal Communities of Andhra Pradesh in Medical Genetics in India*, I.C. Verma (ed.), Vol. 2, Pondicherry: Auroma Enterprises.

Yeats, M.W.M. 1932, Koyas in Census of India 1931, Madras, Part 1, Report, Vol. XIV, Madras, pp. 366–369.

15 Pre-Agricultural Economy, Deprivation and NGO induced Empowerment

The Soliga of Karnataka

S.N. Mahato

The Soliga Identity

The Soliga people inhabit mainly the interior thick forest ranges of southern Karnataka state bordering Tamil Nadu. Other communities are also living in the same ecological setting like the Iruligaru, Kurumbal, Uraligree and so on. According to a popular legend the word Soliga means: "The one who comes from a bamboo." It is believed that the Soliga origin, in some way or other, is connected with the bamboo. Thus, it is significant that the above legend indicates an intimate relationship of the Soliga with the forest. The Soliga's settlements (Podu) are found in the hilly terrain of Billigiri Rangana Betta (BR Hills) Mahadeshwara Betta (MM Hills) and foothills of these hilly tracts. They also inhabit the forests of Heensur and Bandipur in the district of Mysore. A few of them reside in Kushalnagar area in Kodagu district, Malavalli area in Mandya district and Magadi and Kanakapura areas in Bangalore district. The author visited several Soliga settlements in order to select the study village. Hosa Podu Soliga settlement was selected finally for the study. The settlement is located on the BR Hills, in Yalandur taluk in the district of Mysore. Over three months of fieldwork was conducted among the Soliga. Hosa Podu Soliga settlement is one of the nine settlements of the Soliga in BR Hills. The distance between one settlement and another is one to 10 km. In various ethnographic reports the word Soliga is spelt differently, such as Sholaga (Thurston, 1909; Luiz, 1963), Sholiga (Nanjundayya and Iyer, 1931), Sholigars and Soliga (Census of India, 1966; Morab, 1977). The lists prepared by the then state Government of Mysore, 1967 and the Centre (Census of India, 1966) used the terms Sholaga and Soligaru. The latter term is the plural form of the Kannada word Soliga.

The details of B.R. Hills and settlements are as follows:

B.R. Hills: Ecological and Ethnic Background

1. Total geographical area 22,775.32 acres.
2. Extent of cultivated area 630.07 acres.
3. The forest cover in remaining areas.
4. Total no. of families – 499 houses. Out of that 293 families belong to the Soliga tribe with a population of 1540, according to the Census of India 1991.

5. Details of other communities living in BR Hills:

(i)	Pasivara/Nayaka	Other Backwards Class (OBC)
(ii)	Brahmins	Priest, teacher, landowners
(iii)	Lingayat	Priest, landowners, hotel business, shops
(iv)	Agasa	Dhobi (Washerman)
(v)	Uppasa	Agricultural labourers
(vi)	Scheduled Castes	
(vii)	Muslim	

6. One voluntary origination known as Vivekananda Girijan Kalyan Kendra (VGKK) is run by the honorary secretary H. Sudarshan.
7. Temple: Muzarai institution (temple)
   (1) Managed by the government (Ranganatha Swamy Temple) 1
   (2) Temple – Shiva temple (Non Muzarai or non government) 1
8. Co-operative Society 1
9. Police Post/Small thana 1
10. Post office/Sub post office 1
11. Telephone Exchange with 15 connections 1
12. Lower primary schools near the temple and also at a distance of 10 km situated in old hamlet 2
13. Higher primary school – located near temple run by Education Department and another run by VGKK. 2
14. High school and new junior college run by VGKK in the same premise. The college was started in 1995. 1
15. Kaveri Gramana Bank sponsored by State Bank of Mysore, Yelandur. 1
16. Office of the Forest Department 1
17. Sericulture Silk Farm and Training Centre, Karnataka government sericulture department 1
18. Hoticulture Farm 1
19. Ayurvedic dispensary (not functioning properly) 1
20. Dak Bungalows belonging to PWD and Forest Department 2
21. Jai Vijayam Hospital (10 beds) run by VGKK 1
22. Gandhi Ashram school run by Gandhi Seva Shram (for the education of children) 1
23. Distance from Panchayat headquarters at Yaragamballi village 20 km
24. Distance from district headquarters at Mysore 85 km
25. Distance from Railway station 48 km
26. Rain Guage Station. 1

According to the Census of India, 1991 population of B.R. Hills is reported as below:

Table 1

Sex	*Population (all communities)*	*Scheduled Caste*	*Scheduled Tribe (Soliga)*	*Total Literate*
Male	1257	63	840	553
Female	1047	40	700	259
Total	2304	103	1540	812

In B.R. Hills rainfall is recorded more due to the location of the area at the height ranging from 800 metres to 900 metres from mean sea level. Most of the area is covered with thick green deciduous forest. The district of Mysore lies between 11°31′ to 12°50′ North latitude and 75°45′ to 77°45′ East longitude.

Hosa Podu Soliga settlement is a relatively new settlement, formed around the year 1980. The name of the village is significant as 'Hosa' means new and 'Podu' means settlement. Hence, this is known as Hosa Podu. Presently 40 pucca houses have been constructed from time to time under the rehabilitation programme by the taluk revenue department, forest department with the help of VGKK. There are proposals to construct some more houses for the Soliga who are still living in the huts in the same Podu. This apart, a temple of Jadeswamy is housed in a pucca house and an Anganwadi is also functioning in the same house. A borewell is in working condition to supply drinking water to the Soliga. On the outer margin of the settlement one provision shop is run by a Soliga family and one tea shop is also run by a Soliga, who is handicapped. He also sells cheap toffees, bidi, cigarette, match boxes, etc. Another tea and tiffin shop is run by a Pasivara-Nayaka family on the roadside adjoining Hosa Podu settlement.

In Hosa Podu Soliga settlement, there are 44 Soliga households with a population of 203 persons (98 males and 105 females). Other communities have their houses within the area of one to two kilometres. A temple is situated on the hills, dedicated to the God Rangaswamy. It is constructed on a huge rock. 'Billi' means white and 'Giri' means mountain. The term 'Betta' means hills. As this area is viewed from the plains and is nearly at a height of 800–900 metres is regarded sacred the names Billigiri (white mountain) Rangana (Lord Venkatesha, incarnation of Vishnu) and Betta (hills) that is BR Hills, has been given.

The forests on the hills are thickly wooded with huge trees and bamboo thickets. Thus the hills are rich in plants and flowers. Most important trees yielding timber are Arala, Bandeku, Homme, Matti, Herile tegu to name a few. The forests are plentiful with wild plants, bushes and tall jungle grass. The Soliga worship a huge tree nearby which is 200 years-old called Dodda Sampige. Among the fauna, elephant, bison, bear and wild boar are found in large numbers. Previously tigers and leopards were found in the forest but their number is said to be meagre. This apart, other animals like deer, antelope, jungle sheep, jungle fowl and others are found. Several kinds of birds are also found in the hill. Previously, this hilly area was not easily accessible as there were no connecting roads from the plains. Then the mode of transport was only horse. Presently there is a pucca tar road connecting Chamarajanagar from one side and another route is from Yalandur side in the plain areas. The roads are well connected with other parts of the district and state. Now a number of state transport buses are plying to the BR Hills. Light and heavy vehicles are operating in this area, owned by several coffee estates of the area.

Population

The Soliga are a Scheduled Tribe in Karnataka state. These people are enumerated in the Census of India as 'Sholaga' and also spelled as 'Sholiga' in many available works. In the 1981 Census, Soligaru and Sholaga are enumerated at 16,390 and 1902 respectively in the district of Mysore alone. The Soliga were earlier known as semi-nomadic people. They led a semi nomadic life by gathering minor forest produce. At times they tend to trap small animals like rats, wild cat, forest squirrel, wild sheep and pig.

Economy and Food Habits

The Soliga depend on shifting-cultivation. The Podu cultivation (shifting cultivation) involves the selection and clearing of a patch of land keeping in view that the wild animals specially elephants would not come. Several crops, particularly ragi and maize are grown there. The Podu cultivation is done in the particular land for 3 to 4 years as that patch of land becomes less fertile. Thereafter, the Soliga move another virgin land (takkalu) on the hill slopes for cultivation. This practice of shifting cultivation was considered a menace for the growth of the forest. Thus, the forest department of the Karnataka government has forced them to stop. Shifting-cultivation is part of economy as well as culture, hence it is pursued despite ban.

The Soliga are non-vegetarian. Occasionally, they go to trap wild fowl, boar, rats, birds which are consumed by them. They grow vegetables such as brinjal, ladies finger, cucumber, bean and so on for their consumption. Their staple food is ragi and most common pulse is kulthi. Groundnut oil is used as cooking medium. Their non-alcoholic drinks are tea and coffee. A few people were taking alcoholic drinks. Milk and milk products are taken when they are available. Many fruits such as mango, banana, guava and so on are consumed. Fruit trees are found in the forest. Smoking bidi is common and so are chewing of tobacco and betel. Of course, now they are consuming more rice and pulses. Tea and coffee are common drinks. Now bread, bakery product, and biscuits are mainly consumed by their children.

Extension of Education

Table 2

Literacy Level

Literacy level	*Male*		*Female*		*Total*	
	No.	*%*	*No.*	*%*	*No.*	*%*
Illiterate	15	15.31	35	33.33	50	24.63
Signature only	11	11.22	3	2.86	14	6.90
Literate (read & write)	55	56.12	42	40.00	97	47.78
Anganwadi	14	14.29	17	16.19	31	15.27
Infants	3	3.06	8	7.62	11	5.42
Total	98	100.00	105	100.00	203	100.00

Among the Soliga the general trend of response towards formal education is favourable or rather very good in the studied settlement. The above table indicates that illiteracy is only 24.63 per cent (male 15.31% and female 33.33%). Out of this female illiteracy is more than that of the male. Actual literacy level is found at about 54.68 per cent including the persons who know signature only.

Morab has that the literacy level was 4.5 per cent during his fieldwork period in 1965. Presently the trend of Soliga children attending the Anganwadi is increasing. In the settlement, a few infants are left that is 11 babies (5.42%). General literacy level is good at 54.68 per cent due to the availability of education facility nearby. That is due to the existence of a school adjacent to Hosa Podu settlement a residential ashram school from the 1st standard upto 10+2 classes. The school was started in 1981 and further middle, higher and 10+2 classes have been added from time to time. This institution is run by the management of VGKK.

As early as in 1954, Gandhi Ashram school was opened which imparted education among the Soliga. This Ashram still functions there but it has been reduced to a sitting centre for children. Some of the educated persons among the Soliga are employed in forest department in the lower cadre as forest guard, forest fire watcher, and mahabat. Some of them are temporarily employed and a few are permanently employed.

Table 3

Level of Education among Literates

Level of education	*Male*		*Female*		*Total*	
	No.	*%*	*No.*	*%*	*No.*	*%*
Primary with knowledge of signature	38	57.59	30	66.67	68	61.26
Middle	18	27.27	15	33.33	33	29.73
High school	08	12.12	—	—	08	7.21
Pre-University level	01	1.51	—	—	01	0.90
Degree level	01	1.51	—	—	01	0.90
Total	66	100.00	45	100.00	111	100.00

The above table shows that among the literate people, majority of them, that is 61.26 per cent have got educated up to the primary level. At the middle school level, 29.73 per cent have achieved education. At the high school level, 7.25 per cent have received education. One male student was continuing his education under the pre-university (10+2) system while another boy was studying BSc at Bangalore with support provided to him by VGKK.

The VGKK has employed some educated Soligas in its institute, in the different sections of the Kendra in crafts such as carpentry, weaving centre, knitting centre, food processing section, Anganwadi and so on. This apart, four social workers have been appointed by the VGKK from the educated Soligas. These persons are regarded in high esteem by all the Soliga due to their activities. These social workers help the community in several ways. A social worker acts as the catalytic agent between people and forest department, bank and co-operative society for any work that has to be done. The social worker also provides information about the activities of the Soliga Abhivrudhi Sangh.

These social workers are stationed in different places where the concentration of the Soliga are more. They keep their ears and eyes open to gather information regarding any exploitation and any problem arising.

Modernity is observed among the educated people. Their dress pattern including footwear and hairstyle are urban oriented. The old people and illiterates are seen in their traditional dress and hair style. Educated persons have the habit of visiting tea stalls for tea and breakfast along with their friends.

Many girls are employed in VGKK in the health centre as helpers and are also employed in different sections of the training centre that is in the Anganwadi, tailoring and making handicrafts.

Economic Resources and Class Formation

Traditionally, the Soliga are known as shifting cultivators and collectors of minor forest produce. This apart they also pursue some minor economic pursuits such as hunting, trapping and collection of honey, roots and tubers. Morab has reported that the traditional economy of the Soliga is mostly based on shifting cultivation and collection of minor forest produce. There are also other minor economic activities like trapping, fishing and honey collection (Morab, 1977: 36). Morab's statement is based on his fieldwork carried out during 1965. Their traditional mode of production has complete harmony with the natural physical environment where they depend on shifting cultivation by judiciously shifting the fields, and collection of forest produce.

The shifting cultivation is locally known as Podu cultivation. This form of cultivation was practised mainly on the ridges and slopes of the hills. In the forest, podu fields were selected for cultivation by keeping in mind safety from the menace of wild animals, specially elephant. On the hill slopes and ridges several small patches of forest land are cleared through felling of the jungle growth, cutting of bushes, leaving stumps so as to prepare a land fit for cultivation for a few years. There is an elaborate procedure involving ritual performances for the selection of land for shifting cultivation. Though the ritual performances are in vogue, presently, in the new situation, the Soliga perform them in allotted one or two acres of forest land provided as a part of rehabilitation programme. The Soliga have the usufruct rights of use over the forest land provided to them for agricultural purposes with no right of ownership.

The Soliga have a fairly good idea about the types of soil in order to assess the fertility of soil. Those Soliga who have knowledge about soil types, fertility and crop pattern enjoy higher status than the others as many consult them.

In some of the Soliga settlements and specially in Kollegal taluk, many Soliga families have been allotted agricultural land on Patta. These people are referred to as patta land holders, which means landowner. This development has indeed created a clear cut strata of land owners who get better and large yields compared to yields from Podu. Even now a good number of Soligas in interiors depend on shifting cultivation (podu). In B.R. Hills, in the Soliga settlement at Yerakanagadde, some of the Soliga families have got ownership of land that is patta land but many Soligas have not got patta. Hence, there is a clear-cut division between patta land holder and non-patta land holders and this indicates growth of stratified groupings. In Hosa Podu settlement, none of the Soliga has got patta land. Fact remains that every Soliga aspires now to progress and demand from government for making provision to provide patta land to all the Soliga families.

Division of Labour

Women play important roles in agricultural operations, animal husbandry, collection of fuel and bringing potable water. Women engage themselves in operations such as plucking weeds, sowing, harvesting and broadcasting of seeds, specially ragi seeds. Women from economically poor section work as agricultural labour in the land belonging to other communities. Several women are found to work as construction labour and engaged in collection of forest produce. Morab states that various agricultural activities are done by both the sexes, men do the hard task of cutting trees, building fences, harvesting crops, while women do the less arduous works like broadcasting sowing, plucking weeds, etc. (1977: 38). Presently several Soliga women are employed in VGKK as helper in the hospital and health care unit, training centres of tailoring, agarbatti making while males are employed as driver, mess cook, social workers and in carpentry training centre. Generally men are working as forest labour, agricultural farm labour, plucking of forest produce, and collection of honey. This apart, several Soliga men are employed in the forest department in permanent and temporary capacity. Thus, women take up lighter work while men are engaged in labourious work.

Table 4

Distribution of Landholding Household-wise in Hosa Podu Soliga Settlement

Total no. of households	*Landless households*	*Possession of land holders*		
		4 acres	*2 acres*	*1 acre*
44	14	1	1	28

Above table shows that out of 44 households in Hosa Podu Soliga settlement 14 households are landless while 28 are is possession of only one acre of land. Among them, one family each is having four acres and two acres of land. It is reported that landless households have come to this settlement later on after opening of the forest land. The Soliga access forest land but they have only usufruct rights over land.

The person who has four acres of land has developed his fruit orchard with orange and plantain, along with coffee plants. In 1999, he sold out about 10 quintal of coffee seeds and earned a good amount. This Soliga also runs a provision shop in the Hosa Podu settlement. Another person who has two acres of land has also developed a coffee garden. All others are mostly involved mostly involved raising agricultural crops like maize, ragi and pulses. Some families get poor yield which is not enough for even six months supply of food.

The person who has earned money by selling coffee seeds is considered wealthy. Presently his position has gone up in comparison to others. Now a days other Soligas are aspiring to get more land from the forest department temporarily or revenue land for agricultural purposes from the government and to develop coffee gardens. It indicates that the idea of peasantization is slowly growing among the Soliga. In this situation aiming for bigger landholding and hankering to produce coffee are two basic factors which is resulting in the formation of higher economic categories or classes. Further it has also led to status consciousness among the Soliga.

Table 5

Livestock Position Householdwise (in Hosa Podu)

No. of livestock householdwise	*No. of house-holds*	*Total no. of livestock*	*Types of Livestock Possessed*				
			Cow & calf	*Ox*	*Goat*	*Sheep*	*Cock & hen*
35 livestock household	1	35	35	—	—	—	—
22 live stock household	1	22	19	3	—	—	—
18 live stock household	1	18	10	2	4	2	—
10 livestock household	1	10	—	—	6	4	—
9 livestock household	2	18	2	1	2+2	6	5
6 livestock household	2	12	2	—	6+4	—	—
5 live stock household	1	5	—	—	—	5	—
3 livestock household	2	6	1	—	3+2	—	—
2 livestock household	4	8	—	—	—	2+2+2	2
1 livestock household	1	1	—	—	1	—	—
No livestock household	—	—	—	—	—	—	—
Total	16	135	69	6	30	23	7

The above table provides the stock of the cattle and domesticated animals in the Soliga settlement. Most of the cattle, goats and sheep are generally procured through government subsidy or as gift from the government under different schemes of the developmental programmes. Many persons have benefited under such schemes but their cattle died due to lack of proper rearing. Sometimes the hilly terrain is not suitable for some types of cattle and hence animals die. The fact remains that during 1990s when this work was undertaken or during 1970s (when S.G. Morab was working in this area) facilities suitable for settled cultivation could not be availed by most Soligas as majority were still dependent on forest oriented economy. In foothills areas and rehabilitated areas indeed some Soligas could prosper economically, and thus creating a comfortable economic class.

During the field study, the households having more cows and calf were earning money by selling milk to the people belonging to other communities, in the village. As cultivation is not taken up in large scale there are few oxen or bullocks. The Soligas are fond of goat and fowl as they are sacrificial animals, thus many are rearing them. Morab hd earlier observed that, "Among the domesticated animals goat and cow are the chief. Fowls are also raised. The goat and fowl are the sacrificial animals during ritual occasions. The cow and bullock are employed in agricultural operations wherever plough cultivation is introduced. The milk cow gives milk to their owners, but the quantity of milk obtained is sufficient for domestic use only" (1977: 47).

In Hosa Podu, three persons are well known by their wealth of livestock. The household which possesses 35 and 22 cattles are specially known for their cattle-wealth.

During the era of shifting cultivation, one could not think of keeping such larger numbers of cattle. Thus the possession of cattle has also led to economic gain, though very few families could avail the opportunity.

Table 6

Number of Workers Householdwise in Hosapodu Soliga Settlement

			(Sexwise workers)	
Number of workers in household	*No. of households*	*Total workers*	*Male*	*Female*
One worker household	3	3	2	1
Two workers household	27	54	25	29
Three workers household	11	33	15	18
Four workers household	3	12	5	7
Total	44	102	47	55

The above table shows that out of total 44 households in Hosa Podu Soliga settlement, one-worker and four-workers' households are three in each category. Then, there are 11 households having three workers in each household. The maximum numbers of households, that is 27, are two-workers' household. The total workers in Hosa Podu settlement are 102 persons (47 males and 55 females) one female 45 years of age, is getting a pension of about ₹ 750 as her husband died while employed in Forest Department as Mahabat (elephant's caretaker). Thus, she does not go for any daily work for earning. She is staying in the Soliga colony house but does not have agricultural land. Among the workers category female workers are more than the males. The women among the Soliga thus contribute almost rather equally compared to their male partners towards family income.

Table 7

Distribution of Workers Occupationwise and Sexwise

Occupation	*Male*	*Female*	*Total*
Shop and Agriculture	2	2	4
Forest produce collecting, forest coolie, agricultural labour and construction coolie	17	15	32
Firewood collection, forest labour and agriculture, forest produce collection	6	7	13
Only agriculture	1	12	13
Grazing	1	3	4
VGKK-employee and trainer and employee of Anganwadi	13	16	29
Forest department employees temporary and permanent as forest guards and fire watchers	7	—	7
Total	47	55	102

The above table indicates that the Soliga male and female are almost equally engaged in different occupations and earn for a living. Two households own shops – one has a provisions store and another a tea stall, so they are engaged in managing shop but they also work in their fields. The Soliga workers are working as forest coolie, agricultural labour, as collector of forest produce and in constructions. As we see a total of 32 persons are engaged (17 males and 15 females) in this category of occupations. Vivekananda Girijan Kalyan Kendra is also providing employment opportunities to the Soliga men and women as temporary labourer, trainer and some are permanent employees such as social workers, driver of jeep, cook, and helper in hospital and health care unit. VGKK employs a total of 29 persons (13 males and 16 females). There are two females working in Anganwadi of the state government.

Several people are engaged as forest guards as permanent employees while many of them are employed on temporary basis as fire watchers during summer season. In this category only seven males are employed. Twelve females and one male are engaged only in agriculture.

Earlier, the Soliga were mainly semi-nomadic and shifting cultivators. Due to several legislations, they had to abandon the shifting cultivation. Thus, a good number of Soliga became agricultural labourers in the fields of Hindu caste people inhabiting BR Hills. Many Soligas opted to work as forest labourers under the forest department or under the forest contractors for the collection of forest produce. Some status distinction is maintained between ordinary forest/forest- contract labourer and those employed in VGKK on regular basis. There is a striking difference in the lifestyle of different strata of people. The VGKK employees dress themselves in a manner which is similar to that of other non-tribal office-goers. The forest guards and fire watchers are placed below the VGKK employees.

Social Structure and Stratification

The Soliga are divided into six endogamous sub-tribes based on territorial distribution, as described below:

(i) *Male-Soliga*: These people are mainly inhabiting the BR Hills and the MM Hills and their adjoining areas. Male is a Kannada word, which means 'hills'. Those Soliga who are living in the hilly tracts are known as Male-Soliga that is Soliga hill dwellers.

(ii) *The Urali-Soliga*: The Urali-Soliga are concentrated in the hilly regions bordering Karnataka and Tamil Nadu. Most of them are living in the district of Periyar and Salem in Tamil Nadu, whereas in Karnataka, this sub-group inhabits the Kollegal taluk in Mysore district.

(iii) *The Pujari-Soliga*: These people live in MM Hills. They have not been recorded in earlier literature.

(iv) *The Kadu-Soliga*: This group of people mainly inhabit Bandipur forest and the forest of Kodagu district. 'Kodu' means 'forest' and these Soliga have derived their name from 'forest'.

(v) *The Burude-Soliga*: This group of people are inhabiting Heggada Devana Kote (HD Kote) taluk of Mysore district and some parts of Kodagu district.

(vi) *The Urubatti-Soliga*: This group of Soliga are found in Kakana Kota area. The word 'uru' or 'ooru' means village. Those Soliga who are settled in the villages are known as Urubatti Soliga.

All these subdivisions of Soliga are endogamous groups. Earlier there was no much contact between them but now they have regular contact. These people mingle in work places and markets. Presently these people have contacts in the residential school, hotels, VGKK training centres and also through activities of the Soliga Abhivrudhi Sangha, an organization established to fight for their rights in the forest and implementation of other developmental programmes. Some of the marriages have also taken place amongst these groups. These marriages are accepted by the Soliga society.

From the perspective of social structure the Soliga are popularly known as 5-Kula and 7-Kula based people. Male-Soliga and Urali-Soliga have 5 and 7 Kulas respectively. The Male-Soliga people claim to be descendents of mythical hero Karayya while the Urali Soliga's progenitor mythic hero is Bellayya. The Urali-Soliga speak a dialect mixed with Kannada and some Tamil words whereas Male-Soliga and others speak a dialect known as Soliganudu, which is akin to Kannada language. But the Soliga in general use Kannada script for learning and writing.

Clans (Kulas)

The Soliga are broadly divided into 5-Kula as and 7-Kula groups. The 5-Kulas (clans) are found among all groups except Urali-Soliga. These clans are: (i) Shalikiri (ii) Belloru (iii) Haleru (iv) Teneru and (v) Suraru. But a sixth clan that is Baleru has been recorded. There are many tales of origin about the clan Baleru which has been added to the 5-clan fold about 4-5 decades ago. It is believed that a Baleru (bangu seller) might have settled down amidst the Soliga, and then he has married a girl of the 5-Kula group Soliga. The progeny of this couple acquired the name Baleru. The people of this clan have been given a lower status is social structure and are supposed to remove the leaf-plates after the ritual meals during death ceremony or other festive occasions. Presently this discrimination is being ignored. Fact, remains however, that clans are status groups and they enjoy varied privileges. People belonging to the Haleru and Shalikiri clans are higher in the hierarchy and are eligible for headmanship. The other offices of the tribal council are Pattegar, Kolkar and Vhaluvade, which are occupied by the Teneru, Belloru and Suraru clans respectively. These three clans have the equal status while the Baleruclan-members are considered the lowest.

The origin of the clans is not exactly known to the Soliga but clans people of Belloru, Haleru and Shalikiri claim that their forefathers belonged to the occupational groups of silversmith, shepherd and weaver respectively, and thus the clans took these names. But now no one is engaged in such occupations. Their existence is also not found in folk songs.

The origin of Teneru clan has been related with an ear (tere) of Ragi crop. The name of the Suraru clan is linked to the worship of the Sun God. Nanjundayya and Iyer (1931: 593) refer the clan as 'Surya', but the word is pronounced as 'Suraru' which means warrior. In this way, though the Soliga try to associate their clan names with various occupations, but these seem mythical.

The Urali-Soliga have seven clans namely (i) Kodavaru (ii) Padavaru (moon Kula) (iii) Kalkati (iv) Punge (v) Kuppa (elephant) (vi) Poriga and (vii) Kurnaga. The function of the clan is to regulate marriage alliances, as the clan exogamy is the rule of the society. Secondly, the clan people are agnatically related to all those having the same clan name.

Lineage (Gumpu or Budakattu)

Unlike clan members the members of a lineage trace their descent through their ancestors easily. The Soliga are aware of regular formation of lineages. Through the formation of a new lineage, original or remote ancestors are forgotten but immediate ancestors are remembered. During the Hosa Ragi Habba, the family deities (Devaru) are worshipped in different settlements wherein members of each lineage (Gumpu) participate in the festival. It is an obligation on the part of lineage members to share the ritual and to contribute for the celebration, as their ancestor belongs to the same Gumpu (lineage).

Descent System and Status of Women

The descent among the Soliga is reckoned through male line. The tribe is patrilineal in descent and patri-local in residence. The authority in the family is vested with the male who is the head of the household. Nuclear type of the family is prevalent among the Soliga. This type of elementary form of family consists of a man, his wife and their unmarried children. A few cases of extended families are found. After marriage, the son establishes his own residence. The Soliga desire to live nearer to their kins, so that they can seek help and co-operation at the time of emergency and during observance of important rituals and ceremonies.

The Soliga tribe is organized through patrilineal norms. Hence, men play important roles and occupy higher status. However, the status of women is not inferior. They in fact enjoy almost equal status and they play important economic roles. In agricultural operations, Soliga women play dominant role. Besides, they engage themselves in collection of fuel, bringing potable water and animal husbandry. They also work as agricultural labourers and contribute to the family income whenever required, but the women do not have decision-making power. At the family level women are consulted and good interpersonal relation is maintained. Women participate in social functions. The women however do not have role in the performance of rituals and religious activities organized publicly, and similarly they have no place in the mechanism of social control. Presently, under the Panchayati Raj system, women have been empowered to participate in modern political institutions like village Panchayat. Some of the Soliga women are thus members of the Panchayat in BR Hills under Yalandur taluk.

Mechanism of Social Control and Position of the Authority

Social life of the Soligas is guided by norm of kinship. Living in uni-ethnic set-up there is no occurrence of dispute generally. All issues and differences are sorted out by the traditional tribal council known as Kula Panchayat. This tribal council is held in high esteem and is very effective. Intricate problems are solved in a dignified manner. The isolation of the Soliga has helped them in preserving the uniqueness of their culture, social values and the social system.

The Soliga live in smaller settlements and in nuclear families. So the occurrence of disputes is less. But sometimes, disputes of serious nature such as breaches of tribal codes do occur but they are dealt with by the tribal council.

Tribal Council (Kula Panchayat or Jati Koota)

In the BR Hills, the Kula Panchayat has a jurisdiction over nine Soliga settlements spread over the area but the size of each hamlet is small. The headman of the tribal council is known as the Yajaman. This office is not hereditary. He is however, selected by the members of only two clans namely Shalikiri and Heleru, on the basis of attributes such as seniority in age, one's character and ability of the person. These are the guiding principles for selecting a Yajaman. The Yajaman presides over the meetings of the tribal council as and when they are convened.

Other office bearers of tribal council are Chaluvade, Kolkar and Pattegar. Their functions are mainly to assist the Yajaman. These offices are not hereditary, but the Chaluvade is selected from a particular clan namely Suraru, while Kolkar and Pattegar are chosen from Belloru and Teneru respectively.

The Pattegar acts as an assistant to the Yajaman. His presence is required to ask questions and to initiate discussions so as to help the headman to come to a conclusion. This apart, there is one important work of socio-religious nature wherein the Pattegar carries a Kondi-Kolu (a special kind of stick) and visits different settlements of the Soliga in the area and invokes names of the deities. He visits the Soliga house where birth and death rituals are to be performed in order to mark the end of pollution period.

The Kolkar is another office bearer. He moves to the Soliga settlements in order to inform the date, time and the place of the meetings to be held. The Kolkar plays important role in arranging meetings.

The Chaluvade assists both the headman and the Kolkar. He cooperates the Kolkar in various works such as arranging a place for meeting and controlling the culprits if they become violent during the proceedings of the meeting. All these four office-bearers of the Kula Panchayats are responsible for reviewing the disputes and taking a final decision in any case or matter which remains binding upon the concerned parties.

Elderly male members of the settlement are also invited to the meeting of the tribal council. The Kula Panchayat deals with cases relating to the violation of clan exogamy, adultery, entering to a cultivated field by a menstruating woman, taking much alcoholic drinks, quarrels and theft. The case relating to a person who is beaten by boots or chappal is taken seriously by the Soliga. In such a case guilty person is ostracized unless he undergoes an expiation ceremony. Generally the fine is imposed on the offender and the amount increases according to the severity and nature of the cases. The tribal council has been regarded as very effective and powerful, but with the passage of time, this has weakened to some extent. Presently, members are advised to adhere to traditional practices and repeated attempts are made for the maintenance of tribal laws of the land.

The Soliga participate in the Statutory Panchayati Raj elections at the village level. The area of the BR Hills tribal settlement comes under Yerangaballi village Panchayat under Yalandur taluk. Presently six members have been elected (three males and three females) to represent the Soliga at the Statutory Village Panchayat Council.

The traditional tribal council of Soligas survives and it retains authority to maintain the social behavioural code, law and order in the Soliga society. The office bearers have a superior status. The position of the headman (Yajaman) is regarded as the highest position in the four-member council.

The Soliga Abhivrudhi Sangh (SAS)

This organization works for the development of the Soliga in each hamlet. This association has been formed by Soligas drawn from each settlement within taluk and beyond in order to mobilize the Soligas in the struggle against social inequalities and injustices. Since the Soliga's subsistence economy was disturbed due to forest regulation to ban shifting cultivation, the tribals were vulnerable to exploitation, paucity of food, exploitation in the clutches of the landlords. Forest department's negative attitude, led to their indebtedness. Even the tribal development plan of the government failed to improve the economy of the tribals. Soliga Abhivrudhi Sangh is a social work organization of a voluntary nature. Its activities can be broadly classified into four categories namely: (1) land issues (2) government programme implementation process (3) essential services like education and health and (4) a hosts of other problems that emerge from time to time.

The Soliga Abhivrudhi Sangh (SAS) has representation in each hamlet. The village unit is headed by a five member team selected by the people such as:

(i) Margadarshi (a guide – elderly traditional leader)
(ii) Karyadarshi (secretary – a potential youth leader)
(iii) Kajanchi (treasurer – a sincere and honest person)
(iv) Kolkara (organizing secretary)
(v) Sahayaka (helper)

All adult members of the Podu (settlement, hamlet and village) are members of SAS. One or two women are also inducted to be involved in the Sangha committee. At present there are more than 60 Podu Sanghs. These are now grouped under the Taluk Sangha which is part of Maha Sangha and is known as the Soliga Abhivrudhi Maha Sangh. The representatives of all Sanghs form the Maha Sangh, and the members of this Sangh form the tribal district committee, which is a federation of the people controlled from Mysore and Kodagu districts.

The achievement and impact of the Sangha on mental outlook of the Soligas have been numerous, namely:

(i) *Self-confidence*: The Sangha has played an important role in developing the confidence of the tribal people. They can now interact without fear with government officials and other authorities.
(ii) *Recognition*: Sangh office bearers are now recognized by the government officials and other bodies. Thus, the officials discuss matters and often visit Soliga hamlets. Any application or memorandum from the Sangh is immediately responded to by the concerned government department. This has given the Soliga a sense of dignity and has strengthened their unity.
(iii) In Devanahally settlement area the forest department had engaged outside labourers to plant trees in the lands cultivated by the Soliga. There the Soliga women and children protested. The Soliga people were then inducted to do that work.

(iv) *Land encroachment:* In Purani Soliga settlement a few landlords had illegally acquired 65 acres of Soliga land. The Soligas Anganwadi brought it to the notice of the Divisional Commissioner when he visited the BR Hills. Land was returned.

(v) *Exploitation case:* In Budipadaga Soliga settlement and in another hamlet too the tamarind trees growing on land allotted to the Soliga were a source of income for some of the Soligas. Unfortunately a rich contractor was exploiting them by an arrangement whereby he got the crop for a meagre amount of ₹ 15 to ₹ 20 per tree per year, but the actual value would be about ₹ 500. This sort of exploitation had been going on since a decade unchecked. Now the Soliga have got back ownership of their tamarind trees which fetches them ₹ 500 or so per tree per year.

There are numerous incidents whereby the Soliga have sorted out their grievances and benefited from the result.

Here, the function of the SAS is laudable and praiseworthy as the Soliga feel empowered.

Developmental Programmes and Voluntary Organization – VGKK

Under the new forest policies and their regulations, the Soliga were evicted from their abode in the interior forests. In order to rehabilitate them, many governmental welfare schemes and developmental programmes have been launched from time to time to settle them and improve their lot. These programmes aimed to establish colonies, to construct houses for them in a phased manner, and provide forest land for agriculture, one or two acres per family in general. But all these efforts did not make any change. Since 1980s Dr H. Sudarshan, by profession a doctor, has been visiting the Soliga area with the idea of initiating health work. After several visits the felt that the Soliga needed some support in larger perspective. Dr Sudarshan established Vivekananda Girijan Kalyan Kendra (VGKK), a voluntary organization in 1981 with the objective of serving the Soliga of BR Hills and MM Hills and adjoining areas in Mysore district. Instead of mere medical work, a holistic community development work was taken up.

The welfare programmes launched by the VGKK are as follows:

(i) Health Centre: Establishment of Jaya Vijayam Tribal Hospital which is a well equipped hospital with a 10 bed ward in BR Hills. Mobile medical work is also carried out in the Soliga settlements, immunization programme is done under community health, and training is imparted to the traditional birth attendants of the Soliga women. Village health workers, mostly the Soliga young girls are trained to know traditional herbal medicines and to identify the herbs. Child health programmes are also undertaken.

(ii) Establishment of school from primary to SSC (10th class) and upto pre-university level (10+2). Tribal Residential School with hostel for housing about 500 students is established. They receive supplementary food, and hostel students get full three meals a day. Adult Education Programme is also functioning.

(iii) VGKK also launched leadership training and group work. Consequently the Soliga Abhivrudhi Sangh was formed and organized to infuse self-confidence among the Soliga.

(iv) Cottage industry and vocational training programme: After the training many Soligas are engaged in different vocations, such as:

  (a) The Billigiri Agarwathi Sangha: The trained women are collecting materials and after making the agarbatti, they supply to Agarwathi Sangha. One Soliga boy is instructor in the training programme of Agarwathi Sangha.
  (b) Tailoring training: It is very successful. Many boys and girls after being trained in these have started their tailoring shops in BR Hills settlement.
  (c) Training in wood craft and carpentry.
  (d) Leaf cup making.
  (e) Weaving of Kora grass mats.
  (f) Knitting woollen garments.

As a consequence of above programmes many Soligas are self-employed and some of them are employed in the respective trade centres of the VGKK.

The Soliga of the BR Hills in particular and the Soliga of other places in general have much benefited by the VGKK. Several development programmes are in progress and will go a long way towards empowerment of the Soliga.

Besides, the state government has launched many welfare programmes from time to time. These programmes are:

1. To provide drinking water facility by installation of borewells in many Soliga settlements.
2. Under animal husbandry sheep and goat are supplied or sometimes given on subsidy basis.
3. Iron plough and bullock are provided to the Soliga.
4. In the industrial training centre, many Soliga have been given bamboo cane training to make items at BR Hills.
5. For improvement of agriculture, chemical fertilizers and seeds have been supplied from time to time.

Thus, the government department is extending facilities to improve the quality of life of the Soliga. However, there are problems of proper implementation, bureaucratic hurdles which results in deprivation.

Discussion

The Soligas were originally hunter-gatherers and shifting-cultivators. These economic pursuits are still observable in interior areas. The government agencies forced many Soligas to discard shifting-cultivation (podu) and shift to rehabilitation centres in B.R. Hills. Those rehabilitated were given economic assistance. Most Soligas however could not avail proper assistance. Hence majority of them became labourers. Minimum wages and non-availability of works perpetuated poverty among the Soligas. Some Soligas were fortunate to procure Land-grants with patta. Patta holders gradually enlarged their economic activities and they formed a strata of rich peasants, compared to poor section of Soligas and other communities. Landed settled agriculturists and shifting cultivators/Wage-earners/Labourers thus shaped an internal social stratification in B.R. Hills. Last three decades witnessed growth of NGOs, voluntary organizations such as VGKK in B.R. Hills, particularly among the poor Soligas. VGKK taught the Soligas to be self-reliant and use their indigenous knowledge, particularly to depend on their herbal medicines. VGKK, along with government agencies, introduced many schemes of economic development, which had positive impact. The Statutory Panchayat institutions and traditional tribal council side by side helped in maintaining social control. It is the NGOs who have empowered the people to fight for their rights.

References

Census of India 1966, Vol. XI, Mysore, Part V-A, Special Tables for Scheduled Castes and Scheduled Tribes.

Furer-Haimendorf, C. von 1945, *The Reddis of the Bison Hills,* London: Macmillan.

Gazetteer of India 1965, Government of India: Publications Division.

Luiz, A.A.D. 1963, *Tribes of Mysore,* Bangalore: Government Press.

Morab, S.G. 1977, *The Soliga of Billigiri Rangana Hills,* Calcutta: Anthropological Survey of India.

Nanjundayya, H.V. and L.K.A. Iyer 1961, "Sholiga", in *The Mysore Tribes and Castes,* Vol. IV, Mysore: The University of Mysore, pp. 592–599.

Srinivas, M.N. 1942, *Marriage and Family in Mysore,* Bombay: New Book Co.

Thurston, E. 1909, "Sholaga", in *Castes and Tribes of Southern India,* Vol. VI, Delhi: Cosmo Publication (reprinted in 1975), pp. 377–87.

16 Pastoral Clanship, Regional Hierarchy and Social Exclusion

Changing Todas of the Nilgiris

Sibir Ranjan Das

The Toda Identity

The Nilgiris of Tamil Nadu is surrounded by two neighbouring states; Kerala on the west and Karnataka on the north. Coimbatore district of Tamil Nadu is located on its southeast part. The area of Nilgiris is 982 sq. miles. The entire area is hilly and the Nilgiris plateau, a high table land is at an average elevation of 6,000 ft. It has four talukas namely Gudalur, the North West Ootacamund, Coonoor and Kotagiri. Ootacamund is the district headquarters and also a very important centre of attraction for the tourists because of its pleasant summer. Since this is a hilly area, it is not conducive for cultivation. According to Hockings "on the higher slopes the soils are shallow but on the lower land there are deep rich loams and some yellow ocherous clay and black soils. Much of the lands are suitable for grass and timber only". However, at lower levels crops can be grown although tea plantation has been successfully carried out at higher slopes. The Nilgiris as a region has attracted many scholars especially anthropologists and they have been particularly attracted to the Toda. Nilgiris is believed to be the original home of Todas. The Todas believe that their Goddess, created them along with their wandering buffaloes at Nilgiris.

There are other groups like Kurumbas, Kota, Iruvar and Badagas who live in the district. Badagas came about 300 years ago and settled in this place. They not only introduced the art of cultivation, but also brought about remarkable changes in terms of inter ethnic and economic relationships. Mandelbaum reported, "The relations among the four upland groups (that is Toda, Kurumba, Kota and Imlar) mainly their economic and ritual specialization and their exchanges were much like those carried on among jatis (caste and sub-castes) of a locality throughout village India. But of all the people, the Todas are quite distinguished". Scholars from far and near have come to study them, owing to their very different social and ritual organization. Their pastoral life and their hard work evinced a lot of interest among the scholars. It is said that the Toda had certain close relations with Kotas and Kurumbas, but these are no longer strictly maintained. In the past Kota used to play music at the Todas funerals. Kurumbas are very famous people due to their ability for sorcery and black magic and Todas were quite afraid of such acts of Kurumbas.

Todas have a very close relation with the Badagas. Not only do they visit each others' rituals, but Todas also enjoy a respect in the Badaga villages. There are some occasions when the Badagas gift the Toda a basketfull of grain known as Gudlu. However, the traditional relations between Toda, Kota and Badagas are found to be disappearing at present. Until recent times Todas were dependent on their pastoral way of life. Emergence of new economic opportunities, growing economic need and competitiveness have combined effect on their age old inter-ethnic relations. Todas were always a very small population. As early as in 1880 they were estimated to be no more than 1,000 in number. In the early 1950's they were reduced to as many as 488 individuals as reported by Peter. Today they are a little over 1,100 souls. In addition there are also a few Christian Toda, whose number will be a little more than 200. Todas are usually found to be settled in a small village called mund. These munds are scattered all over the district. Due to their pastoral life, the Toda have established several temporary munds and after staying there for a few months, they have discarded many of these munds.

According to the record available in the district office (Adi-Dravida welfare office at Collectorate, South Nilgiris), there are 123 such Toda mund but at present, only about 60 munds are inhabited by the Todas. Their largest concentration is however in Ooty taluka. There are only five munds located at Kodanad area of Kolagiri taluka and only two are located at Coonoor. A traditional Toda settlement comprises of half barrel-shaped semi-circular huts, a dairy and buffalo pen. A dairy is usually located a little far off from the settlement area. But over the years Toda huts have undergone changes and nowadays people seldom have traditional semi-circular huts. State government has also constructed huts for the Todas. At Kandal mund in Ooty taluk, state government has constructed semi-circular-shaped houses with concrete roof. Due to paucity of the raw materials Todas find it difficult to construct their traditional houses and also the dairy temple. This is one of the reasons that many of the munds are devoid of any dairy temple at present. Most of the munds are otherwise located quite far from Ooty town, and since most of villagers are relatively poorly connected, the Todas dependency on Ooty and its market is still very great, in absence of any other market centres nearby.

Toda Social Organization

Todas are subdivided into two endogamous divisions. Walker refers to these as sub-castes. Some scholars refer to them as moiety. They are Tordas and Toivelly. Toda call these subdivisions as Soti. Tordas is a Soti for Teivelly and vice versa. Both the subdivisions are further divided into a number of exogamous clans that is Modol. Tordas have ten and Teivelly have five of such living clans respectively. The names are given below:

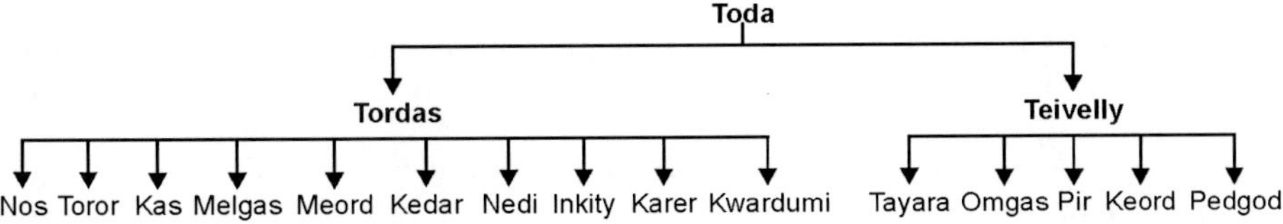

It is believed by the Todas that Toda and their buffalo were created at Nos. Each clan (Modol) has more than one munds. But one mund of each clan is considered as the chief mund, which is known as Edmund. Each Modol has a number of polam that is brother of Head families. There is no fixed number of polam for each clan. The distribution of polam was determined in ancient times, which has continued till today. Polam has a specific function in a clan, that is to build temples and to meet the expenditure of temples.

When several polams are clubbed they form two parts, each part is called Kuoir. For example Kas has three polams but has two Kuoir. Kuoir has a specific role only when a ritual called Ir Warthim that is gifting of a calf to a temple takes place. One of the Kuoir will gift the calf while the other will accept. Although Todas do not admit any hierarchy among its clans, but the Todas refer to Nos followed by Kas. Walker has found out some hierarchy that is maintained among these clans. Todas trace their descent through paternal ancestry but also have certain relation connected with the mother's blood relations. Blood relations from the mother's side are commonly known as Polyol. Walker refers to it as matri-clan and has mentioned a few names of polyol (Walker, 1986). Todas are prohibited to have any sex relations with polyol and can not marry one's polyol. The Toda family usually consists of parents and their unmarried children. The females, apart from their house work, also train their daughters in embroidery work.

Earlier Todas were polyandrous and they attracted the attention of other people because of their institution like polyandry and dairy temple. Most of the earlier writers described them as polyandrous society. Even today they are referred in the same way, but recent trend does not establish that view. Walker (1986) wrote that he could observe only one single polyandrous family. Present researcher has not come across any case of polyandrous family. The Toda pay respect to their seniors by bowing their heads and touching the feet of the seniors with their foreheads. This is a very common scene in a Toda village. In the past Todas were totally dependent on their buffaloes and pastoral way of life. Male folk used to move out to the forest with their buffaloes. But due to the imposition of restriction on the grazing of the buffaloes on the forest lands, the pastoral activities are also steadily declining. It is stated that of late many of the Todas do not have sufficient number of buffalo to maintain their pens.

Buffaloes are part of Toda property. The land as a property has been a recent incorporation in their concept of property. It may be stated that Toda also enjoy the Toda patta land, but they have no right to sell the same. The daughters usually receive gifts or dowry at the time of marriage. They can not have any right over land or buffaloes. Girls' parents may give a buffalo as a part of dowry to their girls, but in many cases such gifts of buffaloes are returned to the parents. This act is known as Kokwriyir. The son-in-law may also give in exchange the money to his father-in-law. This act is known as Mokhwrrpenom. Besides polam the Todas have their own community council called Noym, and it has a very significant role in Toda society. Normally noym, that is council meeting is held on any ritual day but it may take place on any other occasion too, depending on the exigencies. Noym discusses about the ritual day, funeral day, temple thatching day, besides many other matters. Walker (1986: 194) reported that the decision about the abolition of the pollution hut in Toda society was adopted in a noym.

Although Toda have two soti yet while convening a noym they do not maintain any distinction and young and old are given equal opportunity to express their views. Noym can impose fine in such cases where they feel it is imperative. It is said that in earlier days, the unsettled matters used to be referred to the Badaga district head, but such customs do not exist now. It has been observed that in any noym, people from both the soti must be present otherwise such noym may be viewed as procedurally incomplete. Toda life is closely connected with their dairies. The dairies are temples and are considered as the most sacred place in the village. The dairies are classified into five types. They are: ti dairy, worsoly, kudpoly, tordopoly and kogwaly. The ti dairy which is also known as poh is rarely surviving now. There are only three conical poh remaining in the whole of the Toda lands. Among the dairies, poh is the most sacred one. However according to the Toda prescription certain clans can have certain specific types of dairy. It is quite evident that a ranking pattern is present among the dairies, and most of the relatively more sacred temples are situated only in the munds of the clans belonging to tordas and soti. Like the dairy, the Toda buffaloes are also classified into different ranks on the basis of their sacredness.

Ranking of Sacred Buffaloes

1. Ti-ir
2. Kwaglir
3. Worsolir
4. Morthir
5. Nospepir
6. Pennipir
7. Putir

As the buffaloes are sacred, so also is their milk. Certain buffaloes are so sacred that milk of these varieties are not consumed by ordinary persons. There are prerogatives about the consumption of milk. Milk from putir variety is consumed in the common household. However, milk which are normally not consumed, get converted into buttermilk and butter and they are sold for consumption.

Life Cycle Rituals

Todas life cycle rituals are very closely associated with the sacred beliefs attached to the dairies and buffaloes. Todas have a few important rituals such as birth, face opening (name giving) of child, marriage, declaration of fatherhood (bow and arrow) and the death and funeral. Face opening ceremony, Mokh mutartarth of a male child is done with the help of the eldest male who takes the child to the temple in the morning. The temple priest officiates the function. The face of the new born is uncovered at the sight of the temple. Such function is not required in case of a female child. Here face opening may be done near the entrance of the house. A name is given to new one later in the afternoon.

Toda marriage is fixed and performed in the childhood. With the consent of the parents of the eligible bride and groom the marriage is solemnized. Bride remains at her father's place till she attains puberty. Following maturity she is taken to her husband's place. Sometimes girls' parents give dowry to groom's parents, which is called Arpan. After becoming mature if either of the couple refuses to marry, it can be done with adequate compensation to the other party. Compensation is called Thear, which is given in the form of buffalo. Often marriage of Toda is mistaken with the bow and arrow ceremony, which takes place at the groom's house during the 5th or 7th month of the wife's pregnancy. By offering bow by husband to his wife in front of all kinsmen, he actually claims the fatherhood of the baby in the womb. Following the pusorth ceremony, a ritual is also performed in respect of pregnancy which is called Urvansth. This is usually done in the presence of elderly women of the clan. But the ritual is not always strictly followed and may also vary from Tordas to Teivelly.

It may not be out of context to mention about the male-female relation in the Toda society. Although marital relations between the two soti known as Mokh dorth exits, relation is not permanent. Such relation is renewed in case both the parties agree. Following pregnancy, an expectant mother just before giving birth to the child is taken out of her house (before new moon) to the pollution hut referred to as Pisas. In the past, pisas used to be located in the jungle and the wife had to stay there with the new born for a month. This period was called Natesh Pad. But now none remains there for long. A ritual called Moithwozorth or home coming of mother is performed. Nowadays a mother hardly stays at pisas for a day or two.

Todas used to perform two funerals in the past. At present, they have decided to perform only one funeral combining two and many of the functions either have been shortened or avoided. The pressure of money and the buffaloes on the one hand and a social pressure on the other have compelled them to reduce the practice of sacrificing of buffalo in the funeral. Todas believe that after death their soul (Arnotord) along with the souls of buffalo move on to a next world that is Amonord. It is said that the spirit disappears at a specific place called Olxputhae. If a person belonging to one soti, dies, the people from other soti must gather and carry the body. They also dance and sing surrounding the body. The close relations of the individual contribute during the funeral, the contribution is called Tinycomi Pennom. It may be pointed out that no Teivelly woman can participate in funeral of Tordas individual. They however, can go to the funeral place. Similarly for a Teivelly funeral, Tordas women come and wait at a particular place near the funeral place. Teivelly women in a group invite the Tordas ladies to take part in the funeral. It is believed that any one who has tried to violate this rule is likely to suffer in due course.

The Toda Rituals

Other than life cycle rituals, Toda rituals are concentrated on their dairy temple. Establishing a new temple or thatching of new temple as well as old temple is a major ritual. The time and place of thatching is usually decided in a noym. A noym is the council of the Todas where most elderly people from both the soti meet and discuss the matter concerning temples, marriage, disputes and others. A noym is a sort of forum where any one can discuss almost anything. It is usually seen that during all social functions of the Todas, a noym is held to discuss. As a result Todas keep themselves informed about the events that are occurring in the Toda society.

Temple is most sacred in Toda culture and therefore, purifying the temple is an important function in temple ritual. Skin of a Theard plant is used for this purpose. During the thatching only male members participate. Depending on the ritual hierarchy the temple is selected and the rituals performed. The ritual is followed by a mass prayer for the welfare of the temple and the people. Most of the temples have two chambers excepting the Worsoly temple which has one room. Three-roomed temples are seldom found now-a-days. The front portion is less sacred. The rear or the back part is most sacred, and excepting the priest, no one can enter in this part. This second part is further divided into two halves. The first part is used for keeping the sacred utensils and earthen pots which are called Porthat, and pots that are used for storing buttermilk are called Arthat. This Porthat and Arthat can not interchange their fixed position.

There is another sacred object called moni. It is kept inside the temple, but is kept only in Ti dairy, Worsoli, Kurpoly and Kwaguly temple. Thos is not available in any Teivelly temple. Punnus Kristh or dairy purification is also an important ritual. If the temple is polluted because of any internal or external causes, this function is held. All the materials concerning milk clearing, storing and so on are replaced. Priest is appointed on new moon day that is muthod. During, the three days of this ritual, all the females leave the village and they come back only when the ritual is over successfully. Buffaloes are ceremonially offered salt twice in a year. This is also a very significant ritual in Toda life. Salt giving that is Uppadh is done once in summer – this is called Korrupp – and once in winter, which is called Ponaupp. The birth of first calf of a sacred buffalo, Ir workuth is also celebrated with great enthusiasm. Especially in Todar mund (glanmorgan) this is done simultaneously with the function of opening of temple (Warsoly wosh thart).

The concept of sacredness is so deeply imbued in their culture and belief that Todas can always identify the geographical areas, river, stones, hills, villages, buffaloes and so on in terms of its sacred and non sacred-values. Thus the Nilgiri and the Todas have become so interconnected and concomitant with each other. From the brief cultural character of the Todas one can certainly get this feeling that the uniqueness of Toda culture and life is very much centred around their dairy and social organization. The prospect of modernization and economic and political interaction is increasing so much that the Toda culture might lose its colourfulness and rich heritage in the near future. The element of inequality that is existing in Toda culture and life is another important factor which one should try to understand.

Inequality in Toda Culture and Ritual Exclusion of Women

It has already been mentioned that the Todas have two endogamous subdivisions namely Tordas and Teivelly and each division is further divided into a number of exogamous clans. All the sacred and ritually higher grade temples belong to the Tordas and Teivelly people and they are engaged as priests in these temples. Todas in general claim that there is no differential status assigned to the two divisions but in reality it is found that no Teivelly woman is allowed to come to Tordas mund, which suggests that Teivelly women are having unequal status. Tordas do not admit this unequal status of Teivelly women. A few aged informants said that there was no such differentiation in the past, and it was because of a wrong act committed by a Teivelly woman that Toda society imposed such restriction on the movement of Teivelly women. It appears that during one festival a Teivelly lady who came to attend felt very tired after a long walk and sat on the way. She requested that her food should be served there only since she was unable to move. She also demanded an extra plate of food for her child on her lap which was covered by her clothes. But people suspected her and found that she had no baby in her lap. Not only did she lie, but she tried to deceive the people. After this incident it was decided that no Teivelly woman would be allowed to come henceforth in Tordas village. This perspective was refuted later.

Toda women's movement is indeed restricted to a certain area within the village. They are never allowed to visit any dairy temple. Since the temple and its surrounding is sacred, women are considered as a great threat sacredness, and presence of women in temple leads to pollution, it is believed.

Women are not allowed to take water from the temple stream. In case there is no other stream, the women must not use the water in the upper slopes. Women are not even allowed to witness the temple rituals. For certain temple functions, women are not allowed to remain in the village, so long the ritual continues. In all the Toda villages, women use a separate path in case, there is only one way of the village passing besides the temple. This inequality in respect of women is a striking feature of Toda society.

Clan Hierarchy and Ritual Specialization

Todas of Nilgiris present themselves as a very interesting community. They believe in several divisions within the tribe and social exclusion of women is accomplished at various levels. What is significant is that Todas in almost all spheres of their life and culture believe in some form of differentiation. The Toda settlements in the whole of the district have different names, based on its location and distance. For example, settlements which are located very near to each other are referred to as Mozod and those located very far is known as Akuiar and the settlements located in between is called orzed mooth. The district Nilgiri is also differentiated into three parts or areas. Pugod is referred as the places located far east, the western part is referred as Mozod and the central part is called Orzod.

The Toda tribe is divided into Soti segments. Each Soti is differentiated from other Soti. However, there are some situations when they play important complimentary roles. In the bow and arrow ceremony too, making of a hole that is keos in the tree (the place or the hole where the lamp is kept) is made by the opposite soti. Thus soti in actual life cooperate each other in different ways and at different levels, so that the functioning of the Toda society is smooth. As the Toda differentiate their own people in terms of soti; they also differentiate their temple, buffalo herds and priests. Even among the sacred buffaloes there are gradation on the basis of ritual superiority and its association with superior grade of dairy temples. It has been mentioned that Teivelly people perform the job of priest in Tordas temple, but usually they do not perform it for Melgas clan. Melgas people serve as priest in their own temple. In fact Melgas enjoy a special position among the Tordas, because they can do the job of priest in all Tordas clan along with Teivelly priest. But their job is limited to a few categories of temple, therefore as priest among the Tordas subdivision they can not claim their overall superiority over all other Tordas clans.

Similarly in Toror clan of Tordas, they celebrate two temple function, one is Worsoliete, i.e., opening of Worsoli temple and the other is Ir Wolkurth, a ritual connected to Kwaguly temple associated with sacred buffaloes. For both these rituals priests are selected from the Toror clan itself. No priest from Teivelly subdivision will be engaged. Toror priest will be assisted by a Melgas priest. Different priests have different dress as well. A priest of Torwoly temple can wear a white dhoti whereas others wear black (tehoni). Similarly Ti dairy priest will wear only black tehoni and kochch. There is a sacred buffalo known as mother whose milk is totally prohibited. Even a priest can not consume this milk. This milk is converted into buttermilk and consumed. Similarly Ti ir and Kwaqli ir buffaloes are never sacrificed in the funeral.

The common names of the buffaloes are given here as an example:

Teivelly Clan	**Subdivisions**		**Common name for the herd, soft.**
	Keord	Pastir Pastir	Keikk bhatl.
	Burgas	Pastir Pastir	Nalpashir
	Tyach		Kushir kuf
	Morthkeord		Kuserf ir
	Pigod		Kuikk bahtl
Tordos			
Nos	Karahir		
Kas	Tunatwan		
Kerar	Tearthrthe		
Teror	Murchatwan		
Melgas	Narsillee		
Meord	Morchtwan		
Weddi	Chatton kealtan		
Keor			
Inkehy	Chatton kealtan		
Kwarduni	Ital meath anoctwan		

Some of the clans also have similar set of buffaloes in their herds. For example:

1. Keror and Inkity
2. Nos Meord Nedi and Keror

In Toror clan they have a category of buffalo called Kwagulir which is not found in any other clan. Similarly morthir variety is found only in kas. In this manner each clan has certain distinctive characters, so far as the possession of sacred buffaloes is concerned. Although Todas do not admit any form of hierarchical position of their clans, but in their real behaviour they refer always to certain clans as superior than other clans.

Some of the clans enjoy superior status because of the presence of unique temple, a special kind of sacred buffalo and even the presence of funeral temple.

In the past each clan had separate funeral temple, but due to irregular maintenance and absence of priest it became defunct. A few temples are still in existence such as at nos (head mund) at Toror (little away from headmund at pan) kerer etc. In the past during second funeral, a new house was to be built which used to be put on fire. No house is built now for this purpose owing to big expenses involved. We discussed above that there are inequality between clans and that inequality exists in respect of men and women and women are considered ritually inferior.

Inter-Ethnic Relation and Regional Hierarchy

Todas have traditionally maintained symbiotic relation with their neighbours especially with Kota, Kurumbas and Badagas. It is told that Kotas used to play music during the Toda funeral and used to collect the caracas of the sacrificed buffalo. Todas claim their ritual superiority over Kotas because of their sacred status, and vegetarian food habits. Todas did not allow the Kotas to come inside their village settlement. Kotas used to give the Todas iron made implements and used to receive the ghee from them. It is also told that in the past, for any Kota ritual they used to bring ghee from the Todas only. Despite such mutual reciprocity, Kotas are considered low by the Todas. It is told that once a group of Toda while moving around the forest rested in a temporary settlement in a forest. They moved out of the place but on their way they suddenly discovered that they left one of firing stick in the place where they were resting. They rushed back to the place and found that a Kota man is there. They were so upset that they discarded this place for ever since this was polluted by Kota's presence.

Several stories suggest that earlier Toda and Kota were friends, and they became separate because of certain confusion and feuds. At present Kotas come to Todas funeral to play music. Mandelbaum reported that only on the occasion of funeral, Kotas used to bow and touch the feet of the principal Toda mourner (1989: 169). Otherwise touch of a Kota was still a taboo to Toda. Maintenance of social distance between Toda and Kota can be perceived from another incident. There is a tribal school located at Nirrgasimund seven miles on Ooty-Mysore road. This school was started by Servants of India Society. This school was specially opened for Toda and Kota children. When Kota students enrolled, the Toda students threatened to withdraw, but with lot of persuasion the matter was settled. When the residential hostel started again the management had to face the same problem because Todas refused to accept food with Kotas. Many including few Todas convinced the people that, all such social rules are to be followed in village context. A school is beyond sacred village therefore, they should feel they are in a public place and behave as they do in any such place.

The relation between Kurumba and Toda in the past was based on apprehension and fear. Kurumbas are best known for their sorcery and art of black magic. Todas have a feeling that Kurumbas are very powerful in exercising their art and they try to avoid them. "There is a proverb among the Toda that Kurumbas have been created by the God to kill Todas". Kurumbas are also good medicine men. During their pastoralists life the Toda women used to learn from the Kurumba women about such medicines. Kurumbas interaction is restricted to their own village. They rarely visit any Toda village. There is only one occasion during the Toda male funeral, when a Kurumba flag is brought for the funeral. But whatever relation and cooperation existed between them in the past, now they just maintain normal relations with separate identities.

It is told that Badagas came to this place later and they were given the land to settle. But of all the neighbours, Todas are still having very close relation with Badagas. It has been observed that in all the Toda function, Badagas are invited and they also take food with the Toda although separately. There are a few instances from which one can get an impression about the depth of their ethnic interactions. There is a Badaga village called Kikdevily where, every year, during the month of February–March a festival is observed in relation to Lord Krishna (Rangachari festival). During this festival, Todas must send the ghee and the bamboo stick. The stick is used for kindling the light by friction method and the ghee is used for the light and other preparation. During Dhodabba festival too, Toda will supply ghee.

The salt festival is important for the Toda and their buffaloes. At Arsai (arrzaied) near Kotagiri, a salt giving festival is held every year where 14 neighbouring Badaga villages will bring salt. Similarly from Badage village called Taudanad, Kwardwni clan people will bring the moni/kud which they keep in the jungle. After they get this moni to village, festival begins. All such events show that Toda and Badaga have strong inter-ethnic linkages. The Todas used to enjoy a high respectful status in the eyes of the Badaga, and their ritual sanctity is honoured by the Badagas by accepting their ghee as an exclusive item for the ritual.

There is yet another segment among the Todas, formed by converted Christians. The Toda converts during the baptism ceremony keep a Toda name for their children along with Christian names. However, the Toda converts are considered as non-Todas and they are not allowed to participate in any Toda ritual. On the other hand the younger generation among the converts neither bother for their Toda origin, nor they have any great sense of attachment for Toda language and culture. They have fully developed into a separate group.

As one Toda meets another Toda, he is greeted in traditional manner. But when a Toda meets a Toda convert no exchange of greeting from either side takes place. The converted people are relatively advanced in respect of education; they are engaged in different occupations. Some of them are quite well off. Despite the differences both the Toda and converted people enjoy the status of tribe. Converted people also have right over the Toda patta land, therefore, for their own common interest, especially the older people feel the urgency of keeping up interaction, although their cultural ties are no longer strong. Many Toda feel that unless they unite they will disintegrate and be pushed aside, and they will not be able to protect their lands. On the other hand, there are others who feel that, converted Todas should not have right over Toda patta land, because converts are no longer Todas.

Change and Adoption in Toda Culture

Modernity and social change have influenced the Todas considerably. Food habits and dress patterns are also fast changing. Male members are mostly to be seen wearing western dresses. Modern Toda male or female wear such dresses, but during the rituals they wear the traditional dress by covering their body with a long beautifully embroidered cloth called putkuli. Similarly the female also present themselves in their traditional hairstyle. A girl who is not able to do embroidered putkuli is not considered very worth and therefore, each woman learns this art from the early ages. It is told that every woman desires to prepare a putkuli for her husband, and thus this form has been sustained in their culture. Apparently, the old ladies even today retain their hairstyle and wear only traditional clothes.

Todas are vegetarian in their food habits. Their food items are quit similar to the food of the people in the south, such as Rawam and Sambar. Of late they are taking chapattis. Both in their day to day life as well as in rituals they consume lot of ghee. Of late Todas have become quite well acquainted with vegetables such as cabbage, cauliflower, beans, carrot and other.

During the Toda rituals a lot of people consume liquor, but it is told that drinking of liquor has increased in recent years. It is generally alleged that many Toda earn a handful money by leasing out their patta land thus can afford modern life-style. One Miss Ling who came from England took the early initiative for Toda's schooling. It is told that later on Miss Ling also persuaded people to embrace Christianity which created doubts and since Todas became apprehensive, many Todas left going to school.

Despite Miss Ling's missionary activities, she made a good impact among the local people because of her keen interest in educational development of the inhabitants. The Servant of India Society also started their welfare activities and opened a school at Nirgasimund, naming it as Thakkar Bappa Gurukulam. Later on government took over the school. This school is a high school and it has a residential hostel too which is financed by Adi-Dravida Department. At present there are 110 seats in the hostel. It provides breakfast, two meals and afternoon snacks. Hostel supplies only vegetarian food for the convenience of the Toda students. This school has certainly benefited those who want their children should be educated but a single school of this kind is not enough for imparting the education to the people because of several factors such as distance, chances of admission into hostel, etc. People like Kota, Badaga and Christian Todas with their initiatives and enterprising attitude have progressed a lot and Todas are facing a challenge from these communities too. During fieldwork the Toda-Kota school (Thakkar Bappa Gurukulam) had 231 students. There were 88 Toda, 14 Kota and 129 other community students respectively.

In the school, students from VI to VIII standards are given training in agriculture. Tamil language is followed as medium of instruction but English as a subject is taught from VII standard. The District Harijan Welfare Committee sends doctor from primary health centre once in a month for a health check up of the students. In case of emergency medical care service of the doctor from PPI (a factory located close by) is also available. State government has also initiated a number of schemes particularly in relation to education for the local people including the Toda. At present in the district there are 22 government tribal residential schools, of which 19 are elementary schools and 3 are of middle school standard. However, of late many Todas have been attracted by the English medium schools. It has been observed especially among the present generation parents that they are preferring their children to get education in town schools where there are a number of famous English schools. One of them is Breck's School in Ooty town. A few Toda children are residing in this school. Some of these schools are quit expensive yet, a few Toda families are pursuing.

Toda boys are also enthusiastic about the sports, particularly football. They have a football team, which participates in the local tournaments. They have stamina and speed but certainly lack in skill in relation to other players, because of the lack of training and knowledge of proper technique. Despite such shortcomings, they are competing and enjoying themselves. There are a number of Todas, who have participated in the Republic Day celebration in New Delhi, and similar such big occasions. A few of them visited places like Madras, Bangalore, Thiruvananthapuram (Trivandrum) and two of them were invited to construct a Toda traditional hut at the Museum of Man, at Bhopal.

The Todas have become quite familiar with the Tamil movie and often visit the local theatres for watching movies. For Toda males, visiting market, taking tea at a hotel is a good entertainment (those who can afford, also go for drink). The glamour of Ooty town has left a lasting impression on the Toda and at the same time Ooty as a town has enormous importance in their day to day life. An NGO called Nilgiri Adivasi Welfare Association (NAWA) was registered in 1958 (under the Society of Registration Act XXI of 1960) as a voluntary secular, charitable body. It is concerned with the welfare work among tribal people in Nilgiri and adjoining areas, especially extending medical, nutritional, educational and initiating socio-economic activities to the people. Dr Narasimhan, who was a doctor felt the necessity of such activities to be initiated among the tribals and began working with them during the early 1940s and subsequently spending his whole life in their service. NAWA started its operational centre at Kolagiri which is located about 40 km from Ooty. It has other small centres at different places in Nilgiris. There is a women cooperative voluntary organization started in 1950 at Kotagiri. Apart from its help to the destitute women, in recent years efforts have been made to engage and employ the Toda women in the cooperative, so that they can prepare and market their embroidery work. At present there are 60 Tada women members of which 40 are regularly participating in cooperative work.

Concluding Remarks

Todas call themselves as Ord or Od which means man and which distinguishes them from non-Todas. They call non-Todas by their own terms such as Kuef for Kota, Kurumbu for Kurumbas, Muf for Badagas, Arreld for Irular, Phanvi for Paniyans, Pruoned for Tamils and Arzu for foreigners. Certain hierarchy exists thereby Todas consider themselves as superior over the Kota and Kurumba.

The Todas are basically stratified around two social groups, Tordas and Teivelly. In most village affairs they are equal but certain privileges enjoyed by Women of Tordas can not be enjoyed by Teivelly Women. This is a case of traditional social-exclusion.

In Toda pastoral life dairies are regards as temples. Dairies are not equal. Certain ranking exists between them. There are five types of dairies, and among them some are of superior type. Fact that clans are not equal may be seen in division of dairies. Some clans have superior dairies and some clans have dairies of low rank. Buffaloes are also ranked into five types. Despite their adoption of modernization and economic diversification, the Todas continue to attach high ritual significance to their villages and dairies, though economic base of pastoralism is threatened.

The Todas had maintained certain stratification with their traditional neighbours, such as Kota, Kurumba, and Bagada. The Todas generally regarded Kotas as socially and ritually of 'lower' status. They often regarded themselves superior to other communities such as Kurumba and Bagada but they had a symbiotic social relation with them. Thus in each others festivals they participated and offered symbolic gifts, such as 'salt' and 'ghee'. The Todas regard Christian Todas as ritually 'inferior'. This situation may be described as an example of modern 'social-exclusion'.

References

Hockings, Paul, E. 1980, *Ancient Hindu Refugees: Badaga Social History*, New Delhi: Vikas.

Mandelbaum, D.G. 1989, The Nilgiries as a Region. In Blue Mountains. Ed. Paul Hockings, Delhi: Oxford University Press.

Walker, Anthony R. 1986, *The Toda of South India: A New Look*, Delhi: Hindustan Publishing Corporation.

17 Adivasi Solidarity, Social Movement and Empowerment

The Bhumia-Baiga of Madhya Pradesh

R.K. Sinha

Identity and Etymology

This paper discusses the issues of social mobility, Adivasi assertion, political movements and empowerment among the Bhumias of Madhya Pradesh. The Bhumia possess some similarities with the Bharia tribe and Baiga tribe, who are reported to have originated from a common stock namely Bhutiya (Russel and Hiralal, 1916). The etymology of the term, 'Bhumia' is related with Bhumi, meaning land. As they are regarded to be the original settlers of the present Bhumi of Jabalpur, they came to be called owner of this soil. The literature on the Bharia tribe suggests that they might be the descendants of the 'Bhar kingdom' of the Madhya Bharat, who ruled the territory for a long period of time. The present Bhumia believe that they have originated from the sweat of Lord Shiva and are the sons of Mata Sati. Mata Sati is recognized as the first wife of Lord Shiva. The Gond tribesmen are believed to be the children of Mata Parvati who is recognized as the younger wife of Lord Shiva. So, the Bhumia consider themselves as the elder brother of the Gond. The Bhumia are also recognized as great warriors who fought in the armies of the Pandavas of the Mahabharata.

In the whole of Jabalpur district, the Bhumia are recognized as village priests. The Bhumia are variously called by the name of Bhumia, Baiga, Panda and Dewar. The Bhumia are the village priests who alone are entitled to appease and perform the worship of village deities for the welfare of the whole village. The Baiga however are recognized as village priests in the villages of Mandla where they worship village deities. Fuchs (1973) writes that in Dindori Tahsil of Mandla district, the Bhumia prefer the designation, 'Bhumia' or 'Dewar'. Here, the Bhumia are also recognized as one section of Baiga. Fuchs further says that the Bhumia, one of the most important divisions of the Baiga tribe, live in a compact area in Dindori and its adjoining areas. From Dindori some Bhumias have emigrated to Niwas Tahsil in the west and to the former Kawardha state and Pandaria in the south.

It is learnt from the Bhumia themselves that they are distributed mostly in the Jabalpur area on the Jabalpur and Katani road. The areas thickly populated by the Bhumia are Manjholi, Boharbund, Patan, Kundam, Singhora and adjoining Katal. The Bhumia inhabited villages are Manjholi, Khatoli, Semaria, Khagamau, Mohania, Tagbahar, Ranital, Barkhera, Padra, Badera, Silua, Podi and the like. Some Bhumia villages and the approximate number of households therein as stated by them are Ranjhi–40, Mangeli–40, Badera–40, Paheria–30, Belpura–25, Bamhori–25, Richai–25, Kanchanpur–25, Bheraghat–20, Gopalpur–20, Muhas–20, Muria–15, Karmeta–10, Kaliaghat–10, Barakher–10, Barkhera–8, Pathara–7, Piparia–6, Jalgaon–8, Kasahi–6, Kaladubhor–6, Singhaldeep–8, Dodi–7, Lalmati–5, Goda–5 and Khamaria Piparia–5. There is no separate population figure available in the Census report, for the Bhumia tribe. Their population figure is mixed with Bharia-Bhumia, or Bhumihar-Bhumia, including Pando and Paliha. Their mixed population was 1,17,806 according to 1971 Census report which has increased to 1,95,490 in 1981. According to the rough estimation of the Bhumias of Burdagar village, there are about 20,000 Bhumias in the whole of Madhya Pradesh. In Burdagar village, there are in all 395 Bhumias, who live in about 100 households. The Bhumia speak a Jabalpuri Hindi dialect among themselves and with outsiders.

The male dress of Bhumia in the past consisted of langot (loin cloth), lungi, towel and dhoti. Now most men wear dhoti, paint, shirt and baniyan. Their women wear blouse (polaka), petticoat, lahanga and saree (lugra). The children wear half pant and half shirt. The male ornaments are Chura (bangles), Mundari (ring), Luraki (earring), Tahbij (locket) and chain. Their women put on Hasuli (neck), Bedi (metal bangle), Sutia (neck), Hiwal (neck), Khulta (nose pin), Bangari (bangle), Katile (hand), Gajra (hand), Bohara (leg), Jhumaki (ear), Kanphul (eartop), Churi (bangle), Kach (glass bangle), Katdora (waist), Todar (leg), Lachcha (leg),Payal (leg), Mundri (ring), Challi (leg), etc.

Tattooing used to be preferred by both males and females. They believe that by tattooing they go to heaven after death while without tattooing they go to hell and became churel (evil spirits) after death. Another legend has it that during Muslim rule, their girls and women were kidnapped by the Muslims. So, they adopted tattooing the women to look ugly and avoid being kidnapped. Now, their women get tattoo marks on their forehead, chin, and forearms. In the past, the women used to get tattooed in their leg and chest also. Their males also used to get tattooed in their chest, thigh, hand and feet but now their males as also females do not like tattooing. The expenditure of tattooing for the girl or a woman even after marriage is always borne by her parents. The Bandi caste women of Malhagaon undertake the job of tattooing the women.

Due to existence of a number of schools at all levels, the spread of education is good among the Bhumia of Burdagar village where the study is conduced. There is one postgraduate and two graduates who are employed as school teachers. There are 21 males and five females who have passed secondary examination and two males who have passed higher secondary examination. But, the number of primary pass is more, namely, 73 males and 22 females. At the same time, the number of illiterate Bhumias is large such as 120 males and 123 females. The growth of education is result of high aspiration to get better jobs.

Self-Image and Social Status

The Bhumia recognize themselves as the owner of the area and are regarded as the original settlers or the Adivasis of present territory. So they consider themselves to be the true and actual landlord of this soil or Bhumi. Even today they are the priests of Jabalpur villages. They alone are entitled to perform the worship of the village deities. If there is an epidemic in the village in the form of cholera, small pox and so on, it is regarded as the wrath of evil spirits. At that moment, the Bhumia are remembered, and requested to appease and worship the angry deities and spirits by suitable offerings and sacrifices to remove their wrath. This is necessary to bring normalcy in the village.

The priest enjoys a special status and prestige among the villagers on account of his role as sacred specialist and medicine man. On the same account, the Bhumia in general enjoy some prestige in perception of other communities. They enjoy their prestige at the ideal level. Nevertheless in practice the higher caste people treat them as socially lowly placed group in the village. To get rid of their low social position they had taken the path of sanskritization and accepted Janeu (the sacred thread). It may be argued that Bhumia also followed the path of Kshatriyaization by accepting the title Thakur. They also adopted such names as Raghubansi Gond or Rajbansi Gond to avoid the stigma attached to their ethnonym Bhumia. Of late, to get the constitutional benefits, the educated persons claim themselves as Bhumia.

The Bhumia are economically most disadvantaged amongst all communities of the village. They rationalize their poor condition by giving a mythological explanation. They are of opinion that the Lord Shiva cursed them to remain poor because they are guilty of eating up "Nandi", the holy cow Kamdhenu of Lord Shiva.

It is learnt from the oral tradition that Bhumia are believed to be born out of sweat of Lord Shiva. The mother earth (Dharati Mata or Bhumi Mata) brought them up and as such they became Bhumia. They further believe that they are the eldest son of lord Shiva from his first wife Sati, while the Gond tribesmen are said to be the son of Lord Shiva from his younger wife Parvati. Thus they claim themselves as the elder brothers of Gond tribe. Bhumia elite informed that the Bhumia have other ethnic names in other states. To give just a few examples, in Chhattisgarh they are called as Rawat. In Chanda region of Maharashtra Bhumia are known as Baiga. But they regard themselves superior to the Baigas mainly because the Baiga women work as midwives during childbirth. Moreover the Baiga women do not observe the menstrual pollution. The ten days death pollution is also not observed by the Baigas. Those Bhumia who migrated to Nagpur area called themselves as Thakur, and thus lost their Scheduled Tribe status and got re-enlisted as OBC (other backward castes).

S. Fuchs (1968) writes, "according to their own beliefs, the Bhumia are the oldest settlers in the Mandla area. This fact is recognized by the other tribes and castes of eastern Mandla who regard them as Bhumia Malgujar, that is owner of the land. In the Bidrs ceremony, at the beginning of sowing season, the officiating priest, always a Baiga is addressed as "Baiga Raja".

Russel and Hiralal (1916) mentioned that the Bhumia tribe which is a Dravidian tribe residing principally in the Jabalpur district, form half of the total number of the tribe. The proper name of the tribe is Bharia, but they are often called as Bharia-Bhumia, because many of them hold the office of Bhumia or priest of the village gods and the Bharia prefer the designation of Bhumia as being the more respectable. The term Bhumia or 'Lord of the Soil' is an alternative for Bharia. The Bharia have forgotten their original affinities and several stories of the origin of the tribe. One of these say that Arjun, when suffering with the Pandavas in their battle against Kauravas, took up a handful of Bharu grass and pressed it, produced a host of men who fought in the battle and became the ancestors of the Bharias. According to Russel and Hiralal (1916) the Bharia is also a Kolarian caste. In olden times, there was a caste called 'Bhar', who used to rule in the forest and the Bharias are the descendants of 'Bhar'.

Village

The village of Burdagar in the district of Jabalpur was selected for the present study. The name of the village has been given by the Bhumia tribe. But its new name is Gandhigram. There are 910 households with 5,044 population in the village. This multi-ethnic village is located at about 20 km from Jabalpur and 17 km from Singhora Tahsil, on the Jabalpur-Katni road. In the northern side of the village there are some families of Brahmins, Thakur (Rajput), Burmans and Chourasia, while the middle of village is inhabited by some families of Brahmin, Yadav, Chourasia, Lakhera, Rana, Kol, Sahu and Kumbhar (potter). The Basor and Kumbhar live separately on the roadside, and they used to rear pigs. The village is divided into 10 Mohallas, viz., Bhumiana (for Bhumia), Kuriana (for Kors), Kumbharana (for Kumbhor or potter), Gaontena (for Kol, who are also called as Gaotia) Dhemarhana (Dhimar or Baraua), Pansariana for Chamarana (for Vhamaar), Teliana (for Teli or Sahu) and Banjar Mohalla but none of the Banjars live in the Mohalla.

The demographic profile of the area under study is Chourasia–200, Bhumia–100, Kol–150, Vani–70, Teli/Sahu–40, Kori–50, Burman–50, Kurmi Patel–20, Brahmin–15, Rajput Thakur–10, Muslim–10, Badai–5, Lohar–2, Kumbhar–2, Basor–20, Chamar–10, Khare Kayastha–2, Tamera–1, Dahiya–1, and Dorzi–1.

As regards the hierarchical position of different communities, the Brahmin secure the top rank, followed by Rajput Thakur, while the third position is secured by Vani and Khare Kayastha. Rest of the caste and tribal groups secure the middle and lower rank. The Basor, Chamar, Dumar and Kumbhar are ascribed lowest rank by the villagers. The Burdagar village is surrounded by the villages of Kusner, in the south and Marashan, in the western side. By and large, members of similar caste and tribal groups live in the surrounding villages.

The villagers report that the Bhumias are the oldest settlers of Burdagar who came to live here from the neighbouring Mahoba state. Mahaba in the past was recognized as the oldest kingdom of the Chandellas. Thereafter, the Kol tribespeople came here from Riwa state or Desh, so they call themselves as Desha. Thirdly, the Barai or Chourasia caste people came here from Riwa, Allahabad and Benaras and settled here due to favourable conditions for betel cultivation. It is found to be very suitable due to Burdasagar tank from which they used to fetch water for irrigation for betel cultivation. In due course of time the other castes and tribes came here and settled in the village according to their convenience.

The village Burdagar lies 17 km away from the Singhora Tahsil. The village has a bus stop, post office, family planning centre, as well as nursery, primary, middle, secondary and higher secondary schools. The nearest town is Jabalpur which is also its district headquarters where district hospital is located. The

Narmada river is regarded as very holy in Jabalpur town. The village has a sacred centre of its own where in addition to tribal deities there are some temples of Hindu deities like Rama, Krishna, Hanuman, Kheamas, Baba Bhairo and others. The weekly market of the village is held on Friday. The village also has a Statutory Gram Panchayat which undertakes development activities of the village sponsored by the state government. It helps the villagers including Bhumias by getting loans and subsidies for the purchase of cattle, cart, pump set, fertilizer, seeds and the like. By undertaking development works in the area of its jurisdiction, the Gram Panchayat provides employment to the Bhumias as daily wage earners. The Bhumia also get employment in the nearby brick and tile factories and are employed for bidi making. Betel cultivation comes in handy for the Bhumia where they get maximum employment and earn their wages. Some more Bhumia inhabited villages of the area are Badkhera, Pathra, Badera, Bamhor and Ranital in the Jabalpur region, Chapra, Godi, Situa, Indrana, Suhas, and Bohr band, in the Sighera area, Bachaiya, Hotoli, Deni, Pators, Bankheri, Amarga, in the Manjheli region and Bichari, Piprodh, Padua, Akhala, Bistara, in the Katni area.

The present Burdagar village is selected for the study of the Bhumia tribe, because it is located in the middle of many Bhumia villages with about 100 households of the Bhumia. Secondly, it is a multi-ethnic middle-sized village where the inter-ethnic relations with other village communities could easily be observed, noted and understood.

Food Habits

The Bhumia get some rice which they eat in the winter but for the rest of the year, they have to depend on wheat. They call their breakfast as Kalewa, which consists of bread, salt, sauce or *Bhurta* (potato, brinjal or tomato roasted and crushed with salt and spices). In the past, they used to take bread with jaggery. They prefer to take rice and pulse with vegetables as the afternoon food which is named as Khana. The food taken in the night is called Beyari which consists of bread, *thulli, gakade* or *labdua* which are eaten with pulse, *bhurta* and *chatni* (sauce). On festive occasions they prepare *lapta, gorbadi, furra* but now they have added some new festive items like *puri, sewaiya, kodi, ladde* and vegetables. Non-vegetarian food items are consumed during festivals. *Gokade* is also named as *batti* which is wheat flour roasted in the form of balls. It is eaten with pulses or *Bhurta.* Dal is prepared from thin particles of wheat which are cooked in boiled water. This is also named as *thulli* which is eaten with pulse or vegetables. Sweet *thulli* is prepared on some festive occasions by adding jaggery. *Kodi* is prepared from gram flour water, curd and spices. It is a liquid and is eaten with bread or rice. *Lapta* is a gruel like preparation made from gram flour, salt spices. *Labdua* is made from fried wheat flour which is put in boiled water and some spices and salt are added in it. *Puri* is small bread cooked in oil, while *Sewaiya* is sweet noodles cooked in milk. *Gorbadi* is sweet wheat cake cooked in oil. *Furra* is steamed cake like food item prepared from rice and wheat flour, especially for offering to their clan deities and eaten with jaggery.

The Bhumia are non-vegetarian and consume the flesh of goat, chicken, wild bear, fish and egg. Pork was previously eaten, now it is discontinued as most of them stopped sacrificing pigs to their deities. They are very fond of country liquor and get it from government shops. Previously they used to distill country liquor themselves.

Changing Economy

In the past the Bhumia grew Lac. They also collected minor forest produce and practised shifting cultivation. The changing forest laws gradually alienated them from the forest and they have adopted bidi-making as their main occupation now. Although some of them possess some patches of cultivable land, the yield received is very meagre. In Burdagar, the area under betel cultivation is considerably more, so it gives them ample job opportunity. Some of them are also employed in some permanent jobs as teachers, clerk and peon in Jabalpur. The rest of them depend on bidi-making, brick-making and wage earnings in agriculture. Many of them are engaged as permanent labour in the defence factory of Jabalpur, while some others work as school teachers, clerks and peons.

The Bhumia consider government service as the best and they say that those holding some land and also engaged in government service double sources of income. Now, belong to higher strata as they have the Bhumia landholders are attracted towards government service. This is why the spread of education is considerable among the Bhumias of Burdagar. In service, they are secured of a fixed amount of salary without any risk. It is observed that the Bhumia service holders get good amount of money, wear good clothes, eat good and tasty edibles. So, permanent service means double sources of income for them, namely from salary and from agricultural yields.

Division of Labour

In the field of agrarian operations men and women perform respective works. Ploughing is a male activity. The job of cleaning, plastering the courtyard with cow dung and water are done by their women. Their males do not do it in any situation. But, their males plaster the thrashing ground with cow dung and water. The job of cot weaving is always undertaken by their males and their women cannot do it. Again, their women are not allowed to climb on the roof for repairing and thatching, cannot sow seeds in the ploughed agricultural fields. It may be concluded that the hard and strenuous jobs are undertaken by their males while the women do light domestic jobs.

Emerging Social Stratification: Economic Differentiation

The Bhumia agriculturists do not to go to wage earnings. Most of the cultivable lands are in the individual names of the Bhumias. There are 40 Bhumia families who own over 60 Acres of cultivable land. Many of their family members are engaged in government services. In terms of their high income they belong to highest strata. Some of the Bhumias have also acquired some government lands in the village for cultivation. These lands are yet to be registered in their names. Further, five Bhumias of the village have been given about two and half acres of land through Bhoodan, which is located in the neighbouring villages. Only one of them cultivates this Bhoodan land while others do not plough it on the plea that it is infertile. There are some landless families also.

The Bhumia have a local notion of good and marginal cultivators. A good cultivator has more acreage of fertile cultivable lands with some irrigation facilities and grows more food grains. He pays more attention to the cultivation of crops and both the sexes work together for growing more food grains. Again, a good cultivator does not involve himself in gambling and playing cards and drinking. A marginal cultivator has small acreage of land holding and depends more on other economic pursuits for earning a livelihood. Thus two categories of cultivators, good and marginal, are clearly discernible.

Bidi-making is a very popular economic pursuit among the Bhumia. They learnt the art of bidi-making after the imposition of ban on shifting cultivation and lac raising after the independence of the country. At the time of fieldwork they used to get ₹ 15 for every thousand of prepared bidi but the government rate was ₹ 20 per thousand. Both males and females are engaged in bidi-making but females contribute more in this job. There are about 25 women and only 10 men who are fully dependent on bidi work and earn ₹ 20 to 30 per day for their livelihood. There are four bidi contractors in Burdagar village who supply the raw materials and in return give payment on receiving the prepared bidi. At present, most of the Bhumias know the art of bidi-making but only some of them undertake the job of bidi-making. They argue that bidi-making makes their movement very restricted. So, they prefer wage earning jobs.

As we discussed earlier peasant character of maximizing income is noted in the activities of some landholders. Yet another typical peasant quality is seen in case of three Bhumia families who came forward to undertake betel cultivation. Thus, there are three Bhumia families who have undertaken betel cultivation on their own on the basis of lease and share cropping. These families were indeed attracted by high market value of betel. These enterprising families do show the contrast from those Bhumias who did not feel the urge for economic mobility. Indeed majority of Bhumias continue to work as labourer in the betel fields of the Chourasia caste of the village and earn their bread. They work there on a daily wage of ₹ 25 for males and ₹ 20 for their grown-up children, who work on a contract basis. In the earlier times, the women were not allowed to work in betel but now they are also employed. It is very important to observe that up-to the independence of the country, the Bhumias were not interested to work in the betel fields due to its hard nature of work and secondly there were plenty of other economic pursuits available in forest. These three families who fully subsist on betel leaf production may be described as good cultivators while others belong to poor category.

Bhumia are also engaged in the brick-making work. About 15 Bhumias of Burdagar have accepted the job of brick-making in neighbouring villages. It is a seasonal migration in which they migrate after the sowing and the harvesting season, to some nearby villages. They sow the crops and migrate for brick works and return for harvesting. Usually, most of their agricultural yields get exhausted during rainy season hence they undertake the work of brick-making. They get ₹ 60 per thousand bricks and make about 900 bricks in a day, involving individuals of both sexes.

Previously, many Bhumias used to work as 'bonded labourers' with the well-to-do farmers. The Bhumia used to borrow loans in advance from their masters during their marriage, illness and death. But, they were never in a position to repay the borrowed loans, so they were compelled to work as bonded labourers at a meagre payment. They are thankful to the proclamation of emergency in the country, that made them free from their masters with whom they were serving as bonded labourers. Now, they are free to choose the nature of work and their masters. There are about 52 Bhumias who have wage earning as their primary occupation, while 18 Bhumias work as wage earners as their secondary occupation. In the category of permanent service, there are 16 Bhumias who are engaged in service. It is thus seen that clear-cut social stratification based on occupational differentiation exists in this Adivasi society.

Forest Economy and the Bhumia

The Bhumias are dependent on forests to some extent. The nearby forests of Burdagar help the Bhumia to get fuel wood, bamboo and minor forest products for their consumption. They are totally dependent on forests for the supply of their fuel wood. Then, the Bhumia are in the habit of fetching bamboo from the forest without the notice of forest officials and sell them at the rate of ₹ 200 per hundred and earn part of their livelihood. The betel grower Chourasias are the ready buyers of Bhumia's bamboo at half price when the government rate is ₹ 400 per hundred. Again, there are ten Bhumia families of Burdagar who are engaged in mahua collection in the mahua season, for about one month during Chaitra. The dumari is especially cooked during hal-chatta or hal-shristhi, in Bhado month. They also prepare mahua latta or laddoo from fried mahua and wheat and gram flour. The mahua Latta is prepared and eaten especially during rainy season when there is shortage food for the Bhumia. Some of the Bhumias are also engaged in the collection of bidi leaves. There are about 20 Bhumia families who earn part of their living in the summer season by the collection of bidi leaves. These collected leaves are sold to the forest contractors at ₹ 40 per hundred bundles.

Table 1

Amount of Seeds, Fertilizer and Produce

Name of the crops	*Amount of seeds per acre*	*Amount of fertilizer per acre*	*Produce per acre*
Wheat	14 Kuro (70 kg)	20 kg Urea	300 kg
Paddy	12 Kuro (60 kg)	10 kg Urea	400 kg
Mustard	5 Barahiya	10 kg Gramori	3–4 quintal
Alsi (linseed)	5 Barahiya	10 kg Gramori	3 quintal
Masur	6 Kuro (30 kg)	20 kg D.A.P.	4–5 quintal

A total of 3 kuro wheat or 14 kg gram seeds may be sown over 30 decimal land

Table 2

Some Important Local Measurements

One acre	=	14 kuro wheat and 12 kuro paddy
One chattoli	=	315 grams of food grains
One barahiya	=	1.2 kg of wheat or 1 kg paddy
One kuro	=	4 barahiya equal to 5 kg foodgrains
One khadi	=	20 kuro equal to 100 kg or one quintal

Labour Force of Bhumias and Other Economic Classes

A total 52.41 per cent of Bhumias may be categorized as wage earners who are the real labour force of the Bhumia, on whom the village populations depend.

Even though a good number of Bhumias are labourers, they always try to be engaged otherwise. Many labourers thus become self-employed. In the category of self-employed Bhumias we notice three families of cultivators and five families of bidi-makers, who do not migrate for their livelihood. In the wage earning category, there are 42 wage earners who depend on labour works: 24 of them work as labour in the betel cultivation (Bareja), 20 of them are in some kind of regular contract job, 50 of them work as labour in brick-making and one of them is engaged as cattle herder. These 42 Bhumias form economically weaker section among the Bhumias. They may be ranked at lower stratum. In the next rank we notice some poor land holders or temporary job holders who also depend on labour work as their secondary occupation, or they take up agricultural work. Thus, in the category of secondary occupation, there are 33 families who also depend on wage earnings: 12 are working in betel cultivation, one as cattle herder, 22 have taken cultivation as their secondary occupation, three grow food grains on sharecropping basis, four are bidi workers and one is a brick-maker.

The analysis of the economic pursuits presented above shows that the Bhumia society is classified into five layers on the basis of earning of livelihood. There are: (i) service holders with farming, (ii) service holders, (iii) good farmers, (iv) marginal farmers, and (v) landless wage earners. They are hierarchically arranged in terms of the possession of wealth and they lead different life in terms of consumption of food, cloth and other amenities.

Economic Relations

The serving castes used to be called 'Kamin'. Now, all the serving castes serve on ready cash payments for their job. The barber serves on the occasion of birth and deaths charging ₹ 10 and two and half kilos of food grains. In addition, barbers charge separately for shaving and hair cuts. The washerman also charges equal amount of money and food grains for rendering services on death and during Diwali festival. The blacksmith serves them by sharpening agricultural implements on the payment of 5 kures, that is 25 kg of food grains from the Bhumia agriculturists. The blacksmith also visits them during Diwali to put a nail on the main door, with the belief that it drives away evil eyes and diseases. The carpenter also visits them to fix a ceremonial wooden stick (Khutta) on the main door to drive away evil eyes and receives the same amount of food grain. In addition, now, the Bhumias have started purchasing plough on cash payment of ₹ 25 and Khambha and Panch Khambha (wooden articles) for marriage rituals on the payment of ₹ 25. The Khasu or Hijra women visit them on the birth of a child and receive a reward of ₹ 5–25. It is thus seen that the Bhumias are part of village economy and they enjoy the services of all Kamin (Hindu) service castes, without discrimination.

There are some other economic relations in which Bhumias are engaged by way of dealing with other ethnic groups and institutions.

These relations may be described below. The creditor and debtor relation exists involving the Bhumia and Sahukars. It is because of the fact that many Bhumia families do not earn in surplus, so in case of emergency they have to borrow loans from the local creditors. There are nine Sahukars in Burdagar village who charge 3 per cent monthly interest on the borrowed amount. In some cases the Bhumia borrows loans by mortgaging agricultural fields or ornaments.

At present, there are two cattle herders of the Bhumia tribe who have adopted this job as their secondary occupation and charge from all communities ₹ 10 per cattle head for grazing. In the past, the barber (Nai), blacksmith (Lohar) and carpenter (Dada) used to serve Bhumia on the basis of old jajmani relationship twice a year on the payment of food grains that is wheat, during the harvest of Kharif and Rabi crops.

Weekly Market and the Bhumias

There is a small market in the Burdagar village where some shops of cloth, shoes and chappals, cycle repair shop, tea and snacks and sweets, pan and utensils and grocers, exist. These shops serve the villagers including Bhumias by supplying the commodities of their needs. The Bhumias however reported that these permanent shops charge more on the purchase of commodities, so the Bhumia prefer to purchase the commodities of their needs from the weekly market which is held every Friday. The weekly market peaks in the afternoon and lasts upto late evening. On the market day, the Bhumia leave their work in the afternoon for making their necessary purchases. The weekly market has a variety of shops including vegetable shops, grocery shops, tea, snacks and sweet shops, clothes shops, jewellery shops, utensil and earthenware shops, shoe shops, and tobacco shops. Besides the weekly market, one market is held during Chandimela fair held during Diwali.

Economic Cooperation and Specialization in the Village

Burdagar village is a multi-ethnic village where some cooperation and interaction in observed in economic sphere. Some sort of jajamani relations is observed also. The economic cooperation is called as Kam Sadhna or Madad. The Madad is limited for two to three days for the construction of house, roof, harvesting and transplantation. During marriage, several communities cooperate with each other for the cleaning of food grains, fetching of fuel wood and cooking of food. Often the close relatives such as wife's sister, wife's brother, sister, sister's husband and maternal uncle may be called for economic cooperation. At the same time, they are ready to cooperate with other villagers at the time of need.

The Baser castemen serve the villagers by sweeping and cleaning the village. They are engaged in basket-making and serving the villagers by the supply of basketware on cash payment or in exchange for food grains. The members of Biratiya community are regarded as geneology keepers (Bhat) of the Bhumia, and they used to visit the village once in five years. They visit in a group and stay in the Bhumia village for about a fortnight and prepare geneology of new born Bhumias during the stay. The Bhumias used to give gifts to them for their services. In the night, they entertain the Bhumias by karma dance to the rhythm of musical instrument Damaru (small drum) associated with Lord Shiva, Dholak (drum) and harmonium. Since they are the Bhat or bard to the Bhumias they only serve the Bhumias and eat the food and water offered by them. As long as they stay, the Bhumias keep them very comfortable and the expenditure for their stay is met by all the Bhumias.

The Bhumias receive periodical services during life-cycle rituals. Services of Brahmins are limited to some rich families. They also regularly receive services of artisan castes. The Bhumias also serve the higher caste people. They work as labourers in the fields of Brahmins, Thakurs (Rajputs), Kurmis, Chourasias and Banias. They interact with the local Banias (Vanias) while purchasing the goods they need. During Navaratra puja, the Bhumias act as Panda (priest) while sacrificing animals. It is because they are the oldest inhabitants of the village and are believed to know the requirements and preferences of each village tribal deity. The Brahmin priest of the village serves the Bhumias during marriage, death (Ganga Pujan), SatyaNarain Katha and on some rituals and festivals on cash payments ranging from ₹ 11.25 to 25.25 for Satya Narain Katha, ₹ 11 to 51 for marriage, ₹ 11.25 for Ganga Pujan and ₹ 11.25 for other ritual occasions. The Brahmin also receives 'Sidha' in the form of raw food grains, namely, rice, pulse, wheat flour, salt and spices from the Bhumia. Thus, the Bhumias are part of village economy and village religious life. They are not regarded as 'untouchables' but are treated as belonging to lower strata.

Most of the Bhumias are poor and their economic condition is miserable. Their womenfolk are very hard working but the males of the new generation pass their time in card playing, gambling and chit chatting. The set up is such that in each family there is one wage earner and many dependents – that too, the wage earner earns very little. They give their cultivable land on lease or for sharecropping, due to lack of fund for cultivation. Many of them are also landless.

Table 3

Agricultural and Other Economical Calendar of Village

Month	*Activities*	*Festivals*
Falgun	Harvesting of wheat, threshing by bullocks, wage earning	Nan-Dhapa, Jawana
Chaitra	Threshing, wage earnings, harvesting	
Baisakh	Threshing, wage earning, repairing of huts and roofs	
Jeth	wage earning	
Asadh	Ploughing, sowing of paddy	
Savan	Weeding	Raksha Bandhan, Khajlia
Bhado	Stay at home, wage earning	Anant Chaturdasi
Kuar	Stay at home, also go out for wage earning in agricultural works	Dusserah
Kartik	Harvesting of paddy	
Arahan	Threshing	Kartik puja
Push	Wage earning	Sankranti
Magh	Wage earning	Fair in Pori

Note: The month Chaitra lasts from mid-February to mid-March. Each month of the village calendar lasts from the middle of one English month to the middle of the next month.

The Bhumia serve in the agricultural fields of Brahmin, Rajput, Kayastha and Bania, as wage labourers. They also maintain socio-economic relations with Chamar, Nai, Dhobi, Khangar, Gaontia, Bhangi and potters, besides observing festivals together. The Bhumia have also participated in India's struggle for independence. In 1939–40, they took part in Satyagraha. Under the leadership of Laxman Naik, the Bhumia led a march to resist the payment of taxes.

Social Stratification and Clan Ranking

Elders among the Bhumia stated that in the past all Bhumia had a set of fixed clans which had some distinctions. During their long association with numerous communities they came to establish inter-ethnic marriage alliances. Gradually the number of descendents of such unions increased. This situation led to division of the tribe into two classes-upper class or Uttam Shreni and lower class or Nimna Shreni. The knowledgeable persons among the Bhumia report that at present, the Bhumia are divided into two groups, 'Uttam Shreni' and 'Nimna Shreni'. In the former, only pure Bhumias are included. Only those Bhumias who never established inter-community marriage alliances are considered as pure. On the other hand, those who married a non-Bhumia and their descendants are recognized as the Bhumia of Nimna Shreni. However, the practical relevance of this division is very little. In day to day interactions this stratifications does not create any frictions.

The Bhumia are divided into various clan groups, which are functional units of their social organization. The clan groups regulate their marriage alliances as clan is exogamous by nature. The local name for clan is Got or Goti. The members of a particular clan consider themselves as the descendants of a common ancestor, and they are blood relatives who call each other as Goti-Bhai.

The characteristic feature of the Bhumia clan system is that most of their clan groups have a particular set of clan deities who are worshipped in a fixed month and time. The items of offerings and sacrifices are also fixed according to the nature of clan deities which vary from clan to clan. The members of a clan are also recognized as an economic unit as they assist each other during some crisis or at the peak of agricultural seasons namely sowing, harvesting and transplantation. The clan members also work as one unit during birth, marriage and death and at the time of worship of their clan deities. There are some very specific set of functions which are supposed to be performed by the clan members to the best of their ability and resources.

The following clan groups are found in Burdagar village: Rathor, Bade Rathor, Chote Rathor, Telharia, Patelia, Dhemarha, Mareha, Mangarha, Nekha, Naik, Devarha, Kataria, or Katarha, Bamnaha, Govalia or Govali, Chakdaiya, Kukur or Kukarha and Chevalha. There are some other clan groups which are found in the neighbouring Bhumia villages. Mention may also be made of clans such as Dhanbaiya, Marraiya, Dimarha, Deohare, Deorahe, Patelha or Patel, Chandeliya, Gamaliya, Chivalha, Tendua, Marghalia, Parteli, Kamaraha, Jaria, Maravi, Markam, Bharotia, Dhurwa, Saima, Barmaiya and Pakria.

It is reported by the knowledgeable persons among the Bhumia that some new clan groups are also emerging among them. Brijwal or Gowali is new clan which is found in the Katanga, Gada and Jabalpur areas. Markam and Parihar clan groups are reported from Seohore and Jabalpur. Some of the clan names have been adopted from the Gond clans. This may be due to the long association of the Bhumia with the Gond. The Gond associated clan names are Markam, Maravi and Dhurwa. The number of families in each clan of village was Rathor 45, Patelia 9, Mangarha 8, Dhemarha 7, Naik 6, Bade-Rathor 6, Devarha 4, Chakdaiya 4, Nekha 2, Chote-Rathor 2, Telhari 1, Kataria 1, Bamanaha 1, Govalha 1, Kukur 1, Mareha 1 and Chavalha 1.

It is observed that Bhumias of Jabalpur area use 'Ha'as suffix with their clan names, namely Chevalha, Mangarha, Dhemarha, Katharha, Devarha, Mareha, Paveha, Chandelha, Gayakaha, Telhariaha, Patelaha, Kakarha and the like. The Bhumias of Mandla use 'Ya', suffix in their clan names namely Baragiya, Barghariya, Barahiya, Basaniya, Ghatiya, Gopalpuriya, Dangariya, Kamariya, Kaurariya, Jamariya, Marghatiya, Mauchiya, Nadiya, Nauguriya, Panchgaiya, Rathoriya, Sardiya, Sarhiya, Sarjaniya, Surajpuriya, Tamaniya, Khamiya and Udariya.

Again, it is important to observe that the Bhumia believe in the hierarchy and ranking of their clans. They believe and regard Rathor, BadeRathor, ChoteRathor, Mahobia, Chakdaiya and Tendu to be higher in the ladder of hierarchy, followed by Chandeliya, Jhalarha, Marghatia, Muria, Patan, Kumraha, who are lower in the hierarchy. The rest of the clan groups are placed in middle.

Myths of the Origin of Some Clans

Mangarha: In olden time, a Barat (marriage procession) of Bhumia was crossing a river. While crossing the river, a crocodile (Mangar) happened to swallow the groom and other members of the Barat. At that moment, they prayed to the crocodile for life and promised to worship it during their marriages. The crocodile became pleased and exempted them. Due to this occurrence, the crocodile became Mangardeo for them and helped them in crossing the river on its back. Since then, they and their descendants came to be called as Mangarha clan and they started worshipping Mangarahadeo during the marriage of their children. At the time of marriage they prepare a symbolic small crocodile with the flour of gram and present suitable offerings.

Mahobia: Mahobia is a former princely estate on the border of Uttar Pradesh and Madhya Pradesh. The members of the clan believe that their forefathers were the original settlers of the Mahoba estate who spread to other parts of Madhya Pradesh. They prepare the food items in Alsi oil during marriage for offering to their clan deities. The original shrine of their clan deities is located in Mahoba where they go to worship their deities at the time of their marriage. After death of their clan members, their urn is collected on the third day and immersed in the Tirath Sagar tank which is located in Mahoba.

Tendua: The members of this clan believe that their ancestor lived on the Tendu fruits once during the days of crisis, so they are named as Tendu or Tendua clan. During Diwali, the clan members worship their clan deities under the Tendu tree. It is also a taboo to consume the Tendu fruits.

Parteli: During festivals the members of the clan offer cooked food and water on new Palas leaves (Patta) to their clan deities. Not only that, the food and water is also served to the clan members only on the Palas leaves. The clan members thus have some totemic links with leaves though no specific folktale is remembered. When a new bride comes to the house, she also offers cooked food that is Khir (rice cooked in milk) to the ancestors and clan deities on the Palas leaves.

Bamanaha: Its members believe that they got the Bamanaha clan name because some of the local Brahmins started taking services of some members of the Bhumia tribe, who in due course of time came to be called as Bamanaha clan.

Naikha: They believe that once their ancestors were going in marriage procession (Barat) and on the way they were taking rest under a Bat tree during the night. In the morning, all of them turned into stone (Pakhan). They prayed to the Bat tree for escape, with a promise to worship the Bat tree during their marriages. Thereafter, they again turned into living beings and were called as Nok Jana. From this emerged the clan name Naikha or Nekha. Since then, they observe taboo and they do not sleep under the Bat tree, and do not burn or harm it in any form.

Rathor: The members of Rathor clan believe that their ancestors were originally Rajputs who were employed in the armies of the Mahoba kingdom. At that time their male members used to wear sacred threads, while their women used to wear nose rings (Nath), unlike Rajputs. Once they were defeated by the Mughals in war hence they fled away from the war and threw away their sacred threads and Naths of the women with a view to hide their identity and save their life from the Mughals and thus they became Bhumias. Since then, they enjoy a very high status and they even marry within the Rathor clan. They prefer Rathor of another village only. This is because of the fact that the Rathor of other villages are regarded as belonging to different descent group.

Kataria: The clan members of Kataria associate themselves with dagger or Katar (arms). They worship their clan deities at the time of marriage by offering seven symbolic Katars prepared from wheat flour.

Chandel: The married women of this clan do not use vermilion on their hair partings and also do not use other cosmetics. It is feared that application of Kahal (black eye lotion) makes their eyes impure and application of vermilion makes their women widow. They have a mythical belief that their women had to sacrifice their marriage symbols for the cause of protecting their territory. It is believed that their women participated in a war along with Rani Durgavati of Gada-Mandla (Katanga) for fighting the Mughal emperor. At that time, Rani Durgavati came out to face the Mughals in a male dress by deserting all her marriage symbols. So, the participating Bhumia women also followed her and since then they do not use the marriage symbols, even today. They apply turmeric in the partings of their heads in place of vermilion.

The Bhumias lived in large joint families in the past. At present, as the village data suggest 58 per cent live in nuclear families, followed by broken families (27%) and only 15 per cent live in extended families. The reason for more broken families is that there are many families which include widow and widowers and also there are families of married couples who are not blessed with children.

Inter-community Relations and Local Hierarchy

The higher caste people accord the Bhumias a low social status. There were several ups and downs in the pattern of social and ritual spheres. In the past the Bhumias were treated badly, but a long process of sanskritization helped the Bhumias to gain better status. Many of them started using surname Thakur. They referred to themselves as Adivasi, which is a neutral term.

The Bhumia are now largely identified by the term Adivasi. There are some caste-dominant areas in M.P. where the Bhumias were treated as 'untouchables' in the villages, which are located north of Singhora tehsil and in the Katni tehsil. Here the school-going children of these areas are not allowed to sit on the mat (Tatpatti) of the school. The women are not allowed to fetch water from the village well along with the women of the higher castes. Similarly in the remote villages the Bhumia are not allowed to sit on the main cotton carpet (Bichai or dari) of the Panchayat when they participate in the meetings with the higher caste people. Here, they sit by the side of the main cotton carpet and then participate in the meeting. The Bhumia are also not allowed to participate in the Ramayana Mandali arranged by the higher caste people. But the Bhumia themselves are allowed to arrange such Ramayana Mandali. Once in Lakhapatri village of Katni a Purana Katha was going on and some Bhumias were there to hear and participate in it, but they were driven away with the excuse that they are not entitled to hear it. Moreover, the Bhumia are not allowed to take Pan-Supari (betel and betel nuts) from the main communal plates during the Panchayat meetings but are served separately. But, in Jabalpur and Patan areas of the region, the Bhumia do not face such discrimination.

Social Movement and Adivasi Consciousness

Right from the pre-independence era the Bhumia have been involved in various social movements. While in the past ritual mobility and adoption of sacred thread was crucial, in post-independence era they became conscious of their economic deprivation and discrimination as also their constitutional rights. Hence articulation of Adivasi movement became crucial for survival. Thus, historically speaking, to attain better ritual status in 1950, the Gobra King Gulab Singh of Damoh arranged a movement for wearing of sacred thread by all the Bhumias to upgrade their position and status. For that, Bhumia gatherings were arranged in several places and Brahmin priests performed the Janeu ceremony (sacred thread) on the Bhumia. But in due course of time, the Bhumia threw away their sacred thread because it did not permit them to take non-vegetarian food items and country liquor. But, in some villages of Bohribund, there are still some Bhumias who wear sacred thread. After the thread ceremony, many of the Bhumias aspired to achieve the Kshatriya identity and status and started calling themselves as Thakur. This Kshatriaization movement continued for about two years and thereafter they started calling themselves as Rajbanshi Gond or Raghubanshi Gond, which enhanced their position and status. In due course of time, Bhumia elders realized that their educated youth became deprived of the Scheduled Tribe reservation benefits, as they were not getting Scheduled Tribe certificate by adopting name of Rajbanshi or Raghubansi. So, they reverted to their original Bhumia identity and thus they formed a Bhumia society by the name of "Bhoombanshi Bhumia Samaj".

Thereafter, there emerged a second Gond movement among the Bhumias. This movement was organized to enhance the Bhumia position and status equal to the Gond tribe. Several former Gond-Chiefs such as Gobra Naresh, Patan and Katangi Naresh and one Bhumia leader Jodhelal Patel took initiative for the movement. They tried their level best in 1984 to merge the Bhumia tribe with the Gond tribe. They visited several Bhumia villages and addressed them to propagate their ideology and encouraged the Bhumia to merge with the Gond. Bhumia also took a resolution en masse to merge with the Gond and to write their tribe name as Rajbanshi or Raghubansi in all the government records. This movement also failed because their children encountered lots of difficulties in getting tribal certificate for reservation benefits after adopting the new names. So, they once again reverted back to their original Bhumia Adivasi identity.

Adivasi Land and Multiple Religious Beliefs

The Bhumia regard the territory they live as their original home land. This land is regarded as sacred. The tribal deities Bhu-Devta and Dharati Mata and Gram Devta are all worshipped even today by the Bhumia priests, who are called as Baiga also. Even caste Hindus recognise the efficacy of Adivasi deities and Baiga's abilities. The Baiga is regarded as sacred priest of the village and is responsible for appeasing the village deities for the well being and welfare of the villagers. He knows the art of sealing the village boundaries (Gav-Bandhan). This not only prevents the evil spirits from entering the village but also drives them away from the village. When the village gets free from all these evil spirits then only he performs the worship of village deities with suitable offering and sacrifices. A Baiga never harms the villagers through magical charms rather he offers to diagnose and treat the patient suffering from magical charms and evil spirits.

There are other sacred specialists like Gunia and Pand who are slightly different from the Baiga, in the sense that they are sorcerers who may use evil spirits to harm a person by causing disease, ailment and such other sufferings, by magical charms. In reality however they only diagnose and treat the patient and cure him. There are seven Gunias in Burdagar village.

Under the influence and through regular contacts with the Hindus the Bhumia also worship some of the Hindu deities, namely Hanuman, Lord Shiva, NavDurga, Jagdamba, Khermai and Devi. At the same time, they also celebrate some of the Hindu festival and rituals like Ram Navami, Nau Durga, Nagpanchami, Rakhi, Tij, Dusserah and Diwali.

Despite their Hinduization the Adivasi religious beliefs remain intact. Several Adivasi myths survive also. Thus they say that Mata Sati went away in the sky or Asman after her death, so, they worship Asman as Sati happens to be the mother of the whole Bhumia tribe. They also worship 'Por' or 'Porriya' who is recognized as the watchman of the Bhumia deities and who is enshrined on the door of the Bhumia huts. In their language, por means door of the hut and the spirit located there on the door is known as 'porriya', who is equated with the monkey God Hanuman of the Hindus.

Political System of the Bhumia

Traditional Adivasi political system, Adivasi laws and Adivasi elders continue to exist and maintain social control. Modern statutory village councils exist but for the Bhumias their own council is crucial. Thus they are guided by their Bhumia customary rules. The cases of serious disputes, physical assaulting and inter-group rivalry are reported to the nearest police station now at Gasalpur. The traditional Bhumia Panchayat has nothing to do with such cases. They have prescribed set of customary rules and laws which help in the smooth functioning of the Bhumia society. Any breaches or deviation from the customary rules are not tolerated by the Bhumia and the defaulter is taken to task and punished in accordance with their customary norms. Periodically the Bhumia village elders sit together, discuss the issue and decide according to their society's customs. Such assembly of Bhumia elders is called as Panchayat. The head of the Adivasi Panchayat is called as Mukhia or Patel or Sarpanch, while the village elders are called as Panchas.

The Bhumia have a three-tier Adivasi political system to deal with their political affairs and to maintain law and order in their society. First is the village level Panchayat where the area of function is a particular village. This is called as Village Panchayat or Samajik Baithak. The second is Ilaka Panchayat which consists of 13 to 15 Bhumia villages of the area and here only the major problems are discussed and decided. The third is Pargana Panchayat which consists of about 20 to 50 Bhumia villages of the region. When the problems of a particular village of Bhumia is not decided at the Village Panchayat then it is brought to the Ilaka Panchayat and decided by larger gatherings of Bhumia Panchas. The problem is brought to the Pargana Panchayat when the members of Ilaka Panchayat fail to come to an unanimous decision. Here, the decision of the Pargana Panchayat is binding on the defaulter, otherwise, he/she is excommunicated from the Bhumia society, if he/she fails to abide by the decision.

Adivasi Village Panchayat

Most of the Bhumia villages have their own Adivasi Panchayat consisting of one Patel, one Diwan and one Sipahi. In the past, these positions used to be hereditary. The old Patel of Burdagar was Gopal Bhumia, son of Sukhai, while his father-in-law Ramlal was the oldest Baiga and Diwan of the village, and Bhurelal was the oldest Sipahi of the Village Panchayat. Without their consent and acceptance no marriage used to take place. They were also responsible for listening and serving the government officials coming from the outside. They used to call the meetings of the Village Panchayat if any thing went wrong and used to come to a decision. Failing this, the matter was referred to the Pargana Panchayat where the matter was decided by elders drawn from 13 Bhumia villages.

Now, the traditional arrangement of the Village Panchayat has decayed because of some factionalism. So, one of the oldest village Panchas of the particular hamlet (Para) works as Patel and when needed he calls the meeting of the elders of Bhumia. The meeting is called in the house of the oldest Patel, Gopal. In the meeting itself, they select a Patel and Diwan to preside over the function of the Panchayat and try to arrive at a unanimous decision on the issue.

Some important Bhumia Panchas of other hamlets also attend the meeting and contribute towards decision-making.

Adivasi Ilaka Panchayat

The Ilaka Panchayat existed at the time of fieldwork and which consisted of one Patel and one Diwan for the Ilaka or area. The Panchas of each Bhumia village are treated as members of this Panchayat. The head of this Panchayat is also called Mukhia. The members of the Ilaka Panchayat meet on the request of the head of a particular village to discuss a major issue like excommunication and re-admission.

Adivasi Pargana Panchayat

The Adivasi Pargana Panchayat is the largest council of Bhumia elders. It also consists of one Pargana Patel and Diwan and its area of functioning is 25 to 50 Bhumia villages of the area. The Pargana Panchayat meets only to settle major issues like inter-caste marriage, killing a cow, getting maggot in the wound and the like. Having been satisfied with larger Adivasi solidarity the Bhumias of Jabalpur formed a larger body for the whole of the Bhumia community and named it as Shri Bhoombanshiya Bhumia Samaj. Somehow the unity did not last and factions (Gutbandi) have emerged among the followers of different office bearers. In the past, there were no factionalism and all were integrated into one body of the village, Pargana and Ilaka. Adivasi unity existed right from 1910 up to the headmanship of Koradila and Desairam. Trouble started when some actions of a headman were seen as biased and not at par with customary laws.

Norms of Social Control and Recognized Offences

The fact that Adivasi councils exist at various levels indicates that the tribe has a set of norms for social control and a set of recognized offences. The offences are called as Samajik Apradh and the violator is taken to task and punished for violation. Some of their traditional offences are as follows:

1. Marrying a non-Bhumia partner
2. Having sex with non-Bhumia partner
3. Killing a cow, dog, cat and squirrel
4. Removing horse-dung and dead cattle
5. Rearing of poultry
6. Carrying a Palaki
7. Keeping a Bhumia partner without providing food
8. Accepting food and water from lower caste person
9. Eating with his wife
10. Having sex with domesticated animals
11. Adultery
12. Getting maggots in the wound and
13. Returning from prison

Though not taken very seriously, it is very degrading if a Bhumia is beaten by a lower caste person, sits with lower caste person and has food and water offered by lower castes. For the last one, they are fined.

Adivasi Social Reforms

Some of the recognized social norms and new social reforms accepted are as follows:

1. In the past, it was compulsory for the groom to bring a fixed number of sarees when he used to come to marry a bride. Now, they have passed a resolution whereby the number of sarees will depend on capability of groom.
2. In the past, it was compulsory to bring musical band and crackers for the marriage party but now it is left to the wishes of groom party.
3. It was also compulsory to provide a fixed number of gift-items during Pair-Puja marriage rituals, but now freedom is given to provide items such as utensils, money, silver ornaments, cattle heads and the like, in keeping with the economic condition of the family.
4. It was also compulsory to throw marriage and funeral feast to the community at fixed time but now relaxation is given. They have made a provision to even fix an amount of money for feast, according to the economic condition of the family.
5. The amount of food grains (Kharachi) paid to the bride's party in marriage by the groom party is stopped and from now onwards both the parties must divide the marriage expenditure equally. Therefore, it is resolved that such issues should not be brought before the Panchayat for discussion.

The above reforms in Bhumia tribal customary laws were adopted in the meeting of Pargana Panchayat on 26th May, 1989.

Certain customary laws pertaining to marriage have not changed. Thus, upon having some illegal sex relations with a non-Bhumia, male members are firstly warned and pardoned. But, if it is repeated then they are heavily fined. In case of a Bhumia girl having involved in sex relation with non-Bhumia, she is excommunicated and is not readmitted during her life time. If her parents allow her to live with them, they are also outcasted until she is driven out of their household.

In case of illegal sex union between two Bhumias they may be compelled to get married. On getting married, a Satya-Narain Katha is arranged and a feast is given. In case of adultery between married partners, both are fined heavily up to ₹ 1,000 and also forced to give a feast. But, the money charged in fine is given to the husband of the involved woman. If he does not accept her as wife after adultery, he may ask for marriage compensation from the responsible man. The amount of compensation is decided by the Pargana Panchayat which must be accepted by both the parties. A non-Bhumia girl is never accepted as wife by the Bhumia society, even if she is a Brahmin girl.

On killing a cow, cat, or dog, the killer is sent for a holy bath in the Narmada and he returns from there after shaving his head. On his return, the house is cleaned and plastered with cow dung. Then a Brahmin priest comes for reciting the Satya Narayan Katha and a feast is arranged for re-admission. A similar punishment is imposed on return from prison and in case of getting maggot in the wound. On getting maggot, the person is outcasted for a period of six months, then on getting cured, other formalities are performed to re-admit him.

The Statutory Panchayat of the Burdagar village also functions in the village and Nandlal Bhumia is a member of the Statutory Panchayat. Here, no case of customary law of Bhumia comes for hearing and decision. This Statutory Panchayat mainly deals with development schemes sponsored by the government, namely digging of wells, installation of hand pump, works undertaken under Jawahar Rojgar Yojna and the like. It also forwards the villagers applications for loan and subsidy. The Bhumia visit Panchayat office for getting tribal certificate, getting signed their loan applications and for such other reason. The Statutory Panchayat also tries to bring political awareness among the Bhumias so that they can attend political meetings in large numbers when local leaders come to address them.

Several attempts were made by the Bhumias to expand their Adivasi identity and unity. We have referred to some such attempts earlier. Following this tradition the educated Bhumias had arranged a large gathering of Bhumias at Jabalpur on 9th June, 1990 and resolved to establish a Bhumia Samaj for the entire community and named it Shri Bhoombanshiya Bhumia Samaj Sewa. It was formed to attain all round development and to bring integration among the Bhumias who are excluded as backward, uneducated and poor. Other resolutions adopted included to develop friendship and coordination with neighbouring people, educate Bhumias and to grab maximum assistance from the government, remove and get rid of social evils, to maintain integration among Bhumias, to help in seeking loans for trades, and enlighten them about job opportunity.

Concluding Observations

The Bhumia derive their etymology from their association with land or Bhumi. They belong to the same stock to which the Bharia and the Baiga belong. Even today at many places of Jabalpur they are known and recognized as Bharia-Bhumia or Baiga-Bhumia. Bhumia who are certainly Baiga, however, do not want to be called by the name Baiga, but prefer the designation Bhumia or Dewar. In due course of time, the Bhumia became Hinduized with the Hindu identity and re-invention of myth which claimed that they originated from the sweat of Lord Shiva, and are the sons of Mata Sati, the elder wife of Lord Shiva. For sometime they claimed to be Rajbanshi or Raghubanshi Gonds by adopting sacred thread. But they again reverted to their Bhumia identity in order to enjoy reservation benefits by forming Shri Bhoombanshiya Bhumia Samaj.

They are divided into two groups, namely Uncha Shreni or pure Bhumias and Nimna Shreni or 'lower-class' who married outside. The urban or roadside Bhumias hesitate in establishing marriage alliances between the two categories. The urban groom prefers to get an urban life partner. There is also differentiation between educated and illiterate Bhumias. Further stratification is noted at the economic level. Among themselves they are differentiated as rich or good farmer, marginal farmer and landless wage earners. On the religious level, they are differentiated as village priest, namely Baiga and sacred specialists such as Dewar and Panda. At the same time by holding traditional offices in tribal councils they are differentiated as Patel, Diwan, Sipahi and Mukhia. It is apparent that stratification has emerged in the Bhumia society due to cultural contacts in the past and economic and political developments at present.

Acknowledgement

Author is grateful to Dr N.K. Das, Project-Coordinator, for his critical comments and guidance during writing of this article.

References

Census of India: *The District Census Hand Book of Jabalpur,* Madhya Pradesh 1971, 1981.

Fuchs, Stephen, 1973, *The Aboriginal Tribes of India.* Delhi: Macmillan.

Russell, R.V. and Hiralal R.B. (1916) *The Tribes and Castes of Central Provinces of India,* London: Macmillan Co. Ltd.

18 Economic Deprivation, Adivasi Solidarity and Syncretic Religion

The Mawasi of Madhya Pradesh

Tamal Maity

The present study aims to elucidate the process of change among the Mawasi Tribe of Madhya Pradesh. To conduct the present anthropological study two villages, namely Khadbeli and Barosa were selected. The Mawasis dominate these two villages. The village Khadbeli is comparatively more exposed than Barosa. Both are located in the Sausar tehsil of Chhindwara district of Madhya Pradesh. After selecting two villages the fieldwork took place in two separate phases (March to April, 1993 and later March to April, 1995). Data were collected following the revised guidelines on stratification supplied by project-coordinator to members of the team. Indeed the group discussion, participant observation and interview were the methods employed for collecting data. Cross-checking was done to avoid confusion and to establish the authenticity of the data. Other than fieldwork data, many secondary sources data were also collected mainly from the Census handbook, district office records, etc. during 1998–1999.

The selection of the villages for investigations was done on the basis of the project guidelines that instructed that the locations should be in a backward area, with very little communication system and where education and economy levels are both very poor, and another village in exposed area where social economic changes have occurred, to gain comparative perspective of changes. Khadbeli is comparatively more exposed than Barosa village. Of the two villages Khadbeli comes under the Sausar block and Barosa comes under Bichuwa Block. Both are located in the Sausar tehsil of Chhindwara district of Madhya Pradesh. After selecting the two villages namely, Khadbeli and Barosa, fieldwork was done in two separate phases till 1995.

The Village: Khadbeli

The village is Mawasi dominated and it comes under Sausar tehsil of Chhindwara district of Madhya Pradesh. The village is nearly 62 km away from the district headquarters, Chhindwara and 20 km from tehsil headquarter's, Sausar. Hilly slopes and undulating lands mostly surround the village. Plain lands are there in the village and outside the village hamlets which are used for cultivation only. Settlement is systematically arranged on both sides of the centrally located road with the habitation of Gauli, Pradhan, Kumhar, Lohar,

Kirar and Gujar communities. The Mawasi have settled down in the outskirts of the village separately which they call Dhana. The Mawasi reside just beside their agricultural fields. They have their huts closest to the hill tracks, forest and river. Hence unlike others they easily procure needs like firewood and water easily.

There are altogether eight different ethnic groups in Khadbeli village. As per self enumeration in field, there are 606 Mawasis of which 308 are males and 298 are females confined in 108 households. Next to Mawasi, the Gauli occupy the second position with a total population of 118. The following table shows the ethnic composition of Khadbeli village:

Table 1

Ethnic Composition of Khadbeli Village

Ethnic groups	*No. of households*	*Male*	*Female*	*Total*
Mawasi (ST)	108	308	298	606
Pardhan (ST)	4	12	6	18
Gauli	40	65	53	118
Mahar (SC)	5	17	5	22
Lohar	4	10	8	18
Kirar	3	10	8	18
Gujar	2	6	4	10
Kumhar	1	3	1	4
Total	167	431	383	814

For the people of Khadbeli, agriculture is the main source of livelihood, irrespective of tribal and non-tribal groups of the village. Other than cultivation, many are engaged as daily wage labour or in construction work. Education is neglected and the overall literacy rate is also not very good.

Barosa

Barosa is also a Mawasi dominated village which comes under the Bichuwa block of Sausar tehsil of Chhindwara district in Madhya Pradesh. It is nearly 75 km away from Chhindwara district and 28 km from the tehsil headquarters in Sausar. The village is fully dominated by two tribes Mawasi and Gond. The Gonds reside in the village but the Mawasi reside on outskirts of the village which they call 'Buddha Dhana'. The composition of population of village Barosa is given in Table 2.

Table 2

Ethnic Composition of the Barosa Village

Ethnic group	*No. of households*	*Male*	*Female*	*Total*
Mawasi	105	315	266	581
Gond	60	192	140	332
Gond Lohar	1	5	3	8
Maratha	2	6	4	10
Kunbi	50	158	102	260
Teli	4	12	8	20
Sonar	4	11	7	18
Lohar	1	3	3	6
Mahar	7	21	11	32
Dhimar	6	22	12	34
Chamar	2	6	3	9
Total	242	751	559	1310

The village has a total population of 1310 and a total of

242 households. Category-wise Mawasi is the dominant tribal population of the village with a total population strength of 581 of which 315 are males and 266 are females residing in total of 105 households. Next to Mawasi the Gond has a total population of 332 of which 192 are males and 140 are females, accommodated in 60 households. In third position is Kunbi, with a total population 260 of which 158 are males and 102 are females residing in 50 households. Educationally the village situation is not promising. It was observed that 50 per cent of the households are illiterate. In the tribal boys hostel there are 20 seats, but only 5 boys are from Mawasi tribe, rest are from the Gond tribe and the Mahar caste.

The People

The Mawasi are an agriculture-based tribe. They claim to be the autochthons of this area and are at present sporadically distributed in the hilly and forested regions of the district of Chhindwara. The people of the area call them Mawasi or Mowasi.

According to Russell and Hiralal (1975), Mawasi is the subdivision of the Korku tribe and the name is sometimes applied to the whole tribe, while the tract of the country where they dwell was formerly known as Mowas. The 1981 Census shows that the Mawasi tribe exists in 22 districts of Madhya Pradesh. The Mawasi tribe of both Khadbeli and Barosa village speak in their own dialect known as Mawasi. According to Russell and Hiralal (1975), the Korku or Mawasi have a language of their own which belongs to the Kolarian or Munda 'subfamily' and they speak among themselves in the Mawasi language only. The Mawasi people also know other languages like Marathi and Hindi. They have learnt Marathi and Hindi from the local people with whom they interact. So long as the forests protected them in isolation, they were in better position to maintain their own linguistic identity as well as cultural traits. But with the deforestation and arrival of outsiders, mainly Marathi and Hindi speaking people, their relative isolation has broken down and linguistic assimilation has also taken place rather easily.

Though the Mawasi and Gond reside in the same village but in terms of social position, the Gond enjoy higher status than the Mawasi. Among the Mawasi two types of political council has been reported. One is traditional and the other is the modern day Statutory Panchayat. The Mawasi community has in every village a Panch headman (Mukhiya) who heads the tribal council. In the modern Panchayat system, the Sarpanch and members are elected from the villages. As regards changes in the authority structure, it has been reported that the position of tribal Chief among the Mawasi is weakening nowadays because of the lack of solidarity. Thus, statutory Village Panchayat has emerged to be a stronger agent of political change.

Social Structure

The Mawasi tribe is an endogamous group and it has no sub-group. There are exogamous clans which regulate their marriage. The exogamous clans of the tribe are as follows:

1. Bethe
2. Dhurve

3. Tekam
4. Weekey
5. Dhiku
6. Sillu
7. Kayeda
8. Bhosam
9. Ban
10. Zamre
11. Darshama
12. Sakum

In Mawasi language the clan is referred as Kul. Among the Mawasi Sillu clan is dominant, followed by is Ban. It is evident that the Mawasi *kul* names have been derived from many natural and other objects without following any definite pattern. The Mawasi form a patrilineal descent group, and they trace their descent through the father's line. They are patrilineal as well as patrilocal community. Being a patrilineal society, male persons enjoy a higher social status than the women. Right of succession also goes along the male line. This is also true in the case of rule of inheritance that is based on male equigeniture while women have no claim over parental property.

The Mawasi call their family as *kutumba*. They prefer to stay in nuclear type of families. However, instances of extended families have also been reported. The interpersonal relations in a family are maintained cordially. Males are the only inheritors who get equal shares of property after the death of the father. Eldest son of the deceased succeeds as head of the family. The inter-family linkages are maintained harmoniously to foster community spirit and integrity. Moreover, the Mawasi prefer to keep their cultivable lands undivided as far as possible. This is because regular distribution of land reduces the size of land to very small plots which is not at all favourable for high productivity. It is thus found that in both Khadbeli and Barosa villages most of the lands belonging to the Mawasi are still undivided though in many cases sons are living in separate houses forming a number of nuclear families. Undivided parental lands are still cultivated mutually and collectively.

The Mawasi generally prefer to live with their kin members. In Khadbeli village 108 households of Mawasi are living in the outskirt of the village keeping a little distance from each other. In Barosa village also 105 households of Mawasi are living, maintaining a distance from other villagers. The kinship ties among the Mawasi are still very strong and they like to maintain kinship solidarity. At the family level, parents-children relationship is cordial and dependable. Though monogamy is the general rule of marriage and negotiation is the mode of acquiring a mate, it has been found that marriage through love affair and marriage by service (lamajhna) are well established customs among Mawasis. The marriageable age for a boy varies from 15 to 25 years and for girl it varies from 13 to 20 years. They have the custom of bride price. The service rendered by the groom for six months or one year before the commencement of marriage is a sort of bride price in kind towards the bride's side. After marriage the married couple stays at the boys house. They observe patrilocal pattern of residence.

Divorce cases are decided by the tribal Panch or the elders of the community. Divorcees and widows who have children are not allowed to remarry. Some changes are introduced and as per new rules the widows are allowed to stay with any widower or divorced aged males. This is done by social sanction. The officiating authority for a marriage ceremony is a sacred specialist who is known as Parchar. He is from the Mawasi community's Sillu clan. Disposal of dead body is by cremation. The corpse is kept on the pyre and the eldest son offers fire to the pyre. On the third day the son of the deceased or the chief mourner offers rice grain, water and pulses. It is known as offering of *kutchcha khana*. On the 12th day, a special ritual is performed by the Parchar. The Parchar collects coconut wine (home made) and a black cock and visits the nearby forest for ritual. Ancestor worship is performed annually.

Apart from performing some roles in rituals of the life cycle events, the women share responsibility in other household and economic activities. Their role in economic pursuits include collection of fuel, fodder and assistance in the agricultural fields during weeding, transplanting and harvesting of crops.

Some changes in the social structure of the Mawasi are visible in both the villages which are as follows:

(i) The average size of the family is becoming smaller than their traditional family size.

(ii) Marriage-worthy age has increased in recent times.

(iii) Cutting down of marriage rituals mainly because of economic inability and increase in marriage expenditure.

(iv) Instead of bride price, now they have shifted to dowry system and this is a noticeable change in recent times.

Overall educational achievement in both the villages is very poor. Education does not seem to find favour with tribal students. Among the Mawasi and Gond only 102 students out of 207 are found in different educational levels. Educationally the village Barosa is not very conscious or promising. It is evident that only out of the 209 student strength of the village secondary school, 83 students belong to the Mawasi and Gond tribe and 18 students are from Scheduled Castes. Thus we get a very gloomy picture. It is observed that one primary school, one secondary school and a tribal Boys' hostel are located in Barosa village. Despite these facilities, attendance of tribal students in the schools is very low. It is observed that there are only two Mawasi male students in tenth standard, and no girl student was found in school from standard I to X. Only one Mawasi boy was found X standard passed. In the tribal boy's hostel there are 20 boy's seats, out of them only five Mawasi boys are staying in the hostel, rest are from Gond tribe and Mahar caste. It is observed that in the school of Khadbeli village, there are more tribal students studying than Barosa village, though there are more facilities in Barosa for the tribal children. No girl child goes to school in Barosa. This is due to lack of contacts of tribal parents with outsiders or other ethnic population.

The Mawasi traditionally are known for their agricultural economy and also for hunting. But because of the Wildlife Prevention Act, hunting has been banned by the government. So the Mawasi now depend on land as their main economic resource. They completely depend on agriculture and working as agricultural labour. Agriculture is the main economic pursuit in both Khadbeli and Barosa villages. Some families have no land but majority of the Mawasi households have two acres of land, though it is not enough as yields procured are hardly enough for six months. Hence the Mawasis continue to depend on forests because they collect firewood and some other minor produce, for self-consumption, from the forest. Since, this area is dry and has hill tracks they only depend on rain water in the monsoon season for their agriculture. Their main occupation is agriculture and subsidiary occupation is agricultural labour, firewood collection and sale to the nearest market, leaves collection and basket making. The women are equally involved in agricultural operations. Practically, the women spend very little time doing cooking and other activities and they are engaged more in agricultural activities with their male folk. Little girls from the age group of 12 to 14 usually take care of the house, leaving their mothers free from the pressure of daily household activities. The labourers of both Khadbeli and Barosa villages get their wages on daily basis which is not regulated by any government approved rates and often vary from one place to another. Payments for agricultural work may be made either in cash or kind and sometimes in both, depending upon the contract made between the landowner and the labourers. They have some rules regarding transfer of land and other resources. After the separation of joint family the Mawasi people now go to the revenue inspector, who separates their land.

The religious beliefs of the Mawasi is a blend of their traditional tribal form of religion and Hinduism. They call family deity as Kuldevi, which is a form of Shakti (power). Apart from this, they have Kothdeo (boundary god), Mahadeo, Matadevi, Kaladeo, etc. Some of the Hindu gods and goddesses worshipped by them are Shankar, Parvati; Panch Pandava, Satidevi, etc. Parehar (sacred specialist) is from their own community. Various festivals are observed by the Mawasi of both Khadbeli and Barosa such as Nagpanchami, Diwali, Sankranti, Holi, Akshaya Tritiya, Dussehra, Mahasivaratri, etc.

Labour Organization and Statutory Council

There are two types of labour system in these two villages, namely Barsutia (permanent field servant) and Dharki (daily labour). The Barsutia must be ready to do not only fieldwork, but also to go to the forest to cut trees and for other timber work. The contract with a Barsutia is usually made for one year. He is given an annual payment between ₹ 1,200 to ₹ 1,500. The money is often given to him in advance, or in regular instalments. The other system is called Dharki. Dharki means occasional daily labour, the wages of which are paid either in the evening or on the bazaar day. Women and adult children too are employed as dharkis especially during the weeding and harvesting seasons. The Mawasi of both the villages are in direct contact with the weekly markets and now there is no middleman between the buyers and sellers. The Mawasi prepare baskets and collect leaves and some other produce from forest. They sell their products in the market and after selling their goods, they purchase their daily needs on the same spot instantly.

Traditional political system of the Mawasi prevails and customary laws are respected. However, the modern statutory council also plays important role. The traditional system of authority structure comprises a village chief who is elected by voice vote. The Mawasi community in every village has a tribal Panch headman (Mukhiya) and they have their own tribal council. At the level of cluster of five or six villages the Mawasis have a Jat Patel. Women are restricted from attending a Panch meeting unless they are called to give a statement. In the modern Panchayat system, the Sarpanch is elected by the villagers. All the general function and village development work are administered by him and his council. Some changes are noted in authority structure. Because of demands of modern politics the statutory council and its members play major role. The Statutory Village Panchayat has emerged to be a stronger agent of political consolidation. Gram Panchayat consists of nine elected members of whom one post is for the Sarpanch, one is for Up-sarpanch and rest are the elected members of the body. The Sarpanch of Barosa Gram Panchayat is Baliram Sillu, who belongs to the Mawasi community. It may be stated that despite small landholding and lesser educational achievement, the Mawasi have acquired a comfortable status in both villages because of hardwork and economic diversification and forest-produce collection.

Since the Mawasi elites have come to occupy some positions in Statutory councils, it is possible for the common tribespeople to have access to development programmes. Various developmental schemes initiated through Gram Panchayat for the rural people are Indira Awas Yojna under which they are provided built houses for the homeless persons; Integrated Rural Development Programme (IRDP) scheme under which IRDP card holders are given saree, dhoti, goat and support for launching grocery shop, pump set for irrigation, cycle repairing shop, sewing machine, etc. Like other villagers, the Mawasi avail these facilities at 50 per cent subsidized rate and by arranging 50 per cent loan facilities from the banks. Samaj Kalyan, Gobar Gas, Jawahar Rozgar Yogona, Jivandhara Yojana, Adivasi Upo Yojana, Adivasi Yojona, etc., are some important welfare and developmental measures undertaken through the Gram Panchayat office.

Level of Stratification

As per existing oral tradition the Mawasi and Nahal are sub-tribes of Korku tribe. The Mawasi however claim themselves to be of a higher position than Korku and Nahal. They deny their identity as a sub-group of Korku and claim a distinct identity as Mawasi because Korku is a derogatory term for them. The Mawasi have twelve exogamous clans which regulate their marriage alliances. Among the 12 clans 'Sillu' is the dominant clan in the villages of Khadbeli and Barosa. They have a total of 40 and 74 households respectively. Naturally there are more persons in the Sillu clan with higher average landholding (average two acres of land). Because of economic dominance of 40 and 74 Mawasi households in Khadbeli and Barosa respectively these households also play crucial role in social control, and the decision-making power is concentrated in the Sillu clan. Elders of Sillu clan are influential among all tribes and castes. Hence, an elder of this clan became Sarpanch of Barosa village.

Fieldwork reveals that Mawasi speak among themselves in Mawasi language. However, economically rich Mawasi also know other languages like

Marathi and Hindi. They have learnt Marathi and Hindi languages from local people or people with whom they have modern socio-economic interaction. The Mawasi children have also learnt Marathi from school.

Because of better land-holding the literacy rate is better in Khadbeli village in comparison to Barosa. Barosa Mawasis are not very conscious educationally even though there is a tribal boy's hostel situated in Barosa. Despite such a facility few Mawasis attend school. It is found that more children attend up to primary level while in higher classes the student strength is less. During fieldwork only two students were in Class X and one in Class IX. There were three students in Class VIII. No girl student goes to school. Mawasi parents say that they prefer to send their children for working in the field than sending to school. A son can earn money as daily wage labour in the agriculture field. It may be argued that due to poor economic condition parents are not sending their children to school.

The Mawasi live in multi-ethnic villages. In different villages distinct inter-ethnic relations are observed. Since most households among Mawasi have about two acres of land they are forced to work as agricultural labour followed by forest work, road construction or house construction work and so on. Men and women both are engaged as wage labour. They also collect leaves (patta) from the forest and prepare thali or plates at home and sell in the market directly. The Mawasi people are also engaged in basket-making work. They are often employed as daily wage labourer in the fields of Gond, Gauli Kunbi and Maratha people in the village or outside the village during agricultural season. There are poor families among Gond, Kunbi and Maratha. But members of these communities do not work as daily wage labour in the Mawasi agriculture fields since Mawasis are ranked below the other communities in the village social hierarchy.

Concepts of pollution and purity are not important for Mawasi as they are not integral to Hindu caste-system. The Mawasi retain the Adivasi identity. However, other communities regard them 'lower' and do not dine with them. Mawasi accept cooked food and water from Gond and Gond Lohar only. The latter also accept the same from the Mawasi. However, Mawasi do not accept any cooked food from the rest of the village communities even if any Mawasi happens to work in the house of such community. The Mawasi accept only the wage in cash or kind but never cooked food. The Mawasi are never invited during marriages in the houses of other communities excepting Gond and Gond Lohar. This sort of status-distinction does not apply in public places where the Mawasi, Maratha, Kunbi, Teli, Sonar etc., are found taking tea and snacks together in the market.

Economic Deprivation and Evolving Livelihood Pattern

The Mawasi are traditionally known for their agricultural economy and hunting. Hunting was banned by the government with the passing of the Wildlife Prevention Act. So the Mawasi preferred to depend on land as their main economic resource, earning a living from agricultural activities. As land-holding is not enough majority of Mawasis depend on agricultural labour in both Khadbeli and Barosa. They also depend on forests because they collect firewood from the forest. They also depend on various secondary or subsidiary work such as forest work, road, construction work, house repairing work, basket making, collecting firewood for selling in the market, etc.

The Mawasi, specially in Khadbeli village, are economically comfortable as they possess good quality of land. It is also a fact that Khadbeli is more advanced in adapting to modern agricultural technology due to more outside exposure in comparison to Barosa village. Khadbeli is in a position to grow both Kharif and Rabi crops while Barosa village exclusively depends upon Kharif crops as there is lack of irrigation facilities.

The workers of both Khadbeli and Barosa villages get their wages on a daily basis. These rates are not always government regulated and often vary from one place to another. In Khadbeli, wages for male labourers for agricultural work during those days was ₹ 15 to 20 per day while for the females it is usually ₹ 10 to 15, besides a mid-day meal offered to all the labourers irrespective of sex. In both the villages, payment for agricultural work was made either in cash or kind and sometimes in both, depending upon the contract made between the landowner and the labourers. However, during the peak agricultural season when the deployment of extra labour force is essential, wage rate used to be increased up to ₹ 5 more than normal wages. For any kind of labour work, working hours are roughly 8 hours starting from 8 am or 8.30 am to 5 pm or 5.30 pm with a break of half an hour for mid-day meal. There are also some other types of work for which remuneration is paid on contract basis, e.g., digging of well, levelling of land, canal work, carpentry work related to making household structure with logs and woods, etc. Skilled labourers earn better wages than unskilled labourers. Agricultural labourers are treated as unskilled labour. In both the villages, black soil is considered as best in quality, suitable for all types of cultivation including paddy cultivation. But because of the hilly topography of villages, lands are mostly undulating, red in colour with a combination of small stone chips and basically infertile. So the flat lands are very limited in both the villages, specially in Barosa village.

The local people, including the tribals now pay land revenue directly to the government tehsildar incharge of a taluk. A number of such taluks are administered by a Sub-divisional officer who in turn reports to the Collector in charge of a District. Individual families control the resources of land.

Two types of land are found in these villages, namely Barha or low quality land and the other is Unhari Jamin of better quality. The production of crops in Unhari Jamin on an acre of land is about half quintal to one and a half quintal of crop in a year. The crops produced in a year are mainly jowar, thar, and in the rainy season it is paddy. Except these the other products are Kodo, Sana, Macca and Urda (Barbati). There is no agricultural production in the Rabi season, due to lock of irrigation facilities. Agriculture starts from April or May and continues till the months of October–November.

Mawasi mostly use the traditional method for cultivation. They use cow-dung as fertilizer in their fields. Apart from this nowadays they also use fertilizers, insecticides and weedkillers such as urea, aluminum sulphate and 18,180 khad. Of course, a majority of Mawasis are not able to use them due to their poor economic condition. They can use these only when government provides them with seeds, fertilizers and medicines free of cost.

Social Organization

The Mawasi call their family as kutumba. They prefer nuclear type of families. However, instances of extended families have also been reported. The interpersonal relations in a family are maintained cordially. Males are the only inheritors who get equal shares of property after the death of the father. Eldest son of the deceased succeeds as head of the family. However, the Mawasi prefer to keep their cultivable lands undivided as long as possible, since, regular distribution of land reduces the size of land to a very small plot which is not at all favourable for high productivity. It is thus in both Khadbeli and Barosa villages that most of the lands belonging to the Mawasi are still undivided though in many cases sons are living in separate houses forming nuclear families but undivided parental lands are cultivated collectively. Land is still a very important factor in maintaining the emotional bond among brothers and other members of family.

Table 3

Types of Family in Khadbeli

Types of family	*No. of households*	*Total*
Nuclear (0–4) (5–9)	28; 38	66
Joint (0–5) (6–10)	13; 24	37
Extended (6–10) (11 & above)	3; 2	5
Total	108	108

Table 4

Types of Family in Barosa

Types of family	*No. of households*	*Total*
Nuclear (0–4) (5–9)	34; 31	65
Joint (0–5) (6–10)	5; 28	33
Extended (6–10) (11 & above)	2; 5	7
Total	105	105

It is evident from the above tables that in the two separate villages, separate types of families are found. In both the villages nuclear families dominate. The increase in nuclear family is noticed due to a number of reasons such as: (1) disintegration of families because of economic dispute and mal-adjustment of the housewives and (2) shortage of space in the living room, as it is very inconvenient to accommodate more people under a single roof.

Other than land and some domestic animals specially cow, bullock, oxen, goat and buffaloes, the Mawasi do not posses any other valuable material items in general. So, land and cattle constitute the most valuable items of the Mawasi properties.

In both the villages, distribution of property is mutually settled among the Mawasi and never became a very complicated issue. All the undivided lands are jointly cultivated with mutual understanding among the brothers, though many have their own independent family units and are not living in a joint family. The Mawasi prefer to live with their tribespeople. In Khadbeli village thus all 108 households live in the outskirts of the village side by side. In Barosa village also, 105 households of Mawasi are live separately from core village.

Mechanism of Social Control

Among the Mawasi, as we have discussed above, traditional tribal council and modern statutory village council prevail. There are tribal headmen who play role in village and beyond village. The traditional system of authority structure comprises a village chief who is elected by voice vote. The Mawasi village has a Panch headman (Mukhiya) and circle of five or six villages is under the charge of a Jat Patel. It is the task of the Mukhiya to settle all tribal disputes in his jurisdiction, to punish or ex-communicate any member who offends the tribal norms and regulations. Women are debarred from attending a Panch meeting unless they are called to give a statement. In the modern Panchayat system, the Sarpanch is elected from the villagers. He looks after all the affairs of the village. All the general village development works are looked after by him and his Gram-Panchayat. The Gram Sevak is the official associated with the Gram Panchayats at the village level. Other than the Gram Sevak, the Gram Panchayat consists of nine members including one Sarpanch and one Up-sarpanch, who are elected for a tenure of five years. In Khadbeli village out of nine members, four members are Mawasis and the rest belong to Gauli, Mahar and Teli. Like Khadbeli Gram Panchayat, Barosa Gram Panchayat also consists of nine elected members of which one post is that of Sarpanch; one is for Up-sarpanch and rest are the elected members of the body. The Sarpanch of Barosa Gram Panchayat is Baliram Sillu, a Mawasi.

Gram Panchayat undertakes welfare and development works. Gram Panchayat is not responsible for social control. The main functions performed by the Gram Panchayat are maintenance of drinking water facilities and streetlights, allotment of land to landless persons for the construction of new houses, drainage system, distribution of clothes, agricultural accessories, seeds and agricultural machinery through various schemes, providing loan facilities through banks, adult education, giving information regarding family planning, etc. Various developmental schemes initiated through Gram Panchayat for the rural people are 'Indira Awas Yojana' under which shelter is built for homeless persons, IRDP scheme under which IRDP card holders are given saree, dhoti, goat, grocery shop, pump set for irrigation, cycle repairing shop, sewing machine, etc., loan facilities from banks. Samaj Kalyan, Gobar Gas, Jawahar Rozgar Yojana, Jiwandhara Yojana, Adivasi Up-Yojana, Adivasi Yojana, Rozgar Hami Yojana, etc., are some other important welfare and developmental measures undertaken through the Gram Panchayat.

Madhya Pradesh government has introduced the office of the village Patil, now called as Police Patil in all the villages of Madhya Pradesh. The statutory Patil enjoys considerable power that is bestowed by the District Collector for the maintenance of law and order in the villages. Now, all the villagers irrespective of caste or tribe are directly brought under the Police Patil, a village headman holding a statutory post. The villager for this post is selected by the District Collector and the tenure of the post depends upon the efficiency of the Police Patil. The Police Patil is responsible for looking after all village matters and problems irrespective of castes and communities. The post is prestigious, and very important too. Every incident, either social or criminal should be brought to the knowledge of the Police Patil. Recommendation of any case to the police or to any other judicial authority, can be done by the Police Patil only. Police Patil is also responsible for settling all disputes whether inter-community or intra-community. At present, for any kind of offence, punishment is usually cash fine and there is no question of excommunication. Besides the Police Patil,

Sarpanch being an elected member of the Gram Panchayat also enjoys some powers to settle minor socio-cultural disputes in consultation with the Police Patil.

Religious Conversion and Syncretic Practices

The religion of the Mawasi is a blend of their traditional tribal form of religion and some level of Hinduism. In day to day life of the Mawasi villagers, the tribal religion prevails. Thus in every family Mawasi worship Kuldevi, which is a form of shakti (power). Apart from this, they have Kothdeo (boundary god), Mahadeo, Matadevi, Kaladeo, etc. Some of the Hindu gods and goddesses are being worshipped by them. They are Shankar Parvati, Panch Pandava, Satidevi, etc. They worship Bhimsen on Chaitpurnima day, Nagdevi on Nagpanchami day and Matadai in the month of Chait. On the new moon night of Shravan (August) popularly known as Hariyali Amabasya a religious rite is performed. The tribal priest Parehar (sacred specialist) is the officiating authority. He ties a pig with a piece of rope and runs in the village area. The Parehar continues his run to distant places where the pig's grunt is heard, till the pig dies. This ritual is aimed at freeing the village from ghosts. After that he encircles the village and chants hymns. The pig is then slaughtered by the Parehar and offered to members of tribe. The sacred centre which they visit annually is Mahadeo Cave at Raghodevi. On the day of Pitarpaksh Amabasrya, they perform ancestor worship and pay visit to Deola. They worship in front of the memorial post, which is the symbolic representation of dead ancestors.

So, though the Mawasis are not Hindu by religion, the process of Hinduization set in tribal areas, hence the Mawasi were regarded as Hindu. The Mawasi however continue to have strong faith on supernatural powers, tribal gods, dead souls, ghost and witchcraft. Among Mawasi male witch is called Bhutara and female witch is known as Bhutari. The services of the Bhagats (religious mendicants) are still very much sought after as they drive out the bad and evil spirits. They also perform many socio-religious functions including the appeasement of dead spirits. Earlier, among the Mawasi, witches were usually beaten or burnt to death but they can not do that now due to stringent legal provisions. Now, the government is using the media to try to develop consciousness about the non-existence of the witch and to prevent harassment of women. But the Mawasi of both the villages still believe in witches though they usually do not assault any person on the suspicion of being a witch. Now, they simply consult their Bhagat to get rid of witchcraft and go for remedial ritualistic performances including worship and sacrifice.

Development Programmes and the Tribe

There are several schemes of development which are meant for all villagers. The Mawasi try to avail some benefits from these schemes. There are some programmes which are meant for tribals. Thus the Mawasi are in a position to avail economic assistance from various sources. Through Gram Panchayat or Block office the tribal people are getting hybrid seeds, high yielding seeds, agricultural implements, cattle, chemical fertilizer, pump sets of irrigation for their socio-economic development at the subsidized rates and also free of costs. Under the Jawahar Rozgar Yojana, Anti-poverty and Jivan Dhara schemes, total 4 bore wells were provided for those who have some land upto 6 acres while 50 per cent subsidy was granted to 4 tribal farmers for purchasing pump sets and bullock cart under the Adivasi Up-Yojana scheme. The IRDP is another scheme under which 50 per cent subsidy and 50 per cent bank loans are offered to the all IRDP card holders.

Madhya Pradesh State Tribal Development department has launched several major schemes for the betterment of tribals, namely: (1) Monopoly procurement, (2) Consumption finance, (3) General activities, (4) Dwar Vitaran Yojana; and (5) Nuclear budget schemes. The Mawasis reported that they could not get adequate assistance from these schemes. In Barosa village under the 'Nuclear Budget Scheme' a total of six Mawasi persons were given some development facilities in the year 1991–92 and a total of ₹ 24,000 was spent for procuring three pairs of bullocks, one bullock cart, one sewing machine, five female goats and one male goat and one grocery shop. The Nuclear Budget Scheme comes under Adivasi Up-yojana, run by the Madhya Pradesh State Tribal Development Department. Under this Nuclear Budget Scheme, 50 per cent of the total value of an article is provided by the Tribal Development Department while the remaining 50 per cent of the total value is made available by the TDC from banks as loan, to be repaid by the beneficiaries in instalments.

It is true that the overall economic condition of the Mawasi is gradually improving specially in Khadbeli village though not so rapidly in Barosa village because of so many unfavourable conditions. With the introduction and implementation of the modern knowledges in the fields of agro-based economy, noticeable change is visible in the agricultural operations, specially in Khadbeli village. The Mawasis of Khadbeli could procure pump sets, bore wells and many other modern accessories and thus could get more than one crop in the same agricultural calendar year in Khadbeli.

Conclusion

The Mawasis have shown the typical characters of central Indian Adivasi societies who came to be influenced variously by the Hindu castes and Hindu practices. Like elsewhere in Adivasi regions, the Mawasis are accorded a low position in local social hierarchy and through culture-contacts they came to adopt many elements of Hinduism and blend them with tribal religion in syncretic manner (Das, 2003). Some sections of Mawasi tribe used modern agricultural methods in exposed village and improved their status. Education also helped them. Many Mawasi families in both exposed and interior villages remained economically deprived as they had no land and development programmes could not be availed by them.

References

Das, N.K. 2003, 'An Outline of Syncretism', in *Culture, Religion and Philosophy: Critical Studies in Syncretisms and Inter-Faith Harmony*. N.K. Das (Ed.). Jaipur: Rawat Publications.

Russell, R.V. and R.B. Hiralal 1975, *The Tribes and Castes of Central India*, New Delhi: Inter-India Publication.

19 Sectarian Movements, Changing Economic Relations and Inequality

The Dungri and Talat Warlis of Gujarat

Rajendra Sarkar

The Warli Identity and Demography

The Varlis or Warlis inhabit the southernmost part of Gujarat. Some historians have traced the origin of word Varli (Warli). Maratha historian Rajwade describes the word 'Varud', mentioned in Philosopher Katyayan's treatise Vartikas, thus: Varud – Varudaki – Varulai or Varuli and finally Varali. He believes Warlis to be a tribe of non-Aryan origin who lived near the Vindhya and Satpura ranges from where they moved southwards. Dr Willson states, "Varlis, probably originally 'Varalis' or uplanders gave the name 'Varalat' to the sixth of the seven Konkanas" (Save, 1945: 4). He further writes, that the word 'Varal' means a tilled patch of land, and those who cultivated these were called Varalis. Enthoven has described Varalis as a sub-division of Bhils – who are found not only in Khandesh in considerable numbers but also in the northern part of Gujarat. In the present day, Warlis are found not only in Gujarat, but also in the adjoining state of Maharashtra and the Union territories of Dadra, Nagar Haveli and Daman & Diu. All these areas of major Warli concentration were part of the erstwhile Bombay presidency. The southern part of Gujarat especially Valsad or Bulsar – the original home of the Warlis was a part of Maharashtra which came over to Gujarat due to the reorganization of states on 1, June 1964.

It can be seen from the table below that the maximum concentration of the Warlis (89.59%) is in Valsad (Bulsar) district of Gujarat, followed by Dangs (10.07%) an adjoining district. A further analysis of the demographic figures of the Valsad district reveals that approximately 90 per cent of the Varli population of the district is concentrated in Dharampur (60.32%) taluka. As such this could be termed as the Varli heartland of Gujarat. Their habitat, like the majority of other tribal habitats, lies in the forest and hilly terrains of Kumbghat, Mohgadh, Luheri, Peria, Bopi, Gar, Pilao, Nimno, Astol, Kastol and Wilson hillocks to name a few. These mountainous regions are quite rocky, undulating, covered with thick forests, and requires lot of human effort and struggle for existence. The Warli villages are heterogeneous, but the falias (hamlets) within the villages are homogeneous. The other tribal populations living in or near the Warli villages are Kohna and Kolcha. One can also find a sprinkling of communities belonging to other castes residing near their conglomerations. These people are either government field staff, shopkeepers or an occasional doctor, who have come to serve them.

Social Divisions

Population: Warlis in Gujarat

District	*Population*	*Percentage*
Banaskantha	06	—
Bharuch	10	00.01
Dangs	12,688	10.07
Mahesana	02	—
Panchmahal	210	00.16
Sabarkantha	06	—
Surat	173	00.14
Vadodara (Baroda)	38	00.03
Valsad (Bulsar)	1,12,975	89.59
Total: Gujarat State	1,26,108	100.00

The Warlis are divided into two main divisions, the Dungris and the Talatis. Dungri Warlis are the ones who live in the remote forest areas on the hill slopes and are economically and educationally backward, whereas Talat Warlis are one who live in plain areas and are better off both economically and educationally than their brethren. Talat Warlis are mostly found near the urban conglomeration of Dharampur, Valsad, Sansda, Chikli, Pardi and Umbergaon and are also referred as Naikas. Socially too, the Talatis rank superior to the Dungris on account of their better economic position. It has already been stated that Talatis are inhabitants of the plains area. The Talatis own good quality land. Due to fertile soil, the Talatis reap a good harvest of crop twice a year, resulting in more surplus and a good earning. Besides, a good income from agriculture has also helped them to send their children for education. Their proximity to the urban centres have also brought them in contact with outsiders, thereby widening their world-view, and raising their social status vis-à-vis, other Warlis.

Clans: Warlis are divided into approximately 144 exogamous kuls (clans), the names of many of which they hardly remember. R.E. Enthoven (1920) however mentions 24 such clans or kuls. These kuls are named after their *vadeels* (ancestors), trees, birds, animals, etc. All the kuls are equal in status. Some of the kuls like Bhoya, Gavit, Jadav, Mahla, Powar, Bamne are common to the Kolcha, Kokna and Warli tribes. These tribes however maintain distinct identities.

The Warlis now establish marital alliance with the Koknas. This is on account of better economic and social status of the Koknas. Among these three tribes the Kokna and Warli are regarded as higher and the Kolcha regarded as lower in local hierarchy. The Koknas can accept a bride from the Warlis and Kolcha, but a Warli can accept the bride only from the Kolcha.

The Warlis are divided into several religious and sectarian segments. A few of the Warlis who have accepted the Christian faith are known as Is-wale Warlis, and such converts have no 'roti' (food, i.e., commensal) or 'beti' (matrimonial), relation or vyavhar (ties) with the non-Christian Warlis. They are a sort of excommunicated members from the original stock. Other sectarian sections include the adherents of Tulsipuala sect, Dandavat or Mahanubhav and Sanatan Dharmi panth. There exists a segment of original Warlis pursuing their tribal religion. The adherents of the sectarian sections rank superior to the non-adherents for they have become vegetarians and teetotallers and observe cleanliness in their daily life, whereas the non-sectarians continue with their traditional way of life. Two other sects namely the Maksha and the Gangasagar sects are also in existence among the Warlis, but have yet to gain momentum. These sects also functions as marriage regulating groups.

The Warlis regard marriage as essential for every young man and woman of the village. It is believed that bachelors on death become *khains* (ghost) and similarly spinsters become 'hedri' (witches). Monogamy is the prevalent mode of acquiring a mate, but a few cases of polygamy are also witnessed. A study conducted on the Warlis reveals that 95 per cent marriages are monogamous, whereas 5 per cent marriages are polygamous.

Marriage is prohibited between members of the same kul (clan). Parallel and cross-cousin marriages are prohibited. However, alliance between children of maternal uncle and paternal sisters are quite common. A man may marry two sisters, the first married being the senior wife. They seldom look for a match beyond the limits of a taluka, and matches are often settled within a commutable distance.

According to the Warli custom of Nanipen, the Warli boy and girl may start living together without being formally married, and can also raise a family. Such type of arrangements are resorted to when the boy is unable to pay bride price (daja) to the girl at the time of marriage on account of poverty, but no sooner is he in a position to pay the bride price, he must pay it and get married to get a social approval to their relationship. The bride price (daja) is to be paid in cash which ranged from ₹ 150 to 600, besides a certain amount of food grain, i.e., dangar, nagli, tuvar or urad. The food grains are given basically to meet the additional food expenditure. The Warlis mostly get married by arranged marriage, but there are other forms of marriage also, like marriage by service, exchange, elopement and intrusion, which are not of common occurrence. In marriage by service, the boy serves the prospective father-in-law for a period of five years, and thus pays the bride price through his services. This is called as 'bartaney' among them. Marriage by exchange (sate vate) is resorted to between two families who exchange brother and sister as husband and wife. Since there is exchange of girls in the families, no payment of bride price is involved. Marriage by elopement, though rare, occurs when the boy and girl develop a liking for each other. The duo elope from the village and secretly get married. They later return to the village after some days. The Panchayat is convened, which fines the boy and he is also made to pay the bride price. Marriage by intrusion (ghar-ghusili) is a system wherein a girl forcibly goes to stay in the boys house, and forces him to marry her.

This happens mostly in cases where a girl conceives, as a result of premarital relations, but the boy refuses to marry her. Divorce (short-chitti) is recognized among the Warlis, and is effected by their Panchayat. The common grounds of divorce are maladjustment, selling cereals to shopkeeper for liquor or infidelity. The Patels and Kharbari are authorized to conduct the divorce proceedings. This takes place in presence of both the parents and their relatives. Both the parties hold alcohol in khakra leaves and a Kolki (wooden-stick) is broken into two pieces by the Patel or Kharbhari, which signifies that henceforth the marital bond between the two partners which was as strong as the Kolki stick is now broken. They then pour some alcohol around and drink the rest and depart after wishing each other, connoting that they hold no ill will against each other. The expenses of the Panchayat is borne by the party wishing to obtain divorce. Fines are levied by the Panchayat, which is paid to the opposite party.

A divorcee can remarry. Widow or widower remarriage is also practised. A widow (randki) is obliged to marry her deceased husband's younger brother. This is known as Mohtur. Such type of marriages has a socio-economic rationale to it. Firstly, the working hand available in the house is not lost and secondly the expenses which the family will have to incur subsequently for bride price, etc., for the younger son's marriage is saved.

Family: Members of one family share a common roof and a hearth. A survey of the Warli family revealed a dominance of nuclear families (57.27%); which consists of the couple (husband and wife) and their unmarried children over that of extended (37.27%) families and other families (5.45%).

Frequency and Percentage of Warli Family

Type of family	*Family frequency*	*Family percentage*	*Population*		
			Male	*Female*	*Total*
Nuclear	63	57.27	179	180	359
Extended	41	37.27	138	159	297
Others	06	5.45	05	04	09
Total	110	99.99	322	343	665

The extended family consists of nuclear families with their parents, brothers and sisters and the other families consist of members who are either widow or widower living separately or living with their unmarried children. In most cases the members of a family live together in a joint or extended family, to prevent the fragmentation of land. Further, the rough topography, the adverse climatic conditions also necessitate their living together. Some Warlis said that splitting of the family has been because of the economic necessity, so that individual families can move out for other economic pursuits.

The property is divided equally among all sons irrespective of the number of wives. Girls have no traditional right in the parents property. In case of debt on a family, it is the joint responsibility of all brothers to repay the loan. Adoption is resorted to in very exceptional case, when all their efforts to have a natural heir fail, sometimes even by marrying more than one wife. The children of the nearest relatives that is father's brother's children or brother's children are adopted and accepted as ones own and the right of inheritance devolves to the adopted child. The Warli women enjoy equal status as that of men. A women also enjoys the freedom to divorce her husband on relevant grounds. In all such cases she has to return the bride price as also the expenditure of marriage, but more often it is paid by her paramour who is the main cause for divorce. She has the right to bring up the children. As a mother and custodian of the house, she does all household work, cleans the house, cooks food, besides sometimes also collecting fuel for the hearth.

In the economic sphere the woman does all agricultural activities except ploughing. She also works as agricultural labour and horticulture labour, and thus contributes to the meagre family income. The women take part in all social and religious ceremonies. While the male deities are revered and propitiated by the Warli men, the female goddesses Hinay and Kansari are objects of worship by women only.

In the field of politics, the women traditionally did not have any say nor ever had a representation in tribal Panchayat. In the modern statutory Panchayats, it is made mandatory to have representation of two Scheduled Tribe or Scheduled Caste women members through elections.

According to the 1981 Census figures, only 42.30 per cent of the Warli population were returned as workers. More than a decade later, a sample survey of the Warli villages returned 48.2 per cent as workers in 1991. Among them 44.8 per cent were doing self-cultivation and 51.9 per cent were agricultural labour. The other occupations pursued by Warlis are service (2.8%) and 0.6 per cent in teaching. These statistics confirm that Warlis are primarily agriculturists. Traditionally, they did not enjoy rights over land for cultivation. Rather it was owned by non-tribals, who encroached land in these areas, and forced tribals to work as labourers.

A glance at the data on land possession of the Warli reveals that only 25.45 per cent of the households possess land, and out of these 75 per cent have land in between 1–10 acres. These figures are in sharp contrast to the population directly engaged in agriculture. This discrepancy is on account of the fact that as long as the father remains alive, the land remains in his name, as Warlis used to live in a joint family. After the death of the father the land automatically gets transferred in the name of the elder son on official records, even though the respective share in land might have been actually in possession of the individual brothers; who would have separated from the family in nuclear homes.

Some Warlis who do not own land on their own take sir-pattar (fallow land) on lease from the forest department for a particular agricultural season. Others work as tenants of bigger landlords in the area, namely the Koknas. These tenant cultivators are known as 'bathe', and ordinarily half the yield of the crop is to be paid to the landowner as lease rent. The entire expenditure for cultivation is borne by the tenant except the cesses on land, which is paid by the owner.

The area of cultivable land available along with irrigation facilities is only 552 acres (0.11%) of the total of 4,03,908 acres of land in Dharampur taluka – the heartland of the Warlis. The figures of the taluka is quite revealing. Of the total land area of the taluka, 1,40,058 acres fall into the category of uncultivable land, being without irrigational facility, 1,74,901 acres under forest, 29,659 acres as cultivable but barren land and 58,738 acres as uncultivable. Since the land available for agriculture is meagre, the terrain is rocky and heavy rainfall results in soil erosion, hence the life of the Warlis is miserable and full of struggle. These factors and their indigenous mode of farming, lead to poor yield and deficit of food supply. The local Warlis as well as the government have failed to conserve the rain water for irrigation purposes, making the area a single crop area.

Due to deficit production and less opportunity for employment as agricultural labour, the only alternative left for the tribals is to migrate to the adjoining region of Maharashtra to work in vine groves or in cutting grass of the rich Gujarati Seths during the lean agricultural months, to add to their meagre source of income. They also resort to procuring loans from traders in kind, especially food grains on deferred payment with interest. Foodgrain is in great demand

and is essentially needed for the survival of the family. This reason alone accounts for 30 per cent of the loans, other reasons being loan for cattle (28%), agriculture (18%), social and religious ceremonies (17%) and miscellaneous (7%) which includes loans for medical treatment, house construction, etc. These loans are provided by traders, moneylenders, relatives, co-operatives, etc.

In majority of the cases the agricultural land stands as a surety, which is mortgaged to a tribal relative in case loan is procured from them, otherwise benami transaction of land takes place. Another method is that the land actually remains in the name of the tribal but it is used by the money-lender. Thus, the tribal in fact works on his own land as agricultural labour; this results in alienation.

As a consequence of this, the already poor becomes poorer because inequality among the landlord and sharecropper keeps growing larger and larger.

The government has enacted a number of legislative measures, which has helped prevent the alienation of tribal land to a great extent, but still quite a number of cases of disguised misuse of tenancy laws do exist.

"The fear of the supernatural is the key to the Warli religion", says a Warli schoolteacher. Their gods and goddesses are deeply associated with their lives, their animal wealth, their land and their produce. Cosmogenic and natural phenomenon such as sun, moon, earth, cloud, winds, lightening, etc., are considered divine. Cow is held in reverence. Other animals like snake and tiger are also propitiated on a day set aside for them in the Warli calendar, for they are considered harmful. Besides, certain trees are also held in reverence and are considered sacred for the Warlis.

The principal Warli deities are Naran Dev, Hirva, Kansari and Himai. Naran Dev is especially worshipped by the people of the Nimbara clan, for he is their clan deity and is identified with Lord Satyanarayan of the Hindu caste people. He is considered a male and is represented by either a stone or a supari (arecanut), besmeared with red powder, and is placed along with other deities in a basket filled with paddy, fastened to the wall on a wooden pole. Naran Dev is worshipped on all religious ceremonies but a special ceremony is held in his honour in the month of magh (February). Quinquennially, a special festival is also held in his honour after sowing of paddy, in which a he-goat is sacrificed and the entire village feasts. Naran Dev is believed to be born of a bamboo shoot, and hence bamboo skins are not used as a fuel by many Warlis.

All these deities, alongwith Ihmai, Ir, Bagul are considered as family gods, whereas some others like Gaon Dev, Makherdev, Deongar Dev, Wagh Dev, Mavli, etc., are village deities. All these deities are worshipped especially at the time of Holi, New Year, Akhateej and Diwali, as also while undertaking economic activities like sowing, reaping, winnowing, threshing, constructing a new house or buying cattle. Besides these local and native deities, certain gods of the wider Hindu pantheon such as Shanker (Lord Shiva), Ganapati (elephant head god), Hanuman and Durga (the goddess of Shakti, i.e., power) have also found their way into the Warli theology due to Hindu influence as well as their interaction with the outside world.

Warlis also fear the evil spirits. They believe that persons dying unnatural or premature death, become bhut or khains (ghost) if it is a male spirit and if a female she becomes a hedri or sanveri (witch). They are invisible in the day time as they are believed to have nocturnal habits. All these spirits can be controlled by the bhuva or bhagats – who is a very important person of the Warlis. He is a medium, a medicine man, an arbitrator, a divine, a conductor of rituals and above all an enemy of witches. He is gifted with the power to identify the cause of sickness as also failure of crops and to suggest remedial actions. No social or religious ceremony is believed to be complete without bhuva gracing the occasion.

For the last couple of years, certain reformist movements have been going on in the Warli areas, as a result of which there has been a spurt of sects like Tulsiwala, Mahanubhav or Dandavat, the Moksha and the Ganga Sagar. All these sects have been founded by different progenitors, and are identified by a particular sectarian mala (necklace) of each sect. All the sect preachers speak of the same cardinal principle of one God, cleanliness, vegetarianism, universal brotherhood and shunning the old practices.

The village affairs are managed by village Patels, which is a hereditary post and comes from the family of the earliest settlers in the village. Palel's jurisdiction of control extends to a number of falias, and is called as a Khangi Panchayat. There are two other functionaries to help the Patel in his duties. They are Karbhari and Kathia, who hold second and third place in the Warli traditional council. Each falia is managed by a Kharbhari and his position is also hereditary like that of Patel. If the village is small in size, there can be one Patel. The Warli traditional Panchayat is called Zat or Jat and besides Patel, it consists of senior experienced male members of the village and a bhuva. It adjudicates on matters of social offences and the offender is penalized in the form of cash fines. A major part of the fine is paid to the person who has been wronged by way of compensation for damages and a part is utilized towards defraying expenditure of the Panchayat meeting.

Besides the judicial role of the Patel, he also acts as a Jatela and performs the purificatory functions, thus discharging a religious role too. In the event of breach of commensal and connubial norms which effects the social status of the wrongdoer, the Jatela performs the purificatory rites to get the outcasted person (batala manush) readmitted in the community.

While the traditional Panchayat exists among the Warlis, yet another Panchayat, i.e., the Statutory Village Panchayat exists among them. With the enactment of legislation for the formation of village Panchayats, each village, corresponding to one revenue unit, with a population of 1,000 has Panchayat as a local unit of administration. In the event of its population being less than 1,000, however villagers can apply for the establishment of Panchayat.

The legislation of Panchayati Raj has led to the political awareness and political activities of the Warlis. The national and regional political parties take equal interest in the Panchayat elections, in setting up their candidates, canvassing for them, and providing funds for contesting the elections, for it is here that they can motivate the people at the grass-root level.

Stratification in Social and Religious Life

As has been stated in the preceding paragraphs, Warlis do not live in isolation, but share their habitat alongwith Kolcha and Kokna tribes. In terms of social ranking, Warlis occupy an intermediate position between the two. While in earlier days, marriage within the community was strictly a norm, but recently a laxity has been observed in their rules, especially in the families of the affluent tribal groups. Marriage alliances are now established between families of these three tribes. Amongst the three tribal groups, rules of hypergamy is strictly being observed in the matter of exchange of bride.

Stratification is observed among the two geographical divisions of the Warlis. These two divisions are the Dungri and the Talat Warlis. This stratification is based more on economic considerations than on anything else. The Dungri Warlis are the ones who reside in the hilly areas, the forest areas, the hill slopes, etc., while the Talat Warlis inhabit the plains or valley area. The Talatis are educationally and economically better off and consider themselves superior to the Dungri Warlis. This stratification is clearly visible in their marriage patterns. A Dungri Warli man marries only among its own section, but a Dungri girl can be given in marriage to a Talati. The Talatis, marry among themselves, and cannot give a girl to Dungri.

The Warlis are divided into number of exogamous kuls (clans), which is known as 'atak'. There are an estimated 144 clans among the Warlis, but only 29 clans were identified in the village studied. Some of the kuls like Dhusan, Delvi, Rathore, Jagare, Tumbea, Baragi, etc., are named after their 'vadels' (ancestors), whereas some others are named after trees like Sadia, Dhamora, Had, Kalamb, Asan, Taras, Modal, Somar, Amba, Ambali, Khair, Alamb, Karanadi, Jaimura, whereas some others are named after animals like Sambhari, Mohandkar or Mohandi, Vardin or birds like Gore, etc. All these kuls are equal in status and rank at par. Matrimonial alliance with clan member is prohibited. A person attains the membership of a particular kul by birth. Once the membership has been attained, he cannot change it by any means, with the exception of only the female member, who acquire the status and kul of the husband to whom she is married, thereby severing all links with the parental clan.

Religious Stratification

The majority of Warlis are Hindus by faith. About a decade ago, a few Christian missionaries came from Painth on the border of Gujarat and Maharashtra within a distance of about 16 km from the village being studied, and established a church in village Hunda, about 3 km from the village. The missionaries started their work in the village with the help of the priest and a medical specialist. They distributed cereals to the hungry, clothes to the needy and medicines to the sick, took care of the invalid and provided compassion and comfort to the poor and preached that Jesus can alone relieve them of their sufferings. They also ran a free school for the tribal children. The missionaries' act of charity was viewed skeptically by the locals, as they were thought to be alien people and it was believed that they ate beef and pork, things which were a taboo to the Hindus. A few influential people among the locals, which besides the Warli consisted of the Koknas and Kolcha tribals, persuaded their brethren not to get persuaded or lured by the gifts and the largesse being given by the missionaries as it was antithetical to their religious dictates. Some of the people who in spite of all persuasions accepted the Christian faith were termed as Isuwale Warlis and were ostracized from the Warli society. They were considered as low vis-à-vis the non-Christian Warlis and no 'roti' or 'beti' vyavhar were established with them. While the 'roti' vyavhar is the acceptance of food, the beti vyavhar is the giving and taking of brides from a particular group.

While at one stage there was an attempt by the Christian missionaries to improve the lot, but due to certain social constraints it did not meet with much success. The extent of the effect of conversion by Christian missionaries can be gauged by the fact that from the selected village only five people got themselves converted to Christianity. This speaks of the low acceptance of the faith. As the Christian missionaries were attempting to make a dent on the Warli culture through their religion, there developed several sects among the Hindu Warlis, which could be termed as a revivalism of Hinduism or backlash of Hinduism or still better these sects developed to counter the effect of the missionaries' religious zeal.

The momentum of revivalism peaked around 1964, when a saint from Pardhar Pur (Maharashtra) by the name of Vithal Rukmai who lived near Chandra Bhaga river, and who by the dint of his bhakti (devotion) founded the Tulsimala sect. His followers were Tukaram Maharaj, Nameshwar Maharaj, Jana Bai, Mukta Bai, Dhora Kumbha Vandova, Karova Maharaj and Umakant Ram Das Maharaj also known as Bagul Baba, and his wife Tara Bai who were instrumental in spearheading and spreading the saint's message to the masses. By a conservative estimate, there are approximately 10,000 followers of this sect presently. The followers of the Tulsimala sect are devout believers of the family gods and village gods. They are vegetarians and teetotallers and prefer to give and take bride from the same sect, on account of the common ideology. The sect professes cleanliness and reverence to the Almighty; and is characterized by wearing a basil bead necklace.

Another saint by the name of Chakradhar Swamy, originally from the village Ubhoi in Bharuch district of Gujarat migrated to Rudrapur in Aurangabad where he preached Mahanubhav panth or Dandavat panth. From here he went further ahead to the Vindhya mountains where a saint by the name of Kathari Nath saw Swamy Chakradhar meditating. Impressed by his meditation, he accepted him as his disciple and established a sect by the name of Dandavat. The first person to be initiated to the Dandavat sect was a Kokna by the name of Chiman Bhai Gopal Bhai Kharkuti. The Mahanubhav sect has an all-India body by the name of Akhil Bhartiya Mahanubhav Parishad and its president at the time of field investigations was Mahant Shri Nagraj Baba. The Swami preached about the existence of only one God, whom he called Krishana, and said that all other gods are in fact a different name for Krishana. Followers of this sect are characterized by wearing of a sandalwood bead necklace. The followers of this sect too are vegetarians and teetotallers. A person of the Dandavat sect considers himself superior to the other two, i.e., the Isuwales and the Tulsimalawales and would not accept prasad (offerings to god) from them.

The third sect, which also finds a place in a Warli society is the Sanatan Dharma. They too like the Tulsimalas believe in family and village gods, and are followers of vegetarianism and teetotalism. Like the other two, they also prefer to marry within their own sect, but should a person of this sect marry a girl of an other sect, in that event the girl would have to change her sect to that of her husband.

Besides the above, there are two more minor sects among the Warlis, one is Moksha, which has been founded by Vallabh Ram Vyas and is characterized by their members wearing sandalwood bead necklace. The other sect is the Ganga Sagar sect, whose presiding deity is Lord Shiva. Both these sects do not have a significant following as of today in comparison to others. The remaining of the non-sectarian and non-Christian Warlis, still continue to worship their tutelary deities Wager Dev, Mavli, Kansari Devi, Himay, Imahi, Eer, Bagul and Varan Dev, besides also propitiating and revering certain gods of the wider Hindu pantheon like Hanuman, Shiva and Ganapati. Thus, the acceptance or adoption of a particular faith or sect has resulted in the internal segmentation of the Warli society, leading to a stratification in an otherwise homogenous community.

Presence of different sects has resulted in the clustering of the tribal population into different groups and this has led to certain stratification among the different sects in terms of marital preferences and 'roti' vyavhar (commensal norms and acceptance of food). Divisions between the sectarian groups of Warlis have become very sharp, on account of the development of the sects.

The Ritual Hierarchy

Ritual status	*Type of religion*	*Community/Groups*
High	Hindus	All sects
Middle	Hindus	Non-sectarian tribals
Low	Christians	Converts

Another social change that is visible in socio-religious life of the Warlis is the induction of Brahmin priest for the performance of their marriage rituals. In the past the relatives and the Patels played an important role in the performance of the marriage rituals. In the religious sphere Warlis worship various gods, including family gods, e.g., Naran Dev, Kansari Devi, Hirva, Himai, while others like Gam Dev, Makher Dev, Doongar Dev, etc., are village gods. They are worshipped by the village as a whole and the expense is borne collectively. They are worshipped at the time of Holi, Diwali and Akhateej. Doongar Dev is the god of the hills, Himai is the protector of fields, and Kansarimata, is the goddess of corn. Vagh Dev (tiger) and Nag Dev (snake) are some other important Warli gods. With the penetration of the various sects as already detailed, numerous other gods have found their way in the tribal religious life. Though Warli of different sects have changed their social habits, yet it has in no way affected their belief in their traditional tutelary deities. Emerging social stratification is reflected in the fact that while those who are agriculturists, teachers and in service, worship Ram Krishan and Vishnu and Lord Shiva, whereas the landless and a majority of the agricultural labourers continue worshipping their tutelary gods. Due to the impact of the sectarian faith, the non-sectarians have also started worshipping a few gods, but the percentage is not significant.

The fear of the supernatural is the key to the Warli religion, so says a Warli schoolmaster. This statement of the school teacher appears to be quite true and logical, for the Warlis are constantly struggling for survival and try not to offend the supernatural beings. Some of these supernatural beings are gods and goddesses, others ancestral spirits, ghosts and witches. All these spirits are to be periodically propitiated to appease them on appropriate occasions in Warli calendar.

All these spirits can be controlled by the 'bhagat' who is also called as a 'bhuva'. He is a medium, a medicine man, an arbitrator, a divine, a conductor of rituals and above all an enemy of witches. He is thus a man of pre-eminent social position, as such he is respected and revered by all. He performs magico-religious duties. He is gifted with the power to see the past, present and future of a person. He also imparts training in magico-religious rites to his pupil. He can forecast to the people in the event of sickness in a family or a failure of a crop, and point to which spirit is responsible for the cause. He also suggests ways and means of propitiating the deity, so that the evil or harm done can be averted. There is virtually no social or religious ceremony in which a bhagat has no place.

The performance of the special rituals and the acting as a – shaman between the tribals and the supernatural puts the bhuva on a higher pedestal in a Warli society.

Political System

The village affairs are managed by the village Patels or Patils. It is a hereditary post and is vested with one of the earliest settlers in the village. The village Patel has his say in every affair, whether it be individual, social or religious, in the Warli society. The Patels or Patils have the privilege of getting the first invitations on any occasion in a village. At the Warli wedding, there is a custom of turban tying to the Patel. The village always acts under the leadership of the Patel and as such he commands a great respect and honour from his community men.

Every village has a Patel, and the Panchayat which he organizes is called Khangi Panchayat (traditional council). The affairs of village are regulated by council of people from the same community, who are five in number and are called as Panchs. The people in the Khangi Panchayat are, more often than not, selected by general consensus of the village community excepting the Patels and Kharbari. Such people are usually selected (nominated) on the basis of their age, experience and education. A bhuva (shaman) is also an important person to be on the tribal council. If the village is small than a few villages can join together.

The traditional Warli council dispenses justice in matters of grave social offences or on breach of traditional norms. While dispensing justice, not only the views of the 'Panchs' are taken, but at times the Patel invites the views of even the elderly persons present in the meeting. The offenders of the social norms are penalized in the form of cash fines. A major part of such fines is given to the person who has been wronged, by way of compensation for the damages, and a part of the fine is utilized towards defraying expenditure of the Panchayat meetings, including cost of local liquor.

Though the Patel and Panchs dispense justice within the area of their jurisdiction only, but in such cases where the warring factions are members of the same tribal community of two different villages, in that event the Patel and Panchs of both the villages sit and decide the case. Patel or Patil at times also has to perform religious and purificatory functions; and on such occasions he is referred to as Jatela. While the tribal council takes up cases of social disputes in general, the Jatela deals with matters which are connected with the polluting of the status, especially when a person partakes food from a member of a lower strata or has illicit relations with person of opposite sex and has been ostracized by the community. The Jatela in such an eventuality performs purificatory rites to get the outcasted person (batala manush) readmitted in the community. So a Patel is not only a law giver but also a conductor of the ritual for the purification of an outcast person. Since Patel is an important functionary in the village, he enjoys considerable prestige and honour. Any government official visiting the village for any official purpose, calls on the Patel and it is through him that the official approaches a particular person. For obtaining loan and other things from the block office, the recommendation of the Patel is a must, for it is he alone who certifies the credentials of a loan seeker. No loans are sanctioned to a person without the Patel's recommendation. Since more often than not he is also a Sarpanch, he enjoys a double social prestige.

There are two other functionaries to assist the Patel. They are the Kharbhari and the Khathia, who hold the second and the third place in the Warli political system. While the Kharbari is a secretary or a manager of the council the Khathia acts as a messenger and immediate helper to the Patel or Kharbari.

Besides the above traditional council of the Warlis, there also exists the statutory council constituted under the Village Panchayat Act. Though both the statutory, and the traditional council exist among the Warlis, it is the latter which exercises more hold over them. In case of any dispute it is the traditional Panchayat which is approached and not the statutory one. It is generally believed by the Warlis that the traditional council is more aware of their customary laws than the statutory one, and it is for this reason that it is more often approached. Politically, great stress is laid on Panchayati Raj nowadays at village levels, but for the Warlis, the Patel has more authority than the Sarpanch – the head of the statutory council, as the former is a hereditary post and his authority goes unchallenged, whereas the latter is an elected post, and there exists an opposition group.

Social and Economic Stratification

In Warli society social stratification in visualized in terms of economic standards, mainly land-holding pattern. In fact about 25 per cent of Warlis are owners of land and they enjoy high status.

Distribution of Landowning Households

Type of farmer	*Category of land (acre)*	*Landowning household*	*Total land owned (acre)*	*Land owned/house (acre)*
Landless farmers	Landless less – than 1 Acre	82.01	nil – 0.36	nil – 0.36
Marginal Farmers	1–5 acre	10	39.27	3.92
Small farmers	6–10 acre	11	84.03	3.92
Big farmers	11–15 acre – 16+ acre	03.03	40.34 – 87.22	13.11 – 29.07

A perusal of the above table reveals that of the 110 households 83 households constitute landless farmers, which accounts for 75.45 per cent of the population, whereas the marginal farmers rank next with 9.01 per cent population followed by 5.45 per cent population as big farmers.

Big farmers	5.45%
Small farmers	10.00%
Marginal farmers	9.10%
Landless farmers	75.45%

The big farmers are economically well off as the produce of their land is also better than the others. The quality of the land possessed by them is also of comparatively better quality, resulting in better yields. The landholding being large, they also use some amount chemical fertilizers. None from this strata goes to work as agricultural labour. The small and marginal farmers constitute approximately 19 per cent of the population and are clubbed together. Socially and economically their condition is better than the landless farmers. The difference between the two types of strata lies in the fact that while the members of the families belonging to the marginal farmers go to work as agricultural labourers, the members of the families of small farmers do not work as agricultural labourer. Most of farmers have more than one bullock or only one bullock.

The bulk of the population, i.e., 75.45 per cent are landless labourers. However, these people take land on lease from the forest department on seasonal basis, or work as share-croppers for bigger landlords of the area, who are mostly Koknas. Ordinarily half the yield of the field is paid to the landlord as lease rent. The tenant share-cropper has to bear the entire expenditure of cultivation. With the peculiar ecological factors and topography of the region, these tenants cannot expect sufficient produce from the fields for the entire year. Besides, the soil is rocky and barren. Most of them do not have a pair of bullocks or even a well. These people do not use chemical fertilizers as they have no means to purchase it. Since they themselves are workers, they do not engage any other person, but prefer to work on each other's land on reciprocal basis. During lean agricultural months when there is neither any agricultural activity nor any demand for labour, they migrate to the neighbouring areas in search of jobs in vineyards or grasses. There are times when they eat certain edible roots to mitigate their hunger.

A glance at the following table reveals the occupational differentiation in the area.

Distribution of Workers in Different Occupations

Nature of occupation	*Male*		*Female*		*Total*	
	No.	*%*	*No.*	*%*	*No.*	*%*
Agriculture	89	52.66	55	36.18	144	44.86
Agriculture labour	77	45.56	95	62.50	172	53.58
Teacher	02	01.18	—	—	02	0.62
Service	01	0.59	02	01.32	03	0.93

The bulk of the population that is 98.22 per cent males and 98.68 per cent females are directly dependent on some form of agriculture activities. The number of persons involved in agricultural labour (approx 50%) falls short of 25 per cent, who has been shown as landless farmers (75.45%). This is on account of the fact, that these people do sharecropping by taking the land of the big landlord on lease on seasonal basis or by taking the land from the forest department on lease.

It is further observed that 1.77 per cent of the males and 1.32 per cent of the females are in the white-collared profession, and all of these fall into the category of big farmers. They work as teachers and teach in government run schools and ashram type schools while the females work as Sevikas in Anganwadis. These employees earn regular salaries, which is quite high in terms of the Warli idea of income. These people come more in contact with government officials, non-tribals and others and are better aware of the governmental aid to the tribals, and make full use of it. Since the people of this category are educated and economically better off they enjoy higher social status and prestige in their community. They are approached by their not-so-privileged brethren in seeking advice on certain issues, drafting of application for various governmental agencies for obtaining loan, etc.

There is a striking difference in the literacy pattern and lifestyle of the different strata of these tribals.

Literacy Levelwise Distribution

Literacy Level	*Male*		*Female*		*Total*	
	No.	*%*	*No.*	*%*	*No.*	*%*
Illiterate	252	78.26	320	93.29	572	86.02
Primary (I–V)	50	15.53	14	4.08	64	0.962
Secondary(VI–X)	15	04.66	09	2.62	24	03.61
Technical/Prof	05	01.55	—	—	05	0.75
Total	322	100.00	343	99.99	66	100.00

The Warlis are clearly stratified in terms of their literacy, with only 13.98 per cent as literates and 86.02 per cent as illiterates. The small and the big farmers constitute the category who are literates. The bulk of the small farmers constitute the category who are in primary level of education.

A striking difference is visible in the life style of the different strata. An educated school teacher dresses himself in a manner similar to that of other non-tribal office-goers. The uneducated dresses almost like the landless Warli. In terms of food habits the bigger landlords eat wheat flour besides their traditional raghi and dangar, the illiterates who are landless have to be content with raghi and dangar. The educated Warlis, can afford hospitality on the occasion of visit of an official visit, which the uneducated cannot do.

The Warli tribe is divided into three economic strata on the basis of ownership of land and occupation. These are: (1) Rich cultivators (2) Middle-ranked cultivators, and (3) Agricultural labourers and landless cultivators. Agricultural labourers and landless cultivators are at the bottom of the occupational hierarchy. It is the single largest stratum and consists of 75.5 per cent of the households. Such people who do not own land themselves, take forest fallow land (sir-pattan) on lease for a particular season, and grow essential crops on it by means of primitive tools. Others work as tenants of the bigger landlord of the area, mostly Koknas. This share-cropping is known as bathi. Ordinarily half the yield is paid to the landowner as lease rent. The tiller of the soil bears the entire expenditure on agriculture, excepting for the cesses on the land which have to be paid by the owner. The cultivators falling in this category do not have enough infrastructural facilities to make their land economically viable. Their soil is rocky and barren and most of them even do not have a pair of bullocks to plough, which they have to borrow and for which they have to pay 2½ quintals of produce per pair of bullocks borrowed. Whatever they produce is barely enough for their own needs. Those who neither take land on lease nor have land, work as agricultural labourers.

During the slack season of agriculture as the opportunity for regular employment as agricultural labour is not available, the only alternative left for the Warlis is to migrate to the neighbouring region of Nasik in Maharashtra or to Umbergaon in Bulsar district to work for big Gujarati landlords or to work in vineyards for daily wages. Middle cultivators are those cultivators who own land up to 10 acres. They constitute 20 per cent of the population. The family members till the land themselves and are engaged in the entire agricultural operations. With all their hard work they are able to produce a little surplus. During paddy transplantation they take the help of the fellow community members on the basis of mutual exchange of labour. With the little surplus that they are able to generate, they barter things for their necessities in the local weekly market. The rich cultivators constitute 5.5 per cent of the Warlis and they normally possess land in between 10 to 20 acres. These are the people who are not totally dependent on agriculture, rather they are employed as teachers (0.62%) and in service (0.93%). Since they are economically well off they also generate enough surplus, often employ labourers and use high yielding varieties of seeds. They also mortgage land of their fellow tribals, and also increase agricultural assets by buying land. Thus, the three economic strata are quite distinct among the Warlis.

Social Inequality and Its Implications

Above discussion revealed that the Warli tribe is divided into three economic strata on the basis of ownership of land and occupation. These are: (1) Rich cultivators (2) Middle-ranked cultivators and (3) Landless cultivators/Agricultural labourers. Agricultural labourers and landless cultivators are at the bottom of the social hierarchy. The Warlis of different strata possess property variously. The houses of the rich and educated are big in size, with brick walls and tiled roof supported with wooden beams obtained from the forest. The rich and the big farm owners have even three or more rooms and a kitchen but the middle order Warlis had only one or two rooms. Comparatively, in the house of the poor members the numbers of rooms are less, just one room in most cases. Similarly in terms of household utensils, in general it was observed that almost all houses have few earthen pots and iron pans. However, while the poor had only earthen wares and the aluminum wares, the rich had a combination of earthen pots, aluminum wares, brass utensils, china clay and a few glass wares, while the middle order had more of aluminium and less of earthen ware. Cots were not found in any of the houses of the poor people, and the members usually slept on the ground, but in the houses of the rich people one could see wooden beds, the intermediate class of people had a few cots only and that too made out of strips of split bamboo, Chair could be found only in one household that is, the house of the school teacher. The poor did not have any clock or wrist watch, but all the persons who were working in school or other government service had wrist watches. Only the school had a transistor set. Similarly very few households, usually of the bigger and educated landlords possessed electricity while the middle order managed with the lanterns and or chimneys. The poor had none of these facilities and had to get light by burning wood. Thus on the whole, the Warli society appears stratified. It is generally the agricultural labourers and landless cultivators amongst the Warlis who are at the bottom of the local ranking. The discussion and analysis provided here is about the Talat Warlis only. The Dungri Warlis live closer to forests in the interior and are economically backward.

References

Enthoven, R.E. 1920, *The Tribes and Castes of Bombay*, Bombay: Government Central Press.

Save, K.J. 1945, *The Warlis*, Bombay: Padma Publication Ltd.

20 Poverty, Social Exclusion and Culture-Change

Emerging Inequality among the Bedias of Jharkhand

Tilak Bagchi

The Bedia Identity and Social Structure

The Bedia of Jharkhand are a predominantly rural population. Panchpargania, an Indo-Aryan language is the mother tongue of the Bedia inhabiting the region between Golla in the Hazaribagh district to Jhalda in the Purulia district of West Bengal, while Khorta or Sadani, a sub-dialect of Bhojpuri which falls under the Indo-Aryan group of languages is the mother tongue of the rest of the Bedia. They use mainly Devnagari script. However, a few Bedias can communicate with others in Bengali and Odia language and a few of them can write in Bengali and Odia script. It is needless to say that the educated and elite class of Bedia can speak in English language and write in Roman script.

The Bedias are one of the numerically dominant tribes in the entire foothills of the Ramgarh Hill Range of Jharkhand. They believe that they are the descendants of Vyas, the composer of the epic Mahabharata. Bedia is the corrupted form of Veda Bangsi, the lineage from which they are believed have originated. The myth of the Bedia depicts that their dynasty was called by the appellation of 'Veda Bangsi' after the great epic of the Mahabharata, which is also known as 'Pancham Veda'. Their myth has it that their last chief Sampati, along with all Veda Bangsi persons died in the hands of a Muslim Badshah on the day of Sohorai. However, a 'Veda Bangsi' boy and a girl luckily escaped and were reared in the custody of the Munda. The present day populations are believed to be the offspring of that boy and girl. This myth shows that the Bedia have a close affinity with the Munda (Hunter, 1976; Lister, 1917). According to the Kurmi Mahato, a section of Kurmi was outcasted and came to be known as Choto or Shan Kurmi, i.e., wandering Kurmi (Singh, 1994). In Kurmali the word 'Bedho' means misbegotten children and the word 'Bedia' according to the Kurmi Mahato probably stems from the root word 'Bedho'. Rejoining to the Kurmi fold by Bedia or Chhoto Kurmi or Shan Kurmi is allowed by hosting a feast and performing *prayaschit* (atonement). Dutta Mazumdar (1956) and Risley (1891) stated that the Bedia is the twelfth clan of the Santal. But nowadays, no member belonging to Bedia 'paris' (clan) is found in the Santal community. But the ethno-history of the Santal depicts that the clan Bedia, though a secondary clan in the Santal society, was very much in existence among the Santal community when the latter ruled Chai and Champa in the Hazaribagh district. Dalton (1872) observed that the Bedia is a gypsy-like tribe that leads a nomadic life like a Bazigar. Thus it seems that Bedia is a community having heterogeneous origin.

The diet of the Bedia is very simple. They eat cereals like maize, rice, gondli, bajra, makai, wheat and, vegetables of both leafy and non-leafy varieties as well as fruits, all of which are locally grown. They also purchase a large number of food stuffs from the local daily and weekly markets. Mustard oil is their main medium of cooking. They eat fish, mutton and chicken. The Bedia also relish pork but Hinduized Majhi Bedia never rear pig or consume pork, except when it is a sacrificial one. Beef eating is now strictly prohibited in their society but in olden days, they were beef eaters. They also eat flesh of wild game, like deer, hare, wild pig and so on whenever available. They seldom consume milk but are fond of taking tea. Tobacco with lime, betel are also consumed by them. Tapoon i.e., mahua spirit and Haria or rice-beer are the favourite alcoholic beverages consumed by them. The followers of several Bhakti sects, viz., Anandamargi, Satsangi, never consume any alcoholic beverages nor meat with the exception of milk.

The Bedia society is divided into a number of totemic clans namely, Rukhi (squirrel), Kach (tortoise), Solakhi (small black bird), Pecha (owl), Sega (small squirrel like animal), Bami (a kind of fish), Ullu (gibbon-a type of primate), Bar (banyan tree), Dundua (small black bird), Sundi (white bird) and so on. The clans are exogamous and their main function is to regulate marriage. The Majhi Bedia in addition to maintaining their pristine clan affiliation also claim affinity with a gotra namely Kashyap which is mainly used for performing Brahminical marriage rituals.

The Bedia mainly live in nuclear families. However, a large number of Bedia households are extended or joint in nature. Polygynous families are rare in their society. The Bedias are a patrilineal tribe. Within the family, all members maintain economic cooperation in daily life. Normally the father or eldest male becomes the head of the family who manages all family affairs and allots duties and responsibilities to the individual members in the family in consultation with adult males and females. On the death of the father the eldest son or the widow of the deceased in cases of minor and dependent children conducts the family affairs. At the time of inter-village conflicts the elderly persons are consulted to deal with the situation. Intra-family nexus pivots around love, respect, affection, duty and responsibility among different members of the family. Family is also the citadel of the initial process of socialization for both male and female children separately. Avoidance relationship exists between a man and his younger brother's wife or with his wife's elder sister. In such cases physical touch or cordial conversation is not permitted. On the other hand, joking relationship exists between a man and his wife's younger sister. Ceremonial and artificial or putative kinship is also maintained across the ethnic boundary.

Marriage is the basis of a new set of relationships. Junior levirate and junior sororate though allowed, are not a preferred form of marriage. Widow remarriage and polygyny are not prohibited. Life partner can be acquired through marriage by negotiation, mutual consent and capture. Indeed, capture, as a form of choosing better half is extremely rare in their society. They prefer adult marriage. Divorce is not generally seen in their society but separation is not very rare. The

Bedia have a classificatory system of kinship and have borrowed several kinship terms from the neighbouring Hindu communities.

In Bedia society the eldest son succeeds the traditionally held office of the father. Property of the father is inherited by all the sons almost equally. However, in some cases the eldest son gets a little larger share of land known as jesthangsa.

Life Cycle Events

Stopping of menstruation is the first sign of pregnancy. During the advanced stages of pregnancy, women are not allowed to go to unholy places like cremation grounds, burial grounds and so on. Delivery generally takes place in one corner of the room with the help of a dai, i.e., midwife, who generally hails from the Chamar caste. On the very first day of childbirth the father of the newborn baby sacrifices chicken at the sacred altar to appease the ancestral spirits for the well-being of the baby. Chati is celebrated on sixth day after child-birth. On that day a name is given to the child. On the twelfth day the baby is again bathed by the midwife during the rituals known as 'Bari'. At the age of nine months 'Mujuthi' ceremony is observed when the baby is given 'kheer', a kind of food prepared from rice, milk sweetening agent and so on.

In Bedia society two kinds of marriage, namely, Charibarat and Bankhari generally take place. The former type of marriage is solemnized in the bride's house while in the latter type of marriage the bridegroom's party pays a visit to the house of the bride and brings the bride. The actual marriage takes place in the bridegroom's house. However, in anga, i.e., widow remarriage no elaborate ritual is seen in Bedia society.

The corpse is generally cremated. However, the dead body of the pregnant woman, infants or those who committed suicide or died in accident, epidemic, snake bite, etc., are buried. After cremation the 'agmukhia', i.e., the person who first touches fire in the mouth of the corpse, collects four unburnt pieces of bones and keeps them in an earthen pot (*chukka*). A big stone known as 'Bedia Patthal' is erected in a specific area. The chuka is thrown on that stone with the belief that performing this leads to the soul of the deceased to join the ancestral spirits. Lineage members observe mourning period for a period of three days. 'Dashakarma' is done on the tenth day of death. After performing 'Dashakarma' the agmukhia performs Parmeshwari puja with fowl sacrifice. A few Bedias especially Majhi Bedia offer pinda, i.e., rice ball in the name of deceased, with the help of a Brahmin pandit.

Magico-Religious Beliefs and Practices

Menta, Kudra-Kudri, Burha-Burhi, Surjahi, Bhagat, Murakata and so on are some of their benevolent deities while witches, Baram, Pisach, Jin, Dakin and so on are some of the mischievous spirits who can do harm. Gram puja, Sarhul, Shiv puja, Mahabir Jhanda puja, Dhanbuni puja, Rohini Nakshatra puja, Duarshini puja, Karam parab, Chhata parab, Durga puja or Durga Maharani puja, Soharai, Sakhrat, Manasa puja are some of the religious observances celebrated by the Bedia.

In fact 'jeth rayat' and 'mahato' are considered as the traditional headmen of the village. They are consulted by all the villagers before organizing any sort of community festivals. It is obligatory on the part of the villages to invite them during feasts and rituals associated with the life cycle rituals. In the mechanism of social control both 'jeth rayet' and 'mahato' have a definite and decisive say. In the religious observances like Sarhul, Mahavir Jayanti puja and so on they assist the priests and are greeted with special honour. The offered food and flowers are given first to them during any sort of community religious festivals.

Secular and Sacred Specialists

Pargana headed by the 'parganait' is the supreme political body of the Bedia. Dewan and Sardar assist the 'parganait' while 'ohedar' acts as a messenger in the Pargana Council. Nowadays only a vestige of the 'Pargana Council' can be seen. 'Mahato' or 'jeth rayat' is the headman of the village. Presently various organizations, viz., Bedia Jati Sudhar Samiti and so on act not only as a body of reform and development but also contribute significantly towards the mechanism of social control. 'Pahan' is exclusively a religious functionary who comes from Bedia or Munda community. Apart from *Pahan,* Brahmin priest, Vaishnav *baba-ji,* i.e., mendicants also act as religious specialists. The 'sakha' and 'bhagat' are their native medicine men as well as sorcerer-cum-witch doctor.

Economic basis of Social Stratification

Agriculture is traditional means of economy. However, the Bedias are now working in coal mines, various industries and urban sectors as a permanent employee or daily wage earner. Agriculture as well as rearing of lac and collection of faggots from the forest for selling is the main occupation of the Bedias living in the forest-clad foothill region of Ranchi district. The Bedia are also famous as vegetable growers. To a Bedia hunting and fishing are more a recreation rather than a vocation. Communal hunting and fishing are the popular adventure-cum recreation of the Bedias.

Occupational mobility is another factor for social differentiation. In Hesla village which is situated in the vicinity of mining-industrial-urban complex of Ramgarh, it has been seen that the Bedia who are educated and/or involved in some white-collared job, viz., teaching in primary or in high school, service in block office, bank, railway, IFICO and so on as officers or at least Group C employees are treated as elite in Bedia society. As a result they enjoy somewhat higher status. The second group of Bedia whose status is either slightly lower or almost at par with the former group of Bedia are those who are the permanent mazdoors (labourers) of colliers or big industries like Indian Fire Bricks and Insulation Company (IFICO). They enjoy an additional social prestige owing to their outside contact and economic solvency. The second category of the Bedia take a lead under the general leadership of the first group of people in arranging picnics, community rituals and religious observances and so on. Their outside social contact is responsible for the welfare of the village to an extent. All these factors raise their social position to a considerable extent. The lower category of Bedia are those who are temporary workers and labourers in coal mines and various small industries situated in the vicinity of Ramgarh. These groups of people along with a group of Bedias who are involved in some petty trade and business often show reluctance in agricultural activities. On the contrary we see Bedias who are often involved in labour and collection of minor forest resources along with their age-old vocation of settled cultivation. This social differentiation between agricultural and non-agricultural Bedia is apparently not striking but it is very much in existence at the level of cognition. The service class of Bedia conceive the agricultural Bedia or cattle herding or agricultural labour. But outwardly this view can hardly be expressed. The lowest category of the Bedias are those who eke out their livelihood by selling of faggots after cutting these from the forest on regular and permanent basis.

It has been observed in each Bedia village that big landowning families in the olden days had a distinct place in the society. They played decisive role in all the socio-religious affairs of the village. But with the emergence of a new power structure based on formation of a new class of elite who hail from the educated and service class of people, the status and power of the landowning peasants is slowly eroding. This newer class of elite by dint of their nexus with various political parties, administration of the statutory councils and so on, influence several welfare activities in the village. The members of this new class often get direct patronage from the Mukhia, Sarpanch or leaders of the political parties as well as support from officers of various governmental organizations, like Block office, Circle office, Karmachary office and non-governmental organizations. However, as time rolled on, the privileged class of people slowly but steadily consolidated their decisive influence not only over Bedia but also over other ethnic groups like the Koiri, the Munda, the Kurmi and so on. In this connection it may be stated that these Bedias act as a mouthpiece of their entire community and are also involved in the political activities of the Jharkhand Mukti Morcha, Jharkhand Kisan Mazdoor Samity (JKMS) which is a constituent body of CPI (ML) Benod Mishra and are associated with, social activities conducted by the Gram Bikas Samity situated at Hesla and functioning since 1992, Adivasi Harijan Committee and so on, for the welfare of the villagers and Dalits including Bedias.

Solidarity and Social Exclusion

In Bedia society we notice both internal and external solidarity. They express internal solidarity by sharing certain cultural symbols and through cooperation at intra-village, inter-village, regional and community level. Intra-village solidarity is maintained through mutual cooperation, community participation in rituals and festivals and in the maintenance of politico-religious organization. The Bedia maintain inter-village solidarity by clan and lineage affiliation, marriage alliance, exchange of social visits and revisits during festivals, communal singing, dancing and participation in village weekly market, which is not only a centre of economic transaction but a place of social intercourse too. Regional solidarity is maintained through regional council and through the various bodies of the Bedia society stated above. The solidarity at the community level is mainly depicted through their myth of origin already narrated. In the Bedia society external solidarity is maintained through the concept of 'we' and 'they'. It is in the context of inter-ethnic transactions that external solidarity is expressed.

The elements of social exclusion between privileged and non-privileged segments of the Bedia is mainly manifested in their material possessions and in visibility of prosperity. The privileged class of Bedia mostly live in the centre of the village while non-privileged and poorer segments of Bedia by and large live at its periphery though this can-not be considered a rule. The privileged class of people of Hesla village live in houses which have electricity while the less privileged section of Bedia inhabit houses which are devoid of any electricity. In the other two villages under study, viz., Ajaygarh and Piska there is no electricity. The privileged Bedias also possess television set, radio, diesel operated pump set, tape recorder, steel almirah, wooden and/or steel furniture, motor cycle, moped, wrist watch, wall clock, gold ornaments, bicycle, individually owned well, hand pump and so on, while these items are lacking among underprivileged section of the Bedias. Certain social exclusion is maintained between these two categories of Bedias.

Land as a Basis of Social Differentiation

In Bedia society land is the pivotal element which marks social differentiation. A few households are landless while some of them are small farmers or marginal farmers. There are some big land-owning families having land of more than ten acres. Big landowning households enjoy more power and prestige in the society in comparison to their small and marginal counterparts. The big landowning Bedias are called 'Mahato'. The descendants of the families who were enrolled as first 'rayat' under 'korkar' system also enjoy a special status. The families of the original settlers of the village are known as 'jeth rayat'. Both 'jeth rayat' and 'mahato' enjoy special status and privilege in each of the Bedia villages and this forms a major milestone of differentiation. It has been observed that these elites play a decisive role in the developmental activities of the village such as construction of road under Jawahar Rojgar Yojona, selection of beneficiaries who are eligible for getting old-age pension or houses constructed under Indira Awas Yojana and so on. These elite members are often consulted by the members of the Statutory Panchayat, officials of the state administration and so on, before implementing any welfare activities for the entire village or for the Scheduled Tribes only. This elite section, by dint of their western education and social contacts pressurize the administrative machinery or political parties or Statutory Panchayat to implement specific welfare measures that will help the poor.

Education and Political Awareness

Apart from land, education is another factor which is responsible for social differentiation. In Bedia society some are totally illiterate, while persons having postgraduate, medical, agricultural and engineering degrees are also seen. The elite among the Majhi Bedia segment have given a number of memorandums to different departments of the State and Union governments and had several rounds of talks with the administration and politicians to include the Majhi Bedia under the canopy of Bedia and had submitted some write-ups in support of their claim. These educated elites among the Bedias are involved in organizations like Bedia Bikash Samity, Bedia Samaj Unnayan Parishad, Bedia Jati Sudar Samity, Gram Vikas Samity, Adivasi Harijan Samity and Kishan Majdoor

Samity. These bodies are responsible for welfare activities of the depressed classes of people in general and the Bedia in particular. Due to the efforts of Gram Vikas Samity, electricity has reached the village Hesla and a sub-post office has been established in the village. Moreover, a private school was also established in Hesla. In fact, specially the young educated Bedia conceive themselves to be of a somewhat superior status than that of the agricultural and illiterate or less literate Bedias. It has been observed that educated young Bedia often take a lead in all the socio-religious affairs like Sarhul, Orang Grara, Mahivar puja, etc., in the village. They collect subscription and take decision regarding the organizational aspects.

Bedia and Majhi Bedia: Stratification and Exclusion

The Bedia tribe is clearly divided into native and Hinduized sections. The main divisions within the Bedia are Bedia and the Majhi Bedia. The former group of Bedia is purely tribal. A settlement record of 1908 reveals that upto 1908 all the Bedias were referred by a single appellation, i.e., Bedia. But afterwards Bedias who are living in the area between Gola or Goita in the Hazaribagh district of Jharkhand and Jhalda of Purulia with the patronage of royal families changed their identity and took the new nomenclature as Majhi like other neighbouring communities such as Danda Chatra Majhi, Sarak Majhi and so on. At the same time unlike non-Hindu Bedias, they took up the gotra affiliation in addition to their original clan. Thus the Majhi group of Bedia have a Kashyap gotra. This trend of the existence of a single gotra is strikingly similar to many communities with extremely low social strata who are believed to have converted from the tribal fold. The Majhi group of Bedia in addition to their original marriage rituals also follow some sort of Brahminical marriage rituals with the help of Brahmin pandit (priest). In case of death rituals too, the Majhi group of Bedia follow adopted Brahminical and Vaishnavite rituals along with their original death rites. These rituals are administered by the Brahmin priests and the Vaishnav mendicants. Thus, in the life cycle rituals of the Majhi group of the Bedias several Brahminical and Vaishnavite rituals, viz., satpak, subhadristi, etc., during marriage rituals as well as 'pinda dan', Harinam Sankirtan, Brahmin bhojan, Vaishnav bhojan and so on during death rites can be witnessed. Moreover, certain sections within Majhi group of Bedia take guru-mantra from Kanthi guru or Kanfuka guru (religious teacher) once every year. They form a distinct form of Vaishnava through religious affiliation. At least one Vaishnava family is found to be residing in almost all of the Majhi Bedia villages which patronize the Vaishnavas. They not only emerge as religious teachers and religious specialists but they also observe certain religious performances for the general well-being of the village. For those performances the Majhi group of Bedia support them whole heartedly.

The Majhi group of Bedia also use their surname as Majhi in lieu of using the surname as Bedia. They speak in Panchpargania language while their non-Hindu Bedia counterparts speak in Khota or Sadani language which is in vogue in Hazaribagh. The Majhi Bedia also participate in some regional festivals like Chata parab, Tusu and so on. Marital exchange though rare, does exist among these two segments of Bedia. Many elite and affluent families among tribe Bedia follow some Brahminical and Vaishnavite ritual performances not only during life cycle events but also during certain religious observances, like their Majhi Bedia counterparts. Fact remains that the Majhi group of people are debarred from any recognition as Scheduled Tribe. It is the Bedia who are recognized as Scheduled Tribe both in Jharkhand and West Bengal where they are mainly concentrated. Thus the Majhi Bedia are now organizing a solidarity movement to claim their identity as Bedia and not as Majhi or Majhi Bedia.

Social and Economic Differentiation: A Quantitative Profile

The Bedia society is organized around certain clans. Table 1 shows the numerical strength of different clans in the villages. The results obtained from the present study clearly show that some particular clans or a cluster of two to four different clans emerge as dominant clans in all the three villages under study. In Hesla village the majority of the members belong to Solakhi (39.5%) Fecha/Facha (27.5%), Kachuc/Kach (14.8%), and Rukhi (14.6%) clans. On the contrary in Hesla village has less than 4 per cent Bedia belonging to remaining three clans namely Chidra/Chira, Bar/Barwari and Dia. Same is the case in Majhi Bedia inhabited Ajaygarh and Piska villages. In Ajaygarh the largest numerical strength is found among the Kach/Kachchab Kashyap clan (39.0%). Only about 5 per cent villages of Ajaygarh have three-clan affiliation namely Bami, Rukhi and Mahua.

Table 1

Numerical Strength of Clans by Villages

Clans	*Hesla*		*Ajaygarh*		*Piska*		*Total*	
	No.	*%*	*No.*	*%*	*No.*	*%*	*No.*	*%*
Bami	—	—	6	1.9	—	—	6	0.4
Bar/Barawari	9	1.4	—	—	3	1.1	12	1.0
Chirra/Gilahari	4	0.6	89	28.0	41	14.4	134	10.8
Dia	10	1.6	—	—	—	—	10	0.8
Dundua/Dari	—	—	—	—	3	1.1	3	0.2
Fecha/Facha/Pecha	177	27.5	49	15.4	—	—	226	18.2
Herna/Tnar Herna	—	—	—	—	46	16.2	46	3.7
Kachua/Kach/Kachchap/ Kashyap	95	14.8	124	39.0	93	32.7	312	25.01
Mahakal	—	—	40	12.5	—	—	40	3.2
Mahua	—	—	4	1.3	32	11.2	36	2.9
Rukhi	93	14.6	6	1.9	—	—	99	8.0
Solakhi	253	39.5	—	—	—	—	253	20.4
Suiya/Sua	—	—	—	—	66	23.3	66	5.3
Total	641	100.0	318	100.0	284	100.0	1243	100.0

Source: Field data.

In Piska village too about one third of the villagers belong to Kachua/Kach/Kashyap clan and is followed by Majhi belonging to Sua/Suiya

(23.3%), Chirre/Herna/Tnar Herna (16.2%) Chirra/Chidra/Gilahari (14.4%) and Rukhi (11.2%) with only about two per cent villagers belonging to the remaining two clans namely Bar/Barawari and Dundua/Dari. In this connection it may be stated that a section of the villagers living in Ajaygarh and Piska belonging to the Kach/Kachua/Kachchap clan tried to Sanskritize their clan name by claiming that both their clan and gotra name is Kashyap.

Material Articles

Table 2 reveals that the majority of the Bedias are outside the reach of modern amenities. Diesel operating pump set is of paramount importance for artificial irrigation and is mainly needed for the growing of vegetables in the Bedia dominated area under study. Less than two per cent Bedia households of Hesla and Ajaygarh have diesel operated pump sets of their own while pump sets are owned by more than 22 per cent households of Piska. Radio or transistor is the most common and popular mode of entertainment among the villagers. Radio or transistor is found among one fourth to a little more than one third of the Bedia households in all the three Bedia inhabited villages under study. Watch or clock is available in about 40 per cent of Hesla and Piska households while the same is available only among about 16 per cent of Bedia households of Ajaygarh. Most of the Bedia households of Piska had at least one bicycle while about 46 per cent and 32 per cent Bedias of Hesla and Ajaygarh respectively possessed bicycles of their own. About ten per cent and five per cent Bedia of Hesla and Piska possessed tape recorder while the same is available only in about two per cent Bedia household of Ajaygarh. Only three households of Ajaygarh claimed that they have their own refrigerator which are kept in the place of their service. Two wheelers like moped, motorcycle, etc., are available in about 5 to 8 per cent of the Bedia households in all the three villages under study. About 5 per cent Bedias of Hesla village have a television set in the village itself while about ten per cent

Table 2

Householdwise Availability of Some Modern Amenities

Modern articles	*Hesla (N=129)*		*Ajaygarh (N=57)*		*Piska (N=58)*		*Total (N=244)*	
	No.	*%*	*No.*	*%*	*No.*	*%*	*No.*	*%*
Pump Set (Diesel Operated)	2	1.6	1	1.8	13	22.4	16	6.6
Radio/Transistor	43	33.3	20	35.1	14	24.1	73	29.9
Watch/Clock	52	40.3	9	15.8	23	39.7	8	3.3
Bicycle	59	45.7	18	31.6	33	56.9	110	45.1
Tape recorder	13	10.0	1	1.8	3	5.2	17	7.0
Refrigerator	—	—	3	5.3	—	—	3	1.2
Two wheelers	6	4.7	5	8.8	3	5.2	14	5.7
Television	7	5.4	6	10.5	1	1.7	14	5.7
Brick built houses or Pucca houses	16	12.4	16	28.1	5	8.6	37	15.2

Sources: Field data.
N=total number of Bedia households.

Bedia of Ajaygarh and about two per cent Bedia of Piska claimed that they have TV set and most of them kept these at the place of their work. However, a few of them have battery operated TV sets in the village itself. Most of the Bedia live in mud built kachha houses; however, a few Bedias live in wholly or partly constructed mud/stone-walled building or asbestos or tiled roofed houses or fully pucca houses. These houses can be seen in case of about 13 per cent, 28 per cent and 9 per cent houses of Hesla, Ajaygarh and Piska villages respectively. In this context it may be stated that electricity is available only in Hesla and not in Ajaygarh and Piska.

Landholding Pattern

Land is the prime asset of the Bedias since they are basically agricultural people. The landholding pattern gives some idea regarding the degree of affluence. Of late, the importance of landholding has slowly but surely lost its significance because youngsters are now trying to get permanent jobs. Nevertheless even today land is the most vital economic asset of the Bedias because they are basically an agricultural community.

Landholding as shown in Table 3 indicates that most of the Bedias in all the villages under study are marginal farmers since they possess less than 2.5 acres of land. Landless Bedia in Hesla and Piska are found in about 10 to 11 per cent of the total Bedia households of the respective villages. However, less than two per cent of the Bedia families of Ajaygarh are landless. Small farmers having land of 2.50 to 4.99 acre is found among about 13 per cent, 19 per cent and 27 per cent of the Bedia households of Hesla, Ajaygarh and Piska respectively. More than 22 per cent of the Bedia households of Ajaygarh can be grouped as medium farmers since their land is in the bracket of 5.00 to 9.99 acre while merely about 4 to 5 per cent of the Bedias of Hesla and Piska are medium farmers. Less than 1 and 2 per cent Bedia households of Hesla and Piska villages respectively can be clumped under the category of large farmers with 10 acres of land. However, more than five per cent Bedia household of Ajaygarh are large farmers with at least 10 acres of land.

Table 3

Familywise Landholding Pattern by Villages

Category and amount of land (in acres)	*Hesla*		*Ajaygarh*		*Piska*		*Total*	
	No.	*%*	*No.*	*%*	*No.*	*%*	*No.*	*%*
Landless	15	11.6	1	1.7	6	10.3	22	9.0
Marginal farmers								
(a) <0.49	34	26.4	2	3.5	4	6.9	40	16.4
(b) 0.50–0.99	25	19.4	9	15.8	8	13.8	42	17.2
(c) 1.00–2.49	32	24.8	18	31.7	20	34.5	70	28.7
Small farmers 2.50–4.99	17	13.1	11	19.3	16	27.6	44	18.0
Medium farmers 5.00–9.99	5	3.9	13	22.8	3	5.2	21	8.6
Large farmers > 10.00	1	0.8	3	5.2	1	1.7	5	2.1
Total	129	100.0	57	100.0	58	100.0	244	100.0

Family wise per capita land holding pattern gives the economic picture of the Bedia. The variable size of land holding determines the size of the families.

Table 4 reveals that most of the Bedia of Hesla are either landless or have less than 0.25 acre of land per head. The land is not enough to meet even 35 per cent of the energy requirement or 60 per cent of the requirement of rice of an adult person for a complete year, even in the year of bumper crop harvest. This can be proved by the following calculations. Average productivity per acre of land is approximately 500 kg of paddy or approximately 350 kg of rice. Therefore, average yearly productivity from one fourth acre of land is approximately 125 kg of paddy or 87.5 kg of rice. That can yield approximately 302,750 K. Cal energy (assuming 100 gm rice can yield 346 K. Cal energy). Energy requirement of a person for one year is 885,125 K. Cal (assuming daily requirement of an adult individual performing moderate work is 2,425 K. Cal). Thus 87.5 kg rice can only provide 34.20 per cent of the yearly energy requirement of an adult person. Daily requirement of rice of an adult person is 400 gm (ICMR 1981 recommended allowance). Annual requirement of rice for an adult is 146 kg. Therefore 87.5 kg rice can meet 59.9 per cent of the annual requirement of rice for an adult individual.

Thus, it can be said that most of the Bedias of Hesla have non-viable holdings. However, the situation is to some extent better among the Bedia of both Ajaygarh and Piska where most of the Bedia possess more than 0.25 acre per capita as calculated from familywise average holdings. More than 19 per cent Bedias of Ajaygarh have per capita average of one acre of land which is less than 2 and 3.5 per cent among the Bedia of Hesla and Piska respectively. Thus it can be concluded that paddy cultivation in one's own land is a more pivotal element in the subsistence economy of the Bedia of Piska and Ajaygarh in comparison to their counterparts living in Hesla. Grabbing of land for industrial purposes is one of the reasons for less availability of land for Bedia in Hesla.

Table 4

Familywise Per Capita Landholding Pattern by Villagers

Amount of land (in acres)	*Hesla*		*Ajaygarh*		*Piska*		*Total*	
	No.	*%*	*No.*	*%*	*No.*	*%*	*No.*	*%*
Landless	15	11.6	1	1.8	6	10.3	22	9.0
< 0.25	68	52.7	11	19.3	17	29.3	96	39.4
0.25–0.49	25	19.4	23	40.3	17	29.3	65	26.6
0.50–0.99	19	14.7	11	19.3	16	27.6	46	18.9
1.00–1.99	1	0.8	10	17.5	2	3.5	13	5.3
> 2.00	1	0.8	1	1.8	—	—	2	0.8
Total	129	100.0	57	100.0	58	100.0	244	100.0

Occupation: Traditional and Modern

The primary occupation means that vocation which contributes the lion's share of income for livelihood. Table 5 shows several occupations in which villagers are engaged.

Table 5 highlights that agriculture is the primary vocation of most of the Bedias of Ajaygarh and Piska whereas it is the primary occupation of merely about 10 per cent of the Bedia of Hesla. On the contrary more than 10 per cent of the Bedia working force of Hesla is primarily engaged in various kinds of labour, which include both agricultural as well as non-agricultural labour like migrant labour. Contract labourers are employed under various works available under Jawahar Rojgar Yojana, road construction work of P.W.D., job of domestic helper, cook and service boy in food and tea-stalls, temporary night guard, daily wage earners, piece rated workers in coal mines and so on. However, merely about 6 to 7 per cent of the Bedia working force of Ajaygarh and Piska are engaged in the job of various categories of labour to eke out their livelihood. About 10 to 11 per cent Bedias of Ajaygarh and Hesla are engaged in some permanent job both in government and private sectors. The corresponding percentage in Piska is about 6 per cent. It has been reported that many Bedias are engaged in some white-collared or other permanent jobs in bank, railway, health department, block office, Eastern Coalfield Limited, India Firebricks and such other prestigious concerns. Business other than selling of faggots and vegetables or lac is the primary occupation of about four per cent Bedia of Hesla and a solitary Bedia of Piska while two aged Bedia widows primarily subsist on collection and selling of the faggots in Hesla. They collect the faggots not from the jungle but from the neighbouring zone and mainly dispose it in the village itself. Teaching in school is the primary occupation of a small number of individuals in all the three villages. Labour is often supplemented by collection of faggots from the jungle or growing of vegetables in the kitchen garden. Thus

Table 5

Primary Occupation by Villages

Name of the occupation	*Hesla*		*Ajaygarh*		*Piska*		*Total*	
	No.	*%*	*No.*	*%*	*No.*	*%*	*No.*	*%*
Agriculture	20	10.5	94	66.7	78	54.9	192	40.4
Labour including agricultural, non-agricultural, migrant and contract labour job of domestic helper, cook, service boy in small food stalls, night guard, piece rated workers, wage earners and so on.	138	71.9	8	5.7	10	7.0	156	32.8
Service	19	9.9	16	11.3	9	6.4	44	9.3
Business	7	3.7	—	—	1	0.7	8	1.7
Carpentry, woodwork, masonry, tailoring, automobile mechanic and so on.	1	0.5	5	3.5	2	1.4	8	1.7
Collection of faggots	2	1.0	—	—	—	—	2	0.4
Teaching in school	2	1.0	3	2.1	1	0.7	6	1.3
Labour and selling of wood or vegetables or both or selling of lac.	—	—	14	10.0	41	28.9	55	11.6
Automobile driving	2	1.0	—	—	—	—	2	0.4
Quackery	1	0.5	—	—	—	—	1	0.2
Goat rearing	—	—	1	0.7	—	—	1	0.2
Total	192	100.0	141	100.0	142	100.0	475	100.0

labour plus selling of firewood or vegetables or firewood, lac and vegetables are the primary means of livelihood of about 10 per cent Bedia of Ajaygarh and about 29 per cent Bedia of Piska. It is strikingly absent in Hesla as the forest is far away from the village. Various other vocations like quackery, automobile driving and rearing of goats are also present in Bedia society. A few Bedia in addition to their primary occupation are also engaged in secondary vocation not only for sheer survival but often for better standard of living too.

Subsidiary vocations of the Bedia are shown in Table 6. Table 6 reveals that the secondary occupation of most of the Bedias of Hesla village is centred around agriculture because most of the Bedias of Hesla village possess non-viable holding. About one third of the Bedias of both Ajaygarh and Piska retain agriculture as subsidiary occupation as they possess agricultural land which can be categorized as non-viable holding. About 10 per cent Bedia of Piska, about 20 per cent Bedias of Hesla and a little more than 40 per cent Bedias of Ajaygarh are engaged in labour as their subsidiary vocation. About 18 per cent Bedia of Piska and 41 per cent Bedia of Ajaygarh are mostly engaged in selling of lac, vegetables or faggots. Only two households of Ajaygarh are engaged in some temporary or part time service for supplementing their family income. One person of Ajaygarh and another person of Piska is engaged in quackery as well as masonry-cum-construction work respectively. Thus, a good deal of inequality exists among the people in three villages under study.

Table 6

Subsidiary Occupation by Villages

Vocations	*Hesla*		*Ajaygarh*		*Piska*		*Total*	
	No.	*%*	*No.*	*%*	*No.*	*%*	*No.*	*%*
Agriculture	129	78.18	22	32.8	23	35.9	174	58.8
Labour including service boy and cook	36	21.82	28	41.8	6	9.4	70	23.7
Business	—	—	2	3.0	8	12.5	10	3.4
Service	—	—	2	3.0	—	—	2	0.7
Labour and selling of wood or vegetable or both wood and vegetable and selling of lac	—	—	12	17.9	26	40.7	38	12.8
Masonry and construction work	—	—	—	—	1	1.5	1	0.3
Quackery	—	—	1	1.5	—	—	1	0.3
Total	165	100.0	67	100.0	64	100.0	296	100.0

Income Inequality and Poverty

Planning Commission during the seventh Five-Year Plan declared that families with an annual income up to ₹ 1,600 to be considered as extremely poor household. For rural areas Planning Commission declared families with an annual income from ₹ 1,600 up to ₹ 3,500 as very very poor household, families in the income bracket of ₹ 3,501 to ₹ 4,800 as very poor household and families with an annual income in the range of ₹ 4,800 to ₹ 6,400 as poor families. The families with an annual income of more than ₹ 6,400 were regarded as families living above the poverty line (Bagchi, 1994). Familywise income distribution of the Bedias have been depicted in the above light.

Table 7 depicts poverty among the Bedias in all the three villages. Its shows variability at inter-community, inter-family and inter-village level during different seasons, yet most of the Bedia households are not poor, when measured on the basis of subsistence income level. It has been observed that about 22 per cent, 38 per cent, and 19 per cent Bedia households of Hesla, Ajaygarh and Piska village live below the poverty line. However, most of the poverty stricken Bedias of Hesla and Piska villages are only poor households while in Ajaygarh most of the Bedias who live below the poverty line are either very poor household or poor households. Most of the Bedia of Hesla and Piska earn an amount ranging between ₹ 6,401 and ₹ 20,000 annually. In Ajaygarh more than 40 per cent households in a single year earned the same range of money. More than 12 per cent Bedia of Ajaygarh earn more than ₹ 60,000 annually. Annual income amounting to more than ₹ 60,000 is also observed among 3.5 and 0.8 per cent Bedias of Piska and Hesla respectively. Familywise per capita data also shows variability in the income profile of the Bedia and is a measure to find out the income profile in a more authentic way since households are variable in size.

Table 7

Householdwise Income Profile by Villages

Degree of Poverty	*Annual Income (in ₹)*	*Name of Villages*							
		Hesla		*Ajaygarh*		*Piska*		*Total*	
		No.	*%*	*No.*	*%*	*No.*	*%*	*No.*	*%*
Extremely poor household	< 1600	—	—	2	3.5	—	—	2	0.8
Very very poor household	1,601–3,500	1	0.8	4	7.0	—	—	5	2.01
Very poor household	3,501–4,800	3	2.3	7	12.3	3	5.1	13	5.3
Poor house	4,801–6,400	24	18.7	9	15.8	8	13.8	41	16.8
Household above poverty line	6,401–10,000	27	20.9	16	28.0	21	36.2	64	26.2
	10,001–20,000	53	41.1	7	12.3	18	31.0	78	32.0
	20,001–30,000	10	7.7 7.7	—	—	1	1.8 8.6	11	4.5 8.2
	30,001–60,000	10	0.8	5	8.8	5	3.5	20	4.1
	>60,000	1		7	12.3	2		10	
	Total	129	100.0	57	100.0	58	100.0	244	100.0

Table 8 tells that per capita per annum income of most of the Bedia ranges in the income bracket between ₹ 1,000 and ₹ 2,999. However, average per capita per annum income is found to be below ₹ 1,000 in case of 6.9 per cent, 13.1 per cent and 24.6 per cent Bedias of Piska, Hesla and Ajaygarh respectively. Four Bedia households of Ajaygarh and one each households of Hesla and Piska have per capita annual income more than ₹ 12,000.

Table 8

Householdwise Per Capita Average Income by Villages

Annual Income (in ₹)	Hesla		Ajaygarh		Piska		Total	
	No.	%	No.	%	No.	%	No.	%
<–1,000	17	13.1	14	24.6	4	6.9	35	14.3
1,000–2,999	81	62.8	28	49.1	42	72.4	151	61.9
3,000–5,999	26	20.2	6	10.6	7	12.1	39	16.0
6,000–11,999	4	3.1	5	8.7	4	6.9	13	5.3
>–12,000	1	0.8	4	7.0	1	1.7	6	2.5
Total =	129	100.0	57	100.0	58	100.0	244	100.0

Educational Inequality

A wide range of inequality is also observed in level of education and literacy. In the present study a person who can read, write, work with understanding of any language and work out simple arithmetic are considered as literate. All children of the age group of 5 years or less are treated as illiterate. However, there are some children of 5 years age who have started going to school and may have picked up reading and writing a few odd words. Table 9 shows that a large number of Bedias are illiterate. Literacy rate is higher in case of male than that of their female counterparts. The Table further highlights that most of the literates read up to primary (i.e., up to Class IV) or junior secondary (up to Class VI) level. Mainly male Bedias have access to higher education. The Table 9 clearly depicts that though they are not educationally much advanced but among them there are postgraduates, engineers having B.E. degree and even agricultural graduates and honours graduates are found among them.

We have discussed above the 'inequality' in terms of income and educational achievements among the Bedias. We have discussed above how economic inequality and differentiation exists at inter-family, inter-clan and inter-village level. We discussed these issues in terms of clan structure, households, possession of modern amenities, including familywise total and per capita landholding pattern, primary and subsidiary vocations, as well as educational achievements. The inequality is caused by outside interventions like opening of job opportunity, specially through expansion of industries and coal mining operations in the adjoining area of the village Hesla and rural development works in the form of Jawahar Rojgar Yojana, Indira Awas Yojana and so on. Literacy campaigning, opening of more and more primary schools in the rural areas and the growing urge for imparting education to the children were responsible for educational advancement among the children of the present generation. However, social stigma and superstition along with low image profile of the women obstructed growth of female education.

Traditional System of Stratification

The myth of origin, history and mythology do not suggest existence of any traditional system of stratification among the Bedia. During the early part of last

Table 9

Level of Education

Level of Education	*Hesla*			*Ajaygarh*			*Piska*			*Total*		
	M	*F*	*Total*	*M*	*F*	*Total*	*M*	*F*	*Total*	*M*	*F*	*Total*
Illiterate	210 (32.8)	281 (43.8)	491 (76.6)	55 (17.3)	120 (37.7)	175 (55.0)	44 (15.5)	101 (35.6)	145 (51.1	309 (24.9)	502 (40.3)	811 (65.3)
Literate without formal education	7 (1.1)	2 (0.3)	9 (1.4)	5 (1.6)	1 (0.3)	6 (1.9)	4 (1.4)	1 (0.4)	5 (1.8)	16 (1.3)	4 (0.3)	20 (1.6)
Primary level (Class–IV)	61 (9.5)	24 (3.7)	85 (13.2)	23 (7.2)	21 (6.6)	44 (13.8)	21 (7.4)	20 (7.0)	41 (14.4)	105 (8.4)	65 (5.3)	170 (13.7)
Junior Secondary level (Class V-VIII)	32 (5.0)	3 (0.5)	35 (5.5)	31 (9.7)	14 (4.5)	45 (14.2)	31 (10.9)	14 (4.9)	45 (15.8)	94 (7.6)	31 (2.5)	125 (10.1)
Secondary level (Class IX-X)	16 (2.5)	1 (0.2)	17 (2.7)	37 (11.6)	2 (0.6)	39 (12.2)	37 (13.1)	2 (0.6)	39 (13.7)	90 (7.2)	5 (0.4)	95 (7.6)
Higher Secondary level (Class XI-XII)	1 (0.2)	—	1 (0.2)	4 (1.3)	—	4 (1.3)	4 (1.4)	—	4 (1.4)	9 (0.7)	—	9 (0.7)
College/Technically specialized higher education.	3 (0.4)	—	3 (0.4)	5 (1.6)	—	5 (1.6)	5 (1.8)	—	5 (1.8)	13 (1.1)	—	13 (1.0)
	330 (51.5)	311 (48.5)	641 (100.0)	160 (50.3)	158 (49.7)	318 (100.0)	146 (51.5)	138 (49.5)	284 (100.0)	636 (51.2)	607 (49.8)	1243 (100.0)

Figures within parenthesis indicate percentage.

Source: Field data

century, Bedia lived in Panch Pargana regions, which encompassed Bedia dominated Gola region of Hazaribag, Ranchi district as well as Jhalda police station of Purulia. In order to elevate their status not only within the Bedia fold but also in the regional social hierarchy where Kurmi Mahato lived as a dominant ethnic group, the Bedia followed the path of Sanskritization. In fact, during this period several regional communities, like Kurmi Mahato had been transformed into Kurmi Khabiya and Munda into Bhumij. Sarak Tantis had been transformed into Sarak Majhi by adopting Brahminical rituals and by Hindu methods of 'tribal absorption'. By discarding the practice of rearing of pig, pork eating, and taking the help of Brahmin and Vaishnab sacred specialists in life cycle rituals and religious observances and above all by adopting Kashyap gotra and the appellation of Majhi this section of Bedia sought a superior status, i.e., Hinduized Bedia within the greater Bedia fold. However, the indigenous Bedia do not recognize their superior status hence a partial horizontal stratification has been formed between Hinduized and non-converted Bedia. Both Majhi Bedia and non-converted Bedia claim their respective superior positions. In the Bedia tribal social structure certain statuses are considered as birth ascribed status and certain members by dint of their birth enjoy specified power and prestige. For example, the eldest son of the 'jeth rayat' often enjoys the status of the 'jeth rayat'. The 'jeth rayat' acts as the headman of the village. He is often referred to as Mahato which means headman. He is the key person who arranges all the community religious observances of the village in consultation with priest and some influential members of the village. He also often plays vital role in life cycle rituals of the members of the village. The 'jeth rayat' is always invited in any feast and celebration in the village or its vicinity where Bedia inhabit. He resolves both-intra and inter-community disputes with the help of elderly male members. The post of 'parganait' is also hereditary. 'Parganait' is the headman of the Pargana, which is believed to be the traditional supreme political unit of the Bedia. 'Parganait' looks after the moral, ethical and social aspects of the Bedia. Like 'parganait' the posts of 'ohedar' 'dewan' and 'sardar' in the Pargana council are also birth ascribed or hereditary in nature. But they can also be chosen by the 'parganait' from members of other families or clans. Thus, it may be stated that the Bedia have a functioning polity where elders from specific clans enjoy power and prestige, at village level. 'Ohedar' acts as a messenger who sends notice to different villages regarding any meeting convened by 'parganait'. 'Dewan' and 'sardar' help the parganait in his activities. The post of 'pahan' i.e., priest is not always a birth ascribed status but in reality the eldest male son of the 'pahan' often takes the role of new 'pahan' with the general approval of the villagers after the demise of his father.

Besides hereditary positions, now the achieved positions also play crucial roles. Achieved status also is a mode of achieving social prestige. The educated affluent and white-collared job holders or their family members often enjoy special status and privilege in the village. They are often consulted for intra-and inter-community disputes regarding land, property, matrimonial disputes, and ill-treatment towards any members of the family. They are often elected or selected as the members of various bodies of social control or councils meant for the general welfare of the village. Thus we find that most of the office bearers of

Bedia Bikash Samity, Bedia Samaj Unayan Parishad, Bedia Jati Sudar Samity, Gram Vikash Samity, and Adivasi Harijan Committee are either educated or affluent Bedia. Similarly in the political and trade union fields too, leadership is provided by educated Bedia. It has been seen that the leadership of Jharkhand Kishan Mazdoor Society, Jharkhand Mukti Morcha and a political party is mainly in the hands of the Bedia. 'Mukhia' is the elected headman in the Statutory Panchayat system. A few Bedia individuals from the studied villages have been elected as mukhia. Apart from political power, they are considered to be important functionaries for initiating the developmental activities of the government for the welfare of the Bedia in particular and all the villagers in general.

There is another category of achieved status in Bedia villages. The 'gunin' 'sakha' or 'bhagat' by their knowledge and expertise to perform the activities of the sorcerer and native medicine men often enjoy a special position in Bedia society. But since they are believed to possess power to perform black magic, their status in the Bedia society is differently perceived. Certain Bedia women were regarded as witch. Their position is extremely low in Bedia society. The present author however could not meet a single witch in the course of his fieldwork.

Stratification, Culture Contact and Social Change

A search for higher status during last century had prompted a section of Bedias to follow Sanskritization, like some neighbouring tribes. Regional Hindu chieftains also encouraged them to do so, to adopt a new name Majhi. Majhi Bedia became Hinduized by discarding many of their age-old habits like beef eating, participation of women in communal dancing and so on. They also started celebrating Shiv Puja, Mahabir Jhanda puja and so on in Hazaribagh and Tusu, Chata Parab, etc., in Ranchi. However, as in most parts of tribal India where we witness multi-faith coexistence and religious syncretism (Das, 2003), the Hindu Bedias could never give up all traditional religious traits, including belief in supernatural powers. Thus during tribal festivals specially community festivals namely Sarhul, Karam Parab, Sohorai, Sakharat and so on they attend them like other tribal people like the Munda, etc. In fact, in Hesla village their pahan, i.e., priest comes from the Munda community and in this village all the major religious festivals are arranged jointly by the Munda, the Bedia and the Karmali. No distinction is maintained between Hindu and non-Hindu Bedias. Their sorcerers, are also consulted by many non-Bedia tribal and non-tribal people who believe in their magico-religious powers and their indigenous concepts (preserved by the Bedia sorcerers) regarding disease and their methods of treatment.

The Bedia live in multi-ethnic villages, such as Hesla and Piska as also Ajaygarh, and interact with Koiri, Kurmi Mahato, Karmali and Prajapati. They establish gaongar and bartahi-jajamani links with artisans like Karmali, The 'Jajmani' connection is often established between the Bedia and the Vaishnava. Thus, we see that the Bedias have become part of local caste society and some caste norms are adopted, but most of the Bedias are segregated and excluded from the core social and economic activities as they belong to lower strata.

Acknowledgement

Author is grateful to Dr N.K. Das, Project Coordinator, for his critical comments and guidance in preparation of this report.

References

Dalton, E.T. 1872, *Descriptive Ethnology of Bengal,* Calcutta: Government Press.

Das, N.K. 2003, 'An Outline of Syncretism', in *Culture, Religion and Philosophy: Studies in Syncretism.* N.K. Das (Ed.). Jaipur: Rawat Publications.

Dutta Majumdar, N. 1956, *The Santal: A Study in Culture-Change,* Calcutta: Dept. of Anthropology.

Hunter, W.W. 1976, *A Statistical Hand Book of Bengal (Hazaribagh and Lohardga)* Vol. XVI. (Reprint) Delhi.

Lister, E. 1917, Bihar and Orissa District Gazetteers (Hazaribagh) Patna: Government Press.

Prasad, N. 1961, *Land and People of Tribal Bihar,* Ranchi: TRI.

Risley, H.H. 1891, *The Tribes and Castes of Bengal,* Calcutta: Secretariat Press.

Singh, K.S. 1994, *The People of India: The Scheduled Tribes,* Vol. IV. New Delhi: Oxford University Press.

21 Changing Tribe-Caste Stratification and Secularization of a Kokna Tribal Village of Maharashtra

Debesh Roy

This paper elucidates the changing patterns of social stratification among the Kokna and other tribes and castes living in Karanjkhed village of Dindori tehsil of Nasik district in Maharashtra. It describes the stratification at three levels, intra-tribe, inter-tribe and tribe versus caste. The focus is on the Kokna social system in Karanjkhed village. Though the study was limited to the Kokna tribe only, yet information were gathered from other tribes and castes of Karanjkhed village, in order to assess the relative statuses of the communities. Fieldwork was originally undertaken under the project 'Tribal India: Structure, Pattern and Transformation' during 1993 among the Kokna tribe. During next year data on the project 'Stratification and Social Change in Tribal India' were also collected. Fieldwork was undertaken in Karanjkhed, the Kokna dominated village that is 68 km away from the district headquarters Nasik and nearly 40 km away from the tehsil headquarter, Dindori. The village is on the top of a hill and surrounded by a number of small hills of Sahyadri range, with a regular undulating feature.

Altogether, the village has six different ethnic groups namely, the Kokna, the Mahadev Koli, the Teli, the Vaishya Vani, the Mahar and Marwari. Out of these six, the Kokna and the Mahadev Koli are Scheduled Tribes while the Teli and Vaishya Vani are Other Backward Castes (OBCs), the Mahars are Scheduled Caste and the Marwari are in the General category. The total population of the village is 1,025, of which 513 are males and 512 are females, distributed over 186 households. Table 1 indicates the communitywise distribution of the village population.

Table 1

Ethnic Distribution of Village Population

Ethnic Groups	*Male*	*Female*	*Total*	*No. of Household*
Kokna (ST)	427	428	855	146
Mahadev Koli (ST)	37	31	68	15
Mahar (SC)	40	45	85	21
Teli (OBC)	6	5	11	2
Vaishya Vani (OBC)	1	1	2	1
Marwari (General)	2	2	4	1
Total	513	512	1,025	186

From the Table it is revealed that the Kokna are the dominant ethnic group in the village in terms of population with maximum number of households. The Mahars occupy the second position in numerical strength and also in the number of households. The village is named after a kind of local tree called Karanjjhar which had a thick vegetation in this particular village sometime in the past. The village has two broad divisions namely: (1) Orchawadi (upper village) and (2) Khachawadi (lower village). The Hanuman Mandir (Hanuman temple) of the village is situated at the middle point which is also the demarcation of Orchawadi and Khalchawadi hamlets. Settlement from the north and up to the Hanuman temple is known as Orchawadi while from Hanuman temple to down south is known as Khalchawadi. By and large, settlement pattern of the village is systematically arranged on both sides of the only central road which goes from extreme north to southern part of the village. There is no particular settlement area for any particular tribe or castes except in the case of the Mahar community who are exclusively concentrated on the southernmost part of the village, known as Ragwada, which comes under the Khalchawadi hamlet. All other tribal and non-tribal population live side by side without making any particular ethnicity based settlement areas. The important landmarks of the village are: village primary school, Gram Panchayat office, Samaj Mandir (community hall), Hanuman temple, Anganbadi and a water reservoir for the supply of drinking water in the village. All these landmarks are found at the centre of the village, adjoining the Hanuman Mandir. The Hanuman Mandir is a very important spot of the village in front of which there is an open space where day-to-day gossiping goes on besides occasional gatherings for specific purposes.

The economy of the village is mainly based on agriculture. Almost all the Kokna are agriculturists by occupation and they are generally owner-cultivators. It is interesting to note that even the Kokna women are so involved with cultivation that they usually give first priority to cultivation. They undertake their household duties when they are free from their agriculture based duties. So far as religion is concerned, except the Mahars and one Marwari family, the rest of the tribal and non-tribal populations follow Hinduism. All the Mahars are Neo-Buddhists and the Marwari family is Jain by religion.

Kokna: The Identity of the Tribe

The Kokna tribe is also known a Kokni in Maharashtra. It is very well known and one of the primitive tribes of the state, whose constitutional status is Scheduled Tribe in Maharashtra. "Their name indicates that they are a tribe from the Konkan, probably so named upon immigration, and the inference is that they are one of the hill tribes from Thane" (Enthoven, 1922: 265). From their dialect it may also be assumed that the Kokna belonged to the Konkan as their dialect is Kokul, a mixed dialect of Gujarati and Marathi. It is also said that the Kokna were driven northward by the pressure of devastating Durgadevi famine from 1396 to 1408 (Enthoven, 1922: 265).

So far as the distribution of the tribe is concerned the Kokna have some population in Gujarat and in Dadra and Nagar Haveli but are not as numerically strong as in Maharashtra. In the state of Gujarat, the Kokna are found in Surat,

Dangs, Boroda, Kharai and in Ahmedabad. In Maharashtra, they are mainly found in Talods, Navapur, Sakri and Nandurbar area of Dhule district; Jowar, Mokhada and Dahanu tehsils of the Thane district and Dindori, Surgana, Kalwan, Satana and Peth tehsils of Nasik district. In other districts of Maharashtra namely, Mumbai, Pune, Jalgaon, Nanded and Raigarh, etc., their population strength is not very significant. Table 2 depicts the distribution of the Kokna population in some districts of Maharashtra.

Table 2

Distribution of the Kokna Population in Some Districts of Maharashtra

Name of the Districts	*Male*	*Female*	*Total*
Nasik	1,12,011	1,09,930	2,21,941
Dhule	43,425	43,089	86,514
Thane	20,679	20,797	41,476
Nanded	1,152	1,058	2,210
Greater Bombay	855	779	1,634
Pune	165	133	298
Raigarh	56	49	105
Jalgaon	171	194	365
Aurangabad	66	42	108

Source: Census of India, Special tables for S/T, Maharashtra.

The Kokna do not have any sub-group such as sub-tribe, phratry or moiety division. But they practise kul (clan) exogamy and community endogamy. Kul plays a very significant role in regulation of marriage alliances. It is also used as surname by Kokna. Marriage within the same kul is never permitted, because it is their belief that marriage within the same kul is equivalent to a marriage between the brothers and sisters. The origin and meaning of the kul is unknown to most of the Kokna villagers. However, it is observed that there is no fixed object or phenomenon after which kul names are derived. These kul names have been derived from many natural objects, animals, place names and also from occupation. A few Kokna kul names as collected from the field are: Gaikwad (door of cattleshed), Wag (tiger), Wagmare (killer of a tiger). Satpute (seven consecutive sons who survived. This also a place name), Impal (place name), Deshmukh (head of an area), etc. Among the Kokna, lineage is called 'Pirri'. Lineage has some important functions in many socio-religious rites and rituals. Pirri is considered for tracing one's ancestors. The Kokna are aware of their Pirri because all the dead ancestors are worshipped in various socio-religious functions. Making of silver images for all the dead persons that is of 'Pirri' members is a tradition which is called as 'irr'. These silver images are considered as Deo (deity) or Kuldeoti. These silver images are kept in a particular place in the house called Dewara where regular worship goes on, keeping an oil lamp lit day and night. All the 'pirri' ancestors are worshipped during marriage and Holi festival. In some Kokna families, the silver images for the female lineage ancestors are also made, called Supali, but this is not compulsory.

The Kokna of Karanjkhed mostly live in nuclear family and the number of joint families is gradually declining. The Kokna practise both monogamy and polygamy. But nowadays practising polygamy is not very popular in a normal situation though it has usual social sanction even today. Practising polygamy is not a very regular trend. Divorce (Farkat) and remarriage (Gandharva) are allowed for both males and females. Both widow and widower remarriage are permitted in Kokna society. But neither any female divorcee nor any widow is allowed to marry a bachelor, though male persons may go for second marriage with a maiden. In the case of Gandharva, rites and rituals are very simple while in the case of lagna all the regular marriage rituals are performed. Marriage is called by the Kokna as lagna. The Kokna practise Dej (bride price) even today but not *Hunda* (dowry). Paying Dej is a respectful practice, whereas paying Hunda is a shameful practice. Dej is given both in cash and kind. Besides the regular options of marriage, only junior sororate is permitted. Other than mother's brother's daughter, no type of consaguinal marriages are allowed in Kokna society. Property is normally distributed along the male line following the rule of male equigeniture. The Kokna either cremate or bury their dead. But all the unmarried persons and minor children are buried as social norm.

The Kokna practise Hinduism though they have a good number of tribal 'Deos' (deities). They also believe in ancestor's spirits, evil spirits, witchcraft 'Bhutani' and they worship many natural objects. They celebrate many Hindu festivals too. They propitiate many Hindu gods and goddesses like Shankar, Parvati, Laxmi, Satyanarayan, Ganapati, Vittoba, Rukmini, Saptashringi, Jagadamba mata, Tulja Bhavani, Ram and many others. The major festivals of their own are Dongrideopuja, Wagdeopuja and Holi. But now many Kokna have adopted many other local festivals of the Hindu religion. Now they worship their village deity, Hanuman in a very Hinduized way and it is now celebrated for seven days. The celebration is marked as Hanuman puja though the traditional way of propitiating this deity was very simple and it was a single day celebration.

In Karanjkhed, the Kokna do not have any local government of their own. At present they have a local council called Panch for all the villagers, irrespective of tribes or castes. The head of the Panch is Police Patil who is selected by the District Collector. The present Police Patil in Karanjkhed village is a lady who belongs to the Kokna community. The Police Patil is assisted by a Kotwal or Naik who communicates information regarding the meeting, venue, time and date to all the villagers. This post of Kotwal is selected from the Mahadev Koli community who also acts as a messenger for all the villagers in any situation. Police Patil is responsible for maintaining the law and order situation of the village. In some serious cases, intervention of police and local judiciary is also sought.

Stratification and Differentiations at the Intra-tribal Level

The Kokna of Karanjkhed practise group endogamy. They do not have any sub-group. They strictly follow kul (clan) exogamy. The clan plays a significant role in marriage alliances. But there is no hierarchical order among clans and thus there is no differentiation at this level. Some notion of upper and lower exists within the tribe. However, in the overall hierarchical order of lower, middle and upper strata in the Kokna social structure, there is no apparent difference in terms of marriage norms and other norms. There is no recognition of hypergamy and hypogamy in normal marriage alliances. In their society, besides monogamy as a regular practice, polygamy has equal social sanction and is never looked down upon, even today. In the Kokna society, either party can go for remarriage as it is permitted for male or female divorcees, and for widow and widowers. Remarriage in the Kokna society is known as Gandharva while regular negotiated marriage is called as Lagna. The Kokna practise Dej (bride price) but not dowry.

Some economic factors, education, government service and trade are regarded as determinants of higher status. The status of Guruji (teacher) and qualified persons are considered high. Common people have a special reverence and esteem towards the Guruji, who is honoured by showing respect to him. He is also approached for advice from him. The sense of honour towards the Guruji among the Kokna of Karanjkhed is still very high. On the part of Guruji also, his behaviour and dealings with the villagers are modest, honest, sincere, and the Guruji has a charming personality. By virtue of his profession as a teacher, Guruji has occupied a very esteemed position among the Kokna of Karajkhed village.

The Koknas of Karanjkhed are primarily agriculturists and most of them are landowners. Out of total 146 Kokna households in the village, a total of 16 households are landless. These landless people form the lowest strata within the tribe. Agriculture being their traditional as well as present-day primary occupation, having some cultivable land is not just an economic security, it indicates one's economic position too. Having more land as economic resource indicates one's sound economic condition and highest strata in the village. Such persons are popularly known as Shrimonth (rich person). Rich persons hold some social prestige too. They have a distinguished social position as they are Shrimonth, and they belong to high economic class. They maintain their social status by deploying more daily-wage labourers during agricultural seasons, leading a better and comfortable life, donating more money in socio-religious functions and by maintaining more social interaction with the other Koknas who are also economically quite well off having huge landed property. Economic solvency also counts at the time of selecting spouses for marriage alliances. Though it is not a very rigid criterion, however, establishing relationship through marriage often demands a good economic background of both the parties. Economically well-off parents also have more educated and higher qualified children, that helps maintain the social status of the parents. It is found that among the Kokna of Karanjkhed, there is one graduate, two postgraduates of which one is female, one D.Ed. and B.Ed. each and one M.B.B.S. degree holder who are not only the pride of their economically well-off parents, they are also the pride of all the Kokna of Karanjkhed village. Father being the owner of lands, as head of the family is duly honoured. Eldest brother holds the right of succession and thus enjoys more controlling power over the parental lands. There are land disputes between brothers.

Political System and Village Panch

In the traditional Kokna society, the function of Panch is respected. The post of Patil as head of the Panch is of great significance. The post of Patil was a highly honoured post at the village level council and always went in the male line. Patil held a supreme power in the village and was responsible for both rewards and punishment in the village. He was responsible for solving disputes, and resolving critical situations related to the village as well as people. So the post of the Patil was not only an esteemed post, it was a position at the top of the social structure. In due course the process of democratization has taken place. Thus, the village Panch and village council act as statutory council. Village Karanjkhed has a Panch and its head is now called as Police Patil. It is now a statutory post selected by the District Collector and not a hereditary one. The scope of Police Patil as village head is now wider in comparison with the post of Patil in the traditional Panch because of legal support from the District Collector. Now, the role of Police Patil or Patil has been formalized as the Patil is now responsible for maintaining law and order in the village and is directly involved with all legal and statutory functions of the government. As a result the present post of Police Patil is not only more powerful than the Patil of the traditional Kokna society, the post extracts more honour, esteem, prestige and social status among the Kokna and other villagers as a whole. The Police Patil of Karanjkhed is a Kokna lady called Kamala Gaikwad who has been symbol of empowerment of tribal women.

The posts of Sarpanch and eight other elected members of the Gram Panchayat have some special social position in Karanjkhed village as they are the representatives of the villagers and are responsible for the development of the village. Since they jointly act as pressure group for implementing various developmental programmes through Gram Panchayat, they also hold a position of honour, status and prestige. But as soon as they complete the tenure of their service or they are terminated from their posts, the social position of the Sarpanch and other elected members goes down as a common man without any special prestige. Political leaders also hold a special position in the Kokna society as they are capable of mobilizing the common people.

Religion: Old Specialist and New Priest

Deoram Gaikwad, a Kokna man, acts as a Bhagat in Karanjkhed village. He is the traditional specialist. In the Kokna society, the position of Bhagat (religious mendicants) is highly honoured not only as a sacred specialist but also a medicine man. He is believed to have some supernatural powers and is capable of controlling all sorts of evil spirits, ancestral spirits, ghosts and many others by appeasing them through worship and sacrifice. He is the person who has supreme control over the witch-crafts performed by the Bhutari (witch). The Bhagat also specializes in worshipping Dongrideo and Wagdeo, two very important deities among the Kokna. The Bhagat gives medicines during ailments and provides explanation for any unfortunate happenings. So his place in the Kokna society is rather indispensable and he deserves a highest social position. Besides tribal Bhagat, there is no sacred specialist who has that much of social status and esteem in day-to-day life.

In recent years the influence of local Hinduism has decreased the roles and the social position of the Bhagat. At present majority of Kokna in Karanjkhed village are not only under the influence of local Hinduism, they are also getting exposed to the modern ways of living, with the expansion of modern communication and new medical facilities. As a result, the roles of traditional Bhagats have also been curtailed in recent times. Now, the Kokna of Karanjkhed are deploying local Brahmin priests for marriage and tribals are also getting their illnesses treated using modern medical methods. The local Maharashtrian Brahmin priests are now respected by virtue of their sacred performances. However, the position of the Bhagat as sacred specialist in socio-religious activities is still very essential as the Kokna of Karanjkhed still believe in evil spirits, witchcrafts and in many natural and supernatural objects.

Differentiation at the Inter-tribal Level

It is found that in Karanjkhed, there are only two tribal communities namely the Kokna and the Mahadev Koli. Table 3 shows that there are total 855 Koknas in the village of which 427 are males and 428 are females, living in 146 households. The Mahadev Koli on the other hand have a total population of only 68 of which 37 are male and 31 are females residing in 15 households. So, it is very clear that the Mahadev Koli are numerically a very small group in comparison with the Kokna tribe in Karanjkhed.

In fact, though the Kokna are numerically dominant compared to Mahadev Koli but no serious differentiation is visible in day-to-day interactions between the Kokna and the Mahadev Koli. Both the tribes live side by side without maintaining any social distance or forming independent settlement areas. There is friendship among the Kokna and Mahadev Koli boys and girls. However, a sense of superiority always persists among the Kokna. The Mahadev Koli admit this. Actually, to some extent, both the communities are culturally similar to each other. Both have some common Deos (deities) and rituals and there has been a long association between both the tribes. It was reported that the Kokna, Mahadev Koli and the Warli are three major tribes who live harmoniously in all the tribal villages of Dindori, Peth, Surgana and Kalwan tehsils of Nasik district in Maharashtra. It is observed that in villages where all three tribes live the political head, the Panch of village council is selected from Kokna tribe. It was so because of the established superiority of the Kokna over the Mahadev Koli and Warli. On the other hand, Mahadev Koli always provided the Kotwal or Naik in the Panch whose main function was to assist the Patil in any meeting and also to work as messenger for the villagers. Both the posts are hereditary and under no circumstances ethnic identity attached with the posts can be changed. During fieldwork, in Karanjkhed, the post of the Patil (now called as Police Patil) was with the Kokna community while the post of Kotwal was with Babu Nago Dombare who belongs to the Mahadev Koli community.

In marriage and in other socio-religious functions, the Kokna invite the Mahadev Koli who take part in the socio-religious functions and consume foods and drinks offered to them. The Kokna on the other hand also take part in any socio-religious functions of the Mahadev Koli but usually do not take any cooked food, though the drinking of *Daru* (liquor) is not prohibited. But now, some changes are visible in the commensal rules too. Many Kokna now take cooked food from the Mahadev Koli where friendship and intimacy is present. But orthodox people, particularly from the older generations, do not consume any food from the Mahadev Koli even today. Actually, with the influence of modernization and education and because of more interactions with outside world many marginal differentiations are gradually diminishing between the Kokna and the Mahadev Koli, though a sense of superiority is still maintained by the Kokna at the level of social hierarchy.

At the economic level also, there is less differentiation now. The Kokna are always deploying the Mahadev Koli in any agricultural operation and in other types of work and vice versa. The free exchange of labour between the Kokna and the Mahadev Koli under the Palthe system is possible which is not compulsory but obligatory. In this system, service is discharged to a person willingly without taking any remuneration and thus, it becomes obligatory on the part of the service taker to discharge his services to the service giver as a reciprocity. This type of relationship still survives between the Kokna and Mahadev Koli in Karanjkhed village.

Besides the mentioned senior-junior relationship between the Kokna and the Mahadev Koli in the Panch (local council) in Karanjkhed village, no other significant differentiation is visible between the Kokna and the Mahadev Koli in political spheres. Practically speaking, with the intervention of the District Collector for the selection of the Police Patil, the traditional notion of holding the post of Patil exclusively by the Kokna has been changed. Earlier, the post of Patil was always headed by a Kokna which was hereditary too. But now it is not so. Now, even a Mahadev Koli may be selected to the post of Patil if the District Collector finds him suitable. In Karanjkhed, Police Patil is still from Kokna group while in other villages, the Mahadev Koli are also now getting the chance of becoming Police Patil as the post has now a statutory support from the District office. In Karanjkhed, besides the post of Police Patil in 'Panch', three other elected members of the Gram Panchayat are from the Kokna community while the post of the Sarpanch is from the Mahadev Koli, who lives in Sarsale village. There are two more elected members of the Gram Panchayat who belong to the Mahadev Koli group, one each in Eklare and Sarsale villages. So all these Mahadev Koli people, either as Sarpanch or as elected member of the Gram Panchayat, are now in a very good position, as they now enjoy status, prestige and controlling power over the rest of the villages irrespective of being tribes or non-tribes. So, now in the political arena, differentiations are not necessarily ethnicity based. In Karanjkhed, not only does the post of Police Patil, the most powerful and prestigious post at the village level, belong to a Kokna female, there are two more Mahadev Koli women, living in Eklare and Sarsale villages, who have achieved the status of elected member of the Karanjkhed Gram Panchayat. As per Panchayat Raj rules, 30 per cent or 33.3 per cent of the total seat in Panchayats must be kept reserved for the female candidates mainly to encourage the womenfolk in politics. This type of provision has also changed the outlook of the females and common people.

Deoram Gaikwad is the Bhagat of Karanjkhed village. He belongs to the Kokna community, and holds a higher social status in both Kokna and Mahadev Koli societies. Being a Bhagat he not only favours the Kokna people of the village, but the Mahadev Koli also enjoy his favours. For his services, he is given some cash money, rice, nagli and daru (liquor). As a whole, the inter-tribal differentiations between the Kokna and the Mahadev Koli are not very prominent, except certain sense of high and low in their social hierarchical order, perceived by them. A very close interaction between them is seen, during the Dongrideo puja (worship of hill God), Way baras (worship of tiger God) and Hanuman Saptaha (a week-long programme of the village deity).

Tribe Versus Non-tribes

If we look into the ethnic composition of Karanjkhed it is found that among the non-tribal populations, the Mahar community is the next dominant group in the village whose numerical position is just next to the Kokna tribe. The non-tribal communities of the village are: the Mahar (SC), the Teli (OBC), the Vaishya Vani (OBC) and the Marwari (General). For better understanding of the ethnic composition of the village Karanjkhed, we may see Table 3.

Table 3

Distribution of the Tribal and Non-tribal Population of the Village

Ethnic Status	*Ethnic Groups*	*Male*	*Female*	*Total*	*No. of Households*
Tribal	(1) Kokna (ST)	427	428	855	146
	(2) Mahadev Koli (ST)	37	31	68	15
	Total	464	459	923	161
Non-tribal	(1) Mahar (SC)	40	45	85	21
	(2) Teli (OBC)	6	5	11	2
	(3) Vaishya Vani (OBC)	1	1	2	1
	(4) Marwari (General)	2	2	4	1
	Total	49	53	102	25

From the Table 3 it is evident that the Mahar community has a total population of 85, confined in 21 households while the Teli group has only a total of 11 people residing in 2 households. The Marwari occupy the third position with a total population of 4 and the Vaishya Vani, who have only two people in a single household, are placed at the bottom.

If we look into the interactional pattern between the Kokna and four non-tribals in the village, social stratification and differentiation at the various levels are visible. If we arrange all these castes along with the Kokna in a hierarchic order, the following order takes place from the perceptions of the Kokna:

(1) Marwari (upper caste people)
(2) Teli (OBC)
(3) Vaishya Vani (OBC)
(4) Mahar (SC)

Within this hierarchical order, the Kokna place themselves just next to Marwari people but is not accepted by castes. There are many situations when the Kokna and the four other non-tribal communities, both the Marwari and the Vaishya Vani regularly interact mainly as later are running one attachakki (flour mill) and one kirana dukan (small grocer's shop) respectively. Actually, both traders have a very small population and have been living in this village only for a few years just to run their business. Other than the regular business dealings, they are not involved in any socio-religious activities of the Kokna tribe. The Kokna on the other hand too, do not find these communities, particularly the Vaishya Vani, equal to their own social status and position. However, the Vaishya Vani find the Kokna unequal though the Kokna consider the Vaishya Vani group inferior to them in the hierarchical structure. In Karanjkhed, the position of the Teli community among the non-tribal groups is just below the Marwari group and they are placed above the Vaishya Vani group though the status of both the communities in Maharashtra is OBC. In Karanjkhed, both the Teli families are next door to the Kokna households and thus every day interaction happens between the Kokna and the Teli though the commensal rule between these two communities is not very flexible. Both groups can exchange water and other drinks but not any 'kutcha food' (boiled in water). The Kokna consider the Teli group inferior to them in social status as they are pressing oil to earn a living while the Kokna are farmers. The Teli on the other hand, since they are non-tribal feel superior to the Kokna but they do not express it as they are not very old in this village and because of the dominant numerical strength of the Kokna in the village. The Teli are still a minority group who have a total population of 11 persons, confined in two households. So, in the case of the Teli and Vaishya Vani, we see that duration of stay in the village and their numerical strength are not favourable and that affects the perceptions about relative statuses in Karanjkhed village.

The Mahar being the only Scheduled Caste community of Karanjkhed, are found in the lowest strata of the hierarchical order of the village. The Kokna have a very limited interaction with the Mahar on a daily basis. Similarly, the Mahar also do not show any respect towards the Kokna and Mahadev Koli. To them, the Kokna are a lower grade people and thus, they do not have much social interaction with this tribal group usually. On the contrary, the Kokna treat the Mahar almost at the level of untouchables though in present-day situation there is no untouchability at the surface level of village social system. To the Mahar, the Kokna are not only at the lowest rung of society, they are heavy alcoholic too. So, differentiations at many levels are maintained with them and there is no question of social mixing, taking food and drink or exchange of water. To the Kokna, the Mahar are one of the degraded Scheduled Castes in Maharashtra who belong to the lowest occupational category and were earlier the untouchables because of their traditional unclean profession. In Karanjkhed, the Mahar are now called as "Rajparivar" (the kingly families) and their separate settlement in the village is referred to as "Rajwada" (the area of the kingly persons). Despite this, the Kokna and other tribal and non-tribal communities of Karanjkhed still address them as Mahar, though publicly they are referred as Rajparivar. The Mahar on the other hand are usually afraid of loose conversation with Koknas. To them, being even a tribe, the Mahadev Koli are far better in their manners and behaviours and thus, the Mahar always place the Mahadev Koli above the Kokna and many have some social interactions with the Mahadev Koli. Practically, the Mahadev Koli also treat the Mahar at the lowest social position but their approach towards the Mahar is not so antagonistic as between the Kokna and the Mahar.

So if we try to look into the existing social relations, we can see that for all practical purposes, the position of the Mahar in Karanjkhed village is definitely the lowest, and differentiation at all levels are very prominent in comparison with any other tribal and non-tribal population. Practically, the Mahar of the village are quite isolated and they are restricted in there regular interaction with the Kokna. They live in the southernmost part of the village, forming a separate settlement area of their own ethnic group now known as Rajwada. Other than this distinctive settlement area, there is no separate hamlet of any other community. So, excepting the Mahars, all the other tribal and non-tribal groups live side by side without having any separate hamlet. Within the Rajwada hamlet of the Mahars, there is provision for supplying drinking water through taps. Same provision is found in rest of the village too. So, the Mahars do not have to depend on other parts of the village for collecting water. However, the Mahars of the Rajwada settlement often face water problems. This is because, the Rajwada settlement is on elevated ground and thus, non-availability of water due to low pressure is a regular occurrence, particularly during the lean period or during winter when the flow of water comes down naturally. Under such a situation Mahars are forced to fetch water from nearby water taps which are not within the Rajwada hamlet. It was reported that only a decade back, the Mahars were not allowed to fetch water from any public water point. But this type of differentiation is not very prominent now-a-days, because of the government's constant efforts to eradicate such discriminations. Now, the Mahars of Karanjkhed are also getting all support from the government's policies towards this downtrodden people. Earlier, they were not only restrained from collecting water from the public water sources, they were not even allowed to go through the central road of the village. This indicates the nature and extent of social stratification that persisted in Karanjkhed between the Mahar and the rest of the population, particularly the Kokna, the most numerically dominant group of the village. Of course, those days have gone and now, no Kokna has any guts to behave with the Mahar in this fashion any more, though the Mahars are yet to integrate fully with the main stream of village activities.

In Karanjkhed, the Mahar have their own burial ground for disposing the dead. They are not invited to join in the collective village festivals like Dongrideo puja and Hanuman Saptaha. No subscription is collected from any Mahar in any collective socio-religious function at the village level while, the contributions both in cash and kinds are usually collected from all other tribal and non-tribal population of the village. But in all the socio-religious functions, the Kokna take the lead. Social exclusion of the Mahars is apparent in many ways. Fact remains that even today, the Mahars mostly prefer to go through some short cut roads which start from their hamlet Rajwada, and meet the state road Vani – Bhanwar.

However, the Mahar are not totally isolated from all sort of social interactions. Their position in Karanjkhed village as providers of service still bears some social significance. They are often deployed by the Kokna and other tribal and non-tribal groups as and when their service as labourers are required. The Mahars are also paid for their services in cash or kind or both, for their service being musicians in marriage parties and in many other socio-religious functions. For their role as musician, they usually charge ₹ 300 to 500 for each contract. But in the village primary school, there is no such differentiation seen and Mahar students get the same facilities as are applicable to all other ethnic groups of the village. There is no separate sitting arrangement for the Mahar students and there is no humiliation by the other students and teacher. The distribution of the total student strength including the Mahars is shown in a Table 4.

Table 4

Ethnic Distribution of the Students in the Village Primary School

Ethnic-Group	*I*		*II*		*III*		*IV*		*Grand Total*
	Boys	*Girls*	*Boys*	*Girls*	*Boys*	*Girls*	*Boys*	*Girls*	
Kokna (ST)	12	4	6	5	2	4	5	1	39
Mahadev Koli (ST)	2	0	0	0	5	0	0	3	10
Mahar (SC)	2	0	1	1	2	0	1	0	7
Total	16	4	7	6	9	4	6	4	56

Source: Attendance Registers of the School during February, 1993. Practically speaking, the entire interactional pattern between the tribe versus tribe and tribe versus non-tribe is now secularized and stratification and differentiation at various levels seem negligible.

Summary and Conclusion

This article has described the changing patterns of stratification and ritual hierarchy in a Maharashtra village, where the Kokna tribe is not only numerically dominant, they now enjoy considerable social status in village-level political and economic spheres. Some of these changes are result of increasing secularization of village society. Indeed, despite considerable culture change and Hinduization, the Kokna people retain their religious beliefs and tribal institutions such as clan, lineage and traditional leaders. Tribal identity is maintained through veneration of tribal deities, ancestors, evil spirits and through observance of witchcraft. Tribal priest Bhagat still plays important role as shaman-diviner and medicine-man. Rich Kokna however also receive services of Brahmin priests. The Kokna and Mahadev Koli are two tribes of the village Karanjkhed, as we described above. In the traditional village council the head is chosen from the Kokna tribe and the assistant of head is provided by Mahadev Koli tribe. In fact, in all neighbouring villages where these two tribes live with the Warli tribe, the Koknas always enjoyed the higher status as only they were entitled to provide the head. The tribes now live with caste people in the villages. In Karanjkhed village, the Hindu castes regard the tribes as inferior only in ritual sphere. Political dominance of the Koknas on account of the numerical strength and their economic prosperity places them at par with the 'higher' caste people. The Mahar Scheduled Caste belongs to lower strata in the village but many common privileges enjoyed by SC and ST and their specified representation in statutory council brings them closer to each other. Secular factors are more important in day to day village life now.

Reference

Enthoven, R.E. 1922, *Tribe and Caste of Bombay*, Vol. 2, Bombay Mumbai: Central Press.

22 Bhotia Tribe-Caste Cluster, Religious-Secular Ranking and Social Exclusion in Uttarakhand

Mukul Hazra

The main purpose of this paper is to describe the stratification patterns and aspects of social change among the Bhotia of Uttarakhand. The Bhotia cluster includes tribe and caste segments further divided into active clans, which are ranked. To understand the changing patterns of social stratification in Bhotia community, issues like the traditional economy and the impact of Sino-Indian war in the 1960s are taken into consideration, along with the unique ecological circumstances of the Bhotia settlements, specially the system of summer resorts, in the high Himalayas. At the same time the existence of the caste Hindus in their vicinity is also a factor influencing the stratification patterns. Scholars have observed that unlike the plains, in the Himalayan region the twofold division of the castes into Bith and non-Bith is sharply established as a system of stratification. The Bith-category encompasses the upper castes of the region which include 'indigenous Brahmins' and 'Rajputs' inclusive of the Khasiyas (Das, 1995: 146). The Bith includes only the twice born castes while non-Bith comprises other castes, such as the artisans, Halias, the agriculturists and the workers: Lohar, Darji, Auji, Koli, Dhobi, etc. The Bith category includes Brahmins and Rajputs from plains and Khas Rajputs. The Bhotias remained in regular contact with the Biths for procuring various articles of daily necessity. Thus, The Bhotias came to borrow some of the cultural traits of the caste people living in proximity to them in the Himalayas.

The Bhotias in Uttarakhand are mainly found in the Garhwal and Kumaon divisions. Their main concentration is found in four districts, viz., Uttarkashi and Chamoli in Garhwal division and Almora and Pithoragarh of Kumaon division. In these districts the Bhotias mainly live in seven villages viz. Biyans, Chamundas and Darma in Pithoragarh, Johar in Almora, Mana and Niti valley in Chamoli and Bhagirathi valley of Uttarkashi. The Bhotia are not a single unified tribe. They are divided into several groups. In Chamoli the Bhotias inhabit Mana valley nearly four kilometres from the shrine of Badrinath and the inhabitants are Marchha Bhotias. In Niti valley of the same district live both the Marchhas and Tolchas. Upper Niti valley villages like Niti, Bampa and Gamsali are occupied by Marchhas whereas lower Niti valley is occupied by the Tolcha Bhotias. The names of the two Bhotia groups may have been derived from the altitude of their habitat. In local usage "Talla Chhal" means lower part and "Malla Chhal" means upper part. So the Bhotias living in the lower valleys have been named Tolcha and those living in the upper valleys nearer to the snowline and Indo-Tibet border in the district of Chamoli are called Marchha. The Bhotias living in Uttarkashi district are called Jaad. They derive their name from the valley they originally inhabited, before coming to their present habitat in the village of Bageri in Bhagirathi valley, i.e., Jaad Ganga or Janhavi Ganga.

Table 1

Distribution of Bhotia Groups

Bhotia Group	*Division*	*District*	*Tehsil*
Johri	Kumaon	Almora	Almora
Shauka	Kumaon	Pithoragarh	Munsiari
Tolcha	Garhwal	Chamoli	Joshimath
Marcha	Garhwal	Chamoli	Joshimath
Jaad	Garhwal	Uttarkashi	Bhatwari

The Bhotias are primarily a trading community. They used to practise trade with Tibet mainly before the War during summer from their summer homes in the high Himalayas adjacent to Indo-Tibetan frontier. They used to trade through grain. In the past, local Hindus and Bhotias living in higher altitudes had regular contacts with those Bhotias who had friendly relations with the Tibetan people. However, despite their long contact with the Hindus, no serious Sanskritization process of Hinduization ever took place ritually amongst the Bhotias. Thus, the Bhotias of higher altitude were generally considered to be ritually impure, mainly because the Bhotia-Buddhists are beef (yak) eaters. Thus, due to commensal relation with the Tibetans these Buddhist Bhotias living in higher reaches maintained cordial relations with the hills neighbours, but were regarded as degraded for their food customs.

The economic organization of the Bhotias has undergone drastic change after the Sino-Indian war. In fact, the economic order of the present Bhotias is the reoriented and modified form of the old economic order. The Bhotia economy was highly developed through Tibet trade and cultivation on hill terraces. The Bhotia economy thus traditionally depended on trade with Tibet, pastoralism, woolen handicrafts and terraced cultivation.

The Bhotia used to bring grain, sugar etc., from the plains of Uttar Pradesh and used to exchange salt, borax, butter, wool, sheep, horse from the other side. Their trade with Tibet came to a halt owing to the Sino-Indian war. After cessation of trade, the Bhotias started permanent settlements by opening shops of general merchandise at places like Joshimath, Gopeswar and other places and their contact with local caste people became intense.

Sub-Tribes and Social Stratification

As far as stratification is concerned the Bhotias can be stratified in several ways. The major categorization is based on their habitation. Bhotia population of Uttarakhand Himalaya is distributed over seven major valleys, in four districts viz., Almora, Pithoragarh of Kumaon division and Chamoli and Uttar Kashi of Garhwal division. Inhabitants of each valley have their own name depending on the valley they inhabit excepting the Tolchas and Marchas of district Chamoli.

Bhotia society of Kumaon is divided into three endogamous sub-tribes. These divisions practise endogamy at sub-tribe level. They maintain exogamy at clan level. These grouping of the Bhotias are related with their highly differentiated economic structure. Among the Johari Bhotias the three-tier social ranking is witnessed. These three groups of the Johari Bhotias are Bharet, Kunkiya and Nitwals.

Table 2

Internal Hierarchy of the Kumaon Bhotia Cluster

Name of Bhotia Groups	*Status*	*Reason for having the status*
Bharet	Elite	Big traders and owners of large number of sheep and goat
Nitwals	Workers of Bharet Bhotias	Assisted Bharet Bhotias and perform sacred rites and rituals
Kunkiyas	Workers of Bharet Bhotias	Assisted in carrying household articles during migration, look after sheep and goats

There are two other Kunkiya groups who are not Bhotias as such. They are Garhwal immigrants and Khasia immigrants turned into Kunkiyas. The Garhwalis from well-off families migrated to Kumaon from Garhwal to do trading business and got settled. But they could not compete with the Bhotias in trade and ultimately lost their socio-economic status. In such a situation they could not manage to have a spouse from the economically well off and socially higher Bharet Bhotias but gradually they established connubial relationship with Bharet Kunkiyas and got assimilated in Bhotia society as Kunkiyas.

In the same fashion Khasia people coming to Kumaon for earning a livelihood got settled over there and subsequently married Kunkiya girls and got assimilated in Bhotia society as Khasia Kunkiyas. The Johari Bhotias are divided into 14 clans. Their clans are strictly exogamous. These clans have been named after the villages of their residence. Each clan is an original settler of the village after which the clan name derived. One family originally founded the village and the family gave the name of the village with the suffix 'aal' in general which in due course became their clan name.

Following table shows the details of territorial clans of Johari Bhotias.

Each Bhotia clan is further subdivided into several lineages and sub-lineages. The different clans of the Johari Bhotias enjoy various positions in the social hierarchy in terms of heritage, economic prosperity, literacy, etc. Hierarchy among Johari Bhotias now-a-days depends mainly on economic prosperity and literacy. Those having better economic resources and better education are considered higher in social stratification.

Village	*Clan*
Bilju	Biljuw-Aal
Burfu	Burfu-Aal
Khelanch	Khinchiy-Aal
Laspa	Laspa-Aal
Lowa	Lowa-Aal
Mapa	Mapa-Aal
Mertoli	Mertoli-Aal
Ganghar	Ghan Gharia
Paachhu	Paachp-Aal
Milam	Milam-Aal
Ralam	Ralamw-Aal
Rilkot	Rilkotia
Sumdu	Sumdy-Aal
Tola	Tolla

Through constant Hindu contact, caste like stratification based on 'ritual' factor has developed among sub-tribes, though economic factor is also crucial. Thus these three sub-tribes emerges as social classes. Among these social classes the Bharets occupy the highest rung and the Kunkiyas the lowest. In between lies the

Nitwals. Nitwal Bhotias are considered to have equal ritual status with the Bharet Bhotias, whereas the Kunkiyas are often considered to have ritual status lower than the two groups mentioned earlier. The Bharets and Nitwals look down upon the Kunkiyas as they are ritually lower in status. Nitwals are immigrants from Niti valley. They are ritually pure but economically weak. The Kunkiyas are the economically backward and ritually impure. Ritual purity of the Nitwals has given them a better status than the Kunkiyas. In Almora and Pithoragarh the Johari Bhotias are found in Johar valley. Shauka Bhotias are found in Darma, Byans and Chaudans in Pithoragarh district. The Tolchas are found in Dhauli valley of district Chamoli. Marchas are found in Mana valley and upper Dhauli valley. In Uttarkashi the Jaad Bhotias were in Bhagirathi valley in the village Bagari. Their original habitat is in the villages of Nilang and Jadung in Jadh Ganga or Jahnavi Ganga valley of Uttarkashi.

Among the three Bhotia groups under study one thing is common and that is they practise transhumance. All the three groups used to practise Tibet trade or salt-grain trade till the closer of Indo-Tibet or Salt-grain frontier. Among the three groups the Tolchas were best traders and they occupied highest rank and their claim was accepted by the other two groups – Marchas and Jaads. Among the three, the Jaads are considered to be the lowest in social position. Other Bhotias were earlier reluctant to have marital or commensal relation with them. The Jaads follow Lamaistic Buddhism, whereas the Tolchas and Marchhas are Hindus as they claim. But all the three groups claim to be Rajputs. The Jaad village of Bagori has a Buddhist temple. Besides, there is a Shiva temple and a temple dedicated to goddess Kali. The Tolchas and Marchhas have many gods and goddesses for specific purposes and each sub-group of the Tolcha and Marcha has its respective guardian deity. Those deities are mainly mother goddesses worshipped by Hindus in the lower altitude and in plains. The Tolcha and Marchhas claim themselves to be Hindus. All the three groups have their respective 'shilpkars' who annually migrate along with the Bhotias and these shilpkars hold the same status as the other shilpkars in Hindu villages. Therefore, it can be said that each Bhotia locality under study can broadly be stratified into two sections, the Rajput Bhotias as they claim, and the Shilpkars. Among the Bhotias there are further divisions, most of which are named after local Rajput groups, like Kathait, Kandari, Rawat, Bisht, Parmar, Chauhan, Rana, Negi, etc.

The Bhotias remain in contact with local Hindu castes and they are broadly stratified in the same fashion as that of the Hindus. However, even though some Bhotias claim Rajput status but they are looked down upon by the Hindu Rajputs. Actually they are looked down upon by both Rajputs from plains and Rajputs of Khas origin living in the area. the non-Bhotia Rajputs call the Bhotias as huniya, which means 'of Tibetan origin'. The Bhotias who live in the Indo-Tibet border areas carried on trade between India and Tibet from time immemorial. Naturally in connection with their business they visited Tibet frequently. Each Bhotia trader had a counterpart in Tibet with whom he generally preferred to have commercial exchanges. When any Bhotia used to go to Tibet for business he generally used to put up with the Tibetan trader with whom he had trade relations. These Bhotias being non-vegetarian people used to consume Yak flesh which is taboo to the Hindus. Such food habits of Bhotia Rajputs became cause of separation and social exclusion. While ritual factor is crucial in Hindu context, at the level of sub-tribes of Bhotia secular factors only decide high and low status. Among the Bhotia, wealth and political power and not ritual purity determine the higher status in the ladder of stratification. Bhotias being mainly traders originally, still accept the superiority of a wealthy trader. With the cessation of border trade with Tibet during 1960s and being declared as a Scheduled Tribe, the Bhotias found the new opportunity to make up their loss in trade by taking advantage of the new political status as a Scheduled Tribe which entitled them to procure the government service and facilities for education.

Village Clan Ranking and Internal Social Exclusion

We may discuss here the pattern of clan ranking, absorption of a Tibetan group Molfa within the Bhotia cluster as a dominant clan and internal exclusion involving the artisan and other lower 'castes'. Mana village situation will be discussed here. In Mana village a total of 18 clans of the Bhotia is found. These groups in most of the cases have taken the name of a local Rajput group. Of the eighteen clans the one called Molfa holds the highest position in social order, though it is not named after a Rajput group. The Bhotia sub-groups/clans with Rajput names like Kathit, Kandari Rawat, Bisht accept superiority of the Molfa. The Molfas claim to have come from Tibet and claim to have established the village. Thokdari of the region was bestowed upon them by the King of Garhwal who married a Molfa girl, and thus high social position of the Molfa in Mana is backed by political support. Moreover, being the first settlers in the village of Mana the Molfas also had the monopoly of Tibet trade from this region. Thereby they accumulated considerable wealth. Till date the Molfas are the richest people in the village though trade with Tibet has stopped. The Molfas being the earliest settlers of Mana also enjoy the privilege to present the winter woolen cloth to Badrinath during closure of the temple before onset of winter. Further, the Molfas are also given higher position among the Bhotias of Mana as they receive a separate dish of prasad from the temple of Badrinath during the worship of Mata murti. A dish of 'prasad' is also presented to the whole village. The Bhotia clans like Kathit, Kandari, Kankholi, Bankiholi, Jitwan, Jirrwan, Rawat, Badwal and Bisht, have equal status. They intermarry and inter-dine among themselves and also with the Molfa. But clans like Chauhan, Parmar, Rana, Negi, Tikola, Fonia and Gharia occupy lower status compared to them. The Molfa, Kathit, Kandari and other higher groups neither inter-dine nor intermarry with Parmar, Chauhan, Rana, Negi, Takola, Fonia and Gharia. These so-called lower clans generally do not approve such hierarchy. At present secular and economic factors only determine the stratification. Now those who are educated and holding high positions in government are regarded as superior. Such a position may be in the administrative service or police service. Service in bank and government undertaking also have high value and that situates a man or a family higher in the hierarchy. But political power or connection with power is regarded as most valuable and political leaders are the high ranking people.

In Bhotia villages we also witness groups of service class. They are called Shilpkars. They are also Bhotias but were in the past 'untouchables'. Four groups of Shilpkars are found in the studied villages, they are Lohars, Darji or

Auji, Koli and Dholi. Of the four groups three groups, viz., Lohar, Darji and Dholi are found in all the villages of Bagori. The Shilpkars are not allowed by the Bhotia to enter their house.

Among the Shilpkars also there is stratification. The Lohars claim highest status among the Shilpkars. They are endogamous, next comes the Darji. The Dholis occupy the bottom rung. Among the Dholis there are two groups the Badi and the Hurkiya. The Badis are village musicians. The Hurkiyas play on Hurk, a sort of drum. But they are lower than the Badi for the fact that their women offer themselves as 'workers', if needed. In Bagori the village of Jaad has people called as Kolis. The Kolis claim higher status than the Lohar in Bagori. Among the Kolis there are two groups, the higher one called Goukurya Koli (swearing by the cow) and they do not consume pork. The Dom Koli consume pork and occupy a lower position. They also keep fowl and eat fowl. The Gaukurya Kolis do not have marital relation with the Dom Kolis. All these working class and shilpakars indeed continue to suffer from 'social exclusion'.

A Recapitulation

In the Himalayan region of Garhwal the Bhotia community is divided into two distinct layers such as the Bhotias claiming Rajput status, and the Shilpkars, who are somewhat subsidiary to 'Rajput-Bhotias'. In the vicinity are found the caste-Hindus. The Hindu castes are divided into two main groups; the upper castes, i.e., Brahmin and Rajput, comprising the Bith category and the non- Biths, and other castes. The traditional Bhotias who adopted Rajput status are distributed mainly in three valleys of Mana, Niti (lower Dhauli Valley) and Bhagirathi. Mana valley and upper part of Niti valley are occupied by the Marchha Bhotias and lower part of the Niti Valley is occupied by the Tolcha Bhotias. Bhotias inhabiting the higher valleys and living nearer to Tibet border are called Marchha Bhotias and those living in the lower valleys away from the Tibet border are called Tolcha Bhotias. Of these two groups the group living away from Indo-Tibet border at a lower altitude claim higher social status. Thus, the Tolchas enjoy a better position in the Bhotia hierarchy. On the other hand the Jaads who originally belonged to Janhavi valley occupy a still lower position than the Marchhas. Though they claim Rajput status, but their associations with Lamaistic Buddhism pursued till date have assigned them a status lower than the Marchhas. Among the Marchhas there are two sets of clans. One set which claims higher status than the other is called 'Molfa', a clan of non-Rajput affiliation and of Tibetan origin which established the village of Mana and are wealthy Mana Bhotias. On the other hand there are a number of clans with longer ranking with whom the higher clan people do not establish commensal and matrimonial relation. These clans in most of the cases were attached to the higher clans as their employees. But now major changes have taken place and those having political power and government service are regarded superior people.

Reference

Das, J.C. 1995, 'Cohesion and Conflict in a Himalayan Village: A Study of Inter-caste Relations in the Himalayas', in *People of the Himalayas*, M.K. Raha (ed.), Calcutta: Anthropological Survey of India.

23 Kinnaura Tribe-Caster Cluster, Status Ranking and Social Exclusion

Frontier Villages of Himachal Pradesh

Pranab Jyoti De

The Kinnaura tribespeople of Himachal Pradesh have a long history of stratification and exclusion in social, economic, political and religious spheres. The present study attempts to highlight the pattern of social stratification, the level and nature of culture contact and the resulting social change. In order to prepare this paper, fieldwork among the Kinnaura was carried out by the author during late 1990s in Kinnaur district of Himachal Pradesh. Some secondary source materials were added later. The data were collected from the key informants in some villages through interviews, group discussion, and participant observations and from the secondary source, such as the official records. A guideline was provided by the project coordinator for the collection of data. The data were collected from the Kinnaura groups practising the Hinduism, Buddhism and the mixed-faith showing syncretism (Raha, 2003). For the purpose of this study, three villages in Kalpa sub-division were selected at the varying altitudes. They had different degrees of exposure to the urban centres. These villages are Khowangi, Telingi and Kothi. Additional information about the groups has also been collected from nearby villages, e.g., Duni, Chini (Kalpa), followed by crosschecking of data. In Nichar sub-division, Nigani, Wini and Sungra villages were visited for the collection of data. The composition of Kinnaura groups and their household numbers in the above referred villages are stated in Table 1.

Table 1

Ethnic Composition and Household Numbers in Six Villages

Kinnaura Groups	*Household Numbers*	*Kalpa Sub-division*			*Nichar Subdivision*		
		Khowangi	*Telangi*	*Kothi*	*Nigani*	*Urni*	*Sungra*
Rajput (%)	695 (60.38)	80 (11.51)	70 (10.07)	220 (31.05)	45 (6.47)	160 (25.02)	120 (17.27)
Badhi (%)	90 (7.82)	45 (50.00)	—	17 (18.89)	8 (8.89)	12 (13.33)	8 (8.89)
Lohar (%)	91 (7.91)	2 (2.20)	—	73 (80.22)	7 (7.69)	5 (5.49)	4 (4.40)
Koli (%)	266 (23.11)	27 (10.15)	21 (7.89)	83 (31.20)	—	60 (22.56)	75 (28.20)
Nagalu (%)	9 (0.78)	—	—	—	—	—	9 (100.00)
Total (%)	1151	154 (13.38)	91 (7.91)	393 (34.14)	60 (5.21)	237 (20.59)	216 (18.77)

From the Table 1, we learn that the Rajputs among the Kinnaura groups have largely dominated the area followed by the Koli. The Badhi and Lohar have almost equal percentage of households that is 7.82 per cent and 7.91 per cent respectively. At villagewise level, the Badhi are large in number in Khowangi with 50 per cent and the Lohar have 80.22 per cent in Kothi village.

Due to inaccessibility and certain unavoidable reasons, it was not possible to visit any village in Pooh sub-division during the course of field investigation in that area. However, information about various Kinnaura groups of that area who are in service and posted in the district headquarters at Reekong Peo, have been collected. The information has been utilized in the report as a representative data of that area. All the studied villages have developed due to construction of all-weather metalled roads with permanent bus communication between district headquarters and other places in Kinnaur. The above-referred villages are provided with all the modern amenities, like electricity, drinking water, telecommunication services of the post office and so on. The inhabitants of the village get their daily required commodities from main markets at Reckong Peo, Nichar and Sungra. Many families in Khowangi. Kothi, Nichar and Sungra villages possess television and radio sets. In Reckong Peo, there is a cinema hall so that the people of the villages can see Hindi movies. Some also arrange to show movies through the video cassette player. Khowangi village is famous for its temple of Marketing, Telangi for Mahasu, Kothi for Chandika and Nichar for Ukhadevi. Being situated at altitudes varying from 7,500ft to 9,000ft from sea level, all these villages are endowed with the scenic beauty of Kinnaur with high snow covered mountain peaks, green vegetation at the foothills, patches of fertile agricultural lands and fruit orchards.

Before writing about the stratification system of the Kinnaura, a general description of the Kinnaura tribe covering their socio-economic, political and religious aspects is provided. The report is divided in parts. The first part describes the Kinnaura covering all their mythological accounts and the social, economic, political and religious aspects of life. The second part describes the stratification system in the Kinnaura society in terms of their social, economic, political and religious aspects. The last part deals with the stratification system of the tribe in the contemporary situation as also the changes that have taken place in recent times.

The Tribe

The indigenous Kinnaura live in Kinnaur, the north-eastern border district of Himachal Pradesh, situated in rugged and mountainous terrain. The Kinnaura are classified under the Scheduled Tribe category in the entire region of Kinnaur. They do not belong to a single ethnic group, but consist of five endogamous communities having distinct social status as well as different traditional callings and religion. Some groups are now part of Scheduled Caste category. The present name and its spelling as 'Kinnaur' has been officially introduced since the formation of the district in May 1960. In pre-independence period, the name of the state was variously spelt by different scholars like, Kanawar (Victor Jacquemont), Kunavur (James Baillie Fraser), Koonawur (Alexander Gerard and Edward Thornton), Kanaur (H.A. Rose, 1911), Kunawar (Thomson, Thomas,

Andrew Wilson and C.F. Gordon Cumming). The inhabitants of Kinnaur also have their own local name for the place as Kanauring (Mamgain, 1971). Some other names in use are Kanaura, Kinnara, Kinner, Kinnaura, Kinnawarees, Kinnaurese, Kanore, Kinnora, Kunawarees, Kanawari, Koonawur (Raha and Mahato, 1985; Mamgain, 1971). Rahul Sankrityanyan (1956) has also opined that the name Kinnaur has been taken after the Kinnaura community who have been occupying the area since the remote past.

Existing mythology, legends and literature depict the community's origin and history in different ways and forms, but definitely consider Kinner or Kinnaura as a distinct race, somewhere in between human beings and gods. According to Kalhan's *Rajtarangini*, the Kinner were born from the shadow of Brahma; the 'Amarkosha' mentions Vidyahara, Apsara, Yaksha, Kinner, Rakshasa, Gandharva, Pisacha, Guhyaks, Siddha and Bhuta having same origin as the Deva. Another legend says that the Kinnaura have sprung from the toe of Brahma alongwith Yaksha. According to the *Matsya Purana*, Kashyap Rishi had 13 wives among whom Muni and Arista gave birth to 'muni' and 'apsara', and Kinner and Gandharva, respectively. Another legend says that the offspring of Pulastya were Rakshasa, Vanara, Kinner, and Yaksha and offsprings of Pulana were Kimpurusha and Pishacha. In *Ramayana*, the Kinner are mentioned alongwith Deva, Gandharva, Charana, Siddha and Apsara. In *Vishnu Purana*, the Kinner are associated with Gandharva, Yaksha, Rakshasa, Daitya and Danava, as the inhabitants of the mountains and as singers, dancers and merry-making people. The *Mahabharata* mentions Kinner alongwith Gandharva, Yaksha, Siddha and Kimpurusha. Buddhist and Jain literature have mentioned the Kinnara time and again. Gautam Buddha had preached his doctrines to Yaksha, Gandharva, Asura, Garuda, Kinnars and Mahoraga. Buddhist moral code stressed that if Bhikshu had intercourse with Kinnars then they will be guilty of the highest offence that is Parajika. Several stories are mentioned in *Takkariya* Jataka regarding Kinnaura and their physical form, etc. The Kinnar have found a prominent place in Indian and Central Asian art through a number of sculptures, (Bajpai, 1982).

Scholars differ in delineating the area that Kinnars occupied during the ancient period. Vidyalankar mentions that the mountainous area near the Sutlej River where erstwhile Bushahir and other states near Simla Hills exist was known as Kinnerdesh in ancient time. Budh Prakash is of the opinion that the southern part of Kashmir known as Kinnaur is reminiscent of the ancient Kinnerdesh. The region lies along the upper valley of the Jhelum between the Dhaola Dhar and the Zaskar mountains. In course of time and after centuries of change the Kinner, probably alongwith the Kirat in the adjoining region, were gradually pushed towards higher hills. This was done through attacks, one by the Vedic Aryans of the plains going upwards and the another by the Khas, sister branch of the Aryans who penetrated into the region gradually through the hills of Khashgir (Kashmir). In due course, the Khashas became the undisputed masters in this region. The Khas or Khash tribe finds mention in the *Mahabharata* as well as in many works of the writers of ancient history. It is believed that after the extinction of the races of Kinnar, Kirat and Nag, the Khas settled down for the cultivation of land in addition to their patent occupation of rearing and raising cattle. The Khashas were a virile and well-knit community for whom there was no caste distinction. The subjugated tribe became their subordinates. Among the Khashas, affairs of the community were carried out with common consent and the family deities were the guiding hands. An elder of the house was considered a representative of the family deity who spoke for the family in the assembly of the elders of the community. With the passage of time, a few strong leaders must have emerged among the representatives of the individual households and must have found it difficult to obey and yield to a single individual. These leaders thus carved out areas of influence over their own separate holds. The foundation of separate hill states were thus laid down, those who were nearer the plains were influenced more by the Aryan customs and languages strongly prevalent in the Indo-Gangetic plain. The others remaining in the higher hills understandably got influenced by the impact of the Bhot (Bhotia) culture through trade with Tibet. Thus, the history of Kinnaur can broadly be divided into three periods:

1. Pre-Aryan of pre-Khash period.
2. Pre-Bhot period up to 7th century, and
3. Bhot period upto 13th/14th century (Mamgain, 1971).

Mamgain supports Grierson's view that the Kinnaurs speak the Kanowari language under the western sub-group of Tibeto-Himalayan, which belongs to the Tibeto-Burman family of languages. Mamgain also refers to Edward Thornton and Gerards who opined that a number of different dialects are spoken in Koonawar (Mamgain, 1971). Kapoor (1972), following different linguists, like Konow Bailey and Grierson mentions five different dialects in Kinnari language, namely, Lower Kinnauri, Standard Kinnauri, Chitkuli, the Borskad and Samehu. However, speakers of these dialect are at present well-versed with Hindi though many of the grown-up women cannot speak in Hindi or know it very little. A few educated men can speak English well. Besides Hindi, many Kinnaura of Upper Kinnaur (Pooh sub-division) and some areas of Kalpa sub-division can speak Tibetan. With frequent visits to Pooh sub-division areas, many members residing in Kalpa and Nichar sub-divisions have also learnt Tibetan language to some extent. Roman and Devnagari are the scripts of the Kinnaura living in Central and Lower Kinnaur, whereas, Tibetan, Roman and Devnagari scripts are used in Upper Kinaur.

Social division among the Kinnaura are found to be of a different type since the Kinnaura are composed of various ethnic groups, having different social statuses. They are differentiated into two broad categories, namely, the Khosia or Kanet or Rajput (Scheduled Tribe) and the Beru (Scheduled Caste). The Beru category is again divided into three divisions, like, Domang, Chamang and Chanala. The Domang category includes the members of Lohar and Badhi (Ores) who are traditionally the blacksmiths and carpenters respectively. The Chamang includes the Koli who are traditionally weavers, shoe-makers and workers. The Chanala includes the Nagalu who are traditionally the basket-makers.

As shown in following chart, each social category is considered as an endogamous group and, and it follows the rule of group endogamy. Among the Beru category, the Domang members, i.e., the Lohar and Badhi (ores) inter-marry. The Chamang and the Chanala are endogamous. Inter-caste marriages among them are nowadays reported but regarded as exceptions.

Chart 1

Stratification of the Kinnaura

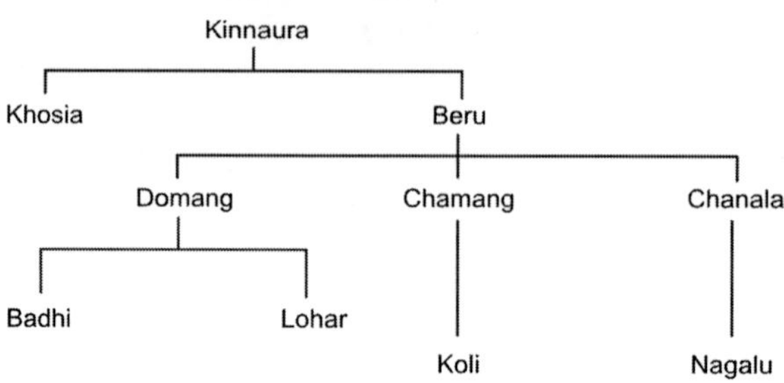

Khel exogamy was strictly followed among the members of Khosia or Rajput Kinnaura in the past, but now such restrictions are overruled. This system is not reported in any other social group under the Kinnaura tribe. Lineage or Khandan is an exogamous unit among members of the Kinnaura whereas, it is altogether absent among other ethnic groups of the district (Raha and Mahato, 1985). Sometimes, these lineages denote the name of place or territory from where the consanguineal kin group originally hailed. Among ethnic groups belonging to the Scheduled Caste category, it is seen that they intermarry among themselves, only avoiding marriage with "children of same set as well as parallel cousin and members of lineages at least for three generation" (Ramesh Chandra, 1992). Raha and Mahato (1985: 169) mention that the Kinnauras prohibit marriage in father's side for seven generations. Cousin-marriage of both parallel and cross variety is not allowed. Sororate is permissible where a man is permitted to marry his wife's elder or younger sister but is not a common feature. Levirate is not reported due to the prevalence of polyandry. Polygyny though permitted is not widely practised. Due to impact of modernization and education, polygyny is not popular and polyandrous marriages are disliked now in most cases. Approximately, three to five per cent of polyandrous families have been reported during the present study. Monogamy is well preferred and accepted particularly by the educated members of the tribe. Educated and affluent members particularly from the Kanet (Rajput) nowadays, arrange their son's and daughter's marriage at the age around twenty-five and twenty-one years respectively mostly on account of their higher education. A marriage is usually arranged through negotiation (zanekang, zandung or zanchang) between elderly members of two families; sometimes, they take the help of mediators (Mazomi or Dermana). Marriage by elopement (Dabdab or Kunchis) is also socially approved and takes place frequently. The 'hari' is another type of marriage by capture where a married woman runs away or elopes with another man. Divorce (Kajnama or Thagchocha) is permissible where both husband and wife have every right to divorce with the approval of traditional Caste Panchayat on grounds like adultery, quarrel, incurable diseases or suffering from contagious diseases, maladjustment, etc. Breaking of a small piece of dry stick by the couple symbolizes the divorce and the act is termed as Shing Tak Shinig or Thagchocha. Widow and divorce remarriages are permissible. The practice of giving, taking or demanding of dowry does not exist. Gifts and presents are customarily given to the bride and these do not constitute a dowry (Mamgain, 1971). But recent investigations (People of India project), show bride price (Dhori) prevalent in the society which is paid in cash. Ibbseston (1911) reports "the dhari ... is a sum paid to the bride's guardian by those of the bridegroom and must be refunded to the latter if the marriage turns out badly, e.g., if the wife leaves her husband and goes off with another man, he was to refund the amount to them".

Among the Kinnaura, Virilocal residence is practised whereby after marriage, a man brings his wife to his parental house and stays with parents and other members of the family. Extended family type is still largely prevalent, though nuclear type is now gradually replacing the age-old system due to impact of education, modernity, ideological differences among members in a joint family and for the sake of service either in distant places or in and around Kinnaur.

Inheritance of property is patrilineal. In case of a division of property in a polyandrous family, the rule of Jathang and Kanchhog is applied. In Jathang, right of elder brother is the prime factor with the share of good part of agricultural field and in Kanchhong, younger brother gets the ancestral house, and thereafter, landed property is equally shared among the brothers. Daughters of a deceased man have no right over the property. Children of non-sanctioned marriage have no right to their parental property, though they have now started asserting their rights through the court of law. A widow however, in absence of sons, inherits the property. Succession right goes to eldest son of the deceased. Descent is reckoned through male line. Children always belong to their father's lineage or Khandan. Adopted son also gets the Khandan of the man who adopts. Apart from Rajputs, other ethnic groups of the Kinnaura also follow the same rule of descent.

Several rituals are associated with birth, marriage and death. A pregnant woman has to observe certain restrictions by not going out in the dark, not visiting a burial or cremation place, not accepting anything from an unknown person and so on. An experienced old woman acts as a midwife (api). The Rajput does not engage a midwife from any community other than their own group. Birth pollution (Sekhar) is observed for a period ranging from seven to fifteen days. During the pollution period, no member of the household is allowed to visit any temple or monastery; to go to any neighbouring house; to perform socio-religious ceremonies, etc. On completion of pollution, purificatory rite (Chokharasemik) is done in which the house is cleaned, mother and child are given a bath. All relatives and villagers come to bless the child with some offerings. A feast is arranged. Rituals are performed by the Pujari. In Buddhist dominated area (Pooh sub-division) or in mixed area (Kalpa sub-division), Lama initiates the rite. Name-giving ceremony is conducted by the Lama in between seven to fifteen days of childbirth. Mundan (head shaving) is done at the age of one year through performance of some ritualistic rites. Marriage is arranged through negotiation.

On fixation of marriage alliance, a Majomi (go-between) with a bottle of liquor and some cash as token goes to the house of the girl and offers the same to the girl's father. After accepting this, village deity is worshipped by the family. With this rite, the marriage alliance is finalized. Marriage date is fixed after consulting a Lama or a temple Pujari. On marriage day, bridegroom goes to the bride's village, accompanied by marriage party. Two feasts are offered to them by the bride's party. On the next day, bridegroom returns to his parental home with the bride. On reaching, worship is first performed. They are received by the bridegroom's sister or mother, holding a container of grain (barley) and lamp (Dewa). The main ritual Oopagey is performed where the groom is asked to sit and a Pagri (turban) is tied around his head by the groom's maternal uncle. The Obal (garland), made of different dry fruits is offered by the bride to the bridegroom. In case of polyandrous marriage, tying of Pagri is done to each and every brother. Offering of cash and kind to bridegroom and bride is followed. A feast is offered to all the invitees. Marriage ceremony in Buddhist dominated area is almost the same with slight variation. Lama acts as a sacred specialist instead of Pujari, Matha or Grokch.

The dead are cremated (Agang) while burial is done in case of a death of a child below age three or persons dying from contagious disease like smallpox etc. Death pollution continues for eight days during which members of bereaved family do not consume non-vegetarian foods, oil, fried food, onion, garlic, turmeric, etc. On eighth day, purificatory rite is done by cleaning the house, followed by a feast. On fifteenth day, another feast is given to the villagers in the temple with Halwa, Poltus, Chilta, etc. This day onwards, they are free from the death pollution.

Hinduism and Buddhism are the two main religions professed in Kinnaur district with dominance of Buddhism in some parts of Pooh sub-division, bordering Tibet. Buddhism is professed with Hinduism in Kalpa sub-division of the central part of the district. The whole of Nichar sub-division is absolutely dominated by Hinduism (Raha and Mahato, 1985: 279). Spread of Buddhism in Kinnaur district was due to frequent visits of Buddhist priests in the past. Similarly, Hinduism in Kinnaur was due to rule of Bushahir Hindu kings in the area for several decades. Central part of Kinnaur (whole of Kalpa sub-division and parts of Morang sub-division and Pooh sub-division) shows an admixture of two religions, i.e., Hinduism and Buddhism (Raha, 2003).

The Kinnaura Hinduism is primarily represented by its numerous gods (devtas) and goddesses (devis). In every household (Kim), the deity is termed as Kimshu. The village deity is known as Gaondevta or Devi. The Ghori is composed of several villages and has Ghori Devta or Devi who has control over all the deities of the villages under that Ghori. Similarly, a Khunt, formed by some Ghors, has Khunt Devta or Devi namely Maheshwar, Chandika, Ukha (Usha), etc. The function of this Devi or Devta is to look after the welfare of their clients. The Kimshu is worshipped in the Santhang or temple. Besides, these native deities several Hindu deities worshipped are Krishan, Durga, Kali and other Hindu gods and goddesses. The temple functionaries are constituted by Pujari (priest), Grokch (who communicates to the villagers on behalf of the deity), Mahas (who communicates to the deity on behalf of the villagers), Kaith/Khajachi (temple accountant), Chalia (palanquin carrier of the deity), Deotu (temple guard), Halbandi (messenger) and Baiiantri (musician). All posts of Pujari, Mathas and Grokch are hereditary.

In some parts of upper Kinnaur (Hangrang tehsil of Pooh sub-division), Buddhism is in dominance. Buddhism is also moderately spread in Kalpa sub-division but in Nichar sub-division, it is least visible. With spread of this religion in parts of Hindu dominated areas of Kinnaur, certain Buddhist cultural and religious elements are also accepted by the Hindu Kinnaura. Services of the Lama is thus requisitioned in death rite and in naming ceremony of a child. Many of the Hindu Kinnaura hoist prayer flag (Tharchok, also spelt as Dorchat) in their houses which is a Buddhist religious characteristic feature. Again many Buddhist Kinnarua in Hindu dominating areas of the district have a tendency to identify and compare some of their Buddhist deities with Hindu deities, like, Nam-chhara with Narayana, Chhok-dak with Ganesha, Tarema with Lakshmi, Paldan-la-mo with Mahakali, and so on (Raha and Mahato, 1985: 301). Many of them keep photographs of Hindu gods and goddesses in the house.

However, with the infiltration of Hindu cultural and religious traits into Buddhist dominated areas of Pooh sub-division, the opening of communication system with rest of the country and the breaking of socio-cultural and religious contacts with the Tibetan Buddhists due to closure of Indo-Tibetan border, changes in their (Buddhist Kinnaura) religious beliefs and practices are very much evident as seen from the installation of photographs of Hindu deities in their houses with regular worship, visit to Hindu sacred paces in connection with death rites and so on. Establishment of marital relations with their Hindu counterparts at upper, central and even at lower Kinnaur areas has gradually been helping them to blend beliefs from Buddhism with Hinduism. People belonging to Buddhist religion are either from Nyingmapa, Dukpa or Gulukpa sects. Representatives from Nyingmapa and Dukpa are, however, more in number than the others. A monastery is headed by the Chief Lama. He is helped by other senior Lamas if the monastery is big. Various works are allotted to junior Lamas and also to Jomos (nuns). They are supervized by their seniors. In the whole of Kinnaur, temple and functionaries, at their respective positions, are almost same. The Lama plays an important role in socio-religious sphere of the Hindu Kunnaura in this region, besides his Buddhist religious commitments.

Socio-political control of very Kinnaura village was under a traditional village council (charbhai), headed by Mukhia. Besides, the Mukhia other members of the council were Char, Halmadi, and Toknya. However, the devi/devta used to provide solution of any conflict or to take any decision in traditional council affair, if the council failed to take any positive decision. Mathas and Grokch play a vital role on behalf of the deity. In contemporary situation, though the charbhai is still in existence, its importance has been reduced due to emergence of Gram Panchayat and Nyaya Panchayat system. Importance of devi/devta as the administrative head is also diminishing because of influence of education, modernity and other related factors. People now prefer to go to the other experts in respective matters in spite of approaching deity through the temple functionaries for the solution. As such, the monastery or the temple functionaries do not have much hold nowadays compared to what they had in the past.

Occupational structure of the Kinnaura is caste-based whereby the Kanet or Rajput are mostly agriculturists, horticulturists, orchard growers and service-holders. Other ethnic groups, namely the Lohar, Bedhi, Koli and Nagalu are engaged primarily in their traditional callings like blacksmithy, carpentry, weaving, shoemaking, scavenging and basket-making. This caste-based occupational structure changed due to advancement of modernity, impact of education and social awareness. As such, diversification of occupation has taken place. The Koli have accepted varied occupations like, agriculture, horticulture, labour job, business, playing on musical instruments in temple during festivals and ceremonies, etc. Educated persons from the group are in government service. Shoe making is nowadays either absent or prevalent at a low rate. Scavenging work is totally discarded. The Nagalu, a very localized group, make baskets from Nagal creeper. They are also engaged now in divergent occupations like agriculture, business, labour works and government service along with continuation of traditional basket-making work.

The Lohar, traditionally blacksmiths, are now acquainted with the techniques of using silver, brass and copper by making ornaments and other decorative objects. Besides this, many of them are engaged in agriculture, labour and in service. The Badhi are carpenters and know the skill of masonry works. Wood carving, making of furniture, construction of house, house-roof, repairing jobs, etc., are their main assignments. They are also associated with divergent occupations, like, agriculture, labour, etc. A few are in government service and some are in gold/silversmith work. The Kanet or Rajput are agriculturists. They are also in business, government service, horticulture, orchard growing and so on. Very few also work as labour. Beside this, they have also additional qualities. In upper Kinnaur, or in places where no artisan castes, like Badhi, Lohar etc, are available, the Rajput themselves undertake such specialized jobs of carpentry and blacksmithy, though number of this category is negligible. A few also know the art of gold/silver work (Table 2).

Table 2

Occupational Categories Among the Kinnaura

Group	*Occupation*	
	Traditional	*New*
Rajput	Agriculture landholder	Agriculture, orchard growing, horticulture, business, gold/silversmith.
Badhi	Carpenter	Carpenter, service, agriculture, labour, gold/silversmith, house construction, masonry work, woodwork.
Lohar	Blacksmith	Tailor, weaving, agriculture, labour gold/silversmith.
Koli	Scavenger, tanner, shoe-maker weaver, tailor	Tailor, weaving, agriculture, business, service, gold/silver, labour.
Nagalu	Basket-maker	Basket-maker, labour, service.

So far as landholding of the Kinnaura groups are concerned, the Rajput are the most dominant landholding group which is evident from the data collected from Kothi village (Table 3).

Table 3

The Landholding Pattern of Kinnaura in Kothi Village

Group	*Below 1 acre*	*1 acre to 2.5 acre*	*2.5 to less than 5 acre*	*+5 acre to less than 10 acre*	*10 acre and more*	*Landless*	*Households surveyed*
Rajput (%)	18 (36.00)	17 (34.00)	3 (6.00)	6 (12.00)	4 (8.00)	2 (4.00)	50
Badhi (%)	5 (29.41)	4 (23.53)	1 (5.88)	–	–	7 (41.18)	17
Lohar (%)	12 (24.00)	8 (16.00)	11 (22.00)	–	–	19 (38.00)	50
Koli (%)	14 (28.00)	7 (14.00)	1 (2.00)	–	–	28 (56.00)	50
Total	49 (29.34)	36 (21.56)	16 (9.58)	6 (3.59)	4 (2.40)	56 (33.53)	167

Social Stratification and Status Ranking: Process of Social Exclusion

The indigenous population of Kinnaur is broadly classified into two categories namely the Khosia and the Beru. The Khosia (Kanet or Rajput) are predominantly spread all over Kinnaur. They, also known as the Zad or Jod in upper Kinnaur (Pooh sub-division), are treated as superior-most group in the local caste hierarchy. On the other hand, members of the Beru category consist of few artisan castes and were labelled as unclean. The Beru category is again sub-divided into three broad divisions which Raha and Mahato mention as status groups (1985). These are Domang, Chamang and Chanala. All artisan castes are included in these three sub-divisions, maintaining hierarchical order based on the concept of purity and pollution. The Domang includes two ethnic groups namely the Lohar and Badhi. The Chamang, represented by the Koli and the Nagalu, are members of the Chanala.

A new nomenclature for the Khosia (Rajput/Kanet) in central and lower part of Kinnaur has been recently coined as 'Sawarn' whereas, the Beru category is sometimes referred to as the Harijan, which the members of Scheduled Caste particularly the Koli have opposed. In this context, Kapoor (1972: 165) states "the Rajput are now known as 'Sawarn' or high castes; and the Domang and Chamang as 'Harijan'. The Rajput in spite of the label 'Sawarn' continue to be listed and enumerated as a Scheduled Tribe, the Domang and Chamang are listed and enumerated as the members of the Scheduled Castes. However, they do not object to be addressed or referred to as Thakur. This is an overall view of the social stratification system that is followed by the Kinnaura throughout the district, obviously with some variations in terms of 'local' situation and socio-religious implications. Members of the Chanal group are very localized and are exclusively found in a few villages of Nichar sub-division of the district. Traditional stratification system among the Khosia (Kanet or Rajput) shows both simplicity as well as complexity, depending on the religion and geographic locale. In his study, Raha (1979: 88) states: 'the culture zones in Kinnaur lead to two distinct types of stratification. As one moves from zone-I to zone-II and zone-III, one witnesses a drift from a comparatively simple type of stratification to a more complex type of stratification in the Khosia (Rajput) society". As such, a complex type of stratification is reported from the areas in central and south-western part of the district. Raha (1979) states them as zone-II and zone-III respectively. In these areas, the Khosia (Rajput) have further categorized divisions in terms of status group (Khel) and lineage (Khandan). It appears that the system of stratification among the Rajputs was based on religion and geographic 'locale'. In the past, the Rajput society was territorially segmented, rather stratified. On account of their socio-cultural and religious affinity and regular trade contacts with the inhabitants of Tibet, the Rajputs particularly living in bordering areas of Pooh division were very much inclined towards the socio-cultural life including dietary pattern of the people of Tibet. They were habituated to take Yak meat and had marriage alliances with their counterparts living in the bordering areas of Tibet. Owing to all these characteristic features of the Rajputs of the Pooh division, their counterparts living in lower and central parts of Kinnaur did not establish any type of connection including the commensal and connubial relationships with them. Religion of Buddhism in Pooh division was not the sole criterion for restricting marriage alliances between these two sets of Rajputs. The intake of yak meat distanced the Hindu Rajput of these areas from the Rajputs of the Pooh division. Here also we sea a process of social exclusion at work.

While coming back to the discussion regarding status group and lineage stratification system among the Khosia (Rajputs), it is found that three distinct status groups (khels) are found in their traditional set-up, namely Orang, Maorang (also known as Orangmech) and Waza. The Orang are, considered as most superior and Waza the most inferior. Members of Maorang enjoy intermediate status. These status groups are strictly endogamous. Inter-status marriage in the past was considered as a social offence. It may be stated that these Khels or status groups are well-developed in zone-II and zone-III but they gradually lose their importance as one moves in zone-I. Fact remains that these Khels enjoy their respective status not only in the social sphere, but in the economic, political and religious spheres also. The status group system is stated to be well organized in Hindu dominated regions like Nichar and Kalpa sub-division. These are well distinguishable from each other since the Khosia (Rajput) practice status group endogamy. This system is in rudimentary stage nearer to Pooh sub-division since "Buddhism does not approve ranking in social organisation" (Raha and Mahato, 1985). In Pooh division, existence of intra-group stratification among the Rajput is seen in two 'class grades' namely the Ponpo and the ordinary Rajput. The Ponpo, a title given by the earlier feudal chiefs, had the special power to look after the village administration in those periods, on behalf of the king. They were superior in social status and rank and no commensal as well as connubial relationships were established with other Rajputs, considering them to be inferior to the Ponpo. Since the status group is associated with an endogamous unit and in marriage alliance, marriage with lower status group by the higher is considered a social offence as well as lowering the status of the higher group. In spite of all these prohibitory rules, there were cases of inter-status group marriages. It is reported that if a man of higher status group marries a woman of lower status, as per the customary law, the man's social position in the status group is degraded. Marriage with a woman of higher status group by a Maorang man upgrades his status but the status of Orang family is lowered. Similarly, these rules are applicable through marriage alliances established with Waza group and vice versa. Rules for inter-status group marriages are now being simplified.

The status groups are again sub-divided into a number of unilineal descent groups, i.e., the lineage or Khandan. Raha states that, "each of the khels has got different sets of the Khandans. The identical khandans do not exist in two different khels. Like Khela, the Khandan are also hierarchically stratified. That means the Khandans of the superior khel enjoy the superior status (1987: 333)". Names of Khandans in most cases are associated with individual, family, or the name of place/village/territory from where the ancestors migrated. In lineage or khandan system we find two types, namely the original Khandan (members should be the original inhabitants of the village) and the immigrant Khandan (member either migrated form any part of Kinnaur and settled in the village or settled as the Gharijawai, that is Makpa).

In present study, these status groups (khels) are differently termed by informants at Nichar village in Nichar sub-division as kul. Very few, however, could give the details of these status group divisions. Several historical factors of past define the ranking today. Thus the members of Waza group, originally the potter castes were later accepted by the Rajput in their society and placed them at the lowest strata.

Among the Orang status group, three categories were reported by informants from Nichar division. These functional groups were working in various capacities under the feudal chiefs in the past. They were Bist, Wazir, Mehta, Bares and Roys. The Bist and Wazir households are now considered as superior and well known by Negi titles. The Bist and Wazirs were royal officers, holding superior key posts under the feudal chiefs. The Mehta households were in the second grade due to their position in the servicing rank, but their social position was not inferior to the Bist and Wazir. The Roys and Bares were the last graded officers and ranked below the Mehta. So far the marriage alliance is concerned, the Bist and Wazir were allowed to intermarry and also have marital alliances with members of the royal families. They accept daughters of the Bist, Wazir and Mehta in marriage. Again, marriage in between the Roys, Bares and Meht was also possible, but the royal families avoided such relationships with the members of the Roys and Bares. This differential system in terms of marriage as well as ranking within Orang status group is less visible today in Nichar and in other parts of the district.

It is understood from the oral statements that during the pre-independence period, a professional group of dancers and musicians and drum-beaters were reported to exist in areas of Chegaon in Nichar sub-division. They were named as the Daki who were ranked below the Koli in the local caste hierarchy. They were also the untouchables and commensal as well as connubial relations even with the Koli were not permitted in those days. In the later periods, the Daki were assimilated with the Koli and the group is now exclusively identified as the Koli. This assimilation was stated to be possible due to their prolonged uninterrupted association with the major group, i.e., the Koli.

In a similar way, another assimilation of a group was also reported from Morang tehsil of Pooh sub-division. The Chouba, a caste of traditional medicine men migrated either from Mathura or Varanasi to this part of Kinnaur under royal patronage during those periods. Later, they mixed up with Rajputs through marital ties and finally got established as Rajputs in the given area.

Besides the Kinnaura, several other ethnic groups live in different parts of the district. They are differently named by Kinnaura. The outsiders are termed by the tribe as the Kocha, excepting the members of Tibet, Lahul and Spiti who are called as the Gnyam. The Nepalis are identified as the Gorkha. The Kinnaura never include these ethnic groups in their own cluster and offer no place in the Kinnaura social hierarchy. If a person happens to marry a girl from the Kinnaura through love affair, then he submits sufficient proof of caste identity from the Mukhia of the Kinnaura traditional council from the village he hails from, in support of his claim. On receipt of proper documents, he would be included in the society and allowed to reside in the village with his wife if he so desires.

A division based on occupation among some of lower castes within the Kinnaura has also been reported. Thus we find rudimentary type of occupational divisions among the Koli of lower Kinnaur. These are Bonu and Sui. The Bonu are those who have weaving as their main occupation, whereas the Sui are the tailors. During field investigation, it has been ascertained that since pre-independence period there is a distinct division within the Koli on the basis of occupation. They are Sudh Koli and Asudh Koli. The Sudh Koli are also known as the Suchcha (real) Koli. The Sudh Koli are superior in rank, involved in tailoring and weaving occupation and as such, these were referred to as Sui Koli and Bonu Koli respectively. On the other hand, members of the Asudh Koli were considered to be impure because of their involvement in leather work, including shoe-making and removing and lifting of dead animals (carcass). Commensal and connubial relationship between these two sub-divisions were strictly prohibited. Stitching of garments and dressmaking for devi and devta of the temple were the specialized assignment of the Sudh (Suchcha) Koli. The Asudh Koli did ploughing for the Rajput in addition to other specified jobs. In Sangla area, a term Jhutha Sonar has evolved on account of acceptance of goldsmithy and silversmithy occupation by few Koli members. They are however, not equated with the Sunars who originated either from the Lohar or the Badhi. When a Lohar (Domang) or Badhi (Ores) takes up the job of goldsmithy or silversmithy he considers himself to be superior to the members involved in blacksmithy or carpentry. Such guild, formed through the acceptance of a new superior occupation, is coined by term 'Sunar'. A 'Sunar' may take-up the profession of goldsmithy, silversmithy or brassmithy through specific skill, technique and workmanship. These criteria have helped the members to make them 'separate' in terms of position in the society among the Lohar-Badhi. And as such, today, a tendency is quite marked within this specific artisan group to maintain its "specialized guild based identity" through making of marriage alliance within the 'Sunar' group. They obviously expect superior status and prestige than the Badhi and Lohar from which they have originally branched out. This notion is gradually growing up among the members of the group. On the other side, when a Rajput turns to be a 'Sunar' by profession, his social identity remains unchanged and he claims himself to be Rajput and not become part of Badhi-Lohar. This is due to the fact that the Rajput 'Sunar' has already achieved the higher social status. But the Badhi or Lohar 'Sunar' may have the lower social status but he aspires to classify himself to be in the higher status by accepting a specialized craftwork. However, a term has been evolved for the Rajput who accepts gold or silversmithy namely 'Suchcha' Sunar in Pooh tehsil area of Pooh sub-division. In Pooh area, the 'Jhutha Sunar' term was also used for castes like Lohar or Koli. There exists no relation between the 'Suchcha Sunar' and 'Jhutha Sunar' so far as the social norm is concerned, because, as reported earlier, the 'Jhutha Sunar' is formed by the Badhi or Koli silver or goldsmiths. In Kalpa sub-division, the term 'Suchcha Sunar' among the Rajput is not present though a few individuals know the art of smithy work.

Though the Badhi and Lohar claim their respective social statuses as equal in the hierarchy, they interdine and also sometimes intermarry. The Rajput and the temple functionaries consider the Badhi as superior than the Lohar as he is allowed entering inside the house of a Rajput or the temple for the sake of work. A Bhadhi carpenter is permitted to go inside the temple with his instruments for repairing job, whereas no other artisan caste and the Lohar in particular is permitted to enter inside the temple. Through this right to perform a job, the ranking positions between the Badhi and Lohar can be established though there has been no basic differentiation found between these two ethnic groups, so far as the concept of purity and pollution is concerned.

In day-to-day social and cultural interactions, there exists a differential pattern between the Rajput on one side and the lower caste groups on the other side, thus forming a sacred demarcation between these two broad classes. This basic differentiation is observed among members of different castes within the Kinnarua in their commensal relationship based on purity-pollution. Acceptance or refusal of cooked food and drinks (water) are the main criteria for consideration of such differentiation. No Rajput accepts cooked food or water from any of the lower castes. He may, however, accept dried food materials, fruits and smoke bidi, cigarette and also accept home-made alcoholic drinks (Rakh) from the lower castes on the occasion of some socio-religious events or on day-to-day interaction. To bring cow's milk or the alcoholic drink from the house of lower caste is not considered 'polluted' by the Rajput. Salt as well as the 'Lassi' (butter-milk) are not accepted from the lower castes. On the occasion of some social events, when the Rajputs are invited by the lower castes to their houses, the former accept the invitation and receive only the raw food materials or ration (ration is the local term from uncooked food materials). They cook the same by themselves in their own utensils in a separate place. When the lower castes are invited in the house of Rajput, they are served with the cooked-food but separate dining place is provided to them. Again, the interdining spatial arrangement between members of the Koli and the Badhi-Lohar differs because there exists disagreement regarding their respective rank and status in the caste hierarchy. No caste group accepts cooked food and water from each other. In other words the Badhi and Lohar do no accept cooked food from the Koli and vice versa. The Badhi and Lohar enjoy an equal social status, and as such, no pollution is observed between them in terms of commensal relationship. The Nagalu are in the lowest position in the social hierarchy and devoid of all such relationships with higher castes because of their socially and economically backward conditions. However, they can accept cooked food and water from all the superior groups. In this respect, it is interesting to mention that the drinking water source in the village demarcates the status rank based on purity-pollution concept as the Rajput have their own separate source of water for drinking purpose than those of the lower castes. The following chart describes the pattern of acceptance of food and water between various ethnic groups under the Kinnaura.

Table 4

Pattern and Extent of Commensality

Ethnic groups under Kinnaura	*Acceptance of cooked food from*	*Acceptance of water from*	*Acceptance of dry food and fruits, etc.*
Rajput	Rajput	Rajput	Rajput, Badhi, Lohar, Koli, Nagalu
Badhi	Rajput Badhi, Lohar	Rajput, Badhi, Lohar	Rajput, Badhi, Lohar, Koli, Nagalu
Lohar	Rajput, Badhi, Lohar	Rajput, Badhi, Lohar	Rajput, Badhi, Lohar, Koli, Nagalu
Koli	Rajput, Koli	Rajput, Koli	Rajput, Badhi, Lohar, Koli, Nagalu
Nagalu	Rajput, Badhi, Lohar, Koli, Nagalu	Rajput, Badhi, Lohar, Koli, Nagalu	Rajput, Badhi, Lohar, Koli, Nagalu

Access to religious places by the lower castes is, no more restricted. The temple functionaries had barred the lower castes from entering inside the temple unless they are permitted on some special occasion. Members of the lower castes are not allowed to enter inside the temples like Chandika of Kothi, Markaling of Khowangi, Mahasu of Telangi, Ukhadevi of Nichar village and so on without prior permission of the deity as expressed through respective temple functionaries. If permitted to go inside the temple premises they are not allowed to enter inside the place where the deity is installed. This is not true in case of the Rajput. Entering inside the installation place of the deity by the members of temple functionaries like, Pujari, Grokch, Mathas, etc., is permitted because they are all Rajput. Other Rajput members are also allowed to enter inside the temple to offer worship, subject to the payment of ₹ 2 to the temple functionaries and subsequent permission from the deity through the Grokch. It is the usual practice that if the deity denies permission, the cash is returned to the subscriber. Similarly, entry to the Bhairon temple, adjacent to Chandika temple of Kothi village, is restricted to the lower castes since the past. It is believed that this temple was built by the Pandavas of *Mahabharata* during their fourteen-year exile. The water reservoir inside the temple premises used to be the source of drinking water exclusively for the Rajputs of the village. It is the usual practice of the temple functionaries since past to get it cleaned once in a year by engaging the lower caste members of the village who constitute the task force for the job. This is stated to be the only chance for these lower castes to enter inside the temple premises. After the work, the site is purified by sprinkling the holy water and thereafter, no lower caste member is permitted to enter inside the temple premises. This is another example how the Kinnaura society maintains social-exclusion between the Rajput and the lower castes on the basis of purity-pollution concept.

Participation in various festivals and ceremonies observed in the villages in different occasions is guided by ritual status as superior and inferior. This differential behavioural pattern is very much visualized, in several village-level functions and games. Some of these games are the Rashakesi (tug of war), Rashimig (throwing of ice-ball to each other by the participant members), Rowlanetowannik (a game of appearing in disguise), Kora (pulling of wooden rod by hand by two sets of participants, one set being the women and other by the men). Some games are exclusively participated by the Rajputs where the lower castes are not allowed to join, excepting the Baijantri (drum beaters and musicians) who beat drums and play musical instruments during the game. The lower caste members of the village concerned simply observe the game from a distant place. During Toshmik festival, the Rajput men and women both sing and dance. Musical instruments are played by the lower castes and men and women from the lower castes are also invited by the Rajputs. Food and 'Ghanti' (local alcoholic drink) are supplied to them. The expenditures incurred on the occasion are borne by the Rajput men of the village. Hu Hu Ka Male (stealing of fruits, vegetables from the kitchen garden of horticulture fields) was another popular village-level game. During the day of the Dakrain festival, the game is played. The Rajput by virtue of their highest social and economic position, used to take the opportunity to steal fruits and vegetables from the garden of the Rajput and the lower castes in fun. But the reverse never happens as the lower castes especially the Koli would never dare to steal from the Rajputs.

A distinct feature of ownership pattern, control over resources, and occupation pattern exists. Traditional occupation of the Kinnaura, viz., agriculture, sheep and goat rearing survive. In addition, the Kinnaura have adopted cultivation of variety of seasonal fruits in most of the areas of the district to enable them to earn a huge amount of cash. The Rajputs thus remain wealthy as they are the large landholders, prosperous, economically sound group and have control over economic resources. On the other side, members of the Beru category are poor, backward and dependent on the Rajput masters since long following the reciprocal Binanas system. The system of Binanas among the Kinnaura is recorded and verified by the present author by interrogating his informants during his field visit. The Rajput being the landowners and agriculturists are not involved in ploughing the land and since time immemorial enjoying a higher social position. They used to employ agricultural labourers (Halas) from the Koli, get their house and agricultural tools repaired by the Badhi carpenters and get their smithy works done by the Lohar. The system through which these works are done is called Binanas. Ultimately, the large landholders (Zamindar) formed one class, the marginal landholders (Zigismi) formed another class and the Binanas are in lower class. They consist of servicing castes like, the Badhi, Lohar, Koli and Nagalu (Nagalu are found only in Nichar tehsil of the Nichar sub-division). We thus notice that the whole occupation structure of Kinnaura economy is shaped by three stratified classes, namely, the former Zamindar (large landholding group), Zigismi (marginal landholding group) and the Binanas (servicing group to the Rajput). Raha (1995) draws parallel between this system and the 'Jajmani' system. Only variation is that in case of agricultural operations this service is known as the 'Hala' and in case of non-agricultural services it is known as the 'Binana'. At the functional interaction level, the Binanas class are further segmented on the basis of type of services they render to the Zamidar class. In the past, agricultural operational activities were in the hands of the Koli 'Halas' who also had some low caste-based occupations. The same group when rendering the services of shoe-and-leather work including clearing of carcass, formed the sub-class Chamang Binanas. In a similar way, the Badhi become the Ores Binanas through their specialized job of carpentry and masonry works. The Domang binanas are a specialized class among the Lohar who are involved in work of blacksmithy and allied jobs. Formation of Chanala Binanas sub-class is not widely prevalent. In the modern Binanas system, cash payment is introduced against work done since price rise and modern education have created such needs. In the traditional system, the service castes used to receive meagre seasonal payment in kind, which was not enough for them to survive.

Table 5

Status of 'Binanas' Among the Kinnaura

Type of Binanas	*Group Involved*	*Traditional Form of Payment*	*Present Form of Payment & Status*	*Remarks*
Ores Binanas	Badhi	Seasonal payment in kind	Cash, kind	Jajmani relation persists
Domang Binanas	Lohar	Seasonal payment in kind	Cash, kind	Jajmani relation persists
Halas Binanas	Koli	Seasonal payment in kind	Cash	Payment immediately on completion of work
Sui Binanas	Koli	Seasonal payment in kind	Abolished	Tailoring work done on cash after the delivery of the garment.
Bonu Binanas	Koli	Seasonal payment in kind	Abolished	Cash received after the delivery of material.
Chamang Binanas	Koli	Seasonal payment in kind	Abolished	—
Chanala Binanas	Nagalu	Seasonal payment in kind	Cash, kind	Delivery of material, cash/kind is accepted

Functionary key posts are held by the affluent Rajputs. Only, the Baijantris (musicians) are represented by the Scheduled Castes mostly from the Koli, followed by the Badhi and Lohar. There are temple functionaries who perform all types of duties concerned with the deity and the temple, and they have a major role to act as the shaman mediator between the villagers and the deity. They solve various socio-political and religious problems. The Mathas and the Grokch are the spokesmen of the deity. As the deity had an absolute control over the Kinnaura society, members of the tribe always approached the deity for solution of any problem, mainly when the traditional council failed to solve a problem. In village council, the Mukhia and Char are two key positions held by the Rajputs. Fact remains that key positions in traditional council and in the temple administration are occupied by the Rajputs.

Stratification: Persistence and Change

The opening of modern communication system, impact of education, new cultural elements and immigration of various ethnic groups in the district have led to changes in the life of the Kinnaura people. As a result of social change the concept of status group or 'Khel' system all over the district is gradually wiped out and it is being replaced by inter-status group marriages. In most cases, the total control by the Rajputs over the economic and political aspects of life is being challenged by the ethnic groups under Scheduled Castes category who are now educated, politically conscious and to some extent economically better off. Differential behavioural pattern between the Rajput and the Scheduled Castes members based on purity-pollution concept is reported to have decreased in many aspects of the Kinnaura life.

In spite of some changes that have taken place in recent years, the structural frame of the social-ritual hierarchy remains unchanged. This is, as reported, due to maintenance of the purity-pollution concept by the dominant and socially higher Rajputs, who control the village/regional deities through the temple priests. As such, the Kinnaura social stratification system of traditional type is still maintained by the ethnic groups who still locate the Rajput at the top of the hierarchy. The Lohar, Badhi, Koli and Nagalu remain at lower strata. As in the past they are popularly termed, as the 'Beru' as opposed to the 'Sawarn' or Thakur.

The terms Shudh and Asudh, based on occupation of the Koli are gradually being discarded. The Asudh Koli, traditionally the scavengers, tanners and shoe-makers, have now totally left these occupations and got virtually mixed up with the Shudh Koli. Sui and Bonu sub-divisions are still existing, but the differentiation between these two groups in practical sense is lost because weaving technology among the Bonu is no more in existence, whereas, tailoring by the Sui sub-division in now considered as one of the major occupations. The term Bonu is still known to differentiate it from the Sui terminology.

It is reported that formation of Sunar 'guild' among the Kinnaura is a recent phenomenon. In earlier days, few members either from the Lohar, Badhi, Koli or even from the Rajput had knowledge in silver, brass or goldsmithy. Subsequently the term 'Sunar' is being used by all who work in such specialized jobs. Formation of such new guild is result of involvement of a section of villagers in smithy training received from the government technical institutes. Thus the professionals from the Badhi and Lohar castes are now referred to as the 'Sunar' on account of their involvement in such specialized occupation.

Social position of the Nagalu in the Kinnaura hierarchical order remains unchanged. This is mainly due to their lowest social position, poorest economic condition, educational backwardness and above all, numerical insignificance.

A major change in the general Kinnaura economy had resulted after closure of the Indo-Tibetan international border in the early part of the sixties after the Chinese aggression. After a temporary setback in their economic pursuits, the Kinnaura communities have achieved economic upliftment in various fields with the assistance from the government and due to improved agriculture, horticulture and many new sources of livelihood. The Kinnaura communities as a whole are now earning a huge amount of cash simply from the sale of seasonal fruits and vegetables. Many of them have become economically very sound and prosperous. Those who were previously either landless or having small area of cultivable land, are now acquiring more new reclaimed lands. With this changed situation, the Kinnaura people are mostly engaged in agricultural and horticultural activities throughout the season. Indeed, the Rajputs who hold the major portion of better irrigated lands are economically sound and wealthier. They have much capital to invest in agricultural and horticultural activities. On the contrary, other caste groups among the Kinnaura have failed to achieve such benefits. The Badhi, Lohar and particularly the Koli marginal landholders are obviously unable to economically complete with the Rajput. As a result, major Kinnaura economy is still in the hands of wealthier Rajput agriculturists. The Koli being the largest dominant social group among the Scheduled Castes have diversified occupations now and hence decline to serve the Rajputs under the Binanas system. Even if a Rajput employs them, they ask for cash payment. Some affluent Rajputs now undertake agricultural operational jobs by themselves, being helped by family members. Sometimes, they employ labourers from the Badhi or Lohar or Koli on daily cash basis.

In political and in religious spheres, supremacy of the Rajput among other social groups in Kinnaura tribe still continues to be prominent like in the past. In Hindu dominated areas of Kinnaur, each and every village deity has a defined area of jurisdiction. The deity has an absolute power and authority to guide and control the villagers as per local mythology. Each temple has the temple functionaries (the Kardars). Among them, the Mathas and Grokch are the spokesmen of the deity. They have the shamanic power to mediate between two worlds. Any problem associated with socio-religious or even political issues, is resolved by these shamans on behalf of the deity. It is quite clear that the rural society is totally in the grip of these temple functionaries. They play very significant role in controlling or guiding the villagers in the name of the deity. They act as the key figure in the village politics too. As stated earlier, the key posts of the temple functionaries are hereditarily held by the Rajput and obviously, they control the whole system in religious aspects. Selection of these key Kardar posts, namely, the Pujari, Mathas, Grokch and Khajanchi are done as per the directives of the deity conveyed through the Mathas and Grokch.

Even though the traditional caste council (Charbhai) has become defunct and the Statutory Village Panchayat has emerged, the supremacy of the Rajputs over other castes has not ceased. Majority of the posts including Pradhan, Up-Pradhan are occupied by the Rajput who are still numerically, socially, politically and economically quite dominant. On the other side, the Koli and the Badhi and Lohar represent the Scheduled Caste category and are numerically less in number, excluded, weak and less educated in comparison to that of the Rajput. They have little scope to assert except having a reserved seat in the Statutory Village Panchayat. They have thus an insignificant voice in the Panchayat. Due to their ignorance in political matters, submissive nature in general, less education and illiteracy, they rarely dare to raise their voice against the Rajput, who are majority in number. Table 6 describes the maximal and minimal political representation of Rajput and low castes respectively in frontier villages. It is reported that low caste members ditto the views expressed by

Table 6

Kinnaura Group's Participation in Statutory Village Panchayats

Statutory village panchayat posts	*Kalpa Sub-Division*								*Nichar Sub-Division*				*Pooh Sub-Division*							
	Khowangi Panchayat				*Kothi Panchayat*				*Nichar Panchayat*				*Sunam Panchayat*				*Chango Panchayat*			
	Rajput	*Badhi*	*Lohar*	*Koli*	*Rajput*	*Badhi*	*Lohar*	*Koli*	*Rajput*	*Badhi*	*Lohar*	*Koli*	*Rajput*	*Badhi*	*Lohar*	*Koli*	*Rajput*	*Badhi*	*Lohar*	*Koli*
Pradhan	1	—	—	—	1	—	—	—	1	—	—	—	1	—	—	—	1	—	—	—
Up-Pradhan	1	—	—	—	—	1	—	—	1	—	—	—	1	—	—	—	1	—	—	—
Members	4	—	—	—	2	—	1	1	5	—	—	1	5	—	—	1	3	—	—	1
Total	6	—	—	—	3	1	1	1	7	—	—	1	7	—	—	1	5	—	—	1

majority of the Rajput Panchayat members, and thus the Rajput enjoy full supremacy in political sphere over the 'caste' people.

In spite of deep-rooted existence of Hinduism in many parts of Pooh sub-division the Hangrang valley still is the stronghold of Buddhism, being situated at the border area of Tibet. However, influence of Buddhism on the Kinnaura tribe is reportedly not very significant so far as the social norms at the tribe-level is concerned. In upper Kinnaura, the Rajput (locally known as the Jad/Zad) enjoy higher social rank and are recognized as the wealthier group among all other castes. The Badhi, Lohar and the Koli, constituted the 'Beru' category. Among the Zad (Rajput), the superior class 'Ponpo' does not exist in recent times as they have totally assimilated with the non-Ponpo (Jad), with no differentiation at commensal and connubial levels.

In upper Kinnaur, many villages do not have the Badhi (Ores) who are experts in carpentry and masonry works. Under this condition, the Lohar (also known as the Zothit in Hangrang village area) undertake jobs of carpentry and masonry in addition to their traditional callings. Again, the Zothit perform weaving or tailoring when the Koli cannot be found in certain villages. In Sunam village under Pooh tehsil, a few families of so-called 'Sunar' are engaged in gold and silversmithy. They are bifurcated from the Lohar caste and try to maintain their identity as Sunar since such assignment is considered to be more prestigious and dignified. Two more Sunar guilds are reported to originate from these areas. These are the Suchcha Sunar and Jhutha Sunar. These are the bifurcated groups respectively from the Rajput and the Koli. All these guilds, though accepted in the same profession are quite different when they are viewed from commensal and connubial angle. Emergence of these specialized guilds are the consequence of training, provided either by the industrial training institutes, sponsored by the state government or by some master craftsmen at individual level.

In spite of all the changes, traditional form of the Kinnaura caste hierarchical structure in the Buddhist dominated areas of Kinnaur is maintained keeping the concept of purity-pollution intact. It does not differ anyway from Hindu upper Kinnaur areas or other parts of central and lower Kinnaur. No castes under Scheduled Caste category are allowed to enter the installation place of the deity in a temple. Similarly, in Buddhist dominated areas, they are prohibited in the same way to enter inside the Buddhist monastery where the image of Lord Buddha is installed. They can worship from the doorstep or sit near the door. Such differential attitude is reported from the central part of Kinnaur also. Restrictions in entering inside the monastery is based on caste features as well as observance of pollution.

The monastery is headed by Head Lama. He is assisted by other junior grade Lamas to look after ritualistic and non-ritualistic works associated with the monastery. In the monastery, seating arrangements of these Lamas are determined on the basis of their seniority and also on their caste affiliation. The seniormost Lama sits on the higher platform in the monastery or Buddhist temple, followed by other Lamas as per their respective status ranking order. According to religious convention, Buddhism does not approve the ranking other than simple seniority or the senior-junior relation between teacher and pupil (Eliot, 1954, quoted in Raha and Mahato, 1985: 317). We thus find that within the Lamahood among the Kinnaura, casteism is considered as important factor for the rank status. Most of the Lamas in Kinnaur belong to the Rajput caste. A few Scheduled Castes, like the Lohar, Badhi and mostly the Koli have, however, achieved Lama positions in the monasteries, particularly in different parts of upper Kinnaur. As reported by Raha and Mahato (1985), Lamas from the Lohar caste in Namgia and Leo villages in upper Kinnaur are not allowed to enter inside the monastery but allowed to sit near the door. Similar cases have also been reported from the Buddhist dominated areas in Hangrang tehsil of Pooh sub-division where the Rajput and the Scheduled Caste have separate Buddhist monasteries. Functionaries in each monastery are represented by the Lamas and also the chomos (nuns) from their respective castes.

The Lama from the Scheduled Caste monastery gives special treatment to a visiting Rajput counterpart by offering him a higher seat in the monastery controlled by the Scheduled Caste. The Lama and other members of this monastery would occupy their seats lower to him, keeping a distance in between them. Offering of puja and anai (vegetables cooked or uncooked and fruits) at the Buddhist temple is restricted to the Scheduled Caste members. Since, they are not allowed to enter inside the Buddhist temple, they offer the dry food articles to the deity through the Lama. They offer the cooked food materials to the deity, only if it has been cooked separately by the Rajput near the Buddhist temple. After offering the same, the 'prasad' is collected by the low caste devotees.

It is thus observed that the Buddhists, like Hindu Kinnaura, pursue the concept of purity and pollution at the interactional level. It is only among the Kinnaura, living in Buddhist dominated area in upper Kinnaura, that not much differentiation in terms of social, political and economical and religious relations between Hindus and Buddhists is observed. Less rigid relations are seen also in central and lower Kinnaur.

Discussion and Summary

In the preceding pages, attempts have been made to evaluate and describe the extent of tribal stratification among the social groups within Kinnaura through their day-to-day behaviour in the socio-economic, political and religious spheres. The groups like the Rajput, Lohar, Badhi, Koli and Nagalu constitute the tribe called the Kinnaura. The Kinnaura tribe is unique in the sense that within this tribe, groups have their caste like identities of clean and unclean castes, following norms of pollution and purity. The tribe is also divided into Hindu and Buddhist categories though native religious customs survive. We have discussed how stratification and exclusion co-exist within the Kinnaura tribe-caste cluster. We have discussed above that the Rajput though marked as 'clean caste' and placed in the highest social order, are identified as the Scheduled Tribe. On the contrary, some Kinnaura groups such as the Lohar, Badhi, Koli and Nagaluare called the 'unclean caste groups' are listed as the Scheduled Caste. Such categorization of groups as 'Tribe' and 'Scheduled Caste' within the Kinnaura tribal fold is considered as unjustified. On account of stratification and differentiation at the social, economic, political and religious level, the Kinnaura tribal solidarity is much affected and has become weak in a broader sense. However, within the Kinnaura tribe the Rajput solidarity is stated to be superb in all social, political, economic and religious spheres. At the same time they enjoy all extra-benefits by being declared and included as 'Scheduled Tribe.' The Badhi, Lohar, Nagalu and the Koli are deprived even though declared as SC because of poor resources and low ritual status.

Stratification among the Kinnaura groups is observed at various levels of interaction. The Kinnaura are traditionally divided into two sections of Khosia and Beru. The Khosia known as Kanet or Rajput have no further sub-divisions, whereas, the Berus have their sub-divisions, viz., the Domang, Chamang and Chanala. Of these, Domang is divided into two groups called the Badhi and the Lohar. The Chamang and the Chanala have only one sub-group each, that is, the Koli and Nagalu respectively. The Khosia claim a higher status in terms of economic, political and religious dominance. Though the rigidity in terms of behaviour has changed, the overall stratified traditional ranks as mentioned still exist. In the present context also everyone recognizes the highest rank of the Khosia and the lowest rank as the Nagalu. Contact exists amongst the Badhi, Lohar, Koli and Nagalu. The Badhi and Lohar have achieved certain higher status and now claim a middle status position in between the Khosia and Nagalu. The Koli, however, do not agree with the status claims of the Badhi and the Lohar.

Acknowledgement

The author is grateful to Dr N.K. Das, Project Coordinator, for his critical comments and guidance and also for his editorial assistance.

References

Bajpai, S.C. 1982, *Kinnaur in the Himalayas (Mythology to Modernity),* New Delhi: Concept Publishing Company.

Chandra, R. 1992, *Highlanders of Northwest Himalayas*. New Delhi: Inter India.

Kapoor, D.D. 1972, "People of Kinnaur: An Essay in the Problems of the Tribe", in *Tribal Situation in India,* Suresh Singh Kumar (ed.), Simla: Indian Institute of Advanced Study.

Mamgain, M.D. 1971, *Himachal Pradesh District Gazetteer, Kinnaur,* Himachal Pradesh.

Raha, M.K. 1995, *People of the Himalayas*. Calcutta: ASI.

Raha, M.K. 2003, "Synthesis of Buddhism and Hinduism in Western Himalayas: A Study of the Kinnauras of Himachal Pradesh", in *Culture, Religion and Philosophy: Critical Studies in Syncretism and Inter-Faith Harmony,* N.K. Das (Ed.) Jaipur: Rawat Publications.

Raha, M.K. and S.N. Mahato, 1985, *The Kinnaurese of the* Himachals, Memoir No. 63, Calcutta: Anthropological Survey of India.

Rose, H.A. 1911, *Glossary of the Tribes and Castes of the Punjab and North-West Frontier Province,* Vol. II, Lahore: Government Press.

Sankrityanyan, R. 1956, *Kinner Desh,* in Hindi, Allahabad: Kitab Mahal Pvt. Ltd.

24 Ritual Hierarchy, Class Formation and Social Exclusion

The Gujjar of a Multi-Ethnic Village, Himachal Pradesh

R. Haider

This paper discusses the historical patterns of migration, social stratification and social change among the nomadic-pastoral Gujjars of Himachal Pradesh. The Gujjars are distributed over different eco-cultural regions in Jammu and Kashmir, Punjab, Haryana, Himachal Pradesh and western parts of Uttarakhand. Some Gujjars live in the plain pockets and some in relatively isolated and hilly tracts. Their highest concentration is in the mountainous regions of Himachal Pradesh and Jammu and Kashmir. They are found in Bilaspur, Mandi, Chamba and Sirmaur districts of Himachal Pradesh. They have been included in the list of Scheduled Tribes in Himachal Pradesh. The major concentration of this tribe is in Chamba of Himachal Pradesh. Normally they live in relatively isolated hilly areas. In parts of western India the Gujars have launched social movements for their recognition as Scheduled Tribe.

The Tribe: Origin and Migration

According to Crook, the Gujjars derive their name from the Sanskrit, Gurjare, the original name of Gujarat. Another interpretation is that they were originally cowherders and were therefore called Gocharg in their earlier habitat. The term got corrupted into Gujjar gradually and remained stuck, although the tribe gave up cow keeping and took to buffalo rearing. There are some other explanations about the origin of Gujjars. Different authors namely Ojha, Vaidya, Verma and Munshi consider Gujjars as being of Indian origin. They hold that the people of Rajputana, Malwa and modern Gujarat and the whole region called Gujardesa was once a tract of homogeneous people residing there, during 5th and 6th century AD, especially after the fall of Gupta empire. The Gujjars living in and around Mount Abu organized themselves and moved in different directions. They believe that Gujjars are one of the oldest races in India and have some relationship with the Yadavas of ancient India. According to a legend among the Gujjars, it is believed that Kshatriya community was destroyed 21 times by the Parashuramji. Parashuramji is regarded as the originator of the Gujjar community. There is yet another popular version of mythical origin found among the Muslim Gujjars. They claim that they are the descendants of the Prophet Ishaque who told his sons Ash and Yakup that whoever could first manage to get food for him would succeed him as Prophet. Ultimately Yakup succeeded. Disappointed, Ash retreated into the forest and engaged himself completely in prayers, with the result that he became a great saint. Following his footsteps, his descendants, the present day Gujjars, love to live in the forest and consider themselves nearer to God (Centre for Research, Planning and Action Report, New Delhi). The Gujjars claim that they have descended from Rajputs. According to Ibbetson (1974) Gujjars are of Rajput descent but Baden-Powell (1972) opines that they have a different racial origin and in the course of time merged with the Rajput community. The Gujjar also trace their origin from Jasoda; mother of Lord Krishna. So they have connection with the cult of the child Krishna of Mathura. The Gujjars introduced child Krishna cult.

Some scholars are of the view that these people migrated to India somewhere during the sixth century from Central-Asia after the downfall of Gupta kingdom, from a place where communication with India was a regular feature via a well established trade route. According to the historian Hocrinte (1905) at that time barbarian tribes attacked India's north-western part through this trade route and the Gujjars had captured parts of north India. In course of time they adopted Hinduism and started worshipping Hindu deities and came to be recognized as Rajput. Those who remained only as Gujjars even today inhabit the western part of India. Later the Gujjars were converted to Islam by Tumar. Later Gujjar entered Himachal Pradesh from the neighbouring plains through isolated and stray migration. The Muslim Gujjars appear to have first set foot in the then princely states of Chamba and Sirmaur and then spread out gradually to other localities. Later, they spread in Uttar Pradesh particularly in the western area in search of green pasture and better habitation. According to a legend about 300 years ago, the marriage of a Raja of Sirmaur in Himachal Pradesh was solemnized with the daughter of the Raja of Jammu. So a large number of her Gujjar servants accompanied her and later were settled by the Raja of Sirmaur in the forest area. Another legend states that the Gujjars were allowed to enter the state of Chamba as a result of the services of an old Gujjar woman who had saved the life of a close relative of the ruling prince of that time.

The Village and its People

The Gujjars numbering over a million, constitute one of the most enterprising tribes, their highest concentration is in the mountainous regions of Himachal Pradesh. This territory is commonly known as Chamba Valley. It is a vast undulating plateau studded with mountain ranges and was once covered with dense forests. The Gujjar village Sahu is selected from Chamba for present study. For limited comparison data collected from village Bamta are used. Village Sahu is situated in a hilly terrain and is nearly 20 km away from Chamba town at an attitude of approximately 850 feet above the sea level. The village consists of 71 households and has 15 different castes and communities. This is still rather uncommon in Chamba. The houses are isolated and the distance between houses of a cluster is often 20 metres. The cluster is visible only from a great distance while within the cluster each house looks isolated and the pattern of living is very scattered. The people are located in two type of hamlets. The land on the roadside is flat and is occupied by the higher communities whereas other communities occupy land on hilly slopes. A Gujjar Muslim male is recognized by his typical dress and can be identified from the distance due to his tall built. The Muslims wear an embroidered headgear tape, coloured jacket, a loose kurta and long beards dyed with mehndi. They are very much attached to their traditional way of living.

Table 1

Ethnic Composition and Family Size

Community	*No. of families*		*No. of members*	*%*
Brahman	3		20	5.03
Miya	2		14	3.5
Rajput	5		23	5.79
Jat	2		14	3.5
Mahajan	3		20	5.03
Arya	9		49	12.34
Jeer/Jheer	9		65	16.37
Sippi	2		14	3.5
Nai	2		14	3.5
Dhobi	1		6	1.51
Kumhar	1		4	1.00
Gaddi S/T	6		39	9.82
Mochi	2		7	1.76
Muslim	4		23	5.79
Gujjar	20		85	21.41
Total households	71	Total population	397	

Village Communities

Brahman

The Brahmans occupy the central place in the village settlement. There are three families in the village with a population of 20 persons and they form 5.03 per cent of the total population of the village. Traditionally they are priests. One family is however, engaged in priesthood. The others have agriculture as their primary occupation. They rank high in the society and render their services on ceremonial and social occasions like birth, marriage and death.

Miya-Rajput

The Miya (Rajput) also occupy an important place in the village. They are descended from the royal family. They enjoyed the power among the village communities in the past, which they continue to enjoy even today. At present they still maintain the same position in the area. Only two families of Miya live in village and they form 3.5 per cent of the village population. They are engaged in agricultural activities.

Rajputs

The Rajputs are traditionally landlords and are engaged in the agricultural occupation. They rank high in the society. They also occupy the central place of the village settlement with a population of 23 people out of the total 397 and they form 5.79 per cent of the total population. They claim that they migrated from Gujarat to this hilly area, as they wanted a shelter to protect themselves from the Muslim ruler.

Thus, these three communities together occupy the best land available in the village and their houses are centrally located. These communities belong to upper class.

Jats

They belong to the upper middle class in the society. There are only two families of this community, which has about 14 persons. They form 3.5 per cent of the village population. The Jats are agriculturist by occupation and both families are engaged in agriculture. Their houses are located adjacent to the upper class people's houses.

Mahajan

Mahajans belong to the business class and all business in Sahu village are carried out by their community. The Mahajans came to this village from Kangra district of Himachal Pradesh. There are three families of Mahajan forming 5.03 per cent of the total population. Business is their primary occupation. However, they are also engaged in agriculture.

Arya

There are about nine families of Arya. All of them are engaged in agricultural activities. Traditionally, they are professional shepherds and migrated to this village from Bharmaur district of Chamba. They account for 12.34 per cent of the total population. Altogether there are 49 persons of Arya community as members of Arya Samaj sect who are vegetarian by food habit. The Arya Samaj is a reformed sect of Hindu religion. When it entered this region, a large number of Hindus were attracted to it and its principles, and the people followed its ten principles. At the time of the census, the Arya Samaj issued a clear directive that Arya Samaj members should have entries separately from the Hindu communities in the Census. The Aryas do not observe Hindu festivals of Janmastami, Ram Navami, Durgapuja and Ganesh Chaturthi because they do not believe in any god. Altogether there are 49 persons of Arya community. Originally they were Sappi or Sipi but due to conversion to Arya Samaj faith they have started calling themselves Arya Samaji. Interestingly, they consider themselves superior to their original Sippi community.

Jeer/Jheer

The Jheer, also pronounced as Jheewar, are traditionally fishermen and migrated from the Salt Range. There are about nine families having 65 persons. They form 16.37 per cent of the population, and are the second largest community in the village. All of them are engaged in agricultural activities.

Sippi

This is one of the indigenous communities found in the hilly region. Traditionally they were shepherds but are now engaged in agricultural occupation. The community is endogamous and divided into a number of classes. There are only two families of Sippi with 14 persons and form 3.5 per cent of total population of the village. Their houses are adjacent to the lower class community that is Nai, Dhobi, and Jeer.

Nai

They belong to the Hindu community and are barbers. They act as messengers of their jajman. They play a very important role in the village socio-religious activities. They are still engaged in their traditional occupation. Only two families are there and they form 3.5 per cent of the population in the village. They traditionally occupy a low status.

Dhobi

They belong to Hindu community and their traditional occupation is washing clothes. None in the village nowadays requires this service. So they have shifted from traditional occupation to agricultural activities. There is only one family of Dhobi, which has about 6 persons and forms 1.51 per cent of the total population.

Kumhar

The four members of Kumhar family prepare large and small size of jars used for boiling, churning and such purposes. In addition to their traditional occupation they have some agricultural land to cultivate.

Mochi

The Chamar/Mochi who by and large do not own any land are leather workers.

Gaddi

The Gaddi enjoy the Scheduled Tribe status in Himachal Pradesh. They migrated from Bharmour to Chamba in search of green pasture and settled at Chamba. Traditionally, they are shepherds and follow a nomadic life.

Muslim

There are only four families of Muslim having about 23 persons and they form 5.79 per cent of the village population. Their houses are adjacent to each other and they are engaged in agricultural activities. One family among them is engaged in religious teaching and other ritual activities.

The Ritual Hierarchy and Class Formation: Process of Social Exclusion

We have discussed above the relative statuses of the communities. On the basis of above discussion the population of the village can be classified under three categories – upper, middle and low.

Table 2
Social Stratification and Ritual Ranking

Communities	*Rank*
1. Brahman	Upper class
2. Miya	Closer to Upper class
3. Rajput	Upper class
4. Jat	Upper Middle class
5. Mahajan	Upper Middle class
6. Arya	Middle class
7. Jeer/Jheer	Middle class
8. Sippi	Middle class
9. Nai	Lower Middle class
10. Dhobi	Lower Middle class
11. Kumhar	Lower Middle class
12. Mochi	Lower class
13. Gaddi	Lower class
14. Gujjar	Lower class
15. Muslim	Lower Middle class

The Brahman community in the village occupies the highest rank in the local hierarchy. Of all the communities in Chamba's village Sahu, ritual status of this community is considered higher than other communities in the village. In commensal rules, dietary observation and occupation a Brahman maintains the traditional image of a Brahman. His service revolves around religion. But he does not render his service to the Mochi community. The other service communities – Dhobi, Nai receive the services of the Brahman in their life cycle ceremonies. Ritually, Brahmans are in a high position, but those Brahmans who plough their own land due to poor economic condition are seen as inferior by the Brahmans who are engaged in religious activities. They are called halbah (ploughman) and are widely engaged in agriculture. The Miyas claim a higher status in view of the economic prosperity. The Rajput occupies the third rank in the village hierarchy. Though the Rajput are politically and economically a stronger and more dominant community than the Brahmans and the Miya they still stand below them in the village hierarchy. The Rajputs do not allow widow remarriage. The data of both the villages, Sahu and Bamta, show that there is not a single incident of widow remarriage among the Rajput. They occupy the higher rank in the village by way of their clean occupation, that is agriculture. In actual practice, agriculture is an open occupation that can be followed by any community irrespective of its rank in the village hierarchy. Next come the Jats. They are ranked below the Rajput. The Jats are the major community in both the villages, exclusively following the occupation of agriculture. The castes that stand below the Jat are Mahajan, Jeer/ Jheer, Sippi, Arya. The Mahajans claim higher status than the Arya, Jheer and Sippi because of their ritual status. The Jats and Mahajan observed all the rituals that the Brahman pursued. Their occupation is agriculture and they are regarded as having a higher status than the other artisan and service classes. The Jeer and Sippi stand below the Mahajan. The lower middle group that consists of Jheer, Sippi, Nai, Dhobi and Kumhar stand below the Jat, Mahajan and Arya. Among these communities the Nai occupies little higher rank than the Dhobi because of his occupation that is less impure than that of the latter. The Dhobi stands below the Nai in the village hierarchy because of his traditional occupation of washing the clothes of the higher communities.

At the lower class are included Scheduled Castes and Scheduled Tribes such as Hindu and Muslim Gujjar (Scheduled Tribe), Gaddi (Scheduled Tribe) and Mochi (Scheduled Caste). They take up labour work during the harvest of crop. Ritually they are considered impure and they always maintain a distance. The Muslim Gujjars also fall in this category and they have Scheduled Tribe status. The Muslims do not consider above mentioned lower class communities as their equal and do not approve any marital alliances with them. Thus we witness that the process of social stratification operates at various levels.

The Muslim Gujjars are in a minority. Cooked food or water touched by them was considered polluted. But their touch does not pollute the clothes. Among the Muslims, a high ranking Muslim like the Sayyed occupies the highest position among the Muslims. People from other communities also pay them respect.

The village may be considered a compact unit. We have noted that the Gujjar by and large live by themselves. The Gujjar clans through which the tribal society operates extend beyond the boundary of the village. A man has greater obligation to his clan than to his village. It is observed that the major occupation of the communities is cultivation of land. However, not all these communities have uniformity in the ownership of land. The Brahman and Miya are the communities having a major ownership of land in that order. Rajputs also have a major ownership of land.

Communities, Occupation and Social Relationship

The various occupations could be broadly divided into three categories. They are land based occupations, village traditional services and non-agricultural labour.

So long as the traditional jajman system prevailed in the village traditional relationship between the master and the servant, between the patron and the client existed. But such a system is fast disappearing in the rural areas. The labourer is paid mostly in cash and his work in confined to the farm only. So far as the Nai and Kumhar are concerned jajmani relationship is still found in the village. The Nai is paid in kind and also sometimes in cash.

Discrimination and Political Participation

The caste council or the Jat Panchayat has absolutely nothing to do with the political participation of the village because there is now awareness among lower classes. Earlier, when elections were held, the village elders held a meeting and nominated the candidates giving due weightage to candidate of higher community based on its population. Now, low class communities raise objection to this and they also admit that in the past they were guided by the advice given to them by the higher class villagers, particularly their employers.

Lower class people now take part in organization of Village Panchayat through the system of reservation of seats for them.

Now the Village Panchayat has a tremendous role to play in shaping the social and political life of the village people. No exclusion is seen now. Chairs and benches are kept in the Panchayat hall; but no discrimination of any sort is made in the sitting arrangement. Those who come first take the chairs and late comers take the benches. The higher class people sit by the side of lower class member now in the Panchayat hall. It is observed that the lower class people come better dressed in the days of the meeting.

When the lower class people offer their suggestions and raise their problem the other community members from the higher classes do not oppose them. While addressing each other due respect is shown. However some discrimination is noticed while admitting the lower class people to Panchayat hall.

Religious Communities

The various religious groups found in the village are Hindu, Arya Samaj sect and Muslim. Hindus dominate the scene, with a little over 72.80 per cent of the population. The Muslims generally were on the side of the higher caste, but the Gujjar were on the side of the lower communities and this was a big gain for the lower communities. The relation between the Hindu and Arya Samaj sect was cordial and involved no suspicion, tension or conflicts.

The villagers particularly Gujjar have been living in close and active contact with the Hindu caste groups for a long time. The Gujjars are the least conservative in the area and follow the Hindu way of life. Now the Gujjar religion is of composite order. The Gujjar mix up with the Gaddi, joining in their festivals and public worship.

Interaction, Interrelation among the Gujjar

The Gujjar form an ideal tribal society. The cooperation among the Gujjar families is an enduring aspect of the reality of the social life of the Gujjar community. When a birth, marriage or death occurs in a family the Gujjar members cooperate and participate in the appropriate rituals. This type of help and cooperation may be termed obligatory cooperation. Another type of cooperation is concerned with the everyday life and activities in a household. After a birth has taken place in a family and the period of pollution is over, each family brings cooked food for the mother and father of the child. This is done perhaps as a sign of welcome to the new member of the fraternity. At the time of marriage every household in the community must also bring a gift, and starting from the negotiation stage to the final occurrence of the marriage the community members help and cooperate with the concerned family in many ways. In the case of death. They come to carry the body to the village burial ground and bury it. No one from any other community touches the corpse.

In the daily life of the community, mutual cooperation and help is discernible. The community members live close to each other and there is sufficient interaction among them. One may feel free to enter the house of another family and ask for his favour and children spend a good part of their time together. They play together and when they grow up a little they go to the forest to collect leaves and other things. A woman freely goes to another house of the same community.

Social Structure and Clan System

The Gujjar are divided into two endogamous religious segments of Hindus and Muslims. The village has large section of Hindu Gujjars. The Muslim Gujjars are also divided into Syed Gujjar, Pathan and Shakh Gujjar. The Syed Gujjars are regarded as descendants of the Prophet's daughter Fatama and command respect and occupy a high social rank. Pathan, ranked third are considered to have come from Afghanistan. However, it is observed that the Muslim Gujjar maintain no distinction of hierarchy at present and they marry among themselves without any hesitation.

The Gujjar are divided into various clan groups. The important clans are Paswan, Khatana, Chauhan, Bainaya, Finda, Gorsi, Kalas and Kasana. Some clans Khatana, Gorsi, Kasana and Chauhan are common among the Hindu Gujjar and Muslim Gujjars. The exact number of clan among the Gujjar is not known and it is also surprising that none of the natives could trace the origin of their clan but they know they belong to a particular clan. There is no clear-cut hierarchy found among the clans of the Gujjars. Nevertheless Chauhan, Gorsi, Khatana and Kalas consider themselves high in rank as informed by the Hindu Gujjar residents. The Gujjars usually claim equality of all clans. They do not marry inside the clan and they follow the rule of clan exogamy. The members of a clan are believed to be related as brother and sister and therefore clan exogamy is a norm. In case of a conflict taking place between the members of two different clans, the clan elders settle and help its members in a body. Thus, clan organization has a very important role to play in the social life of the tribe.

Family

The social life of an individual is very closely related to his family life. Out of 71 households of the village the Gujjars have 20 households and form 21.41 per cent of village population. The Gujjars are a patrilineal tribe with mainly patrilocal residence. The father is usually the head of the family and is respected by all the members of family. The wife of the head, is also held in reverence by male members of the family, who also consult her on important family, social and religious matters. Sons and daughters are expected to show respect to their parents and all other elder members of the family. Sons are entitled to equal shares. The eldest son cannot claim any larger share among the Hindu Gujjar. On the death of the father, the property is equally divided among the sons and widow. If a person has more wives the property is equally distributed between the wives; afterwards each part is sub-divided according to the number of sons from each wife. A daughter even if she has been living with the parents or is a widow has no right to inherit the property. However, she may get some portion of property if she is unmarried or if she is married to a very poor family.

The status of the women is lower than men. The woman controls her family both socially and economically. Milking of buffaloes in the morning is her first duty. Then she extracts butter from the milk. The domestic responsibilities for pounding paddy, cooking, fetching water and firewood are entirely borne by the woman. Sometimes she can allocate a particular job to her daughter. She is supposed to plan the training of the children, specially of the daughter which is special duty of the female head of the family. Although ideologically the Gujjar community pay much respect to individual freedom but in reality a woman does not enjoy such freedom. In some important matters her advice may be taken into account, but this is neither obligatory nor is the male head bound to accept her advice.

Marriage

Monogamous marriage is most preferred, however polygynous marriage is sometimes practised. Earlier polygynous marriage was very common among the Muslim Gujjar but nowadays it is totally abandoned. Clan exogamy is still strictly followed in Gujjar society. Secondary marriage like levirate, sorrorate and widow remarriage are practised. Marriage nowadays is performed in adulthood, by negotiation. The following types of marriage are very common among the Gujjar of Chamba:

(i) Marriage by bride-price: A price is fixed which goes to the father of the girl.

(ii) Balta-Salta (exchange marriage) is also very common among the Gujjar. In this system a man can marry another man's sister in exchange of his sister who marries the man.

(iii) Marriage by services is also a common type of marriage among them. Under this category of marriage a boy is expected to stay in the girl's house with the other members and help the family in various economic activities.

Negotiation

Among the Gujjars the first lead in marriage negotiation is taken by the father of the prospective bridegroom through a go-between. He is often a relative of the groom but he may also be a common friend to both the parties. As soon as a girl is spotted in a different village the go-between informs the father of the groom and they decide to pay a visit to her home. Both the parties settle down and discuss about the virtues of the girl and boy, their respective families, bride price and such other points of information. Marriage is arranged at the bridegroom's residence. Dowry is not prevalent among the Gujjars. The father of the bride-groom receives some cash and gifts from the bride's father as token. The amount is negotiated before the marriage. It is paid in the presence of an elderly person from both the sides before the marriage is performed.

Several old norms are declining. Considerable decline in the absolute authority and exclusive decision-making power of the head of family or eldest male is seen. The head of a family is no more sole final authority in the decision-making process of the family. Now it has been observed that the members of a family many sometime rebel against the decision of the head. Moreover, members sometime resort to independent judgement and action. The decline in the authority and decision-making power of the head is also associated with changes such as legal, civil and social rights of sons and daughters.

Economic Activities

Traditional Nomadic Life

Traditionally the Hindu and the Muslim Gujjars migrated from one place to another as a part of their traditional economic habit. The total lifestyle was revolved around the cattle and cattle rearing. But now this is changing. One of the reasons for this is the increasing contact with the other communities. The Hindu Gujjar at present follow a settled life and pursue agriculture as the main occupation, in place of cattle and cattle rearing. In this way they have lost the characteristic of being nomadic and pastoral. For a few Hindu Gujjars agriculture has become a secondary occupation. Due to their involvement in agriculture, they are now mixing with other agricultural communities of the area. The Chamba Gujjar are very different from the Bilaspur Gujjar. Pastoralism is still regarded as an important means of subsistence among Bilaspur Gujjars, who still migrate from one place to another through a variety of routes in search of green fodder with cattle and other belongings. In view of graze and settlement problem faced by the Muslim Gujjars the government tried to settle them in Chamba and other areas of Himachal Pradesh. In 1962, the government provided each household five bigha of free land along with house for their survival. According to government rules the transfer of land from tribal to non-tribal is not permitted. In this way the Gujjar of Chamba district who originally had no home as well as cultivable land in the area, have abandoned their nomadic way of living and settled down permanently in the area and started cultivating. There are a few families who are still continuing their traditional occupation of pastoralism.

Now almost all the Gujjar families of both villages are engaged in agricultural activities and have a well settled life though a few Muslim Gujjars of the area still consider pastoralism as an important economic resource.

Agricultural Activities and Landholding Pattern

It is a fact that the village Sahu is inhabited by 15 communities and each community has a traditional profession. The Brahmans are priests of the village and similarly the Mochi and the Nai have their traditional occupations, but all these communities having specialization in different trades, now prefer to be identified as agriculturists first and anything else only afterwards. All communities of the village are hard working agriculturists and have maximum attachment with their cultivable land.

The condition and quality of the land which was provided by the government in 1962 is not considered good land for agricultural activities. The whole of the area is hilly with barren soil consisting of stones. Majority of the fields are on the hill slopes. Year after year the soil is being washed away during the rains. At this rate the land has become uneconomic for cultivation.

The lands of traditional agriculturists are owned by the families in the Sahu village and right on land is traced through the man's ancestry only. After his death, the land is shared equally among sons only. Gujjars can sell land or transfer the land to the kin or tribal people only. The land is a very important part of Gujjar life. It acts as the security for borrowing money from the money-lender or bank or from among the co-villagers at the time of any important occasion like agricultural activities or socio-religious and domestic activities.

Generally, they take only one crop in the season due to the environment and because the villagers of Sahu are totally dependent upon the rain. There are no other irrigation facilities available in the hilly areas. The method of cultivation is very different due to the fact that the soil is on the hill top where the slope is steep and no ploughing is done, only the hoe and the spade are used. The hoe and spade are purchased from the Chamba market where the Gujjars come for purchase. The field having been thoroughly dug with the spade are cleared of weeds and grasses. In terrain held in the more level place particularly in the Bamta village of Bilaspur district the plough is used twice. After the first ploughing the women remove the weeds and grasses with the help of a hoe and then a second ploughing is done and then the field is dressed. Every alternate furrow is then sown with the seed. For agriculture, normally they use hand made agricultural implements in the field. They are as yet unable to adopt the modern technology for agricultural operations because of the nature of the hilly areas they live and due to and the lack of means of transportation.

Pastoralism

Pastoralism earlier formed one of the important part of the Gujjar economy. Gradually the Gujjars adopted agriculture as main activity. However, many Muslim Gujjars still largely depend on this occupation. The Gujjars keep cattle in the part of the house in which they themselves reside. They graze their cattle in the forest.

For pastoralism, few families form a group and roam from one place to another place, from lower to higher altitude and vice versa, in search of green fodder. The migratory journey starts in the second week of April from lower altitude and continues till the first week of October at higher altitude every year. The Gujjars follow a definite route which came to be demarcated by the forest department. The metalled roads restrict their journey during day time. Gujjars usually cover a distance of 10 to 12 km in a day. They camp at night near a water source. Generally, their journey period varies between one month to three months.

Route of Migration

The route of migration and locations where the Gujjars make their camps are as follows:

1. Sahu village: Mondi (Himachal Pradesh), Mangles – Hurad (Himachal Pradesh), Thanda-nala (Himachal Pradesh), Dorikund (Himachal Pradesh), Ladoo (Himachal Pradesh), Chakki (Punjab), Pathankot (Punjab).
2. Sahu village: Mondi (Himachal Pradesh), Mongles (Himachal Pradesh), Hurad (Himachal Pradesh), Thanda-nala (Himachal Pradesh), Dorikund (Himachal Pradesh), Ladoo (Himachal Pradesh), Marthal (Himachal Pradesh), Uchivasi (Himachal Pradesh), Dusava (Punjab), Paniyar (Punjab), Rajbi Bagh (Punjab), Gurdaspur (Punjab).

The Gujjars of Chamba areas revealed that they follow a single route up to Pathankot and there one portion goes from the Ladoo areas to the Gurdaspur forest areas. The six Muslim Gujjar families depend entirely on cattle economy. The milk is the main source of income in the family. They maintain the number of milking cattle (she-buffaloes) in such a way that every half of the cattle herd continues to produce milk. The cattle which do not produce milk are sold out in the market or to cattle agents. They also purchase the milking cattle from kin groups or from the market through cattle agents.

So the Gujjar economy, though directly dependent upon agriculture, also has a very important pastoral economy component. The present study was carried out on 20 Gujjar families in the village Sahu. The families have been categorized here on the basis of their landholding.

Levels of Income from the Land

Landholding of Gujjar Families

Landholding in Bigha	*No. of families*	*Percentage*	*Economic Gain per month*
Less than 3 Bigha	9	45%	111.08
3–5 Bigha	5	25%	258.43
5+ Bigha	6	30%	564.48
	20 families		

The nine Gujjar families hold less than three bigha of land. They form almost half of the total number of Gujjar families residing in the village.

It is seen from the table that the majority of the households accounting for 45 per cent are in the lower category of income group then earned ₹ 111.08 per month per family, followed by 25 per cent in middle status with ₹ 258.43 per family, and 30 per cent in the higher income category who earned ₹ 564.48 per family.

Average Income from She-buffaloes (Cattle wealth) among Gujjar

S. No.	*She-buffaloes*	*No. of families*	*Percentage*	*Average income (₹ per month)*
1.	Less than 1–2 buffaloes	10 families	50%	432
2.	3 to 4 buffaloes	8 families	40%	963
3.	5+ buffaloes	2 families	10%	1,395

The per family average ownership of buffaloes was calculated for all the three categories of families mentioned above. Ten families of the low income category together own 16 buffaloes, the average being 1.6 per family. In the middle income category, the eight families owned 31 buffaloes, that is 3.9 per family and income from the she buffaloes was ₹ 963 per month. There were only two families in the higher income category owning a total of 11 buffaloes, being 5.5 buffaloes per family, with an income of ₹ 1,395 per month.

One buffalo gives an average of 3 litres of milk per day, which then fetched a price of ₹ 3 per litre. So the maximum cash that can be gained from one she-buffalo was ₹ 270 per month.

Milk and milk products are the main source of earning for these families. It is observed that as far as the marketing of milk is concerned they offered it to the shopkeeper or agent at a certain rate, because they have traditional ties with the shopkeepers and totally depend on them. For example Mata Datta, a shopkeeper of Chamba town had a very old relationship with the Gujjar. His fore-father had established contract with Gujjars and they still maintain those traditional relations now. This shopkeeper in exchange provided the entire domestic and other requirement of families of Gujjar. Because of such historical link the Gujjars were bound to sell milk products to the shopkeeper. Another factor is that due to their isolation and distant hilly terrain and lack of means of transportation they found it convenient to have a fixed customer, though they got a cheaper price.

Only one family of the Gujjar works as labourers, which includes both agricultural as well as non-agricultural labour, to eke out a livelihood. The family has no agricultural land.

Education and Gujjar Community

Formal education among the Gujjar in both villages is at low level and that too, it has started only recently. Gujjars have their own unwritten system of knowledge which includes, religious belief and knowledge about their immediate environment. The children are taught moral vows, tribal etiquettes and community behaviour. Besides these, children also learn from the jungle-lore and acquire other practical knowledge about the types of food, the means of preparing them, the place of their occurrence and so on. They learn by going on excursions with their parents Thus, one finds that this transhumans community has a holistic system of education.

In 1956 Adim Jati Vikas was founded to initiate welfare activities along with education among the tribal population of the area. The Adim Jati Vikas has started work in socio-cultural field as well as education. The main objective of the organization is to impart formal education to the Gujjar community. To fulfil its prime objective it has opened a school in the Sahu village area. The second major objective of the organization was to encourage people's participation in diverse economic activities.

There are many causes of the failure of the education system. First reason is the remoteness of the village from the main town of Chamba. The village is about 20 km away from the Chamba town and has very poor communication system. The inhospitable terrain further aggravates the situation. The second, is the poor infrastructure in the region. Owing to these reasons, teachers are unwilling to come to this place as they find it difficult to live a decent life. Consequently many posts of the teachers are lying vacant. Those who are there in the school are also on the lookout to get themselves transferred since teachers do not consider this place fit for staying for a long period. They have failed to establish any intimate relation with children as well as the people of the village. As a logical corollary people in turn, also do not have a good opinion about the attitude of teachers. The third cause of failure of education system is the high drop-out rate among the children. After second or third standard (classes) the drop-out rate is very high. This is because children are taken to the field or jungle to help parents in their work. Tribal population is of the view that more hands mean more earning. For them, formal education is only of limited use for their children as it does not help them in earning their bread. The girls are not going to school.

Political Life of Gujjars

Gujjar Biradari

Traditional community council organizations are found among the Hindu and Muslim Gujjars through which social control is effected in the village. Such tribal councils also help to prevent the exploitation of its members at the hand of outside agencies.

The Gujjar also have a traditional Biradari Panchayat. The Panchayat elders have common responsibilities, function effectively and manage their collective affairs following customary laws. There is no written record of customs. Community council was also entitled to settle disputes.

Gujjar Panchayat spreads over a forest range and cut across the village boundaries and is inter-village in nature. The people of the same community from adjacent villages that is Thalla, Mashu, Muhal, Meto become the members of such Biradari. It is headed by an elderly person called Numberdar leader. According to tradition the oldest member of the community becomes the Numberdar. No other qualification would be taken into account for filling this post because it is an ascribed position occupied by the oldest man of the village. At present seniority is not the only criterion for selection of the Numberdar.

Numberdar's Privilege and Power

Election of the Numberdar was dependent on personal qualities, but the economic standing was also an important ingredient. Landholding is the only source of a sound economic standing for a person. But usually the village members sit together and settle the election of the Numberdar. A number of names are proposed for the post by different villages and one who secures the highest number of votes is declared elected. The leader acts as a political head, he commands respect and authority of all villages. The Numberdar has a voice in village development programmes where the government needs to consult the villagers. In terms of judicial power the Numberdar settles all petty cases of the village with the aid of his office. The Numberdar is very particular in maintaining the birth and death registers. The Numberdar acts as a representative of the community. He acts as a community judiciary supported by the elders. His decision is regarded as final and the parties have to abide by his decisions.

Usually the cases of land disputes, violence, intra-and inter-family quarrels, theft, inheritance, divorce disputes and so on are decided by the Numberdar and justice is given to the deserving individuals. Upon getting a complaint the Numberdar used to convene a meeting on an appointed evening. The village chowkidar had the responsibility of informing all the community people of the village. When the community members assembled, the parties had to narrate their arguments and counterargument. After listening arguments and through consulting the elders the Numberdar conveys his decision, which remains binding on both the parties.

However nowadays the Biradari council is not considered to be conducive in view of social and occupational mobility. Indeed modern forces of change have weakened these age-old institutions. A gradual disappearance of this institution has been seen in the light of growth of Statutory Gram Panchayat also.

Gram Panchayat

The modern state sponsored Gram Panchayat was established according to the Panchayat Act of 1947. The government introduced Statutory Panchayats in entire rural areas of Himachal Pradesh. But this act did not come into force until

1956. Since then every three years the Statutory Panchayat body is renewed through fresh election of the Numberdar/Pradhan. The Panchayat has two wings, one is known as the executive committee with nine members headed by the Pradhan/Numberdar. The other wing is know as the Gram Cutchery or the village court consisting of nine members headed by the Sarpanch. The Pradhan of Sahu Panchayat is of Rajput community. He has landed property in the village and his primary occupation is agriculture. Of the other members of the committee two are Hindu Rajput and Jat, two are service class that is Jheer and Dhobi and there are two members of Gujjar, one member of Gaddi and one from Muslim community.

Role of Pradhan

All the power and functions of Gram Panchayat have been recorded in a separate register. The Pradhan takes care of village requirement like lighting of public streets. Primary education, registration of birth, death and marriage records, improving the breed of cattle and medical treatment of cattle and prevention of cattle disease are some of the duties performed by the Panchyat. The Pradhan also takes care of construction of new wells or ponds and tanks and provides assistance in the development of agriculture. The main objective of the Pradhan is to maintain unity among the communities residing in the village. Some major offences where the Pradhan can play a deciding role to settle, includes breaching of endogamy and exogamy disputes, divorce without mutual consent and so on.

It was observed that despite the statutory power granted to the Panchayat it has not made significant inroads into the Gujjar political system. This has happened because of two reasons. First, the Biradari of the Gujjar still functions and though the structure has weakened Gujjars prefer to get their disputes settled traditionally keeping away from Statutory Panchayat. Also, the Gram Panchayat is village based, unlike the Gujjar Biradari, which is community based. Gujjar are oriented to depend on Biradari institution which includes the tribe spread across villages. Moreover, from the point of view of the traditional pattern of tribe life the Gujjar remain as a closed community in the sense that they have limited contact with the non-Gujjars. But in spite of all these facts the Statutory Panchayat has the legal authority recognized by the government. The Gujjar recognize this fact.

Religious Life of Gujjar

The religious beliefs and practices prevailing in Sahu of Chamba district and Bamta village of Bilaspur district are reflective of mixed population of Hindu, tribal and Muslim. In addition to these three main categories, there is the Arya community which forms separate religious identity. The Gujjars are divided into two endogamous religious sections. The Muslim Gujjar with a small number of families are settled in Sahu and Hindu Gujjar exclusively live in Bamta village of Bilaspur district.

The Muslim Gujjar and Tribal Beliefs

The Muslim Gujjar who are at present settled in Sahu village trace their migration to Chamba from Jammu & Kashmir. They are very keen to offer prayers five times a day. They are from Sunni sect. Their sacred specialist is maulvi who officiates at life-cycle rituals. Exorcists are from their own tribe.

Traditionally they do not have any festival peculiar to their own tribal religion. Now being a Muslim they take part in all fairs and festivals which are related to their religion. They observe Muslim festivals. The most important are Id-ul-fitr, Idul-Zuha and birthday of Prophet Mohammad.

As per prevailing folklore the Muslim Gujjar claim that they are descendants of Rajput Hindu caste. Some of Rajput influences remain. Despite a clear and distinct impact of Islam on their beliefs, the Muslim Gujjar continue to have a deep faith in the essential ingredients of tribal religion. It is observed that the Muslim Gujjar have still retained their clan organization and several other rituals and traditions of their ancestors, which are not generally observed by the Muslims. In course of time they have slowly imbibed the Islamic tradition but elements of original tribal and Hindu religion affect their life.

There are a number of tribal deities, who are venerated by the Muslim Gujjar. The village deity known as Khera devta is propitiated every six-month. Every family of the community contributes ration which is cooked and served to the local people. The offerings are made to the Khera devta for welfare of the community members. Muslim Gujjars have faith in the local gods, goddesses and regional deities also. Among these deities Panja Parida is most important. The community pays great respect to the deity. There are some other deities such as Gogga Aiavbal and Gugga Jahar Peer (snake deity). They believe that by prayer or worship to these deities they may be saved from snake bite. Gugga Minja Peer, Gugga Panja Peer, Gugga Nani and saint Lakhdevata are all important deities among the Muslim Gujjar.

The Hindu Gujjars

The Hindu Gujjars trace their origin from Mand and Jasoda. They worship major gods and goddesses of the Hindu pantheon. Important among them are Shiva, Ganesh, Lakshmi, Kali, Rama and Krishna. Their principal god is Shiva. A small place for worship of the deities is demarcated by a Brahman in a corner of the room. Sometimes an earthen lamp is lit at the place. Hindu Gujjars keep religious books like *Ramayan, Gita, Sukh Sagar, Prem Sagar* in their houses. They believe and worship the peepal and tulsi tree. They observe fasts on Puranmasi, Ekadasi, Shivratri and Janmasthami.

It is observed that the Hindu Gujjar like Muslim people believe in hell and heaven. The Hindu Gujjars are very liberal and broad minded in their attitude towards other religion too and many Hindu Gujjars hold Muslim saints in great reverence and worship Muslim pirs and saints.

Like the Muslim Gujjars, the Hindu Gujjars continue to worship tribal deities and village deities. The deities are Panja Parida, Khera devta, Baba Garibnath, Panja Peer, Gugga Nani.

Conclusion

The Gujjar tribespeople have a rich folk tradition of their nomadic-pastoral social formation and migration. The Gujjars were variously influenced by cultural and religious beliefs of the Hindus and Muslims. Some states such as

Himachal Pradesh have accorded them the status of Scheduled Tribe. In this village study we saw that they live with many castes and are subjected to some deprivations and social exclusion. The village Sahu has communities belonging to three class-Upper, Middle and Lower. The Gujjar, Mochi, Gaddi and Muslim belong to lower class. The Gujjars, divided into the Hindu and Muslim sections, have many common religious beliefs. Both sections continue to venerate many 'tribal' deities. In present era the Gujjars have been facilitated with many schemes devoted to their development. They have also been encouraged to adopt agriculture as means of livelihood. They are provided with land to lead new economic life. In village political set-up also they have good position but in broad social-religious sphere of village life they remain excluded.

References

Baden Powell, B. 1972, *The Indian Village Community,* Delhi: Cosmo Publications.

Bhatia, A.K. and A. Saran 1984, *Tribe in Contemporary India: Gujjar of Himachal Pradesh,* Dehradun: Anthropological Survey of India.

Crook, M. 1896, *The Tribes and Castes of North Western India* II, Delhi: Cosmo Publications (Reprint 1974).

Hocrinte, A.F. 1905, "Some Problem of Ancient Indian History: The Gujjar Clans", *Journal of the Royal Asiatic Society*, London.